New Selected Letters

Hugh MacDiarmid

New Selected Letters

*Edited by Dorian Grieve, Owen Dudley Edwards
and Alan Riach*

CARCANET

First published in Great Britain in 2001 by
Carcanet Press Limited
4th Floor, Conavon Court
12–16 Blackfriars Street
Manchester M3 5BQ

Copyright © 2001 The Estate of Michael Grieve
Introductory material, selection and notes copyright © 2001
Dorian Grieve, Owen Dudley Edwards and Alan Riach

All rights reserved

A CIP catalogue record for this book
is available from the British Library

ISBN 1 85754 273 8

The publisher acknowledges financial assistance
from the Arts Council of England.

Set in Monotype Bembo by XL Publishing Services, Tiverton
Printed and bound in England by SRP Ltd, Exeter

To Deirdre
and to the memory of
Michael

Contents

List of Photographs
viii

Introduction
ix

Library Abbreviations and Acknowledgements
xxxii

Hugh MacDiarmid (C.M. Grieve): A Chronology
xxxv

PART ONE The 1920s
1

PART TWO The 1930s
37

PART THREE The 1940s
175

PART FOUR The 1950s
261

PART FIVE The 1960s
353

PART SIX The 1970s
447

Appendix: Biographical List of Recipients
535

Index
563

List of Photographs

CMG, Valda and Michael, Whalsay, summer 1933	*frontispiece*
CMG and Michael at the cottage, Sodom, Whalsay, June 1933	vi
The Duke of Montrose, Compton Mackenzie, R.B. Cunninghame Graham, CMG, James Valerline and John MacCormack at the first public meeting of the National Party of Scotland, St Andrew's Halls, Glasgow, 1928	2
CMG returning to Shetland from hospital, October 1935	36
Valda and Michael, Whalsay, summer 1937	38
CMG, Whalsay, August 1935, a week before his breakdown	174
CMG working in the copper shell band department of Mechan's Engineering Company, 1942	176
CMG, R.E. Muirhead and Valda, *c.* 1952	262
Brownsbank Cottage, near Biggar	354
Edwin Morgan and CMG at the launch of EM's book on Hugh MacDiarmid, 1977	446
Ezra Pound and CMG, St Mark's Square, Venice, 10 November 1970	448

Introduction

Owen Dudley Edwards, Dorian Grieve and Alan Riach

1. *Lover, Soldier, Husband*

The letters we have collected here are published for the first time. They were not available to the late Alan Bold, editor of *The Letters of Hugh MacDiarmid* (1984), to whom our debt is incalculable. We have benefitted enormously from his indefatigable industry in quest of biographical and other relevant information, by his zeal and love for his subject, and by his wonderful knowledge of the ramifications of the CMG world whether as shown there, or in *Hugh MacDiarmid: Christopher Murray Grieve – A Critical Biography* (1988), or elsewhere. Michael Grieve bestowed on Alan Bold the same endless generosity, patience and thoughtfulness that he gave to all other scholars. But Michael's mother Valda, CMG's second wife, was still alive when the *Letters* were published. She, too, was generous with her time and patience – not always her most visible virtue – and in aiding Bold write his biography she seems to have spoken freely enough of marital complexities in CMG's life. But the store of family correspondence was not available to Bold for use in the *Letters* and little could be seen from the then sealed archives. Valda's death removes an obvious discretionary barrier against premature release.

CMG's letters are thus divided between Bold's volume (largely the public man's correspondence) and our own, whose primary theme is charged and suffused by the hopes, fears, comedies, tragedies, weeping and laughter of his family life. For the first time the world is given the Christopher Murray Grieve who lived behind Hugh MacDiarmid. The letters published here chart more deeply something of the Odyssey of his mind and heart, in addition to the physical Odyssey whose journeyings Bold's biography and his chosen *Letters* so faithfully described.

We have nothing from before the 1920s, but a hilariously flickering rear light radiating its uncertainties back to 1913 has surfaced from the Grieve MSS:

Edinburgh 5th Sept. 1962

Dear Hugh,
I hope that you have not forgotten me, Minnie Punton, after all these

long years. But now I think you have all your life been a great silly braggart, boasting always about yourself. You have not got the brains of a hen, and all your writings are stupid, and not worth reading.

If only you knew GOD, you would be a much better man, but then you seem to think that you are GOD yourself.

When the Lord Jesus Christ comes down from the sky to remove His own people into the Heavens, it will not be you who are suddenly taken away thither. You give yourself all the praise, instead of giving it to GOD ALMIGHTY. That proves that you are an utter FOOL.

Minnie Punton.

Minnie Punton can hardly have known CMG as Hugh (did anyone?) and he had passed out of her life, so far as we can tell, after 1 January 1916 when (in Bold's brutal words) 'she celebrated the New Year ... by breaking off her engagement ...' Their understanding apparently went back at least to 1913, when he dedicated to 'M.P.' a poem, 'The Curly Snake' (reproduced in Bold's *MacDiarmid*), apparently from a manuscript formerly in the holding of CMG's brother Andrew.

> Sweetheart of mine, I hope that there will be
> A Curly Snake for us in Paradise
> (Oh! All true lovers go to Paradise)
> That goes up darkly unexpected-wise,
> Behind the gardens of felicity
> – A Curly Snake that takes its curious way
> Through heavy woods where night still lingers
> On to dark hills (unknowledged of the singers,
> Who prophesy an endless-shining day)
> – Dark hills and broken stars and ravelled skies
> Else Paradise will not be Paradise.
>
> If it be roses, roses everywhere
> And stirless waters and a constant sun
> (Dearer the moon to lovers than the sun;
> Better than moon a night when there is none).
> Sweetheart, we will not be all-happy there
> For you and I must have a crooked way
> And wild things crying strangely in the night
> And cold winds on the hillside, and the play
> – The unintelligible daring! – of stars' eyes
> That shine out suddenly still-bright
> Through loaded branches – just as here!
> But ah Beloved, there can be I fear
> No Curly Snake for us in Paradise.

Bold notices the 'fundamental features of Grieve's art: the desire for difficulty ... the fondness for the dark ... the excitement of the unknown'. The Freudian may find his phallic symbol in the snake – though if that reading had been open to the dedicatee she would have broken off the engagement long before 1916, or else she must have recovered some virginity by 1962. It certainly relates to the winding path in the wood near Langholm, the Langfall: the path was called the Curly Snake and was one origin – and a subtitle – for *To Circumjack Cencrastus*; and there they courted. Its sentiments, one might disgust the later CMG by pointing out, are those of Harry Lauder's 'Roaming in the Gloaming' (which may, indeed, have been an origin, as may Byron's 'We'll go no more a-roving', and Lewis Carroll's opening of 'The Walrus and the Carpenter', and, as Bold says, Ernest Dowson). Anyhow, it is beautiful, and deserves a place in any anthology of 1890s verse, had the 1890s not run out when the author was seven. Bold elsewhere cites *To Circumjack Cencrastus* ('North of the Tweed'):

> And hoo should I forget the Langfall
> On mornings when the hines were ripe but een
> Ahint the glintin' leafs were brichter still
> Than sunned dew on them, lips reider than the fruit,
> And I filled baith my basket and my hert
>   Mony and mony a time?

Minnie Punton as a schoolteacher may have had more to do with the education of CMG than mere eroticism. It also seems likely that her awareness of CMG's having become increasingly identified with and as Hugh MacDiarmid, arose from some knowledge of the poems. Otherwise her letter would be guilty of pronunciation ('all your writings are stupid') on texts she had not read, a heinous if far from unknown crime in an academic. CMG had just been appearing at the International Writers' Conference at the McEwan Hall at the Edinburgh International Festival, where he denounced Alexander Trocchi to his face as an exponent 'of an entirely spurious internationalism' but at least admitted he had not read Trocchi's work. (The letters to Trocchi collected here suggest a mutual respect beyond this serious public jousting.) What would have activated Minnie Punton, after all these years, may have been the session on 22 August 1962, exactly two weeks before the date of her letter: CMG had arisen to proclaim himself a Communist when Norman Mailer and others had been talking about 'commitment'. This gave an opportunity to radical American writers such as Mailer and Mary McCarthy to distance themselves from him, only to be later distanced from their Kennedy-era selves when they turned against the war in Vietnam. CMG was much denounced, as Hugh MacDiarmid, by patriotic anti-Communists: Minnie Punton may have been aroused through pieties terrestrial as well as celestial. Her letter also gives strange echoes of early MacDiarmid poetry, written only a few years after their breach. It may merely be response to the first edition of his *Collected Poems*, issued in 1961 (with time enough for Minnie Punton to read it in the interval) or it may have been a remembrance of something long, long ago, the germ of things that would mature, as in 'The Following Day', from *Annals of the Five Senses* (1923), where a soldier is imagined, singing of Christ:

> 'I nailed Him high
> 'Twixt earth and sky
> And Heaven shut
> Its flaming eye
> But
> Be nights as Hell
> I know full well
> My way to you, oblivious slut,
> Who all my roaring blood shall glut,
> Shall glut,
> Who all my roaring blood shall glut!
>
> 'And when they loose Him from the tree
> At break of day
> I shall not care and shall not see
> – At break of day.
> My snoring head between your breasts
> Will snugly lie,
> Will snugly lie,
> My snoring head between your breasts
> Will snugly lie.'
>
> Every time when morning came
> Caught and held a flying flame,
> But between her breasts he lay
> Lost to day,
> And between her spent breasts fell
> Spent, to Hell!

That was still C.M. Grieve, a very good young poet obscured by the advent of Hugh MacDiarmid who in *Sangschaw* (1925) famously anticipated the day of judgment with a child's-eye view of Langholm, plain to any who knew of Crowdieknowe:

> Oh to be at Crowdieknowe
> When the last trumpet blaws,
> An' see the deid come loupin' owre
> The auld grey wa's.

> Muckle men wi' tousled beards,
> I grat at as a bairn
> 'll scramble frae the croodit clay
> Wi' feck o' swearin'.
>
> An' glower at God an' a' his gang
> O' angels i' the lift
> – Thae trashy bleezin' French-like folk
> Wha gar'd them shift!
>
> Fain the weemun-folk'll seek
> To mak' them haud their row
> – Fegs, God's no blate gin he stirs up
> The men o' Crowdieknowe!

If Minnie Punton had been as God-fearing in 1912 as she was to declare herself fifty years after, did her qualms play a part in striking the first poetic notes from Hugh MacDiarmid, in addition to those which her charms elicited from Christopher Murray Grieve? It was no small achievement to inspire the best poem on the Divine Assize since Byron's 'A Vision of Judgment'. But it was probably a very fortunate day for Scotland and Humanity – and above all for their reconciliation – when she turned him loose.

That her successor in his affections – already on the scene in her time – Margaret Skinner, later Margaret Grieve, would strike the chords of Hugh MacDiarmid is historical fact. Minnie Punton, in her own self-portrait, would be Nausikaa in her virgin innocence: Heaven forfend we should bring her in as Kalypso in whose arms Odysseus lay so long and (on non-Homeric evidence) so productively. The French young ladies whom CMG encountered in the First World War, when both parties were doing their patriotic duty, may count as Kalypso. We may multiply Kalypso among them.

Margaret Cunningham Thomson Skinner was married on 13 June 1918, in Edinburgh, by the forms of the United Free Church of Scotland, to CMG, a Sergeant in the RAMC. The bride was a typist in the WAAC at Perth. She might be described more exactly as Circe, who transformed her lovers into strange and different beings. 'Valda' said CMG to Norman MacCaig, 'is a wonderful woman, but Peggy – she made the poetry.'

It began simply enough, with 'To M.G.':

> Whether you are fairy or flesh
> I may now know never.
> A shimmer of rose in my eyes
> And a song in my ears for ever,
> You and the haze of my dreams
> I cannot dissever.

> With a rattle and whirl of drums
> You carry the heart of me,
> Or lure me with elfin pipes
> The ends of the world to see, –
> In batlight and noonday blaze
> My mistress and mystery!

But the first surviving words from Hugh MacDiarmid – after the title 'The Bonnie Broukit Bairn' – are, 'For Peggy':

> Mars is braw in crammasy,
> Venus in a green silk goun,
> The auld mune shak's her gowden feathers,
> Their starry talk's a wheen o' blethers
> Nane for thee a thochtie sparin',
> Earth, thou bonnie broukit bairn!
> *– But greet, an' in your tears ye'll droun*
> *The haill clamjamfrie!*

Bold in his *MacDiarmid* reads this, perfectly reasonably, as 'Feeling the force of Nietzsche's declaration of the death of God', portraying 'the bleak chaos of a Godless world' by addressing the earth as a 'forsaken child on the point of weeping'. There may be another, more domestic, origin.

After their marriage CMG remained in service, posted to Sections Lahore Indian General Hospital near Marseilles in 1918 and was not out of the army until July 1919. Peggy Grieve was now living in St Andrews, working as a secretary in a firm of solicitors: she would have been surrounded by the heads of households whose wives of necessity cut a fine figure in that ancient, noble, and pretentious town. Her husband returned from the war, possibly revealing the existence, if not the effects, of occasional adultery induced by a life stifling under immersion in the paraphernalia of death. Bold notes that previous employment on the *St Andrews Citizen* in 1913 ending in a row would have cut CMG off from journalistic livelihood there. The *Montrose Review* employed him in 1920, ending in bitter recriminations against his employer later enshrined as the epitome of business spite in *To Circumjack Cencrastus*. Peggy had to say goodbye to the job that conferred status on her in her own right, and depart with him to Alness, north of the Cromarty Firth, where Scotland begins to thrust her head above the Aberdeen peninsula. Ardross Castle, near Loch Morie, owned by C.W.D. Perrins, the Worcester Sauce millionaire, required a caretaker and under-housemaid for its Kildermorie Forest Lodge. Perrins let the Lodge to grouse-shooters whose wives and maids displayed their finery and their fidgets while their husbands accounted for other feathered friends. Hardly surprisingly, Peggy took a five-week holiday in October 1920 as CMG worked away on *Northern Numbers*, his anthology of Scottish poets to be published in November. Its poets, apart from himself, included John Buchan, Violet Jacob, his former minister the Revd T.S. Cairncross, his school friend Roderick Watson Kerr, and his brother Andrew: they also included its dedicatee, the Kailyard novelist Neil Munro, whom CMG would be vigorously denouncing in *Contemporary Scottish Studies* six years later. The Edinburgh publisher T.N. Foulis appeared (illusorily) to be ready to launch *The Scottish Chapbook* under CMG's editorship, with contributions from Lady Glenconner (cousin of Lord Alfred Douglas), General Sir Ian Hamilton (patron of Winston Churchill) and Sir Ronald Ross (discoverer of the mosquito cycle in malaria): Ross and Hamilton were present in *Northern Numbers Second Series* published in October 1921 (Hamilton by a fine verse about a child's fear of ghosts and a lament for Gordon to rhyme with 'the Cross they fastened our Lord on').

Whatever existence Peggy Grieve found among these hopes and possible acquaintances – and she would have received the more patronising end of the patronage – our evidence has little to give. Grieve wrote to his former English teacher at Broughton School, Edinburgh, George Ogilvie, on 2 November 1920: 'Do you think that [my literary activity] matters to my wife ... I may dedicate my poems to her but do you think she reads them? And if she did do you think she would understand them, or me?' She seems to have loved their surroundings at the Lodge, as he wrote about November 1920 – significantly naming the sonnet 'Rivals' – with dedication 'To M.G.':

>The multitudinous and various hills
>Court thee. Shyly at dawn attending thee
>Or bending in the twilight tenderly
>They vie to pleasure thee, and my heart fills
>(In silence there beyond each dawn whereon
>Your eyes with passion seize, beyond each night
>That thrills you with enchantment and delight)
>With mingled pride, and grief for dreams foregone.
>
>You do not greet me as you welcome these,
>Though kind your smile and intimate your nod,
>I know too well with what bright mysteries
>Your eyes on Braeriach turn: and how you run
>To where Schiehallion standing like a god
>Turns me to dust and ashes in the sun!

This is pleasant in its way: a mountain as a partner in a wife's adultery we may now recognise as an ominous foreshadow but at the time it was merely a somewhat artificial conceit, reminiscent – probably consciously – of the mountain that chased Wordsworth for stealing a boat. But it is hard to reproach the shade of Peggy for undue indifference to poetic effusion that had so little reality. Not being Quakers, they did not address one another as 'thee' (as indeed the switch to 'Your' and 'You' makes awkwardly clear). Her enthusiasm for Schiehallion seems to induce in the poet a self-image as Lot's wife, or the minor characters in *The Last Days of Pompeii*, but it is hard to see the poems winning any warmer response from her than kindness of smile and intimacy of nod.

But what produced 'The Bonnie Broukit Bairn'? Was it return to Montrose, away from her mountains, in late April 1921? CMG once more became a reporter on the *Montrose Review* and (after some flitting between a couple of other addresses) domesticated in a council house at 16 Links Avenue, Montrose. Peggy had had a few unpleasant rounds of 'flu (the frightful post-war 'flu that took so many lives) and there was a minor operation late in 1921. Did 'The Bonnie Broukit Bairn' originate from Peggy's tears at lost St Andrews gentilities and lost Ross-shire mountains, condescending neighbours and luxuriant acquaintances? The journalist's occupation left CMG more vulnerable to alcohol. Could the poem have originated in an assurance that she was all the world to him, and that however shabby her dress, she eclipsed all their more flamboyant and fashionable female neighbours, especially when – as now – she was weeping? Willa Muir remembered her 'looking up shyly through dark eyelashes'; she also remembered Peggy complaining of the gossip of neighbours against which she put up extra net curtains. As a term of endearment for a weeping wife, 'ma bonnie broukit bairn' (my lovely neglected child) would be obvious enough, paternalistic though a feminist would term it. It might also help her to laugh: when neighbours suddenly become planets, a strutting Mars, a complacent Venus, a feather-shaking moon, absurd in their 'wheen o' blethers' and contemptibly inferior to the earth they ignore. It would also explain a strange point about MacDiarmid's Scots. CMG did not talk in the language in which MacDiarmid rapidly found his poetic voice, but he might very well have talked in that of 'The Bonnie Broukit Bairn', especially in reassurance and endearment. Even the reduction of the wife to child status is relevant: the playground was the place where the Scots language was and is most alive. MacDiarmid evangelised Scots as an act of love.

Peggy may have played Circe by enchanting mountains into lovers, and CMG into Hugh MacDiarmid, but for the letters in our collection she remains initially silent, to be addressed when tragedy reaches catastrophe in the 1930s. We have to think of her as there, frustrated, oppressed, bewitching. We say 'oppressed': CMG may not have been a particularly oppressive husband in the active sense but the whole climate and culture conspired against Peggy Grieve, reducing her from career woman to kitchen drudge. Willa Muir, recalling their friendship in 1924, took her somewhat derisively for 'an embodiment of the "wee wifie" loved by

Scotsmen'. From the first there was clearly more to her than would justify the term, but Muir's use of it reminds us of what was expected from women in her situation – unless they happened to be Willa Muir. CMG in any case did not seek submissive womenfolk – Minnie Punton, whatever her other disqualifications for the role of Mrs C.M. Grieve, had no shortage of assertiveneness – and Peggy must be construed as a strong woman sidelined by her husband's many careers and her schizophrenic times. Henrik Ibsen's first British publicist, William Archer, was from Perth but his gospel reached London more rapidly than Montrose.

The poetry Peggy made quickly moved beyond Montrose and the Grieves moved to London, for CMG to edit Compton Mackenzie's pioneering radio magazine, *VOX*. *VOX* failed, and CMG's attempt to establish his cultural imprint by participation in publishing as Eliot was doing in Faber's failed also; the Unicorn Press absorbed and then rejected him. Far worse, his marriage fell to pieces. Peggy in London became the mistress of a cultural coal-merchant named William McElroy while CMG was a publicity officer in Liverpool in 1930. She had also been finding her own links with Celticism, and in summer 1931 had an abortion of a pregnancy apparently fathered by Louis N. Le Roux, a Breton nationalist. CMG lost his job through drinking bouts desperately trying to fight the horrors raining down on him: his Odyssey had now driven him among the Laistrygones, with every ship in his fleet apparently smashed to pieces around him, and his people devoured by monstrous, unforeseeable distortions of nature.

Few letters survive from these hideous months, and those which do carry the pain, deflected somewhat to his brother and mother. One poem, 'Charisma and My Relatives', dedicated with bitter homage to McElroy, concluded in lines the recipient would understand better than the audience reading it in *First Hymn to Lenin*:

> And yet – there's some folk lice'll no live on,
> I'm ane o' them I doot. But what a thocht!
> What speculations maun a man sae shunned
> No' ha'e until at last the reason's brocht
> To view acceptable, as the fact may be
> On different grun's to them and me.

Peggy made the poetry all right. Humiliation, rejection, the imminent removal of his children, the denial of the future he had been making in politics and poetry – all lay behind the dignity and forbearance of his letter to his mother in January 1932. Revolted nature abhorred the emptiness into which he was being consigned. In September 1931 he met a 25-year-old girl from Cornwall called Valda Trevlyn. She sympathised over CMG's tragedy, whose culmination in a divorce court now appeared irrevocable. CMG, formerly a voice fashioning itself for an entire people, could now only obliquely speak for himself, but his dumb honour demanded he give Peggy the evidence she would need in the only way she could obtain divorce. He could have divorced her, of course, but honour and truth alike prevented it: he would not shame her, he would not deny the marriage he so longed to continue. He arranged with this new and sympathetic friend to give Peggy grounds by what was in fact a chaste night together in late September. There had previously been such a night – possibly consummated – with another woman. In fact Peggy Grieve would use all of these facts not only to gain her divorce, but to do so (in January 1932) with denial of parental access by CMG to the children Christine (now aged seven) and Walter (now three). By the end of October 1931, Valda had conceived a child with CMG when they had known each other less than two months. Michael would be born on 28 July 1932. What followed was the building up of love with Valda until after long years it became the centre of CMG's life. But the 1930s cannot be fully understood for him without the realisation that neither of them could be sure of permanence.

To Valda who was then and remained thereafter very much her own woman, of warmth and grandeur, of pride and temper, married life was unprecedented. To CMG the hope of reunion with Peggy would take a long time to die, co-existing, however unbidden, with the second marriage for some years. We have only to look at the terrible letters or drafts to Peggy which are printed now, to get at least a sense of the wound still open or a shaft from the nerve still raw. The decade was expiring on its own funeral-pyre, blazing itself into the Second World War before CMG began to abate his self-torture. His bitterness against his innocent children is its own proof of how he still hungered for them – and for the enchantress who had befouled him. That was his view: it may be that he was far too big a creator for Peggy to share with his poetry and politics in any comfort, and that however divine or diabolical she might seem to him, she was simply a frightened fugitive taking refuge from a genius she could not understand. Even the Scotland he was inventing may have been alien to her – more so than it was to Valda, who knew nothing of Scotland when she met him and at the end of his life would still finish an argument with a triumphant 'Bloody Scotchman!'. Peggy had been a girl with a lost career, but her background was conventional Cupar. Valda, rebelling against her Cornish upbringing, was big enough to take CMG on. Despite being haunted by memories of Peggy, Christine and baby Walter, CMG would labour throughout the later 1930s on his *Cornish Heroic Song for Valda Trevlyn*. He got the right word. 'Heroic' describes her perfectly. And Valda was his Penelope, for whom – and increasingly with whom – he would make the long voyage home.

2. Son, Brother, Father

> An' I think that mebbe at last I ken
> What your look meant then.

In 1924, 'The Watergaw' proved CMG's means of confronting the death of his father, James Grieve, the Langholm postman, on 3 February 1911. He was franker in 'Kinsfolk' – written in Liverpool in 1931 while his marriage was falling to pieces and he wondered how his children Christine and Walter would remember him, as he now thought of his own father:

> Afore he dee'd he turned and gied a lang
> Last look at pictures o' my brither and me
> Hung on the wa' aside the bed, I've heard
> My mither say. I wonder then what he
> Foresaw or hoped and hoo – or gin – it squares
>   Wi' subsequent affairs.

In 'The Watergaw' the sight of the indistinct rainbow shimmering beyond the coming rain makes the poet think of the last wild look 'ye gied / Afore ye dee'd!' Grieve senior had died of acute lobar pneumonia contracted six days earlier, at the age of 47. That puts the date of infection on the morrow of CMG's departure from Broughton School following a prank to which he had been an accessory. It seems to have been an administrative overreaction: the victim, if anyone, was the master George Ogilvie who remained a friend, correspondent, mentor and probably most seminal senior influence on CMG for the next twenty years. But the grim thought remains that Grieve senior may have known of the apparent disgrace, and its destruction of his hopes of his elder son's security in the teaching profession: and that this destroyed in him the will to live. The Scots language became the means of confrontation, but both more bluntly and less clearly than English would have meant. Even the memory/metaphor of the 'Watergaw' is indistinct by definition: the poet is facing/avoiding what he knows/thinks/guesses/denies of his father's last judgment on him.

But the last look had not only been at CMG's likeness: the dying man had also looked at that of the younger son, Andrew Graham Grieve, to whom the first letters printed here are sent. Earlier correspondence is extant with Ogilvie, some in Bold's *Letters*, the whole of the surviving exchanges admirably edited by Catherine Kerrigan in *The Hugh MacDiarmid–George Ogilvie Letters* (1988), nothing, fortunately, having eluded her vigilance to necessitate inclusion here. So we have no Nestor for our Odyssey, although Kerrigan's edition is indispensable for all students of CMG as 'prentice and poet. The original Nestor appears in Homer's text as advisor to Telemachos, but Homer's *Iliad* shows him also as teacher to all the Greeks of Odysseus's generation. Such is Ogilvie's role, certainly, in the Odyssey

CMG made of his life, even more so, it seems, after the end of their formal relationship than before. This also explains a crucial fact about CMG himself. He always remained a great teacher, however little formal teaching he did (he was so employed on the side in his days as factotum at Kildermorie in Easter Ross); his polemics and his promotions must be seen first and foremost as teaching. Ogilvie became an obvious surrogate father, more aesthetic and more political, but with a paternal austerity corresponding to that of the dead James Grieve.

CMG's relationship with his mother fluctuated, but its stability may be shown by his presence as best man to James Dawson when the then 61-year-old Elizabeth Grieve married him on 1 June 1918, thirteen days before the Grieve-Skinner nuptials. 'The Watergaw' assumes its other dimension with the fourth figure in the family, little brother Andrew; also included in James Grieve's 'wild look'.

MacDiarmid might be ready enough for self-similitude with God, as in 'Focherty' in *Penny Wheep* (1926) or Christ, as in *A Drunk Man* (line 117), but CMG might have been less enthusiastic, if likened to one of the characters in Christ's short stories known as parables: the Prodigal Son. He had horrified his parents by threatening to set up as a poet, and perhaps as a tramp. Meanwhile Andrew had gone in 1909 to work in Burton-on-Trent as a 15-year-old clerk in the Inland Revenue, to which institution he gave his life. There was no father left to whom Andrew might speak the words of the non-Prodigal Son, but they seem almost to lie in wait for him:

> Lo, these many years do I serve thee, neither transgressed I at any time thy commandment: and yet thou never gavest me a kid, that I might make merry with my friends:
> But as soon as this thy son was come, which hath devoured thy living with harlots, thou hast killed for him the fatted calf.
> (Luke XV: 29–30)

The bitter and final break between the brothers in summer 1942 and CMG's dismissive 'he and I never got on together' (to J.K. Annand: 6 January 1970, Bold, *Letters*) might seem to validate such a role for Andrew, and no doubt so it seemed in retrospect: yet as Annand pointed out to Bold (ibid.), Andrew, contrary to CMG's recollection, was very helpful to his elder brother, drawing him to Cupar, Fife, when posted there by the Inland Revenue in 1912. In Cupar, CMG met Peggy. (There is perhaps a macabre echo to Allan Breck's proverb in Stevenson's *Catriona*: 'he that will to Cupar, maun to Cupar'.) CMG's letters to Andrew tell a strong story of mutual fraternal affection and understanding. 'A scrappy and egoistic letter – but what other do you expect?' writes CMG at the close of the first printed here: it suggests confidence such as he shared with nobody save George Ogilvie. Andrew may have been less enthusiastic about the relationship – he is less prompt in reply than CMG hopes, but then CMG seems to expect response by return.

Ever since their father's death, the Prodigal seems to be assured that his brother will kill the fatted calf for him as and when necessary. CMG's marriage may have been all that prevented his living off Andrew for a year on his return from the war, as he had told Ogilvie he anticipated. Their early relations seem both affectionate and fairly honest. CMG included Andrew in the first *Northern Numbers* anthology but vetoed his verse for the second, and the letter here is a fine piece of hard-hitting teaching from someone who knows his craft and is sure of the receptivity of his pupil (much the same way Ogilvie seems to have written to CMG). We then break after the return to Montrose from Easter Ross: the brothers could meet during CMG's visits to Edinburgh and when calling on their mother in East Lothian. That Andrew was one of the first to be told the identity of Hugh MacDiarmid in 1923 indicates that no serious break had occurred. The 'Love – Chris' sign-off suggests that if anything the brothers were even more relaxed than before. But the emergence of infants within each family dissipated such cultural common interests as remained.

By the 1930s Andrew had moved closer to the role of the Prodigal's brother, and in his anguish at the utter collapse of his own family, CMG denounces the good and faithful servant of the state which he himself abhors. As his letters become his *Odyssey*, Andrew from time to time seems cast in the ugly role of Antinoös, the usurper of Odysseus's home. He disliked the peculiarities of CMG's marital situation in the early 1930s – divorced from Peggy in January 1932, Michael born to Valda Trevlyn in July, Valda and CMG married two years later – and they denounced one another over the death of their mother. Yet while an income-tax man has little chance in a popularity contest with a poet, especially a poet-liberator of his own country, the Good Brother deserves kindlier obsequies than the Bad Brother would concede. If Andrew was not prepared to advance all the funds CMG found it necessary to seek from him from time to time, he seems to have been far more generous than one would expect from a figure of so respectable a life. His good nature seldom failed, however much his manner took its severe coloration from his occupation. In mid-July 1942 the final break seems to have been at CMG's instance rather than Andrew's.

In *A Portrait of the Artist as a Young Man* James Joyce salutes the old Father, old Artificer, old Dedalus, that Joyce's wings may not melt in his flight towards the Sun of Artistry. *Ulysses* salutes Odysseus, father of Telemachos, and the artificer of artificers, wordsmith and diplomat. The Telemachos of our story is Michael Grieve.

Father and son were like enough in many respects. Michael unleashed much of the propaganda of the Scottish National Party through his own uncredited writing. His hand was behind innumerable election addresses. His party's victories time and again came in constituencies he had evangelised. Michael's politics were combative in style but constructive in character, where his father's defied the universe. Dad (CMG was always 'Dad' to Mike) was a poet, and functioned in ideal terms: the rest of us had to do the best we could with what we had. In certain respects, son was more radical than father: Michael went to jail in the early 1950s rather than accept conscription which Scottish nationalists believed contrary to the Treaty of Union of 1707. CMG had served in the First World War in the Royal Army Medical Corps with no reservations and with much more ideological reluctance accepted labour service in the Second World War. It had advantages: martyrdom gave immunity to the reproach of moderation. The old man would murmur that nothing but violent insurrection would ever gain results from the English, and Michael would smile with appreciation at an old family joke, equivalent to remembering the days of Santa Claus.

The present volume of letters has shaped itself into a book in which Michael Grieve becomes a very vital character, to be met and watched in its course, and as such he is the Telemachos who emerges at the close of the story to guide his father to vindication, and stands at his side. Michael Grieve's life-work was establishing his father's reputation and enabling his achievement to come into its own. This Carcanet series was intended to be the crown of that devotion and labour. Michael helped carry his father's voice to its appointed audience in his own century and the one that has followed. Like Telemachos, hospitality was his first thought in commencing his work. Michael was the guardian of his father's reputation and estate. He guided it, as he guided his father, gently, encouragingly, far-sightedly. In CMG's final years he would make a silent third or fourth or fifth as the old man met with his beloved Norman MacCaig or Sorley Maclean or Sydney Goodsir Smith in Milne's Bar in Edinburgh, a place whose name and reputation they had made but into which they slipped with no Johnsonian authority. It was nevertheless their club. Yet the silence, for Michael, had no unease. The styles themselves stood in their integrity: CMG would vary from the mellifluous grunt to the lilting elfin mischief, Norman turn some well-savoured irony drawn in a schoolmaster's clear word, Sydney quip in a courteous late Victorian elegance, Sorley assent in ruminative post-Gaelic head-nodding. Their nothings might suddenly be everythings, as when a solitary figure entered the bar and the old man looked up and Norman said that was Gavin Muir and the old man said 'Excuse me' to his friends, and walked down the bar, and his tones carried greeting and the offer of a drink and its acceptance and ten or fifteen minutes of unheard talk and Norman murmured that he was very glad Chris was doing that and Sydney agreed and nobody said another word about it. It must have been a third of a century since CMG's friendship with Gavin's parents, Edwin and Willa, had dissolved in bitter recrimination over Edwin's denial in *Scott and Scotland* (1936) that there could be a vernacular literature in Scots for the future. The whole identity of Hugh MacDiarmid had come into being in the resurrection and proclamation of that vernacular, and the Muirs had once seemed allies in that exhausting struggle. CMG's greeting and hospitality to Gavin was another expression of what Michael made of his stewardship: that the younger generation should be a sign of the retention of integrity but also the healing of harms.

3. *Odysseus*

And so to Odysseus, much-devising, much-enduring Odysseus.

The likeness is exceptional, appropriate but self-evident. CMG was an idealist, a worker, a martyr and an artist; he was a trickster, a contriver, a deceiver, a magician. (Does Homer intend us to imagine that Odysseus told nothing but the truth in his reminiscences of his voyage to Alkinoös, although deception elsewhere is almost a matter of principle with him?) Folklore abounds with the trickster-hero across the centuries and civilisations. Norse Loki, whose child the Midgard Snake coiled around the surface of the Earth MacDiarmid would address in *To Circumjack Cencrastus*; Gwydion fab Don, whose adventures conclude *Pedair Cainc y Mabinogi* (otherwise known as the first four tales in the Welsh *Mabinogion*); Fionn Mac Cumhail of Fianna legends, although losing his more anti-social deviousness in their eighteenth-century recension and respectablization by James Macpherson in *Ossian* where he is Anglicized as Fingal; Pau-Puk-Keewis, descended from Amerindian legend to dance at the wedding of Longfellow's Hiawatha who ultimately hunts him to death; Brer Rabbit, of black slave lore in the United States South whence Joel Chandler Harris drew his Uncle Remus stories. All may be mythical, but actual historical characters became commemorated among their people by imposition of trickster legends on their memories: Ferdinand of Aragon, Richelieu, Robert Burns, Daniel O'Connell, Abraham Lincoln, David Lloyd George. The hero figure will usually be from an oppressed, poverty-stricken or intimidated people, and much of his success lies in taking the existing resources of civilisation (which by definition he opposes) and turning them so that they entrap and enchant the stronger ruler to do their will, remaining within conventions he may secretly despise. He is not invulnerable, either within the fullness of his existence or in the working out of a specific episode. But he cannot be trapped by intelligence inferior to his own: if a stupid person defeats him, it is through the acquisition of cleverness, however momentary.

In Eric Linklater's novel based on the author's experiences as a National Party of Scotland candidate, *Magnus Merriman* (1931), CMG is Hugh Skene. CMG quoted the passage in his own autobiography *Lucky Poet* and was delighted with it: 'His suit was unremarkably grey, but he wore a purple collar and shirt and a yellow tie with red spots. Apart from his clothes his appearance was sufficiently striking to suggest genius. He had a smooth white face, dwarfed by a great bush of hair, and in brisk, delicate, rather terrier-like features his eyes shone bright and steady. His hands were beautifully shaped and somewhat dirty ...'

'Magnus' is Linklater (he later named his eldest son Magnus, from Orkney's patron saint, martyred in 1117: the boy would become the *Scotsman*'s greatest editor in living memory). CMG's own comment on the foregoing was 'That's me to a T. The dirty hands are, of course, due to my going with my hands constantly in pockets full of loose black tobacco.'

In Chapter 7, Linklater also describes a moment of confrontation:

> Skene said: 'You're a successful novelist, Merriman. But what are you aiming at? What do you think the future of writing is going to be?'
>
> Magnus, who had never given much thought to the matter, promptly declared that he was a traditionalist. He was beginning to enunciate a conservative philosophy for literature when Skene interrupted him.
>
> As if it were a pistol he aimed his slender and rather dirty forefinger at Magnus and said, with cold and deliberate ferocity: 'You're feeding on corpse-meat. In all its traditional forms English literature is dead, and to depend on the past for inspiration is a necrophagous perversion. We've got to start again, and the great literary problem confronting us today is to discover how far we must retract the horizontal before erecting a perpendicular.'
>
> The solemnity with which Skene enunciated his last sentence persuaded Magnus of its importance, but as it was also somewhat obscure he hesitated to reply until he had elucidated its meaning.

As he wrote and rode the 1920s CMG was Odysseus in the Aeolus episode, now carrying the winds of the world in his bag, now buffeted far and wide by their release. Linklater again:

> In Scotland the chief exponent of literal revolution was Hugh Skene, and he ... attempted to revive the ancient Scottish forms of speech. They had this advantage, at least, that they were fully as obscure as Joyce's neologisms or the asyntactical compressions of the young English poets. But as Skene's genius matured he discovered that the Scots of Dunbar and Henryson was insufficient to contain both his emotion and his meaning, and he began to draw occasional buckets from the fountains of other tongues. At this time it was not uncommon to find in his verse, besides ancient Scots, an occasional Gaelic, German, or Russian phrase. The title poem of his new volume, *The Flauchter-spaad*, was strikingly polyglot, and after three hours' study Magnus was unable to decide whether it was a plea for Communism, a tribute to William Wallace, or a poetical rendering of certain prehistoric fertility rites.

'Necrophagous' is crucial. CMG emerged from the Great War overwhelmed with the sense of a dead world. Many of Hugh MacDiarmid's first poems contemplate the idea of a dead, meaningless Earth (in a very different spirit to the celebration of an Earthchild/Peggy), of doomsday, of lost identity, of songs from worms, of empires and nations in ruins, of howling mobs and chaos of thought, of darkness where the faintest of memories recall that a world existed once. It was from this abomination of desolation that he called Scotland into existence once more, first in reviving its Scots language, then in politics. From the beginning, his nationalism was ferociously positive and overwhelmingly constructive. He was making: he was, after all, a Makar. In Scots, as in Greek, a poet is one who makes.

His account of himself to us through these letters begins the process of rebuilding in his own house, to his brother, then to his native if long-left home town, Langholm where his cousins the Laidlaws remained. John Laidlaw is the first correspondent here apart from brother Andrew: John's niece Jean would be his last, shortly before she, alone of Langholm's worthies, welcomed his body in its final return. After John he is off on his voyage, showering correspondence as he showers art and polemic across the cultural, artistic, ethnic, political, economic divides to draw what he can where he can in his work to find a new meaning for life in Scotland – and hence for the world. As a modernist he is experimentalist, whether toying with the new politics of Communism and Fascism, or discovering new meanings to music through Sorabji and F.G. Scott. He encounters nationalists old and new, makes some friends and loses others. He seeks to found journal after journal, some dying unborn, some struggling to life for a few tumultuous ferocious, fascinating issues. His politics are intensely literary, his literature fundamentally political. His 'Recreations' in *Who's Who* listed 'Anglophobia' but from the first his heart was open to English as to any other friends. What enraged CMG, and supplied the fire for the cross of his crusade, was the Scots self-consumption on the embers of the dying Empire. Scots horizons were still darkened by the goggles of an outworn imperial chauvinism, Scots perceptions still stifled by the gentilities of empty shrines. The future depended on Scottish fire, not on an English torch with a dead battery By Appointment to His Majesty. The Empire whose sun never set from the Boston tea-party to the Indian Mutiny might survive, half-ghost, half-toast, in east-coast thrift ('ye'll have had your tea?') or a postcard of a red-nosed, kilted Scotchman providing the last Scottish Enlightenment. Even Scotland's national identity expressed in the cult of a folk-poet and song conservationist, the Burns Supper had become its own form of self-prostitution. The very love and literature whence it derived alike screamed against its synthetic profanation: and here Hugh MacDiarmid began his new Scotland with *A Drunk Man Looks at the Thistle*. CMG had begun teaching Bible classes at

Langholm South United Free Church in 1905, and now he charged his country with having sold her birthright for a mess of pottage (chapter-heading for Genesis XXV, Geneva Bible, 1560).

He made allies and acquaintances in his cause, from the philanthropic, resourceful R.E. Muirhead, to the visionary moral renewer A.G. Pape, from the amiable marine engineer sixth Duke of Montrose to the veteran Socialist writer and former MP R.B. Cunninghame Graham. With the novelist Compton Mackenzie he built up a passionate unity against English and Scottish parochialism alike, addressing an audience of 3,500 people in Glasgow together in October 1928, and an audience of one early in 1929. He identified Compton Mackenzie not with native Scots such as Linklater (born in Wales but firmly indigenised in Orkney) so much as with displaced Scots of sophistication and elegance such as Hector Hugh Munro ('Saki') and Norman Douglas whose barbs of humour crackled off the page. They mutually inspired one another. In a radio broadcast in November 1929 Mackenzie spoke of 'our wild Scots rose ... white, and small, and prickly, and possesses a sharp sweet scent which makes the heart ache' which CMG turned (only later signing it Hugh MacDiarmid) to:

> The rose of all the world is not for me.
> I want for my part
> Only the little white rose of Scotland
> That smells sharp and sweet – and breaks the heart.

Mackenzie quoted the poem at a Bannockburn rally with Cunninghame Graham in June 1932, noting that MacDiarmid's 'lyric has been perhaps the best loved of all he wrote' (*My Life and Times Octave Seven* 1931-38, 1968). (It now anonymously graces the identifying cards attached to 'Jacobite Roses' on sale in Scottish garden centres: there's immortality!) Both CMG and Mackenzie relished their literary crusade of 1928, including CMG's journey to the newly devolved Irish Free State in August with the veteran nationalist, the Hon. Ruairi Erskine of Mar. (It was the beginning of a life-time's individual success in fighting Irish parochialism towards Scotland, whether he knew it or not.) He met the Opposition leader Eamon de Valera, had tea with the Minister for Defence (Garrett Fitzgerald's father Desmond), stayed with Joyce's Mulligan-Antinoös Senator Oliver St John Gogarty, made friends with the editor of the *Dublin Magazine* Seumus O'Sullivan, and walked through the street of Dublin with an admirer of his poetry, W.B. Yeats at 1am on a Saturday morning, jointly urinating in the middle of the street ('I crossed swords with him', i.e. they played the schoolboy trick of bisecting one another's streams). It legitimised Scottish nationalism as a revolution of the intellectuals, indeed of the creative artists. CMG may not have reflected that Irish nationalism in its present phase had disposed of its poet-founders in the Easter Rising of 1916 and Censorship Board and Catholic clergy were teaching the rest their place. He rode on the winds, and they blew him and what he was founding in all directions.

John MacCormick's memoirs *The Flag in the Wind* (1955) would describe CMG as 'politically one of the greatest handicaps with which any national movement could have been burdened', instancing his 'love of bitter controversy', his 'extravagant and self-assertive criticism of the English', and his mingling of the Social Credit philosophy of Major Douglas with the doctrines of Karl Marx. Historically, both CMG and 'King John' were necessary for Scottish nationalism. MacCormick could have made a stronger case against CMG: Major Douglas and Karl Marx made less peculiar bedfellows than CMG's campaigning for a party solicitous of electoral votes while hurling out experimental pronunciamenti that Burns was as out of date as democracy. MacCormick worried, as a good machine politician should, that 'the more sober-minded of the Scots' would find CMG 'sufficient excuse to condemn the whole case for Home Rule out of hand'. It was well for Scotland that MacCormick's eyes were fixed on something as nineteenth-century as Home Rule. It was much less dangerous than Sinn Fein, with or without Gogarty in his Senate or Yeats cross-culturing his urine, or than the discarding of democracy. It was thanks to MacCormick, in part, and to Home Rule's derivation from non-violent agitation, that Scottish Nationalism avoided the tragedies of twentieth-century Irish nationalism. In fact Scottish Nationalism would take major ideological steps in personal rejection of war regardless of imprisonment, as exemplified by Douglas Young, and later Michael Grieve (stances with which the defender of violence CMG would sympathise more than did its opponent John MacCormick); and the groundswell of support for Scottish Nationalism in the 1950s won its activist spurs – and blisters – through marches against nuclear installations and rocket-ranges destined for the islands and the Scottish west coast. But the apathy that ground down the spirits of Compton Mackenzie and CMG in 1928 and even more in the deeper world depression year of 1929, only blanketed without extinguishing the awakening of modern Scotland in response to CMG's multi-layered, multi-natured, multi-ideological explosions, challenging everything in all possible forms. MacCormick was entitled to show with pride that he had raised his flag: but the winds in which it flew came from MacDiarmid's bag. 'You will find where Odysseus wandered,' said Eratosthenes, the geographer from Alexandria, 'when you find the cobbler who stitched the bag of winds.' You may also find where Odysseus's country wandered too.

But the winds dropped. Scotland may have been shaken to its foundations, especially when the young party came within 36 votes in 1928 of electing Cunninghame Graham Rector of the University of Glasgow whose successful candidate was the Prime Minister Stanley Baldwin: and these votes were from students, a testament to the future, especially in the subsequent battle in the same field where Mackenzie would win. Muirhead in the May 1928 West Renfrewshire election received 1667 votes as an Independent Scottish Nationalist, and Lewis Spence had 800 votes in a 40,000 poll in North Midlothian. Muirhead and MacCormick lost their deposits in the 1929 General Election. As MacDiarmid had written before the heady days of 1928, in a poem 'Ulysses' Bow':

> Better violer never screeded on a silken coord,
>   Or kittled a cat's tripes wi's finger-en's,
> But the lift is yalla as biest milk,
>   And the eagle roosts wi' the hens,
> And the licht o' life is lourd,
>   And the voices nocht but men's.

In the despondency of 1929, CMG heard less human voices: he heard the Sirens, in fact, with their customary disastrous effect. T.S. Eliot's Prufrock had doubted whether the mermaids (who in his version seem to be offspring of the Sirens) would sing to him: but CMG was more optimistic – or, as it would prove, pessimistic. Eliot would indeed be one of the Sirens, the thought of whose music drew CMG to London. Eliot was human, certainly, despite the severity of his attire as an English banker which he showed little desire to discard having become the poetry editor at Faber's; but Eliot was an institution as well as a person, editor of the *Criterion* as well as publishing director, self-transformation from a son of Missouri via avant-garde Bostonian into the High (Anglican) Priest of the Modern establishment.

Yeats was evidently one of the makers of the new Ireland (discounted by its rulers by now, but CMG's ebullience and emulation would not realise that). Poets were on the rise; and (tell it not in Gath) residence in London seemed a stage in their progress. Yeats and Eliot saluted MacDiarmid as their fellow, and each of them had won their place in the literary world partly because of London residence and media links. Compton Mackenzie became the most immediate Siren in offering to CMG the editorship of *VOX*, the journal of radio criticism he had promoted. It seemed modern, influential, a means of capturing Scotland which so far remained resistant to more than transient preachment of Scottish nationalism. CMG liked the attachment to the modern medium. Unlike him, neither Yeats nor Eliot were at ease in public speech, least of all with their own verse. But CMG knew well enough that the critic is but a judicious step from the creator, as Shaw had shown for the theatre. He saw that radio could command a nation, as Joyce recognised the potential in cinema, twenty years earlier. He would be proved right in the 1930s but by then *VOX* had failed, as Joyce's cinema speculation had proved comparably premature. Radio might well have been improved by a well-established independent critical journal, but the BBC wanted no such thing. Ironically, MacDiarmid's very last regular journalism was in the Scottish edition of the *Radio Times*, in which his reviews of the week's programmes in the late 1970s outshone all of his colleagues in occasional flashing of tooth and nail.

4. *All Fools' Eve,* 2001

Of Seamus Heaney's book of poems *Electric Light* (Faber, 2001), the *Guardian* reviewer complained that the poet's approach 'to find in the myths and bogs of Ireland metaphors and symbols of tribal violence' meets critics 'who find these symbols and metaphors ill-judged, too easily finding an artistic resolution of the acute and insoluble problem'. Which problem? Northern Ireland. Since the reviewer goes on to dislike Heaney's use of Greek legends, shall we denounce Homer for making the siege of Troy artistically intelligible?

Heaney's sonnet on the Augean stables ends in news of the murder of a friend in a Gaelic Athletic Club grounds:

> And imagined
> Hose-water smashing hard back off the asphalt
> In the car park where his athlete's blood ran cold.

Heaney has crusaded for the celebration of an Ulster larynx drawing its intonation and affirmation from English, Irish, Welsh, Scots origins, and if there is one Greek image the Ulster of his time would recognise and regurgitate, be the users Pape or Prod, it would be the Augean stables. Prods would use it about Papist squalor, Papes would use it about Prod corruption, and neither would even notice its familiarity in the other's mouth. Heaney's 'Augean Stables' suddenly takes the comfort of the old myth, sure in the efficacy of its cleaning, and shows the Heracles of his time – the athlete – become part of the 'deep dung strata' to be cleansed with a force whose very violence is mere cosmetic.

'Over and again', downsizes the *Guardian* reviewer, 'Heaney vigorously affirms the role of the poet, while remaining vague as to what that role is'. As Yeats asked, how can you tell the dancer from the dance? Heaney's vagueness is the vagueness of God in creation: does the maker define? MacDiarmid, venerating and violating the icon of Lenin, defined the art of being a poet in gigantic measurement much as Heaney in his whole practice defines it:

> Ah, Lenin, you were richt. But I'm a poet
> (And you c'ud mak allowances for that!)
> Aimin' at mair than you aimed at
> Tho' yours comes first, I know it.

The thunder of MacDiarmid's polemic hid the gleam of schoolboy absurdism. His engagement in ideological supremacy would have won singularly little enthusiasm from Lenin, had such propaganda fallen within his jurisprudence, and he does it with a rhyme blatantly impudent in its doggerel. And then the gloves are off, Celtic identities are declared, and Lenin is suddenly juxtaposed by the arch-counter-revolutionary of all time, Edmund Burke, followed by the James Joyce who so indignantly refused to see him off from Zurich as he embarked for the Finland Station in St Petersburg in 1917:

> An unexamined life is no' worth ha'in'.
> Yet Burke was richt; owre muckle concern
> Wi' Life's foundations is a sure
> Sign o' decay; tho' Joyce in turn
>
> Is richt, and the principal question
> Aboot a work o' art is frae hoo deep
> A life it springs – and syne hoo faur
> Up frae't it has the poo'er to leap
>
> And hoo muckle it lifts up wi' it
> Into the sunlicht like a saumon there,
> Universal Spring! for Morand's richt –
> It s'ud be like licht in the air –

In the last lines of the 'Second Hymn to Lenin' MacDiarmid's affectionate mockery reduces Lenin to a mere runner-up, indeed a necessarily inadequate and dwarfed yardstick for the poet's work:

> Unremittin', relentless,
> Organized to the last degree,
> Ah, Lenin, politics is bairns' play
> To what this maun be.

Damn right. The unacknowledged legislators have far greater constituencies than the acknowledged. But *Pravda* would not have cared for such sentiments, had it become aware of them. The *Guardian* review concludes by admitting Heaney's 'spiritual optimism, a sense of celebration and hope. Heaney's poems say "yes"... But yes to what, exactly? In a postmodern age, confronted with pressing and global ethical and political questions, this is a premodernist, nostalgic poetry reaching back to romanticism: nature, God, the ineffable, the sublime. Reliable, reassuring: yes, yes. But something more, surely, is required.'

Is there a finer 'postmodern' epiphany of the absurd than poetry eliciting the question 'yes to what, exactly?'?

What is at stake here is that Heaney wants us to work our way out of mutually destructive political and cultural lethal chambers, and that in so doing he is calling on our ancient roots, roots in common to unite us instead of parasite growths with which we can stifle and strangle one another. Common Christianity has become our means of self-destruction, however valid its foundation. CMG might agree, even at his most atheistic: he universalised Christ and wrote of God with more affectionate humour than any poet since Byron. Heaney offers the classics, whether Greek, Roman, Anglo-Saxon, middle English, Scots, as common ground for Ulster rivals in quest of identity. His poetic agenda is so big, in fact, as to be invisible to the parochial metropolis. Like MacDiarmid and MacCaig, he enlists with élan, whether in the formal challenge of the former or the quiet ironies of the latter. Fundamentally he offers the hope of real identity within his own poetry. If Ulster cannot find that identity, it is doomed, and nothing will grow on its waste land.

What CMG as MacDiarmid, as himself, as so many others, fought for, was what Heaney fights for too. He was reinventing Scotland, as Heaney now seeks to reinvent Ulster, and like all good reinventions the work is composed of much of what formerly was known and visible and has only been lost to sight in recent years. The issues which dominated the life and works of Hugh MacDiarmid, Christopher Murray Grieve, are as much before us as ever.

A Note on the Text

All editorial material in the text is given in square brackets. In most cases, texts of the letters have been transcribed from manuscript sources whose library provenance is noted; occasionally we have used printed sources, noting the periodical in which the letters were published, where that is known. The form used for dates has been standardised. CMG often dated months by number and separated the numbers of the days, months and years at various times by dashes, obliques or dots. The dates are also located at different places on the page. Our standard is to give the month in full and the full date, to the right of the page. Where letters have no date, we have tried to establish one and we have given such dates in square brackets. In the line addressing the recipient, we have left commas, full stops, or a lack of punctuation as written. For the most part, we have observed CMG's idiosyncrasies of spelling, only noting [*sic*] where there is a likely confusion that may make the text resemble an editorial rather than an authorial curiosity or error. Inconsistencies such as reference to *A Drunk Man Looks at the Thistle* as, variously, 'a *Drunk Man*' or '*The Drunk Man*' are CMG's. Where a small word has been omitted we have, very occasionally, inserted it in square brackets.

Acknowledgements

Our first thanks are due to Deirdre Grieve, for her aid, advice, encouragement, patience, inspiration, knowledge and kindness.

Acknowledgements to individual correspondents who supplied us with letters received are due to Ian Campbell, Morag Enticknap, Nancy K. Gish, Christopher Grieve, Walter Grieve, Betty McEwan, Robert H. McGavin, Alistair Macintosh, Christine Macintosh, Donald and Ann Macintosh, Edwin Morgan and Desmond O'Grady. Ewen MacCaig has kindly given us permission to reproduce the poem 'Slow Twilight Ended' by Norman MacCaig as a note to the letter dated 8 December 1952, but asked us to point out that Norman MacCaig did not preserve the poem in his own later collections.

Our thanks are due to the Institute for Advanced Studies in the Humanities at the University of Edinburgh where Alan Riach held a Fellowship from February to April 1995 and December 1996 to February 1997, working on MacDiarmid; and to the University of Waikato (New Zealand) Faculty of Arts and Social Sciences Research Committee and the Dean and Pro-Deans of the Faculty, who have generously supported work on the 'MacDiarmid 2000' project. The Department of Scottish Literature at the University of Glasgow has also supported the publication of this book with a generous subvention towards the cost of indexing, a task accomplished by Helen Lloyd, to whom we are very grateful; Mrs Jean Anderson, School of English and Scottish Language and Literature Information Technology Development Officer at the University of Glasgow provided invaluable computer support.

Thanks for personal kindness and generosity towards the project are due to the late W.R. Aitken, Kenneth Buthlay, Angus Calder, Professor David Daiches, Professor George Davie, Professor Douglas Gifford, Professor Duncan Glen, John Manson, Professor Edwin Morgan and Glen Murray; Professor G. Ross Roy and Dr Patrick Scott of the University of South Carolina; Captain J.A. Riach and Mrs J.G. Riach; Mrs Rae Riach; and Professor Marshall Walker and Dr Jan Pilditch of the University of Waikato. Thanks are also due to the late Elizabeth Balbirnie Lee; Bonnie Dudley Edwards; Sara Parvis; Dr Paul Parvis; Caroline Cullen; Rosemary Gentleman; Gloria Ketchin; Gordon Wright; Christopher Grieve; Lucien Grieve; Walter Grieve; Christine Grieve Macintosh; Morag Enticknap; Nicholas Enticknap; the late Norman MacCaig; the late Timothy

O'Keeffe; Catherine Lockerbie; Llew Gardner; Neal Ascherson; Richard Demarco; Tom Nairn; the late Father Anthony Ross; Professor George Shepperson; the late Valda Grieve; Dr Murray Simpson; Sir John Drummond; Sandy Neilson; Hamish Henderson; Bob Tait; Dr Isobel Murray; the late Matthew P. MacDiarmid; Billy Wolfe; Dick Platt; Dolina MacLennan; Dr Margaret Bennett; Colin Franklin; Dr Leila Dudley Edwards; Dr M.A. Edwards; Dr Jennifer Litster; Professor Alastair Fowler; Dr Roger Savage; Professor Cairns Craig; Dr Ronald Stevenson; Arnold Kemp; the late Dr Robert McIntyre; George Bruce; Maurice Lindsay; the late Sorley MacLean; the late Sydney Goodsir Smith; Hazel Goodsir Smith; Angus Pietz; Jim Haynes.

We would also like to make grateful acknowledgement to the trust of the MacDiarmid Estate, and to the professionalism, commitment and patience of Carcanet Press, especially Michael Schmidt and Robyn Marsack, and that of the typesetter, Grant Shipcott.

Most grateful thanks are tendered to the staff and Trustees of the National Library of Scotland (Edinburgh) and to Edinburgh University Library (letters published with permission), especially Ms Jean Archibald; the Mitchell Library, Glasgow, particularly Hamish Whyte; Tessa Ransford, Robyn Marsack, Penny Duce, Elizabeth MacGregor, Angela Blacklock-Brown and to all the staff of the Scottish Poetry Library (Edinburgh); Lorna Knight, Curator of Manuscripts, Division of Rare and Manuscript Collections, Cornell University; Courtesy LLIU Lilly Library, Indiana University, Bloomington, Indiana

Alison Fraser, Principal Archivist, The Orkney Archives, Laing Street, Kirkwall, Orkney; Brian Smith at the Shetland Archives, Lerwick and Mrs Jacqueline Irvine, Shetland; the University of Waikato Library, particularly the indispensable services of the reference and interloans department. We are particularly grateful to those who typed the book from CMG's hand: the staff of the University of Waikato IJK Word Processing Centre, particularly Gail Bidois, Samantha Fitzpatrick, Lois McMillan, Christine Mackness, but most of all Lorraine Browne-Simpson: their professionalism, expertise, understanding, encouragement and good humour have been more than equal to all that has been demanded by the material, its author and his editors.

The Scottish Arts Council generously awarded Dorian Grieve a Travel and Research grant and we are thankful for that.

Above all, the editors thank Michael Grieve, as the guardian of his father's reputation, as a friend, and as a father.

Library Abbreviations

BMT	Biggar Museum Trust
CUL	Cornell University Library (The Division of Rare and Manuscript Collections, Cornell University)
EUL	Edinburgh University Library
HRHRC	Harry Ransom Humanities Research Center, The University of Texas at Austin
LLIU	Lilly Library, Indiana University, Bloomington, Indiana
McMUL	McMaster University Library (The William Ready Division of Archives and Research Collections, McMaster University Library, Hamilton, Canada)
NAS	National Archives of Scotland, HH 55/557
NLS	National Library of Scotland
NLS DFF	denotes the Drafts and Fragments file of letters which were found among CMG's papers
The Orkney Archives (The Orkney Archives, Kirkwall, The Ernest Walker Marwick Collection, reference number D31/61/6)	
SUNYB	State University of New York at Buffalo
UDL	University of Delaware Library, Newark, Delaware
ULL	University of London Library, MS 978/76/254
URL	University of Reading Library
WUL	Washington University in St Louis (Special Collections, Washington University Libraries)

Our gratitude is due to the staff of all these institutions and to the many others – including private holders – whose MacDiarmid MSS were either not used or non-existent but who kindly met our enquiries and selflessly helped us in our search. Librarians make work such as ours possible; without them we are nothing.

Hugh MacDiarmid Grieve (C.M. Grieve): A Chronology

1892   Born Arkinholm Terrace, Langholm, Dumfriesshire.
1899   Moved to house in Langholm library. Entered Langholm Academy. Age 7.
1908   Pupil teacher, Broughton Higher Grade School and Junior Student Centre, Edinburgh, age 16.
1911   Death of Father. Journalist in Wales. 19.
1912   Returned to Langholm. 20.
1913   Met Peggy Skinner when journalist in Cupar. Moved to Fife to work on *The Forfar Review*. 21.
1915   Enlisted in RAMC. 22.
1916   Served in Salonika. 23.
1918   Invalided home with cerebral malaria. Married Peggy Skinner. 26.
1919   Moved to Montrose. 27.

1920   Moved to Kildermorie, Easter Ross & Cromarty. Edited *Northern Numbers*. 28.
1921   Returned to Montrose, worked on *The Montrose Review*. 29.
1923   *Annals of the Five Senses*. 31.
1924   Daughter Christine born. 32.
1925   *Sangschaw*. 33.
1926   *Penny Wheep*, *A Drunk Man Looks at the Thistle*, *Contemporary Scottish Studies*. 34.
1927   Founded Scottish centre of PEN. *Albyn*. 35.
1928   Founding member of National Party of Scotland. Visited Ireland; met Yeats. 36.
1929   Son Walter born. Moved to London to edit *VOX*. 37.

1930   Separated from Peggy. *To Circumjack Cencrastus*. Met Eliot. 38.
1931   *First Hymn to Lenin*. Met Valda Trevlyn in London. 39.
1932   Divorced by Peggy. Moved to Thakeham in Sussex. Son Michael born.
      Second Hymn to Lenin. Scots Unbound. 40.
1933   Moved to Whalsay in the Shetland Islands. Expelled from National Party of Scotland. 41.
1934   Joined Communist Party of Great Britain. *Stony Limits. Scottish*

	Scene. At the Sign of the Thistle. 42.
1935	Breakdown. Hospitalised in Perth. 43.
1936	*Scottish Eccentrics*. 44.
1938	Expelled from Communist Party. 46.
1939	*The Islands of Scotland*. 47.
1940	*The Golden Treasury of Scottish Poetry*. 48.
1941	Conscripted for National Service. 49.
1942	Left the Shetlands for Glasgow. Joined SNP. Final break with brother Andrew. 50.
1943	Worked in Merchant Service. *Lucky Poet*. 51.
1944	Unemployed in Glasgow. 52.
1945	Worked for the *Carlisle Journal*. 53.
1947	*A Kist of Whistles*. 55.
1948	Left SNP. 56.
1950	Visited USSR. Moved to Dungavel House, Strathaven. 58.
1951	Moved to Brownsbank Cottage, Biggar, Lanarkshire. Met Neruda and Hikmet in East Berlin. 59.
1952	Son Michael jailed for objection to conscription. 60.
1955	*In Memoriam James Joyce*. 63.
1957	Rejoined Communist Party. Visited China. *The Battle Continues*. 65.
1958	Visited Bulgaria. 66.
1959	Visited Czechoslovakia, Rumania, Bulgaria, Hungary. 67.
1961	*The Kind of Poetry I Want*. 69.
1962	*Collected Poems*. 70.
1964	Visited Canada. Communist Candidate for Kinross and West Perthshire. 72.
1966	*The Company I've Kept*. 74.
1967	Visited the USA. 75.
1971	Visited Italy and met Ezra Pound. 79.
1973	Visited Ireland. 81.
1976	Visited Canada. 84.
1978	Visited Ireland for Hon. Litt.D. from University of Dublin. Died 9 September, aged 86. Buried in Langholm 13 September. *Complete Poems* published.

PART ONE

The 1920s

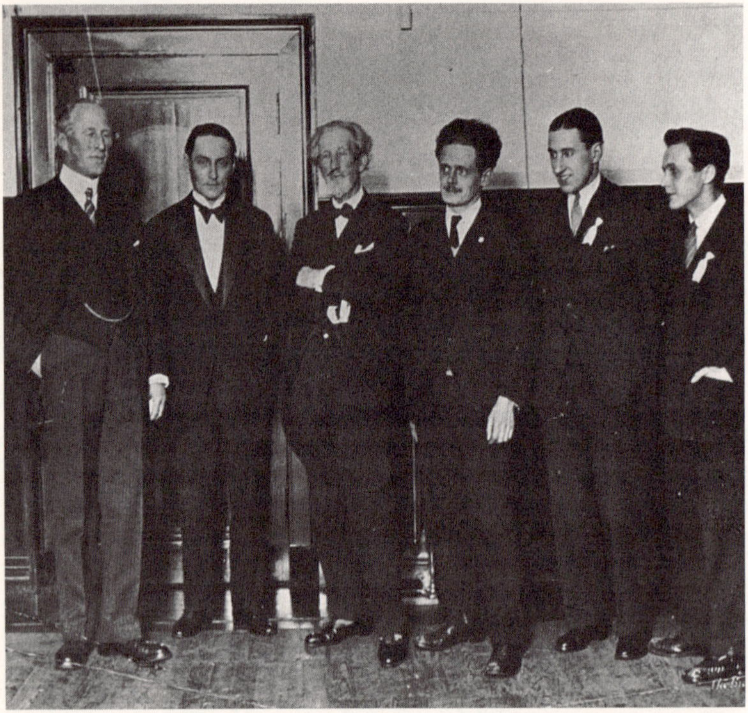

1. *To Andrew Graham Grieve (EUL)*

Kildermorie Forest Lodge, Alness, Ross-shire   29 October 1920

Dear A: –

What has happened to you? I am beginning to wonder if you still survive.

Peggy[1] has been away for a fortnight today, and I do not expect her back for another fortnight at any rate.

I have been very busy. I think you know I am, inter alia, schoolmaster here – hours 9am to noon, 2pm to 4. But apart from that, I am engaged upon three books: –

1/ *In the Tents of Time: Post War Essays* edited by me.[2] Contributors Joseph Lee, L.A. Pavey, R.W. Kerr & self, with critical intro. by John Buchan – to be published in the Spring.[3]

2/ *The Road To Spain*. A description by Pavey & I of our Pyrennean trip – practically completed – full-size book – partly travel, partly political, partly literary: with two sequences of poems.

3/ *Certain Contemporary Scottish Writers* – a book dealing with Neil Munro, John Buchan, Charles Murray etc. etc. which I am busy writing, for publication by Leonard Parsons in the Spring.[4]

In addition I think Foulis will publish my *Cerebral & Other Studies*[5] (the first of a sequence of 10 similar volumes – presenting aspects of current psycho-analytical and aesthetic speculation in imaginative form) in the Spring; and he is at present considering the proposition of issuing *A Scottish Chapbook* monthly under my editorship.

I have just completed a series of 4 articles – on T.S. Cairncross, John Ferguson, Joseph Lee, and R.W. Kerr – for the *National Outlook*, an Edinburgh weekly you perhaps know. I expect that on T.S.C. to appear next week or next again.[6]

Negotiations are also proceeding happily for the launching of *The New Scotsman*, which will be similar to *The New Statesman* in get-up.[7] Foulis[8] was coming up to see me this month about it again: but hasn't managed yet. I am hopeful that the first number will be out about Easter.

Poetical dramas by me will shortly appear in *London Mercury* and *English Review*. I had a most encouraging note from J.C. Squire[9] the other day.

During the past fortnight I have also turned out 41 sonnets of a projected sequence of 50 – to be called 'Sonnets From the Highland Hills'.[10] Competent critics assure me that these include some of the finest work I have done: and will give me a premier place in contemporary Scottish poetry as soon as they are published. Blackwell, Oxford, will publish. But the majority will appear in various periodicals first.

I have other irons in the fire: but that rapid outline may be sufficiently interesting to you to go on with in the meantime.

What of yourself?

I am anxious to secure without delay 3 small volumes of translations by Jethro Bithell, viz.
> Contemporary French Poetry
> Contemporary German Poetry
> Contemporary Belgian Poetry

published by Walter Scott Publishing Coy. (I think) at 9d originally.[11] They will probably cost 1/3 or so each now. Will you please make every endeavour to secure copies for me in Edinr. – Thin's or Baxendine[12] may have them – & send them on: and I will refund cost and postage.

If you see an article in *Edinr. Evening News* on 'Scottish Literature After the War' the initials A.K.L. will be recognisable.[13]

A scrappy & egoistic letter – but what other do you expect?

Write soon and give me your news.

Love to Ciss & Betty.[14] Yours Frat., Chris

P.S. Enclosed proofs (which you needn't return) may interest you.

P.S. You might also please look up *Who's Who* for me and see if you can find the addresses of: – William Canton. James Bryce. J. McDougall Hay. Sir George Douglas. Sir Ian Hamilton. Ronald Campbell McFie.[15]

---

1. Margaret Cunningham Thomson Grieve, née Skinner (1897–1962) CMG's first wife; see Appendix.
2. Neither this work nor *The Road to Spain* was published, nor have their MSS come to light.
3. Joseph Lee (1878–1949), acquaintance of CMG from his army days; several volumes of his war poetry were published and a selection from these appeared in *Northern Numbers* (1921). Leonard Arthur Pavey (1888–?), British writer and journalist. Roderick Watson Kerr (1893–1960), sub-editor of the *Liverpool Post* and founder of the Porpoise Press (1922) with John Gould and George Malcolm Thompson, who, with Kerr, had attended Broughton School under MacDiarmid's mentor, George Ogilvie. John Buchan, first Baron Tweedsmuir (1875–1940), best-selling novelist, Tory MP for the Scottish Universities (1927–35), lawyer, poet, critic, editor and biographer – eventually Governor General of Canada.
4. Neil Munro (1864–1930), Scottish popular novelist, poet, journalist, editor of the *Glasgow Evening News* (1918–27), to whom *Northern Numbers* was dedicated. Charles Murray (1864–1941), Aberdeenshire-born poet, writing chiefly in Aberdonian dialect. Individual chapters of the proposed book appeared in *The Scottish Educational Journal* in 1925–6; it was eventually published in expanded form as C.M. Grieve, *Contemporary Scottish Studies* (London: Leonard Parsons, 1926).
5. Eventually published by CMG himself as C.M. Grieve, *Annals of the Five Senses* (Montrose: C.M. Grieve, 1923).
6. Thomas Scott Cairncross (1872–1961), Minister of Langholm South United Free Church (1901–7), novelist and poet. The young CMG attended his Sunday school. John Alexander Ferguson (1879–1928), Scottish poet and author, occasionally writing in Scots, editor of the *Fortnightly Review*. These articles appeared between December 1920 and March 1921.

7. Although advertisements for subscription appeared in the *Scottish Chapbook*, no periodical was launched under this title.
8. Timothy N. Foulis, eponymous owner of the Edinburgh-based publishing company.
9. Sir John Collings Squire (1884–1958), English author, literary editor of the *New Statesman* and editor of the *London Mercury* (1919–34). CMG's poetical dramas did not appear in either of the journals to which he refers.
10. Sonnets I–V appeared in *Northern Numbers*, Second Series (1921), and VI–XI in the Third Series (1922); no others from the cycle survive.
11. Jethro Bithell (1878–1962). His *Contemporary German Poetry* (1909) first introduced CMG to poets such as Rilke and Carl Spitteler, and it was from these volumes that many of his translations into Scots were made.
12. Edinburgh bookshops.
13. 'Scottish Literature after the War' by A.K.L. (Alister K. Laidlaw – one of CMG's pseudonyms) appeared in the *Edinburgh Evening News*, 28 October 1920. There he writes, '*Northern Numbers* is not merely a book, but a movement'.
14. AGG's first wife and daughter.
15. William Canton (1845–1926), author of religious and children's books, poet. James Bryce, first Viscount (1838–1922), British jurist and statesman, Regius Professor of Civil Law at Oxford (1870–93), a supporter of home rule and university reform. John MacDougall Hay (1881–1919), Scottish novelist, father of the poet, George Campbell Hay. George Douglas, Scottish literary critic, commentator and anthologist. Sir Ian Hamilton (1853–1947), General in WWI, leading the Gallipoli expedition. Ronald Campbell McFie (d. 1931), poet, concerned with the synthesis of science and poetry, writer and doctor of medicine.

2. *To Andrew Graham Grieve (EUL)*

Kildermorie Forest Lodge, Alness, Ross-shire   1 February 1921

Dear AGG.

I am surprised not to have heard from you again ere this. It is curious that your search should still be proving so fruitless. Reviews are still coming in. There was a five column special article signed W.J. in *Glasgow Bulletin* 17/1/21 – classing Buchan, Munro, etc. as the old school – singling out Cairncross as the worst of the lot – and Kerr, Ferguson, Lee, V. Jacob[1] & yourself & myself as the heralds of a Scottish Renaissance. I had 'more talent and latent power than any other contributor to *N.N.*'[2] but got a slating for the use of words like 'inoppugnable' etc.

I am now anxious to get material in for second series as rapidly as possible. It is to be published in November next: so time is short. Space should run to about 3 poems each. New contributors will, I think, include Lewis Spence, Isabel K. Hutchison, Sir Ronald Ross & General Sir Ian Hamilton.[3] Please forward any MSS as soon as possible.
[MS ends]

1. Violet Jacob (1863–1946), Montrose-born poet and novelist, best known for her poems in Angus dialect.
2. *Northern Numbers*, being representative selections from certain living Scottish poets, [ed. C.M. Grieve] (Edinburgh: T.N. Foulis, 1921).
3. Lewis Spence (1874–1955), Scottish poet and a founder member of the National Party of Scotland (1928). Isobel Wylie Hutchison (1889–1982), Scottish horticulturist, Honorary Editor of the *Scottish Geographical Magazine*, published four volumes of verse and a novel. Sir Roland Ross (1857–1932), Nobel Prize-winning Scottish physician, and author.

3. *To Andrew Graham Grieve (EUL)*

Kildermorie Forest Lodge, Alness, Ross-shire   5 February 1921

Dear AGG

You are an Invisible Sphinx these days. What has come over you? Have you taken a vow to write no letters until after a given date? Or what?

Did you see A.K.L.'s articles on the Bolshevist Robert Burns in the *Edinr. Evening News* of 18th ult. – about a column? They seem to appreciate my stuff, as Peggy points out, when they can't keep an article written to appear on the 25th longer than the 18th.

Have you seen the splash in *The Nat. Outlook* (February) – my article on Ferguson, amounting to about a page, and then, following it, a review of *Northern Numbers* about 1½ cols. long? From internal evidence I guess that the reviewer is the Rev. Lauchlan MacLean Watt. I think he is after inclusion. Will Ogilvie writes suggesting that he should be given it. I don't quite see my way however.[1]

Nice letter from W.O. He's coming in again. So is your bête noire, and my good friend, John Buchan – who writes a most encouraging letter and who, incidentally, is doing me another favour by writing a preface to a volume of Post-War Essays.

Cairncross is going strong. My article in *N.O.* seems to have done the needful. I think he will soar into an appropriate fame shortly. On my recommendation Foulis read C's latest vol. of poems *The Contented Man* – and is, I think, likely to publish it. It will broadbase C's work in a desirable way.

I too have been in a good vein recently: and have completed (and despatched to John Lane[2]) another vol. of poems – mainly vers libre and longer flights in the genre of 'La Belle Terre' – entitled *The Following Day: and Other Poems*.[3]

This makes 5 volumes now in hands of publishers – exclusive of the Essays: and the next series of *N.N.* with which I am now anxious to make headway.

Please let me hear from you on the matter shortly – if not enclosing

MSS then indicating what you are going to do.

This 2nd *N.N.* must mark a big advance. We are all determined that it shall. I hope that you will manage to get the necessary time to let me have something really good and significant. I shall be glad to see whatever you care to send, in first draft if you like, and give it both editorial – and fraternal – attention.

My special object in writing however just now is with reference to another project.

The New Scotsman.

Quotations for a monthly or weekly are out of all bounds. To finance the former capital to the extent of £40000 would have to be sunk. Foulis is unwilling to do this in the meantime: and of course even at the best compensating profits could hardly be secured. The matter will be reconsidered as soon as costs of production fall. Even the most enterprising publisher has to ca' canny in the meantime.

I am however convinced that the times are favourable in every respect save the commercial – and not unfavourable in the latter in the sense that provided the initial capital is low ventures are clearing themselves. A Scottish Literary Revival is coming beyond question – and we must be in the forefront of it. If we can get first in the field there is going to be a rich harvest in a few years.

Accordingly, leaving over to a more convenient season the flotation of a monthly or weekly, I have decided to start a periodical miscellany of Scottish prose & verse – *The New Scotsman.*

Blackwell, of Oxford – one of the best, most enterprising and most artistically distinguished of contemporary publishers – is really taken with the idea and is willing to publish – provided that the first issue is subsidised to the extent of £100 – £150.

This is only fair. More reasonable terms could not be procured anywhere. The subsidy is of course only a contingent one i.e. an undertaking to recoup possible losses up to a sum not exceeding £150. I am not able just now to take up this myself altogether. I have too many other irons in the fire. So I want help – in £25s.

I know you have had a great deal to do lately. What your present position may be I do not know. But of course if you took up one £25 any loss would not have to be made good until next Autumn – i.e. until the book had been published and a sufficient time had elapsed to see how it went.

I can promise a particularly strong first number.

Please let me know whether you can or can't come in as soon as possible. Profits would be divisible in proportion of course.

Love to Ciss & Betty and yourself from both. I was glad to hear from Mother that Ciss was better. Hope that betterness continues.

Yours, Chris

1. Reverend Lauchlan Maclean Watt (1867–1957), poet, minister of Glasgow Cathedral (1923–34), moderator of the general assembly of the Church of Scotland (1934). Will(iam) Henry Ogilvie (1869–1963), Scottish poet.
2. John Lane: a London publishing company.
3. No such volume was published. 'The Following Day' appeared in *Annals of the Five Senses* (1923).

4. *To Andrew Graham Grieve (EUL)*

Kildermorie Forest Lodge, Alness, Ross-shire   Sunday [1921]

Dear AGG.

MSS for the 2nd Vol of *NN*[1] are now arriving. Everybody is doing his 'damnedest' to excel. I have already received several splendid things. I am determined that by hook or crook – preferably the former – you will again be represented, and I am going to extend your time limit – I will give you another 6 weeks. This is a prelude to my criticism of the poems which reached me yesterday. None of them will do – none of them come within miles and miles of doing. Believe me I am most particularly vexed to have to say so. I have some idea of the sacrifice of time – of the patient wrestling with material – of the difficulties of all kinds – which have gone to their making. No one will be more anxious than I am that you should do well – no one will ever more readily recognise merit of yours when it appears. But – they simply won't do. If I printed one of them even as it stands I should become not a target for criticism – which wouldn't matter – but a laughing-stock. I am anxious that you should ascertain that in these remarks even I am giving you not only the fullest justice but tempering it fraternally. I have just had the unpleasant experience of having to return Kerr's submitted work for similar reasons. If you doubt my judgement in the smallest particular – in justice to me let me send on these poems to Cholly, not saying whose they are but simply asking him for a detailed criticism of them.[2]

Your 'three main ways' of writing poetry will never produce a poem or anything else in the form of art, leaving out the difficult matters of inspiration, freedom or limitation in the choice of metrical vehicles, the qualities of diction in so far as they inhere with predilections and antipathies which suit or unsuit them for various forms and various subjects, poetry consists of

1. Having something to say.
2. Saying it poetically – that is to say with the maximum beauty, clarity and appropriateness. Poetry is the literature of power and the most concise medium man has devised for the expression of emotion. Any figure of speech that is not absolutely relevant, any work which either in its sound, shape, or suggestions is not strictly congruous, to the business of creating

a given impression is out of place and utterly impermissible. Every word, every figure of speech, every associated idea should, as it were, emit convex rays which go to build a dome of thought or feeling.[3] The adjectives must 'shade' together – the whole must be a harmony – with 'grace-notes' if you like: but without interruptions, digressions, irrelevancies.

It would take far too long to try to explain in writing what precisely is wrong with a hundred and more words and images in these poems. I question even if I have the analytical skill to do so – or if you have the desire or ability to follow me in subtle artistic arguments.

To be brief however, the following lines are all right: –

> 'Forget-me-nots abloom within him still
> But rooted by the well-springs of his tears.'

> 'The pillars Time, Eternity the span.'

> 'The shallow streams go, babbling on their way,
> What deeper waters hesitate to say.'

But no other phrase or line in the whole is either passable poetry or prose. 'Hill-Track' is painfully pedestrian. Poetry cannot deal with ethics or morals by way of such images as 'searching steeps of Truth' or 'tracks of wayward youth'. They are poor pulpiteering even.

Poets do not ('Earthbound') kiss 'chastely' – nor are they 'High Rulers'. The lines that follow in this poem are reminiscent of a melodramatic moment in a Sexton Blake detective story. Here – as in most other places – your work is hopeless because of an utter absence of reality. What poets whose biographies you know ever fell over crags, etc.? It is no defence to say that you are using the image metaphorically – metaphors must be congruous. These are incongruous – 'lied and foully cursed' is bathos, 'driving by grading lust' suggests on the writer's part either an amusing instance of terrified innocence or prurient puritanism, while what the poets were doing in these labyrinths with 'scutcheons' on is inconceivable. 'Beasts of low estate' is in the worst tradition of the general echo.

Take 'Love of Remembrance' – what relevancy has the bit about Time, oars & fragile bark – to the dreamful words of love with which you began, or to the fruited autumn hill at the end? It must be a land-ship. Take it from me that, no matter what the symbols are, they must taken together form a sequence of ideas – one suggesting the next – each springing naturally, or at all events *possibly* from the other – and each in its turn serving to bring out more clearly the underlying idea or emotion and each moving with art, with spontaneity, and advance in beauty & power to a climax, or gracefully & appropriately receding from one. And there is something radically wrong if the whole sequence cannot be envisaged as an effective, easy continuity – unless, that is, the subject flows through the poem as a river flows and each metaphor or word or idea is reflected in it or seen on the banks with precisely the same naturalness and orderliness with which the various but harmonising colours & images in and [*sic*] trees, hills, flowers etc. by a beautiful river are seen by a beauty-loving eye.

An instance of this impossible incongruity: –

No one thing can wing like wayward gulls & sail like Byzantine ships. And why B. ships? – a word is not poetical because it is foreign or fine-sounding. How do B. ships differ from others?

Another incongruity, or worse: –

How can words 'express' a weft or threads?

When is a poet laurelled – why do you make him 'sing the furnaced sun'. Poets don't do that sort of thing. Druidic bards once did, perhaps.

How can a song be 'spun' from colours? An Irish bull! How can your voice be *on* your *breast*?

Moonlit streams are, in actual fact, the reverse of luminously clear.

How can you guide the course of a quenchless flame – or a swung censer – the fact that you are really referring to your soul simply shows that you cannot, once you have likened one thing to another proceed to deal with attributes or aspects of either which both do not (to some extent) share – if you do you achieve if not a mixed metaphor, the effect of one. And such an effect once destroys a poem – such an effect several times (as in all these poems) renders it not merely not poetry: but not sense.

An obstectrical point – when is 'an infant fain for birth'? 'When all the best is yet to be' is ludicrously familiar & would ruin 'The Hound of Heaven'[4] or *Paradise Lost* if interpolated therein.

The second last stanza of this poem ('Beauty') illustrates all your vices at once. You ask to be soaked in spray: to have flowers sown on your lips: to have your art made a target (and 'soaring art' is grotesquely immodest): and to be decorated with seaweed – now you cannot be a person standing by fountains of music and a shore at the same time: – the images clash in all directions at once.

The last stanza again illustrates the impossibility of evoking an incongruous image & then passing without giving time for its assimilation in the current of your thought to another – a thing can't be a sunset, a bridge and a painter. You cannot pass from particular to general, from abstract to concrete, from personal to impersonal – just as your vocabulary dictates. You must be unfailingly coherent – scrupulous in the choice of words, bending them to your needs not letting them run amok. And in the final analysis of a poem you must express pointedly with apt and cooperating illustrations something substantive.

Now if you will take my advice, adopt a simple verse form, avoid abstract conceptions as you would the very devil; express sensible human feelings – not grandiose sensations in regard to great art, love & the like: be concrete, particular, definite, and in every verse see that you embody a substantive idea expressed with economy and effectiveness – and see that each succeeding verse carries the same idea or mood a stage further in a natural reasonable progression of thought or feeling.

Try short things – regular verse forms – model on poems in books you have handy – if you find say a poem on 'Sunset at Dover' in precisely the same verse-form and with precisely the same manner write one on 'Sunset at Langholm' – paraphrasing the former into your own words and changing placenames etc. to suit. Such exercises will help you greatly.

I wish I could have a long talk with you.

I am far sorrier perhaps than you will believe to have had to write this – do something short, simple, pointed, and *true*: and give me a real chance to congratulate you.

I will return your poems one of the days this week: and write then also on other matters.

Love – Chris

---

1. *Northern Numbers*, 2nd Series, ed. C.M. Grieve (Edinburgh: T.N. Foulis, 1921).
2. Cholly. A nickname for George Ogilvie (1871–1934), English teacher at Broughton Junior Student Centre under whom CMG studied to become a teacher (1908–11). A number of his pupils were inspired by him to go on to have careers in the field of literature. He acted as mentor to CMG and kept in correspondence with him from 1911 to 1932.
3. 'And the winds and sunbeams with their convex gleams,/Build up the blue dome of the air' – Shelley, 'The Cloud'.
4. 'The Hound of Heaven': popular poem by Francis Thompson (1857–1907).

5. *To Andrew Graham Grieve (EUL)*

[March 1921]

Dear A.

I am sorry to have been so long in writing. I greatly appreciated the spirit of your reply to my last letter. My willingness to initiate you into whatever I know is only conditioned by my difficulty in keeping abreast of my correspondence – a growing one! However send me stuff whenever you like. I'll not fail to be faithful with it.

Before I forget

1/ Review of *N.N.* appeared in a recent *Spectator* – I did not see it. Can you hunt it up and tell me the terms of it? I understand that it was a trifle cavalier.

2/ Review of *N.N.* Squire tells me in early *London Mercury* if it did not appear in Feb. or this month's one. Failing these, will you keep your eye on the April issue.

3/ Please try to get me particulars of the battle-histories of the flags in

St Giles – which battalions bore them, in what wars.

I enclose two attempts, both of them successful – particularly the first – to fit your two finest phrases in appropriate forms. The last five poems you sent me show an advance, I think – they have the same faults as the first ones but in much less flagrant terms. They fail because they are not organic – they do not achieve any real synthesis – and they do not come to life round any fine figure or splendid phrase as all real poetry must. The two lines I marked as good are still jewels set in tin.

You fail because you do not carry your preliminary thoughts far enough – until you induce the necessary hyper-aesthesia to raise your conception to the nth degree and clothe it in that rhetoric which cannot be used in ordinary consciousness. Amongst the errors you should be particularly careful of are: –

1/ Failure to carry any comparison to its logical conclusion.

2/ Carrying a figure too far – as in your reference to slopes and seas of love – the effective extendibility of such a phrase is distinctly limited

and 3/ Any tendency to permit mere words to lead you away from your original intention. Whatever else you may achieve you will never achieve poetry if you alter the sense as you go along to suit the words in the matter of rhyming or anything else. You must bend your words to your will. And do not try to say too much at once. Stevenson well said 'There is only one art – to omit'.

Do not be discouraged. Out of Miss [Agnes] Falconer's two volumes – and practically all her work appears in *Glasgow Herald*, *Westminster Gazette*, etc. – I could only find one short poem worthy of *N.N.* and told her so. [MS ends]

6. *To John Laidlaw (EUL)*

[December 1921]

Dear Old John

Delighted to hear from you.

Difficulty of living on 24 hours per day still my main one.

Enclosed our rag! But it doesn't disclose anything of my output. If you get *Edinbr. Evening News* 'AKL' is my old nom-de-plume. I have had a variety of letters, poems & articles in there lately. Also Aberdeen, Dundee and Glasgow papers.

N.N. 2 has gone splendidly. My own book is coming out shortly.

Will write you a decent letter in course of week.

In haste now.

Kindest regards to all, from both.

Chris

7. *To John Laidlaw (EUL)*

The Scottish Chapbook, 16 Links Avenue, 24 January 1923
Montrose

Dear John: –
I was delighted to have yours.
I really expected to hear from you some months ago: because I thought you would note that I must have lost your and Mackay's[1] addresses – which I did: hence my device of sending to 'Laidlaw, printer, Lockerbie' and 'Mackay c/o Laidlaw etc.'. At the same time I lost the cuttings of Mackay's verses you gave me, and which I meant to reproduce in the local paper here. I am glad Mackay is going strong still. Has he abandoned the idea of putting out a book? I had thought to have heard from him anent this.
Glad the *Chapbook*[2] continues to interest you. It is finding increasing favour in lots of directions: and I am quite satisfied with the support it is receiving. You will observe that that rude half-relation of yours and half-MacConachie of mine – A.K. to wit, of the clan – has been abominably rude again in the current issue. He's a wild chap.
Many thanks for interesting note reproduced from *Sunday Chronicle*. This 3rd series of *N.N.*[3] has lifted the venture definitely out of the rut. Reviews have been all I could wish for. Even the *Times Literary Supplement* gave us over ½ a col. The result was immediately appreciable in orders. I see pars have been appearing in all sorts of papers to which no review copies were sent. Some were sent to the *Sunday Chronicle*: and I've no notion who was behind that particular little puff.
The first time I can give M'Diarmid a holiday I'll make him do some of the more modern Scots verse you suggest. In the meantime he is hopelessly held. His 'Kist o' Whistles'[4] instalments are generally written in an accidentally free half-hour. You'll see F.G. Scott (who used to be a teacher at Langholm Academy and is now as Mus. Doc. and a composer of considerable powers) has set the 'Country Life' verses to music: and that I intend to give his setting with an early *Chapbook*.
I'm speaking in London on 12th Feb. Intend going up about 3rd: but am very sorry that will not be able to come your way this time either going or coming. I have other breaks to make which will necessitate taking the other line. Needless to say, I should have immensely enjoyed another crack – but we must just postpone that to the summer time, when you visit us here! Don't forget!
You did not congratulate me upon my safe return to Montrose Town Council. Yes, the electors put me in quite comfortably. They also returned me unopposed to the Parish Council. So I am on practically every public Board here now. What a life!
Glad Willie and Nellie[5] landed safely in Australia & hope that you have had good news of them by this. Maggie would feel their going-away

intensely, I know. I hope they do well: and believe they will.

Excuse more in the meantime. This is a scrappy letter: but I am up to the eyebrows and this new weekly paper is an overwhelming task. I hope to launch it in mid-April: but am completing arrangements when in London.

Bar colds we are both well and hope you both are too. Also Mackay to whom my best respects.

With kindest regards from Peggy & self.

Yours as ever.

Chris

P.S. But for the fact that you are an experienced printer I should almost have had to apologise for my handwriting – which certainly doesn't improve with keeping.

Tell Maggie Peggy has just got a new set of clubs – in readiness.

---

1. Eneas Mackay. See Appendix.
2. A monthly periodical edited by CMG, running August 1922–December 1923.
3. *Northern Numbers*, Third Series, ed. C.M. Grieve (Montrose: C.M.Grieve, 1922).
4. Poems 'From "A Kist o' Whistles" By Hugh M'Diarmid' appeared in *The Scottish Chapbook* from November 1922. Some reappeared in *Sangschaw* and *Penny Wheep*, others only in *Complete Poems*, but none were in *A Kist of Whistles* (1947).
5. John Laidlaw's son, and daughter-in-law. Maggie Laidlaw née Cairns, John Laidlaw's wife, worked at Langholm Library where the young CMG had been voracious reader.

8. *To R.E. Muirhead (EUL)*

Scottish Home Rule Association,   24 February 1923
Local Secretary: C.M. Grieve, 16 Links Avenue, Montrose

Dear Sir: –

I have now gone very thoroughly into the whole question of launching the new Scottish weekly (which will be called, not the *New Scotsman* – owing to copyright difficulties, which would only be surmountable if we took the matter to the House of Lords – but *The Scottish Nation*) and I have reason to believe that the moment is exceptionally opportune for such a project and that a thoroughly-well-run-and-well-produced periodical devoted to Scottish interests, on the lines, roughly, of the *New Statesman* but slightly more popular in tone, will command a very considerable measure of support throughout Scotland and among Scots abroad.

The first thing is to determine exactly what line the new paper will take. I have discussed this very fully with all sorts of people and come to the conclusion that we shall be on a very sound basis if while essentially nationalistic and devoted in particular to the Scottish Home Rule issue (i.e. giving space weekly to well-written articles advocating Scottish Home Rule from various angles, in addition to emphasising the need for this apropos of current events in our 'Notes of the Week' and leaders), the new paper is radical in politics, sympathetic to Labour but in no way committed to the political Labour party and stressing Scottish social and economic issues from the broad angle of comprehensive nationalism rather than in any party-political way. That is to say – the new paper will be non-party but progressive and devoted to all Scottish social-reform, liberal, and advancing tendencies. So much for the 'Notes of the Week', leaders, and special articles on political, social, economic and industrial issues. Apart from these this paper will be predominantly a literary one – written in a bright, interesting and fully-informed way, with emphasis on the Scottish national point of view and its differences from the English point of view, and giving space to a poem or two, a literary article or essay, a short story, book-reviews, and musical, art, and dramatic criticism. These will be mainly by Scottish writers – the poems and stories will have for the most part Scottish subjects and settings – and the various critiques will emphasize Scots music, Scots plays, etc. rather than English.

The second thing to determine is if a sufficient supply of articles, etc., of good enough quality will be forthcoming and in this connection I have been fortunate enough to secure promises of contributions, etc., from all the right people. I am confident that we can give Scotland an entirely worthy organ in every respect. Nothing of this sort exists at present.

What is proposed then is a 24 pp weekly, 3 cols. to page, with one or two line or wood-cut illustrations by Scottish artists – well-printed, on excellent paper.

The cost, all included (i.e. production and distribution) would be roughly £100 per week for 25,000.

Suppose we had net sales of only 10,000 – and judging by the experience of similar periodicals elsewhere we shall be very ill-supported if we cannot secure more than that – at 3d per week, that would mean a weekly revenue of £125 from sales alone.

One of the best advertising agents in London (for the type of advts upon which we would mainly rely – publishers etc.) is prepared to risk his reputation, given a 10,000 circulation, upon a minimum from advts from sources outside Scotland of £20 a week for the first year.

I have an extensive knowledge of Scottish advertising and know that with such a circulation an equivalent sum at the very least can be secured from Scottish advts.

That means, then, a weekly expenditure of £100 and a weekly income of £165, with 25,000 copies distributed each week.

I propose to form a limited liability company and to complete the arrangements in order if possible to launch the periodical early in May. We shall not require a great deal of capital: and you will note that the basis indicated above is equivalent, if it materialises even on what may be regarded as the minimum of the probabilities, to at least 25 per cent (allowing for cost of initial advertising, cost of blocks, certain payments to contributors etc.) profit on the turnover.

I am putting the formation of the Company into the hands of Mr J. Cargill Cautley, solicitor, Town Clerk of St Andrews: and I do not think we shall have very much difficulty in raising the necessary amount. We shall, however, require a certain amount of outside help and I venture to hope that you will see your way to invest in the venture. We are, however, issuing no prospectus just yet: and if you or any of your friends desire to come in financially I shall be glad if you will let me know at your earliest convenience. There may be other prominent members of the Association who might like to have a financial interest to a small extent in such a project. If so, I shall be happy to communicate with them.

Apart from that I hope to secure the solid support of the Association as a whole and beg to thank you for your offer to bring the matter before your Executive.

As I have indicated besides being nationalistic throughout, I propose to run a regular weekly article (all articles will be signed) dealing with a given phase of the Scottish Home Rule question. These articles will be about 1500 words each. Not only will they be complete in themselves, however, but they will be part of a programme – taken together they will cover the whole field from, in the course of a year, fifty-two different angles. This will represent a very large extension of the output of Scottish Home Rule propaganda literature. Arrangements can be made at nominal cost to reproduce certain of these in pamphlet or booklet form.

I am also prepared to devote a page (as the *New Leader* for instance devotes a page to 'The ILP at Work') to 'Towards Scottish Home Rule', summarising and commenting upon important meetings during the week or other propagandist developments, and giving a certain number of launch reports – if secretaries will send paragraphs in.

In return perhaps your Executive would be prepared to suggest to branches that they might take a certain number of copies weekly? I have no idea of course what the circulation of *Scottish Home Rule*[1] is: but if your Executive would circularise the branches and, ordering in the aggregate, distribute to the branches in the same way as you now send out the News-Sheet, I would, of course, be willing to give the Association the same terms as are given to newsagents – 6d in the dozen.

I shall be glad if you will put the matter in this way before your Executive. Although I have marked this letter private and confidential you will, of course, use the information contained in it as you may consider necessary, and if you think any of your friends would care to join the proposed Coy. you may disclose the whole of the details to them provided they in turn regard them as confidential.

Hoping to hear from you at your earliest convenience and thanking you in anticipation.

Yours faithfully, C.M. Grieve

---

1. The monthly news-sheet of the SHRA, funded by Muirhead.

9. *To R.E. Muirhead (EUL)*

The Scottish Chapbook, 16 Links Avenue, Montrose   20 March 1923

Dear Sir: –

Many thanks for yours dated 16th inst. I sent you a dummy copy of proposed new paper yesterday: so you will see exactly the lines upon which I hope to go. You will notice that we had to take another name than that at first intended. We would have had to carry the matter to the House of Lords before justifying our right to call it *The New Scotsman* – and the game wasn't worth that candle.

I know, of course, how very busy you are: and I am indebted to you for the interest you have taken in this matter. But for a plethora of claims upon my own time, too, I would have come to Glasgow in the hope of talking the whole thing over with you. I note that you have not yet had an opportunity to discuss the project with many whom you think might be interested.

Given a good initial publicity campaign I do not think it will be difficult to secure a circulation of 10,000 and upwards. I have taken the *Forward* for years and there are, of course, reasons for the comparative delimitation both of circulation and advt revenue of labour and socialist papers. That is why I propose to give this new paper the tone of, say, *The New Statesman* or *The Nation* rather than of *The New Leader*. A well-known London advt. agent told me that he could do absolutely nothing for me if I made the new paper an out-and-out Labour one: if I made it a radical one with labour sympathies, but predominantly a literary rather than political organ, he thought it would do very well indeed and he would certainly be able to attract a good deal of advertising our way.

I know the outs-and-ins of *The New Tribune* and *The National Outlook*. The reasons for their failure were threefold 1/ inadequate publicity (probably owing to inefficiency of initial capital); 2/ the fact that they did not secure good advt. representation (if *The New Tribune* had secured proper advt. representation *at the outset*, as they were endeavouring to do just when the collapse came, they would have been going yet); and 3/ the fact that the literary standard was simply not high enough to command attention.

The Scottish Nation will be all right as far as 2/ and 3/ are concerned. In the estimates I gave you, I gave expense of producing 25,000 copies (if the circulation was only 10,000 this would be very considerably less), whereas, on the revenue side, I gave the bare minimum for advts. Even if only 5000 copies sell per week the paper will clear itself. Office and editorial expenses, generally a heavy item, will be practically non-existent, for the first year at any rate, on the lines I propose to run it: while I am in a position to get 9/10ths of the contributions free, – and from all the best writers available.

As to other papers overlapping, the Hon. R. Erskine[1] assures me that when the proposal to start a new paper for the SNL in place of the *Standard* comes up at the National Council this month he will urge that instead of doing so the SNL should financially & otherwise accept and support the *Scottish Nation*. He assured me himself in London that he will not restart the *Scottish Review* until he sees how the *Scottish Nation* goes.[2]

I welcome the unofficial suggestion you throw out all the more because if both the S.H.R. Assocn. and the S.N.L. could unite to the extent of concentrating upon making this one organ serve both their purposes it will go a long way to guarantee its success.

Please do not imagine that I am heedless of your advice. I know perfectly well what a fight it means to establish a new paper. But I believe it can be done in this case – given adequate capital. Eleven out of every twelve papers (which have a chance on the face of it even) fail because they have not enough capital to keep going until they can turn the corner.

There is no periodical in Scotland at present which deals with art, letters, music, etc., from the national point of view: and in regard to politics I think that the time has come to make a very bold bid – to try to clinch matters – and that can only be done if we have as good journalism on our side as there is on the other side. As the question of Scottish Home Rule comes nearer practical politics there is ever increasing need for the discussion of Scottish internal affairs, economic and administrative problems, etc., in a way for which no existing periodical affords scope.

    Yours faithfully, C.M. Grieve.
P.S. I shall hope to write to you again shortly on this matter.

---

1. Hon. Ruaraidh Stuart Erskine, of Mar (1869–1960), founder of several periodicals, the Gaelic Academy, the Scottish National League (1922) of which he was also president, and a founder of the National Party of Scotland (1928).
2. A weekly periodical, edited by C.M. Grieve, running 8 May 1923–25 December 1923.

10. *To Andrew Graham Grieve (EUL)*

16 Links Avenue, Montrose   Wednesday [27 June] 1923

Dear Old A.

    This is 3 am and I am not through yet but my prolonging inability to find time to reply to your welcome letter is getting on my conscience and as I am not anxious to put any undue strain on that tender organ here goes – and you must just excuse haste, pencil, and other defects.

    I was unfeignedly glad to hear from you and will be to see you when opportunity permits. I hope you'll all avail yourself of the first chance you have to come up here. I'm pretty well tied just now and only get anywhere on business rushes. I'm off on Friday to London – returning again on Monday. I won't smell holidays this year: but am packing Peggy off for a month or so. But I have found it absolutely essential if I'm to keep up the pace to get some outdoor exercise – so I've taken up golf au serieux – 18 hole round or as many holes as possible every night barring Sunday.

    Yes! I'm working pretty hard – and not for money either. The lucre will come in course of time if things go all right: but in the meantime it's a profitless and thankless task. Otherwise I would not have it. But things are developing otherwise. I mean a Scottish Renaissance *is* coming. The pioneer stage is almost over: the solid conservative stage is beginning. The foundations appear to have been well laid: we've builded better than we knew, *vide* Saurat's interpretation of one of my poems in next week's (3rd July) *S.N.*

    Also, as Hugh M'Diarmid, I am making a name for myself – being set to music – translated & appearing in all sorts of Continental papers etc.

    Add to local *Review*, *Chapbook*, *Nation*, original writing, articles in *Glasgow Herald*, *Scots Pictorial*, and *Forward*, arduous labours as a Town & Parish Councillor, member of School Management Centre, trustee of various charities & manager of several Institutions, & peripatetic chairman of I.L.P. and Unemployed Union indoor & outdoor meetings, and you have all the personal details about me that are to be had.

    I keep fairly fit on the whole – have a more fiendish temper than ever – just as much hair – and even more, *vide* Beard – and Peggy also keeps pegging away. Our domesticities are singularly uneventful.

    There isn't much in this letter. But at least I have replied to yours and that's something. I like getting letters and detest replying to them – which is not ununderstandable in view of the fact that I get so many more letters than I could possibly answer anyhow that my powers of replying are being slowly sapped altogether.

    I'll make no brotherly-in-law or avuncular advances in the meantime. I'm not any better at that sort of thing. But this conveys every good wish from P & self to you all – and I hope I haven't forgotten anything important I should have said – but if I have write in & complain & I['ll] deal with

the matter in due course.
    Love, Chris

11. *To R.E. Muirhead (EUL)*

The Scottish Nation Editorial Offices: 4 July 1923
16 Links Avenue, Montrose

Dear Mr Muirhead: —
   I have come back from London to find your letter awaiting me. Stewart is right. The paper has really fallen between two stools. Certain articles — Spence's and Lee's — did us a considerable amount of harm both with readers and advertisers. As you will see by our July 3rd issue we have remodelled a little. I am as convinced as ever that there is a good field for a Scottish weekly paper of this kind, predominantly literary, but its public takes a little time to find, and we began at a bad time.
   I went into matters thoroughly in London. I find that my advt man there is in a position to guarantee a minimum revenue from advts for the year beginning 1st Sept next of not less that £1200, — from London publishing houses alone. I made independent inquiries amongst publishers and found that he absolutely is the best literary advt. agent in London and thoroughly trust-worthy.
   That means that even with our present circulation we will be able to keep going at a slight profit for twelve months at any rate, *if we can survive this month and next*. To do that however I need £120 more than I can yet reckon upon. The £30 (£5 per week for 6 weeks) which you so generously offer would be a quarter of it: but unfortunately I cannot hit upon any source for the other 3/4s so far.
   It will be all the more unfortunate if the *S.N.* goes down in face of these facts — for, for a venture of its kind, it has really done splendidly all things considered, and given a little time on the lines we are now adopting it can make good apparently.
   Money is, of course, very difficult to get just now and I am afraid that I have scant hopes of securing that £150 in time.
   If I could get a loan of that £120 I would be in a position to repay it by Christmas whatever happened: but I have no security to offer and I know of no one who will lend me that sum at present merely on my personal promise to repay.
   Still £120 is not a great deal of money and since it would put us right for at least 14 months — by which time the paper would have had a proper chance in every way — I shall do my very utmost to raise it and will greatly appreciate anything you can do to help me. Again thanking you for your most generous offer.
   Yours faithfully, C.M. Grieve

12. *To R.E. Muirhead (EUL)*

The Scottish Chapbook, Editorial Offices: 1 November 1923
16 Links Avenue, Montrose

Dear Mr Muirhead: —

Many thanks for your encouraging letter of 29th ult. I have received various promises of help but by no means sufficient yet, although I have yet to hear from a good few folks, and Col. John Buchan, Mr Will of the *Graphic*, and others are working to secure help.

I should be greatly indebted if you could broach the matter to Sir Daniel Stevenson.[1] Then if he was inclined to consider it and wished to see me, I would make a point of coming through to see him at Glasgow at any time convenient to him and going into the matter with him fully. As matters stand I am badly tied: but, given a definite appointment and a fair chance of help, I'd manage to get away.

Please treat the following facts as confidential but quote them to Sir Daniel or read him this letter. The paper would require very little to be self-supporting — but 'it's just that little, and how much it is!' Five hundred more readers and a couple of columns more advts per week would do it. We are only losing about £9 per week. Circulation (average during past 6 months 3500) brings in about £30. Advts. have averaged about £6. Total cost is just over £45. 3500 is *net sales*. Gross circulation is about 5000 now.

Our circulation both at home and in the colonies has been restricted through lack of publicity, due to want of money to advertise. Almost every post brings letters to show that the writers have just heard of the existence of the paper. A few judicious advts in home and colonial papers would almost secure us the necessary increase. Colonial subscriptions keep dribbling in. Even at the present rate if it continues for a few more months we will acquire a substantial overseas mailing list. It is only a question of time.

3500 does not seem a great circulation: even so, it compares favourably with London literary papers like *The Saturday Review*. Especially so considering the short time we have been in existence and the lack of preliminary booming.

As to advts we antagonised advertisers at the outset by our insistence on Scottish national politics and by labour sympathies. But the ring of hostility so set up has now been broken: and if we keep going advts. will come. It isn't a question of circulation only. Quality of circulation counts. Fisher Unwin and other advertisers already find that advts in the *S.N.* bring them business.

£500 will, I am quite sure, enable us to continue till we turn the corner. Even £300 may do it: but £500 would enable us to seek an increased circulation more quickly than the rate at which — very slowly but surely — we are acquiring it. On the whole we have, I think, done well all things considered: and a little assistance now will enable us to carry through our experiment to success. Surely the *Scottish Nation* is almost unique in the history of journalism – I do the editing, proof-reading, book-keeping, despatching, correspondence and a great deal of the actual writing single-handed in an already-limited leisure.

I am extremely sorry to hear that the Scotland's Day Demonstration did not pan out well financially. The whole movement hangs fire in a way that is simply inexplicable to me.

I sent you cuttings – you would see that I raised the question of affiliation at Montrose Town & Parish Councils. Better luck next time. As soon as I can possibly find time I shall start a branch here – I know of at least a dozen prospective members now.

You mention that you could send me a few names to which I might apply. I should be glad if you would. I want to exhaust every possible avenue before giving up. But, in the meantime, it will be a great favour if you could see Sir Daniel and put the facts I have stated before him.

Thanking you in anticipation, and with every good wish.

Yours faithfully, C.M. Grieve

---

1. Sir Daniel Macaulay Stevenson (1851–1944), Lord Provost of Glasgow (1911–14), head of D.M. Stevenson & Co., a coal export business, founded Chairs of Citizenship, Spanish and Italian at Glasgow University.

13. *To R.E. Muirhead (EUL)*

The Scottish Nation, Editorial Offices: 27 November 1923
16 Links Avenue, Montrose

Dear Mr Muirhead

I am infinitely obliged to you for all that you have done, and tried to do, for *The Scottish Nation*. I am sorry, however, that Sir Daniel Stevenson did not see his way to ask me to meet him and go into the whole matter with him. I think I could have proved to him that we had a fairly good chance of winning through on half £500. Or at any rate that the experiment was worth making and that £250 would have enabled us to go on long enough to make it.

As matters now stand I am afraid that the *Nation* must be stopped just at the moment when it seems to be turning the corner and prospects are becoming good. I believe I can get the £400 he stipulates – but not in time! That is the trouble. If Sir Daniel, however, will go just one better and give his £50 now, it will save the situation and give me time to get decisions from others likely to help.

Erskine of Marr has discussed the whole position of the *Scottish Nation* with a friend in London who has intimated his willingness to help: but who cannot see me until after the General Election is over to go into detail. I am confident of substantial assistance from this source if I can [keep] carrying on for a week or two pending my interview with him.

John Buchan is very keen on not letting the *S.N.* drop: and is taking the matter up with wealthy friends. But here again matters cannot materialise in time – unless something is forthcoming this week to enable us to continue pending the result of these efforts.

Dr Macgillivray[1] and many other well-known Scots are keenly interested: and very anxious indeed that the *S.N.* should not go down at this juncture. Mr Will, Managing Director of *The Graphic*, has promised financial assistance himself, and is taking the matter up with well-known London Scots.

So you see, many efforts are being made to save the *S.N.* The pity is that unless something is forthcoming this week (pending the result of other efforts) these effects cannot develop in time.

There is every probability that I shall be able to meet Sir Daniel's conditions: but it will take me a week or so to do it, and that delay is only possible if I get at least £50 now. I earnestly hope that a chance along these lines may be given me. I ask for it simply because I am confident that even that would enable me to pull through yet. If you can continue that I shall be tremendously obliged. If not the paper must discontinue now, at the very moment many friends are mobilising to save it.

Again thanking you & Sir Daniel most sincerely.

Yours faithfully, C.M. Grieve

---

1. (James) Pittendrigh MacGillivray (1856–1938), Scottish sculptor associated with the 'Glasgow School' of artists, nationalist and poet.

14. *To Elizabeth Grieve (EUL)*

The Northern Review[1]   4[August/September 1924]
23 Paternoster Square, London, E.C.

Dearest Mother

I've been intending to write to you for several weeks: but have as usual been so busy that I simply couldn't write any letter I could get out of writing.

Peggy's mother came again yesterday: and we are busy getting packed up to return to Links Avenue on Tuesday. Peggy is splendid so far. Living here has done us both a power of good. I'm feeling exceptionally fit: and have all sorts of irons in the fire. I'm concentrating steadily on my Scottish verse – the Hugh M'Diarmid stuff – as Buchan has promised to see about publishing a volume of it for me as soon as he comes back from America (early in November); and Scott is always clamouring for more of it to set to music. Buchan's new anthology of Braid Scots poetry, *The Northern Muse*[2] is now out and contains a poem of mine – no little honour as only eight living poets are represented and the standard of selection was very high, only the very best that has been produced in the whole literary history of Scotland having been included.

I am still hoping to get to London soon. In any case I intend working harder than ever this winter, and I have given up all my public appointments – Town Council, Parish Council, etc. – to leave me free to go at it hammer and tongs. I'm getting old, and it's time I was getting a regular move on at last.

I'm to be in Edinburgh on 17th Oct. delivering the inaugural lecture to the Edinburgh University History Association & later on I am addressing the English Association in Glasgow.

How are you getting on with Otto Kahn[3] at Whittey-hame? He's a great man.

Did we tell you Wallace had started in business in Dundee as a wholesale stationer?

I had a visit from Mrs White from Langholm. Jim has done well at the Academy: and Jean is doing well too.[4]

You didn't say a great deal about your trip South, but I hope you enjoyed it. I'd like a run around the old scenes again too: but I'm afraid it won't be for a while. But perhaps I'll get a run down to see you sometime this back-end. I'd love to.

I wrote to Jenny Aitken, poor body, as nice a letter as I could.

We hope that Jimmie will beat even his own last year's record and win the Medal at the Show. Don't forget the snapshots. We're looking forward to seeing them.

Remember us to all friends,

With love from all here, Your loving Son, Chris.

P.S. I'll wire you all right when the time comes.

---

1. A monthly periodical edited by C.M. Grieve, running May–September 1924. CMG was actually writing from the Kincardineshire village of St Cyrus.
2. *The Northern Muse: an anthology of Scots vernacular poetry*, ed. John Buchan (London and Edinburgh: T. Nelson, 1924). It included 'The Bonnie Broukit Bairn'.
3. Otto Hermann Kahn (1867–1934), German banker, resident in America from 1893, Director of the Metropolitan Opera Company; in England during the war he was Vice President of the English Speaking Union and rendered conspicuous service to the Allied cause. Presumably Kahn was staying with A.J. Balfour at Whittingehame, where EG, as a nearby resident, may have met him.
4. Margaret (Maggie) Helen White née Laidlaw (1879–1962), CMG's cousin and John Laidlaw's sister, and her children, Jim and Jean White: see Appendix.

15. *To Chryssie and Andrew Graham Grieve (EUL)*

Montrose   Thursday [1924]

Dear Chryssie & Andy[1]

Sorry I haven't been able to drop you a line sooner. You'll be glad to know all's going well here so far; and that your niece, who arrived in the world with the substantial weight of 8 lbs and the quite considerable length of 21 inches, is evidently finding it to her liking to judge by the fact that she has put on an extra ½ lb since.

Peggy is also as well as can be expected.

What's in a name? A good deal apparently judging by the difficulty of deciding upon one: our decision is a compromise based on Peggy's name, my name & the two grannies' name, and will run Christine Elizabeth Margaret.[2]

Many thanks, A, for your prompt letter of congratulation (one of a pile that now I set to answering them seems interminable), and to you, Chryssie, for the fine warm frock etc. (I am writing this downstairs & without going up purposely to ask Peggy what to call it I am not sure I am referring to it properly), it is so good of you to have sent.

Excuse more at the moment. We're glad to infer from your letter that you are all well despite the disappointing weather.

Baby hasn't said anything yet about her uncle, aunt and little cousin,[3] but judging from her expression at times I'm sure she should.

Love from all to all. Yours, Chris.

---

1. Chryssie Grieve, Andrew Graham Grieve's second wife.
2. Christine Elizabeth Margaret Grieve, born 4 September 1924, CMG's first child; see Appendix.
3. Andrew Graham Grieve's daughter, Morag; see Appendix.

16. *To William McCance (NLS)*

16 Links Avenue, Montrose   22 November [1925]

Dear Mr M'Cance

I hope I have not been too egregious or gauche and wide of the mark in enclosed article. But it is difficult writing about people and people's work one doesn't know, and an art other than one's own. That matters little, however, against the fact that it's just this sort of thing Scotland needs said and 'thrieped' into it today. But let me know if there's anything too badly out of the drawing, as this article is to form part of a book which Leonard Parsons are publishing next Autumn. I can alter it here and there if you want me to: but not radically, as the type is being kept 'standing'.

On Scott's suggestion I have pleasure in asking you to accept enclosed book.

The Muirs[1] are here just now: and I'm hoping to have Scott down one of these weekends. I'm anxious to get on with the ballet business: but that needs talking over together, not writing about. I haven't been in London this year: but may manage down to a PEN Club dinner ere long, and, if so, will certainly give myself the pleasure of meeting you and Mrs M'Cance as you so kindly suggest.

Muir tells me you have photographs of most of your work. I wonder if I am asking too much if I ask to see one or two of these.

With every good wish to both of you.

Yours sincerely, C.M. Grieve

---

1. Edwin Muir (1887–1959), Orkney-born poet, novelist and critic and his wife Willa Muir née Anderson (1890–1970), novelist and translator.

17. *To William McCance (NLS)*

16 Links Avenue, Montrose   12 March 1926

Dear M'Cance

I have just heard from Scott. You are quite right about having somebody like Burt[1] to keep the Movement going. That's where it has failed all through. I established scores and scores – probably hundreds – of useful connections, but could not maintain and develop them. I am by nature an impossible correspondent and by circumstance even more impossible. I have extremely little spare time and in it is a choice between writing poems, articles etc. or writing letters. I can't do both. In consequence I am devilishly rude to almost everybody.

I was delighted to get the photos: and like some of them immensely. I am looking forward to seeing a great deal more of your work and Mrs M'Cance's at the first opportunity, and hope that by then the Steel Man will be a fait accompli, and that arrangements may be well forward to encourage brighter tombstones for Presbyterians.

The whole idea of a Scottish Renaissance has reached a stage when – even more than a connecting-link correspondent – it needs those capable of forwarding it being in close personal touch with each other.

Scott tells me of your proposed *Socialist Review* article. Curiously enough I have intended writing Strachey[2] myself (I don't know him personally) to offer him an article – not on the Scottish Renaissance business quite – but on The Case For Scottish Home Rule. But I've never found time.

My papers are in a deuced disorder but – in accordance with Scott's suggestion – I have hunted out, and herewith enclose, various things which may help. Scott told me he had sent you others.

I have three books coming out this year – *Penny Wheep*, a companion volume to *Sangschaw* this spring; and in the Autumn *Contemporary Scottish Studies* and the *A Drunk Man Looks at The Thistle* of which I sent you a column of extracts which appeared in the *Glasgow Herald* (and is the worse of sojourning since in my pocket-book!)[3] I'll send you copies of each in due course.

In connection with the latter I was wondering if you might do me either a frontispiece or some cuts or something. I haven't suggested anything of the sort to the publishers yet, but I am sure they'd be very agreeable.[4] You'd need to read over the thing in full first before deciding though: and it isn't quite ready. I want to touch it up here and there and add a little yet. Then I'll have copies typed and send you one and you can see what you think.

I expect you'd see the Muirs when they were passing through London.

Every good wish to Mrs M'Cance and yourself. I'll look forward to the *Soc. Review* article.

Yours, C.M. Grieve

---

1. William Burt (1883–1949), a former English teacher at Langholm Acadamy with F.G. Scott; he arranged a reunion of Scott and CMG in 1923.
2. (Evelyn) John St Loe Strachey (1901–63), editor of the *Socialist Review*, Labour MP (1929–31) before resigning to give his support to extremist political organisations, Minister of Food (1946–50) during the post-war food crisis and Secretary of State for War (1950–1) during the time of the Korean War.
3. Extracts from *A Drunk Man Looks at the Thistle* appeared in the *Glasgow Herald*, 13 February 1926, under the following titles: 'Hurricane' (ll. 2216–2235), 'Denoument' (ll. 369–376), 'Beyond Life and Death' (ll. 377–384), 'The Thistle' (ll. 309–316), 'The Better Part' (ll. 385–400), 'The Skeleton in the Cupboard' (ll. 2327–2334).
4. No frontispiece was included.

18. *To Khaikhosru Shapurji Sorabji (NLS)*

16 Links Avenue, Montrose   25 May 1926

Dear Sorabji: –

I have forgotten your private address and so am sending this through the *New Age* to you.[1] I should have written you long ere this, but for the Strike, which involved me in all kinds of unexpected difficulties and while it lasted completely monopolised my time and thoughts.[2] But though I have been long in acknowledging your kindness in sending me a copy of your great Organ Symphony, I am none the less grateful and appreciative. On the contrary. It was exceedingly good of you and I thank you heartily for it and for your inscription to my two selves.

Scott and I often discuss you and your work, generally on the basis of something you are currently saying in the *New Age* (in which, of late, you have been appearing all-too-infrequently for my taste). Indeed I was on the point of going through to Glasgow for a few days with Scott when your Symphony arrived. Naturally it is difficult for me to arrive at any real notion of your work in the absence of hearing it played. But I profoundly believe in it none the less – on the score of your whole general position as displayed in your criticism and in what I know of your compositions. For my own benefit I wish your 'arrival' were nearer than it is and that there was any probability of hearing your work in the near future: and yet, to encompass that, I would not have you abate your position in the slightest. I would have you always 'all out' – working at the Nth degree – on a plane beyond the furthest vista of the contemporary musical public – in a further dimension even. That, indeed, is what you do appear to me to be doing, and I can envisage no time at which a suspicious public (in Great Britain at all events) will come up to such a level as will make your compositions practical propositions. It is just a question whether, in all the arts, those who are really of any consequence today are not working on planes beyond the destiny of mankind as a whole – beyond what all but an infinitesimal percentage of the people can ever attain to any consciousness, let alone comprehension, of ... But I do not intend to bore you with such a discussion. I have complete faith in your work – in your whole general position as an artist – complete faith in its sheer rightness from the standpoint of art, into whatever region of permanent incomprehensibility that may lead the hoi polloi. For the rest, I shall venture to hope that I may yet, either in London or Glasgow, be so fortunate as to have an evening or two, with you on the piano.

In the meantime, please accept my congratulations and thanks, and every good wish.

Yours sincerely, C.M. Grieve

---

1. *The New Age*, a radical weekly periodical edited (1907–22) by A.R. Orage, and to which CMG contributed one early article (1911) and numerously between 1923 and 1931. Other contributors included Sorabji, Ezra Pound, George Bernard Shaw and H.G. Wells.
2. The General Strike, called by the TUC, occurred 4–12 May 1926 and included transport workers and printers.

19. To Mr McCreath (EUL)

16 Links Avenue, Montrose   6 December 1927

Dear Mr M'Creath

    Many thanks for your kind and most interesting and encouraging letter. I entirely agree with you that a definite big scale move such as you suggest, if properly taken, may appeal to the imaginations – and purses – of our countrymen in a way that what has been attempted hitherto has wholly failed to do. As you probably know things are moving and it is almost certain that the Scottish National Convention at its adjourned meeting on Saturday will agree to form a Scottish Nationalist Party – then the question of finance arises and it seems to me that your scheme is the way-out and that every effort should be made to get the necessary 3000 at £20 each.

    I mentioned the matter to Mr R.E. Muirhead, the Secretary of the Convention, and he writes today: – 'The extract you give from Mr M'Creath's letter shows that he at least has the right spirit. He has been a member of the SHRA since 1921 and I imagine he will be beginning to feel that things are not going on fast enough. To this view I most thoroughly agree, but would add that things just go on as fast as they are pushed! The scheme which friend M'Creath outlines might be carried out, but it would require a few competent enthusiasts who would button-hole our supporters up and down the country. So far we have not found a single one of the type required amongst the friends of the SHRA i.e. a "voluntary pusher" for funds to fight for our cause, one who will not be denied save some support from whoever he singles out as prey. I shall of course endeavour to make use of the extract (I suggested he should read it at Saturday's meeting – in case I can't be there to press it in person). If the Scottish National Convention decides to form a Scottish National Party the way will be open to make a new all-Scotland appeal for funds.'

    The time has undoubtedly come for a big fight and I shall personally do my utmost to ensure that the plan you propose is tried – that it gets adequate publicity – and I and my friends are, I assure you, as ready to do our share towards it as you are yourself.

    There is one other thing. I, like yourself, am a journalist and while I have perfected certain publicity arrangements in Scotland which ensure nationalist material of all kinds access to the majority of our Scottish local papers etc. and have, moreover, a wide free-lance connection which enables me to maintain perpetual propaganda in one form or other, I am cognisant of the fact that the national reawakening that is taking place in Scotland, and the widespread controversy aroused by Thomson's book and mine,[1] is creating a definite counter-propaganda now and an organised effort – especially on the part of the daily papers – to deny publicity of any kind to our propaganda; and this leads me to hope that you will do what you can – and use your colleagues as best you can – to prevent this move and to keep a continual stream of paragraphs and articles of all kinds about Scottish arts and affairs going in every possible quarter.

With every good wish. Yours sincerely. C.M. Grieve

---

1. George Malcolm Thomson, *Caledonia: or the Future of the Scots* (London: Kegan Paul, Trench, Trubner, 1927); C.M. Grieve, *Albyn, or Scotland and the Future* (London: Kegan Paul, Trench, Trubner, 1927).

20. *To Compton Mackenzie (HRHRC)*

16 Links Avenue, Montrose   9 January 1928

My dear Compton Mackenzie

When writing you c/o The Savile Club today to say how sorry I was that I could not get to Inverness after all, I forgot to ask a great favour of you.

With a view to having it out in good time for the Election, I have nearly completed the writing of a comprehensive volume on *The Scottish National Movement*, (70,000 words or so) and hope to get the typescript off to Allen & Unwin in the beginning of next week.[1]

The scheme of the book is as follows: –

Chapter I   1707–1925
Chapter II   The Scottish Renaissance Movement
Chapter III   Scottish Problems; Facts and Figures
Chapter IV   Emergence of the National Party; Programme, Personnel and Prospects
Chapter V   Analysis of Representative Opinions (in which I deal with Sir Robert Horne, Earl Balfour, Ramsay Macdonald etc.)[2]
Bibliography
Index

I think this will be very useful to have on the market prior to the Election.

Now for my request. I want Forewords from Cunninghame Graham and yourself, please.[3] I'll see Cunninghame Graham in Edinburgh on Saturday: so I'm writing you. I hate asking you knowing how busy you are but it means a good deal and I feel sure that if you possibly can you will string together a couple of thousand words or so.

My point of view throughout is, of course, that 'Home Rule isn't enough' – that we must develop an effective sense of difference in accordance with our ancient traditions – that we must seek to replace the Anglo-Saxon ascendancy in our internal, Imperial, and international affairs by a predominance of neo-['Catho' crossed out]Celtic influences by allying ourselves to this end with Ireland, Wales, and the Scots, Irish and Welsh elements throughout the Empire and elsewhere.

Above all, my book is intended to prevent the domestication of the issues.

Do let me know that you will come to my help with a rousing foreword, and (alas! that I have to importune so busy a man so unmercifully) the earliest possible date at which you can let me have your MSS.

Every good wish. In great haste. Yours. C.M. Grieve

---

1. No such book was published.
2. Robert Stevenson Horne of Slamannan, first Viscount (1871–1940), Conservative MP for Glasgow, Hillhead (1918–37), Chancellor of the Exchequer (1921–22). Arthur James Balfour, first Earl of Balfour (1848–1930), Scottish philosopher and Conservative MP, Prime Minister (1902–6), author of the Balfour Declaration promising Zionists a homeland in Palestine. (James) Ramsay Macdonald (1866–1937), Labour politician and Prime Minister (1924, 1929–31) of the first Labour government.
3. Robert Bontine Cunninghame Graham (1852–1936), London-born author of travel books, essays and short stories, Liberal MP (1886–92), first President of the SLP (1888), first President of the NPS (1928), and first President of the SNP (1934).

21. *To Compton Mackenzie (HRHRC)*

PEN (Scottish Centre), 16 Links Avenue, Montrose   4 May 1928

Dear Mr Mackenzie

I have delayed a day or two replying to your last – thinking that further word from you might come in the interval. But perhaps the Glas. Univ. Nat. Assocn haven't yet been able to fix a definite day for their meeting. Is Cunninghame Graham actually back in this country yet – and has he definitely consented to stand? I hope so. And I am delighted that they have asked you – and that you have agreed – to introduce the Nationalist Candidate. I note what you say about being unable to come here on the 10th, but able to come on the 12th. If any change in the Glasgow arrangements permits you to revert to the earlier date, all the better; if not – in the absence of further word – we shall expect you on the 12th. Just drop a p.c. or send a wire saying what train you're coming by.

Mrs Grieve and I are exceedingly pleased that you are willing to act as one of the godfathers to our little son.[1] I know, of course, that you are a Roman Catholic – but that does not affect the matter either from the point of view of the Scottish Episcopal Church or your own Church.

We are looking forward immensely to your visit. Excellent weather has set in after an undue extension of quite wintry severity: and if it continues you will spend your holiday under most congenial conditions.

Yours. C.M. Grieve

---

1. Walter Ross Grieve, born 5 April 1928, CMG's first son; see Appendix.

22. *To Compton Mackenzie (HRHRC)*

PEN (Scottish Centre), 16 Links Avenue, Montrose   15 May 1928

Dear Compton Mackenzie: –

Many thanks for your kind notes to Mrs Grieve and myself. It was a very great and memorable pleasure to have you here: and we will be exceedingly glad at any time to have another visit from you – especially if by then our circumstances are a little less difficult and our domestic economy less like a species of very congested 'general post'. We do hope that your sciatica will ease away to such an extent at the very least as not to further impair your holiday.

I stupidly forgot to tell you before you left that I had duly posted on the key to the Central Hotel first thing on Monday morning. No further correspondence has come here for you.

I enclose notice of the forthcoming dinner which I forgot to give you when you were here, and which will serve to keep you [in] mind of the place, time etc.

I have written lengthily to Muirhead along the lines we agreed upon and have suggested that he should see Ben Shaw anent this prior to your own interview with the latter. I also mentioned to Muirhead the desirability of a swap over of constituencies between M'Diarmid and yourself.

F.G. Scott's address in Glasgow is: 103 Woodville Gardens, Langside, Glasgow.

I have a letter today from Erskine. He suggests my going over to Aboyne, too, when you are there. I'm not sure now whether your arrangements will enable you to take in a night or two at the Forest of Birse Lodge or not: but there are certainly aspects of matters I'd like to hear discussed with you and Erskine.

With kindest regards and every good wish.

Yours. C.M. Grieve

23. *To Compton Mackenzie (HRHRC)*

16 Links Avenue, Montrose   21 July 1928

Dear Compton Mackenzie

What a beautiful quaich and silver spoon for baby! Even if good porridge were available an ordinary bowl must serve, and this porringer be reserved for nothing short of Atholl brose – that wonderful mixture of porridge, honey, and whisky in equal proportions. Accept on behalf of the boy (who is thriving immensely and brown as a berry) the best thanks of Mrs Grieve and myself.

I was sorry you did not manage down to Stirling (a really encouraging meeting) and Aboyne. Your telegram was excellent – put the whole position in a nutshell. Glad you approved *Glasgow Evening News* article[1] – although it was botched by an unfortunate misprint which connected the Workers' Commonwealth as commonly conceived and the Gaelic Commonwealth with an 'and' instead of opposing themselves to each other and suggesting that the latter was more in keeping with our national genius than the former. However, in *Forward* and elsewhere[2] I have been beating up the Scottish Socialist Movement extensively along these lines. I am speaking in Dunfermline on Sunday, and in Glasgow early in September, and, again, (on behalf of Mr Cunninghame Graham's Rectorial candidature) at Glasgow University in October. I note you expect to be North again in October. I hope to see you then, and if you can and care, Mrs Grieve and I would be delighted if you could come to Montrose again for a night or two.

I'm wondering if you are going over to Dublin for the Games. I haven't heard definitely yet whether Erskine is going or not, but he said he meant to, if possible. I'm going over on the 9th, and looking forward to it immensely.

Although I'm dating this letter from Montrose, we have been living all this month away in the country beyond Brechin. I travel back and forward to Montrose from Brechin daily and have a three-mile walk first thing in the morning and again at night – and am, as a consequence, immensely fit. All of us are much the better of this Arcadian retreat.

I trust you are in good form, despite accumulated arrears of work: and am looking forward keenly to your *Extraordinary Women* which I note has been postponed in publication.[3]

By the way, there is an article in last week's *Inverness Courier* on you and your work by J.M. Reid, a young poet – one of a series he is running on 'Present Day Scotsmen'. (He dealt with me in surprisingly eugolistic [*sic*] terms the previous week).[4]

Again thanking you, and with every good wish from all here.
Yours, C.M. Grieve

---

1. 'Guthrie-itis', *Glasgow Evening News*, 27 July 1928.
2. *Forward*, 5 November 1927; *The Outlook*, 12 November 1927; *The New Age*, 10 November 1927 etc.
3. Compton Mackenzie, *Extraordinary Women: themes and variations* (London: Martin Secker, 1928).
4. John MacNair Reid (1895–1954), journalist for the *Inverness Courier* and later for the *Glasgow Herald* and other Glasgow papers; in the 1930s he became a poet and novelist. 'Present Day Scotsmen III' on MacDiarmid appeared in the *Inverness Courier*, 10 July 1928, and 'IV' on Mackenzie appeared on 20 July 1928.

24. To Compton Mackenzie (HRHRC)

16 Links Avenue, Montrose   28 August 1928

Dear Compton Mackenzie

Just a line to say that Mrs Grieve and I are looking forward very keenly to seeing you again in about a month's time.

I got back from Ireland last week after a splendid fortnight with Gogarty, Yeats, A.E., and the others.[1] It was my first holiday for three years: I needed it and felt I had earned it and enjoyed every moment of it: and incidentally Erskine of Marr and I were, I think, able to make certain arrangements which will help the Scots National Party to the Irish vote at the General Election.

Although I was sorry that you, too, couldn't be in Dublin, you certainly did the right thing in reserving yourself for Inverness and Glasgow. With the end of the summer season the National Party should take a great leap-forward: and certainly the preliminary organisation for a grand drive is going ahead in no uncertain fashion. I trust you have been keeping fit and have managed to overtake all your accumulated arrears of work and that you will find it possible to come North again with a light heart. I am looking forward to your *Extraordinary Women* and trust it will be a great success.

A matter I have always meant to write you about is this – you mentioned that Count M'Cormack, the singer, was a friend of yours and that you might receive a little financial help for the Party through him. I know how extraordinarily generous he is in singing for charities etc. Wouldn't it be possible for him to give a special concert in Edinburgh or Glasgow this Autumn (when he is to be in Scotland anyway in the International Celebrities Concert Series, I think) on behalf of the Party funds?[2]

Although I am addressing this from Links Avenue we won't be returning there till Friday – we are still in our country cottage. Rural life suits your godson and he is brown as a berry and in topping form.

Mrs Grieve joins me in every good wish.

Yours.

C.M. Grieve

---

1. Oliver St John Gogarty (1878–1957), surgeon, writer, Senator of the Irish Free State (1922) and a friend of James Joyce whose character Buck Mulligan in *Ulysses* (1922) was based on Gogarty. William Butler Yeats (1865–1939). A.E. (George William Russell) (1867–1935), Irish poet, painter, writer, and economist, editor of the *Irish Statesman* (1923–30).
2. Count John McCormack (1884–1945), Irish singer, naturalised American (1919), Freeman of Dublin (1923), claimed to have sung in every country in the world apart from Russia and the South American countries.

25. *To A.G. Pape (EUL)*

PEN (Scottish Centre), 16 Links Avenue, Montrose   23 January 1929

Dear A.G.P.

Delighted you have got the draft out.

Was to have been in Edinburgh speaking at Nat. Party Rally on Friday night, but something has come in way and that is off! So I am coming up specially tomorrow (Thursday) by 4.46 from here, arriving Waverley about 7 (I think). You will have seen Compton Mackenzie, no doubt; and I have just written to him to this effect too. Will you and he arrange where I am to meet you?

Mackenzie should get hold of M'Cormick.[1] He'd know where to lay hands on him I fancy. But I've written to M'Cormick too in the hope that he can join us sometime between 7pm on Thursday night and breakfast time on Friday.

Kindest regards to Mrs Pape.

Yours. C.M. Grieve

---

1. John MacDonald MacCormick; see Appendix.

26. *To A.G. Pape (EUL)*

16 Links Avenue, Montrose   25 January 1929

My dear Pape

After a full discussion last night Mackenzie and I decided to try to have a Council meeting called in Edinburgh on Sunday first. You stipulated Saturday. But Sunday makes no difference from a legal standpoint. We'll do our utmost. If we don't succeed you will have to take your own course. So far as Mackenzie and I are concerned we are for your Policy,[1] and other things: and if we do not get our way we will wash our hands of the business and take independent action.

You'll probably hear further from me by wire or 'phone tomorrow (Saturday).

At latest you'll know what's what on Sunday.

Yours, C.M. Grieve

---

1. An education policy, dependent on the adoption of a Social Credit economic policy, aiming to encourage full and creative use of citizens' abilities through economic security of the individual.

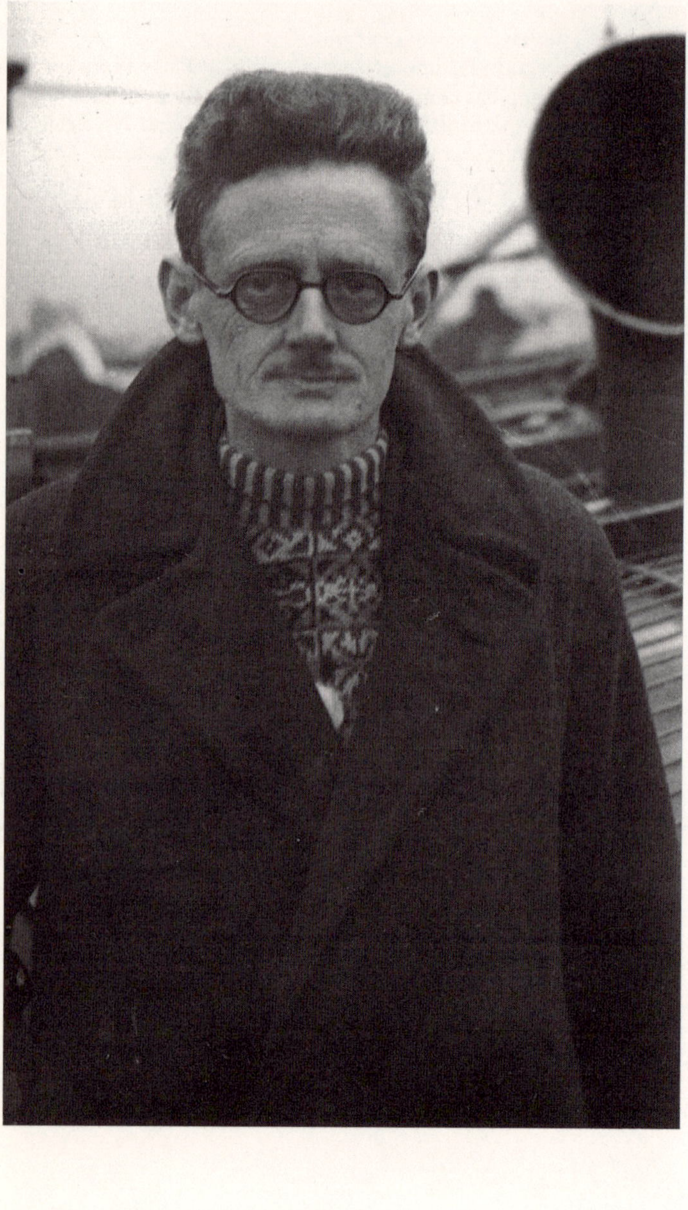

PART TWO

The 1930s

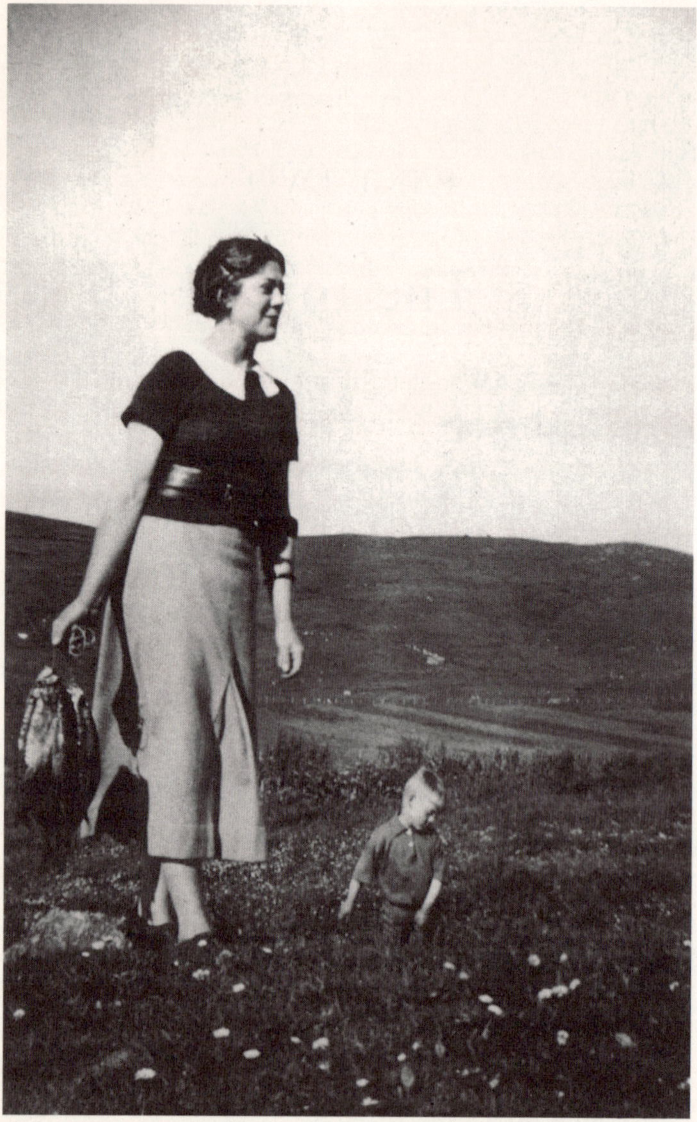

1. *To Compton Mackenzie (HRHRC)*

VOX: The Radio Critic and Broadcast Review[1], 10A Soho Square, London

5 February 1931 [1930]

Dear Mr Mackenzie

Mrs Callis went to get hold of Mr Filson Young[2] to write an article about him for *VOX*, and in the course of conversation he said 'strictly confidentially – the BBC is out to kill *VOX*.'

I have had no doubt of this for some time and grudge them the opportunity. Above all, I am sorry for your sake that it has been necessary to cease weekly publication. For my own part I have worked hard and done my best. I have made a mistake or two: but on the other side – advertising, publishing, and business – greater mistakes have been made, and I cannot help feeling that if all others had concentrated on their work and been as regularly and continuously in the office as I have things might have been better.

As to the Burns article, I had no intention of writing anything in *VOX* beyond a note on Rosslyn Mitchell's broadcast which was one of the items allocated to me at our weekly conference. But Mr Thomson's action in kicking up a row with Mr Maschiwitz[3] struck me – and the others here – as below the belt. And we needed copy – that was the reason why I wrote 3 articles.[4] Mr Jordan was away over the weekend and did not return till the Tuesday afternoon, and Mr Burns and Mr McLaurin were also away over the weekend. So I had a rush and had to write as and what I could to fill space, since my instructions were to accept the irreducible minimum of outside contributions.

Mrs Grieve joins me in every good wish to yourself – and regret for this partial failure of *VOX*.

Yours. C.M. Grieve

---

1. *VOX*, Compton Mackenzie's weekly radio review for which CMG was London editor, running 9 November 1929–8 February 1930.
2. (Alexander Bell) Filson Young (1876–1938), composer, critic, novelist, essayist and joint adviser on programmes at the BBC from 1926.
3. Eric Maschiwitz (1901–69), editor of the *Radio Times* (1927–33).
4. CMG articles in *VOX* vol. 1, no. 13, 1 February 1930 were 'The Cult of Rabbie Burns' by Stentor, 'Mrs Grundy of Savoy Hill' by A.K.L. and 'The D.G. throws his weight about and loses some of it in the process' by a Yes Man.

2. *To Andrew Graham Grieve (EUL)*

Unicorn Press, 321 High Holborn   10 October 1931

Dear A.

I did not deserve a senseless preachment from you. I have my own ideas and a very different mode of life from yours and although years ago I sowed a few wild oats and although I still have my faults, which I probably know better than anyone else, so far from having anything much to be ashamed of I have won to all sorts of distinction to which you could never aspire and which could never have come to a mean and selfish spirit. Circumstances have given you a securer life and latterly kept you nearer Mother, but they do not justify your self-righteous attitude. I only wrote because I wanted to get something fixed up quickly, knew it was perfectly safe and that I could speedily return the loan, and thought the matter a perfectly reasonable proposition. So much is this the case that immediately I got your telegram I was able to arrange the matter elsewhere. As to what I, or you, may have had from Mother at any time my memory is just as long and exact as yours and neither in that respect, nor in doing in return what one could all the factors being considered are you in any position to throw stones. Many of your stupid remarks are due, of course, to ignorance of the situation. This is particularly so where you refer to Peggy, as I fancy you will speedily have some cause to realise.

As to my attitude to Mother I am content to leave that to a far better judgement than yours. On the surface yours may appear to have been more dutiful and loving; but the surface is relatively little. I am concerned about what you say of Mother's health and will write her myself in the beginning of the week.

Yours, Chris

I am carefully preserving your letter and attaching to it for the use of whoever has ultimate charge of my papers a very complete reply, particularly with reference to your purely libellous declaration that you would 'never invest' etc. in a Coy. with which I was 'remotely concerned'.[1] You haven't been asked to; other people have and haven't regretted it and whatever peccadilloes of long ago lie to my account, and whatever personal and domestic difficulties I may have had at any time, I have led at least as honourable a life as you have and have proved myself, as I can abundantly demonstrate at any time, thoroughly trustworthy alike in public and private matters.

CMG

---

1. CMG had been offered a directorship of the Unicorn Press in return for £500 investment and had asked AGG for a loan towards it.

3. *To Andrew Graham Grieve (EUL)*

321 High Holborn, London W.C. 1   22 December 1931

Dear A.

Do not imagine because I have been so long in replying to yours of the 6th inst. that I did not fully appreciate yours – and Chryssie's – kind offer. On the contrary. I received it in the spirit in which it was given. But (though such a holiday would undoubtedly have delighted Christine and done her good) the children are not in my custody and it would have been impossible to have arranged this. Christine, who is heavily colded, travelled up on Sunday and will be with Peggy's people.

Please excuse a short note. I am up to the eyes trying to clear my decks here for a few days out of town over Christmas.[1] I am glad you acknowledged a certain venom in your previous letter and note that you attribute it to a feeling of '*fancied* slighting of one dear to you'. Fancied is right – slighting was not responsible; but a complete difference of temperament, interests and associations. However I hope we've buried that hatchet now and however little we see of each other continue to entertain such friendly feelings as prompted this last letter.

I was extremely sorry to hear of Angus's accident[2] and hope he is fully recovered.

Every kind wish and seasonable greeting to Chryssie, the children, and yourself. Please accept enclosed as a little Christmas gift.

Yours, Chris

---

1. As a delegate to the PEN Congress in The Hague, where he met Karel Čapek.
2. Angus, AGG's son.

4. *To Elizabeth Dawson (EUL)*

321 High Holborn, London W.C. 1 /   Friday [January 1932]
63/64 Chancery Lane, London W.C. 2

Dearest Mother.

You will understand that I have had worries enough and have been in no mood for letter-writing. Apart from that I have been off and on ill for the past week or two with a heavy dose of flu' I am only now managing to shake off, and this came at a bad time when I was up to the eyes in business and had to carry on somehow or other.

I quite understand your feelings about the divorce case. Believe me, there is no help for it. Peggy and I have been exceedingly unhappy for years, and all the effort to keep together came from me. I wanted her – she did not want me. That was why she would not come to Liverpool.[1] I did my very utmost to win her round again and was prepared to make all manner of compromises and meet her far beyond half-way to maintain some sort of relationship. The whole matter has been a desperate blow to me. It is useless my going into details as you do not know the circumstances. Suffice it to say that I exhausted every possible means before I did the only thing left and acted in such a way as to enable her to claim her freedom and divorce me. I am passionately fond of her and would have given anything in the world to have retained her.

It was extremely good of you to send me the socks and I am sorry you have had to wait so long for an acknowledgement. So, too, with regard to Christine. I have not seen her for two weeks but probably will tomorrow. She was down with a bad cold but is keeping better. Walter is at Methil. Peggy is no longer at 18 Pyrland Road and I do not know her new address. I have a flat at the second address given above – the top one is my office address. My new book ought to have been out last week but has been delayed at the binders, but will be ready on Wednesday when you will get a copy sent on at once. I hope you will like it. I am sorry Father has been troubled by his pains again, and also to hear of Angus's misfortune from which I hope he is recovering all right. Are you in good fettle yourself? I hope so but the weather is very trying.

Love and kisses, and kindest regard to all friends. Your Loving Son, Chris

---

1. That is, she preferred to stay in London with William McElroy; see Appendix.

5. To Thomas Sturge Moore (ULL)

321 High Holborn, London, W.C.1 /　　　　　　　　8 January 1932
63/64 Chancery Lane, London, W.C. 2

Dear Mr Sturge Moore

I hope to come to see you next Friday morning. May I bring Austin Clarke, the Irish poet, with me? He has long been a great admirer of your work and was responsible for the review of Vol. I of your Collected Editions in the *New Statesman* and also for reference to it in his review of the verse of the year in Lord Sainsbury's *Observer*. Please do not trouble to reply to this if it is all right for me to bring him along with me.[1]

Yours sincerely, C.M. Grieve

---

1. Austin Clarke (1896–1974), Irish poet and dramatist, working as a journalist in London, 1922–37.

6. To Elizabeth Dawson (EUL)

'Cootes', Thakeham Sussex   12 May 1932

Dearest Mother,

    I am having a very busy time. I do not know if you have been seeing my activities in various Scottish papers – the *Record*, *The Sunday Mail*, *The Free Man* etc. I am enclosing in case you have not seen it a cutting of a long poem I had in *The Scots Observer*. You will see it is about Esk, Ewes, and Wauchope. I had another long one on Wauchope in *The Modern Scot*, and have just written a very long one – one of my very best – on Tarras.[1] All the first volume of this huge new poem of which these are all parts deals with Langholm and my boyhood days.[2] I have been in extraordinarily good mood lately and during the past six weeks have actually written more and better poetry than all the rest of my previous poetry put together. I have done nothing else I could possibly avoid; such a tremendous rush of poetry doesn't come often in any lifetime and one has to seize it when it does. My 'Second Hymn to Lenin' which is several times longer than the first one is appearing in the next issue of *The Criterion* and very shortly afterwards I am publishing it in volume form with a line drawing of my head by one artist and a frontispiece portrait of me by another artist. I will send you a copy.[3] Another very long poem of mine 'The Oon Olympian'[4] is appearing shortly in *The New English Weekly*, and *The Scottish Educational Journal* are to serialise a new book I am writing of essays on Scottish poetry.[5] So you see I have my hands full. I am in excellent health. This country place suits me splendidly and I do not go up to London – 50 miles away – any oftener than I can help. I haven't seen Peggy for a long time but hear from her every now and again. Both the children are very well. I had a nice letter from Christine last week. She is very happy and getting on extremely well with her schooling. I had a report about her from the School saying how intelligent she was. I am hoping to go up next week and see her. I have no more news – living here I am out of touch with people – tho' I correspond regularly with Scott (who has been setting more of my poems to music) and others on literary and business matters. I hope Father and you are both well and that you have good news of all friends.

    With love and kisses. Your loving son, Chris

---

1. 'Water Music', *The Scots Observer*, 5 May 1932; 'By Wauchopeside', *The Modern Scot*, April 1932; 'Tarras', *The Free Man*, 25 June 1932.
2. *Clann Albann*. The poem was never completed. Its structure was outlined by CMG in *The Modern Scot*, vol. 2, no. 2, July 1931, as follows: Dedicatory Poem, Prologue, I The Muckle Toon, 1st Interlude, II Fier Comme Un Eccossais, 2nd Interlude, III Demidium Anima Meae, 3rd Interlude, IV The Uncanny Scot, 4th Interlude, V With a Lifting of the Head, Epilogue. An explanation of the poem appeared in the *Scots Observer*, 12 August 1933.

3. Hugh MacDiarmid, *Second Hymn To Lenin* (Thakeham: Valda Trevlyn, [1932]), limited to 100 copies, cover drawing by Flora Macdonald and frontispiece by William Johnstone.
4. 'The Oon Olympian', *New English Weekly*, vol. 1, no. 14, 21 July 1932.
5. The series, written under the pseudonym James MacLaren, ran from 1 July 1932 to 21 July 1933 and, although not in any way exclusively composed of articles from the *SEJ*, nor relating solely to Scottish poetry, *At The Sign of the Thistle: a collection of essays*, by Hugh MacDiarmid (London: Stanley Nott), appeared in 1934.

7. *To Seumus O'Sullivan (HRHRC)*

'Cootes', Thakeham, Sussex   17 July 1932

Dear Seumus O'Sullivan

I sent Gogarty a poem some time ago and asked him to pass it on to you in case you would care to have it for the *Dublin Magazine* but I have been writing a great deal lately and I now enclose two others which I hope you may like.[1] I'd like to send you an article soon too – about 2500 to 3000 words – breaking a lance in favour of Corkery's position against P.S. O'Hegarty, Sean Faolain [sic] and others – not in reference of some of Corkery's specific judgments but of his basic position, and not of course written in any personal way.[2] It will be an interesting article, I think, and if you care to consider it – without of course commissioning it or committing yourself to it at all until you have read it – I will send it to you in the course of a week or ten days after hearing from you.

I hope you are well. Kindest regards to your wife, yourself, and all friends.

Yours sincerely, C.M. Grieve

P.S. I have two new books of poetry come out [sic] almost immediately and will send you copies in due course.[3]

If you are using the poem I already sent you you can either use these two also – or hold them over for another issue.

---

1. 'Milk-Wort and Bog Cotton' dedicated to Seumus O'Sullivan, and 'Lynch-Pin' dedicated to A.E., appeared in the *Dublin Magazine*, vol. 7, no. 4, October–December 1932.
2. Daniel Corkery (1878–1964) had written *The Hidden Ireland* (1924), exploring the eighteenth-century remnants of an Irish-Gaelic literary language which had been ignored by the dominant Anglo-Irish histories, and believed that new Irish literature should be written in Gaelic. In *Synge and Anglo-Irish Literature* (1931), Corkery called for a Catholic, peasant and nationalist Irish literature. The novelist Sean O'Faolain (1900–91), dissented in a review in *The Criterion*, vol. XI, no. 42. Patrick Sarsfield O'Hegarty (1879–1955) was also hostile in *The Dublin Magazine* (January–March 1932), but ironically became Ireland's leading Gaelic publisher.

3. Hugh MacDiarmid, *Tarras* (Edinburgh: *The Free Man*, 1932), limited to 20 copies, and *Second Hymn to Lenin*.

8. *To Seumus O'Sullivan (HRHRC)*

'Cootes', Thakeham, Sussex   23 July 1932

Dear Seumus O'Sullivan

Many thanks for your letter. I am glad you like the two poems. I will send on the article re the Corkery case in a few days. I quite understand the financial difficulties of running a review like your splendid *Dublin Magazine* and whatever rates you are in the habit of paying will suit me. I will leave it entirely to you. I am enclosing a copy of my latest production.

Every kind regard to your wife and yourself and all friends.

Yours sincerely, C.M. Grieve

9. *To Eneas Mackay, Publishers (NLS)*

'Cootes', Thakeham, Sussex   23 July 1932

Dear Sirs: –

I have two books of poetry coming out this autumn, and two books of prose under consideration, by different firms of publishers: but I am anxious to put out another small volume of poems, entitled *Scots Unbound and Other Poems*, with, as frontispiece, a photograph of the bronze head of me by William Lamb in the current Royal Scottish Academy. As you know I have long admired your enterprise in publishing Scottish books and I will much like to have your imprint on one of my books.

This book contains, in the view of leading judges, some of my very best work, and if you can consider publishing it – to appear, if at all possible, (and it should be, as there is not much setting up) about the end of September – I will immediately send you the complete MSS, and a copy of another book with which I wish its format to be uniform. I know the exigencies of poetry publishing, of course, but, though I have an established public for my work, I will be willing to guarantee the book to the extent of £25 against any loss shown six months after publication.[1]

With best wishes, Yours sincerely, C.M. Grieve

P.S. I am again doing a weekly literary causerie on Scottish topics in *The Free Man* and shall be glad to give notices there to any books of which you care to send me review copies.

---

1. Hugh MacDiarmid, *Scots Unbound and Other Poems* (Stirling: Eneas Mackay, 1932).

10. *To Elizabeth Dawson (EUL)*

'Cootes', Thakeham, Sussex   27 July 1932

My dearest Mother

I have only time for a brief note to accompany enclosed copy of my latest productions.[1] I hope you'll like the very modern portrait of me which serves as frontispiece – not the cover drawing which, while good enough of its kind, is not nearly so interesting a piece of work. Johnstone, the artist, is a cousin of F.G. Scott's, and Flora MacDonald, who did the cover drawing, is Johnstone's wife. I had another even longer poem in *The New English Weekly* last week but I haven't a copy of it by me.

I was awfully glad to hear that the Doctor thought you were keeping a bit better and do hope the improvement will continue. I suppose it is too much to hope that you may not have to go into the infirmary after all, but if you have, whatever the treatment there may be, you will be able to stand it all the better if you can build up your strength in the meantime.

I will write you again in a day or two. I am in splendid form myself and as usual extremely busy. I haven't heard about Christine again for a little while – she will be going on all right or I would have heard.

Love to Father, Maggie, and all friends, and kisses to yourself.

Your loving son, Chris

11. *To Eneas Mackay (NLS)*

c/o Highway Press, 1 India Bldgs.,   31 August 1932
Victoria St., Edinburgh

Dear Mr Mackay

Many thanks for the galley proofs which I herewith return corrected, plus 'The Scott Centenary' poem. I prefer MacDiarmid to McDiarmid. I have no objection whatever to a cream antique laid paper and am content to leave all details of this sort to you with perfect confidence. I will look forward to receiving specimens of binding linen, paged proofs etc. Please note my new address, which holds till further notice.[1] I enclose a brief note on the book which may suffice for a prospectus. Along with it you may care to use a block of the photograph I sent you – or I can send either the block of the AE portrait which appeared in my *First Hymn to Lenin*, the Johnstone drawing which formed the frontispiece of my *Second Hymn*, or an entirely new and hitherto unreproduced photo for the purpose.

Will you please tell me approximate date of publication as I would like to arrange in advance for certain auxiliary publicity in certain quarters?

If you would prefer a longer summary or description for prospectus I can get Compton Mackenzie or someone else who is well-known to do this. Please let me know.

With kindest regards and best wishes.
Yours sincerely, C. M. Grieve

Scots Unbound and Other Poems
by
Hugh MacDiarmid

In this important new volume of poems Hugh MacDiarmid not only gives us a few more of the highly concentrated lyrics with which he established his reputation, but a series of longer poems in which he carries to a new stage his work for the revival of the Scots Vernacular. We have here the maturest work of a poet who has achieved a world-wide reputation and evoked such tributes as these: –

'Where Burns turned back, McDiarmid has plunged deeper and faced the problems of the times'
    Naomi Mitchison[2]

'Since ever I came into contact with your poems I have recognised you as one of our few poets of the modern European world in any English dialect.'
    Prince D. S. Mirsky[3]

'A poet of genius, with wide intellectual interests. I can think of scarcely no contemporary poet whom I find more intellectually exciting.'
    'A. E.' (G.W. Russell)

'No one can send me anything I am keener to see.'
    Gordon Bottomley[4]

The volume has for frontispiece a photograph of the bronze head of MacDiarmid, by William Lamb ARSA, which was shown in the Royal Scottish Academy Exhibition this year.

---

1. CMG was now working as Assistant Editor of *The Free Man*. He had told Helen Cruikshank that he could make ends meet if he could earn £2 per week, a matter with which she approached Robin McKelvie Black, the editor of *The Free Man*, and Dr. Stanley Robertson, its financial backer, who agreed to take him on.
2. Naomi Margaret Mitchison (1897–1999), Edinburgh-born novelist, socialist and feminist.
3. Dmitri Petrovich Svyatopolk Mirsky (1890–1939), literary historian and critic to whom *First Hymn to Lenin* is dedicated. A Russian prince, he emigrated after the October Revolution and lived in England (1922–32), working as a lecturer on Russian literature at London University and the Royal College and as a literary critic for *Criterion*. He returned to Russia, died in imprisonment at Magadan and was 'posthumously rehabilitated'.
4. Gordon Bottomley (1874–1948), English poet and playwright.

12. *To Compton Mackenzie (HRHRC)*

The Scots Free Press, 1 India Buildings, Edinburgh 1   11 October 1932

My dear Compton Mackenzie

I think, if possible, we should arrange an early meeting in Edinburgh which follows very different lines than any previously employed. What I would like to suggest is that yourself, F.G. Scott, Moray McLaren, Cleghorn Thomson, Dewar Gibb, Major C.H. Douglas[1] and myself should stage a meeting, say in the Usher Hall, where the procedure is as follows:—

  1. That you state in a very succinct way some point which appears to you to be vital in regard to the present position and potentialities of Scotland.

One of the others of us seizes upon that point and makes a relevant remark and in sequence all of us follow on. My idea is to get completely away from the ordinary debate business and to ensure that if six or more of us appear on the platform, if one of us sets the ball arolling the others are quite prepared to chip in on an appropriate plane and in this way we may have six or more Scots joining in in what would not be a formal discussion but would be a case of one person (preferably yourself) giving initial stimulus to a discussion that would incite all the rest of us to say something of more or less moment and give you a subsequent opportunity of replying, while at the same time allowing the audience free scope to interject in the way of either questions or discussion.

If you have a free date early in November for this purpose please let me know as soon as you possibly can. Pending hearing from you I shall not proceed any further in the matter.

With kindest regards, Yours sincerely, C.M. Grieve

---

1. Moray McLaren (1901–71), on staff of *The Listener* (1929), first programme director for Scotland (1933), popular writer and journalist, author of Penguin Books' accessible introduction, *The Scots*. David Cleghorn Thomson, regional director of the BBC (1929), a nationalist who edited *Scotland in Quest of Her Youth* (1932) and went on to run a Scottish literary agency in 1935. Andrew Dewar Gibb (1888–1974), lecturer on Scottish Law at Cambridge, becoming Regius Professor of Law at Glasgow in 1934, Chairman of SNP (1936–40). Major Clifford Hugh Douglas (1879–1952), Social Credit theorist, construction engineer, Assistant Director of the Royal Aircraft Works at Farnborough during WWI. The central dogma of Douglas's Social Credit was that money had become divorced from the measure of man's labour it proposed to represent, that banks by obstructing the circulation of money and imposing charges created a situation where the 'sum of the wages, salaries and dividends distributed in respect of the world's production … would not buy it, since the price includes nonexistant values'. CMG and Ezra

Pound were converts to the theory which fell into disrepute as it became increasingly associated with anti-semitism. Using his position at the Unicorn Press, CMG privately published C.H. Douglas, *Warning Democracy* (London, 1931).

13. To Compton Mackenzie (HRHRC)

c/o Highway Press, 1 India Buildings,   11 October 1932
Victoria Street, Edinburgh

My dear Mackenzie

I am with you all the way. I am booked up every night almost for weeks ahead with National Party meetings – sometimes several per night – and everywhere I go I am confirmed in the readiness of most people for a real lead – they rise like fish to a bait to any out-&-out no compromise talk. Even detached men – like MacPhail, editor of the *Edinburgh Evening News* – who was at Usher Hall meeting had absolutely no use for any of the speakers except yourself – 'We want more fireworks' he repeated again and again to me, 'Vivid personalities – real drive – none of your flat-footed statistical and platitudinous blethering but the fire from on high.'

I don't know whether I can possibly get through to Glasgow on Thursday night but think I can – where can I get in touch with you if I arrive late and stay overnight? Please let me know and I will do my damnedest. The council have taken exception to my rejoining the Party and are writing the Area Council here to that effect and thence it will pass to the South Edinburgh branch which has admitted me to membership when it will be for me to explain and insist on my title to rejoin – but that will take some weeks and in the meantime I am a member – besides which I am *ipso facto* a member through being an office bearer of the Glasgow & Edinburgh University groups which are affiliated to the NPS. So I am going to hang on, speak all over the place, and defy them to get rid of me before I do the necessary damage.

It was a great joy to see you again and I do hope we may be able to meet and have a talk in Glasgow on Thursday night.

Kindest regards to Miss Boyte & Mrs MacSween.[1]

Yours, C.M.G.

P.S. Please do not forget little contribution to *Free Man* Symposium – we have some splendid stuff in – all along our line.

---

1. Nellie Boyt and Chrissie MacSween, Mackenzie's secretaries.

14. *To Eneas Mackay (NLS)*

1 India Buildings, Victoria St., Edinburgh   23 February 1933

Dear Mr Mackay,

Many thanks for sending me the copies of Dr Lauchlan MacLean Watt's letter to you and your reply.[1] I am exceedingly sorry that you should have been troubled about this matter but do not think you are likely to be bothered any further. I have had no communication from – or on behalf of – Dr MacLean Watt myself. I cannot understand how he failed to put the same interpretation on the matter as you yourself advanced in your reply to him. I have myself taken advice, and am assured that there is nothing actionable. In any case, should proceedings arise—which I have reason to believe extremely unlikely – I, of course, hold myself entirely responsible to indemnify you if need be.

With best wishes. Yours sincerely, C. M. Grieve

---

1. In *Scots Unbound*, CMG published 'An Apprentice Angel', a satirical poem in two parts, dedicated to 'L.MacL.W.' (the Reverend Lauchlan Maclean Watt, an Edinburgh divine). In part one, the Reverend is imagined trying on a pair of angel's wings and flapping around his study like a drunk crow; in part two, he is likened to the pupated moth whose former, pre-larval stage, haunts his transformed, ariel life, as the Reverend's earthly existence might haunt his heavenly one, when or if it should ever come. When the book was offered for review to the Reverend Canon MacCulloch, it was declined, a letter to the publisher (27 October 1932) saying that the prospective reviewer 'could not speak favourably of it': 'I have tried to extract some meaning from the poems, but have failed. And there seems to be no music or beauty in the lines; and a very defective sense of rhythm is noticeable. I daresay certain people like that kind of writing, but I can't get up any enthusiasm for it.' Rather than write an entirely negative review, the Reverend Canon MacCulloch offered to return the book. On 15 February 1933, Lauchlan MacLean Watt himself wrote to the publisher to say that CMG had written a letter to him to alert him to 'An Apprentice Angel' in *Scots Unbound*, and having read the poem, Watt was now obliged to complain to the publisher: 'There is a certain limit for the decencies and criticisms which law protects; and I suggest you should look into your position in regard to these, as affecting a man in my position, with reference to a book published by you. I am taking legal advice on the matter.' The publisher Mackay replied to Watt on the 18 February, suggesting that it was impossible for him to conceive of CMG's poem as being anything other than praise. Watt responded on 25 February, emphasising that when the 'objectionable' verses had been drawn to his attention by CMG himself, the poet had told Watt that 'he had "put me in my place". He also said that he would "by every means in his power" show me up as being "the conceited vain skunk" that I am.' Watt continued: 'Of course, the verses are the poorest, most vulgar balderdash that any semi-idiot could have written' but maintained that they were nonetheless 'objectionable'. However, he concluded, 'There is no use of writing to Mr Grieve on the matter, as I do not consider that he is entirely sane.' When CMG introduced a reading of the poem

on BBC Radio Scotland about forty years later, he referred to this incident by saying that he thought the second part of the poem was a particularly good example of his aim of bringing science and poetry together, and that when the poem was originally published, its dedicatee took exception to it and promised to sue the author; 'I replied, "Very well! Go ahead, then."' Promptly thereafter, the dedicatee 'was sequestrated, and died'.

15. *To John MacCormick (NLS, DFF)*

1 India Buildings, Victoria St., Edinburgh   10 April 1933

Dear Mr MacCormick[1]

I have your letter of 10th inst. regarding my desire to make a personal statement of my case at the Annual Conference in May.

I would now point out that it was you yourself who stated, publicly and officially, that I was entitled to do so, and I therefore wrote you intimating my intention of exercising this right.

Your subsequent letters are before me. I am cognisant of the fact that despite these you yourself moved at the last council meeting that I be not heard.

I regard this, in view of what had gone before, as entirely characteristic of your disgraceful dealings: and I also regard it as characteristic of the Council as at present predominantly composed that 1/ an attempt should be made to cheat me of my right to appear before the Conference on a thin argument that I am not actually a member of the Party, and 2/ that (as I foresaw) the Council should attempt to arrogate to themselves the right of dealing with the matter instead of leaving it to the Conference. I have no expectation of fair play from the former and no fear of not getting it, despite all the manoeuvres of the Council, from the latter.

I regard as an insult your request that I should write informing the Council that as an applicant for membership I accept and am prepared to adhere to the declared objects and policy of the Party and am not a member of any other political organisation; since I have already stated clearly in the public press that I am fully eligible under the Party's Constitution and since my becoming a member of the South Edinburgh Branch implied my readiness and ability to accept the necessary obligations of membership.

I adhere to the above and formally reiterate that (despite whatever hearsay the Council may have been relying on) there is no bar to my membership under the Constitution of the Party. I do not believe that any of the Council ever imagined there was but chose to pretend so for ulterior reasons which may be in the interests of their own petty personal ambitions but have never been in the interests of the Party.

Apart from the fact that there is no ground whatever for raising the point in my case, I would ask you to refer me to any clause in the Constitution requiring members of the National Party of Scotland not to be members of any other political organisation; and, if such is forthcoming, I would ask why this is not enforced in certain other cases.

I shall be glad to hear what the Council has to say in reply to this letter as quickly as possible; and herewith give you notice that, irrespective of any decision they may come to or the result of any appeal I may be permitted to make to the annual conference, I am instructing my lawyers [MS ends. Following page has notes for the poem, 'Scotland, when it is given to me ...', from 'Ode to All Rebels', *Complete Poems*, Vol.1, p.489.]

---

1. The letter is addressed to J.M. MacCormick, Esq., Hon. National Secretary, National Party of Scotland

16. *To Andrew Graham Grieve (EUL)*

1 India Buildings, Victoria St., Edinburgh   26 April 1933

Dear AGG

I was extremely sorry to hear from Mother about Chryssie's illness and trust she has made a good recovery. I do not know whether you have yet flitted to Liberton (?) but am sending this to old address on off-chance. You will not have misinterpreted not seeing me for so long – I have been having a difficult time – but I am going off on Tuesday to Shetland for some months to get some new books written and would like to see you before I go. Can I come round any time tomorrow (Thursday) evening – or any time on Sat. (Friday is impossible) – or (it could only be for a couple of minutes) tea time on Monday? Please 'phone my office tomorrow and leave word if I'm not there.

Love to all – Chris

17. *To Andrew Graham Grieve (EUL)*

2 May 1933

Dear A.

Haven't managed round after all. So sorry – especially as I had copies of *Modern Scot* etc. containing some new poems of mine, principally about Langholm I wanted you to have. But I'll post them on to you. I have had a hell of a rush and have still all kinds of things to do before I board the boat about 7pm tonight. Arrive Thursday forenoon. My address will be c/o Dr Orr, Whalsay, Shetland Islands. I'll be there for a couple of months at any rate but how much longer depends on a/ whether I like it, 2/ how the books I am writing progress.[1] I'll be coming back to Edinr. in any case and have just written Mother telling her I've stored her stuff which I had at Longniddry in a flat in Bruntsfield I intend to occupy on my return. The stuff is perfectly safe – in a dry place, free from mice etc. – and I only pay a small storage rent in the meantime.

I trust Chryssie is much better. Love to all of you.

Yours, Chris

P.S. I've meant over and over again to call for the underthings with which I could be doing very well, but something has always come in the way – could you possibly post them on to me at Shetland address? I expect they'll come in very handy there: I'll refund you postage by return.

Valda & baby[2] are going tomorrow to Cornwall for month and will then join me in Shetland.

---

1. Helen Cruickshank, concerned with CMG's heavy drinking and poor financial situation in Edinburgh, helped arrange for the Grieves to move to the Shetland island of Whalsay. David Orr, the resident doctor, agreed to accommodate them with Valda working as a housekeeper.
2. (James) Michael Trevlyn Grieve, born 28 July 1932, CMG's only child by Valda; see Appendix.

18. *To Valda Trevlyn (NLS)*

[Whalsay, Shetland Islands]   Monday Morning [8 May 1933]

Dearest Valda

I thought I'd have had a letter this morning, you naughty girl, but there isn't one and I'm hoping that all's well with you and the Young Man. I got here all right last Thursday about mid-day after an excellent passage up. Dr Orr was at Lerwick to meet me when the boat put in between 6 and 7am. We had time for a welcome bit of breakfast there and left again on the little Whalsay boat about 9. It is incredible that I should have been away from you practically a week already. Time passes here as elsewhere at an unbelievable rate; I had meant to have a good long time yesterday writing letters in time to catch the mail today but here I am with only about an hour before the mail goes – and several letters to write – and only the above written so far.

The Dr has delightful digs; there's the Geological Survey man[1] here too; and we're all being fed like fighting cocks. The only previous experience of similar gastronomic achievements I can recall is the holiday I spent at Bude. I like the island immensely – it is very bare, not a single tree, the very minimum of animal life (just a few sheep and a cow or two), no real village anywhere – only scattered crofters' cottages. But curiously beautiful with several splendid walks. I think you'll like it too. The people are very simple and quiet and happy-hearted. The Dr's house is nearing completion and is fully modern – with bathroom and all conveniences. He'd have had to get a housekeeper in any case, but the idea as long as we are here is that you may care to act in that capacity (with the help, probably, of a little day girl) – and it seems to me an excellent arrangement, although no doubt you'll be a bit dubious at first of your functions of managing (quite unnecessarily dubious – you'll manage all right).

I can't think at the moment of anything else I ought to say – but didn't you let me away without my trunk keys? I haven't succeeded at all events, even with the Dr's help, in getting my big trunk opened, nor my other bag either for the matter of that. I did not think they were locked and I've a horrible suspicion that they may not be after all – but in any case our joint efforts cannot get them opened and we've tried one or two bunches of keys belonging to the landlady and others in vain. The book, comb and penknife arrived all right this morning but no keys.

My appearance on arrival at Lerwick was so appalling that I had perforce to buy another comb as soon as the shop opened.

I feel sure you'll like it immensely here. The island – all the group of Shetland islands – are completely Dry (non-alcoholic) by the way; there are practically no shops; one has to make one's own entertainment – but the islanders are good at that and let people like us join in. I was at a whist drive on Friday night – and may possibly be at a concert this week! Which is good going for me; and once we get settled in what with dances and the like you'll get on all right, I fancy. Orr himself is just a mountain of jollity.

The weather has been splendid since I came up and you'll probably have a good spell for the first few weeks after you come. There'll be plenty of chances for bathing for you – and we'll make a sailor of you too I fancy. The herring fishing starts in a fortnight or thereby and I intend going out with the boats. Besides there are little voyages planned to some of the other islands and towards the end of June Orr projects taking me to the Faroe Islands (look up the map, you lazy girl).

I hope there's a letter on the way from you by now; if so I'll get it on Wednesday – if not, I'll be really alarmed. I hope James Michael behaved himself nicely and was none the worse of his journey and that you hadn't too trying a time going down. But do write and give me all the news. I hope your mother and aunts – to all of whom my best love! – are in good form and getting used to the progress in the house of Master Baly.

The Muse by the way is beginning to work all right. I've got several things done – and one longish poem (4 verses of 12 lines each) which I think is particularly good. But it's too long to copy out now. I'll enclose it in Wednesday's letter perhaps. I wonder if you are really missing me as much as I am missing you – not that I am miserable in any way; I am extremely glad I came up here and only want to share the happiness of it with you, as soon as possible. You've had a pretty trying spell with your

Wild Man; Whalsay will make it up to you, I fancy.

Kisses, darling, – and give James Michael an appropriate ration too, and remember me to them all at home with every affectionate regard.

Ever yours, Chris

---

1. Thomas Robertson, one of HM Survey geologists, was carrying out research on Whalsay; he and CMG became close friends and remained so till his departure in August, CMG often accompanying him on excursions to outlying islands.

19. *To Valda Trevlyn (NLS)*

Whalsay   Thursday [11 May 1933]

My dearest V.

I was very glad to get your p.c. the other day and know that little J.M. and you had arrived safe and sound at the other end of these islands from myself. I thought there might have been a letter from you by today – tho' I knew it was barely possible so soon – especially as you probably did not receive mine till today (and no doubt were feeling very hurt about my being seemingly so indifferent – tho' as a matter of fact I sent it to you by the first post after I came here).

Delightful weather here. I have been away all day on a cruise to the Outer Skerries – remote islands where the schoolmaster is a reader of the *Modern Scot* and not only that but a personal friend of the late Donald Sinclair[1] – and had a glorious time – in a haddock boat. There are great times in store for you here, lassie – speed the end of the month. I will write you details of the voyage up from Leith in plenty of time before that, but the single fare Leith to Lerwick (where I will likely meet you) is 37/6 (get a first-class cabin and you'll have a very comfortable bed and excellent conditions), while you change boats at Lerwick for Whalsay, 4/6 single fare.

You'll like your new house (heaven hope we can stay on here for as long as possible) –

Ground floor; scullery, with two fitted sinks and large boiler.

Kitchen; with a splendid type of stove that is of grey colour and requires no polishing or blacking; with big hot-water boiler and nice shelved cupboard, larder etc.

Sitting room.

Dr's consulting room, with Dispensary off.

Bathroom, w.c. etc.

Upstairs: five rooms (bedrooms – one may be furnished as additional sitting room). Fitted with ample cupboards. Lumber room. Linen cupboard etc.

So you see it's thoroughly modern and the h. and c. throughout will be splendid for you; besides having a maid to help you. But take it from me you'll have all the chances for cooking, baking etc. you want. We fare splendidly here and will expect ditto with lots from you. Landlady here is excellent cook and gives us wonderful variety. Sample menu yesterday:

Breakfast. – Porridge. Bacon & Eggs. Marmalade. Bread and Butter. Oatcakes.

Dinner. – Tomato Soup. Roast mutton, baked & stoved onions with sauce. Stewed rhubarb and baked rice pudding. Coffee and biscuits.

Tea. – Bread and butter, boiled eggs, muffins, scones, jam, cake.

Supper. – Cocoa, biscuits and cheese.

So now you know the sort of thing that's expected of you, my hearty, and remember – never the same thing twice in one week, and always plenty of everything.

I'll write you again on Monday. I hope you are behaving yourself, and that the Boy is fine, fat, and flourishing. Tell him Da-Da-Da sends love and kisses. Every kind regard to your mother and aunts. Wearying to hear from you. Do hope you're O.K. – apart from missing me, of course!

All my love. Yours, Chris

---

1. Donald Sinclair (1886–1932), Gaelic poet, essayist, and playwright.

20. *To Valda Trevlyn (NLS)*

Whalsay   Tuesday 16 May [1933]

My dearest Valda

I was sorry to get yesterday your wee note dated 9th inst. showing that even by then you had not received the first word from me of my safe arrival in these remote parts: but you will by now I hope have had not only that first letter but another long letter and a post-card. I should have written you again in time to catch Monday's (yesterday's) boat: but I let any question of writing letters slide over until today instead for the simple reason that I was in the throes of writing a new long poem, which I have *finished*, and believe will be regarded as one of my most important things. It is called 'Ode to All Rebels', and is more than twice as long as the 'Second Hymn to Lenin'. I intend to have it published as a separate book as quickly as possible and to this end will write out a fair copy of it tonight or tomorrow and get it off to Gollancz – whom failing I will offer it to Boriswood Ltd.[1] But – first of all – I must write this letter to you in time to catch tomorrow morning's mail-boat. (I cannot send you a copy of the poem. It would take too long to write it all out. But you'll see it when you get up here, and, praise the Lord, more than half the time of our separation has now passed.)

Apart from wearying for you and J.M. (whom I am delighted to hear has won favour with the Cornish folk), I am having the most wonderful time – boating, wandering about in uninhabited islands, eating, talking to Dr Orr and the geologist man and reading and writing to all the hours of the morning. The weather is glorious and I am in the pink of condition.

I've had quite a little deluge of books since I came here. Helen sent me a new *History of Scottish Literature till 1714* as a parting gift; Gibbon's *Sunset Song* arrived, and his *Cloud Howe* will shortly; Aeneas Mackay sent me a couple of books for review; and Gawsworth his *Collected Poems*, and I've had letters from Neil Gunn, Whyte,[2]

[MS ends]

---

1. Objecting to its obscenity, Gollancz refused to take the poem and instead it was included in *Second Hymn to Lenin and other poems* (London: Stanley Nott, 1935).
2. Helen is Helen Cruickshank. The books are: Agnes Mure Mackenzie, *An Historical Survey of Scottish Literature to 1714* (London: Alexander Maclehose & Co., 1933); Lewis Grassic Gibbon, *Sunset Song* (London: Jarrolds, 1932), *Cloud Howe* (London: Jarrolds, 1933). John Gawsworth: see appendix. Neil Miller Gunn (1891–1973), Highland novelist (CMG had published his early work in *The Scottish Chapbook*); James H. Whyte, a wealthy American who ran the Abbey bookshop in St Andrews, founder of *The Modern Scot* (1930).

21. *To Valda Trevlyn (NLS)*

Whalsay   20 [21] May 1933

My dearest Valda

I was delighted to get your letter (and the key of the trunk) at last and to know that both you and J.M. were well and that you were enjoying your well-deserved holiday. I have written fully to Michael at Thakeham and the accounts etc., which have not yet been sent to you at Bude I understand, will, if they were not dispatched before he got my last letter be sent on to here to await your arrival instead, as I thought that by the time he gets my letter and got the accounts I sent to you, you might – since correspondence takes so long from here – have left Bude.

Now I'm not going to write a long letter tonight for, in addition to the fact that I have walked over 12 miles today in perfectly glorious weather and am now pleasantly sleepy, I have a good few other letters I must write before I go to bed and have to make an early rise. I am leaving here tomorrow (Monday) and may not be back until Thursday or Friday. I am going out to the herring fishing in a sailing boat – to about 100 miles North West of Shetland Mainland, and the boat I am going on will not be returning for at least a week, but I can go back I understand on one of the other Whalsay sailing boats or steam drifters we will encounter on the fishing grounds which is returning earlier. The herring fishing has just started and all the islands are now very busy with it, hundreds of crans arriving daily and being expeditiously gutted, salted, and barrelled by the girls, enveloped in clouds of gulls swooping and clamouring around them for the odds and ends.

Now as to your coming up here, for which, of course, I am now all agog, the house is not quite ready yet (though it is practically) and the Doctor's plans have been a little put out of smooth running by his sudden and unexpected marriage. At present he is not living here but at the Schoolhouse a mile or two away with his bride. The geologist is still here but is going away towards the end of this week to other islands and will be away for a fortnight when he will return here. But the position is this.

1) We will definitely come to some arrangements by Thursday or Friday.

2) If these are O.K. for you to travel north on Monday (29th inst) I will telegraph you to that effect on Friday or Saturday.

3) If you do not get a telegram then you will understand that I think it is better for you to wait at Bude for a few days longer although that will involve your paying excess on the return half of your ticket. In this event I will get a letter off to you on Friday again; and tell you exactly what has been arranged.

4) Whether you come North on Monday first or a little later I think what you should do is 1/ arrange to spend a night in Edinburgh and get the Atlas Carrier people to collect the stuff from 8 Westhall Gardens you want sending on here and instruct them to put it aboard the Shetland boat at Leith (as they did with my stuff) and 2/ instead of joining the boat at Leith yourself travel up to Aberdeen by railway and catch the boat there instead – you will find out what time the boat leaves Aberdeen and arrange to catch a train which will enable you to board the boat before it sails – the advantage of this being, for both baby and you, that the sea voyage will not only be shorter but that you will only have one night instead of two to spend on board.

I hope all that is clear – and of course I sincerely hope – and will do my utmost to secure – that it is Monday first you are coming up. I am wearying to see your funny little face again.

You will find a marked difference in mine – I have got quite sea-tanned; and cut quite a dash I can tell you with my blue bonnet.

Now I have another piece of good news for you. You need have no fear of my not doing my very damnedest up here so far as work is concerned, – so far, at least, as my own real work as a poet is concerned. I am just thoroughly into my vein again, and in addition to the poems I have told you of previously, I have had an extraordinary stroke of luck these last two days – I have completed no fewer than 20 lyrics and have notes for a lot more and am perfectly confident that I will be able to run this particular lot up to 50 or 60. And they are real McDiarmid lyrics – nothing forced about them – but a genuine recovery of the kind of impulse that created those in *Sangschaw* and *Penny Wheep*. So there you are! Some people who think me played out will be horribly disappointed shortly when these appear. And F.G. Scott will be up in the air.

Love to all at 28 King St: and kisses to the little Man, and yourself.
Yours, Chris

22. *To Andrew Graham Grieve (EUL)*

Whalsay   20 [21] May 1933

Dear AGG

Many thanks for your letter and for the winter underwear. Although we are having a spell of glorious weather here, the latter will come in extremely useful immediately as a matter of fact for I am off tomorrow morning on a sailing boat to the herring fishing, which has just commenced, about 100 miles North West of Shetland Mainland, and a pair of 'heavies' are highly desirable for that. I expect to be back here on Thursday or Friday provided I can get a lift on one of the other Whalsay sailing boats or steam drifters which is returning earlier, as the particular boat I am going by will not be coming back for a week or longer. As you say, this is just the type of holiday I have been needing – you would scarcely know me already – sun-tanned and well set up again in every way. And the change is proving equally beneficial to my work. I do not know if I told you in my last that I had already written since I came up here a new 900-line poem – 'Ode To All Rebels' – which will be published as a separate small book: but since then I have had a remarkable access of real MacDiarmid lyrics – something after the *Sangschaw* or *Penny Wheep* kind and not inferior to them in quality, but yet not a mere repetition of my older mode but a genuine new development. Of them I have during the past two days completed no fewer than 20 to my satisfaction and have notes for so many more that I am confident this series will pan out to 50 or 60 in the course of the next few days. It is certainly the richest vein I have struck of this sort of thing for years.

I note what you say about the Income Tax people. I will try and get all that cleared up shortly; I thought – since I got no reply, though months elapsed – that my last letter regretting all the trouble they had been put to, owing to my frequent changes of address and pointing out that the amount claimed did not take into consideration the deduction to what I was entitled in respect of wife, children, etc., had ended the matter. I am sorry it has cropped up again and that incidentally you have been troubled about it.

Now – to get to it at last – the real object of this letter is to say that I am writing by this post to Mrs Craik, 8 Westhall Gardens, to ask her if she can take in Mother's stuff all right and saying that you will probably call shortly after she gets my letter to see if it is all right. I think it will be as there isn't much of it. From what you say I am sure it isn't worth fetching up here – especially as boat freight rates owing to monopoly, are deuced heavy both from Leith to Lerwick, and from Lerwick to here.

Sorry you are having such a busy time again officially, and a flitting on top of that. Wish you could have a change like mine for a while. I hope you will pull through all right till your own holidays, & that Chryssie will not be overtaxed again with all the dirdum of the removal.

Love to you all, Chris

23. *To Valda Trevlyn (NLS)*

Whalsay   27 May 1933

My dearest Valda

Now I am back from the herring fishing, really brown as a monkey and feeling extraordinarily fit. Damn the *Daily Mail* and its stupid articles. The life is undoubtedly a hard one and certainly impossible for women – even as visitors: as there is no place for them on such boats and even if there were they would see life in the raw. Apart from other little inconveniences there are of course no lavatories in these sailing boats and one has to hang on the wire rope and do it – both kinds – over the side of the ship which isn't an easy matter when the ship is pitching and rolling and a strong wind blowing. But I got quite expert at it. It is one of the most marvellous sights in the world to see the thousands of herring wriggling about as the nets are hauled in. I came back from Colla Firth in a little motor boat and on the way down we spent some hours line-fishing in some of the lonely inlets, and caught, amongst other things, two halibut, each nearly three quarters of a cwt. & as big as table tops – also caught skate, scallops etc. A great game.

Sorry to get your snotty little note. I wasn't in the least irresponsible about the furniture. I got Miss Veitch in the office to phone up Guy's and arrange it and was there – as was Black – when she did and they said the stuff would be delivered at Craik's at the time I stated. Not hearing from you to the contrary I of course assumed that it had arrived all right. Mrs Craik should have let you know of its non-arrival sooner. I hope it is O.K. now.

I wired you today to come on boat of 6th inst and will do my best to meet you at Lerwick when you arrive there. But I may not be able to get a boat down there the previous day – I will if I possibly can. But otherwise it would mean spending two full days in Lerwick, hotel exes, etc., and I won't do that – I will only be awaiting you if I can get down to

Lerwick the previous evening. If I happen not to be there go to one of the hotels in Lerwick and have a wash-up and some breakfast and a rest for an hour or so till time for the Whalsay boat.

In any case, wire me time you are arriving in Lerwick from Edinburgh or Aberdeen just before you go aboard.

And send on any stuff you can – pram etc. – to me at c/o Dr Orr.

Dr Orr and his wife are off today for a month's holiday: the geologist is away for a fortnight; Dr Orr's locum – a lady doctor – is staying here. The arrangement is that pending the completion of Dr Orr's house you come here for a few days, and then we are going to live for a week or two in the Schoolhouse at Broch.[1] By then Dr Orr's house will be ready. He is to be sending up furniture etc. while he is away and we are to take delivery and install it against his return.

Inter alia – in case of eventualities, and because I am absolutely determined to stay here as long as I possibly can – I have just rented a cottage *for a year* myself.[2]

Homes are practically impossible to get here and the opportunity of securing this one was too good to miss – I secured it while it was going.

I enclose a letter from Whyte (which please keep as I want it back) which may serve as corroborative evidence to you that I am doing some good work. The flow is continuing unabated. I have had a really exciting spell of poetry-making.

I have bought you a nice Shetland jumper (you should have a grey skirt to go with it) – I had to buy something from a sale of work here – but I feel now you will like it and find it lovely and warm later on. But I will keep it here for you.

I am so glad you are having good weather, bathing, and a happy time generally, and that J.M. is so full of beans. I'll discipline the little beggar all right once I get him up here, and you too!! Darling, I'm wearying very much now to see your funny little face again. Love to all, and kisses to JM and yourself.

Yours, Chris

Yes, I wrote Michael all right and have written him again. Will get all that fixed up once you arrive here.

---

1. Broch, the spelling CMG consistently uses referring to Brough, a hamlet in the north-west of Whalsay.
2. The cottage was located at Sudheim (Sodom), east of Symbister, Whalsay's main harbour, and had at one point been a booth of the Hanseatic League. As a child of the previous tenant had died of tuberculosis, nobody had wished to live there and CMG rented the cottage from John Anderson for 26/- a year, plus 7/- in rates.

24. To Andrew Graham Grieve (EUL)

Whalsay, Shetland Islands   24 July 1933

My dear A.

Delighted to get your letter. Congratulations to Morag; I am glad she is doing so well. But I wouldn't worry if Angus doesn't show a similar bent; he may come away – and late ripeners are often the heaviest croppers – or he may find a different bent altogether. Schools aren't very useful to certain types who are none the worse for that.

Thanks for sending on Inland Revenue letter, and to Chrissie for her adroit parrying of their importunity. I can't understand why they didn't write me in acknowledgment of my own letter which simply pointed out that I had notified them on first notice that due allowances had not been deducted, that if these were I wouldn't owe them anything, and that I had at that time applied for an appeal form which I thought I had duly completed and sent them. I regretted any trouble the Department had been put to – mainly owing to my frequent changes of address – and expressed my willingness to fill up another form if need be showing that the deductions to which I was entitled at the period in question cancelled any alleged indebtedness. It is queer that they should persist in following me in this way rather than reply to that letter, and in the circumstances I cannot see how I can do any more at the moment than continue if possible to keep them from learning my address. I want if possible – in the meantime at least – to avoid every avoidable expense. At the same time I do hope you are not further troubled in any way over the matter.

You will probably have heard from Mother about my alarming illness and likelihood of an operation. It is an anal fissure of long standing; these things sometimes lie quiescent for years or keep recurring at intervals and gradually getting worse. Finally an operation is the only way to get rid of them and it happens to be a particularly painful and troublesome operation. When I wrote to Mother I happened to be in the throes of by far the most extensive and excruciating manifestation of it I have had – after such a long period of quiescence that I half thought it had made up its mind to lie doggo for good. But apart from the pain I was panicky about the cost of the operation and the fact that it might throw me for some time off the work I am doing and that just at a crucial juncture too when the maintenance of a particular psychological temper is a *sine qua non*. Since then however there has been a very considerable retraction and the pain is gone. An operation will be necessary but happily not at the moment – unless I have another severe recurrence. I can choose my own time though the severity of this attack renders it inadvisable to delay this too long now. I have written Mother again by this post unless she is worrying unduly or rather still more unduly than she will do in any case.

In the relief from this impending embarrassment I have decided to go off on Wednesday to the Faroe Islands, where the Faroese National Festival is on and representatives will be present from Iceland and Denmark too. The *Scots Observer* have been good enough to commission a couple of articles and that will cover my exes. and I may get one in the *Edin Evening News* too for a spot of bunce.[1] I will be away for just over a week. I had originally intended to go on from the Faroes to Iceland to see some friends in Rekjavik but have abandoned that project in the meantime because I had not time to fix up enough sure commissions to cover exes, because to get back I'd have had to travel via Bergen and Leith, and finally because I am busy with certain work at the moment which does not permit of such a lengthy interlude cutting into it without a probably disastrous discontinuity of mood.

We are into our own cottage now – 4 rooms (26/- per year rent, plus 7/- rate) – standing on a hillside overlooking the sea and the islands – away from all other cottages – and have acquired as pets 1/ a scoury (or wild herring gull chick), 2/ a wild cat. I got up a few things of Mother's, but otherwise – apart from bedding etc. – have so far bought the minimum, but have made bookcases etc. out of boxes. We are very comfortable with an open hearth fire, though I have to carry the peats in a basket from a stack I bought over quarter of a mile away; draw water from a well about a quarter of a mile in the opposite direction and so on. I am very sorry you find a holiday out of the question this year but hope you may bear Whalsay in mind next summer – you will find it one of the most delightful places you ever struck and once the fares are paid (and they are not so very heavy) it is a very cheap place indeed and Valda and I could put the lot of you up very comfortably and would be delighted to have you. You could put in a nice month here at an all-in cost for the four of you of not more than £12.

I've rambled on. There was something else I wanted to say – apart from being glad you like your new place, sympathising with the heavy garden work, and hoping your office duties are abating a bit – oh, yes, it was about the bookcase; that might be very useful here, which one is it? I'll let you know once I hear from you again – that is if it's really no use to you.

Love to you all. I hope you are all O.K. Valda and baby are – I'll send you more snaps next letter – and so am I except for that posterior nuisance I mentioned above.

Yours, Chris

---

1. 'Faroyar: Impressions of the Faroe Isles and the Festival of St Olaf', *Scots Observer*, 19 August 1933.

25. To W.R. Aitken (NLS)

Whalsay, Shetland Islands 29 September 1933

Dear Mr Aitken

Very many thanks for your letter of 25th just to hand. I greatly appreciate the attitude you manifest – both generally and in regard to my own work. Naturally I welcome the opportunity to 'chip in' on the chorus in question. You do not mention what your closing date is: but – seeing your letter has taken a few days to reach me here (this will be my address all winter) – I have dashed off the enclosed just to try to be in time for you. It is perhaps too discordant a note (I know that whatever your own sentiments you may have to observe certain proprieties in the conduct of the *Student*); but, if so, – just to make sure that the point of view finds expression – I will leave it to you entirely just to tone it down or cut this sentence or that out as you think fit. I will be glad if you will in due course send me a copy of the issue in question to the above address.[1]

With best wishes, Yours sincerely, C.M. Grieve

So far as payment is concerned at least 75 per cent of my work always has been, is, and, failing a revolution in Scotland, is always likely to be gratuitous. That wouldn't matter, if only one could get adequate ingress to express one's views even free, gratis, & for nix.

P.S. My message may be too long also. It occurs to me that it will both shorten it and cut out disparaging references to the others which you may scarcely feel you can print, if you cut out the part beginning 'I dissent – ' on page 1 right down to the paragraph ending 'chorus of gratulation' on page 2. The remainder probably says or implies as much as we can hope to 'put across' on such an occasion. But I leave it to you; you may care to retain par. 3 beginning 'Without exception' and ending 'centuries ago'.

The inclusion of my contribution could of course be 'justified' by an editorial paragraph pointing out the unanimity of the others and a consequent desire to hear at least one expression of 'the other side'.

---

1. Bill Aitken had entered Edinburgh University to study English, and was editing *The Student* magazine, which, on 25 October 1933, published a number commemorating the 350th anniversary of the institution. Aitken had read MacDiarmid's work of the 1920s, was stunned by its brilliance, and shocked and saddened to hear that its author was being so much held at bay. The special celebration number of *The Student* (vol. 30, no. 2) attracted birthday salutations from many eminent contemporaries: J.M. Barrie, Ramsay Macdonald, John Buchan, Sybil Thorndike, Stanley Baldwin and Winston Churchill all sent their congratulations, which were printed in the journal's opening pages. Then, by invitation, at the end of the magazine, 'C.M. Grieve ("Hugh MacDiarmid")' threw 'A Stone among the Pigeons'. MacDiarmid's two-column polemic came from so far beyond the constellation of warmth generated by the high-and-mighty that it must have felt as though a switch

had been thrown to shut down the national grid. This was discordance amuck:

> Edinburgh University may be celebrating its 350th Anniversary; it is safe to predict that before it reaches its 400th it will have undergone radical changes representing a complete overthrow of all that my co-contributors are so satisfied about, and that its past history and the reputation of its 'distinguished sons' will be subjected to a correspondingly different estimate ... All our so-called 'progress' has landed Scotland in a mess, the excruciating horrors of which cannot be exaggerated, and any attempt to gloss over our predicament can only be due to wilful or constitutional blindness to all the facts.

This might seem merely strident egomania, but it was grossly offensive and evidently effective. For daring to publish it, the young student was emphatically invited by the authorities to surrender his editorship of *The Student*. He did so proudly. He was almost sent down from the university, but press support of free speech dissuaded the authorities from such disciplinary action. The friendship between CMG and Bill Aitken was to be sustained through the rest of their lives.

26. *To Stanley Nott (EUL)*

Whalsay, Shetland Islands   19 October 1933

My dear Stanley

Just a note at the moment – I'll write you later on in reply to yours to hand yesterday – to say that I've suggested to a friend of mine that he should call in and make your acquaintance. He is a young Scottish writer, J. Leslie Mitchell, who has published histories of Mexican antiquities etc. but also novels and imaginative romances over his own name, the latest being an historical novel, *Spartacus*, well-reviewed in last week's *Times Literary Supplement*, while over the pseudonym of Lewis Grassic Gibbon he has lately scored a great success with *Sunset Song* and *Cloud Howe*, the first two volumes of a trilogy of novels. His publishers are Jarrold's, and Faber and Faber for a biography of the explorer, Mungo Park.[1]

He and I are collaborating in a miscellany on Scotland.

Excuse haste. This is just being dashed off in time to catch the mailboat.

Every best wish for your success in the Ita matter – and everything else.

Yours, C.M.G.

---

1. J. Leslie Mitchell, *Spartacus* (London: Jarrolds, 1933); *The Life of Mungo Park* (Edinburgh: Porpoise Press, 1934). Faber and Faber were then Porpoise's London distributors.

27. To Stanley Nott (EUL)

Whalsay, Shetland Islands   20 December 1933

Dear Stanley

This is just a line from Valda and I to wish Rosemary, the children, and yourself – and the firm of Stanley Nott Ltd – all the compliments of the season and every good wish for a happy and prosperous New Year.

I have been going to write you for ever so long – ever since you sent us the snap of your little James Michael – but got caught up in a whirl of diverse activities. How strange that your baby should have the same unusual combination of Christian names as ours! I did not know your baby's name and though Valda now thinks she was told she had not remembered. I called our baby James after my father and Michael after the Patron Saint of Cornwall.

How are things going? Is your first list of publications available yet? I shall look forward to it eagerly.

Love to you all, Chris

28. To Professor Schlapp (NLS, DFF)

Whalsay, Shetland Islands   26 January 1934

Dear Professor Schlapp

You may remember me. I have had the pleasure of meeting you several times, at Miss Cruickshank's at Corstorphine and elsewhere. And you may know of me as a fairly well-known Scottish poet, through my pseudonym 'Hugh MacDiarmid'.

I have a favour to ask of you. I have been told you are a great Rilke enthusiast and I read with great appreciation your letter in the *Times Literary Supplement* about the Sackville-Wests' very bad mistranslations in their sumptuously-produced volume of renderings of the *Duineser Elegien*.[1] Well, my difficulties are in connection with these wonderful poems and the still more difficult, I think, 'Orpheus Sonnets', and I wonder if you will help me. The type of difficulty – or one of the types of difficulty I am encountering is similar to that to which A.W.G. Randall drew attention in his review of the Sackville-Wests' book in the *Criterion* when – apropos the 2nd Elegy – he said: '"redoubtable" hardly seems happy for *schrecklich*, the epithet applied to angels at the beginning of this second elegy; "terrible" or "fear-inspiring" might be suggested alternatives'.

May I list just a few of the difficulties I have in mind in this initial letter? It is presumptuous on my part to seek your assistance in such a matter and you may have neither the time nor the inclination to assist me in regard to these details. But I shall be very grateful if you can – rather that than such a letter later on as you administered to the Sackville-West efforts!

Here we go then: —
1st Elegy: — und andern eigens versprechenden Dingen — *particularly* promising sounds ridiculous in English, but what else can it be?
2nd Elegy — göttliche Körper — does he refer to the *actual* bodies of Gods, or the Attic statues?
3rd Elegy — die leicht sich verschob — clouds verschicken, but what do they do, equivalent to that, in English?
— das den Keimenden leicht macht — to put 'embryo' is barbaric; I understand that in German this is a colloquialism corresponding almost with our own 'my trouble' but I am puzzled to get an exact and acceptable rendering.
4th Elegy — O Stunden in der Kindheit, da hinter den Figuren mehr als nur — *what* is the Figur?
5th Elegy — Kommt das Brennen der Futssohln ihm, seinem Ursprung, zuvor — Grammar is clear, but the sense isn't — is the schmerz the origin of the burning of footsoles, or vice versa?
6th Elegy — uns rühmt es zu blühn — a *very queer* construction. But how about the English? (Blossoming praises us?) It is (praise) for us to blossom?
Sixth Elegy cont. — anstehn — stand in a queue — the difficulty is to get a translation which will bring out the eagerness to be served as soon as possible.
Seventh Elegy — innigen Himmel. Wie er — really is untranslateable; it is so essentially German, like Gemut — apparently a calm, cordial, intense, deep fervency gives the meaning — 'rapt' is too weak.
an dacht is in the same category — devotion is the nearest I can get to it — meditation won't do — it must be *giving* and of the senses.
— wie der spannende Drang — he means, I suppose, electricity — tensioning — the tension of stress is a poor compromise.
Unfasslicher — a double-meaninged word is it not? — unseizeable, both mentally and physically — it means using two words in English for Rilke's one.
Ninth Elegy — Menschliches — Mensch again is untranslateable — 'human being' is not enough.
Schwelle — just what is this schwelle? — transgressing the boundaries or merely the word itself, like for Krug etc.
Vertrauliche Tod — intimate *with us*?
Tenth Elegy — nicht in euer gelöstes Haar nich gelöster ergab — Rilke is fond of gelöste — see 'Sonnets to Orpheus' — in all cases the word is ambiguous and very difficult to render into English.
Aber ihr Schaum, hinter dem Pschent-Rand hervor, scheucht as die Eule. were they (if it is they; the ihr, could it not, could refer only to die Klage) looking from behind the Pschent-Rand, or did the owl fly out from behind the Pschent-Rand — in German it can be both — only the es referring back to Schaun is unusual, almost ungrammatical — the usual way would be es scheucht.

doppelt aufgeschlagenes Blatt – what is this? steigendes Glück – this is difficult – felicity is appalling; ecstasy too inconstant, but I can't think of an English word for enduring ecstasy.

I am very conscious of my temerity in asking you about all this, but Rilke is so very difficult, and so incomparably worth while any and every expenditure of time and trouble, I think.

With compliments and every high regard.

Yours sincerely, C.M. Grieve

---

1. Rainer Maria Rilke, *Duineser Elegien – Elegies from the Castle of Duino*, tr. V. Sackville-West and Edward Sackville-West (London: Hogarth Press, 1931).

29. *To J.B. Caird (NLS)*

Whalsay, Shetland   8 February 1934

My dear Caird

Excuse a very brief and business like letter. I am also too infernally busy for any verbal embroideries. I was glad to have your note today for I was just on the point of writing to you, or one of you, being anxious to know how things were going with your group and alas – as you will see – to find out something else. I am delighted the book is shaping out. As to *The Free Man* I should certainly like the articles to appear there first – the circulation so reached would not affect the subsequent prospects of the book – the only point is how many weeks it would take to serialise the whole thing in *The Free Man*, as I feel that time matters a great deal the way things are going and am particularly anxious if it is at all possible that the book should appear in April or May. But as to the publication of the book – while I think to serialise it in *The Free Man* and keep the type standing will help matters greatly and cheapen the eventual publication – I think that it would help the book (and the objects for which the book is being written) to have it published by a publishing firm with a good sales organisation and pull with newspapers etc. through being Advertisers. This could be either an Edinburgh firm like Oliver and Boyd, if an Edinburgh firm will take it up, or a London firm. In the latter case it might be possible to arrange a basis of formal publication with them and the Scots Free Press as the Porpoise Press used to with Faber and Faber, or as the Moray Press now does with Messrs Harrap. In either case having the type standing should result in receiving a much bigger royalty percentage than is usual. Where they probably had to pay the cost of the type setting and part of this – say 5 per cent if the royalty is fixed at 20 per cent – might be allocated to the Scots Free Press. In the event of your deciding either to try to manage journal publication with the Scots Free Press and a London firm or entire publication by the latter a/ using type left standing or b/ setting *de novo* my services are at your disposal – and I have in mind a London firm likely to be willing to agree to one, and perhaps to any of these three alternatives.

You might perhaps read this part of my letter to R.M.B. [Robert McKelvie Black] and discuss it with him. He will understand that it is written in view of the pros and cons of the publication question as you have put these to me in today's letter.

The next point is that if you want any prefatory and/or concluding article for the book either Gibbon or I – or in the latter case both of us – will be very willing and so would Naomi Mitchison. Just let me know when you are ready and I'll write Gibbon and/or Naomi.

Perhaps you will have seen by *The Free Man* by the time you get this that both Gibbon and I have these books coming up this spring – one a big book in which we have collaborated.

Now the final matter is a very private and urgent one upon which I am particularly anxious that you should not breathe a word to anyone, so we'll go on to a new page to discuss it. [MS ends]

30. *To Andrew Graham Grieve (EUL)*

28 King St, Bude, North Cornwall   Thursday Night [12 April 1934
                                                 – date noted in AGG's hand.]

My dear A

I got your wire at 7 o'clock tonight; can't get telegram off till tomorrow morning; couldn't get to London till 4.30 tomorrow, not to Lockerbie and Laurie's Close till Monday sometime. You will have seen my last letter to mother – which I gather she can't have got.[1] I delayed writing her because I was unsure from day to day when I could get north. I was to have spoken in Edinr. on Monday but at last moment was held up *sine die* over certain legal difficulties concerning a new book of mine, so came down here pending developments. I need not tell you – and perhaps you can't even imagine or believe – how sorry I am this has precluded my seeing Mother again before her death. I had, of course – though Ann[2] said (in a letter I received very belatedly after it had been repeatedly redirected to different addresses) she was *very poorly* – no idea the end was so near. I, of course, reproach myself for at least not even writing to her oftener – tho' I had improved in this respect of late. Yet my sense of failure in this respect would have been very greatly mitigated if I had known that she had received my last letter in time. I can imagine some of the reflections that are passing through your mind. Chryssie said to me last time I was in Edinburgh that she thought I was only concerned with one thing – my own self-glorification. She was wrong – because what I do, irrational as it is from ordinary standards, isn't even concerned with that but often dramatically opposed to the advancement even of my own reputation. I do serve certain ideas – quite disinterestedly, and to my own loss; and at the moment and for some time back I have been involved in very difficult matters; it has taken me all my time to keep going at all. If occasionally this has led me (and I am in no way apologising for it) into ways of living of which you would for one reason or another have disapproved, and which admittedly were disapprovable on both general and particular grounds, that does not mean that I was unconscious in any way, or failing to meet, my major problems, as is proven by the fact that I have no fewer than seven books coming out this year and others contracted for in advance. My troubles (apart from acute legal difficulties with two different firms of publishers involving the very considerable rewriting or alteration of two books due for immediate publication)[3] were greatly added to on my arrival in London a week or two ago. I found that Peggy's husband – who is extremely wealthy – had not only been suddenly beggared but that the papers in an intricate civil case had been passed on to the Public Prosecutor.[4] I saw him and Peggy last Friday – the Public Prosecutor had just given his fiat – and the upshot is a criminal case on a fraud charge due for hearing on 22nd inst. I like the man – I am as fond of Peggy as ever – and there are my two children to consider. You can imagine from this briefest of summaries how on this score alone I have been worried and how it was one of the reasons that upset my plans for returning to Scotland and dropping off at Lockerbie to see Mother.

I am very sensible how impossible it is for Chryssie and you (and I greatly appreciated your kindness & was delighted to see you again) to understand the factors that are operating in my case and dictating – or at lest accounting for – my apparently unconscionable and irrational behaviour.

I will say no more of that. I can only say that I hope Mother had an easy and peaceful passing. My regrets and reflections are my own. But I would have given all I possess – and that wouldn't have paid my fare – to have seen her before the end, and it was a mere damnable fluke that I didn't.

I will be grateful if you will send me a letter to above address telling me about her end and about the funeral. You will have been involved in all sorts of expenses and of course I will share these with you if you will tell me the amount. So in regard to anything that requires to be done in adding to the inscription on the tombstone or otherwise in attending to her grave. I did not know what to do tonight but I am wiring you first thing tomorrow (didn't know if you'll get wire tomorrow before leaving Laurie's Close) and at last moment I thought of Bob Laidlaw[5] and am writing him too to have nice wreath from me at funeral. I hope this can be arranged.

I can say no more, pending, I hope, a letter from you. I have to go back to London tomorrow on urgent business and will be there several days,

but letters here will find me for some weeks yet.
    Love to you all. Yours, Chris

---

1. Elizabeth Dawson died 11 April 1934.
2. CMG's cousin, Ann Barnfather; see Appendix.
3. Hugh MacDiarmid, *Stony Limits and other poems* (London: Gollancz, 1934). The publishers had claimed that 'Ode to All Rebels' and 'Harry Semen' were illegal under obscenity laws and also wished the removal of several pro-Communist poems; all were excised and substitutions made.
4. William McElroy and Peggy were not in fact married.
5. Robert Laidlaw (1882–1949), another of CMG's cousins and brother of John Laidlaw.

31. *To Valda Trevlyn (NLS)*

c/o Scott, 44 Munro Road, Glasgow   Thursday, 3 May 1934

My dear V.

　Just a line to show you that I have returned to the land of my fathers. I made up my mind very suddenly and came up with the overnight train. Please send any correspondence here till further notice. You'd get my wired money order all right. My resources at the moment are at the lowest possible ebb, but I think that will speedily rectify itself now and that the general situation *in re* the Shetlands, my return there (which will take place as soon as ever it possibly can), and your maintenance in Bude will turn out quite satisfactorily after all. But I'll write you again in a day or so, and by that time expect I will have definite news and some 'dibs' to send you. Excuse this very short note at the moment. I am exceedingly tired after my journey, but I'll be O.K. by tomorrow. Mr and Mrs Scott asking for you and sending their love.

　Kisses to Mike and yourself, and every kind regard to your mother and aunts and Mrs Fellowes.

　Yours, Chris

32. *To Andrew Graham Grieve (EUL)*

c/o Scott, 44 Munro Road, Jordanhill, Glasgow   7 May 1934

Dear Graham

　I have nothing to say in reply to your last letter which is, from that particular point of view, quite understandable. My own point of view as you recognise is entirely different and the fact that yours is a far more commonly accepted one means nothing to me. Suffice it that apart from remissness in letter writing I have little or nothing to reproach myself with; my inability to carry out what I had hoped re weekly payment was simply a real inability – 5/- a week is 20 per cent of my unmortgaged earnings for the past year and more and I have three people to keep on these; and I totally deny your oft repeated assertion that I in any way got more than my share from Mother. Your first letter urging me to come up on account of Mother's serious condition did not reach me until *the Tuesday after her funeral*. Re the rest of your letter I have only to say that I shall await news of your dispositions. Above address will get me for some days.

Yours, Chris.

P.S. You will understand that I write this 'without prejudice' and that it is in no way to be construed as consenting to any intromissions you may make with Mother's estate or an agreement to forego any of the rights under Scottish law of a son in relation to an intestacy.

33. *To Andrew Graham Grieve (EUL)*

c/o Scott, 44 Munro Road, Jordanhill, Glasgow   Saturday
                    [12 May 1934 – date postmarked on envelope.]

Dear Graham

I am sure that – apart from real differences of opinion – you will appreciate that the nature of my last note to you (like some of my previous actions) was determined by the desperate situation in which I am placed and did not reflect any ill-will to you personally. Like yourself I would have wished that our renewed relationship might have led to a happier issue, and no fault of yours, but my circumstances, prevented that. However, this is only a note to say that I shall be in Edinburgh on Monday and that if there is anything you would like to discuss with me we can meet anywhere you care if you send a message to *The Free Man* Office, 1 India Bldgs, Victoria St.

My movements after Monday will be very indefinite.

Yours, Chris

34. *To Valda Trevlyn (NLS)*

The Royal Hotel, Woburn Place,   Saturday [1934]
Russell Square, London W.C.1

My dear V.

I agree we have a lot of things to talk over very seriously. But do believe – despite my subsequent behaviour[1] – that I am *very* fond of you and regard our last Cornish week as one of the happiest times in my life. I am very short of cash myself but want you to have the outing (to a place I can't make out from your writing) if possible, so enclose 10/- herewith. The delay in my Mother's matter is *not* due to the extent of her estate but to complications ensuing on her last illness and burial. My libel action is proceeding merrily – I have spent most of today with lawyers etc. – and have had (in order to prosecute the case) to implement them in funds to the extent of £20 which I had a devil of a job raising.[2] I want you to send back the bedclothes to Whalsay as soon now as you can – and tell Maguire I want the peats & will pay for same immediately I get back there which won't be long now. Sorry you are having difficulties with the aunts – conscious that I have been largely responsible therefor.

Glad J.M. is growing up such a fine little fellow.

Love to you all. Yours, Chris

---

1. CMG had arranged to meet Valda in a London pub, The Plough, on Monday 21 May and had wired her the fare; presumably he did not turn up, as Valda later claimed she had found him, drunk, at the Royal Hotel, where he had brought a woman (who was staying in a separate room).
2. The proof of *Broken Record* (London: Boriswood, 1934), by the South African poet, Roy Campbell, contained a reference to CMG which he had seen and considered libellous and which was removed before publication.

35. *To Valda Trevlyn (NLS)*

Northumberland Hotel, 9, 11 & 11a Euston Road,   Sunday [1934]
King's Cross, London, N.W.1

My dear V.

I wired Anderson at once – 'Definitely buying cottage. Arranging early payment. Returning next week.' And also wrote him in full about it. I am annoyed about the whole thing as he already had my definite agreement in writing to purchase the cottage at the figure he asked. Also I don't understand why he is worried about firing. I thought Mrs Arthur was seeing to that for us.[1]

The real trouble is that I cannot yet get hold of the necessary dough to go back – complete the purchase – pay for the peats – and get the few chairs etc. we need. In fact at moment I cannot pay tonight's hotel – I have only 4/- left. I may be able to raise the wind tomorrow. But in case not please wire me £1 if you possibly can to c/o Lahr[2] – and make it payable at Chancery Lane Post Office (which is the nearest one I remember the name of). If I get money elsewhere I'll at once send it back. If I don't and you can't send it I'll be on the streets. I have not heard from my brother or the *Scottish Educ. Journal* or the Edinburgh *Evening News* – Gollancz seems to be dodging me – and so on. The week in fact has been a blank and I wish I hadn't come to London at all. I greatly enjoyed my Cornish week – greatly regret my behaviour to you here – and am very anxious about the future and eager to get back to Whalsay as soon as possible.

Love to all and kisses to little J.M. and yourself.

Yours, Chris

---

1. Harriet and Hugh Arthur were the Grieves' neighbours at Sudheim.
2. Charles Lahr; see Appendix.

36. *To Valda Trevlyn (NLS)*

33 Great James St., W.C. [London]   Monday [1934]

My dear Valda

I agree that from your point of view my conduct must appear callous and inconsiderate in the extreme. But the explanation is simply that I do not know which way to turn myself. I have the very utmost difficulty in keeping going at all – have had no money myself except the 30/- you sent me. Have not heard from my brother yet about the settlement of Mother's estate tho' I spent my last two bob on Friday wiring him about it. If I hear I'll write or wire you at once and then we can make plans. I worked out a scheme for acquiring Mrs Crosskey's house all right but can go no further for lack of cash – till my brother or Gollancz or somebody ante up.[1] As to my books the advance copies must all have gone to the Shetlands – I'd have got a few others and sent you samples if I could have managed it, but I couldn't buy them – and if I could, couldn't have afforded to post them. As you say – what a life! I got the first whisper of the Henson business on Saturday. Grant has obviously forged the receipt – I'll get on to him as soon as I get a bob or two. He got the money all right, damn and blast him.[2] I'll have to get parked down to hard work very soon now so, pending anything else, I think you should look around for Cornish cottage – furnished one – we could take if necessary for a couple of months or more. In any case be sure I'll send you any cash I get at once – and if I'm slow in writing be sure it's only – or mainly – because I haven't the stamps. I am really dreadfully sorry about all these infernal difficulties but simply can't get out of them.

Love to Miky Fike[3] and all friends, and kisses to yourself.

Yours, Chris

P.S. McElroy was acquitted.

Scottish Scene is going well, I understand.[4]

I've no Scottish news – or cuttings or anything.

---

1. 'Auntie Betty' Croskey lived at Anchor cottage, between Hamister and North Park. In the event, CMG purchased John Anderson's cottage which he had

previously been renting.
2. Seeing an advertisement for *Scottish Scene*, a certain Mrs Henson from Thakeham had written to Valda, saying that she hoped it would sell well so that CMG could repay the £5 he owed to her. The Grieves had paid the £5 in question to Grant, also an inhabitant of Thakeham, and assumed it had been passed on to Mrs Henson as she had returned the MSS she had been holding as ransom.
3. Fike, to trouble or vex.
4. Lewis Grassic Gibbon and Hugh MacDiarmid, *Scottish Scene: or The Intelligent Man's Guide to Albyn* (London: Jarrolds, 1934).

37. *To Valda Trevlyn (NLS)*

[London]   Wednesday [12 June 1934]

My dearest V.

If you had only sent my brother's letter on right away – instead of saying it had been knocking about in your bag for some days but you'd send it on if you remembered – we'd probably have been in considerably less desperate straits ere this. Immediately I got it I spent every remaining cent I had wiring him (I'd sent the receipt for the £5 – part of which you had – immediately I received it) and following it up with a detailed letter. I'm disgusted to have had no reply yet. He promised settlement by 1st week of this month. I only suggested the Cornish cottage because I must complete books for the autumn I've contracted for; have no earthly chance of doing so here where I am in really desperate straits to keep going on absolute minimum existence level, without laundry and conveniences of any sort or more than one meal per day; and can't possibly go back to the Shetlands until I have money 1/ to go, 2/ to pay Anderson, 3/ to pay peats etc. The libel case is dragging on; they haven't compromised yet ... but will, I think, tho' that may take long enough (Cathy Carswell's libel case has been dragging on for 9 months).[1]

I have my faults and am not trying to extenuate them – but I am not lying; I thought I saw a way re the Crosskey house but that depended – and stills depends – on my getting money from Gollancz and in respect of my autobiography (from Jarrolds – whom I think I may make final contract with this week). As to Mrs Henson I can do nothing at the moment.

I will send you copies of my books as soon as I have postage for them. I enclose a few reviews. Did Whyte send you a copy of the *Modern Scot*? It is virtually a Grieve number.[2] You'd get Helen's *Up the Noran Water*?[3]

I'll write again – and send some – the moment I get any cash. I'm extremely sorry you are so ill-off and wish I could do anything but at moment I am powerless. (You ought, by the way, to have had *Educational Journal* cheque.) I really do love you and am wearying to have you with me again – you and Miky, to both of whom kisses.

Yours, Chris.

Can't understand reference to Midge – have not seen her to my knowledge – wouldn't know her in any case unless she told me who she was.

---

1. Catherine Roxburgh Carswell née Macfarlane (1879–1946), Glasgow-born novelist and literary critic.
2. *The Modern Scot*, June 1934.
3. Helen Burness Cruickshank, *Up the Noran Water* (London: Methuen, 1934).

38. *To Andrew Graham Grieve (EUL)*

c/o Gawsworth, 33 Great James St [London] 14 June 1934

My dear AGG

I hope you duly received my telegram (sent immediately I got your letter re the £5) and subsequent letter. I have been waiting to hear from you. If I remember rightly you expected to settle Mother's estate by last week. No doubt some belated a/c or something has delayed matters, but I am extremely anxious to receive the balance as soon as possible, and will be glad if you can let me know by return definitely when I shall have it – as it will just serve to bridge me over a difficult period until I get certain other monies which I am due to receive on completion of new books by or about the end of July.

I hope Chryssie is much better and all the others of you fine and fit.

Excuse this short note. You will receive copies of my 4 Spring books in a day or two.

Yours, Chris

39. *To Valda Trevlyn (NLS)*

c/o Gawsworth, 33 Great James St [London] 14 June 1934

My dear Valda

They say – what say they? – let them say.

These rumours and scandals must of course make things very unpleasant for you and create difficulties with your mother and aunts; but so far as I am concerned I not only trust you implicitly but I do not expect you to be inhumanly circumspect nor – if you deviated on occasion from conventional conceptions of fidelity – would I be unduly disturbed. I want you to be yourself and as long as you care for me and want to rejoin me I have no reason – and no right – to try to repress the free play of your personality in other directions.

I think I'll be able to send you the copies of my books today or tomorrow.

You ask me to trust you. Trust me too, darling – in essentials; in detail I am – well – uncertain.

Love to Mikey & all, & kisses.

Chris

40. *To Valda Trevlyn (NLS)*

[London]   Saturday [1934]

Dear V.

Your letter arrives – as did your telegram – at moment when I'm absolutely broke; not even fare to Edinburgh. I wrote Black but have had no reply from him. Nothing whatever has turned up yet and I'm at my wits' end. However things must develop soon. So far as the cottage at Widemouth is concerned the thing to do is to tell the owner you've been in communication with me – that I'm agreeable, and want a month's option, in order to realise some shares and receive the necessary cash. This is true because I have already written Captain Matthew Heath MP who is the Chairman of the Unicorn Press and a very wealthy man about his taking over my holding in that company.[1] Also I have not heard yet about my mother's estate but that cannot be long delayed and I will certainly have something coming there – my brother is handling the matter but I have already impressed him that while he can go ahead, I only let him do so without prejudice to my rights, which in the case of an intestate state are considerable under Scottish law and that I reserve the right to disapprove of any dispositions he may make. Gollancz – *New Britain* – etc. are all still in the air;[2] and I have completed another contract with Macmillans to issue a volume of 50 of my best lyrics at 1/- this autumn (I don't get any money on that however till the book appears).[3] Excuse this hasty scrawl – I know you will be dying to hear – I would have written you ere this only I have been waiting day to day in hope of some definite news. I will write you again as soon as anything happens. I have your shoes, and all my stuff, but cannot afford to post you the former yet. Delighted to hear of J.M.'s progress in speech etc. – bless his little heart. Sorry the snaps of me were not better. Many thanks for the flannel trousers etc. Now just go and get a month's option on that cottage (which certainly seems just the very thing) and – while not promising any more – I will at least do my very utmost to be in a position to take it up at the expiry of that period. Love to your mother and aunts, and Mrs Fellowes, and kisses to yourself.

Yours, Chris

---

1. In fact, Captain Michael John Hunter (1891–1951), Tory MP for

Brigg/Lincolnshire.
2. *New Britain*, a periodical to which MacDiarmid had contributed October 1933–March 1934.
3. Hugh MacDiarmid, *Selected Poems* (London: Macmillan, 1934).

41. *To James Leslie Mitchell (Lewis Grassic Gibbon) (NLS)*

c/o Lahr, Bookshop, Red Lion St., [London] W.C.   Saturday [1934]

My dear Mitchell

Greetings to you, and to your wife and family. I am still in town (and will be for another couple of months at least) – or, in Hale's phrase, unable to tear myself away from the fleshpots. I've just heard from Mirsky – letter was forwarded by *Moscow News* to an old address and had just run him to earth when he wrote. Thinks *Spartacus* the goods and intends writing about it shortly. Do you ever come up to town these days? I've been wanting to talk to you about *Scottish Eccentrics*.[1] If you are to be up one day this week let us meet for a little – phone Lahr and leave a message fixing a rendezvous (say in that pub we visited last in Ludgate Hill – but *not* at Lahr's, and *not* at The Plough). You probably subscribe to a press-cutting agency – if so, if you've a collection of *Scottish Scene* reviews you might let me have a look at them. I've only seen one or two – including that silly bitch, Agnes Mure Mackenzie's in the *Times Lit.*[2] I hope the book has sold well – and that all your other affairs are prospering. I'm hard at work again.

All the best. Yours, C.M.G.

---

1. Hugh MacDiarmid, *Scottish Eccentrics* (London: Routledge, 1936).
2. Agnes Mure Mackenzie (1891–1955), historian and novelist.

42. *To Andrew Graham Grieve (EUL)*

c/o Woodhead, 12 Petherton Road, London N.5   Tuesday, 11 July 1934

My dear A

You'll have received by now the three books I think – *Scottish Scene*, *Stony Limits*, and *At The Sign of The Thistle*. The first has sold very well – I'm looking forward to a nice cheque from it in the Autumn which I wish was here, for I am still having an excruciatingly difficult time, one of those infernal between-times till more money is due to come in, which seem perfect eternities of short commons and anxiety. The second is one of my best and most varied volumes of poetry: I have only seen one review so far – in the *Glasgow Herald*; about a column – extremely laudatory. The third is the best prose book I have done; full of solid stuff, and far better written than the bulk of my current journalism – from which it is largely drawn. I'll be pleased to have your candid views of them anon – when you get time to read them and marshal your impressions.

As I say I'm still having a devil of a difficult time. I've taken on some film work for the GPO Film Unit under John Grierson[1] – to fit poetic libretti in vers libre to 3 new films instead of prose captions: but they aren't ready for me yet and I can't get money from that source until I've evolved these verse accompaniments. I'm busy too with my new books for the autumn but there again there's nothing doing in the cash line till I actually hand over the goods. I don't want to worry you but things being in this rather desperate pass I'd be very glad indeed if you could possibly send on any more that may be coming to me – or part of it – by return post. I need some money by Friday and, tho' I may have a little coming in from another source that is uncertain to arrive in time and I must mak' siccar if I possibly can. It's a devil of a business this trying to bridge these horrible gulfs between the times when cash comes in – something beyond the ken of those who enjoy a regular weekly or monthly income.

Tho' thus worried and cudgelling my ageing wits all airts, I am in good form physically and thoroughly enjoying the splendid hot weather. I trust Chryssie is now fully recovered and that you are all well.

Every kind regard. Yours, Chris

---

1. John Grierson (1898–1972), Scottish documentary film producer and the 'father' of the genre in Britain, worked with GPO film unit from 1934 to 1938.

43. *To Sorley MacLean (NLS)*

c/o Woodhead, 12 Petherton Road, London N.5   9 August 1934

My dear Maclean,

Your letter of 27th ult. has just run me to earth here. I am delighted to have it. A variety of causes – also responsible for my unexpectedly protracted stay down here and my inability to get back to the Shetlands for a month or two yet – have prevented me from getting on with the anthology[1] as quickly as I had hoped and forced me to concentrate on other matters first. But I have pretty well cleared my decks of these now and am ready to work double tides in order to complete the anthology by the contracted time. The bulk of the material must be in the hand of the publishers within the next fortnight but so long as that is done it won't matter although a few items are not delivered until a week or two later. I am immensely grateful to you for all your help and will be extremely glad if you will post off to me all you have ready right away. I am particularly anxious that the Gaelic side should be thoroughly well represented, but those poems you name – Macintyre's 'Ben Dorain', MacDonald's 'Moladh Moraig', MacCodrum's 'Mavis of Clan Donald', and MacDonald's 'Birlinn' – seem to me an excellent start to that end. I should certainly like the others you mention by MacDonald, Rob Donn, Roderick Morrison, and Ross.[2] And above all I am anxious to have Livingstone represented by a characteristic piece, also Donald Sinclair. Re the latter I still have some of his stuff in the Shetlands but there is no one there to look it out and send it on to you; the bulk I sent on to Sheriff MacMaster Campbell, but I will try at once to get hold of some of it for you. Have you seen Watson's book of Mary of the Songs?[3] Is there anything there we could use? Also is there anything you know of really good by a living writer? I don't want to give the impression if I can help it that good Gaelic poetry is a thing of the past and that we have no one today worthily carrying on the great tradition. I wonder if there is anything we could use in young Aonghas Caimbeul for example?[4]

This is not a considered letter. I am just dashing it off immediately on receipt of yours to say how eager I am to have anything you can send right away and to take you at your word and enjoin all the speed-up you can possibly manage with regard to the rest. But there are other points I will mention when I write again in a day or two.

What a glorious Summer it has been! I hope you are in good form and having a thoroughly enjoyable holiday. Every kind regard,

Yours sincerely, C.M. Grieve

---

1. *The Golden Treasury of Scottish Poetry*, ed. Hugh MacDiarmid (London: Macmillan, 1940).
2. The Gaelic poets Duncan Ban Macintyre (1724–1808), Alasdair Mac Mhaighstir Alasdair (Alexander MacDonald) (c.1700–70), Ian MacCodrum (1693–1779), Rob Donn MacAoidh (c.1715–78), Uilleam Ros (William Ross) (1762–90) and Roderick Morrison (c.1656–1714).
3. *Gaelic Songs of Mary Macleod*, tr. J. Carmichael Watson (London and Glasgow: Blackie & Son, 1934).
4. Aonghas Caimbeul (1908–49), an aspiring Gaelic poet, was not included in the anthology and seems only to have had one volume, *Gaelic Songs* (1943), published in his lifetime.

---

44. *To Sorley MacLean (NLS)*

12 Petherton Road, London. N.5   31 August 1934

My dear Maclean

It is too bad my being so long in acknowledging your translations; but I have been absolutely up to the eyes. They are just the very thing I wanted and so far as I have gone everything seems clear enough. I have completed the translation of the 'Birlinn' and am extremely pleased with it; you may not be so satisfied – but it is at least very close to your translation and at the same time a thoroughly good poem in the English (which were the two considerations I was striving after), while, also, I have been able to give such faint suggestions of the original structure and the assonance and other technical devices as are practicable in that antipathetic tongue. I will send you a copy as soon as I can get one typed. Two points only occur to me – in the second verse of the Ship Blessing is it the blessing of holy Eruine or holy Gruine [in fact, it is Truine] that is invoked and (forgive my ignorance) who was she? And in the tearing sounds towards the end – *Tise, Taise*, – are they rightly given just so? I ask because you seem to have an accent over them.

I am busy now with the 'Ben Dorain' which is a very very much more difficult proposition.

Excuse this very short note. But I could not delay longer in letting you know I'd got your letters all right, that they were just what I wanted, and that I am busy on them.

Every good wish. Yours, C.M. Grieve

45. *To Andrew Graham Grieve (EUL)*

12 Petherton Road, London N.5   18 September 1934

My dear A.G.G.

I herewith beg to acknowledge your cheque for £9.10.1, in final settlement in respect to my share in mother's estate.

Valda and I have just got back from spending a few days with 'Lewis Grassic Gibbon' at Welwyn Garden City, where we had a glorious time, sleeping in a three-sided (i.e. open at one side) glass-roofed shed in the garden – although we got the full benefit of the big thunder-storm. We are both the better of the change tho' Valda is still far from her usual form, and I am still afflicted with infernal headaches.[1]

There are numerous misprints in this book, alas, but I have not time to go through it just now and mark them for you; you will spot the most important ones (i.e. those that affect the sense – where any!) at any rate as you read. I'm busy trying to conclude a few more contracts here and get off back to the Shetlands now as speedily as possible. Hope you are all well. Love from Valda and I.

Yours, Chris

---

1. CMG had married Valda on 12 September 1934. The witnesses were Charles Lahr and Margaret Bressler. On the occasion, Lahr presented them with a wedding gift of a book, *Songs of the Army of the Night* by Francis Adams.

46. To A.J.B. Paterson, Sales Manager, Routledge (URL)

12 Petherton Road N.3 [London]   21 September 1934

My dear Pat

As promised I have written tonight to Lewis Grassic Gibbon, suggesting that we lunch together one day next week. I will get into touch with you as soon as I hear from him and then we can fix hour and place.

I am as I have already told you greatly taken with the idea of your Scottish section. I am dead certain that this is timely – you are on a rising market and all sorts of good books about Scottish subjects will undoubtedly be written in the next year or two. As you know I am in touch with practically every Scottish writer of any quality or promise today and also with the students at all our universities. The latter are more and more concentrating on Scottish subjects and some of us are directing them along useful lines. I give particulars of four books on attached page; these can if you care be contracted for Autumn publication and would I think give your Scottish list a thoroughly good send-off. There are others I have in mind or know different writers are either working on or contemplating, and there is also as you know the question of suggesting subjects to likely writers. I will of course be glad to help in all these directions, but I confine myself to these four suggestions in the meantime because I hope it may be possible to fix up a definite arrangement such as you indicated before I leave town (which I fancy will be about the end of next week). I would also be quite willing to give your firm the option on two other books in addition to the possibility of a second volume of *Scottish Eccentrics*.

I have been thinking about the question of a name, and suggest the following for consideration along with those you have already in mind, viz.,

 Caledon Press
 Abbotsford Press
 Albyn Press
 Burns Press
 Scottish Publishing Company

Others will probably occur to me. This question of a name is of course a very important one and not to be rushed.

Expect a phone call from me on Monday or Tuesday.

All the best from Valda and myself. Yours, C.M. Grieve.

I'll let you have Walkinshaw back in the beginning of the week with a few notes that occur to me thereanent.

1. *The Soul of Scotland* by Matthew J. Moulton. This is an anthology of extracts dealing in different sections, each of which is arranged chronologically, with the essence of the Scottish character, Scotland's historical function and particular contribution to the world, the qualities of our

various intranational elements, our regional differences and the changing character of our principal cities down the centuries; and the salient comments on Scotland and the Scottish people of foreign visitors (e.g. Chopin, Dr Johnson, Dorothy Wordsworth, Shelley, Keats, Bret Harte, Edgar Allen Poe, Karel Kapek etc.) Curiously enough this has never been done in regard to Scotland and Moulton has levied on a great range of books throughout the ages and the bulk of his material is from little known sources, and makes very vivacious reading, while his method of arrangement results in a complete picture – a unity of effect which is of a very lively and entertaining kind with a splendid sardonic edge. It is not a scrappy book but reads right on, each quotation being shrewdly interrelated.

2. *The Ceol Mor.* Or *Big Pipe Music.* By Francis George Scott. Mr Scott is Lecturer in Music in Jordanhill Training College, Glasgow, a pupil of Roger Ducasse, and the only composer of international calibre Scotland has produced. As an art-song writer he ranks with Hugo Wolf. The Ceol Mor were the bagpipe compositions of the great period and until Mr Scott went thoroughly into the whole matter during the past three or four years had never been the subject of that systematic study against the whole background of musical evolution and in particular that of oriental music they require. What usually passes for bagpipe music is tuney stuff of the post-1800 degeneracy period. The Ceol Mor are of a very different sort, and call for a thorough understanding of, for example, the Gregorian Chant or plainsong and use of the neuma in Roman Catholic music, and also of Arabian music. The necessary qualifications for such a study are rare. Any useful writing on the matter so far is buried in obscure German musical magazines. This will be an important book of permanent value, and would require to embody a fair number of illustrative passages in music type. If you think of this book – which it seems to me you are the ideal firm to publish – arrangements should be made at once as there is a danger of it going elsewhere. You should let me approach Mr Scott on your behalf in the first instance, and then I will put you in touch.

3. *Expression In Scotland.* By James MacLaren.[1] This is a very interesting study of Scottish literature and other forms of expression from the point of view of their relationship to changing social conditions and the extent and conditions of their appeal to the general public. It is not directly concerned with purely literary or aesthetic values, but has of course a shrewd bearing alike on the problems of distinctive Scottish culture today and tomorrow, and on the more general issues which are being so widely canvassed at present of popular art and ways and means of bridging or obviating the gulf between the arts and the masses. Mr

MacLaren (who is a regular contributor to the *Scottish Educational Journal*, and other organs) had not quite completed the book when I saw him a few weeks ago, but it will run to some sixty thousand words and is not treated in any heavy pedantic style but in a racy fashion likely to appeal to a big public. Here again you have a study of an important subject which has not previously been tackled at all.

4.*West Highland Boy*. By R.M. Black. These vividly written pages of reminiscence transport one into a fascinating world which has completely disappeared within living memory. The late Neil Munro touched on it but in fictional form. Mr Black's recollections of Oban and Argyllshire thirty to forty years ago recreate an atmosphere that is already half legendary; he not only describes the development of a singularly attractive personality in some of the wildest and most beautiful scenes in Europ, but his book is peopled with extraordinary characters and informed throughout with an intimate knowledge of Gaelic culture and characteristics. Several books somewhat of this sort have scored notable successes recently e.g. Sullivan's *Twenty Years A-Growing* (an account of a boyhood on the Blasket Islands) which was the book of the month alike in this country and in USA.[2] Nothing equivalent has yet come out of Scotland, but I am confident that Mr Black's book is a first-class item in this category.

1. One of CMG's pseudonyms. None of the proposed books was published.
2. Maurice O'Sullivan, *Twenty Years A-growing*, tr. Moya Llewelyn Davies and George Thomson (London: Chatto and Windus, 1933).

47. *To Stanley Nott (EUL)*

Whalsay, Shetland Islands   27 November 1934

My dear Stanley

I was very glad to get your letter of 21st inst yesterday. I was completely puzzled by your long silence, tho' of course I knew that following Orage's death you would be overwhelmed with grief and no doubt busy giving your help in the winding up of his affairs.[1] The news of Orage's death, which I got here over the wireless, came as a terrible blow. I have, of course, had no details yet at all, although some one sent me a short newspaper cutting which said that he had been off colour for some time before the end. I wrote immediately to Mrs Orage expressing my very real sorrow and sympathy with her. Is the *New English Weekly* to carry on or not, and, if so, under whose editorship? I have not seen it since I got back here but if in one of the issues since his death there has been any memorial article about him it would be awfully kind of you if you could send me a copy. Are you thinking of bringing out any little commemorative volume or memoir of him? I should think that a book of personal impressions of him by men like A.E., Edwin Muir, Michael Arlen,[2] and others, with a prefatory biographical note giving the facts of his life and career, would be a very good idea. As to my poems I shall of course be very happy to have you publish the selection, as you suggest of the best of those in the MSS you have, at a cheap price. But two points arise in connection with this. The first is the question of title – would *Forty New Songs* still suit the selection and be a true description of it?[3] I would have to see your selection first to know that, and (this is the second point) I want to see it and consider it carefully in any case, to make sure that it is the best possible with the material at my disposal and thoroughly worthy of me. You see with the whole collection I sent you I was calculating on the long 'Birlinn' translation and other things to balance out the rest and make it an important book, but without that, and falling back on a choice of the shorter pieces, I want to be quite sure of my ground both for your sake and my own. So I think the best plan is for you to send me back the whole lot at once, indicating those you think of including in the volume and giving me your opinion on the title question. I will return them immediately to you with any suggestions that occur to me. It will then be all plain sailing and we will know exactly where we are.

I am sorry you are not having the 'Birlinn' as it is an important bit of work certain to attract considerable interest and to have a very definite influence. I have now arranged however, that this is to appear in the January issue of *The Modern Scot* and that then a limited edition of 100 signed and numbered copies at 10/6 each is to be struck off.[4] In connection with this I intend to use as a prefatory note the account I sent you of the technique of the Gaelic original, which you have with my other MSS; and this is another reason why I want the latter back at the earliest possible moment.

I am very distressed indeed at the still-birth of the *At the Sign of the Thistle* and cannot understand this at all. I do not believe that it is at all due to people not wanting them because of having read them already, as you suggest; they appeared originally in so many different quarters that I am perfectly certain that exceedingly few people had previously read half of them. I know of course that the critical positions for which I stand are very unpopular and that most people are inclined to brush them aside with impatience, but I am not daunted by that. I am convinced that the book is a good one and will surely, no matter how slowly, pull its weight. This, of course, is poor consolation for the loss you have sustained and I shall be very glad indeed if the poems help to recoup that.

As to the big 'Glasgow' poem I am very glad you are interested in that, but it is a matter that must be gone about very carefully, as undoubtedly it is against the law and liable to very severe penalties. I am determined to have it published by hook or crook (and anxious too to complete it and publish it while the Disaffection Bill trouble is still acute) but whether there are ways and means whereby you could be associated with it without undertaking undue risks is a very serious consideration and one that we cannot decide until I complete the poem.[5] I will write you fully about it later on when I see how it is shaping as a whole and if we can then find means of bringing it out which will not implicate you too seriously I shall be very glad indeed. In any case I will certainly give you first option on it as soon as I have it ready.

I hope that your other projects are all proving successful and that Rosemary and the children and yourself are all in good form. Valda joins me in every kind regard.

Yours, Chris

By the way Valda tells me that she has still 50 copies of the signed *Second Hymn to Lenin* and wants to know if you still wish to take these over.

---

1. Alfred Richard Orage (1873–1934), editor of *The New Age* and *The New English Weekly*. Both periodicals had been focal points of the Modernist movement.
2. Michael Arlen (originally Dikran Kouyoumdjian) (1895–1956), Bulgarian-born British novelist.
3. No such book was published.
4. The poem appeared in *The Modern Scot*, vol. 5, no. 4, January 1935, and the book subsequently appeared as *The Birlinn of Clanranald (Birlinn Chlann-Raghnaill)* by Alexander MacDonald, tr. from the Scots Gaelic of Alasdair Mac Mhaighstir Alasdair by Hugh MacDiarmid (St Andrews: The Abbey Book Shop, 1935). Limited to 100 copies.
5. The Incitement to Disaffection Bill proposed to grant the police greater powers to search private property and was the subject of heated debate.

48. *To A.J.B. Paterson, Sales Manager, Routledge (URL)*

Whalsay, Shetland Islands   27 January 1935

My dear Pat

I know you are busy; and hope that the success is equal to the industry. Many thanks for the Spring catalogue; you've some splendid stuff in it – if I were a popular novelist (but then if I were I don't suppose I'd have so much sense!) I'd send it back to you with ticks against the books I specially want and a cheque for £10 to cover cost and postage. All good luck with it. I'll be particularly interested to hear how Walkinshaw goes – and don't forget I expect copies of each of the Scottish books!

I've just written Mr Warburg[1] and given him the contents list for the *Scottish Eccentrics* (varied somewhat from the original proposal with a view to a second series later). You'll see I've included MacGonigal.[2] I'll be sending in two or three of the essays by an early post, and the remainder of the book will follow very quickly thereafter. I am desperately busy – somewhat overfilled my schedule for work that must all be completed before the end of March – and conditions aren't too conducive; heavy snow followed by iron frost. Just come up and try prizing a few peats out of a frozen stack with your finger tips, or breaking ice to draw water out of the well etc. It's a rigorous life, but I'm in fine form. Valda is a prey to a racking cold, so I have most of the household duties temporarily on my shoulders as well as my own preoccupations.

I don't think you need be the least little bit apprehensive of losing the contact you've established over the meanings series through the unfortunate business with L.G.G.[3] But I'm relieved to know I'm to read the MSS of these books as they come in.

One thing Scotland badly wants (especially now since the old Oliver and Boyd's *Almanac* is gone – tho' it never quite filled the bill) is a good Scottish Year Book, giving in handy form all the useful personal business and statistical information and with good articles on leading aspects and issues of Scottish affairs. I've devoted a lot of thought to this and come to conclusions as to what it ought to contain to be of maximum utility and yet of ready size and easy for one man to edit and put together (tho' of course the various special articles could be by different – and most of them well-known – writers, acknowledged experts in their various subjects) and if you are interested I will send you a full memorandum on the matter.[4] There is nothing of the sort on the market at the moment; it would meet a real want; it would, I am certain, become a very valuable property; and, incidentally, it would be an invaluable focus for your Scottish interests, because the special articles would put you in contact with leading Scots of all kinds and the chance of their books would follow. Let me know what you think.

There's been quite a spate of anthologies recently (*The Year's Poetry* – Lane; *Modern Poetry* – Macmillan, etc., etc.) and it seems to be going to continue judging by the applications I am receiving for poems of mine – and I think the time is rife to put contemporary Scottish poetry on the map again. There may not be any money to speak of in it, but it would be a useful thing to have on our list. What I am thinking of is a *Scottish Poetry, 1935* – not a big book; two or at most three poems (and most of these short lyrics) by fifteen to twenty writers; and a prefatory note expressing the hope that if adequately supported the thing may be an annual. My experience is that there is no risk of loss nowadays on this sort of thing; it funds a sufficient sale at the very least. The poets I could have in it include Edwin Muir, William Soutar,[5] William Montgomerie, Naomi Mitchison, Marion Angus, Arthur Ball, Kenneth Muir, Wm Jeffrey etc. – and myself. Poems to be not previously published in volume form. Fee to poets represented 10/6 per poem.

Finally, as you probably know (or, if you don't my section in the forthcoming *Scottish Country* – Wishart's[6] – on the Shetlands will show you) life has changed completely within living memory in the islands and only the older fishermen remember the pre-motor-boats, pre-drifter, pre-trawler days, – living here was then an extremely hazardous and Spartan business. That old life is being rapidly forgotten – there is no good book about it – the old skill of the six-oared boat with the square-sail is quite unknown to the younger men. Now I've got hold of a man who has the whole thing at his finger-tips (a great six-foot-four deep sea fisherman himself, of the proper Viking breed) and he's willing to talk it all to me. I know I'm on a rattling good thing here and that he has any amount of splendid material to yield up. I want a commission for this – *Life of a Shetland Fisherman* – about 60,000 words.[7] For publication next Spring. That's looking ahead, but it means having a few hours' steady talking time with him every week, making dead sure of all the details to get the vital hang of everything, working hard on the actual writing up to make it as racy and realistic as possible. So I've got to have a good while in front of me for the job, but I want the contract settled so that I'll really get down to it – instead of keeping on saying 'some day we'll put our heads together and do it' and getting no forrader. There's nothing like a fixed date.

The *Week* is reaching me all right and I look forward eagerly for it. Many thanks.

Hope you are all well.

Valda joins me in kindest regards.

Yours, Chris

P.S. I've other matters afoot – but not ready to put up to you yet as formal suggestions. Still waiting to hear from various people. Lazy hounds at writing. Must have a trip down to Edin. and Glasgow soon and look them up in person.

---

1. Frederic John Warburg (1898–1981), joint managing Director of Routledge until 1935.
2. A.J.B. Paterson had remarked that McGonagall was a conspicuous omission from CMG's list of Scottish eccentrics.
3. Gibbon had asked for his fee for editing the 'Meanings in Scotland' series to be raised from £100 to £200.
4. This volume did not appear.
5. William Soutar (1898–1943), the Perth-born poet, had contributed poems, including his first in Scots, to the *Scottish Chapbook*.
6. *Scottish Country: fifteen essays by Scottish authors*, ed. George Scott-Moncrieff (London: Wishart, 1935).
7. The book was not commissioned.

49. *To A.J.B. Paterson, Sales Manager, Routledge (URL)*

Whalsay   Sunday [17 February 1935]

My dear Pat

Very many thanks re Dicks. By all means; I'll return this out of my next quarter's dough, if not before then; at any rate out of the first monies that come in. But go ahead with your splendid plan, and put me down as a foundation member of your Mutual Rescue Guild.[1]

Meanings For Scotland series[2]
Thanks for list of 7 definitely fixed up; all good ones too! Let me know as soon as you find out whether Mitchell really did approach Cunninghame Graham or not. If he didn't I will tout suite, simply explaining the nature of the series, mentioning the titles already arranged, and asking him to suggest a subject he'd be willing to do one on. The Burns one (I assume Mitchell hadn't done much or any of it) I think might be passed on to Cathie Carswell; I know she is pretty busy at the moment but she has the subject at her finger ends, and can write. I am writing her by this post saying that she will probably be asked to do it; and, if you agree, you might drop her a line on receipt of this saying I had suggested her for it and asking if she will do it. Her address is 17 Keats Grove, Hampstead (Mrs Catherine Carswell). Then there's Mrs Naomi Mitchison, Riverside House, Hammersmith Mall (check this address in telephone directory – it may be Riverside Court or Rivercourt House; I forget). I think you might drop her a letter, outlining the nature of the series, mentioning the titles and writers already arranged for, and asking her if she will come in (say I suggested her – she's a great friend of mine) and if so if she will request a subject she would care to tackle which comes within the scope of the series. T.D. MacDonald (who writes over pseudonym of Fionn Mac Colla) could do a good one on 'What Gaelic Has Meant To Scotland' and, provisionally, without committing myself in any way, I am writing him by this post. Finally there is Norman Douglas; the only way to get hold of him is, I think, to write Compton Mackenzie saying you do it at Grieve's suggestion and asking him if he could possibly write Douglas and use all his influence to induce Douglas to write a book for the series on any subject coming within its scope he cares to take. Anything by Douglas is well worth getting and will both sell and enhance the prestige of the series. (If Cathie Carswell can't do the Burns, Naomi Mitchison could and probably would – if Cathie does take the Burns, Naomi could do 'What Religion Has Meant to Scotland' very brilliantly and provokingly.)

Rats, Lice, & History[3] – and Mirsky[4]
I am looking forward to these very eagerly. Many thanks.

Year-Book: and Scottish Poetry 1935
See separate pages attached to this letter.

Eccentrics
I enclose herewith first batch of copy; the remainder will follow in additional batches by every other mail or so. Thanks for arranging re typing; I'll pay this on completion of job.

Children's History of Scotland
I think the best man to approach re this is Dr G.P. Insh, lecturer in History, Jordanhill Training Centre, Glasgow.[5] Say I suggested him; put the idea before him; express the hope that he can see his way to do it but if he can't ask him if he will be so kind as to suggest someone else who might. He knows everybody in this line, but I hope he does it himself – he has the right touch for writing this sort of thing, is one of our best authorities on Scottish history, and knows all about the Scottish Board of Education. Besides he has a big pull with the Educational Institute of Scotland.

Re Donald Carswell[6]
If you can find time you should also fix up a meeting – say, in the Chapter pub, any lunch-time – with Donald Carswell. He's an awfully decent chap and a jolly good writer. I've spoken to him about Routledge's idea of expanding a Scottish books section; so you might talk to him about that and see if he has anything suitable on the stocks or any book on a Scottish subject he'd like to do.

Little Scottish Classics
As you probably know there are a considerable number of very interesting Scottish books – real classics – extremely difficult to get hold of, the need for new editions of which is widely felt; also the Burns Federation and other bodies are constantly stressing the desirability for school use and other purposes or good selections of our older poets. My idea is a little library of such books at a popular price. They only want a little careful choosing, editing, and competent prefacing, and as I go along I am making a list of these desiderata and a little later will send you full particulars and make a definite proposal, in the hope that you may care for the idea and that we could fix it up so as to initiate the series in question early enough to get out the first batch for next Spring season. This is really the end of the letter, tho' I accidentally finished it off in the margin of the previous page instead.
[In the margin of the previous page is the following:]
Trust p.c. reached you O.K. Many thanks re Dick. You're a brick. Valda sends all the best.
   Yours, Chris.

[On separate page:]
The Scottish Yearbook 1935
Edited by C.M. Grieve

Population Statistics.
Vital Statistics (births, deaths, marriages, etc.)
Parliamentary and Municipal Electoral Statistics.
1/ Summary of the year's events in Scotland.
Industrial and Commercial Distribution figures (showing the number of workers employed in different industries, etc.)
Useful facts and figures (a few pages of short paragraphs giving all sorts of useful miscellaneous information in regard to current Scottish affairs and interests).
List of Public Holidays, Common Ridings, and other Festivals, etc.
Who's Who of Leading Scots.
Directory of Principal Scottish Societies at home and abroad.
Public Health and Unemployment Statistics.
2/ Current Legal and Legislative Changes; by A. Dewar Gibb.
3/ Recent Scottish Literature (a review and check list of all the worthwhile Scottish books published during the year).
4/ Scottish Land and Agricultural Problems (including afforestation and land settlement).
5/ Scottish Affairs at Westminster (summary of speeches and acts, orders, etc. relating to Scotland in Parliament).
6/ The Development of the Scottish Drama Movement.
7/ In Memoriam (obituary notices of leading Scots at home and abroad deceased during period in question).
8/ Scottish Authors' and Composers' Guide (article on Scottish editors' requirements – how to place MSS – how to market songs, etc.) by David Cleghorn Thompson.
9/ The policy of the BBC in Scotland.
10/ Trade Development and National and Civic Planning and Publicity Activities.
11/ The Trend in Scottish Education.

Note: –
Though in regard to 2 and 8 I have suggested probable writers it remains to be seen whether they would do it, but in any case all these 11 features would be written by experts in their subjects, and 5 probably by a leading Scottish M.P. while Joseph Duncan would probably do 4, Dr Wm Boyd or Thomas Henderson 11, Moray McLaren or Andrew Stewart 9, and myself 3.

1. The Mutual Rescue Guild was conceived by Paterson as a fund which would provide financial assistance to writers or their dependants in times of crisis. (Its immediate occasion was perhaps to benefit Mrs Rhea Mitchell after the untimely death of Lewis Grassic Gibbon on 7 February 1935.)
2. CMG had taken over the editorship of the series after Gibbon's death.
3. Hans Zinsser, *Rats, Lice and History: being a study in biography, which, after twelve preliminary chapters, indispensible for the preparation of the lay reader, deals with the life history of typhus fever* (London: Routledge, 1935).
4. Dmitri Mirsky, *The Intelligentsia of Great Britain*, tr. Alec Brown (London: Gollancz, 1935).
5. George Pratt Insh (1883–1956), teacher and writer of popular history books. This book was not published.
6. Donald Carswell (1882–1939), Catherine Carswell's husband, worked as a journalist and critic and had published various works of history including a study of Scots Presbyterianism and a biography of Walter Scott.

50. *To Andrew Graham Grieve (EUL)*

Whalsay   18 March 1935

My dear A.

If it were not that it would almost certainly only provoke a sarcastically and interrogatively inflected repetition of the word 'going' on your part, I'd open this note by asking, 'Am I going dotty?' For in yours you say: 'We are relieved to hear that the box we sent you from Cooper's reached you all right.'[1] I can hardly credit you heard this from me, for until I got your letter I was totally unaware that you had sent any such box – tho' now that you mention it I acknowledge that it was safely received, and highly appreciated, and would have been promptly acknowledged with due thanks but for the following circs: –

Last year we got a nice box from Cooper's. It transpired that the donors were Mr & Mrs F.G. Scott. This year a box arrived from Cooper's. There was nothing to indicate who had sent it. We arrived at the conclusion that it had come from the Scotts. About ten days later calling at the Island Store Valda found that another box from Cooper's had arrived about a week earlier but had by inadvertence not yet been delivered to us. On being opening it proved to contain – amongst other things – a *carte de visite* of F.G. Scott. I then wrote and thanked him for the two boxes. He had written me since but did not refer to the matter, having doubtless concluded that I had made some mistake. So now it appears that Box No. 1 was from you. Please accept our belated thanks and our regrets that we should have been so long in tendering these. I can only imagine that in my last letter I phrased my acknowledgement of your Christmas book-marker card in terms which you thought referred to the box.

I've been badly off colour, as after effects of a chill, since I wrote you last and am consequently in desperate arrears with books I ought to have had finished and off to the publishers by the end of February. I'm keeping better but not yet capable of much sustained effort. Sort of nervous and mental prostrations. I'd been overdoing it, of course, and the weather has been damnable ever since we came back here. Sorry you had a brush with the flu', and have had so much illness and consequent short-handedness in the office. Trust you're O.K. again and Chryssie and Angus clear of their colds.

Gibbon, poor fellow, had been ill a couple of months with what was supposed to be severe gastritis. But you know how difficult that sort of thing is to diagnose properly and how suddenly it can develop into something much worse. He was apparently recovering nicely when he had a haemorrhage, was rushed to hospital, operated on for peritonitis, and died. He'd had a perforation. It was a great shock. He'd had a stiff struggle and was on the upgrade to make money and established himself and his wife and family quite nicely. But death came too soon to give him time to clear his feet, and his wife and children were left very poorly off. The Scottish PEN, however, have raised a fund, and there's also likely to be a grant from the Royal Literary Fund.

Re Hugo McDownall, you probably know I'm also in two other novels – Christine Orr's *Immortal Memory* and Eric Linklater's *Magnus Merriman*. A good discussion, from a sympathetic point of view, of my Bolshevist poems appears in *A Hope For Poetry* by Cecil Day Lewis, one of the best of the younger English school.[2] I'm going to lecture on myself at Manchester University on 10th May.

Again with thanks, and love to you all from all here.

Yours, Chris

---

1. Cooper's: a supermarket chain.
2. Christine Orr, *Immortal Memory* (London: Hodder & Stoughton, 1933); Eric Linklater, *Magnus Merriman* (London: Cape, 1934); C. Day Lewis, *A Hope For Poetry* (Oxford: Blackwell, 1934).

51. *To Ernest Marwick (The Orkney Archives, ref. No. D31/61/6)*

Whalsay, Lerwick, Shetland Islands   22 April 1935

Dear Sir: –

How kind of you to write me! I am glad to know that you find poems which interest and please you in my *Selected Poems*. An author who has written so much, and in so many different kinds, as I have done has no little difficulty in seeing his work in perspective and cannot anticipate the final winnowing. But this particular selection has been fortunate in winning a considerable measure of appreciation and has served to introduce my work effectively enough to many who had not previously encountered it, scattered as it is through many different books some of which were issued only in small limited editions at high prices. I am interested too to know that you have been following the recent developments in Scottish matters and share that weariness and dislike of the smug conventional stuff which has been so long approved by Scottish taste (or want of taste) alike in verse, and, I think, in all the departments of our national life. To overcome this and establish higher standards is a slow and difficult matter and those engaged in it are apt to make many mistakes; but I think that we have registered substantial progress during the past decade and laid a worthy foundation for truly nation-size developments in the near future, astonishingly meagre as the substantive achievements of contemporary Scottish writers are when carefully scrutinised.

If headway is to be made it is only by enlisting the interest up and down the country of individuals like yourself, and in that way it would seem an adequate public, in quantity and quality, is now emerging. It is as one other welcome little sign of this reorientation that I am pleased to receive a letter like yours.

Again thanking you and with compliments and best wishes.

Yours sincerely, C.M. Grieve ('Hugh MacDiarmid')

52. *To A.J.B. Paterson, Sales Manager, Routledge (URL)*

Whalsay Thursday [25 April 1935]

My dear Pat

I do hope you can manage a run up to Manchester. My speech there is on the evening of Friday 10th May. I'll arrive in Manchester either on the night of the 9th or early on the 10th. If you can't let me know before I leave here – on 6th – a letter or a wire to me c/o Professor Barker Fairley, University, Manchester will get me. As presently planned I'm to spend the week-end with Fairley, not in Manchester, but at Buxton, where he lives. But if you come up we'll arrange something else. I don't know Manchester and your guidance will be helpful. I wish I could have come on down to London, but alas! That's out of the question just now.

I'm not surprised at either Routledge's or your brother's attitude re the Scottish Year Book idea. I believe such a thing is extremely desirable and would justify itself, not perhaps the first year, if only it could be got together and launched. But I recognize it's a big proposition and would involve sinking a considerable capital.

Cathy Carswell's idea of a Scottish Week-End Book is tip-top. I've only just received your letter and haven't had time to think the matter over, but I will do so and make what comments and suggestions I can in my next letter, or verbally to you if you do come to Manchester.

By the way George Scott Moncrieff[1] in a recent letter outlined to me a book he'd been planning for some time – on the actual signing of the Act of Union; a dramatically written description of the historic scene, with vivid pen-portraits of the principal men involved. It would certainly make a very interesting book and Scott Moncrieff could do justice to the theme. I asked him to write you direct thereanent and hope he has done so.

I am enclosing herewith 18 of the *Thirty Stories*, and hope you'll manage to place them for me.[2] I'll try to get the balance of the copy off to you by Monday's mail – if not, I'll certainly manage to do so later next week, before I go South. Also, by Monday's mail I'll send you the suggested illustrations for the *Eccentrics*.

Excuse this hurried note. I'm up to the eyes getting all sorts of tasks finished off before the 6th. Am looking forward keenly to this break, which I badly need; I'm considerably run down and need a change – besides I must get my eyes seen to in Edinburgh before I am back here.

Trust your teeth are all right now.

Valda joins me in kindest regards.

Yours, Chris

---

1. George Scott Moncrieff (1910–74), wrote travel books and various works on Scottish cultural history.
2. *Thirty Stories*: The book was not published.

53. *To Andrew Graham Grieve (EUL)*

Whalsay   Friday [April 1935]

Dear A.

Glad to get your note today, and to hear you're getting clear of flu' and all perking up. Here we're in throes of wildest of weather and snow again. Am much better and extremely busy. Have to speak Manchester University 10th May; will be in Edinr. to get eyes seen to etc. but can't say definite date yet – will let you know.

Herewith *Five Bits of Miller* – you'll appreciate that the dedication is 'writ sarcastic'; the coupling of such a story with Agnes Mure Mackenzie as dedicatee was almost a constructive libel.[1] A little literary feud.

Love to you all. In haste, Chris

---

1. This letter was found in Hugh MacDiarmid, *Five Bits of Miller*, 'now for the first time set up and printed from the manuscript', published by 'The Author, 1934'.

54. *To Sorley MacLean (NLS)*

Whalsay   21 June 1935

My dear Maclean

Many thanks for yours to hand yesterday. I note the various little points you raise. What you say of the translation generally pretty well expresses my own feeling about it. I am glad that, on the whole, you think so well of it. I am not bothering about changing the lines about the butt-iron's kick for the *Modern Scot*. But I'll put this right later on for the *Anthology*.

My wife and I are extremely pleased you're coming up and will expect you about the 20th of July or thereabouts. But send me a wire as soon as you know when the boat you are coming by is due in at Lerwick. The North Isles steamer only comes up from Lerwick twice a week and if it so happens that you don't reach Lerwick the night prior to one of these sailings you might have to stay (if so, stay at the Grand Hotel) a couple of nights – but, on the other hand, I might know of a means of getting you a lift up in one of the fishing boats and thus obviate the delay in Lerwick, or failing that I might come down and meet you in Lerwick. We'll be looking forward eagerly to seeing you.

Sorry Campbell does not seem as promising as I had hoped. I'd give a good deal to know any young Gaelic poet with a big intellectual background. Campbell, I take it, is quite untutored; probably since he is so young he could be influenced and developed a good deal if one were in close touch with him and had time to devote – provided, of course, he were of the temperament to welcome and profit by such intercourse.

You'll see I'm standing for the Edinr. rectorial.

Yours, C.M.G.

P.S. Bring up any Gaelic poetry books you have – I haven't any here just now.[1]

---

1. Shortly after Sorley MacLean's visit, CMG was admitted to Gilgal Hospital, Perthshire.

55. *To Valda Grieve (NLS)*

Gilgal Hospital, Perth   Monday 9 [September] 1935

[As with all the letters from Gilgal, the script is legible and the incoherences are as MacDiarmid wrote them.]

My darling Valda

Others tell me I have registered an amazing improvement even since Monday – Dr Chambers[1] and his assistants express themselves as pleased with my progress. I have not had a definite report, however, on the findings of the lumbar puncture. All appears to be going favourably and the rest, and treatment etc. are clearing up a lot of my obscure but important processes and I certainly feel greatly revitalised. I am delighted at your returning to St Andrews and seeing the Muirs etc. *That* is awfully good of Pat and I trust to H–ven Mr Warburg has consented and that Mr Jas. Arthur is wearing a more satisfied smile. I certainly have not written to Pat or the Rou[t]ledge's or anybody like that.

Can't understand this passage! Chambers will assure that I have proved a very model of a patient in all respects and have not undone anything of the good either Orr or Chambers have done me by any ill-advised conduct.

I am certainly glad you should not both by sending on my letter you do not feel important. Letters are few and far between. I enclose a nice from Saurat which please keep amongst my stuff. I'll reply to this by this post as this. I'll also write to Orr at last – I ought to do have do ages ago but simply have been in fettle to do any writing I could possibly avoid at all. I am extremely sorry I am missing Robin's visit to which I have asked for so often and looked forward so keenly. However.

I'll write to R.M.B. today too – I am extremely set on the Oban job and feel it will give us – our little domestic outfit, a real chance of security and comfort, good schooling for J.M., at last; what in short, it has hitherto almost rocked[2] and whence it has been so precarious. God bless both of you. I am longing to see both of you again. I cannot help wondering and worrying constantly about you.

F.G. came through alone one day and I was delighted to see him and he said he'd fetch you along with him again at least. I don't suppose circumstances permitted. Probably F.G. himself will (this isn't far from Glasgow). And he's on a holiday till next month.

All love and kisses. Yours, Chris

Enclosed fragment puzzles me because I can't make out the words in the sentence I've put (?) behind.

Trust you are O.K. yourself definite all the perils of the deep and the monotonies of the Island life and landscape.

Yours, Chris

P.S. Do hope you wrote Wisharts in reply to this kind letter about *Red Scotland*[3] – regretting Mr Grieve was seriously ill and in hospitably and he asked to reply that he still more regretted that the matter he alas prematurely in one sense put to them now unfortunately fell to the ground since on the question of Messrs Rou[t]ledge taking objections to any of the matter in it on grounds of Incitement to Disaffection Messrs Rou[t]ledge had now assured that them they do nothing of that sort.

---

1. Dr Walter Duncanson Chambers, Physician Superintendent at the Murray Royal

Hospital.

2. Presumably, CMG means 'always lacked'.

3. Originally entitled *What Lenin Has Meant to Scotland*. On 25 November 1934 CMG had made a contract for its publication with Routledge. Suspecting they would object to its seditious content he subsequently offered it to the publishers Lawrence & Wishart, but in a letter of 7 August 1935 Routledge assured him 'we have no objection to the work on account of its revolutionary nature'. However on 15 January 1936 Routledge expressed their desire to break the contract on the grounds that over 50 per cent of the MS consisted of quotations and that it was libellous to various members of the Royal Family.

56. *To Andrew Graham Grieve (EUL)*

c/o Dr Chambers, Calgil [*sic*] Nursing Home, Perth   12 September 1935

My dear A.

I am sorry to have been so long in writing to thank you for your welcome letter and large surprise – but exceedingly welcome supply of cigarettes. I am improving rapidly and Scott is pressing now as hard as possible for my earliest possible discharge. But I have not been in a writing mood. I would not have been so churlish, however, as to delay so long in thanking you for your splendid gift, and especially to pen a word or two of genuine congratulation on Morag's and Angus's school successes hearing of which pleased me immensely did writing not present certain little difficulties here – the need, inter alia, to secure permission, to borrow paper pen and ink and to have an envelope and stamp credited to one's small sundries A/C.

Love to you all. I trust you are all in the best of fettle, and that I may pay you a flying visit on my way to Leith – which, please God, be soon.

Your loving brother, Chris.

57. *To Valda Grieve (NLS)*

Calgil [*sic*] Nursing Home, Perth   16 September 1935

My dearest Valda.

Delighted to have your letters – one on Saturday, one today Monday.

The first was an exceedingly kind and cheering document – a real sweetheart's letter – tho' I was greatly worried to hear about the peat-bags and the aching back. Do be very careful, lassie. Take it – if at all – in much smaller doses. Get Orr to give or get you some Winter Green liniment and massage your back. It is excellent stuff, and massage with it this week has practically put my own racked back all right.

I had an unexpected and very pleasant visit from my brother this afternoon and he had a good chat with Chambers, who is highly pleased with the way I am going.

By the way that business I had about my first visit to Soutar's is all wrong – I immediately challenged him with it, and he said it was a misapprehension entirely due to the fact that he did not know that I had motored ¾ of the way there and the whole way back in Soutar *senr's* car.

Dr Orr by the way has far graver views of my condition than the facts warrant. I did not and could not (so old was my own infection) in any way, and I am not likely to have any recurrent trouble with the matter following my treatment here. Dr Chambers would have been able to detect any sign of a more recent infection of myself (e.g. A. McN. Duff) than the 1915 I admit.

The Matron of course has nothing whatever to do with the male patients. Whoever replied to H.B.C. on the phone was a God-sent joker. Even if she had come up and been shown into the waiting-room I would not have consented to see her. Scott came through on Saturday bringing me black tobacco and a fine new big-bowled pipe. He strongly urged me to stay on here for another month or so (I resisted because he is paying the entire expense – tho' I'll need cash to get back).

And Dr James Valentine (second in charge here and just back from a Canadian holiday) who is an old friend of mine (along with myself he was one of the five or six founders of the National Party of Scotland) had been strongly urging me in the same direction in the forenoon. Valentine presented very cogent technical reasons. I saw Dr Chambers and he urged the latter even more strongly; I agreed finally to stay other 3 weeks in order to have the first four of a series of arsenical intravenous injections. I refused to stay any longer (provided of course all keeps going on satisfactorily in the interval) because the whole series would mean waiting here other 2 months or 10 weeks and I cannot possibly consent to Scott paying the account for any such period. Drs Chambers, Valentine and F.G. himself were entirely satisfied with my decision; I really have made astonishing progress lately and now get up and out for walks in the forenoons. So alas, it is to be a little longer, my dear, but not so long. The injections will stop – and remove any further danger of – any such invasion (as Orr feared and as the mere contingency of horrified me unspeakably) of the horrible thing into the nervous system.

Kisses and all love to J.M. and yourself, and very best regards to Dr Orr whom I have never got written to yet – but will very soon now (as soon as I think he'll have received Chambers' next letter.

Yours, Chris

P.S. My brother will help you financially if you are in desperate straits – before the advances arrive.

58. To Valda Grieve (NLS)

Gilgal Hospital   Friday, 20 September [1935]

My dearest Valda

I have just written a long letter to Dr Orr and want to repeat to you certain points I made in it.

First of all, however, I want to say – the copies of *2nd Hymn* you referred to have never arrived. Perhaps you changed your mind.

Second, I wish you could look out the red notebook in which I was writing my new poems – including the Stefan George translation: 'A Woman's Son Comes Home'. You'll remember it – how he'd gone to sea a boy and returned a man and how her arms were now too short to go around him. If you find it, please tear it out of the notebook and send it on to me at once; I need it urgently.

I am in great form now. I had my first arsenical injection last Monday – and crikey, it was sore; I've had all kinds of injections in my life – anti-typhoid, anti-tetanic, anti-bubonic, anti-cholera, innumerable intravenous injections of quinine etc. etc. but this was by far the worst. I thought it had knocked me out completely. Dr Valentine said it would have a tonic effect in a day or two. He was right. I felt infernally shaky, and down-and-out for a couple of days, then my old vigour began to come up like milk on the boil, and yesterday and today I've felt restored to full energy and everyone has been commenting on how splendid I was looking.

The only other point I want to impress on you is that I was not unfrank to Dr Orr in any way, because I had no earthly reason to suppose that my old trouble of 20 years ago could possibly be responsible, and he was continually attributing my condition to the striking up of the cold and damp through me from the floor while night-working. *That* seemed perfectly feasible to me and I took it in perfect good faith. With regard to Peggy and you suspecting my trouble, you could not possibly – for I had no suspicion of it myself, never a single moment's, and no reason to have any. I knew that in 1915 I'd had a slight dose of Gon. I'd driven underground with violent boozing and that I'd no notion where it had gone – but there is no proven case of suppressed Gon. turning into Syph. and of Syph. I never had the slightest sign – chancre, rash, etc., all of which are invariably present. So how on earth could I suspect?

As to abstention for long periods from sexual intercourse between married couples, weakness or temporary or longer impotence on the man's part is not always due to venereal causes. It was not – as it happens – in my case.

Next time you write Pat I wish you'd find out if he has no further word of the 30 Short Stories.

I hope – against all likelihood – that you are suffering less from wind and weather generally than most of Great Britain. We've had some wild days and nights here recently.

It must be pretty eerie for you lying alone – even with Little J.M. – in our rattling loft. I do hope you are taking good care of yourself – eating – good fires etc. – and not finding time too terribly weary on your hands.

Love and kisses (I really *do* love you all the same, you know – and always did) and ditto to Mike.

I hope the money has come in to let you relieve matters and carry on more comfortably.

Finally, there is one more thing I wanted to remember – please write Mr J.D. Turnbull c/o Dr Stanley Robertson, Parsonage House, Musselburgh, near Edinburgh and explain to him that I fell ill and have now been in hospital for over five weeks, hence reason for my not replying to him re socks – then tell him about the gross of pairs of socks question.

Again all love and longing my dearest.

Yours, Chris.

59. *To Valda Grieve (NLS)*

Gilgal Hospital   Sunday [22 September 1935]

My dear V.

It was a great disappointment to me to gather from your last that *Red Scotland* has been postponed (so please send on enclosed note to Pat) and also that you have apparently not received yet the *Eccentrics* £40 nor the Sept £13. The October and final £13 is due on Oct 1st – the September £13 nearly a month over due. No wonder you are so deplorably short. I feel sure you are underfeeding etc. Re fare home I'll arrange that myself. The Oban thing is *sure* to come off; that's why I want to come straight back to Shets from here, I'll wire you which boat I am coming by. Scott was here again on Saturday and he and I had a long and most enjoyable walk on Corsiehill. Poetry is bubbling up in me again; I'm in good form and getting it jotted down. Best of love to Michael Fikle and yourself, little Funny.

Yours, Chris.

60. *To Andrew Graham Grieve (EUL)*

Gilgal Hospital, Perth   22 September 1935

My dear A: –

I hope you are settling down nicely at home again after your holiday. It was a great pleasure to have your call here, and to see you looking so fine and fit. I managed to keep the cigs, all right.

I'll have to take advantage of your kind offer, after all. I find from her

latest letter that V. has let herself run deplorably low but she has misman-
aged matters so badly that one of my books has been postponed while £40
in respect of one book due weeks ago and a sum of £13 due 1st Sept have
not come to her, whence she is unable to send me the money I need for
my fare back etc.

Please lend me £10; I'll send her £5 and use £5 for above-mentioned
purposes. Meanwhile as you may well believe I am taking the strings into
my own hands and will repay you as soon as I get back and have either of
these or any of the several other considerable sums due in respect of book
contracts safely garnered in, I hope you can manage this; I am very anxious
about it. A cheque will be no use to me here of course; please send registered letter with money in one-pound notes.

Love to you all and every kind regard.

Yours, Chris

P.S. I'll postcard you as soon as ever I know date and time of discharge
and of arrival in Edinburgh etc.

61. *To Andrew Graham Grieve (EUL)*

Gilgal Hospital, Perth,   Tuesday [24 September 1935]

My dear A.

Very anxious now about matter of which I wrote you a few days ago.
Hope you can manage it, very quickly now. My good progress is continuing. A matter of which I have spoken to you before is advancing rapidly
– viz. my reunion with my first family. Peggy (who left the man she has
been living with since our divorce) is coming to see me here this weekend
– with, I think Christine. That means (I know because of the terms of our
recent correspondence) she is now prepared to remarry me as soon as matters
can be arranged. In view of this I urgently need money at once. I must for
example make myself presentable with a new shirt and pair of flannel bags
(my present shirt – the only one I have with me – having been laundered
into a most ragged condition), while as matters stand I haven't a halfpenny
to give them a cup of tea. These small outlays will leave me with enough
for my Shetland fares next week) with[out] trenching [these last two words
are unclear] on Valda's half, if you can lend me the sum stated.

Love to you all, Chris

62. *To Valda Grieve (NLS)*

Gilgal   Saturday [28 September 1935]

My dearest Valda

Returning next Saturday – a week today – this is (today) Sept 28th –

by train to Aberdeen and thence by boat leaving Leith, Monday week. Please tell Dr Orr, and also that I will need to have him continue my arsenical injections and that Dr Chambers says he will give me to take back with me the remainder of the stuff necessary to complete the course. Reverting to your last extremely kind letter, in which you say you realise that you are of great importance to me. That, my dear, is putting it mildly. A terrible crisis developed here this week which, Peggy visiting me here today, in a complete and final understanding between Peggy and I, which involves, owing to my mad 22 year-long obsession for you,[1] and absolute abandonment of any question of my reunion with her and the children, Christine and Walter. I will tell you all about it – fully and frankly – when I see you.

Trust you and Mikey Fike are well. Yours Ever, Chris.

---

1. CMG met *Peggy*, in Cupar, in 1913.

63. *To Valda Grieve (NLS)*

Gilgal   Sunday [29 September 1935]

My darling Valda.
    Coming now by hired boat from Leith, leaving Leith Thursday first.
    All my love to Mike and yourself.
    In haste. Yours. Chris

64. *To Andrew Graham Grieve (EUL)*

Gilgal Hospital, Perth   Tuesday [1 October 1935]

My dear A.
    It is true, as you say, that 'the ugly matter of money' has cropped up each time we've met lately; the reason for this of course is simply that I've been in extreme economic straits and you'll agree the sums have been very small. My last two letters were written in a complete misunderstanding as to what you said and because I was in a particularly urgent and excruciating predicament. Don't you believe for a moment I have no other use for you. Others know me better. I would have been dead a month ago without any peradventure if I had not been enabled to undergo the positive miracle of specialist treatment I've undergone here; it was utterly beyond my own resources and the whole thing was arranged without my knowledge between my friends Dr Orr, Whalsay, and F.G. Scott. Scott took the whole financial burden on himself; Orr offered to go halves but Scott wouldn't let him (Orr has helped Valda all the while and would have

telegraphed the cash I asked you to *lend* me by return if I'd had or cd have got enough to wire him the request). Nor would Scott tolerate any question of repayment; said he would regard it as an insult to the spirit in which he had undertaken to do it. Scott has visited me every Saturday here; brought two or three ounces of black tobacco every time latterly; and a fine, big-bowled new pipe. I've this moment received from him registered letter containing the amount I asked you for. Scott's in your position. A salaried man, with like you a lately acquired house to keep going, a wife, and 4 children at good schools. He could not have done it at all but for the fact that he had happened to receive payment for some extra inspectorial duties he'd done apart from his ordinary work. It has cost him at least (apart from railway fares, keeping Valda and I in St Andrews, paying the 'Chief's' – Dr Chambers' – £15/15 – fee for motoring through and inspecting me there when it was decided I needed hospital treatment, and apart from papers, tobacco, pipe etc. he's given me) – £31.10/- to my knowledge and likely more. So there you are. Orr is in like position but only one of family. He'd have done the same and prior to getting in touch with Scott kept me in his own house for a week on special diet etc. I fully recognise and respect your position and would not wish to, and could not willingly, harm it in any way. Be assured I have real fraternal affection for you and yours and the more we can see of each other the better pleased I'll be – yet there's no getting away from the simple fact that at this crisis but for friends I'd have passed out weeks ago.

As it is I've made a miraculous recovery tho' I'll have to be extremely careful, and undergo further treatment from Dr Orr, for many moons – so remarkable a recovery that I am dropping you this note to say how sorry I am that I'll not see you – I'm travelling right through from here on Tuesday to catch direct boat Leith that evening. But I'll be in Edinburgh this month again for Rectorial. Hope see you then. Love & best of luck to all of you.

Yours, Chris

P.S. What Valda was thinking of when she spoke of travelling London, Cornwall etc. was arranged before I left – idea being (as is still case – but little later in coming off owing to my illness) I'm taking up editorship of new Oban paper very soon and for a while, while we're merely in rooms there, I wanted Valda to take the boy to Cornwall first and leave him there for a month or so – and of course she thought these monies would come in and enable her to do so.

65. *To Peggy Grieve (NLS)*

[Whalsay] [Noted in CMG's hand: 'Copy of letter written 12/10/35, and posted 14/10/35'.[1]]

My dear Peggy
 Valda's courage is perhaps indeed beyond comprehension to you, for it turns upon the little word 'love' of which you know nothing.
 This must be my last letter to you. You were still dishonest to me at that last tragic meeting at Gilgal. You persisted that I was wrong in representing that I could with better cause have brought a divorce action against you than you against me.[2] This was a mere discreditable quibble if it only meant that I wrongly suspected MacDonald[3] or MacElroy. It was your blame if I blamed the wrong man – and in the circumstances I could certainly have won if I had brought an action against MacElroy. But while you were persisting in this, you were dextrously sliding over the fact that when I returned home from Liverpool you were carrying the child of my false friend La Roux[4] under your heart. And yet with that guilty knowledge you do not hesitate to quibble with me still any more than at the time you hesitated to accept my sacrifice[5] and on the strength of it deprive me of a wife I idolised, children I loved dearly and who loved me, my home, my books, everything. Nor since then have you ever betrayed the slightest regret, or shown the least affection, let alone any lingering flicker of love, for me. You spurned all the years we had together as if they had never meant anything. And yet, even at this last, at Gilgal (after, I believe, deliberately sending me that laughing photograph because you knew it would recall to me the one I so greatly loved and lost) when I press you for your real reason for all this hellish and unrelenting cruelty to me and ask what I had done to deserve it, you admit I had done nothing and declare you do not know why you did it. You even deny that you knew you had driven me to utter desperation – and yet in long letter after long letter from Liverpool I poured out my heart to you and pleaded with you as only a true husband, father, and lover could do who felt that his marriage and fatherhood were imperilled. There was no lack of precision and clarity about these letters to leave you in any ignorance of the state to which you had driven and were driving me. In other words, here again you lied. What a genius for self-justification you must have had to stand by and coolly witness a man having, owing to your fault, to sell the custody of his children to another man just because the latter was better off and so could better provide for the children in material ways.
 All that is over and done with. You saw me tear out of my heart forever root and branch all hope and desire for reunion with you and our children. But even then I clung to the idea that we might be friends and that I would help you and the children in any way I could. That letter was a

genuine prompting of the spirit – as, I believe, was your impossible offer to pay Valda's fare to Cornwall. But it will not do. Even friendship between us is out of the question now (tho' I do not go back on my promise that if I should ever be in a position to help the children financially I will only too gladly do so), and it is the final good-bye. I shall not see you or correspond with you, or see or correspond with the children, ever again. La Roux you can leave to me if I ever come across the beastly little coward; I will look after him better than the Political Section (who, I realise, weren't after me at Pyrland Road, but after him).

Love blinded me to an awful lot, but now I see the whole thing from beginning to end and it is an utterly ghastly and repellant sight from which I gladly turn away my eyes forever at last. I accept at last the dreadful words of the divorce decree and agree to be as 'one dead' to you and the bairns.

Yours, Chris

---

1. All of the letters to Peggy and William McElroy included here and the undated letter of 1938 to CMG's daughter, Christine, came to the National Library of Scotland from CMG's own papers. They may be copies, drafts, letters returned undelivered by the Post Office or that were simply never sent. We have no independent means of determining whether any of these letters was, in fact, sent.
2. The instances of adultery cited in the divorce case against CMG post-date the period when Peggy must have committed adultery by at least four months.
3. Most probably Thomas Douglas MacDonald (Fionn Mac Colla). See Appendix.
4. Louis N. Le Roux, Breton nationalist, author of *La Question Brettone pour le Separatisme* containing the manifesto of the Breton Nationalist Party (1911); while living in Ireland, wrote *L'Ireland Militant: la Vie de Patrice Pearse* (1932), translated by Desmond Ryan; Le Roux later moved to London. He wrote a study of Ramsay Macdonald in 1919, translated his *Socialism and Society* in 1922 and also wrote *La Ligues de Gaelique: Son Origine et sa Mission* (1934), *Relations Inter-Celtiques* (1935).
5. CMG had agreed to spend the night of 26 September 1931 in a hotel with Valda in order to allow Peggy to bring a divorce action against him. He had also spent the night with another woman earlier in September and this too was cited in the divorce case.

66. To Sorley MacLean (NLS)

Whalsay   25 November 1935

My dear Maclean

Sorry to have been so long in dropping you a line since my return here in the beginning of last month. But, apart from the ordinary exigencies of life here, trying enough in themselves unless one is perfectly fit, and from the special difficulties due to the almost unbroken continuance of the world's worst weather, my situation has been greatly complicated by the fact that we have all been ill; Valda went down with nervous exhaustion, Michael with what was at first diagnosed as fracture of the base of the skull but turned out not to be, but a very painful ear-trouble which has kept him in bed for a month now – and a deuce of a handful he is; while I completed the unholy trinity with exceedingly painful and disabling accidents first to one arm and then to the other, and finally collapsed with a dose of flu' specialising in sore throat and swelling of the supertonsilar glands. We are all much better, but Valda's nerves and mine are all to pigs and whistles. While conditions have thus scarcely favoured my convalescence I have gone on all right in not incurring any relapse of the grave illness which took me to hospital, or, I think, lost any of the essential benefit my sojourn there conferred.

Literary work has been out of the question and a couple of books of mine (*Red Scotland* and *Scottish Eccentrics*) had perforce to be postponed publication until January. All the same I am ready for any more translations you have managed to make, and hope to get that *Golden Treasury* finished in the next few weeks. My contract only gives me to the beginning of March anyway.

I hope you are having a better time, and are in good form. You will understand that I can scarcely recall the circumstances of your visit here or appreciate how far short I must have fallen as a host. But I know you understood at the time that I could not help myself. I became very much worse, losing all responsibility for my actions, after you left, and it is in fact a miracle that I am still alive.

Valda encloses the snaps for you, and joins with me in sending you all our love. I hope that we may have a chance of a holiday together some time again and greatly regret that my developing illness gave you such a poor time and prevented you from making much more of your first visit to Whalsay.

Ever yours, C.M. Grieve

67. *To Andrew Graham Grieve (EUL)*

Whalsay   17 February 1926 [1936]

My dear A.

Glad to get your last letter. I'd have written sooner but have been very busy. I expect *Scottish Eccentrics* this week and will send you a copy. *Red Scotland* is hung up owing to certain allegedly seditious etc. elements which I refuse to excise or moderate; I'll probably have to transfer it to other publishers. We're all in pretty good form again and – this is the point of present note – hope to return to Edinburgh about the end of next month. We're keeping our cottage up here, of course, and leaving our furniture etc. only bringing down what we need. Valda is looking forward to meeting you all; and I fancy it will be very amusing to see Michael in juxtaposition to Morag and Angus.

By the way before I left hospital I had completely finished my relations with Peggy. You will probably have seen references in the papers to the big enticement suit in which she is presently figuring.[1] You will, of course, not mention any of these things in Valda's presence.

I hope you are in good form. Tho' you were well when you wrote the inspection and stiff programme of work for the next month or two are bound to take it out of you.

Love to you all from all here. Yours, Chris

I may be in Edinburgh shortly – I'm supposed to be broadcasting (from Aberdeen) in beginning of March but don't know exact date yet. I'll p.c. you.

---

1. William McElroy's wife, Kate, had taken Peggy to court for obtaining money by enticing McElroy away from her.

68. *To the Editor,* New Scotland *(Alba Nuadh)*

In Reply to Mr Kerrigan

Dear Sir, – In reply to Mr Kerrigan[1] all I have to say is that I accept Comrade Stalin's definition of a nation, and that one unsupported statement is at least as good as another. He says that, asking above-mentioned definition, Scotland is not a nation. I say that it is. I have as high an opinion of Comrade Dimitrov's record and abilities as anyone;[2] that does not alter the fact that he has no title whatever to be classified as a thinker, and that Mr Kerrigan should imagine that the various qualifications he adduces prove the contrary – instead of being completely beside the point – shows an incapacity for the very simplest reasoning on Mr Kerrigan's part which, to say the least of it, renders it highly unlikely that he is capable of any real perception of the dialectical process. I regret that I do not consider him worth wasting my time trying to argue with, and that this letter therefore represents the conclusion of this controversy so far as I am concerned. – Yours sincerely, Hugh MacDiarmid (C.M. Grieve)

---

1. Vol. 1, no. 20, 22 February 1936.
2. Peter Kerrigan (1903–85), one of the CPGB's most significant organisers of the 1930s (see Appendix). Kerrigan's article was entitled 'The Errors of Mr C.M. Grieve: Scotland is Not a Nation', vol. 1, no. 17.
3. Georgi Mikhailovich Dimitrov (1882–1949) Secretary-General of the

Comintern, 1935–45. Bulgarian Communist politician, best remembered for his skilful defence and acquittal in the trial following the burning of the Reichstag (1933).

69. *To Valda Grieve (NLS)*

Whalsay   Wednesday [20 May 1936]

My dearest Valda

   Arrived home all right on Monday morning at the usual godless hour – after a deuce of a tossing in the *Earl*, following on a particularly bad Kirkwall to Lerwick crossing on the Saturday before.[1] Home did I say? What a terrible difference from my returns hitherto. It was a cruelly cold and wet morning (the first rain after a drought lasting all the time we've been away) and I toiled up to our house carrying a plethora of parcels – only to find that the door was locked. It was impossible to get in by any of the windows; it was impossible to try to knock up Harriet at that hour; I put the parcels in the dunnigan pro tem, returned to the Doctor's, rang his bell urgently till he got up thinking it was a confinement case, and here – at the Doctor's – I'm remaining, at least for a week or two, alike for bed and for all meals. So set your mind at rest on that score, lassie. I saw Harriet later and also the house – she had the fires on and my bed made – and will keep on fires for a few days longer anyhow. But the house is in splendid state owing to the long dry spell that has been obtaining.

   My first job has been to try to begin to cope with a truly tremendous accumulation of mail.

   Item first. Four letters. I have already – much more deeply sorry and ashamed than you'd credit perhaps – apologised for my non-writing to you, my poor darling. I'll make up for that yet. As to the Peggy business I don't blame you for your outburst. But remember I've had an equal dose of it all the time I've been away, wherever I went, with all my own friends, and am just as utterly sick of it all. It wasn't that you were the 'softy' in the matter – it was simply that the poet in me prevented my putting the matter as effectively behind me for good and all once you and I met, and flamed in love for each other, as I would have done if I had not been cursed with my poet's psychology. But you won't be bothered with it any more once you and I get together again and you'll pan out best of all concerned in the long run, for I deeply and truly do love you, my darling. And I know how deeply and truly despite your occasional not surprising outbursts at my periods of recurrent foolishness you love me. 'We'll have moonlight on the Borders again.' And we'll have our holiday.

   Item two. Two letters in my mail pleased me very greatly. One a letter from Lady Brooke (maiden name, Cunninghame Grahame) thanking me specially for coming all the way from the Shetlands to Cunninghame

Grahame's funeral.[2] Another from Butchart, the literary agent who's fixing up my *Autobiography*, suggesting that I do – if I can get the permission of the family (and Lady Brooke will come in useful here) – the official Cunninghame Grahame biography. I'll step on that to some tune and do my damnedest to fix it up at once. There's money (tho' money is the least of it really) in this idea.

I suppose you realise that General Allenby's death means another Edinburgh Rectorial this Autumn and that I'll be standing again. I saw the students – Davie[3] and others – about it, but I intend to go to Raasay, and I think take you, by hook or crook, in July or August – I had a long letter from Maclean. I'll reply to this by this mail too to that effect. I'm going to do my utmost to write my Universities book[4] and have it published in time for this Rectorial (October). So I'm going to be devilishly busy. Both the Shetland (Jemima) story and the Cornish story are to appear in *Outlook*, and did I tell you the passages of *Cornish Heroic Song* I was able to read to the students and others at Manchester scored a great success.[5] It was agreed on all hands that this is magnificent stuff. I've a lot to do to it too to get it all into final shape; also to my Anthology, which I must get down to thoroughly as quickly as possible now.

Another great bit of news – the Doctor is here beside me wearing his Macnab tartan, a magnificent affair, a more sensationally showy kilt than mine and he looks splendid in it. I'm desperately afraid you really do fall for him now once you see it.

I cannot hope to overtake in this one letter all the items of news I ought to deal with to make up arrears. I'm in active correspondence re increased journalism. And yes – if the Canadian thing comes off – you'll come too.

The photos of my Manchester portraits haven't come to hand yet; I'll send you copies as soon as they do.

Did I tell you I've brought back this time all the necessary materials to get on with my water colour paintings, as I said I would?

Switching back for a minute to the Canadian project, the reason why I say so definitely yes – you must come too – that is an essential condition – is that I am determined if there is any means whatever of preventing it that you and I are not going to be separated again for more than the briefest of periods. I do need you and want you all the time, darling.

What I ought to have commented on at the very outset of this epistle perhaps is that I am extremely glad there is a prospect of your mother having perhaps a good term of years yet even without being able to work and perhaps with an aneurism. We must do all we possibly can to ease things for her remaining years.

I need not say again how I hate and rebel against the idea of you having all that hard work and horrible drudgery to do; but from now on I'm going to redouble all my efforts to build up a lucrative business as a journalist etc. and get completely out of the mess we've been in.

It gave me quite an ache at the heart to read what you wrote of Mike and his old tricycle, tho' I may have seemed very grumpy and impatient with him often while he was here I do love that boy and I simply could not bear anything happening to him. I'm really worrying both about his ear business and his tonsils, and will be very anxious till I know how they go off. Also I'm desperately anxious to hear what the verdict of your own overhauling has amounted to, because I've really been worrying about your health all along.

While still on health matters I think your Aunt Agnes should try – or find out from her medical advisers – about the new Anahaemin injection treatment for pernicious anaemia. You remember I saw in a paper about it and cut it out and gave it to Orr re Glibie's Kirsty.[6] She was very far down – almost at death's door – yet the Doctor got in and from the first injection it has produced very favourable results. The cost of the stuff is only about 5/- per injection and only one injection per month is given, so the cost is only 5/- plus the fee of the doctor for giving the injection per month.

Finally – to complete the health comments – I've come back in excellent form myself, and I'll go into the question of the utility of further injections with the doctor at once.

I have a whole pile of new books and would send on the copy of Romains' *The Body's Rapture* I got for you, if you'd like me to rather than await your return.[7] I got it for you because it is a great masterpiece in the literature of passionate married love and because, my dearest, circumstances have starved and limited our life together in that way and we've got to make it all up as soon as possible now.

I've dated this Wednesday since it can't go off till then but I've written all the foregoing this (Monday) afternoon and will add anything I think of in postscript form.

Love to all of you at 28, and kisses and all loving-kindness to your dear little self.

Yours, Christopher

In all above I am not forgetting *Red Scotland* – far from it. And will get that off very quickly now.

I came ashore today with boat off *Earl* containing coffin and remains of old Jimmie Leask who died suddenly in Lerwick Hospital after cancer operation.

Mrs Bruce is away in Lerwick just now. Harriet and others here asking very friendly about your mother and about Mike and yourself.[8]

Enclose herewith Cathie's review of *Eccentrics* which please preserve and bring back for scrapbook.[9]

Also enclose Paisley's a/c. Please send them a cheque.

I am attending to Phoenix request for 5/- due – by sending them P.O. for that amount – & also joining Left Book Club. Also attending to my lost Communist Party Card and question of paying arrears. Will also pay Andrew Patterson the 14/- for which he has now re-rendered account.

No other letters here for you – only circulars and samples, which I presume you do not wish sent on?

---

1. S.S. *Earl of Zetland* (built by John Fullerton & Co., Paisley, in 1877), the 120-foot steamer ship which ran between Lerwick and Whalsay. It was decommissioned in 1939 and replaced by a new diesel-engined ship, the M.V. *Earl of Zetland*.
2. Lady Brooke: see Appendix.
3. George Elder Davie (b.1912), a student of Classics and Philosophy at Edinburgh University when CMG first met him, he went on to teach Philosophy there until 1939. After a period at Queen's University, Belfast (1945–59) he returned to Edinburgh, publishing his seminal study of Scottish educational philosophy, *The Democratic Intellect* (1961).
4. Universities book: no such work was published.
5. Hugh MacDiarmid, *Cornish Heroic Song for Valda Trevlyn* (Glasgow: Caledonian Press, [1943]), first published in *The Criterion*, vol.18, no.71, January 1939.
6. Glybie was the nickname of John Irvine of Saltness, Whalsay, the skipper of a sail drifter, the *Valkyrie*; Kirsty was his wife.
7. Jules Romains, *The Body's Rapture*, tr. John Rodker (London: John Lane, 1933), sent with the advice 'not to leave [it] lying about!'.
8. The Bruces were the lairds of Whalsay and lived at Symbister House(the Haa).
9. Catherine Carswell, 'Speakable Scots – *Scottish Eccentrics* by Hugh MacDiarmid', *Spectator*, 3 April 1936, p.946.

70. *To Sorley MacLean (NLS)*

Whalsay   22 May 1936

My dear Maclean

Sorry I missed you; I did go back to the Shetlands but only to return South with Valda and Mike. They are in Cornwall where Valda's mother has been seriously ill – tho' now happily improving. I was down in Manchester and elsewhere talking to the students, and subsequently in Glasgow and then – as you may have heard from your brother Calum – in Edinburgh; Davie and Aitken saw me off back here and I understand there is to be another Edinburgh Rectorial and that I am to stand again – but this time I think with the advantage of having a book out first on the question of Scottish University problems. Besides I have now the emphatic commendation of Sir J.M. Barrie behind me.[1] We'll see. Anyway these peregrinations account for my delay in receiving yours of 11th inst and replying to same ere this. I am in great form again – I've taken to regular kilt wearing (as has Dr Orr) and you'd scarcely know me for the same man as you saw last year. I am infernally busy, and inter alia have now *Red Scotland* adjusted and appearing shortly,[2] and the *Anthology* (on which I got a 6-months extension of time) to finish as one of my earliest tasks.

I note all you so kindly say about my coming to Raasay and unless something unforeseen happens I will certainly come. I do hope your mother is speedily restored to complete health. (Phlebitis – and thrombosis – is what's wrong with Valda's mother too.) When we went South, we did not know anything about Valda's mother's illness; the result was unfortunately that Valda who very badly needed a thorough holiday and rest just landed home in time to be saddled with all the work and worry. The original intention was that she should leave Mike down in Cornwall, rejoin me in Scotland herself, and that she and I together should then have a jolly good holiday. That programme still holds, only the time schedule has had to be shifted ahead almost indefinitely. However, as matters now stand, it is likely that Valda will return to Scotland in July and if we can then park Mike somewhere we will be free. From what you say about the accommodation available at your home I wonder if I might dare to suggest bringing Valda up with me; if so I would certainly do that, tho' I cannot give you a definite date yet. In any case you can certainly rely upon my coming up some time towards the end of the Summer.

I hope this finds you in good case yourself. I'll look forward very keenly to seeing you again. What are your own plans for July and early August?

Scottish Eccentrics was extraordinarily well reviewed; I have my big new poem *Cornish Heroic Song* almost finished; and have piles of other work on the stocks.

Every kind regard (Orr joins me) – and, again, I do hope your mother is now securely on the upgrade.

Yours, C.M. Grieve

---

1. Sir James Matthew Barrie (1860–1937), Scottish playwright and novelist, author of *Peter Pan* and Chancellor of Edinburgh University (1930–7). In the spring of 1936 Barrie, along with many other prominent writers, had been signatory to a public testimonial to CMG, praising him for 'bringing [his] own country into vital touch with the main currents of world thought'.
2. *Red Scotland*: now placed with Lawrence and Wishart.

---

71. *To Valda Grieve (NLS)*

Whalsay   Saturday evening [1936]

My darling Valda

You said the other day that I did not, in the letter you had just then received, seem quite so sanguine and hopeful as in a previous one. But, bless you, these things take a little time to arrange, and I have an enormous number of things on foot. I am up to the neck – literally! – in papers, and my output of letters trying to negotiate this, that, and the other is really astonishing. But I have hardly any doubt at all that we will speedily now fix up 1/ the Autobiography 2/ the Cunninghame Graham book 3/ a book, for American publication, entitled *Speaking for Scotland*[1] and consisting of carefully arranged extracts (from all my previous books and uncollected articles etc.) illustrating the whole range of Scottish problems, needs, prospects and potentialities, a preliminary essay – by *you* – on the whole range and significance of my work, about twenty selected poems, two or three essays, two or three short stories, two plays, and a specially written 4000 word epilogue in the form of 'An Open Letter to American Scots'. Also arrangements are definitely in hand for several broadcasts. So I am not wasting my time.

But I am wearying very badly to have you with me again. And do hope you are having a better chance now to enjoy the sun and to go bathing etc. – that things are much easier in every way; that you are responding splendidly to your treatment; and that Mike is O.K.

I'll leave this letter open and probably add more to it tomorrow. I am going over to Broch tonight for Lizzie's brother to cut my hair! – which badly needs cutting. It is glorious weather, and I'm in great form.

The mirror wasn't in my room, but Harriet has it all right and I'll leave it with her in the meantime. What has happened to our little clock? – I can't see it anywhere – I borrowed a watch from Auntie Betty and am going by it and by my own wrist-watch, when either or both of them are going and I do not forget to wind them.

I got off *Mature Art* to Dent's all right this morning. It is *some* poem, believe you me – in about fifteen languages; putting in the accents etc. and marking the necessary italicizations, indentations and so forth was a deuce of a job in the wee sma' hours between midnight last night and breakfast time this morning; but I think I made it fool proof for any printer.

I have snaps of you stuck in the corners of your Coia[2] drawing and Ayrton's etching of myself – just to create the illusion that you aren't far away; and I find myself every now and again trying to picture just how you are looking and what you are possibly doing. As John Burns said 'a man should always have an opportunity of reminding his wife that he is her sweetheart still'. Darling, I love you better and better. See and take all care of yourself and come back to me safe and sound – and soon! Kisses on your eyelids and the pulse in your neck, and on your mouth in case you think I am silly and it tries to laugh at me!

Yours, Christopher

I didn't forget about my will, but have had it properly fixed up and engrossed and registered in due legal form.

Sunday
Meant to go sketching and painting today but it was windy – with quite

a cold touch in it – and later developed into Scotch Mist and thick small rain. Walked over to Hool to the Doctor's for tea and then to Isbister with him. He has fifteen confinements just happening or about to happen. Also wrote several thousand more words of *Autobio*, and since letters.

Monday
No letter from you yet!! –
Very worried!

---

1. Hugh MacDiarmid, *Speaking for Scotland* (London: The Lumphen Press, 1939).
2. Emilio Coia (1911–97), pre-eminent Scottish caricaturist. Numerous depictions of CMG include those reproduced in Gordon Wright, *MacDiarmid: An Illustrated Biography* (Edinburgh: Gordon Wright, 1977), *Akros*, vol. 12, nos. 34–5, August 1977 and *Emilio Coia 1911–1997: Memorial Exhibition [Catalogue]* (Glasgow: The Glasgow Art Club, 1997).

72. *To Peggy Grieve (NLS)*

Whalsay   1 June 1936

My dear Peggy
   There is no reply from you yet (of course I know you may be away on holiday) to my letter regarding the children. I shall wait until 13th inst before taking proceedings. You are acting in this matter again with the incredible callousness and inhumanity that had characterised you all along. That you could not love me was nothing, since love is not a matter of the will, but that you showed me not the slightest loyalty, fair play, affection, friendship, or minimal human decency is another matter, and in this question of the children (whom you never loved)
   1/ you cannot have the hardihood to imagine that the Court removed them from my control owing to my adultery (with a woman I have since married) in order to give them into the control of a woman living in open adultery with the husband of another woman. That would surely 'take the cake' altogether.
   2/ You know I was extremely fond of the children and had done nothing at all to deserve to lose them, compared with what you have done – and yet in addition to all your fiendish cruelty to myself you have for five years denied me all access to the children and kept me in ignorance of their address to such an extent that when Christine sent me a postcard last year (which postcard bore no address) I could not even reply to it.
   3/ And yet you yourself at Gilgal said you had nothing against me, but attributed our divorce to your 'having been ill at the time' and with another reference to your famous ignorance or innocence of what marriage meant

when we married in June 1918.

You have frequently come over this last matter. I must tell you I do not believe it; I have always believed on the contrary that you were not a virgin when we married and also that you were unfaithful to me during the period between our marriage and my demobilisation. If either or both of these beliefs are well-founded they amply explain all that has happened since and that, on any other assumption, is frankly inexplicable.

I mention this because I am dealing with the whole matter in my *Autobiography* which I am under contract to publish this year.

Though I go into the whole hellish business fully, frankly and fearlessly – with what I am sure even you will recognise (though you may not admit) as an ample admission of my own imperfections – you and everybody else who reads it will recognise that it is fair and utterly without vindictiveness and again proves how deeply and truly I loved you.

I have nothing whatever to fear from the utmost publicity. My drinking habits are frankly and fully acknowledged – and not apologised for. I shall contrast you – as you emerged out of the enticement suit proceedings with myself, without the slightest fear – from the point of view, inter alia, of my claim to the children! And my national and international reputation today stands clear and unchallengeable. You have doubtless heard of the handsome testimonial presented to me recently together with an album signed by hundreds of well-known writers and celebrated men and women at home and abroad. The man to whom (no matter how excruciating may have been the difficulties, economic and psychological, through which he has had to pass) such a public testimonial can be presented can hold his head high and secure anywhere. I remember you once wrote, after our divorce, expressing the hope that I would yet be a father of whom the children could be proud. You need have no fear – but I would surrender all my literary reputation gladly if I could undo the last few years and make you again a mother of whom, legitimately, they could be proud too.

Another thing; you had the hardihood to tell me, apropos venereal disease, that you had not even reproached me for what was a crime against the children. A pretty sentiment from a callous aborter – a matter which is not extenuated even if the murdered baby were mine – which I know to have been (and, despite the difficulties of proof in such matters, think I can even now *prove*) not to have been mine.

If there is any bitterness in this letter it is excusable in view of your treatment of me generally, and in regard to the children, particularly, but that does not alter the fact that, poor infatuated fool, I cannot even now feel vindictive against you – any personal agony of spirit you have caused me is swamped at once in deep pity and concern for you and in a host of memories – if you think just for a second on how kind I tried to be to you, and how I pleaded with you to live for me and the bairns, just before your operation when I had newly had that horrible shock of seeing you almost at the point of death as the result of aborting what I then believed – and still believe – to be another man's baby; or how although I was down and out and heart-broken I could yet go Christmas shopping with you and buy things for the bairns tho' I knew I was unlikely ever to see them again – perhaps some little understanding and kindness may even yet break through the damnable crust of callousness and cruelty which surrounds you and deafens you to even such a simple appeal for decency to me in this matter of the children; a crust of callousness and cruelty which makes me think at times that I wrote better than I knew in the last line of a love poem I once wrote you, 'The Herd of Does' – 'a golden movement of your dreams' – but that the emphasis should have been on 'golden' in a different way, since it is only lack of money that has made me unable to defend my interests, first as a husband and second as a father, or has enabled you to treat me as you have done.

But do not dismiss this contemptuously as another of 'poor old Chris's outpourings'. I must have the children back. Please write me at once about this.

Yours, Chris.

P.S. I do not fear the revelation in Court of the fact that I have unable to pay the alimony the Court allocated.[1] It has always been more than double my total earnings in every year since our divorce. Besides I was denied all access to them and they were being maintained by monies derived, directly or indirectly, from your paramour, who was jolly well entitled to pay through the nose for all the bearings of the situation he – an avowed libertine – had on his own admission in court set himself out to bring about, when he could not help me with a £50 overdraft (you knew damned well the filthy £10 he gave you was outside my knowledge all together) but almost immediately after could give you hundreds and then thousands to seduce you from me – and then found you a £1000 a year job and all the rest of it at a time when you kindly gave me 10/- and a note (which I shall quote in *Autobiography*) advising me to go to a Rowton House,[2] or commit suicide. I may add I shall deal fully, fairly and fearlessly in *Autobiography* with Mr McElroy, Sean O'Casey,[3] Gogarty etc. etc. – and that I will have the volume thoroughly 'vetted' by first-class lawyers to ensure that there is no loophole for any libel action. My literary skill is quite adequate to enable me to tell the full truth (where necessary in any detail against myself too) without being actionable.

Yours, Chris

P.P.S. There is one other matter which you might please tell me out of mere rudimentary decency. Do you still possess the books, and papers – including letters from R.B. Cunninghame Graham, Neil Munro, etc. etc. – and if so, can I have access to the latter? With regard to the former I should not be surprised if you had long since sold them for the few shillings a lot of second-hand books bring (and perhaps destroyed most of the latter too), but the books were my tools and were intimately associated with my work, and the changed nature of my poetry was intimately connected with my loss of them, in ways I feel it necessary to explain in considerable details, in this *Autobiography*.

I shall be glad if you will let me know if these books and papers are still held by you, if I can have access to them, and if you have my list of the titles of the former since that would be very useful indeed in detailing my sources and checking and illustrating the stages of my mental and spiritual evolution.

Finally, let me say that I have no interest whatever in washing dirty linen in public – it is necessary however for the first and last time for me to tell my side of the case honestly and clearly in regard especially to 1/ our divorce, 2/ the children, 3/ money, and 4/ drink, 5/sex – and also to give as full an account of my intellectual development and personal contacts as possible. I am actuated by no revenge motives at all. What I say of intimate matters between you and I will be strictly conditioned solely by its bearing on my poetry and both in regard to Mr McElroy and yourself, if I have to say hard things, these will be amply balanced by gratitude for any incidental little kindness that either of you have ever shown me and by a passionately expressed acknowledgement of whatever I know of good in the characters and careers of both of you. If I deal in what you may regard at times as base suspicions and cruel surmises you must remember that you have not been in any way frank or fair with me and that what I do know for certain justifies no confidence, and my need to surmise and suspect is due to bitter necessity.

---

1. Alimony was awarded at the rate of £100 per annum for each child and expenses.
2. A doss house.
3. Sean O'Casey (1880–1964). The Irish playwright was friendly with William McElroy, who had been best man at his wedding to Eileen O'Casey in 1927. CMG had written to O'Casey around the time of Kate McElroy's enticement case, asking whether he should stay with Valda or go back to his first wife. O'Casey, feeling he could offer no useful advice, ignored the letter and communication between the two lapsed till the late 1940s.

73. *To Valda Grieve (NLS)*

Colla Firth, (Aboard *The Valkyrie*)　　　　　　　　Tuesday [2 June 1936]

Dearest V.

Went to sea yesterday in hailstorm at Symbister. Very cold up Yell Sound but turned splendid night. Shot nets about 10 to 11 pm about 20 miles beyond Ramna Stacks and Muckle Flugga lighthouse and drew up again about 4 am – light fishing; about 8 crabs. All boats had small catches.

Just going to sea again – noon Tuesday. Hope I'll see catch tonight. Noise of capstan etc. did not wake me last night at all. I went to bunk about midnight – after rattling good game at Bridge – and fell asleep at once and slept like a log till 8 am. I was very tired, but I'd been up to 3 am on Monday morning playing bridge with Dr Orr, Auntie Betty and a Dr Calder.

Was glad to receive your letter on Monday before I sailed. Down to 70 blood is happily not very bad. The prescription is for the most part just the usual stuffs – quinine, and arsenic – good blood tonics. The Oppenheimer thing is a special blood treatment. Hope your blood will respond all right and that you soon be up to 100 again. Incidentally Dr Orr doesn't think that should take long, and if your Bude doctor says five weeks there is no need – unless you want to – to stay there so long. The treatment can easily – and more cheaply – be continued up here.

The Cunninghame Graham official biography is off – owing to a clause in the will. But that doesn't debar one writing a book; Butchart thinks I should go right ahead with a 40,000 word memoir. I will. I'll get off outline particulars to him in day or two and see if he can place contract.

He is delighted with my outline of proposed *Autobiography* and I ought to know very soon now about contract. In any event I've been rattling up the material good and plenty.

Dear little Mike! I do hope he comes through all right. It would break my heart if anything went wrong and he had a bad time of it. Please give him an extra dose of kisses and tell him these are from Daddy away out at the Atlantic fishings on the west of the Shetlands.

And give my love to your mother and aunts. I am so glad your mother is keeping on keeping on.

My poor darling! What a terrible time the holiday we so looked forward to has turned out for you. Illness – nightmares – your own overhauling – just one damned thing after another. But – *sursum corda*! There's a good time coming. Get well and strong again – and we'll have a great time together yet.

I am in splendid fettle myself; and just going to sit down to a fine dinner of fried herring and tatties.

Hope you got parcels all right; also letter I posted on Monday.

The sea gives you an appetite. I breakfasted heartily off stewed steak and chunks of bread soaked in the gravy and a big mug of black tea. And I'm as hungry as a hawk again. God! These herring frying smell the goods all right.

Wednesday
North Rew
Second night out last night. Glorious weather, not too good for the fishing

and far too calm for a sailing ship. Put into North Rew this morning and had some good fun with the fish girls there – me being in my kilt and balmoral. Small cottage to let at Sandvoe – N. of Rew – only 10/- a year rent. Think I'll take it if I can. Handy for a change now and again.

Dinner just coming up. Praise the Lord. Fried herring and tatties again. I could eat a couple of whales.

Wednesday night
Out again 20 miles S.W. of the Flugga light and about 10 due West of the Ramna Stacks, and just about to shoot our nets. Big fleet all about us – fifty or sixty sail-boats, motor boats, drifters etc. Hope we get a big shot tonight. Wrote two good lyrics today, lying up on the deck on the herring-nets in the sun. But it's dashed cold now. However we will be getting our supper-time porridge soon.

Thursday morning
Colla Firth
No luck again last night – fewer herring than we could eat ourselves. Made less per man than I made myself if the *Outlook* takes my two lyrics[1] – one of which now runs to about 30 4-line verses. Lovely morning here again, with a little light rain. Was on deck most of night, and when I did turn in simply couldn't get off to sleep – too much poetry in my head, I fancy, for otherwise I am feeling fine. Think now you should, when you are ready, come back here first; then we can see about the Borders and Raasay a little later. I'll feel happier about you when I (and perhaps Dr Orr) has had a look at you again. And if we can't fix up Mike down South for a week or two we can always do so in Whalsay. In any case after this week at sea I'll have to set myself down to a spell of damned hard writing for a few weeks at any rate.

In sight of Foula
Thursday night
Casting our nets again under a perfect weatherhead. Hope for better luck tonight.

Friday 4 am
Hauling our nets since 1am. Nearly finished now. Much better catch. Deck littered with fish. Was helping to haul myself for a while. Lovely red sunrise. Soon the cabin will be a snug little place with a fine smell of smoke, steam, cooking, and sweaty socks. No doubt I'd prefer to be with you in our own little house; but this suits me A1 to go on with.

Friday night
Colla Firth
Very high wind-storm, and dense small rain. Conditions quite impossible on the West Side grounds especially for sailing boats. The motor-boats and drifters even tried to go out but had to come back. So we'll lie here tonight and go home to Whalsay tomorrow if conditions permit. Spending our time playing bridge, whist, laut etc. But before rain got too heavy went up the hill with Johnny Glibie, jnr., and angled in the mill-stream, getting 4 nice trout we've just eaten for supper (following 2 platefuls of gruel each).

Saturday morning
That is to say – to Whalsay, *if* we can win. It is blowing a furious gale up here at the top of Colla Firth, but the wind and tide may suit us once we get into Fell Sound. Anyhow we've had to put three reefs in our sails.

No doubt you are wearying to hear from me. I have had no chance of posting any of this before returning to Whalsay, but, tho' it is now out of date news, I enclose it because it proves at least – if you needed any proof – that there hasn't been a day of time or day all week I haven't been thinking of you, and I'm wearying for letters too. We'll see what the mail at Whalsay has for me. At the moment we're having a devil of a job to leave Colla Firth Harbour at all. Heaven only knows what like it'll be out in the open.

– Came down with sails three-reefed. A most exciting experience – but not for any except good sailors.

– Landed at Whalsay in fury of wind & water.

In haste. Getting this off by post (Saturday) just few minutes after my arrival back.

Love & kisses. Yours ever, Christopher
Splendid letter from Lady Brooke re Cunninghame Graham project – a letter which I think is almost certain to work the oracle.

---

1. 'Off the Coast of Fiedeland' and 'The Wreck of the Swan'.

74. *To Valda Grieve (NLS)*

[Whalsay]   Tuesday [1936]

My dearest Valda
The Doctor removed to the little cottage at Hool Grind on Monday and I went home. Everything is fine and dry; I have plenty of coal; and I got in adequate provisions – bread, bully, bacon, eggs etc. So I'll be all right. But I find it difficult to settle – I get nervy sitting there writing all by myself, and will be extremely glad when you return to me.

I am enclosing for your perusal an article from the *British Medical Journal*, as it contains important information along lines upon which I feel every wife ought to be thoroughly informed.

Had a wire from Whyte yesterday wanting 1000 word review for next issue of new volume of poems by the Scottish American Communist and poet Norman Macleod.[1] So I must get that off by this mail too.

The weather continues very patchy and has been windy and showery this last day or two.

Mary Lou[2] has been having her meals at Harriet's, along with Ginger.

Was at Whist Drive on Monday night, and had 95 in first half but slumped badly in the second half and was well out of the prize list.

I was so glad to get your wire on Tuesday and do hope poor little Mike has had no post-operation trouble and that the operation was not too terrible a shock to him. Give him heaps of kisses from Daddy.

Everybody always asking most kindly for you and your mother.

You'd get Auntie Betty's epistle.

No word yet from Dent's re *Mature Art*.[3]

Hope – if it is warm and sunny – to do a little sketching this week-end.

Wednesday

Many thanks for letters and parcel. The shirt looks O.K. and the sizes should be all right, but I'll try them on and if necessary return one or both. But I do not think that'll be necessary. I do not propose to wear them here; but to reserve them for special occasions.

I will take the jumper and letter down to Mrs Mainland. Ina, who is away from Crosskeys, is off on holiday for a few weeks.

Sorry my letter re cash struck you as less full of luck and beans. But that's just the nature of my job. I have a devil of a lot on, and anything may happen at any moment. I certainly hope to fix up both *Auto.* and Cunninghame Graham books. The only question is when – and when the advances will come in. Please do not worry; I'll do all the worrying that is necessary. But I'd work better if you were here now. I simply can not get off to sleep here living alone. It is of course just too absurd as I am in splendid health, but there it is.

If I seemed a little less hopeful it is just because negotiations from here take up such a devil of a time. I had hoped things were going to move much more quickly. But I feel sure things are going to pan out all right.

I was horrified to find on coming up here on Monday that instead of sending you my other red shirt etc. by mistake along with the unfinished white knicks for which you asked, I'd got even more mixed up – for the white knicks themselves were still lying here. So, with all due apologies, I am forwarding them now.

I have added the two oil-paintings (the others haven't come on yet) to the collection on our living room walls, and they look tip-top.

The plants all look fine and green and healthy, and I have just taken a stroll out and had a look at the honeysuckle, which seems to be flourishing nicely, while the wire netting is still intact. I'll keep an eye on it henceforward.

Do not worry about tone of *Autobiography*. After all my journalistic instinct *is* part of my life and has been a very important and indeed determinant part of it. I have now made up my mind to call the book *Lucky Poet*.[4] That'll be some indication of how I intend to treat the business, for, despite all my ups and downs and the many unfortunate aspects of my life, on the balance I have undoubtedly been lucky – 1st of all in my own gifts, 2nd in having despite all had a very varied and interesting life and meeting all sorts of people, and 3rdly and conclusively in meeting you when I did – just in the nick of time – and winning your wonderful selfless love, you splendid little darling. My *Autobio.* is certainly not going to be anything in the nature of a whine for pity.

I'll have to stop now. I do hope Mike isn't suffering from any psychological upset as the results of his hospital experience and that his physical condition is all right.

But above all I remain very very anxious about yourself, and longing to see you with my own eyes again to satisfy my mind that you are safe and sound.

Please give my love to your dear little mother and to your aunts, to Mrs Fellowes, and with heaps of kisses to dear little Michael (with whom I fancy you'll find me very much more patient and understanding than before) and to yourself.

Yours, Christopher

---

1. For MacDiarmid on Norman Macleod, see *The Raucle Tongue*, vol. III, pp. 550–2.
2. Marie Lou: the Grieves' cat.
3. *Mature Art, an exercise in Schlabone, Bordatini, and Scordattura*, referred to as a work of some 20,000 lines, it was accepted for publication by Jack Kahane of Obelisk Press, Paris, in 1939. His death and, shortly after, the Fall of France made publication impossible. Much was eventually published in *In Memoriam James Joyce*.
4. *Lucky Poet: a self-study in literature and political ideas, being the autobiography of Hugh MacDiarmid (Christopher Murray Grieve)* (London: Methuen, 1943).

75. *To Valda Grieve (NLS)*

Saturday [20 June 1936] (to go by Monday's post)

My dearest Valda

Did not get mail (owing to *Earl* being held up by fog all day yesterday and until dinner-time today) until this afternoon. Was so glad to get your letter – and so vexed to hear you are still having such a dreadful time. Please pay no attention at all to my last – and other complaining – letters. It's just the nature of the beast, to get all worked up about nothing at all. And I do love you very truly and completely.

And what a mail I have had! I'm still swamped under it. Davie is coming here on Wednesday to stay with me – I'll put him up at Auntie Betty's, however – and has just wired me he is bringing me an offer of nomination for Edinr. University Rectorial Election – in the name of the United Front. A great deal has been happening; but it's far too complicated to go into in a letter. I certainly seem to be in for the most important fight of my life. I have still the universities book to write. I've been busy instead with my *Autobiography* and *Cornish Heroic Song* etc. and various articles (the Langholm articles unfortunately fell through – Anderson of the *Record* and others blow hot and then cold in the most disconcerting way).

Church of Dent's has been on holiday, and I've only had a formal acknowledgment of *Mature Art* yet.

I'm not going to let you see the typescript of the *Autobio.* at all. I want you to trust me in this – to do the fair and generous thing by you and all concerned. If you see only bits you'll almost inevitably come to the wrong conclusions; the thing can only be appreciated as a whole. It will be devastatingly frank and fearless.

Do trust me, darling. Though I write you a stupid letter or two at times, you have really nothing to fear. I love you, and only you, passionately and completely; and you would be surprised if you only knew how completely I have got rid of the Peggy obsession at last – much more completely than I myself had dared to hope; as I have had cause to find out in the very thorough heart-searching and psychological cross-examination I have had to subject myself to in connection with this *Autobiography*.

Mr Mainland has just been in with my brogues he was heeling for me, and your jumper. Do you want it sent on?

I'm going to fry myself a couple of herring in oatmeal. Perhaps that'll put me in a better frame of mind.

———

Just had them, with a pot of tea and a couple of slices of brown scone; and toddled down through the fog to have a word with Charlie who is busy furring the earth up round the cabbages. I met little Mary Jean too and gave her a penny to buy sweets. I'm doing not so badly – both Harriet and the Doctor's Lizzie have made me oven scones, and I've had umpteen meals at the Doctor's, Auntie Betty's, and the Ha'. Lerwick was closed yesterday, owing to a big glut of herring (over 31 crans average for each of 260 boats). I haven't heard whether the boats are to win out tonight or not – probably not, owing to the dense fog.

If only the mail would come now – but it will be at least an hour yet, damn it!

I water your plants every day and they are in splendid condition. Ditto the honeysuckle. Marie Lou only comes to see me, for a second or two, at rare intervals – tho' I always give her milk and often fish, when she does come.

I hear the *Earl* blowing in Symbister Voe, so it has come – at last!

You've never even said a word about whether you liked Romains' *Body's Rapture* or not! I've just gone up to the shop and got a new bottle of milk; also 1 lb of Sugar – and with some of the latter I have just eaten a bowl of milk that has gone thick with the heat.

I am sending you with this letter *Out of the Night* (be sure and bring it back with you.)[1] I would like you to read it carefully and get all its information and ideas thoroughly into your head – as I am increasingly interested in all these vital matters and anxious to have you able to discuss them with me if you too are interested, as I hope you will be.

On second thoughts I am also enclosing the jumper which has come back from Mainland's today – just in case you want it. (I do not know whether there is, or should be, anything to pay in respect of it – I paid for the heeling of my brogues – but forgot to ask if I owed Mrs Mainland anything for whatever she's done to the jumper.)

9pm

Waited hour after hour for the infernal mail. Finally have just gone up and seen the Arthurs. It wasn't the *Earl* after all blowing in Symbister Voe – the *Earl* left Lerwick all right about 3pm but has had to anchor somewhere between here and there. The fog is worse than ever. So I'll get no letters tonight. I'm terribly worked up. I expect I'll get no sleep tonight again.

And there are *three* Mondays *yet* before you come – *three* at least. How absolutely hellish!

I do not know how the devil I'm going to last all that time. I was never any damned good at waiting.

I hope, however, that when you do come, you don't have one of these foggy passages and have to lie out at sea for Heaven only knows how long.

Yours, Christopher

---

1. H.J. Muller, *Out of the Night: A Biologist's View of the Future* (London: Gollancz, 1936).

76. *To Valda Grieve (NLS)*

Whalsay   Thursday, 25 June 1936

Darling Valda

How extraordinary, for Cornwall of all places, that your p.c. should report only one really good day since you went there. Here for the past few days the heat has been really Mediterranean; brilliant sunshine all day – too hot and light all night for sleep. There was no weather like this up here last year at all – it is even better than it was that first summer we came to Whalsay. Difficult weather for steady application and hard work. Davie arrives tomorrow (I am writing this Tuesday evening, tho' I put Thursday up above as that is the day the next mail goes out). The Doctor and I are going up to the Ha' tonight to play bridge. I had a letter from H.B.C. She is holidaying this week on the Island of Lismore off the Argyllshire Coast. She says 'I have not heard of Valda for weeks'. I explained how little time or energy you had had for letter-writing.

I was out – over to Broch – this afternoon and inadvertently left Marie Lou in the House. When I got back she had upset my jug of milk all over the papers on my table. Damn her! I caught her, smacked her tail, and put her out.

Been tidying up – washing pots and pans and dishes – sweeping floors etc. – ready for Davie's arrival. Have arranged for Auntie Betty to put him up. And Charlie is to waken me in time to go down to meet *Earl* tomorrow morning – can't waken, or rather can't get up if I am woken, these mornings. Charlie woke me about 10.30 today but it was nearly noon before I got downstairs. Of course I was reading etc. till about 5.30 am.

Hope you've received my last letter and forgiven me for the stupid state I could not help your non-writing putting me into. There were some turns of expression that were just too bad, and I am very sorry indeed for them. Somehow I just could not help myself. Yet I did understand all right. Only it has been such a very long time and I have wearied dreadfully to see you again. I've always told you you should not have married a poet – it's no joke – either for the poet himself, or anybody else.

Sunday.
Couldn't find this – to get it away yesterday. So sorry you had to wire me over my stupidity. Was glad to get your long letter. Forgive me, darling. I am a silly ass.

Davie is here and we are having a great time together – getting everything thrashed out.

All love and kisses to you and Mike; and kindest regards and best wishes to your mother and aunts.

77. *To the Editor,* Daily Record, *Glasgow (NLS)*

Whalsay, via Lerwick, Shetland Islands [1936]

Dear Sir: –
Since many people all over Scotland have been eagerly awaiting my book, *Red Scotland*, which presents my final conclusions on the Scottish

political questions to which I have devoted my life and is the first comprehensive survey of Scottish affairs from the standpoint of the majority of Scottish electors, viz. the Left Wing, may I ask you to spare a corner of your paper to intimate that the publication of this book has been indefinitely postponed owing to the fact that Mr Edwin Muir took the extraordinary step of intervening with the prospective publishers and inducing them not to publish my book? Mr Muir was actuated in an action happily extremely rare in British literary circles by the fact that the book contained a few sentences of adverse criticism of his (Mr Muir's) work. It is a remarkable and significant fact that his personal vanity and his fear of criticism should have led him to this unique act of literary sabotage against a fellow writer whose reputation and influence is, to say the least of it, not less than his own. The suppression he has effected can, of course, only be temporary and I have little doubt that I shall be able to secure another publisher very soon, but I think that on general grounds the widest publicity ought to be given to Mr Muir's unprecedented action which, in any other profession than that of letters, would undoubtedly arouse widespread indignation as a case of 'infamous conduct in a professional respect' and meet with the drastic punishment it deserves.

Yours sincerely, Hugh MacDiarmid

78. To William McElroy (NLS)

c/o Macdonald, 6 West Claremont St, Edinburgh   29 December 1936

Dear Mr McElroy

I do not know whether Peggy told you of the letters I wrote her early in the year none of which she answered – I do not even know what your relationship with Peggy is now – but I take the liberty of writing you because the matter involves you too.

I made no trouble at the time Peggy and I separated – and I have raised no actions since, though my lawyers advised me that I could – mainly because I was thinking of Christine and Walter. I had done nothing whatever to lose them – to be denied not only any chance to see them but any knowledge of their whereabouts and welfare. I could not possibly imagine at the beginning that this could be done to me. It is so absolutely fiendish. I thought we could be friends – I wished you and Peggy well. I could not help being destitute – unable to defend my rights or to do anything for the children. But even after we separated, Peggy and I went shopping together and I bought Christmas presents for the kiddies. But Peggy has never allowed me to see them – not even when I was at death's door in hospital two years ago. Nor do I know their whereabouts.

I write now – after standing this merciless cruelty for five years – to say that I will stand it no longer. If you are still in touch with Peggy will you speak to her about it? If I do not hear very soon now that I may correspond with and see my children I shall have no option but to raise an action to review the divorce proceedings and to have access to the children – who would never have been put into Peggy's custody by the Court if the Judge had known the facts. And at the same time I will lodge an injunction with the Director of Public Prosecutions against Peggy and yourself for perjury during the enticement case and conspiracy to defeat the ends of justice. I have in my possession sworn statements of responsible witnesses with regard to the points about which I am concerned. I am not anxious to bring actions against you – though you ruined my life I have no desire to do you any harm now I can avoid – but I must have means of hearing about and seeing the children or I shall have no alternative.

I have no ill-feeling whatever against you. Nor had I at first against Peggy either – but my feeling in regard to her changed completely after seeing her in Gilgal Hospital in 1935 – when she told a man who had just escaped death by the skin of his teeth and was utterly down and out a pack of the most atrocious lies; and when, also, she failed to bring Christine with her although I had been eating my heart out for years with longing to see her and that might well have been my last chance.

I appeal to you as a matter of ordinary humanity to use any influence you may have with Peggy to put an end to this diabolical injustice.

Yours sincerely, C.M. Grieve

79. To Sorley MacLean (NLS)

Whalsay   15 January 1937

My dear Maclean

I can only thank you on behalf of us all for your far too generous parcels. Mike – who had a bumper Christmas – was vastly delighted with all his presents and sends his love to 'the big man'. I myself am specially indebted for the books. Babette Deutsche's very useful and intelligent survey was on my own list to purchase and I am particularly glad to have it.[1] I don't agree with you about Yeats's anthology.[2] He could of course have made a more representative selection of my stuff – and that of most of the poets he includes – but that would not have suited his special purpose – to give a very shrewd thrust from an unexpected quarter at the 'English-English' view of poetry in the English language. And his thrust has been telling enough – witness the bad press the book has had from all the stuffy little English Ascendancy reviewers.

My health has been causing me some anxiety again, but I think I am now over that hurdle – it was not unconnected with a proper log jam of work I'd developed. But that is now beginning to clear away nicely, and things are opening out for me in a way that will in turn be the best possible tonic. Enough that this year is to be one of my very busiest and most productive. That is already assured.

I cannot write you at any length just now – but will soon. There is one thing however. *Inter alia* I am doing a book on *The Islands of Scotland* – Hebrides, Orkney, Shetland etc. and I want to come over to Skye – probably next month or March; I'll know definitely in a few days' time.[3] Whether I bring Valda with me or not will depend on the weather etc. But would that be convenient for us – or me – to come to Raasay? Don't hesitate to say no, if it isn't, because in that case we'd just stay in Skye. I'll write you as soon as I am able to make definite arrangements.

Hope this finds you – and all your people – in good form. Orr joins me in kindest regards. All the best to all of you for 1937. And again, our warmest thanks.

Yours, C.M. Grieve

---

1. Babette Deutsch, *This Modern Poetry* (London: Faber & Faber, 1936).
2. *The Oxford Book of Modern Verse 1892–1935*, ed. W.B. Yeats (Oxford: Clarendon Press, 1936).
3. Hugh MacDiarmid, *The Islands of Scotland: Hebrides, Orkneys and Shetland* (London: Batsford, 1939).

80. *To Andrew Graham Grieve (EUL)*

Whalsay   8 February 1937

My dear A.

I was very glad to get your letter – tho' sorry you had to tell of various illnesses and other difficulties. You seem however to have got hold of a nice – and nicely situated – house and I hope that by this you are all O.K. and greatly enjoying your new circumstances.

I have been unable to write sooner. For nearly three weeks we had no mails in or out here owing to a succession day after day, week after week, of the most terrific storms within living memory here. Then – just as the weather moderated a little – all of us, like almost everybody else on the island, went down with flu' and are just crawling slowly out of that horrible condition again now. This is our first day up for several; and we are all feeling very seedy and shaky and light-headed. So please do not expect more than the merest note tonight. Valda says she will write Chryssie one day soon. If all goes well I hope to take her to Skye, Glasgow, and round about for a little holiday as soon as we are fit to travel, and then I must park down and work like blazes, for all my work has got dreadfully into arrears.

I do hope that on top of the ailments you mentioned in your letter you have not also been afflicted with flu', and that this finds you all in good form and liking your new circumstances, in the office (you seem to have put yourself at the head of a whole Department judging by the battalion of your subordinates), in the home, and at school.

Please thank Morag and Angus very sincerely if alas so belatedly for the splendid big story-book they sent Mike for Christmas. He was a very lucky little boy again – at that age you and I fared well enough with a well stuffed stocking full – but Master Michael, forsooth, had a pillowcase and ½ another pillowcase bulging beside his pillow on Christmas morning.

His attendances at school have been few and far between this winter – the weather has been so atrocious and the usual wind, going at about 80 m.p.h., being a bit too much for him to exercise the art of walking in.

All the best to you all.

Write soon. Yours, Valda, Chris and Mike

P.S. Reminder re photo. duly noted and securing attention.

81. *To W.R. Aitken (NLS)*

Whalsay   18 February 1937

My dear Aitken

I have been wondering about Central Library for students' facilities. Perhaps you can tell me. The Rural Library Scheme here is in charge of an old dodderer in Lerwick and is moribund. There is no branch on this island. I understand that the Central Library forwards books to applicants on their paying postage back and forward: but what I don't know is

1/ if applications can be sent direct, or must be sent through the librarian of the local Rural Library Scheme;

2/ how many books can be had at once, and

3/ how one knows what books are in stock and readily available, i.e. whether there is a catalogue to be had or not.

I'd be glad if you could tell me these things. I need urgently to get as many books about the Western Islands as I possibly can – descriptive books, historical books, guide books, maps etc. If I could get what the Central Library has in batches of five or six at a time I'd work through them quickly. If I can only have one at a time it would take me too long to get all I want and I'd require to supplement what I could procure in that way by trying to borrow others from other libraries and – I am afraid – by buying quite a number too. I don't want to do the latter if I can help it as I have no permanent use for them – all I want is to go quickly through them and take the necessary notes to serve my immediate purpose.

Trust you are O.K. and hope to hear from you soon, with any cuttings you have accumulated for me. I hope you got the p.o. for the printers I sent you some days ago.

All the best. Yours, C.M. Grieve

82. *To W.R. Aitken (NLS)*

Whalsay   25 February 1937

My dear Aitken

   Very many thanks for your letters and the Catalogue. I hope you, and the other members of your family, are now all clear of illness or its after-effects. We are O.K. here now. I'll – in the meantime at any rate – get some of the books about the islands via Mr Ratter. It is good of you to offer to get me a book or two I want quickly in this way through you personally – and while I do not want to make myself a nuisance to you in any way, I am afraid I must take advantage of your offer too – I, of course, refunding you the postage hither. In addition to the islands book I have, amongst other things (and please do not mention these matters to anyone) a contract – calling for early delivery of complete typescript – for a 80 to 90,000 word book which will be partly a history of medicine and surgery in Scotland, partly a study of the relations of public health, disease, and other factors touching on physiological history, problems of stature, energy, reproductivity, population in relation to physical surroundings etc., and, finally, discursive somewhat in the manner of *Scottish Eccentrics* and giving particulars of the life stories, eccentricities, curiosities of scientific interest etc. of several hundred of the chief Scottish doctors through the last 3 to 4 centuries.[1] I note what you say about the Central Library, getting books from other libraries, also buying books not in stock; and I have a very long list of books, mostly recent, none of them in the Catalogue, which I must have a look at once (or before) I get thoroughly into my stride with this opus. In this connection if you could I'd be glad if you could have a look at Stubbs (S.G.B.) and E.W. Bligh's *Sixty Centuries of Health and Physick* and tell me if the index has many (or any) reference to Scotland or Scottish doctors.[2] Could you also do the same with MacLaurin's *Mere Mortals*? There is no hurry for this – any time within the next 2 or 3 weeks. But in the meantime can you send me the same author's – MacLaurin's – *Post Mortem* (catalogue, p.134, under Medicine)? I will post it back without fail within a week of receipt. And then – if it is not too much to ask of you – I'd like (catalogue p.175) Vivante's *Intellegence in Expression*.[3]

   I can't say at moment just when I'll be down, but it won't be long now. I have, amongst other things, several broadcasts coming off ere long, but I think April 16th will be the first of these. Each of these broadcasts will mean a trip to Scotland and on each of these trips I'll try to get about as much as possible and kill as many birds with one stone as I can. Either at these times – or at others which will involve additional trips South – I understand that I'll have engagements to address in succession as many of the Left Book Club Groups in Scotland as I can get round in the time.

   I am delighted to hear of your – and Davie's – papers on Doughty;[4] and of course I'll be only too happy to autograph *Adam Cast Forth* and *Cencrastus*.[5]

Hope Davie and you will have a pleasant day or two together in the beginning of March – wish I could have been with you two, despite the 'two's company, three's none' saying. I am delighted to hear of your brother's intentions re Buchanan;[6] if he has any difficulty in securing a publisher later on I may be able to help, which of course I'd be extremely glad to do.

I quite understand about the cuttings, but I'll be glad to have whatever you cull once you get time to go through the *Herald*s you've stowed away for ultimate scissoring.

All the best. Yours, C.M. Grieve

---

1. Although completed, this book was never published. A portion of it survives in the NLS.
2. S.G. Blaxford Stubbs and E.W. Bligh, *Sixty Centuries of Health and Physick* (London: Sampson Low, Marston & Co., 1931).
3. Charles MacLaurin, *Mere Mortals* (London: Cape, 1925); *Post Mortem* (London: Cape, 1923). Leone Vivante, *Intelligence in Expression*, tr. Prof. Brodrick Bulloch (London: The C.W. Daniel Company).
4. Charles Montagu Doughty (1843–1926), English travel writer and poet whom CMG greatly admired.
5. Charles M. Doughty, *Adam Cast Forth* (London: Duckworth, 1908); Hugh M'Diarmid, *To Circumjack Cencrastus or The Curly Snake* (Edinburgh and London: Blackwood, 1930).
6. George Buchanan (1506–82), Scottish Neo-Latin poet, scholar, tutor to Mary, Queen of Scots, and James VI, among other things he wrote *De juri regni apud Scotos* (1579), an attack on the divine right of monarchs, justifying the deposition of Mary, and a twenty volume history of Scotland. James M. Aitken, *The Trial of George Buchanan before the Lisbon Inquisition* (Edinburgh: Oliver and Boyd, 1939).

83. *To Peggy Grieve (NLS)*

[March 1937]

If I say bitter and unworthy things you must remember how horribly I have suffered – and how utterly undeserved and unjust I consider that suffering to be.

I never understood – and probably never will understand – what came between us. I knew of course that you did not love me. But you never loved McElroy either – you couldn't possibly love so inferior a man, and that from the very beginning there was a tragic sense of impermanence and insecurity about our marriage, and later on as the years passed I was always worried and sick at heart by your lack of response.

I did not blame you for that. But I did seek to earn your respect and loyalty. For health reasons – ever since I left Gilgal – I have been wearing the kilt – what tartan does Walter wear? and there is a feeling it gives one, a sort of unconscious bracing up and pride of carriage, that is like what I always felt about you. I was so proud of you and so deeply in love with you and knowing that you did not love me I did my utmost to weld your friendship by my loyalty and kindness and constant considerateness. I was a good husband and loved my home and our children as much as a man can – though, of course, I did not earn much money and was mainly concerned with totally unremunerative things. But what money I got you got and as married people of the working class go I do not think you can say that we were not happily enough married – we had few quarrels and these for the most part very trivial ones all the years we were together. And I was as proud of you and as fond of you after we went to London as when I first married you – until the cleavage showed itself again and I realised that a break was likely, if not inevitable. But I did plead hard against it and there was nothing I wanted less. If you think hard of me in the face of all that, in the name of God why? I know I have my faults – but I cannot see that I deserved this disaster and dishonour in any way; and I have certainly paid bitterly enough since for any fault I ever had – and will go on paying to the end. It is six years now but I haven't got used to it yet. I have never lost a friend but you, and I have won wide respect and esteem – except from you, from whom I always coveted it most.

All that punishment for one act of adultery after so many loyal years – and then you go and give yourself to a habitual adulterer!

(I am to be down broadcasting on 16th April – why don't you let the children have tea with me in Edinburgh on the Saturday?)

84. *To Peggy Grieve (NLS)*

Whalsay   26 March 1937

Dear Peggy

Please excuse my writing in pencil. What tartan have you put Walter in? (You see though I had to return the photo I have not forgotten he was in a kilt.) I ask because for health reasons I have worn the kilt myself ever since Gilgal. I work well in it, and it always reminds me (not that I ever need any reminding) of you because it gives me a feeling of being braced up, that is exactly like how you and my love for you made me feel for all those years. I wear the red Murray – Murray Tullibardine – tartan. I'll send you a photo if you like.

Talking of the kilt, did you see Colonel Cuthbert was drowned last year – trying to rescue a lamb from a river in Sutherlandshire? Perrins has sold Ardross and Gildermorie.[1] Also, did you see that John Edwards (who lived opposite to us in Links Avenue) was killed – run down by a train at Broomfield Level Crossing? He was married and left a young widow.

I am hardly surprised that you did not reply to my last letters – for of course you knew I would not take action against you if I could possibly help it. I have never done you any deliberate injury – I have never wished you ill but always (even when I was most angry and hurt) success and happiness. But I have wished you would wish me well too and not injure me – and that you would think ahead, of the children. Because you know how very fond I was of them and how impossible it is as long as I live that I should reconcile myself to being kept from ever seeing them or hearing about them. I cannot believe that you do not realise how terribly cruel that is; am I to believe that you mean to keep them from me in this way as long as you possibly can? And if so, in Heaven's name, why? You admitted at Gilgal that you had nothing against me. If I have written some very bitter letters since, surely I have had cause enough – even if it were only McElroy's damnable perjury in the Enticement Case. I was always dead straight with you, and far from deserving treatment of this sort. When I saw how we were drifting apart I tried to prevent it not only for my own sake but for the children's sake – and (in my opinion – perhaps I was wrong) for our sake. It was largely the same feeling that impelled the letters I wrote from Gilgal – the desire for family reconciliation, for, on the whole, despite our poverty, we were a happy family. You have given me no credit whatever for all those years when I was a loyal, devoted, and hardworking father and husband. You may report that I should have thought of that at the end. But I did. You must reckon with the fact that (coming as it did on the top of our long alienation and your refusal to live with me as husband and wife) I honestly believed your illness was the end of things – that it was not due to me but to someone else – McElroy I thought. And in the circumstances I do not see how I could possibly think anything else. In any case I was in an absolutely insupportable position. But I acted as I did largely for the children's sake and for yours. I believed you wanted rid of me, and had already betrayed me, but I knew I was in a desperate state financially. That was why I did not oppose the divorce. I discussed it with Gogarty and he agreed it was the best thing to do; so did Scott. If I had raised the question of your illness and your relations with McElroy – and also the fact that you had conduced to my adultery by refusing me all marital relations for so long – you would hardly have got your divorce and we would all have been in a proper mess. You must remember that the thought of forgiving me for my one solitary offence after all these years of faithful love never entered your head, although you knew you were yourself to blame for driving me to that action. It has always seemed terribly hard to me that you should punish me in this way for a single act of adultery – and then go and live yourself with another woman's husband, and one who was a habitual adulterer. Surely that is far from fair play. You must also remember that while I thought McElroy responsible for your illness (and so, naturally 'phoned him up, and so interpreted his readiness to pay)[2] I was not then able to prove anything and was far too distressed to think clearly and act in a responsible way. I know you have told me McElroy was not to blame. Well, Peggy, all I can say is that I have now carefully checked the medical evidence – times etc. – and am absolutely satisfied that I can *prove I* was not to blame.

Why do I not go ahead, then with the actions I threatened, to recover the children and lodge information re McElroy's perjury? The reason again is the same reason that led to my giving you cause for divorce instead of taking action against you for divorce or for restitution of conjugal rights. I am thinking of the children. I do not want to jeopardise their living – or yours. Nor either for their sake or yours do I want to wash more dirty linen in public, whether you believe it or not – though I often feel very angry – I do not feel revengeful towards you even though I think you got your divorce on fraudulent grounds. I have suffered far too much hardship myself to wish to make anything harder for anyone else, and I cannot bring these actions to vindicate myself for fear (not knowing what your position is, what your relations with McElroy now are) of hurting you financially – affecting your livelihood, and the children's – as long as I myself am destitute, and so ill that it is extremely unlikely that I will live very much longer. I am perfectly satisfied that I would succeed in the actions if I brought them – but I do not really need to do it, because I know I am sure of ultimate vindication in any case, I know I do not need any vindication so far as my real friends are concerned, and therefore I have no need to care a damn what anybody else thinks. But the children are the question. Although I have written you all these letters and got no reply you must appreciate that I have served my other object – by keeping careful copies, I can prove to the children that I never forgot them but kept on asking to be allowed to see them and protesting against our separation for which I was in no way really to blame – and which in any case was utterly unfair and undeserved.

I am anxious, Peggy, to let all the other fleas (the question of McElroy's perjury, your illness etc.) stick to the wa' – if only you will let me see the children again while there is yet time. I do not want to see you; that could do neither of us any good. If you refuse to let me see the children you will have to reckon with them later on – it is monstrously unfair to them – and they will inherit my papers setting out the full story with all the necessary proofs. I do not see why you should not let me see them. In any case, the opportunity won't last long and you may be sorry – or the children may – when it is too late.

I do not intend to write you again. I will certainly raise no actions as long as I may cause you or the children any financial harm, while I myself am so poorly off that I could not make good any such damage to your livelihoods. But – and you cannot blame me for this – all my papers will be found in order at my death, and I have arranged for Christine and Walter and certain other persons to receive copies setting out the full facts with all the necessary corroborative evidence.

I have only to add that in my extreme bitterness of spirit I have said certain things in my letters to you for which I am very very sorry. Please forgive me. I gave you that love that no man can give twice and few men can ever give, and though since Gilgal I have tried hard to finally disentangle myself from that thrall I am afraid I have not wholly succeeded – and never will. Our rupture has not only cost me dear – but Scotland dear, for it destroyed the pith of my poetry and the very core and kernel of all my work. Our rupture was the last thing in the world I wanted and if you had loved me as I loved you it would never have happened. No doubt I was to blame too – but not deliberately. Now that we have gone our separate ways and there can be no coming together again, please do let bygones be bygones – let us forgive each other as much as ever we can. And do let me see the children again – (I am very seldom and then very briefly in Scotland and could very rarely have any chance of seeing them even if you were willing, but we might arrange something, that is if they are in Scotland) – or, at the very least, do please write and tell me how they are getting on.

With best wishes, Chris

P.S. The hardest thing of all for me to understand – even harder than your refusal to let me see or hear about the children – is your retention of my books and papers. Surely that was not necessary. They could be of little use to you, they were worth little or no money – but they were invaluable to me, absolutely essential to my work, and you knew I was completely down and out and had not the wherewithal to buy others to replace them. Indeed that has been one of my greatest difficulties up here – the lack of books. However! Let that flea stick to the wa' too.

P.P.S. In any case – if you can't agree to let me see the children, or don't even reply – please accept as my parting gift to all of you the self-sacrifice of not raising an action against you although I know beyond the shadow of a doubt that I lost my home, my books, my right to my children, all through a fraudulent action, for which I could have you severely punished and recoup myself heavily in damages, since I can absolutely and conclusively prove that I was not in London and that you were not in Liverpool at or anywhere about the date of that impregnation, while your letters in my possession also show that there was no question of access on my part.

Another point I ought to mention – since the suggestion was utterly unworthy of me – is that, of course, I have said nothing to hurt you in my *Autobiography*. I have written of what you meant to me just in a simple straightforward way, express my gratitude for all the help you gave me at Montrose, and just barely mentioned our divorce and expressed my regret at the way in which circumstances forced us apart. I have nearly finished writing it. I have over 20 books on the stocks altogether – several of them for early publication – and several of them very big books indeed.

29 March 1937

Since I wrote the foregoing I have been checking over everything connected with matters between us as carefully as possible.

In particular I have been trying to account for your denial that your pregnancy was due to anyone but myself, in face of the fact that you know perfectly well that I know I could have nothing to do with it. It is of course natural that you should try to stick like glue to that story now – as otherwise our divorce was a frame-up and I can have you for criminal conspiracy. But I think there is even more in it than that – that you probably double-crossed McElroy too, and had been simultaneously carrying on with someone else to whom the pregnancy was due.

However that may be, it was certainly not due to me.

There are divorce cases and divorce cases. Ours you have made a particularly foul one. Apart altogether from the question of criminal conspiracy (and McElroy's subsequent perjury supports that conclusion) there was no reason on earth but sheer lust of cruelty why you could not let me have access to the children and remain on amicable terms with me. You never had a shadow of excuse for the utterly damnable and inhumanly cruel way you treated me. I know I went to Hell with booze finally, but that was your blame – a very little decency on your part would have put a stop to that. I can only conclude that even by then association with that leprous swine McElroy, who has all along fouled everything he has come in touch with and betrayed everything he could betray, had wrought a corresponding degradation in you. I have always been slow to believe any evil of you, and perhaps this is another instance of it – i.e. blaming McElroy, and not just yourself. Whichever is true, it is at any rate even yet incredible to me that you should refuse to let me see or hear about the children in this way. As if I would ever consent to that state of affairs as long as I was alive. And even if I die, the children will then learn the true state of affairs and know that you betrayed their father – the straightest, kindest and most intelligent man you ever knew – for this rotten old libertine, and that they were brought up on your immoral earnings. For make no mistake. Whatever your £1000 a year Secretaryship may involve the primary qualification was sexual, and you'd never have had a chance of getting the job if you hadn't been willing to gratify McElroy's senile lusts.

I do not blame McElroy. Probably it's only a question of his prostate gland. But why the Hell doesn't he have it seen to and an end put to his senile lusts? Even if he died under the anaesthetic it would be no loss to civilisation. Certainly, if you had ever been fit to be my wife, you would have been incapable of ever giving a second look to so patent an inferior and utter outsider.

You must be morally insane to punish me for a single act of adultery (to which you drove me) in this fiendish way, while yourself living in flagrant adultery with another woman's husband older than your own father – old age creeping over you. You once reminded me that one good turn deserves another. I immediately agreed to give evidence for you,[3] and this was one of the things that worried me most at Gilgal, in case I wouldn't be well enough to travel to London & keep my promise. Poor fool! I wasn't wanted and the whole case was unscrupulously rigged to throw unjustified slurs on my poetry, my Communism etc., and the whole concoction topped off with the most damnable perjuries.

Do you think you are going to get off with this sort of thing much longer? You know perfectly well that you have no right whatever to stand between me and the children – that if the Court knew it had vested their custody in a woman who had since then been in open immorality and whose only resources are the proceeds of her shame, the children would be taken speedily enough away from you. I do not want that. Lost to all decency as I consider you to be, I would never do what you have done to me – and refuse to let you see your children. But on the other hand, you have no good ground whatever for treating me in this hellish way either. There is not a single thing in the whole of my record at which you or anybody else can point a finger except the fact that your abominable cruelty drove me for a while to alcoholism.

I do not want to see you ever again – I marvel indeed at the utter brazenness which has enabled you to face me at Gilgal and elsewhere clad in the fur coat and other things which were the price of your dishonour.

Chris

Even despite all that, I have never spoken against you – or allowed any one else to do so in my presence. I defy you to bring any evidence whatever to the contrary. But although in the circumstances not one man in a hundred thousand would have told you, I told you about the Gilgal business (in the letter I gave you then) – for your sake and the children's – and you had to go and blab even that about (although any decency whatever, or even any thought of the children, should have put a seal on your vindictive and utterly unscrupulous lips).

---

1. Charles William Dyson Perrins, of Worcester Sauce fame, was the owner of Kildermorie Forest Lodge where CMG had stayed (1920) working for him as a caretaker. Lt. Colonel Thomas William Cuthbert was his factor.
2. In conversation with his daughter-in-law, Deirdre Grieve, CMG said that he had gone to see Peggy off to the Nursing Home from the train station; he arrived to find McElroy already there and, having no money at the time, had to agree to his paying for the nursing home and expenses.
3. CMG and Oliver St John Gogarty were to be witnesses against Peggy in Kate McElroy's enticement case. In a letter to CMG of 18 July 1935, Peggy wrote asking

'would [you] be willing to come down to be a witness for me', to which request he evidently agreed.

85. *To William McElroy (NLS)*

[1937?]

Dear McElroy

So you think you will just lie low and say nothing now, do you, you leprous swine?

You may have been a great gambler but you've backed the wrong horse this time with a vengeance.

You have never allowed any consideration of human decency or honour to stand in the way of gratifying your lusts. So my plea for access to my children was naturally one you thought you could just ignore. But I have you now and by the living God you're at the end of your tether.

Peggy and you jockeyed me out of my home and my children and even out of my books and papers which were vital to the continuance of my work tho' of little or no money value and of no earthly use to mindless creatures like you.

I knew at the time of the divorce that there had been a conspiracy to defeat the ends of justice, but though I knew that when Peggy aborted her pregnancy was not due to me and believed it was due to you I could not prove anything and was far too distressed to be other than a helpless victim of your machinations.

But your deliberate perjury in your wife's enticement suit against Peggy cleared the way. I saw why you had to tell that monstrous lie. I immediately put myself in a position to prove that you had paid the expenses of Peggy's illness and succeeded in getting full and conclusive evidence. I have also pieced things together from the medical and other evidence, from Peggy's letters to me while I was in Liverpool, from my employers and others in Liverpool; and I can now absolutely prove a complete and conclusive alibi with regard to Peggy's pregnancy.

I had nothing to do with it. It follows – and this has been within your knowledge and Peggy's all along – that I was divorced and robbed of my children and my books etc. on entirely false grounds. Also that if any enticement suit should have been brought it should have been brought by me and against you.

And yet in the face of all that you have the bloody hardihood not to reply to my letter.

At bottom I do not suppose you are really to blame – I expect it is a question of your prostate gland. But why don't you go through an operation and have an end put to your senile lusts? Even if you died under the anaesthetic it would be no loss to civilisation. I would prefer of course that you met a different end – through my hacking off your genitals and stuffing them down your throat.

Au revoir, Chris

You'll not buy me off for a million times all the money you ever owned.

86. *To the Editor,* The New English Weekly *(NLS, DFF)*

Whalsay, via Lerwick, Shetland Islands [1937]

Sir: –

I notice a letter from Count Potocki de Montalk[1] in your issue of April 29th which has only reached me thus belatedly. In an account, captioned 'Whited Sepulchres' describing his trial and imprisonment, in *The Right Review* for last October, Count de Montalk, says, concerning Mr Douglas Glass who was prosecuted along with him, 'Finally a certain Scotch Nationalist, Social Creditor, and Communist (three persons in one poet) who wanted to lease my house in Thakeham in the event of my going to gaol, and was consequently willing to impress me with his wealth, bailed Mr Glass although he did not know him from a soapy bar'.

Nor had I ever heard of Count de Montalk! As he knows very well, I bailed Mr Glass because I was approached and asked to do so by Mr Charles Lahr, and there was no question whatever of my wanting to lease Count de Montalk's house in Thakeham. I had never heard of Thakeham or the house there, called 'Cootes', at that time; and it was not Count de Montalk's house in any case.

In the article mentioned above Count de Montalk also says of Mr Kingsley Martin that although he 'had supported me in the *New Statesman*, he had as low an opinion of me and my poetry as Sir Ernest Wild had'. So far as I am personally concerned, if I had seen Count de Montalk's 'poetry' beforehand, I would certainly not have had anything to do with his precious case, not because the 'poetry' was obscene, but because it was so obscenely bad in every other respect that capital punishment on its perpetrator would not have been too severe a sentence by any means. If Count de Montalk's writings are to survive anybody's by centuries or millennia – or seconds, for the matter of that – he must be relying on an idiotisation of some part of the future reading public which – far from sanguine though I am – I regard as no less incredible and repellent than the Count's activities in all the other relations of life.

Yours, Hugh MacDiarmid (C.M. Grieve)

P.S. I also – God forgive me! – contributed substantially to a fund raised to meet the expenses of Count de Montalk's defence, and my only souvenir of this utterly misguided generosity is a photograph of the Count in the nude half-hidden behind a *penis erectus* (*half*-hidden, not because of any specially brave proportions of his sexual equipment, but because of a skinniness in the rest of his physique which consorts better alike with his pretensions to anything but the most nominal nobility and with any difference between his literary abilities and those of any urinal-scribbling devotee of (to use the late Robert Ross's phrase) 'the Fifth Muse'[)]. I may add that I have failed to find anyone – except Count de Montalk himself – who has any higher opinion of Count de Montalk's 'poetry' than the late Sir Ernest Wild's, Mr Kingsley Martin's, or my own.[2]

---

1. Count Geoffrey Wladislas Vaile Potocki of Montalk was a New Zealand-born eccentric, claimant to the Polish throne and founder of a reactionary periodical, *The Right Review*. Along with Douglas Glass, a photographer, he was prosecuted under obscenity laws for trying to print a pamphlet entitled *Here Lies John Penis*.
2. Robert Baldwin Ross (1869–1918), Canadian art critic and sometime consort of Oscar Wilde. Sir Ernest Edward Wild (1869–1934), the Recorder of London, had attacked the book vigorously in his summation at the Old Bailey. (Basil) Kingsley Martin (1897–1969), Editor of *The New Statesman and Nation*.

87. *To The Richards Press Ltd. (HRHRC)*

Whalsay, via Lerwick, The Shetland Islands   25 June 1937

Dear Sirs

I have to thank you for your letter of 18th inst re my poems and regret that you do not find these suitable for your series of *Shilling Selections*. I am afraid I went as far as I could in trying to meet what I understood were your requirements. I knew of course that you might take exception to one or two of the satirical pieces and was prepared if necessary to agree to the omission of these. But, of the more than thirty pieces I sent, your readers only note nine as suitable – plus two Mr Gawsworth had by him, 'Coronach for the End of the World' (which I would have been quite willing to include) and 'A Mountain of Music' (to the republication of which I can never agree).

I note that in forwarding these poems to you Mr Gawsworth also sent you my explanatory letter addressed to himself. I should have thought this made my attitude sufficiently clear. To publish a collection of new lyrics similar to those your readers regard as suitable would not only be of no advantage to me but a grave disservice to my reputation and an act of treachery to my position as a poet. I can only agree to publish such poems as sops to the conventional if they appear in a collection consisting for the most part of poems of a very different sort. I am not willing to make more than an occasional genuflection of this sort in the direction of traditionalism, just to show I can do that sort of thing too, and above all I am not willing to publish any collection which does not include at least a proportion of morally, technically, and intellectually revolutionary pieces and also at least one or two pieces of a definitely pro-Communist political character. (I would point out that pieces of this kind appeared in my selected lyrics published by Macmillan.)

I cannot agree to your suggestion that I should permit a new selection from my previous books. This would not be fair either to you or to myself. These books contain no other lyrics of equal strength to those in *Selected Poems*; and I have no wish to serve up 'cold kail hot again' when it is a matter of common knowledge to all who are interested in my work that my aesthetic position today is completely at variance with work of that sort. I could not agree to the suggestion even if I had at my disposal an ample number of lyrics of equal calibre to the Macmillan selection, nor if it were a question today of issuing the latter would I agree to it unless with the inclusion of a considerable proportion of pieces of a very different kind.

I would have suggested, however, that I might shortly send you another batch of new poems and that from these you might select a sufficient number to meet – together with those of the present lot your readers regard as suitable – the requirements of the series. But I am afraid it is no use my trying to meet you in this way, since it appears that you are confining the series not only to lyrics in an exceedingly narrow definition of the form, but to kinds of subject-matter to which I am definitely unwilling to be confined. I cannot understand save on these grounds the exclusion of 'Why I Choose Red', 'Why We Choose Red' and 'Choosing Red Again' – especially the last named, which, though of some little length, is pure lyric. Even less understandable except on the most conservative (i.e. politically prejudiced) grounds is the exclusion of 'The Glen of Silence'.

The collection would have sold well; the objection is therefore to the kind of poet I am – an objection which admits of no compromise on my part.

Kindly return my MSS in due course, and oblige.

Yours sincerely, Hugh MacDiarmid

88. *To The Richards Press, Ltd. (HRHRC)*

Whalsay, Shetland Islands   14 July 1937

Dear Sirs: –

Many thanks for your letter re your 1/- series of poetry. I will have pleasure in sending on to you a further batch of poems in the course of the next few days.[1]

With best wishes. Yours sincerely, C.M. Grieve ('Hugh MacDiarmid')

---

1. A further letter dated 10 August 1937 encloses seven additional poems: 'The

Glass of Pure Water', 'Have You?', 'Advice to a Young Poet', 'Choice of a Grave', 'On the Fishing Grounds', 'To My Friend, Miss Ruth Pitter', and 'Two Scottish Boys'. CMG says that 'The Glen of Silence' should be included and emphasises that so should the *three* 'choosing Red' poems, because they form a sequence. This is curious because only the first of the 'choosing Red' poems survives in the *Complete Poems* – the others are yet to be discovered. In a final letter dated 13 October, CMG regrets that further lyrics are required and hopes that he might provide them by the end of the year, but meantime requests the return of the MSS. The matter seems to have ended there.

89. *To The Chairman, Welsh Nationalist Meeting to welcome the released prisoners. Carnarvon Pavilion, Carnarvon, Wales.*

Whalsay, via Lerwick, The Shetland Islands   23 August 1937

Dear Sir: –

I write on behalf of a considerable number of young Scottish writers and Republican Nationalists to join with you in welcoming back the three released prisoners – Rev. L.E. Valentine and Messrs Saunders Lewis and D.J. Williams – and in congratulating them on the intrepid action which landed them in a foreign gaol and which has been a great joy and inspiration to fellow-Gaels in Cornwall, Ireland and Scotland in their struggle against the English Ascendancy.[1] More power to their elbows now they are back in their beloved Wales, and may the good fight proceed with redoubled vigour and determination. Direct action is the only way, and I hope that ere long now we may see an effective 'common front' in Scotland, Ireland, Wales and Cornwall against our common enemy – the callous and unscrupulous English, the cruellest people in the history of mankind.

Yours sincerely, Hugh MacDiarmid

---

1. Saunders Lewis (1893–1985), Welsh playwright, poet, novelist and critic, co-founder (1925) and president (1926) of the Welsh Nationalist Party (later Plaid Cymru). He and the others mentioned had been imprisoned in 1936 for an act of arson against the building materials for a new RAF bombing school at Penyberth.

90. *To Valda Grieve (NLS)*

Whalsay, via Lerwick, Shetland Islands   Wednesday, 15 September [1937]

Dearest Valda,

You must have been wondering what had come over your wandering boy. I wired you today – we have been in Eigg with MacNair Reid and his wife, Dr Shepherd, since Monday and are going on tomorrow by steamer to Skye where I'll see Maclean to whom I wired today also; and then we are going on to Lochboisdale to stay with a cousin of McColl's[1] and thence to South Uist. I hope to be home about the end of next week but will wire you as soon as I know exactly. I have had the holiday of my life – a great deal of walking in some of the very grandest scenery in Europe; long sail 20 miles down Loch Shiel; visited Alasdair Mac Mhaigstir Alasdair's grave where we had photos taken; stayed one night with Gunn in Inverness etc. etc. This is a glorious island and we have had a splendid time here. I have seen and learned heaps and this will make all the difference to my islands book. I do hope all is well with you and Mike. When I wired you my address from Arisaig I had hoped to hear from you in case anything had turned up, but in the absence of news I can only assume that all is well. I wish to God you'd been with me – but never mind, you will yet – you really must see this part of Scotland. It is breath-taking in its sheer beauty. On the whole we have had good weather – at first it was cold and broken but since we had had heaps of sunshine, and only occasional showers.

I have some detective stories for you – no; I may parcel them up with this letter, no, sending them later, also some little white rose of Scotland bushes which grow here very plentifully – please set them in beside your honeysuckle at the corner of the porch. They need damp conditions. I hope they grow.

All news when I come. I am in splendid form. Hope you and Mike are well and not wearying too much. I may be out of touch for a day or two after I leave Skye, but if possible will send p.c.s.

All the best to Orr, and love and kisses to Fikel Michael and the Hen Bird.

Yours truly, Chris.
Hope good news from your mother.

---

1. W.D. MacColl, Scottish nationalist and Gaelic revivalist, expelled from the National Party of Scotland along with CMG in 1933.

91. *To Valda Grieve (NLS)*

Raasay Hotel, Island of Raasay,   Monday, 19 September 1937
By Kyle of Lochalsh

Dearest Valda,

Spent Thursday night with Sam Maclean's people. Then came on to Portree in Skye where we have had a wonderful four days. Yesterday for example we motored over 100 miles in Sleat in the South of Skye – thanks to Mr Macleod of Skeabost who drove us and gave us a delightful lunch

by a burn side in glorious sunshine. Macleod is an extremely wealthy man; I met him and his wife in London years ago and they were delighted to see me again and gave us great hospitality. Today we sail back to Mallaig and catch another boat for Lochboisdale in South Uist. I do hope all is well with you. I am worried about not hearing about you at all all this time. But I have certainly had the
[MS ends]

92. *To Valda Grieve (NLS)*

Lochboisdale Hotel, Isle of South Uist   Tuesday [21 September 1937]

Dearest V.

Arrived here last night. Dr Shepherd, going to Canna, joined our boat at Eigg. She handed me your letter enclosing Peggy's. I was very sorry to get it. I do hope this old question is not to be reopened. It was a pity to get such a note from you as the only communication I have had since leaving home. It was too bad of you. I had been wearying to hear from you; but certainly not this type of letter. There was no need to send on Peggy's letter. You must have known it could only hurt me – which it did – badly. I did not send Peggy any photograph of me either in the kilt or the nude. Please try to think kindly of me. I do love you very dearly and truly. I have no regard for or interest in Peggy – apart from Christine and Walter.

Love and kisses to Mike and yourself. Yours, Christopher

93. *To Valda Grieve (NLS)*

Post Office Telegram   [postmarked] 22 SP 37

Going Barra till Friday then Poste Restante Tobermory till Monday thence Leith home.

Love, Chris

94. *To Valda Grieve (NLS)*

[Picture post card, 'Main Street, Tobermory', 1937]

Had splendid time in Barra with Donald Sinclair's brother, Neil Sinclair, Father John MacMillan,[1] Compton Mackenzie etc. Glorious weather. Will be home soon. Love Chris. Kisses to Michael.

---

1. Father John MacMillan, a priest on Barra on whom Father James Macalister in Mackenzie's *Whisky Galore* (1947) was based.

95. To W.R. Aitken (NLS)

Whalsay, via Lerwick, Shetland Islands　　　　　　8 October 1937

My dear Bill

　Sorry to have been so long in writing; and especially hope that the delay in sending on Albert's *6000 years of Gaelic grandeur*[1] and the two books of Ireland's from Edinr. University library has not involved you in any trouble. I have had a great time – in Eigg, Barra, South Uist, Raasay, Skye, Iona etc. So my islands book will be a much easier proposition now.

　As you will see I got the notepaper O.K. But no account with it.[2]

　I am greatly diverted by what you say of Prof. Calder – Kemp Smith etc.[3] I'll deal with these 'gentlemen' in my own way later. In the meantime I'm extremely glad Davie is going to France instead of Germany.

　Many thanks for all the trouble you've taken in re the *Chapbook* poem. I'm extremely interested in what you say about Brough and the quarterly magazine project. I will of course gladly do anything I can for it – and above all look forward to seeing it.

　I enclose the letters to Mairet[4] and Cathie Carswell for Miss Robertson.

　I'll be glad to have both Davie's – and, later your own – essays on Doughty.

　Excuse this scrappy letter. I'm not in a writing mood – still hopelessly beclouded by piles of work to do and with which somehow I cannot make the progress I ought to.

　Valda and Mike are both O.K. but would be the better of a good holiday. Perhaps I'll be able to contrive that for them ere very long.

　All the best. Yours, C.M.G.

P.S. I also enclose note to Saurat.[5] Miss Robertson should see him. He's the centre of a very brilliant, very cosmopolitan crowd, and a man of great influence in many directions.

P.P.S. By the way, Bill, I wonder if you could look up the voters' roll for Cupar-Fife and find out for me the address of Mrs D. Skinner. The house may be in her name, or that of her husband (now dead), D. Skinner, or that of Mrs Margaret Grieve, or, perhaps even, that of William McElroy. I hope looking this up won't be a nuisance to you. If you happen to find it, please just add it to one of your letters – the bare address, without saying in which of these names it is entered, and without making any comment or using any such phrase as 'Mrs Skinner's address is …'. I'll be very glad if you can procure this address for me.

---

1. L. Albert, *Six Thousand Years of Gaelic Grandeur – Unearthed* (London: W. & G. Foyle, 1936).
2. The letter is written on paper with the printed heading 'from Hugh MacDiarmid (C.M. Grieve)' and the address.

3. Norman Kemp Smith (1873–1958), Professor of Metaphysics at Edinburgh University (1919–45). It had been reported that Smith would not give his backing to George Davie's career as a student unless he ceased his association with CMG though he later denied that anything he had said could be thus interpreted. CMG was, at the time, refraining from correspondence with Davie and receiving news of him through W.R. Aitken.
4. Philip Mairet: see Appendix.
5. Denis Saurat, Lecturer in French at Glasgow (1918–21) and King's College London (1926–50). A contributor to *The New Age*, he had been early to recognise the Scottish literary renaissance and had translated some of CMG's early lyrics.

96. To Sorley MacLean (NLS)

Whalsay, via Lerwick, Shetland Islands   21 October 1937

My dear Sam,

I caught a bad chill on the way back, about a fortnight ago. Hence my delay in writing – prior to that, after leaving you, I was of course too busy and too much on the move. Altogether it was the most wonderful holiday I ever had – a perfect revelation – and I saw almost everybody I wanted to see, alike in Scotland and in the Islands. Everybody was extremely kind to us. And it was an especial happiness to visit Raasay and meet your father and mother and the other members of your family. Please give them all my love, and my warmest thanks for their hospitality.

McColl and I had a great time in South Uist – visiting Staoiligery and the Four Pennies of Drinisdale, etc. etc. – and then on Barra, where we saw Compton Mackenzie, Annie Johnston, Father John MacMillan, and Donald Sinclair's brother, Neil, who is the schoolmaster at Northbay.

I was sorry not to see Jock Stewart again. Please remember me to him – and the others we met, including Miss Flora MacDonald and her sister!

I am not in a mood for writing tonight (indeed, I wouldn't try were it not that I have already been so long in doing so), but I'll write you at greater length soon and send you my versions of the different translations etc. If you have any more for me please send them on as soon as possible now, as I am busy putting the whole job ship-shape and want to get it off to Macmillan's now as quickly as I possibly can.

George Davie didn't go to Germany after all – but to Montpellier in France instead. That is certainly a great deal better; Fascist Germany was a hopeless place – indeed a damned dangerous place – for George.

Again, with best thanks and all good wishes.

My remembrances to your landlady and all the other kind people we met.

And love from Valda and Mike, Yours C.M.G.

Would you please remind me again too when you write of the point you raised about a mistake in the 'Birlinn'? I have your previous letter about it somewhere but can't lay my hands on it yet, and it is of course desirable to correct this for the *Anthology*.

97. *To Peggy Grieve (NLS)*

Whalsay, via Lerwick, Shetland Islands   17 November 1937

Dear Peggy

I have given you every conceivable chance to show me even a modicum of decency. But I am going for you now. I have put the whole facts before Messrs Myers and Wills, Montrose, and they only await the word 'go' to start the necessary proceedings — against you and McElroy for criminal conspiracy, perjury, and defamation of my character; against Ina for criminal libel;[1] and against you to give me access to the children (and if need be I'll take complete custody of them) on the ground that you only secured custody of them by fraud, have wrongfully denied me all access to and knowledge of them, and are a woman of flagrantly immoral life unfit to have anything to do with them.

So far as you are concerned — not for your sake but your mother's and the children's — I will let the other matters go provided you agree to my having access to the children at once, arrange to send me all my books and papers immediately, and pay me the cost of the furniture etc. that was in the house — at Pyrland Road (and it's no use telling me any cock-and-bull stories about McElroy's money paying for any part of that furniture etc. at all. Try that on, and you'll find yourself in Queer Street at once). I hope — again only for the children's sake — you will have the decency to accept this very generous offer, now that you know McElroy has given the whole dirty game away (unwittingly, but none the less completely). I'll give you a week from above date; if I do not hear from you by letter or telegram before then agreeing to my conditions and advising me of the dispatch of my books and papers, I'll wire Myers and Wills to go ahead. And in that case I'll also sue for damages in keeping with the hellish injury you have done me.

I am, of course, going to tell the whole story in my *Autobiography* and elsewhere. I am not offering to keep the matter secret in any way. But I am giving you the chance to avoid financial ruin, newspaper publicity, and a spell in gaol. That's all. I am not making any such offer, however, in regard to McElroy and Ina and have already written to Myers and Wills instructing them to go right ahead with proceedings in these cases.

You will know that I have written to your mother. That is only a foretaste of what is coming to you, you rotten lying fornicating bitch.

Chris

1. Ina Skinner, Peggy's sister, who had accompanied the Grieves to London and stayed with them at Pyrland Road, doing secretarial work for *VOX*.

98. *To Christine Grieve (NLS)*

[1938]

My dear Christine

I have not received so far any reply to the letter I sent you. I do not know whether you mean to reply yet or not. Please do not. If you reply now I will return your letter unread. I will not write to you or Walter, or to your mother or grandmother again whatever happens or have anything at all to do with you.

I do not blame you, but your grandmother says that, like herself, you have decided against me – without hearing my side of the story. Well, you will hear it yet and realise that you did me a terrible injustice – but it will be too late then to put matters right. I will vindicate myself completely and show clearly and incontestably that I did nothing whatever that was wrong or dishonourable or unfair. I will not do it through the Law Courts – because I do not believe in them, and because once before when I felt I could not avoid legal proceedings your mother asked me not to and I was glad to agree, for her sake and yours. Though she had no hesitation in asking this great favour of me, your mother herself has steadfastly refused to give me the very slightest meed of justice or even elementary human decency, let alone generosity of treatment.

She is about to pay for that now – and so, alas, will you. During the past few years a dozen books have appeared dealing, amongst other things, with me and my work. By different authors in this country, and Germany, and France, and America, that all pay tribute to my high character and great kindliness of nature. Do you think all these writers are wrong – and only your mother and grandmother right?

When I was very ill and seemed about to die over two years ago, all the leading British newspapers had long articles about me ready to publish. All these articles agreed that I was one of the most vital spirits and greatest poets Scotland had ever produced, and a man of honour and life-giving knowledge of whom Scotland should be proud. Isn't it queer that only your mother and grandmother and stupid people like them who don't know anything about anything worth knowing should think ill of me?

My life is an open book and the truth of the matter will be easily seen once I am dead and my biographers get to work. It is twenty years ago this year since I married your mother and I am celebrating it by publishing a big *Autobiography*. All the facts are set out in that, supported by an abundance of independent evidence, which will prove up to the hilt that I loved you and your mother very dearly and truly and was in no way whatever to blame for the break-up of our home. That book will also prove that your mother, who was to blame and who took the course she did despite the clearest warnings and most passionate entreaties, has treated me since – without any reason that could bear a moment's examination – with the most incredible cruelty and callousness. And amongst other things she has not hesitated to come between me and my own flesh and blood and treated you and Walter as mere pawns in her horrible game.

It will be seen that all the years we lived together she was responsible for a man who was engaged in great and most difficult tasks – that she cared nothing for these things, but preferred her own wretched ambitions, and betrayed him and the high interests to which his life was dedicated in the most shameful and abominable fashion. She did not believe I was a great poet; she thought she was just as important as me, or more so. She was not interested in poetry or Scotland or Socialism – but in rotten things like money and Mr McElroy. But history will demand an account of her stewardship and condemn her. My own *Autobiography* has chapters which contain by far the most utterly damning indictment of her that any writer has ever had to pen of a wife or ex-wife. Two other great British writers had their children taken away from them, though in both these cases with better cause as the world or the law phrases it than in mine. Like me they suffered terribly. Has it hurt their reputations? Not a bit. But the verdict of history has condemned the miserable wretches of women, and the stupid Judges, as it will now condemn your mother and the stupid Judge who gave her divorce. My letters show that I appealed to your mother with all the earnestness and clarity I could command, not only on your behalf and my own, but for the sake of Scotland and my work as a poet – and she was deaf to all my appeals; her heart was set on her own ignoble ends and on men – rich perhaps, but of no human consequence whatever – like McElroy and Milne. She chose the fleshpots of Egypt – and she chose for you as well as for herself, and sold your birthright for a mess of potage.

All the years since I have striven to undo this great wrong. But I might as well have spoken to a stone wall. A great man of letters was nothing to your mother in comparison with a wealthy coal and iron merchant.

Very well, my dear. I can do nothing but make the matter utterly clear. When that book is published, or when I die, the whole situation will be open to the public view and you will be involved in immense publicity. It will be too late then for any reconciliation between us. Remember again, I do not blame you. I know the pressure, the atmosphere, in which you have been brought up. But while I can set out the facts and be sure of winning the verdict of other people, one does not prove things in that way to one's own children. One expects their unswerving love and loyalty and it is in that you have failed me, if, as your grandmother says, you have chosen against me. But perhaps that is only the evil lie of a stupid and malignant old woman, and you still love me, difficult though it must have been for you all these years. It is a terrible business altogether, Christine. It will be years yet before Walter and you understand just how terrible – but when you do, and read my *Autobiography*, and the many poems in which during all these years I have expressed my longing for you and grief and anxiety about you, you will understand just how deeply and truly your Daddy loved you, and what a horrible web of treachery and fraud was set between him and you by a ruthless and vindictive woman capable of no loyalty to any principle, since she has always been wholly absorbed in her own base desires.

99. *To W.R. Aitken (NLS)*

Whalsay, via Lerwick, Shetland Islands   Friday, 28 January 1938

My dear Bill

I am returning herewith the Lawrence and Powys books: and – since my friend Taylor[1] has today arrived and can type out the passages I want, – I'll send the Buchanan next post. I'm awfully sorry about the latter; I meant to send it with that last bundle and thought I'd done so till I got your letter asking lest it had gone astray in the post. I failed to find it here for some time – it had got buried under an avalanche of papers – I only retrieved it a day or two ago and then decided to hang on to it for a day or two longer until Taylor could make the extracts I want.

Now Taylor has come, I am anxious to get back some of these doctors' books as soon as I can – particularly Comrie and Ireland. I wonder if you could tell me whether these are in again and so available or when they are likely to be; then I'll write for them through the Lerwick librarian. Also I am anxious to get – if the Central Library has it – 'Christopher Caudwell's' (Christopher St John Sprigg's) *Illusion and Reality*; and also Tschiffaly's *RB C-G*.[2]

My letters tend I am afraid to degenerate into a sort of succession of requests: but I would also like if possible another print of one of your Whalsay photos; the one of Valda, Mike, and I in which I look a particularly hefty Highland-Games sort of figure.

There are also a few particulars I'll give you a note of in an early letter which perhaps you will be so kind as check for me – dates etc. in connection with various poets for the Macmillan Anthology.

I'm looking forward to hearing from you what Davie's news is and how he is faring in the now-so-very-inaccurately-named Freiburg.

All join in best regards to you. We're in the throes of another big blizzard of snow. Hope you're more comfortably placed.

Yours, Chris

1. Henry Grant Taylor (1914–99), graduate of Edinburgh University (1936) where he had studied German and French. Unable to get a full-time job after leaving University, he had been told by Robert Garioch Sutherland of CMG's need for a secretary and went to work for him, unpaid, from January 1938 until his conscription in 1940, living as a member of the household.
2. Christopher Caudwell, *Illusion and Reality* (London: Macmillan, 1937); A.F. Tschiffely, *Don Roberto* (London: Heinemann, 1937), a biography of Cunninghame Graham.

100. *To Sorley MacLean (NLS)*

Whalsay   Tuesday, 28 March 1938

Dear Sam

Please excuse a pencil scrawl. I was very glad to get your letter at last. Though puzzled at your continued silence, I somehow or other guessed what had happened – i.e. that you had left Skye – and I was worrying as to what had happened to you. I knew you had had an interesting and enjoyable time there and was sorry that your pleasant little group had been broken up. I spent a few days in Tobermory with MacColl and liked it greatly, and I hope you will have a good time there too and meet congenial spirits. But in many ways I am afraid it will not suit you as well as Portree – and, of course, you won't be able to get home so often! I hope all your family are well and would be particularly glad to hear that some suitable post was presenting itself at last for your brother John. Please give them all my kindest remembrances and best wishes when you write.

Here I am absolutely bogged in work, but tackling it systematically at last with the aid of a very competent secretary-typist – an MA honours French and German, of Edinburgh. So I am hoping if no unforeseen snags develop to get all the books I have on the stocks polished off at last. While I have not yet delivered to the publishers the actual copy for the *Golden Treasury of Scottish Poetry*, I have given them the full contents-list, the MSS of my Introductory Essay, etc. So I am afraid it is too late now to add translations of any additional poems. But at the same time I am anxious for another reason to have any such you care to send me. This other reason is the fact that I am going to launch very shortly (I hope to have the first issue out in the beginning of May) a new quarterly[1] devoted to Scottish Literature and Politics (i.e. Scottish Republicanism à la John Maclean[2]). So do send me anything you can as soon as possible. I suppose you wouldn't care to see if you could give me a quarterly letter for this magazine – covering anything you thought of special interest in relation to the Gaelic movement, the land question and other public affairs in the West Highlands and Islands etc., written from the angle mentioned above – i.e. Marxist-Nationalist? I'd be awfully glad if you could. It wouldn't have to be long, of course – but, say, about 700 words.

Excuse this short letter. I have no news of any kind – save that I had a letter from Davie, who seems to be having a very good time of it in Freiburg. We're all O.K. here and all of us, including Dr Orr and Auntie Betty, send you our best love. Mike still refers to you as his Big Man. By the way, we'd be only too happy to see you here again any time you could come. Write soon again.

All the best. Yours, C.M. Grieve

---

1. *The Voice of Scotland; a quarterly magazine of Scottish arts and affairs*, ed. Hugh MacDiarmid, vol. 1, no. 1, June–August 1938. Although interrupted by the War, it ran till vol. 9, no. 2, August 1958.
2. John Maclean (1879–1923), Marxist-Socialist and teacher. Sacked for his support of the Glasgow rent strike (1915), he devoted his time to giving lectures on Marxism and advocating workers' education. Lenin appointed him Bolshevik consul to Glasgow in 1917. He was arrested six times between 1916 and 1923 for his political activities.

101. *To Sorley MacLean (NLS)*

Whalsay, via Lerwick, Shetland Islands   9 May 1938

My dear Sam,

Just a very hasty note to thank you for your poem and article. Both are admirable and exactly the sort of thing I want for the *Scottish Republic*. I'll very gladly use them both in the first issue, and you'll probably receive proofs before we go to press. I'm busy getting a good first number in shape, but am still waiting to hear from various people I want stuff from. But I expect to have the first issue out early next month all right.

I am very sorry you find things so uncongenial in Tobermory and about these periods of lassitude or loss of will or whatever it is – probably just a question of your age, a love (or need of love) matter. I hope things will even out for you; and fancy they may do so via writing – especially poetry. I cannot tell you how glad I am to have this excellent poem of yours and how keenly I will look for more. The all-absorbing interest of the development of a genuine creative faculty in you may well dispose of your other problems in the most satisfactory way.

I am extremely glad to hear that John has a post in the Royal High, hope he is enjoying life, and that this post will lead on to still better things.

Love to you all. All here send their warmest regards. I'll write you soon again.

Yours, Chris

102. *To J.F. Hendry (SUNYB)*

Whalsay   10 September 1938

Dear Mr Hendry

Many thanks for your letters. And my best wishes to your good lady and your young son. 'David' is a fine poem and I'll be proud to print it. It's too late, however, for our second issue, but will be all right for the third (for which I have also excellent poems by Ruthven Todd, Donagh MacDonagh, and others). Proofs of the second issue have [not] come to hand yet. I'm not sure how many poems of yours I'm managing to get in – but two at any rate. I'm cramped for space and so haven't been able to find room for short stories yet. I've a lot of very heavy political stuff following on the Red Scotland Thesis in No. 1 I must get printed somehow – but I may manage to put out most of it in separate pamphlet form. We'll see. No. 1 has done fairly well, but it will take a few issues to get the thing on a proper footing. I'm more than delighted that further issues of *Albannach* are likely. A little later when you, and Russell, are arranging that, there are one or two additional poets I'd like to suggest to you – young fellows not hitherto printed, some of whose poems I'm going to use in the *V. of S.*

I'm very vexed about your not receiving your copy of No. 1. I can't understand how this has happened. I gave Dunfermline a list of names and addresses to send copies to – and this list of course included you, and all the other contributors. I enclose a copy now and will be interested to have your opinion of it.

About the International Brigade article, this too is now too late for No. 2; but I'm very keen all the same to have it, even if you feel you have rather slight material to go on and the article must consequently be a bit thin. It doesn't matter how short it is – it's the essential fact I want put across, since it fits in with my general line with the C.P. here and against certain elements in London Communist thought and Left-Wing literary organisation there.

By the way, what's happened to Keidrych Rhys?[1] I wrote him to his old address, Penybout, and that was forwarded to a London address and returned to me marked 'Gone away. Address unknown'. Then I tried to have a letter forwarded to him via the distributors of *Wales* in Parton Street. But that came back too.

I read your story in *Seven* and was much impressed by it.

I hope you greatly enjoyed your holiday in Italy and are fine and fit. More power to your elbow.

With warmest regards, Yours, C.M. Grieve

---

1. Keidrych Rhys (1915–87), Welsh poet, writer and journalist.

103. To the Editor, The Criterion *(NLS, DFF)*

12 October 1938

Dear Sir:

I am greatly interested in what you say in your Commentary on what being fundamentally wrong being the urbanisation of mind, and on the need that the greater part of the population, of all classes (so long as we have classes), should be settled in the country and dependent upon it, and think it is worth while to point to some evidence that all the available scientific data on the regional distribution of mental capacity supports your conclusions. Professor Raymond B. Cattell in *The Fight for our National Intelligence* (1937) says (*op.cit.* p.15): 'Basing my conclusions partly on proven results and partly on indications known to research students I should describe the regional distribution of intelligence in Great Britain roughly as follows. It is in general higher in towns than country villages, but in very remote villages never tapped by the towns it is a little higher than in the towns. It is higher in Scotland than in England, but the Scottish towns are lowered by Edinburgh and especially Glasgow which has had a big influx of Mediterranean Irish. East Anglia and the home counties are probably slightly higher than the rest of England (excepting Yorkshire), whilst Greater London itself may well be as much as three points higher than the rest of England.... It is interesting to notice that Thomson ("The Northumberland Mental Tests", *Brit. J. Psychol.*, Vol. XII) found a good, normal level of intelligence in villages too remote from towns to be affected by migration.'

Yours sincerely, Hugh MacDiarmid

104. To W.R. Aitken (NLS)

The Central Hotel, Glasgow   Monday 28 November 1938

Dear Bill

I duly arrived here last Friday after a very long and rough journey. Crossing the Pentland Firth from Stromness to Scrabster was quite an ordeal, as — of a different sort — was the subsequent 18 hours' railway journey from Wick to Glasgow.

I got here to find F.G. unfortunately down with an attack of tonsillitis. That meant I couldn't stay, as arranged, at 44, but have had to put up instead at the above, which, plus the extra expenses of coming via Wick etc. has run me so very short of cash that I am writing to ask you to lend me £3 to £4, if possible, of the *V. of S.* money. I will repay this, of course, when I return home, but in the meantime it will save me from a difficult situation in which I have no other recourse if on receipt of this you will please *wire* me the amount in question (presuming you have so much in hand) to c/o Scott, 44 Munro Road.

I am wondering if I'm going to see you. I should like to very much. I expect to remain in Glasgow till towards the end of next week. The PEN function is on Saturday 3rd.

All the best, Yours, Chris

105. *To The Secretary, The Cornish Gorsedd (NLS, DFF)*

[1938]

Dear Sir: –

I venture to write to you on a matter of, I think, unique interest to Cornwall and in particular, to the association of Cornish bards.

Hugh MacDiarmid, the famous Scottish poet, whose work (as you will see from the enclosed leaflet) has already been the occasion of a Scottish national testimonial, and who was also honoured a few years ago by being the guest of the Irish nation at the Tailltean Games, has written a very long (as yet unpublished) *Cornish Heroic Song*. This great poem – one of the longest poems written in modern times – is the crown of his work and undoubtedly the greatest poem ever written on a Cornish subject. Its theme is the Gaelic genius and it not only presents a wonderful historical and literary picture of Cornwall itself, and of Cornwall in relation to Scotland, Wales, Ireland and Brittany, but of the landscape and geology of Cornwall.

It is difficult for even a distinguished poet to secure publication for such an enormous poem in these days. The financial burden is too great for most publishers to contemplate in such unpropitious times. But Mr MacDiarmid will probably be able to secure publication of portions at a time ere long in volume form. In the meantime certain small parts of it have already been published in American and Canadian papers.

If Mr MacDiarmid's quality as a poet is unknown to the Cornish Gorsedd, it would be vouched for by two of the greatest poets in the world today – Mr W.B. Yeats, and Mr T.S. Eliot, the world-famous modernist poet and literary critic.

The occasion of this great poem is the fact that Mr MacDiarmid is married to a Cornish lady, and himself knows Cornwall well and is a great lover of it.

I write entirely on my own initiative but knowing Mr MacDiarmid's life-long enthusiasm for all branches of Celtic scholarship, my object is to venture to suggest with all humbleness that some recognition of Mr MacDiarmid by the Cornish Gorsedd would be a very appropriate and useful thing. I do not know if you confer honorary memberships, but if so I am sure that recognition in this way of Mr MacDiarmid's great work – which will rank as one of the outstanding celebrations of the glories of Celtic civilisation, Celtic literature, and the various Celtic languages, in the whole of poetry – would not only redound to the honour of the Cornish Gorsedd, but would delight admirers of Mr MacDiarmid's genius in all parts of the world and in this way serve to attract a great deal of attention to the Cornish language and literary movement.

Please pardon my temerity in venturing to write to you on this matter. I do it entirely on my own responsibility and would ask that in any communication you may make to Mr MacDiarmid you do not refer to the fact that you have received this letter or mention my name. In the event of your writing to Mr MacDiarmid, he should be addressed c/o Messrs Macmillan & Co. Ltd, Publishers, St Martin's Street, London, W.C.2.

With compliments and best wishes, I remain,
Yours very sincerely, (H. Grant Taylor)[1]

---

1. The MS, including the name of CMG's sectretary, is all in CMG's hand.

106. *To W. R. Aitken (NLS)*

Whalsay   Friday, 20 January 1939

My dear Bill
    Additional to the letter and batch of MSS I sent you last mail.
    1/ Please excise from the text of 'Dìreadh III', as it is to appear in the *V of S*, the long passage beginning
    'I love the universality and solitude of places like this'
down to, and including the lines about the Feadan a' Cloiche, the 'chanter of stone'
    2/ And kindly substitute enclosed verse, which is to go in – as a separate verse – following the verse in which reference is made to Georgia, Stalin's native country and the first home of the Scots.
    3/ Address, as promised
        George Campbell Hay,[1]
        14 Carlton St.
        Edinburgh.
    4/ If you are using in next issue the anti-Chamberlain poem[2] dedicated to Karl Capek[3] and Catherine Carswell, please just footnote as follows: –
    * This poem was written a few weeks before news was received of Capek's tragically untimely death from pneumonia.
    5/ I hope that it may also be possible to use in this issue the George Buchanan-Corneille poem. If you do, please give it – as also the above-mentioned anti-Chamberlain one – as by A.K. Laidlaw, not Hugh MacDiarmid.
    I think I have sent you now virtually all that is required for the next issue, except 'Notes of the Quarter', a page or two of Book Reviews, and

a poem called 'The Stepping Stones', celebrating the essential forerunners of the new Scotland. Both these two prose articles I will keep as short as possible.

You will note that additional copy re Berriedale Keith[4] will be sent by next mail – but if necessary hold over this Keith bit of the Forerunners so long as the Burns, Wolfe of Badenoch,[5] and Scott bits go in.

If – with what is still to come – you have too much prose for next issue, Fraser's article on St Andrews Verse should be held over – I am anxious to get all the forerunners article in.

You would notice that in the note I appended to Douglas Young's[6] letter I used the phrase 'the keepers' – because I could not remember or lay my hands on the well-known Latin question, 'who is to guard (or watch over) the guardians?' You could perhaps substitute the Latin for this?

---

1. George Campbell Hay (1915–84), Scottish poet, writing in English, Scots and in Gaelic, of which he was not a native speaker, as Deòrsa Mac Iain Deòrsa.
2. 'When the Gangs Came to London', an uncollected poem printed in *The Scotsman*, 25 November 1999, after its discovery by Margery McCulloch among the papers of Catherine Carswell.
3. Karel Čapek (1890–1938), the Czech author who brought the word 'robot' into its present use with his play *R.U.R.* (1921).
4. Arthur Berriedale Keith (1896–1941), translator of Sanskrit, author of books on various Indian subjects and a prominent commentator on Commonwealth Constitutionalism. See *The Raucle Tongue*, vol. II, pp. 432–4.
5. Alexander Stewart Wolfe, Earl of Buchanan and laird of Badenoch (c.1343–1405), son of King Robert II, nicknamed 'Wolfe' for his continued harrassment of the bishopric of Moray. See Sir Thomas Dick Lauder (1774–1848), *The Wolfe of Badenoch* (Stirling: Eneas Mackay, 1930), a hefty and portentous historical adventure novel first published in 1827; the 1930 edition had a Foreword by R.B. Cunninghame Graham and was well-known to the Scottish writers of the time.
6. Douglas Young (1913–73), lecturer in Greek at Aberdeen University (1938–41), chairman of the SNP (1942), he published the first of three collections of poetry in 1943 and translated two of Aristophanes' plays into Scots.

107. *To W.R. Aitken (NLS)*

Whalsay   Wednesday, 25 January 1939

My dear Bill

I enclose additional 'copy' for Notes on Our Forerunners. There probably won't be room for it in next issue as I've already indicated – but in that event just hold it over, and put Burns, Scott, and the Wolfe of Badenoch in.

I'll write you again on other matters at the week-end and send on then the *Mind In Chains* and *Orchardford*.[1]

Very many thanks for the books, all of which I'm glad to have. I'll try to return them in a few days. I'll apply via Ratter for MacNeice and also again for 'Poetry and Scepticism'.[2]

Love from us all, Yours, Chris

---

1. *Mind In Chains: socialism and the cultural revolution*, ed. C. Day Lewis (London: Muller, 1937). John Smellie Martin, *Orchardford*, from which CMG quarried many of the words which became the 'In the Fall' section of *In Memoriam James Joyce*. (See Kenneth Buthlay, 'The Ablach in the Gold Pavilion', *Scottish Literary Journal*, vol. 15, no. 2, November 1988, pp.39–57.)
2. Louis MacNeice (1907–63), Northern Irish poet, associated with the British left-wing poets of the 1930s, lecturer in Greek at the University of London (1936–40). D. G. James, *Scepticism and Poetry* (London, Allen & Unwin, 1937).

108. *To W.R. Aitken (NLS)*

Whalsay   Wednesday, 8 February 1939

My dear Bill

Many thanks for your letter and enclosures. I'll be delighted of course to give you the Light Verse book, and am ordering it to be sent to you.

I haven't succeeded in getting into touch with Orr again, but have just written once more. My last advice was that he was still somewhere in the West of Canada.

Re No. 4.

Very many thanks for your offer to help financially if the last issue of Vol. I were made a little larger. But I think we'd better hold our horses. I'd like very much of course to adopt the suggestion and get a good swatch of the material we have in hand printed and done with. But I'd rather reserve any little cash we have till the continuance of the venture is assured. Even if I don't get things settled up with Orr as quickly as I desire it may be possible to put out a Vol. II No. I before adjusting matters finally with him, and I'd prefer that to enlarging Vol. I No. IV.

As to stuff in hand, I hope the following can go in our next issue. (The provisional measurements quoted are yours.)

Poem by McCaig	½ page
Poem by Brodie	½ page
Poem by Treece	½ page
Poem by T.E. Nicholas (Welsh)	½ page
Poem by T.E. Nicholas (English)	½ page (I'll send this)
Six poems by Geo. Campbell Hay	3 pages
Poems by Norman MacLeod (Two if at all possible)	
Poems by J.F. Hendry (One if at all possible)	

When the Gangs Came to London[1] (Laidlaw) 1 page + ½ (with footnote re Karl Capek's death).

Carry forward	8½pp.
Notes on our Forerunners Burns	4
Wolfe of B.	5
MacGillivray	1
(i.e. Hold over Scott, Keith, and Paterson)	
The arts of Scotland	1
Readers' Sign-Post	4
Notes of the Quarter	8
[Scottish Poet and Gaelic metrics	5]

Also

Poem by Galloway	½ page
	37 pages
Leave out also Gaelic metrics article	5
	32

That's as near as I can make it, I am afraid. I am particularly anxious to have Hay's six poems in – I have other excellent stuff from him, in hand now.

Let me know what you think.

I have got my Islands Book finished now, and am on the last lap of the Doctors' one, but I am absolutely bung-fu' of verse I am writing or itching to get down to writing.

I'm enclosing the Sir Ronald Ross and the *Orchardford*.

Love from us all. Yours, Chris

P.S. I think we'll have the 'Brief Survey of Modern Scottish Politics' pamphlet ready for distribution with the next issue of the *Voice* all right. It's a 32pp. pamphlet.

And in addition, I want by hook or crook the Buchanan-Corneille thing (1½pp) in!!! Also I *must* somehow get in Douglas Young's letter and my reply to it. Afraid therefore you must keep out the Readers' Sign-Post.

And I am also very anxious to have in the 1707 over again re Dewar Gibb. My dear chap, you'll just have to do the best you can – and I know you will – along these lines.

---

1. Title chosen from eponymous novel by Edgar Wallace.

109. *To W.R. Aitken (NLS)*

Whalsay   15 March 1939

My dear Bill

1st Congratulations on getting through your examination.

2nd We're all delighted to hear you are beginning to think of your Shetland trip again and will be extremely glad to see you whenever – and for however long – you can come.

3rd I'm extremely pleased about what you say you've succeeded in arranging for our next issue of the *Voice*. I'm not sure yet (I may know before this letter gets off tomorrow – i.e. I may hear by tomorrow's mail) if the pamphlets are to be ready for issue with this number. I hope so; but it's a biggish job. The pamphlet runs to over 16,000 words and makes itself 33pp. like the *Voice*. I've corrected and returned the proofs a week or so ago, but have not heard how the job progresses since.

4th I think I told you the *Islands* book is now being printed.

5th I'm awfully sorry to have been so long in writing you. I've been desperately busy. *Inter alia*, Grant is going off in a day or two to France on holiday, and I've been anxious to get as much work polished off before he went as possible. But the real reason for my exclusive absorption recently has been that I've been writing a poem, from the point of view of the extreme left, in reply to Roy Campbell's Right Wing *Flowering Rifle* on the Spanish War.[1] If it was to be done at all it was desirable to strike while the iron is hot – i.e. to strike at the present juncture in Spanish affairs, and also while the controversy aroused by Campbell's Fascist poem was still raging. Victor Gollancz was eager to have such a poem; and there is a possibility that it might be issued to the Left Book Club. I got it off to Gollancz a few days ago – over 4000 lines of it! So, as you can imagine, that fully took up all my time and energies. Whether Gollancz will like it and publish it now it is done is of course another matter. But that's one of the risks incidental to this peculiar business of authorship – and especially *in re* poetry! However, I'm glad to have written it, whether I succeed in getting it published or not; it certainly contains some very good work.

6th Finally, re Ross, I thought I had sent you this. Since I got your wire I've hunted high and low for it, without success. However I'll make absolutely sure by next mail, when, also, without fail I'll return Manson and Mackenzie. Mistral like Ross seems at the moment to have vanished; for it too I'll institute a thorough search and send it if I find it by Friday's mail too – or, if not, let you know. Pushkin, Griffin etc. I also send you now.

Flu' is raging in the Shetlands. So far we've escaped with mere colds. Mike has been off school a week or thereby with an inflamed inner ear. Trust you are O.K. yourself.

Love from us all. Yours, Chris

---

1. Roy Campbell (1901–57), *The Flowering Rifle* (London: Longman, 1939). CMG's swift response was not published for nearly twenty years: Hugh MacDiarmid, *The Battle Continues* (Edinburgh: Castle Wynd Printers, 1957).

110. *To William White (NLS, DFF)*

Whalsay, via Lerwick, Shetland   24 March 1939

Dear Sir:

I am sorry that illness and pressure of work has prevented my replying before now to your letter of 21st Feb.

With regard to your poems (which I now return), I am afraid they are not of a nature upon which I can usefully comment. I see no evidence in them at all of a genuine poetic talent at work, and they seem wholly lacking in what Rossetti called that 'fundamental brain work' indispensable to creative art. I have no doubt at all that many people would deem them poetry, because they are constructed of the kind of phrases which form the common denominator of a great deal of the poetry of the past, and are ostensibly concerned with the kind of subject-matter most people regard as synonymous with that of the poet. But, as someone has said, one does not become a master violinist simply by being put in possession of a master violin, and in the same way mere manipulation of the clichés of past poetry does not constitute poetry. In so far from producing poetry you seem to me to be engaged in producing a kind of anti-poetry which almost any literate person could turn out indefinitely. But you communicate no vital experience at all, and express no authentic reaction to your subjects, while your verbalisms are throughout quite appallingly trite and unilluminated by any flash of personal vision or first-hand feeling at all.

This may seem a very severe judgment, but you asked for my frank opinion and I therefore give it. Bogus poeticising of this kind is very common and forms perhaps nine-tenths of all our hopelessly miseducated people are capable of recognising as poetry. It is nothing of the sort, but the very antithesis of poetry. I think your trouble is largely due to an utterly false idea of the nature and functions of poetry, evidenced in the atrocious hooey of many of your notes – e.g. 'I have reached forth on my own and have written down the whispered words of the Muse as she spoke them to me.' This indicates to me only a sentimentalism of the spirit which is utterly incompatible with the production of any decent writing. For while I say this utterly false idea of the nature and functions of poetry accounts for the deplorable characterlessness of these MSS, it is necessary to recognise that beneath that is the question of what makes you entertain that utterly false idea; and when one reaches that point it seems to me clear that the responsible factor is a radical defect of your own nature, and that there is therefore no ground at all for hoping that any little guidance or detailed criticism can make good such a basic deficiency and offer any probability of your ever being able to produce poetry of the very slightest value at all.

Yours sincerely, [Unsigned]

111. To Frank O'Connor (EUL)

Whalsay, via Lerwick, Shetland Islands, Scotland   21 June 1939

My dear Frank O'Connor

Two good friends of mine – George Davie and W. Angus Sinclair, both lecturers in the Philosophy Department of Edinburgh University and thoroughly sound lads in every way – are to be in Dublin shortly on holiday and have written asking me to put them in touch with some of the Irish writers, and, in particular, Higgins[1] and yourself. I've just written to Higgins too. I'll be very glad if you can see them and give them the freedom of literary Dublin. I wish I could be with them too, but alas! I am pent up here on the edge of the Arctic Circle and cannot get away. How many years ago is it now since Geoffrey Phibbs and yourself came to see me in Dublin? You've done a great tale of work since then; I've read all your books I think, with vast appreciation. Please accept my kindest regards and best wishes, and if you are in Dublin during their time there and not too busy with other things do let my friends meet you and help them, in the American phrase, to 'see a good time'. I haven't your address – or Higgins's address, but am telling my friends that they'll be able to find your whereabouts from the *Dublin Magazine* office or from the Cuala Press.

Yours ever, Hugh MacDiarmid

---

1. F.R. Higgins (1896–1941), poet of the Irish literary revival, friend of Austin Clarke and Yeats, director of the Abbey Theatre, 1936.

112. To W.R. Aitken (NLS)

Whalsay   Monday, 10 July 1939

My dear Bill

I am so sorry you did not get that job, but glad you were on the short list and feel sure too that this will stand you in good stead and that ere long you will land a really substantial and important appointment all right. I had a very nice letter from Bain, which I'll enclose with this if I can lay my hands on it.

Very many thanks for all the books and for the photos, some of which are really excellent. I like the exceedingly Leninesque portrait of myself.

The book I am most anxious to get hold of soon (apart from the Women as Men one) is the *Early German Art and its Origins* by Harold Picton (Batsford).[1]

I mention this because I am not sure if it was one of those you said you got Rattar to order – or whether I will apply for it now through Rattar.

I am also very anxious to find if possible what biographical or critical study of Milton gives the fullest account of the epic of *Isle Britain* he planned but never carried out; and to lay my hands also on the available information regarding the similar intention or views thereanent of Geo. Buchanan.

The other Vaughan Cornish book is the one – *Ocean Waves and Kindred Geophysical Phenomena*.[2]

I am also anxious to have anything bearing on the bathymetrics of the Hebridean and Shetland waters.

I am in short taking the plunge, and going right ahead with the epical novel of early Gaelic-Norse Scotland I spoke of.

Re the *Voice*, A.K. Laidlaw please for the Gangsters in London poem; and I have not yet been able to give a fresh beginning to the Scott article in the Forerunners, but I'll send this without fail next mail (i.e. Wednesday). And I'll also return several of the books then – I'm practically finished with the Arthurian legend, also Powys's *Autobiography* which I've read with enormous relish.[3] I really must procure copies somehow of the *Glastonbury Romance*, *Wolf Solent*, *Bridlegoose* etc.

It is good of you to think of giving your paper on my work, and of course I'll be very glad to send you copies of the parts of *Mature Art*, constituting a sort of Ars Poetica I read you here, which you want. I'll try to get these off to you this week too.

Glad you got your copy of the *Islands* book all right. It seems to have created a very favourable impression in most quarters. The reviews to hand so far are very satisfactory.

I'm glad you are feeling – and looking – so fit after your holiday here. The weather since you left has been deplorable and now it is more like November than July – a howling wind, and wet, and cold.

Barbara and Ernest[4] come just after 17th inst, and later we're to have Alasdair Alpin McGregor, and a friend of his – Presbyterian minister of Muswell (London), a Mr Christie.

Valda will write you ere long. She is very pleased that Miss Aitken liked the brown jumper and that the other items of hosiery sold to the benefit of the Sale of Work funds all right.

I hope I haven't forgotten any of the points I should reply to you about, but in any case I'll be writing you again next post.

I enclose a note to John Brough (I've mislaid his address you gave me – but I've said in the note that I had forgotten his address so was forwarding the letter to you to address and post for me).

Love from us all. Yours, Chris

---

1. Harold Picton, *Early German Art and its Origins* (London: Batsford, 1939).
2. Vaughan Cornish, *Ocean Waves and Kindred Geophysical Phenomena* (Cambridge: The University Press, 1934).
3. John Cowper Powys, *Autobiography* (London: John Lane, 1934).
4. Barbara Niven and Ernest Brooks; see Appendix.

113. *To the Editor*, The Shetland Times *(NLS)*

Whalsay   18 July 1939

Sir:

A supply of newspapers usually reaches Whalsay by the *Earl of Zetland* on Sundays. Every now and again, however, as happened on Sunday last, the *Earl* carries these on instead of putting them off at Whalsay. There is no excuse for this sort of thing. It is an intolerable nuisance and can only be due to unmitigated carelessness and the absence of any effective checking system or proper attention thereto.

It is bad enough when newspapers are delayed in this way; it is a more serious matter altogether when mail matter is also carried past. This also happened on Sunday last. Under certain circumstances it is obvious that remissness of this kind might involve addressees of the correspondence in question in a great deal of hardship and loss. Certain letters call for immediate action and the speediest possible reply, and allowances are not made for belated delivery due to the *Earl*'s vagaries.

Mistakes now and again are unavoidable perhaps, but, in the case of the *Earl*, recurrences of this sort of thing are altogether too frequent and must be stopped. Heavy damages might well be exigeable against the North of Scotland Steamship company in respect of the hardships and losses sustained through such gross carelessness, and so far as the mails are concerned it is high time the PO authorities took the matter in hand and stopped this nuisance. The delivery of mail intended for elsewhere to Whalsay, (and a consequent delay of several days involved in returning it to Lerwick and having it sent out then to its proper destination) is only another indication that things are being very inefficiently run, and that it is high time the system was looked into and a much higher degree of efficiency insisted on.

Yours sincerely, [Unsigned]

P.S. To cap the farce, having failed to put off the papers at Whalsay and carried them on its northward trip on Sunday, the *Earl* again failed to put them off when it returned on Monday and carried them back to Lerwick again.

114. *To Thomas Johnston, County Assessor (NLS)*

Whalsay   18 August 1939

Dear Sir

Reference your personal valuation of £3.10 on my house, I beg to appeal against this on the grounds 1/ that this proposed valuation is higher than that on similar subjects on the island 2/ that I am a blind person receiving 10/- a week pension under the Blind Persons Act and, since I am wholly dependent on that, unable to discharge such a liability without serious hardship. The house is only a but and ben, with an annual rent of £1. It is within my knowledge that other cottages on the island rented at £1.6/- per annum – some of them with four rooms – are only paying 6/- to 7/- in rates, whereas you state that if the proposed valuation of £3.10/- is enforced I shall have to pay about half of that, i.e. about £1.15/-. This seems out of all proportion to what others are paying.

I will be glad to supply any further information desired.

Yours sincerely, [Unsigned][1]

---

1. In spite of a disastrous fishing season and impending war, the Assesor had increased the assessments on cottars' houses in Whalsay. CMG formed a defence commitee and invited cottars to his office where he dictated, and H.G. Taylor typed, their letters of appeal. CMG had begun renting this office as soon as Helen Cruickshank had secured a Royal Literary Fund award of £75, which was to help him pay off shopkeepers, and a further £50 at £5 per month. See Laurence Graham and Brian Smith, *MacDiarmid in Shetland* (Lerwick, Shetland: Shetland Library, 1992), p.58.

115. *To Guy Aldred*

Shetland   28 August [1939]

Dear Comrade, –

As a revolutionary poet and critic, of whose work a leading American poet and critic recently said, 'It is my conviction that you started the whole revolutionary trend in poetry in Great Britain and remain its most significant example – if not its only significant expression, which I believe you are as far as Great Britain is concerned', permit me to congratulate you on the most interesting and valuable copies of *The Word* which have reached me, and to offer my most cordial and comradely greetings for the continuance and development of the paper and the USM[1] generally.

I agree in particular with your castigations of Willie Gallacher[2] and Peter Kerrigan, and your exposure of the infernal monkey tricks of the CPGB with regard to Conscription, etc. I have had occasion in recent issues of my own quarterly, *Voice of Scotland*, to show up the shameful intellectual incompetence and spiritual bankruptcy of the CPGB and its auxiliary, the London leftist group of writers headed by Auden, Spender and MacNeice in belles lettres and John Strachey and the Left Book Club, and the Penguin Books, in political controversy; and my analysis of these elements has attracted a great deal of interest and approval among writers in Wales, Ireland, America and elsewhere.

I am not now a member of the CPGB, from which I was expelled in ludicrous lying pretexts as, indeed, any one with a scintilla of genuine

socialist integrity is always sure to be.
   Christopher Murray Grieve ('Hugh MacDiarmid')[3]

---

1. United Socialist Movement.
2. William Gallacher (1881–1966), leader of the shop stewards' movement on Clydeside during WWI, arrested and deported for his militant activities in 1916, a founder of the CPGB, Communist MP for Fife West (1935–51).
3. The text of this letter, published in *The Word* (vol. 1, no. 5, October 1939), was supplied by John Manson.

116. *To W.R. Aitken (NLS)*

Whalsay   Wednesday 13 September [1939]

My dear Bill
   Your news came of course as a complete surprise, but we are delighted to hear it. Please accept for your wife and yourself the heartiest congratulations and good wishes of all here – with the rider that we will expect your annual visit as usual, and Mrs Aitken (whom we will eagerly look forward to meeting) with you.
   I do hope that you won't have to join up, but fear it is inevitable. I cannot conceive that this war can be a short one. And no matter what its issue will be in this or that direction it can only make for a bestial submergence and perhaps final dissolution of all decent values. I have had little or no news since it started – no papers, few letters and these belated, etc. etc. I have no idea what's going to happen to myself. Barbara and Ernest went off yesterday but are hung up for want of steamer services in Lerwick till tomorrow afternoon anyhow. In all the circumstances I am extremely anxious to carry on *The Voice of Scotland* for a while till we see how things go. I was much surprised at your news about the printers. I thought they had been paid up – with the exception of the last issue. I gathered that from Orr when he was here. He will certainly pay them all right if he hasn't already done so. As to the new volume, I'd have been in a position now to have paid for the last issue and an advance for the one now in hand but for this war business. I have monies overdue from USA and Canada – and am working desperately hard to complete my *Autobiography*. Probably as matters stand this will now be more difficult to market in this country than it would have been a month or so ago, but two American publishers are very keen and I'll certainly get enough from one of them to enable me to carry on the *V of S* all right – and to keep us going for a year or so ahead too. So I do hope the printers will get this issue out on my promise to give them a really substantial payment before the next. I'll get in touch with Orr at once.

As to the books, the need to drive ahead with the *Autobio*. has sidetracked my concern with the Pibroch book – and also my work on the other 'novel that is not a novel' for which I wanted Mackenzie and Bremner, and of which I have already completed – and Grant has typed – over 40,000 words. But I'll send them on to you next year. Tillyard by the way I think I returned. I may be wrong – I'll have a hunt round the other cottage tomorrow – but I intended to send it back with my last parcel.

Until the arrears of mail come in and bring with them some of the monies I am awaiting, you must please not mind that Valda and I do not send you and Mrs Aitken a wedding present yet, and let us mark the happy event in that way a little later when it is more convenient. If you will go marrying in war-time this is what happens. Love and warmest good wishes to you both from all here.

Yours, Chris

117. *To Peggy Grieve (NLS)*

Whalsay, Shetland   21 October 1939

Dear P.

As I showed clearly when I agreed to MacNair Reid's and Power's[1] appeal not to raise an action for perjury at the time of the Alienation Case, I did not want to take action against you or wash dirty linen in public if I could possibly help it – i.e. if I could get any sort of decent human consideration out of you with regard to the children any other way.

But you have refused me anything of the sort, tho' you know you have no good ground whatever for treating me in this inhuman way. Even murderers are allowed to see their children in the condemned cell. And most children are only too anxious to see their fathers even if the latter *are* murderers. But I committed no crime. You simply betrayed me most foully and then in the most cowardly way let me appear as the guilty party and obtained custody of the children by fraud.

And then your lying hag of a mother wrote me that I could see the children whenever I wanted!

Well, all my appeals to you have been ignored and tho', as I told you, I long for the children as much as ever, circumstances have been too strong for me and now I have been forced to realise that there is no use in appealing further. But I also told you I would clear myself and publish the true facts at all costs, and that I am now on the point of doing. I have managed to finish the writing of my *Autobiography*. It will be published simultaneously in this country and in America. And in it I have told the whole story – abortion, perjury, and all the rest of it.

I have done this not only to ensure my vindication (for I supply proofs of all I say, and the whole account has been carefully vetted by lawyers) but because I am determined that the Scottish Courts' practice of allowing both parents – both the 'guilty' and the innocent – access to the children – will not be flouted as you have flouted it, but cease to be optional and become a definite rule. And also that no divorce petitioner securing the custody of the children on the ground of the other parent's adultery will be allowed to keep that custody if subsequently committing adultery too. Friends of mine in the House of Commons are to take the matter up. There will be plenty of publicity as a consequence. Legal proceedings will probably follow: but I won't instigate them, but leave the authorities themselves to do that.

But I write now to make one thing clear – and that is: no matter what the upshot is I will not seek or take custody of the children either now or again, nor will I *ever* now consent to see them, correspond with them, or have anything whatever to do with them. I do not blame the children, though they are old enough now for them to have seen through your damnable treatment of me and for their natural instincts to have asserted themselves and made them get in touch with me and hear my story. But I know the sort of pressure you have exerted and the way you and your infernal mother have poisoned them against me. And in any case too long has elapsed now and they have been brought up in a way and in an atmosphere which makes it out of the question altogether now for me to join up the broken threads of our relationship in any way.

So you will have the satisfaction of knowing that your vile plot has succeeded and can never be undone.

But I will have my own back in every way, and I will certainly make it impossible for the children not to know exactly what sort of a woman you were and how you won their love by fraud and lying and inhuman cruelty, and they will be forced to see how you have treated me – but they will not be able to do anything about it so far as I am concerned, since even if they have the decency to make any overtures to me, I will never now consent to have anything whatever to do with them.

Chris

P.S. I have always been aware that the very strongest circumstantial evidence can be entirely misleading, but I have given you countless opportunities through all these years to explain matters in such a way that the conclusions to which I was otherwise driven would be shown to be wrong. You have not availed yourself of any of these opportunities. If any injustice has been done to you it is therefore entirely your own fault.

What cannot be denied in any case is that despite all my desperate pleas to you from Liverpool, you gave me no warning whatever of your pregnancy and abortion.

Nor can you deny that gross perjury was committed when it was stated that 1/ I knew of the £200 that MacElroy gave you, and 2/ that I paid for your operation and nursing home expenses.

Apart from that your treatment of me has shown that you had no love or affection for me whatever nor any sense of ordinary human decency or you could never have denied me all access to (and not only access to, but any news about) the children all these years. Our letters set side by side in themselves condemn you absolutely, whereas my constant plea to be allowed to see the children and my acquiescence in not going on with the Perjury Action etc. all bear out my side of the matter.

There is also the fact that if you had been worthy of having the custody of the children you would have considered their interests which were undoubtedly reconciliation with me, instead of poisoning their minds against me, at the very time you were leading a shameful life and committing the very offence for which you took them from me, but without being forced to do so as you forced me as the only means of escaping from an intolerable position in which you and your sister jeered at my plight.

However there is no use in going into all that. I have done so finally and far more effectively in my book. You ruined me – completely disoriented my work – were not content to drive me out of my home, reduced to beggary, but had to take from me the only thing I had left, the affection of my children – and did not hesitate even when I was dangerously ill to buoy me up with the hope of seeing Christine again when you had no intention of allowing me to do so at all, but simply visited the hospital in passing on the way to a vulgar intrigue.

You would never have been able to wreak your evil will but for my poverty. Keeping the children from me can have had only one object – to inflict the maximum of pain upon me. In that you have succeeded all right.

---

1. William Power (1873–1951), Scottish journalist and author, founder and editor of the *Scots Observer* (1926), president of Scottish PEN (1935–8).

118. *To Andrew Graham Grieve (EUL)*

Whalsay   3 November 1939

My dear Graham

I was delighted to have your letter from Reading – as previously, your p.c. from Achiltibuie, and to know you had had such a delightful holiday; and are now having an interesting time on your various itinerant duties. I remember Reading; I was there for a day or two – last War.

Since the present War started I have, of course, been practically marooned here – with infrequent, very uncertain and always belated mails; ditto papers. So I scarcely know what is going on and have great difficulty in keeping my various interests active. Worst of all, War at once affects journalism and book-publishing seriously and at first it seemed that my position here would speedily become untenable, and, since a long War seemed certain, I made tentative – but unsuccessful – efforts to get some sort of remunerative employment in Scotland or England. Since then, however, the position has improved a little and I think now I may manage to keep getting a small trickle of income which despite the rise in prices may enable us to continue to exist on short commons.

I've just finished writing my *Autobiography* – it's a big book and has been the very devil to write but I think I've succeeded in putting the whole writing of modern Scotland and my own psychology and position as a poet, on paper much more effectively and fully than has yet been done anywhere. So I have hopes it'll pan out well. The *Islands* book has done well, and has had uniformly favourable reviews both here and in America where it has been published separately. I'm glad you liked it: but of course the word-limit cramped me, and so I agree with you that there was a lot that could – and should – have been said that I was unable to touch on for space reasons.

My big poem (over 20,000 lines) I had hoped to have had published by the Obelisk Press in Paris, but the death of the proprietor of that business seemed to knock the proposition in the head. A longish interval elapsed and I'd given up hope. However I've just heard from his son who is to carry on the business and he's keen to go on with the publication provided I can secure a certain number of advance subscribers. He's writing a prospectus for me and I think I'll manage – so we'll see.

In America Professor G.K. Anderson and Eda Lou Walton have just put out a magnificent conspectus and anthology of literature in English since 1914, nearly 1000 pages of the best poems, short stories, plays etc. with critical interchapters, strongly stressing and representing the swing to the left in creative writing both in this country and America during that ¼ century period. I am the only Scot represented – by five of my poems and a good critical notice. This is a great book to have, and if you can lay your hands on it you should do so.[1]

A new quarterly – *The New Alliance* – has started in Edinburgh and I had four poems in the first issue.[2] Apart from that and my own quarterly *The Voice of Scotland* (the current issue of which is overdue but hung up by war-time exigencies in the printers' office – I'm mainly contributing to Welsh periodicals these days, and have longish poems appearing in both *The Welsh Review*[3] and *Wales*.

Winter weather has set in here, very snell and gurly: but apart from the inconveniences etc. of irregular and infrequent steamer services, mails, and dearer provisions of all kinds, – and seasonal colds – we are all pretty well about the bit. And do not envy you people in the South at all. I trust you are all well and that conditions (apart from black-outs, ubiquity of sand-bags and other ARP contrivances etc.) are not affecting you adversely in any way.

In your letter you mentioned being at Langholm. But didn't say who – if anybody – you saw there. I'd like any Langholm news you picked up. I had hoped (as indeed I have hoped for years – for I am very fond of Langholm and/or round about it) to have got down there myself this last summer, but alas! I haven't been there now for just over 21 years! I'd like to see Aunt Maggie too. But somehow it never becomes possible.

Love from us all to all of you, Yours, Chris

---

1. *This Generation*, ed. Eda Lou Walton and G.K. Anderson (Chicago, 1939).
2. 'Bonnie Birdie A' Aflocht', 'Under the Hallior Moon', 'The Black Rainbow Over the Minch', 'The Auld Howff', *New Alliance*, vol. 1, no. 1.
3. 'Diamond Body', *Welsh Review*, vol. 12, no. 4, 1 November 1939.

119. *To Andrew Graham Grieve (EUL)*

Whalsay, Shetland   18 December 1939

Dear A.

Many thanks for your welcome letter. You certainly had a whirlwind tour. Lucky dog. It is splendid that you should be having a spell of such diversified interest. I am particularly interested of course in the possibility you mention of your being located for some years in Scotland again. But that will mean all the upset of changing your home again and resettling in a very different atmosphere from your present one. And I cannot gauge of course how this is likely to pan out in regard to Morag and Angus if by that time they have matriculated at London Univ. Salutations to both of them. I am delighted to hear of their progress and hope they both go through with flying colours – as I have no doubt they will. Angus must have fairly shot up. Mike is in one of those stages of arrested growth. A good deal bigger than when you saw him of course, but still not tall for his age though fairly sturdy. He is making such headway as is practicable at his age perhaps, but not seriously at grips with education yet. The other night he did well in the character of Twinkle Toes in a fairy play at the School Concert.

The *Autobiography* is finished. Some 200,000 words of it. It may require a little cutting and reordering before publication. It is of course a poet's autobio. – and a political poet's at that. That is to say it is a psychological and intellectual self-portrait – concerned far more with the evolution of my ideas and technical processes and the inside story of the development of my works than with what are usually regarded as the facts of one's personality and career. So I am afraid it'll not be much use to you so far as comparison of recollections goes – though there is a good deal about Langholm and the Borders in some of the earlier chapters, about our father and mother and early home life and school and kirk. But most of the chapters are concerned with my mental life – my life inside myself rather than in contact with other people, or, in other words, myself as poet and politician rather than as human being. So far as other people are concerned most space is given to my friendships with and reminiscences of such people as F.G. Scott, Kaikhosru Sorabji, A.R. Orage, W.B. Yeats, Professor Patrick Geddes,[1] A.E., and various European writers like Jakob Wasserman,[2] Karel Capek and Chaim Nachman Bialik.[3] But I think you will find it all very interesting if not just what you may be looking for.

Publication is not definitely fixed up yet. Several firms both in this country and USA are interested and the matter is in the hands of my agents. I must get as much money at this time as I possibly can and the negotiations may take some time, as apart from this being a bad time the work itself is not only full of difficulty, but highly controversial and full of political dynamite. So we'll see. I think it will appear in the Spring all right, and of course I'll send you a copy when it does.

My first book to appear now will be my *Golden Treasury of Scottish Poetry* via Macmillan's. I'll send you a copy of this too. It is at the printers now. You must, I am afraid, rely upon copies of these books in lieu of any Christmas remembrance this year, for we will not be able to send any presents this year. It is good of you to be sending us a parcel. We'll be writing you again when it comes to hand.

I am not sure that your willingness to subscribe for my poem was expressed with a clear view of what this would entail – in other words, I am not sure that I gave you an indication of what the cost of this great work would be. I enclose a prospectus now with due apologies for administering such a shock in war-time. I'll need all the support I can possibly muster to ensure publication of this huge poem. It is a very serious matter for me and my future will largely depend on the success or failure of this project. I do not suppose that you know of any other likely subscribers – people able and willing to pay 2 guineas for a poem (even if it is as long as 3 novels at one whack) don't grow on every tree, of course. But if you do know any such, and can round them up by hook or crook, please let me know and I'll be only too glad to send them – or you – additional copies of this prospectus.

Before I got off on the theme of my books I was speaking about Morag and Angus and what I meant to say was this – if they go to London University I may be able to do a little to ease their path which I'll be very happy indeed to do, since I am on very friendly terms with quite a number of the professors and lecturers. Morag I think is strong on languages. Well, the French Prof. (Saurat) is one of my oldest and best friends. Rose, the German Prof, is another very good friend of mine. Well, we'll see when the time comes, but a little pull in such connections can be very useful and I'll be very glad if I can exercise it on behalf of Morag and Angus.

Love to you all from all here, and best wishes for a happy Christmas and a bright and prosperous 1940.

Yours, Chris

---

1. Patrick Geddes (1854–1932), Scottish pioneer of town planning.
2. Jakob Wasserman (1873–1933), German novelist; CMG particularly admired his *Christian Wahnshaffe* (1919), authorised translation by Ludwig Lewisohn as *The World's Illusion* (New York: Harcourt, Brace and Co., 1930).
3. Chaim Nachman Bialik (1873–1934), Ukrainian, regarded as the greatest early modern Hebrew poet.

PART THREE

The 1940s

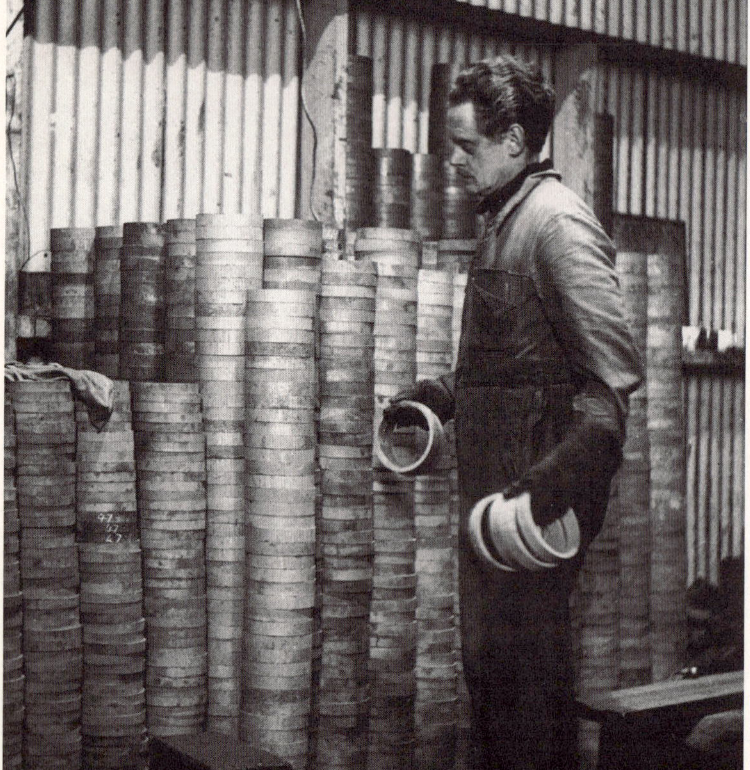

1. *To Andrew Graham Grieve (EUL)*

Whalsay   8 January 1940

Dear A.G.G.

Valda will be writing Chryssie very soon; time goes on, but mails are so uncertain, infrequent, and belated that one's disposition to write letters is depressed to a minimum, so – since we cannot allow longer to elapse without making due acknowledgment of your Christmas gifts – I am writing just this brief note as a stop-gap.

We were all three delighted with the beautiful presents. Valda will probably express in her letter more effectively her appreciation of the beautiful brush, comb, and mirror set. Mike was greatly bucked with his watch. A previous cheaper specimen (and sans chain) I gave him had a sad fate. He had it loose in his breast pocket. He and his mother were down at the shore fishing – he had occasion to stoop down to reach at something. And plop went his watch into the briny – with disastrous results to its internal mechanism. Poor little beggar! He was very cut up about it. The leather guard with yours will prevent any such occurrence again. Altogether he had a very successful Christmas, but since then he has been having a thin time of it. He pricked himself with a needle under one of his finger-nails and the thing festered and became very inflamed. We were very much afraid of septicaemia setting in; the Doctor thought the nail would have to be taken off – but wouldn't do it himself for lack of proper facilities, and that meant sending Mike to the Lerwick Hospital in which case Valda would have had to go with him, and with the uncertain steamer services might have had to stay there 3 or 4 days. Altogether it looked as if the matter was going to mean the inside of a £10 note. However assiduous poulticing and the application of glycerine fomentations has cleared the matter up – the nail may come off of its own accord, or may require to be removed later, but the suppuration and inflammation have ceased.

Valda and I are O.K. but the weather is atrocious and for lack of news, infrequency of mails, shortage of papers and other reading material, feel as if we were jailed in a nasty damp cold little cellar.

The *Autobiography* isn't definitely fixed up yet. Gollancz is eager to publish, provided I'll condense the thing to 150,000 words from its present 200,000. That isn't too easy; besides since I sent off the MSS I've written another 20–30,000 I want to add! Another publisher – Hale – has it just now: it'll be arranged all right soon in any case.

Again with love to you all and best thanks for the lovely gifts.
Yours, Chris

2. To Andrew Graham Grieve (EUL)

Whalsay   5 February 1940

My dear Graham

Your telegram received here today came as a terrible shock to us. Before you get this you will have received our telegram expressing our sorrow and heart-felt sympathy. At the moment we are without details, of course, and had no idea Chryssie was ill or anything. If an illness preceded her death you may have written to us but in that event your letter will still be in course of post because there have been no mails in here for nearly a fortnight. I mention this because in the event of your having so written you may not have allowed for the difficulties and delays of circumstances just now, and imagine we have been careless. For the same reason I am just sending you this short note just now, but even so it may be long enough before you receive it. Steamer sailings are very uncertain and a few days without them at this end may make a difference of as much as a week or longer in the receipt of a letter in England or Scotland.

So you will understand. Until we have your letter and can write to you at greater length with some knowledge of the circumstances we can only express the hope that this very sore and untimely bereavement took place with a minimum of suffering to Chryssie and as little shock to you and the children as possible. One wonders if you were at home, or away on one of your official itineraries. And what we hear of the death-toll due to accidents in the black-out makes us wonder if Chryssie too has been the victim of such a fatality. Another friend of mine – the Scottish writer, Donald Carswell, who was employed at the Home Office, was killed in such an accident early in January.[1]

But it is no use speculating. We must just await your letter with what patience we can command. We are at any rate dreadfully sorry. Your last letter said you were all well and though we have not corresponded very frequently we had understood that Chryssie was in good health and that life down South was suiting her very well. Neither Valda nor myself had seen much of Chryssie as you know yet we both liked her immensely and feel a real loss. What it must be to you and the children hardly bears thinking about. It is tragic that she should have been taken from you just when the long years of struggle were past and you were so much better off. Happily the children are no longer just bairns but well grown-up. Love and every good wish to all of you, and may you have all the comfort possible in such circumstances.

Valda had been intending to write Chryssie as I told you in my letter acknowledging the lovely gifts you sent us at Christmas. But circumstances here have been for many reasons singularly unconducive to letter-writing – hence her delay which alas! can never be made good now.

I am wondering if you will be taking her home to Edinburgh for burial.

But in any case I could not manage to be there. Even if I could get down to Sumburgh and catch a plane there (and getting down to Sumburgh might not be manageable within a week anyhow) I could scarcely get to Edinburgh in time – and the expense makes that mode of travelling (the only possible one in the circumstances) out of the question.

Apart from seasonal complaints we are all well and trust this finds you, and Morag and Angus in good health too. We will await your further news with deep concern.

Yours affectionately, Chris, Valda, and Michael

---

1. Carswell died in a car accident while driving home in the dark.

3. *To Sorley MacLean (NLS)*

Whalsay   11 February 1940

My dear Sam

I was delighted to hear from you again, to receive the little book of your verse and Sutherland's, and to note with pride your inscription of a poem to myself.[1] I had been wondering what in the world had come over you, but I note what you say thereabout and I am the last person to underestimate the value and necessity of the harsh and dark rigours of winter to the subsequent seed-time and harvest; and I am immensely cheered to learn that the spell of sluggish repression to which you refer has already resulted in such a rich yield of poetry. I will look forward very keenly to the eventual publication of the whole Cuillin poem you have so kindly dedicated to myself, coupling my name with the great name of Alexander MacDonald, and the collection of poems to Eimhir, and to the English thereof you promise me.[2]

Fancy you being in Hawick which as probably you know is only 20 miles from my own birthplace of Langholm and a town in which I used to have uncles and aunts and still have cousins, and, to boot, a town that is the birthplace of F.G. Scott. I hope you got to Glasgow all right at the end of last month and saw F.G. (who would be delighted to see you) and that your address to the Gaelic Society there went off all right. I wish I could get down to Inverness and be present on the occasion of your paper on the poetry of Livingston there next month: and indeed if steamer sailings had been normal I think I would have managed it – but as matters are with war-time curtailments and uncertainties of sailings it is out of the question.

I note Hood is with you in Hawick. Please give him my greetings. He asked me last year to lend him my material on John Maclean. I had hoped to have been in Edinburgh in the autumn and to have stayed with Hood and meant to take the material in question down with me then and give it to him. But the advent of War knocked all my arrangements sideways. Later I asked Davie if Hood was ready for the stuff, but I haven't heard from George since. So will you now ask Hood if he still wants it. If so, I can post it to him right away.

Talking of Hawick, my friend H.G. Taylor (who has lived here with me for a couple of years and acts as my secretary and typist) was in Hawick a few weeks ago seeing a friend of his – a Miss Tait, a school-teacher, whom perhaps you also know. Perhaps he met you too. Taylor is still holidaying in Dumfries but I expect him back soon now.

I note Calum[3] is in Dublin and hopes to meet Higgins. I do not expect he will have any difficulty but if he liked I would be glad to send him letters of introduction to Higgins and any of the others he'd like to meet. Please give Calum my kindest regards – also your brother John and his wife, whom I have pleasant memories of meeting at Edinbane.

I am very busy myself. I enclose a prospectus of my huge new poem. In addition to this 'enormity', I have also coming out this Spring my *Golden Treasury of Scottish Poetry* (via Macmillan) at long last, and my autobiography, *Lucky Poet*, which Messrs Victor Gollancz are publishing. As you will know the *Voice of Scotland* is temporarily suspended but I hope to restart it soon now.

Mike and Valda are both in good form and join me in warmest greetings to you, as does Dr Orr (here as *locum tenens* again for a while *vice* Dr MacCrimmon). I have written to Sutherland separately.

Yours, Christopher

---

1. Robert Garioch Sutherland (1909–81), poet and school teacher, wrote under the name Robert Garioch. Somhairle Mac Ghill-Eathain and Robert Garioch, *17 Poems for 6d: in Gaelic, Lowland Scots & English* (Edinburgh: Chalmers Press, 1940) was each poet's first collection.
2. They were to appear as *Dain do Eimhir agus Dain Eile* (Glaschu: W. MacLellan, 1943) – a book which is recognised as a major turning point in the world of modern Scottish Gaelic poetry.
3. Calum Iain MacLean, Sorley's brother, folk-song collector and author of *The Highlands* (London: Batsford, 1959).

4. *To Andrew Graham Grieve (EUL)*

Whalsay   18 March 1940

My dear Graham

Forgive me being long in writing. Both Valda and I have been down with flu' and are still feeling like deserted houses in a blizzard. Many thanks for your letter. I was glad so many friends were able to rally round you in your sorrow. And from the sad particulars you gave of Chryssie's illness and death one at least gleaned a little comfort from the knowledge that she passed unconsciously and therefore with less pain of mind and body than might have been the case – though even this little comfort is tragically offset by the fact that this very unconsciousness made it impossible for you to get through to her real self again. We felt very deeply from your letter the appalling shock that sudden collapse must have been to you – and our hearts were wrung by the thought of that long helpless wait you had by her bedside till the end came. Chryssie's death has affected me far more deeply than you can possibly realise. It seems out of keeping with my own attitude to things and I do not quite understand it myself; these things go very deep and at such depths few people have any real knowledge of themselves at all and the little they are ever able to glimpse often cannot be brought into line at all with their habitual conceptions of themselves and others. In any case, if, alas, we were unable to be with you or to give any of the ordinary practical tokens of our feeling, both Valda and I have felt Chryssie's death and your bereavement just as keenly as if it had happened in our own home, and I have had you and Angus and Morag constantly in my most anxious thoughts ever since. I do hope that physically you have all been able to sustain your ordeal without serious effects from the shock and all the readjustments you must all have had to make. I noted what you said about Morag – her reserve, her consequent difficulty of relieving her feelings. And that made me feel anew how little I really know of any of you – how poorly equipped I am to gauge how any of you are fitted psychologically or physically to cope with such a crisis; and that lack of knowledge gives an added edge to my anxiety on your behalf. Especially in these most unsettled and difficult times. I do not know how things are in the London area, but I have heard there is a great deal of flu' etc. in some parts of England and Scotland. So I hope you are all immune from whatever troubles may be rampant in your neighbourhood, since this lowered vitality you must all have been suffering from as a result of the shock you have sustained would render you more than usually liable to fall victims to such illnesses. Apart from bodily health, I appreciate that as matters stand at present all the ordinary routines of life must be exceptionally difficult – homekeeping, cooking etc. – and of course I don't know how these may be further complicated in your case by the exigencies of travelling – into and out from London, or perhaps, on wide official itineraries. At any rate, what these rather futile speculations are trying to express is a very real concern as to how things are with you in every way, and I will be glad if you can find time to write me. These are not good times for much corresponding – and up here I am so cut off from knowledge of all sorts of things that letter-writing of any useful sort is very difficult: but I think we should try to draw a little closer together and write each other more regularly than we have done in the past.

My various books are going ahead (not without war-time difficulties of all kinds too, of course) and you'll hear about them in due time. At the moment I am literally drowned in proofs, and proof-reading is a peculiarly vexatious business to a fluified head.

Love to you all from all here.

Yours, Chris

5. *To Douglas Young (NLS)*

Whalsay   Friday [Postmark 22 March 1940]

Dear Douglas Young

I have just received your latest letter. I have an idea that I failed to reply to an earlier letter of yours. If so, I am very sorry; the discourtesy was quite unintentional and due solely to the pressure of circumstances, the endless difficulties the War multiplies in the way of keeping activities like mine going from a remote place like this.

I see the *S.I.* [*Scots Independent*] regularly of course and am delighted to know that its sales are going up so much – though I must add that I find much of its matter simply imbecile, e.g. my friend Gunn's article in the last issue on a Scottish view of Stalin. Just another appalling revelation of one of those semantic blockages which are responsible for humanity's chronic un-sanity.

I'll look forward to the new series you write about however, and will be very glad to contribute to it. I should like, if I may, to take both Thomas Muir[1] and John Maclean. Will you let me know by what date you would like to have these articles in hand, and I will see to it.

At the moment I am bogged in proofs – with three big books coming out. 1) *Golden Treasury of Scottish Poetry*. 2) *Autobiography*. 3) A huge poem called *Mature Art*.

I mean to revive the *Voice of Scotland* at the earliest possible moment but cannot yet say just when that will be. I believe that ere long things will be not only much worse than they are with us just now but worse than we can possibly conceive – sheer and apparently bottomless chaos!

I am delighted to hear of your – and Hay's – projected gallimaufry, and will look forward eagerly to this. You do not need my permission to use in this any material either of you contributed to the *V of S* but if you did need such permission it would of course be only too gladly given.

How is Hay? I knew he was 'on service', but have not heard from him again. I am anxious to keep in touch with both him and you, and if you too are caught up in this infernal business and feel like writing me once in a while I'll be very glad and make a point of replying to you promptly. In any case please accept my warmest good wishes for your safe re-emergence from this beastly business and the speediest possible resumption of those infinitely more important services typified by your recent work for the *S.I.* and the Scottish Cause generally.

Yours for Scotland, C.M. Grieve

There is another article I'd like to send you – long enough to make 3 of 1500 words each – and so it would have to appear in three or more instalments. It is a wide-ranging view of a great tract of little-known Scottish biography – insisting upon the significance of elements hitherto misprised and misrepresented because incompatible with the Anglo-Scottish set up – and bringing out in a remarkable way not only certain key differences of Scottish temperament and tendency compared with English, but showing a strong strain in successive generations of leading Scottish medical men of anti-English feeling and a sense of the way their scientific work was frustrated by the great English professional organisations and of the very different and mutually exclusive lines upon which really significant Scottish thought must proceed in regard to these subjects as compared with English thought on them.

---

1. Thomas Muir (1765–99), Scottish Advocate and radical reformer transported for sedition in 1793.

6. *To F.G. Scott (EUL)*

Whalsay   13 July 1940

My dear F.G.

I wonder what you are doing with yourself this vacation, and wish to God I had you here. Taylor is away, Aberdeen local Tribunal turned him down and he's appealing – like Hay and Douglas Young.[1] Orr has just gone South too. So I am very much alone. I've been wondering how you found Saurat whose projected articles in the *Times Lit.* events outran – anxious to hear how Burt is keeping – and to hear how the Michael Bruce commemoration passed off. The other book contract I mentioned in my last materialised all right: and there are fresh hopes of the *Autobiography* being published. Macmillan's latest catalogue gives September as a provisional time of publication for the *Golden Treasury* the delay of which has of course nothing to do with me at all but is purely a matter of trade difficulties through war time exigencies. I'm very busy and in good form but feeling hellish cut off and desperately short of reading matter and news of all kinds. Valda and Mike are O.K. I hope you are all well.

Love to you all. Yours, Chris

P.S. Re enclosed, verse 3 line 3
    'All, all is beautiful, but what we men
    oorsels think and dae when we forget'

gives my thought much clearer than the shorter 'we oorsels think and dae wha forget' but is, I suppose, hopelessly cumbrous.

And verse 4, line 4, my first draft reads
  'through the windas o' a body that isna free'
which seems better in some ways than the shorter 'o' a body no' free', which I first thought of as 'o' a body no' yet free' but felt wouldn't do either.

Also, verse 2, lines 2 and 3, could end *lust* and *dust* respectively instead of *power* and *stour*, and instead of *coup*, we might put *whummle* or just *lay* or *ha'e*.

I see advertised in *Times Literary Supplement* a book on the *Scots Literary Tradition* by John Spiers (Chatto and Windus 7/6). I haven't seen it yet but it may be good. It claims to cover the whole field up to today. I knew Spiers in London. He's an Aberdeen man; Cambridge graduate – one of Leavis's group – subsequently Lecturer in Latvia.

I note what you say about the slithy Edwin.
  'The slithy toves did gyre and gimble
  And the mome raths outgrabe...'
I was pleased to read his unspeakable long 'Refugees' poem in the *New Alliance*. If this is the kind of poetry he'd rather be writing he'd a thousand times better concentrate on nothing but his BBC talks. I re-read my own 4000 line Spanish War poem with great satisfaction after reading his 'Refugees'.

---

1. All conscientious objectors. Young and Taylor were imprisoned and both Taylor and George Campbell Hay saw military service overseas.

7. *To F.G. Scott (EUL)*

Whalsay   Wednesday, 28 August 1940

My dear F.G.

So, as the Shetlanders say. The French *si!* I am glad to have your letter and am of course extremely sorry to hear of Saurat's domestic troubles. As to the rest, it is pretty much as I of course knew it would be – only I hadn't realised that the Gaulle show had been abandoned – I thought a terrific much ado about nothing stunt would be still in full blast, and pictured Saurat in the heart of it, in a hell of perpetual phone calls, conferences and what not! Circumstances do not permit me to comment on the state of affairs you report but in any case there's no need – you know my view. As to the religious business I'm not surprised – you'll remember how in the *New English Weekly*, reviewing his *History of Religions*, I pointed out his Fascist and 'religious' destination![1] And his shocked and amused disclaimer which he gave you in Glasgow and you conveyed to me at Gilgal. Well, well! And now here's Muir with his ridiculous autobiography about his little personal psychological Whipsnade, where, indeed, it's brillig all the time! A beastly book in every sense of the adjective.[2]

Well, I'm certainly having no luck with that sort of thing at all.

I'd heard Tonge was with Reid and Lefevre in London.[3] Indeed he met a Communist friend of mine in London and said he was an old friend of mine. My Comrade wrote post haste to tell me of that (to him) preposterous claim – he simply couldn't believe I'd ever known Tonge or had two minutes use for him. Honest to goodness fellows like this Comrade haven't any idea what strange bedfellows we who are working on the intellectual and aesthetic fronts have to put up with. I wrote Tonge twice I think after his Scottish Art book appeared, congratulating him on it and suggesting that he might let me have his news now and again. But he never replied. Not a cheep!

As to Johnstone, of course, the boot has been on the other foot. I felt that he might think I'd let him down over the proposed Johnstone issue of the *Voice of Scotland*, with blocks of his pictures etc., though I wasn't in any way to blame, and couldn't help, the sudden emergence of the war time difficulties which inhibited that issue and brought the venture to an end. I'll drop him a note now, if I haven't done so before it's simply that letter writing nowadays is for the most part so futile.

I have been fully alive all along to the Chisholm-Dunedin Society-MMM-Celtic Ballet-Willa Muir racket. Alison Shepard keeps me *au courant*. I've given her the low down on the whole business several times – but it's no good. God only grant I never have to see and hear any ballet with which the egregious Willa has had anything to do! The Chinese death of the thousand cuts would be a little playful tickling by comparison. But never mind how Chisholm[4] thinks he's using you and camouflaging the subsidisation of the publication of a symphony of his by letting a fraction of the money that costs go to the publishing of a new selection of songs by yourself. Get anything you can out of the blighters.

I hope that Vol VI of *Scottish Lyrics* comes off all right.

I enclose Speirs' book. (My Spain typescript – only copy in existence – is still in Manchester. I've written for it urgently 3 or 4 times during past month or so, but can't evoke any reply let alone return of poem yet. If it comes by next mail I'll enclose it with Speirs book – if not, I'll send it to you immediately it does come.) [Added in margin: Later – no! It hasn't come yet.]

As to Speirs book I'm saying nothing just now: but I equipped my *Golden Treasury* with a fairly longish essay, supplementary to the prefatory one, in front of the notes in which I state the facts as to the continuing prevalence of Scots, on school teachers' and employers' evidence published in various quarters, etc., the extent to which the children 'think' in Scots and translate into English, the scientific findings in regard to the relationship between thinking and language, the actual testimony of writers themselves who use Scots (testimony which Speirs, Muir and all such so loftily ignore – because they do not know where to find it and are neither intelligent enough nor honest enough – if intelligent and honest are not completely invisible in this and most other connections! – to appreciate the implications of these confessions and see them in their proper literary historical and political bearings.) All this sounds pretentious enough. But in fact I've done it quite succinctly and with a lighter touch than usual, and it is a thoroughly effective reply in brief to the Muir-Speirs position.

I'll send you some more poems shortly – one of my troubles just now is that the sort of poems apropos the world situation I'm writing just now cannot pass through the mails. But I'm accumulating a fine body of stuff through which anger goes like a blast from a furnace – that will at least stand as a testimony that there was a brain or two in Scotland completely immune to all the dopes.

---

1. Denis Saurat, *A History of Religions* (London: Cape, 1934).
2. Edwin Muir, *The Story and the Fable: An Autobiography* (London: Harrap, 1940)
3. John Tonge (A.T. Cunninghame), author of *The Arts of Scotland* (London: Kegan, Trench, Trubner & Co., 1938). Along with James H. Whyte, Tonge was involved in the production of *The Modern Scot*, a progressive periodical of the 1930s. Whyte was the dedicatee of *On a Raised Beach* and, along with Prince Dimitry Mirsky and Tonge, shared the dedication of *In Memoriam James Joyce*. Reid and Lefevre were London art dealers.
4. Erik Chisholm (1904–65): Glasgow-born composer, appointed Professor of Music at the University of Cape Town in 1945.

8. *To F.G. Scott (NLS, DFF)*

Whalsay   Monday, 23 September 1940

My dear F.G.

Many thanks for the Shaw. I am so short these days of reading material of any kind at all that I have been glad to re-read it too. But I have certainly not got much out of it. Not nearly so much as out of the Saurat typescript even. What I object to in the latter is that a wealth of extremely interesting material is handled owing to an innocence of or antipathy to scientific method in precisely the same way as the moon is handled by someone who insists that it is made of green cheese (which is exactly the order of thing upon which the quarrel between Science and Art is maintained – and no doubt the assertion, that the moon is made of gorgonzola, is essentially poetic as distinct from factual in a way that my intermissions with lunar geography, e.g. [in 'Stony Limits']

> ... Save where Arzachel or Langrenus allures
> Such spirits as ours, and the Straight Wall Stands ...

are not well-founded). It is certainly in keeping with Saurat's own anti-aesthetic predilection for poets like Blake and Hugo — a wonderful couple to serve up to me in this particular connection of my 'verse indistinguishable from prose'! I read Valda a couple of swatches of Blake just now; but she missed my point because she did not understand that they purported to be poetry at all, and took them as prose. And I certainly do not agree for a moment that Blake and Hugo paint on any stupendous canvas. On the contrary! They manipulate all the Big Words of course — but all the Big Words died in the *last* war.

Excuse my scribbling in pencil: but I have quite a lot to say and I have neuritis in my fingers and find pen and ink troublesome. First of all then a poem. [CMG encloses here the poem 'Two Memories', *Complete Poems*, vol. 1, p. 671.]

You probably saw the damnably malignant review of Eliot's *East Coker* poem in [this or last] week's *Times Literary Supplement* — the product of one of their infernal spinster-bitches, and certainly in keeping with the tone and matter of their putrid patriotic leaders and the notion that there is matter for epic in the current exploits of the RAF — Shaw's 'Boy Scout romanticism', all right.

This attack on Eliot's 'bare bones' poetry forgets amongst other things that the thing by no means began with Eliot but with one of the panjandrums, one of the great established names to whom the *T.L.S.* is wont to kowtow. These mindless swine do not even know their own English Literature. This is what Matthew Arnold said — and I say it again, and nail it as a branch to my mast in this matter: —

'More and more I feel that the difference between a mature and a youthful age of the world compels the poetry of the former to use great plainness of speech as compared with that of the latter; and that Keats and Shelley were on a false track when they set themselves to reproduce the exuberance of expression, the charm, the richness of images, and the felicity of the Elizabethan poets. Yet critics cannot get to learn this, because the Elizabethan poets are our greatest, and our canons of poetry are founded on their works. They still think that the object of poetry is to produce exquisite bits and images — like Shelley's *clouds shepherded by the slow unwilling wind*, and Keats *passim*; whereas modern poetry can only subsist by its *contents*; by becoming a complete *magister vitae* as the poetry of the ancients did: by including, as theirs did, religion with poetry, instead of existing as poetry only, and leaving religious wants to be supplied by the [MS ends]

9. *To A.D. Mackie (NLS)*

Whalsay   8 March 1941

My dear Mackie

    When I wrote you a few days ago I forgot one thing I had meant to write about. As you know I have been up here 7 to 8 years, living off writing books – not a fat income at best writing the sort of books I do – plus a certain amount of free-lance journalism. The latter, which was very useful, had, however, dwindled to next to nothing before the outbreak of this War, and as soon as War was declared I recognised that I was in for a very bad time unless I could find some way of augmenting my earnings. So I cast about to see if I couldn't get back into regular journalism, or find something else – clerical, secretarial or such – that might do, temporarily at least. But of course I found that newspapers were cutting down, free-lance contributions being practically cut out. One or two said they might need men later on as men being called into the Army etc. reduced their staffs, so they'd put me on the waiting list and communicate if and when anything offered. I have heard no more. A column a week for a couple of papers would have seen me through all right and enabled me to remain here and carry on my own work at the same time; but I couldn't get it. Papers like the *Glasgow Herald* and the *Scotsman* simply wouldn't give me anything at all – not even a little reviewing.

    One of the difficulties of being way up here is that one doesn't see any useful advts. in time to apply, but I've had several friends on the look-out for anything of that sort that might be offering and ready to wire me at once so that I might apply timeously. But there have been no such jobs ongoing it seems.

    As the time has lengthened out since the start of the War things have got steadily more and more difficult and I can't hold on any longer unless I get hold of something. I don't want to bother you with this, but it occurred to me that you'd at least be in a position to know how matters were going with Scottish newspaper staffs and possibly even outside of Glasgow itself to hear of any local paper job that might be offering. If so, I'd be mighty glad if you could put me wise or out of your own knowledge suggest anything you think I might try. I recognise that it will be no easy matter for me to get a job in any case. Most of the Scottish papers wouldn't have me in a gift in any capacity. But there may be some niche I could fill – even in a temporary capacity. In this connection I should add that I'm not looking for any big job – editorial chair or even sub-editorship. What I'd like best would be a reportership on a local weekly paper. But I would pro tem be willing to take absolutely anything. If you know or hear of anything, be a good fellow and send me the necessary particulars in a telegraphic letter – the postal service is a very unreliable quantity; if you wanted to advise me of anything you could not be sure I'd receive any letter you might send, other than telegraphic, in less than 10 days.

Apart from any specific vacancy, I'd be glad if you would
[MS ends]

10. *To Sorley MacLean (NLS)*

Whalsay, Shetland   2 April 1941

My dear Somhairle

It was a great treat to get your letter. I remember well how in my own experience last War the conditions of army life (congenial in many ways as I found them – more congenial than anything I've had since) militated against letter-writing and literary pursuits etc., but such a fallow time may prove later to have been no bad thing. I read all you say about the political situation with great sympathy and in detail not without agreement with you, tho' on balance I regard the Axis powers, tho' far more violently evil for the time being, less dangerous than our own Govmt. in the long run – and indistinguishable in purpose if not in the present pace of that purpose, tho' in some vital respects the greater speed is being shown now by our own rulers.

The Conservatives have now practically every section of our people 'in the bag', and the labour movement has scarcely a vestige of any effective minority who realise how completely – and perhaps irreversibly – they have been sold. No wonder the P.M. can go out of his way to express the profound satisfaction he and his cronies feel at Britain's possession of a strong Trade Union body, under Gauleiter Bevin.[1] For reasons you will realise I cannot go into these issues fully here – I may try to do so in a form that will pass in a longer letter ere long. So far as Scotland is concerned I am glad that there is one healthy development – the steady if subterranean progress of the Workers' Republican groups. Not only Miller's paper and Arthur Donaldson's[2] *Scottish News and Comment*: the latest is the fact that whereas at the People's Convention meeting in London nothing was said at all about Scottish Independence, despite a strong resolution to that effect from the subordinate Scottish People's Convention, now the London people have been compelled to agree to a considerable measure of Scottish autonomy in this organisation, Miller and others have won on to the Executive, Pearson of the Mineworkers and others (mainly C.P.ers) have been won over to a recognition of Scottish Independence, and all is now set fair for the establishment of the Scottish People's Convention equal in status to the English body. It is along these lines that the real and only hope so far as we are concerned is moving, and moving at last I think to some purpose.

As to the *Golden Treasury* I enclose a copy of the *Times Lit. Supp.* review in case you haven't seen it, because it is the best the volume has evoked and because as you will see it pays special attention to the Gaelic translations. In its view that I make out my case against Muir in the Scots being a better medium for Scottish writers than English – and in its welcome of the possibility of live developments in Scots literature – it is at one with most of the more important reviews in English papers (many of them by well-known writers) e.g. Louis MacNiece in the *New Statesman*, Edmund Blunden in the *Book Society News*, and Naomi Royde Smith in *Time and Tide*. In contrast to this generous recognition of and welcome for the differences of the Scottish tradition and the possibilities of Scots and Gaelic in the English papers, the Scottish papers' reviews were not only very short and quite inadequate, failing to recognise the importance of the book, quite hostile to any such developments, and in most cases went out of their way to condemn me personally while taking good care not to join issue in any genuine debate on the contentions I put forward. In a word they showed themselves plus royaliste que le Roi – more English than the English – and completely neither more nor less than reactionary Eng. Lit's Fifth Column in Scotland. In general this did not surprise me: but the virulence of the attacks on myself, and the total dismissal of the book, did – tho' it is a welcome measure of the alarm of these people and their recognition that they have failed, and despite all their efforts will probably continue to fail, to arrest the developments (associated with my name) which they detest so much.

I think the book has probably sold very well: and I understand that Macmillan's are now putting out an American edition of it.

In other ways America is coming more into my orbit. Two American firms wrote me recently with proposals to issue selections of my poems. I accepted the proposals of the Colt Press, San Francisco, and that book will be out this autumn – prefaced by Horace Gregory, the Irish-American Socialist poet and critic, and strongly supported by Edmund Wilson[3] of *The New Republic*, the ablest Marxian literary critic, I think, in the English-speaking world. The other firm was New Directions, Norfolk, Connecticut, and I am still in correspondence with them but in any case they are to publish a long piece (1000 lines or so) of my big unpublished poem in *New Directions*, 1941 (which comes out this back-end) a big magazine-book of advanced prose and poetry they issue annually. Some of my Left Wing poems have also been appearing in the *New Tribune*, Canada, which, however, has just been suspended for a warning period of three weeks.

My *Autobiography* was to have been out this Spring, but the publishers (Methuen's) have found, no doubt owing to the London blitzes and other war conditions, that they cannot have it ready until September. I think I told you my total MSS amounted to over half a million words – hopeless proposition just now, and, perhaps, at any time – and it was finally decided to split it up into 3 separate volumes of 150,000 words each. This is the first of these and consists of the parts dealing with myself as poet, my ideas on poetry etc., leaving to a second volume my reminiscences of Yeats, A.E., etc. etc. and to a third my personal and domestic revelations. So it will be a big book and with all the proofs to read and many matters to consider carefully since the cutting about of the original means that unless I watch the transitions carefully this volume will be hopelessly lacunous and disjointed, I am glad publication is to be later. I'll need all the time.

I am of course busy too with my Faroes book – a sort of companion volume to my book on the Scottish Islands.[4]

We've had a very long trying winter here but are all fairly fit. All join in kindest love to you. My best wishes also to your father and mother and all your family. Write soon again and I'll try to respond with a less scrappy reply.

Yours, Chris

---

1. Ernest Bevin (1881–1951), Secretary of the Transport and General Workers Union, 1921–40 and Minister of Labour and National Service in Churchill's coalition government.
2. Harry (James Harrison) Miller (Wheeler): see Appendix. Arthur Donaldson, poultry farmer, editor of *The Scottish News and Comment*, founder of the United Scotland Movement, Chairman of the SNP through the 1960s.
3. Horace Gregory (1898–1982), American poet and critic. Edmund Wilson (1895–1972), American critic and author of the landmark of literary criticism *Axel's Castle* (1931), edited the *New Republic* 1926–31. James Laughlin edited *New Directions in Prose and Poetry 1941*, including MacDiarmid's 'The Divided Bird', pp. 220–9.
4. This book was never finished.

11. *To the Rt. Hon. Thomas Johnston, P.C., M.P., H.M. Secretary of State for Scotland (NAS)*

Sudheim, Whalsay, via Lerwick, The Shetland Islands   25 May 1941

Dear Comrade

It is a good few years now since I wrote you – in connection with the Dundee Burghers bye-election, at a time when I was a member of Montrose ILP and a Socialist member of Montrose Town Council and JP for the County of Angus: but you may recall my name perhaps, if not in that connection, at least as that of a well-known Scottish writer.

I am writing you today in the hope that you may be able to do something for me with regard to the seizure of an important typescript of mine of about 20,000 words – 'A Brief Survey of Modern Scottish Politics in the Light of Dialectical Materialism'. This was seized during the recent raids and domiciliary searches on Scottish nationalists and republicans in Glasgow, Edinburgh, Aberdeen etc.[1] It was in the possession of Mr H.J. Miller, the editor of the *Scots Socialist*, whose home address is 54 Arrowsmith Avenue, Glasgow W.3. There is no excuse whatever for the CID seizure of this MSS, which I am anxious to recover as speedily as possible. It is a historical survey and analysis, was written before the War, and does not deal with the War in any way.

Neither I nor any of the Scots Republicans who have been raided have had any subsidisation from or dealings with the German Nazis – nor any subsidisation from any other foreign source. The whole thing is a base English Imperialist manoeuvre to throttle and libel the now rapidly growing Scottish Socialist Republican Movement – and to divert public attention from the pro-Nazi Fifth Column traitors who are not to be found in our ranks but in the ranks of our aristocracy, plutocracy, and the Government itself, where there are plenty who will sell us out to Hitler if they get a chance – tho' they are posing meanwhile as the most active and vocal of 'patriots'. English Imperialism (the interrogations of those raided show) is specially anxious about, and eager by hook or, more likely, crook to destroy the affiliations many of my associates and I myself have with the Breton, Cymric, Irish and Indian movements.

Apart from the purely political aspect of the matter, the seizure of my MSS calls for the strongest protest and immediate action, as does the utterly unwarrantable interference with Free Speech and Scottish cultural interests represented by the raids on *The Scots Socialist*, the *Free Man*, and *Scottish News and Comment*, and the internment of Arthur Donaldson, the editor of the last-mentioned, in Barlinnie. Douglas Young, of Aberdeen, is another Scottish author who has been raided, questioned, and grossly victimised in this way by the English Gestapo, and further cases are those of Mrs Hay of Edinburgh, mother of George Campbell Hay, the Scottish Gaelic poet and literary essayist, and – worst of all – the Rev John MacKechnie[2] of Glasgow, whose houses have been twice searched and who has had seized from him invaluable Gaelic MSS by great 18th Century Scottish poets like Iain Lom and Alasdair Mac Mhaighstir Alasdair, simply because they are in Gaelic and ipso facto objects of suspicion to our ignorant English and Anglo-Scottish CID people.

Apart from these matters, as yourself a distinguished Scottish historian, you must be aware that all the legislation under which conscription and other war-time measures are being applied in Scotland, is utterly illegal[3] and represents a deliberate and systematic violation by the English Government of one of the safeguarding clauses of the Act of Union. In this connection I beg to conclude this letter by entering my most emphatic protest against your Government's illegal detention without trial, and removal furth of Scotland, of Matthew Hamilton, the Scots law student, who has done invaluable work in exposing the way in which the English Government has illegally subverted the Scottish Law, violated the solemn undertakings of the Act of Union which must therefore be now considered abrogated, persisted in applying in Scotland enactments which it has no shadow or right to impose and which are utterly opposed to the interests of the Scottish people.

Yours sincerely, Christopher Murray Grieve ('Hugh MacDiarmid')[4]

1. In a co-ordinated action at 6 am on 2 May 1941, acting on instructions from MI5, police raided the homes of seventeen Scottish nationalists.
2. Afterwards lecturer in Celtic at the University of Aberdeen.
3. In a letter of 18 June 1941, the Secretary of State replied that 'Defence Regulation 88A authorises the issue of search warrants if ... there is reasonable ground for suspecting that evidence bearing upon the commission by certain persons of acts prejudicial to the public safety or the defence of the realm will be found on the premises specified ... I have had the most explicit assurances that the action taken had no connection with the advocacy of Scottish Nationalism.'
4. CMG's letters in the NAS were revealed by Arnold Kemp in an article in the *Observer*, 22 February 1998, p.4.

12. To The Lord Chancellor *(NLS, DFF)*

[Whalsay]   [1941]

My Lord[1]

As a Scottish magistrate and member of HM Commission of the Peace for the County of Angus I write to ask your ruling in a grave matter which has been giving increasing anxiety to me, and, to my knowledge, to many other magistrates all over Scotland.

It is this. That owing to the deliberate, systematic, and unscrupulous violation by the authorities of the safeguarding provisions relating to Scottish Law in the Act of Union (under which alone Westminster legislation is applicable to this country), this amounts to unilateral repudiation of the basis of Union, and there is therefore no law in this country and the Union must be considered null and void and in particular the enactments applying conscription, censorship, and other war-time measures to Scotland are wholly *ultra vires* and while the presently established authorities may have the right to enforce these, and to penalise Scots for non-obedience, they are, in enforcing them, acting illegally and have no tittle of right other than brute force to act in this way.

In particular the prolonged imprisonment without trial and removal in custody furth of Scotland of Matthew Hamilton, the Scots law student whose brilliant researches and splendid courage have exposed the utter illegality of the present legal system in this connection is a grave scandal cutting at the root of all justice in Scotland, and in that connection I beg leave to protest to you in the most emphatic fashion, while on the general issue which seems to entirely undercut the authority of all judges and magistrates in Scotland today I earnestly beseech you to favour me with your considered ruling and advice in this most serious matter.

I have the honour to be, Sir,
Your faithful servant, Christopher Murray Grieve.

P.S. As your Lordship probably knows, a number of the Scottish objectors to military service have based their pleas to exemption on the grounds of the illegality of applying the Military Service Act and other war-time measures to Scotland, and it seems to me, and to many others, that in enforcing such legislation and dismissing the appeals of such protestors and subjecting them to compulsory military service and (or other) penalties, the Judges and Tribunals have been acting quite indefensibly and disregarding the fundamental rights of the Scottish people as by law established and expressly guaranteed in the Act of Union.

This matter has not only engaged my attention as a magistrate and citizen, but as a professional author with an international reputation, who has written and published many books on Scottish matters.

I have recently been invited by the Bar Association of several foreign countries and by leading journals in these countries to submit to them memoranda on these matters, and am taking steps to do so.

If your Lordship cares, I will be happy to send you a detailed statement embodying the results of my researches into this matter, and/or to answer any questions or submit to you any further information to the best of my ability which your Lordship may desire to have.

C.M.G.

---

1. Sir John Allsebrook Simon, first-Viscount Simon. See Appendix.

13. *To J.H. Miller, Editor,* Scots Socialist
[Copy sent to the Ministry of Information] (NAS)

Ministry of Information/Postal Censorship/Terminal Mails/
(Private Branch)
Submitted to M.I.12, London/M.I.12, Edinburgh/S.O. Scottish Command/S.O. No.2 P.A./Date of letter submitted 24.6.41

<u>COMMENT</u>
<u>Letter Sent On</u>
Letter reads as follows:

'I hope that the dislocations and difficulties in which recent events have involved you are now straightening out and that the *S.S.* [*Scots Socialist*] will forge ahead and become the power in the land it ought to be. I was glad to get the current number. Congratulations. It is a very effective issue. Full of excellent stuff.

'I hope the Mutual Aid Committee[1] will now be able to get on a solid footing and play a very active part. Also the Scottish Civil Liberties Council. I've never heard anything further about this since I wrote accepting the request that I should become Vice President.

'I particularly wish something could be done to force forward the legal issue. Couldn't this systematic violation of Scots Law by the Executor – and the monstrous injustice of the Matthew Hamilton case – be dealt with by means of a Petition to the King over the head of the Government altogether. That would force the whole issue into the open.

'I sent you a copy of my letter to the Lord Chancellor and hope you got this all right. Lord Simon replied simply that he could not give me any advice on the matter! I do not intend to let it rest at that. Scottish Magistrates should not consent to administer the law in minor matters while the Executors violate it in major matters!

'I have just had a letter from the Secretary for Scotland. He says that my essay "Brief Survey of Scottish Politics" was never in the hands of the Police and that he has learned that you posted it to me early this month. Is this the case? Because if so it has not reached me. I'm sorry to bother you, but perhaps you registered it or even if you didn't this notification that it hasn't arrived there may enable you to take up the matter with the Post Office people.

'All the best. I hope you are in good care and that your home is again intact and all your papers, books etc. restored to effective working order after CID handling.

'Yours for Scotland.'

---

1. The Mutual Aid Committee was set up by a group of nationalists to assist objectors or their families.

14. *To Douglas Stewart (NLS, DFF)*

[Whalsay] [1941]

Dear Douglas Stewart,

I am delighted to have your brief note and eager to know your news in all the detail that may be possible. As you will understand, I am virtually marooned up here and get little or no news. I have no idea at all of the matters to which you refer, but if there are any developments afoot I am keen to hear about them and to associate myself with them in any way I possibly can. I have had no cause to imagine that letters to me are interfered with in any way – nothing in my mail so far has borne any signs of anything of this sort – on the other hand, I know that letters going out from here are subject to surveillance.

I had hoped to have been in Edinburgh about the end of this month, but the various engagements I had to speak in Edinburgh, Glasgow and St Andrews under the auspices of the Verse-Speaking Association and other bodies have been cancelled, and their usual writer syllabi abandoned owing to war-time exigencies.

I am in good form and busy with several new books I have in hand. I am glad to hear from your note that you are in fine shape too, so in the meantime I will conclude with kindest regards and best wishes for the success of yourself and your friends in the matters in question.

Yours for Scotland [Unsigned]

15. *To Oliver Brown (NLS)*

Sudheim, Whalsay, Shetland   12 July 1941

Dear Oliver Brown

Many thanks for your two splendid pamphlets, *Hitlerism In The Highlands* and *War For Freedom or Finance*.[1] It was very kind of you to send them to me. My trouble here is that I am so cut off that I don't see about lots of things I would like in time to procure copies. I expect there are other pamphlets of yours I have missed; if you could let me have a list, I could send for those I haven't got, if still available. Your Highlands pamphlet is a most useful store and contains a lot of items new to me, and otherwise difficult of access, which I am exceedingly glad to have. There is a better revelation in one of Wolfe's letters of the cynical murderous attitude to Scottish soldiers traditional of English militarism; and no less a figure than Oliver Cromwell expressed himself of the same sentiment with like brutal frankness on one occasion.

Re the other pamphlet I noted recently in the *Labour Monthly* in one of Palme Dutte's editorial notes an excellent exposure and condemnation of the machinations of Sir James Lithgow in 'concentrating' the shipping industry after the last war – with the incisive and wholly justified conclusion that if Britain lost the Battle of the Atlantic Sir James Lithgow would be very largely responsible.[2] A quotation of this would have been a useful addition to your armoury of facts in this most effectively compiled pamphlet.

I am delighted that you find it possible to keep on putting out such things under present conditions and hope (and have no fear) you will be able to keep on keeping on in this way. Owing to paper shortage and publishing trade difficulties a lot of my work is presently held in a log jam: but I am hoping that some of it will break away soon. My *Autobiography* should be out in September (via Methuen's) unless conditions worsen in the interval; and I have a biggish volume of new poems (provisionally scheduled for August publication) being put out by the Colt Press, San Francisco, and other long poems appearing this Autumn in *New Directions* (Norfolk, Connecticut, USA).

It's a long time since we met. I haven't been off this little island for three years now. I wish I could get to Glasgow and have a long talk – or series of talks – with you and Miller and Donaldson, etc. But that'll have to wait alas! I do hope the *SS* [*Scots Socialist*] can keep going, also Donaldson's *SN & C* [*Scottish News & Comment*], (though – in regard to the former – Archie Lamont was badly 'off his eggs' in his comments on Russia, Finland etc. in last issue).

You'll understand why it is impossible, in lieu of actual talk together, for me to attempt to go into matters at all in this letter.

However, please accept my thanks and heartiest congratulations and earnest hope to be further greatly indebted to you in like wise.

Yours for Scotland, C.M. Grieve

---

1. Oliver Brown, *Hitlerism In The Highlands* (Glasgow: The Author, 1940). *War For Freedom or Finance* (London: Independent Labour Party, 1941).
2. Rajani Palme Dutt (1896–1974), Stalinist, leading theorist of the CPGB. Sir James Lithgow (1883–1952), Port Glasgow shipbuilder. After inheriting their father's business in 1908, he and his brother Henry made a series of acquisitions and diversified the company into areas of coal, iron and steel, marine-engineering and ship-owning.

16. *To The Editor,* The Shetland News *(NLS, DFF)*

Sudheim, Whalsay   15 September 1941

Sir: –

As you explained in a recent issue you refused to print certain letters of mine written in reply to violent personal abuse published in your columns, because you did not agree with my interpretation of the 'criticisms' in question. This is a novel editorial doctrine. When a man is thus publicly vilified it is surely his interpretation of the attacks made upon him – and not yours – that counts and he ought to be allowed to reply. Presumably, since you have published it, you agree with the 'interpretation' made of my personality and work by your correspondent who signs himself 'Contemptuous' (it ought to be 'Contemptible', since he lacks the courage to attach his name to his precious effusion). I agree with it too, in the main. I am an impenitent highbrow, utterly contemptuous of public opinion, concerned almost exclusively with matters which are 'caviare to the general', intolerant, quarrelsome, and, no doubt, inordinately conceited. I make no bones about any of these things, since I do not subscribe at all to conventional morality, and your correspondent must just 'like it or lump it'. It is customary humbug to pretend that arrogance, intolerance, and conceit do not consort with true greatness, but the fact of the matter is, as literary and artistic history in all countries and all ages shows conclusively, that most writers and artists are overweeningly vain, self-assured, and intolerant – and that these faults of character (if such they be) are very far from being incompatible with the highest literary and artistic gifts. Hypocritical humility which is really only a very similar vanity – but in this case unaccompanied by sterling gifts – is, on the other hand, the great stand-by of irremediable mediocrity, and this your correspondent exemplifies to the full, together with the characteristic inconsistency of rebuking another man in public for 'rudeness' in a far ruder letter than any the latter wrote.

Your correspondent also errs in suggesting that I am contemptuous of the Shetland people. This is not the case, as my writings about them abundantly attest; my contempt is confined to certain sections and in certain connections.

Your correspondent asks where I have made any detailed criticism, destructive or otherwise, of Shetland literature. He will find a good deal of it in a 300,000[-word] volume of autobiography which a leading firm of London publishers are producing in the Spring – a book, incidentally in which all my other notorious 'faults' are exemplified to the full. It would be a good idea to let your correspondent review that book in your columns, and then compare his findings with those of the leading critics in the principal
[MS ends]

17. *To Andrew Graham Grieve (EUL)*

Whalsay, Shetland   21 October 1941

My dear Graham,

It's a long time since I heard from, or wrote to, you – whether I'm to blame in the sense of it's being my turn to write I dunno. One loses track of things in the cut-off-ness of conditions here. And I have no news anyway. Owing to conditions in the publishing and printing trades my autobiography in this country and one of the two volumes of poetry I have appearing in America are held over now to Spring; the other American volume I've had no news of for months but I'm afraid it's in like case. Such delays and disappointments – and the detail worries of all kinds attendant upon them – are the sum total of my days just now.

I hope you all had a better summer and contrived good holidays of some sort, and that this finds you all in good shape.

Some year or two ago you said something in one of your letters about some books (school-books I took it) of Angus's and Morag's which might be useful for Mike. But probably most of these got 'dumped' at Woking. What I'm wondering is whether amongst such things no longer of use to Angus and Morag there is such a thing as a good Geography book or two and a serviceable Atlas. These would be very useful indeed if you have such lying spare about your establishment. Mike is just beginning Geography – and the book they use in the school here is the very worst primer of its kind I've ever seen, and the maps in it hopelessly bad (as well as badly printed, with microscopic lettering of place names – and Mike's eyes aren't strong and the light here in any case poor, i.e. oil-lamps). So if you can dig out anything of this sort it would be very useful. I don't happen to have any geography stuff among my own books, nor atlas nor gazeteer; and of course I've been out of touch with that sort of thing for far too long now to have any idea of what the best current textbooks on such subjects are. But don't worry, of course, if you haven't superannuated specimens on the premises. I'm just mentioning this on the off-chance.

Mike had just gone back to school after his Tattie holidays a few days ago when a prevalence of whooping-cough on the Island necessitated another three weeks' closing of the schools – and the weather is foul and the days very short and the nights very long and black so he is not having a very happy time, poor fellow. Things were a bit better during the aforesaid Tattie vacation: and he put in a great deal of stout work fishing, and kept us in plenty of fish. Not like our days in the Esk and Ewes when to catch anything was a nine-days' wonder: here close inshore there are hosts of fish they call 'sillocks' (1st year Saithe) and it is these mostly (but occasionally codling etc.) Mike catches. And with sillocks it's a poor two hours' work if you catch fewer than 3 to 4 score.

Write soon and give us your news. Angus will be back at school, of course, very robust I hope after his forestry: and I hope Morag is still managing to cope with all the rationing and clothing coupon complexities and has good news of her John (whose appearance as I think I said in my last, on the snap you sent me, secured full measure of my avuncular approbation, as did that of his girl and her brother, both so greatly grown that I'm afraid I'd hardly know them if I bumped into them in Sauchiehall – or, for that matter, of course, any other – Street).

Love from us all to all of you. Yours, Chris

18. *To Andrew Graham Grieve (EUL)*

Sudheim, Whalsay   23 December 1941

My dear Graham

Just a very brief and hasty line to thank you for the parcel of generous Christmas gifts and to wish Angus, Morag, and yourself all the compliments of the season and best wishes for 1942 from Michael, Valda, and myself.

I had hoped that one at least of my new books – from America – would have come in time to fill a corner in your Christmas stocking; but there is no sign of a transAtlantic parcel here yet, so my reciprocal gift will be a little (I hope only a little) belated – but in any case I have three books coming out and you will duly receive copies of them as and when they do reach me.

The meshes of National Service are closing over me as I write; and I expect to be located in Glasgow on war work shortly. Final details are not yet to hand but as soon as they do arrive I will apprise you of my arrangements (Valda and Michael will not be accompanying me – for some time at any rate).

So I will be looking forward to seeing you ere very long if all goes well: and in the meantime I hope you are all well and full of Christmas pudding and what not.

Yours, Chris

19. *To Valda Grieve (NLS)*

Benachie, 70 Grenville Drive,   Tuesday, 10 February 1942
Cambuslang, Glasgow

My darling Valda,

You would get the wire I sent yesterday – the first time I possibly could, as we got into Glasgow late on Saturday. The boat went via Kirkwall where it joined a convoy which went extremely slow. We had an alarm with some German aircraft in the Moray Firth and had to don lifebelts etc. The passage down was not only extremely slow (Thursday morning – I had to stay overnight in Lerwick – till Saturday forenoon when we reached Aberdeen; but it was desperately cold. The whole of Scotland was still very heavily under snow, and the Aberdeen-Glasgow train was late in reaching Glasgow. I spent the weekend at F.G.'s, and he and I did not get to bed at all on the Sat. night but talked right to 9 am. They are all in good form and send Mike and you their love. George is now considerably taller than I am, and Malcolm very little short of me.

I reported to Thornliebank Training Centre on Monday morning. I found they knew all about me and had special instructions regarding me. They want me for inspectors' work directly under the Ministry. To this end I have to do a month first of all in the engineering shop, to learn the routine, furbish up my mathematics etc., then 16 weeks learning inspecting and viewing, and a final month at Chilwell, near Nottingham. Then, if I pass the periodical tests all right, and become duly qualified, I'll be posted to an ordnance factory, or to a private ammunitions firm. What the work then means is that the munitions made by the factory or firm are not accepted by the Government until I have inspected and OK'd them. This is special work and means that I begin at considerably higher remuneration as soon as I pass through.

At Thornliebank there are three shifts – 7 am until 1 pm (the shift I am on this week), 2 pm until 10 pm (which I do next week), and then the nightshift, 10 pm to 6 am (which I'll have the third week), after which the same three shifts in rotation. I am staying meanwhile at any rate at Graham's, though that means that one has to be up and out an hour before the time the shift starts in order to clock in on time, which is of course essential. So this week on the early shift means rising at 5 am, being out and down to Cambuslang Station at the back of 6, and thus arriving at the works on the tick of 7. All that is of course done in pitch darkness. However I managed OK today, and expect to get into it all right. Coming home – from that early shift – is in daylight fortunately, but it takes a full hour; because I have to take the 'bus into Glasgow Central Station and then a train out to Cambuslang.

The works are huge and employ a vast army of workers. Today we began learning how to cut metal bars with a hacksaw and then put them in a vice and polish them with a file. In the afternoon we had to listen to lectures and do workshop calculations involving vulgar fractions, decimals, and geometry and trigonometry. I got on all right; the other trainees, drawn from all parts of Scotland, are a very cheery lot, two-thirds of them girls and the rest men. I am in blue dungarees now and look the part quite well.

I'll tell you more about it all in subsequent letters. You'll have to excuse a short one this time. I hope you were not worrying too much about me before you got my wire. My head is screwed on all right and I am determined to do well for all our sakes and think I have struck a very lucky and promising line indeed.

Before I left Lerwick I signed a note to the Lerwick Labour Exchange asking them to have payments due to me made out to you, so that you can sign for the money and receive it. You are *not* allowed to sign my name in my absence, nor would your own signature get you the money without my authorising it in this way. What that means is that you will get the backpay due from the Labour Exchange all right. With regard to my pay here we get paid on Wednesdays – not starting tomorrow but a week tomorrow, when I'll get the week and a half's pay due me. So I'll be posting you money every Thursday if possible; that is to say if mails are running regularly you should receive my letters enclosing the weekly money every Monday, or, at latest, by the Thursday mail.

I hope this is all clear. It is very complicated but you'll soon understand the system and then things will go on smoothly.

I do hope all's well with Mike and you since I left. Having Grant for the week you'd miss me a little less – or at least have less time to feel lonely.

If you have been anxious to hear from me, please remember it seems just as long to me since I saw you last and that I am anxious to hear from you too.

Please tell Mike I am not forgetting about the bicycle bell etc. I can't do anything this week, but may manage next week to have more time – and perhaps a spare shilling or two – when I am on the afternoon shift.

There is of course a canteen at the Training Centre and we have dinner there – potatoes and meat, a sweet and a mug of tea, for which we are charged 1/-.

Now, darlings, this is all I can manage to scribble tonight, but I'll write to you regularly – and frequently – hereafter. I hope Mike is getting clear of his cold and will soon be back to normal and able to get out and enjoy his cycle. See and look after yourselves well, both of you. Give Mike my love, and a kiss from me, and tell him I hope he is being very good to Mummy. My own love and kisses are enclosed to yourself, and my kind remembrances to Mary Shearer, and Mary Hughson.[1]

Yours, Chris

P.S. You'll appreciate that if there isn't much news in this letter that's just because I haven't had much time yet, and because of the particularly awkward hours of the shift I am on this week. But the following two weeks I'll get round more and see people – and tell you all about it. I'm in splendid form and quite encouraged by feeling I've made a good start and that the whole thing promises to pan out very nicely.

There's just one thing I want you to do. You know the four volumes of old Scots poetry I got from that bookseller in Edinburgh. They are on the third or fourth shelf of my bookcase – the one at my right hand when I'm sitting in my chair. Well I want you to parcel them up, and along with them the pamphlet of your poem of Burns's we got once from Mary Shearer if you can find it – the one about twirling at the cannister etc. – and send that parcel to F.G. Scott, 44 Munro Road, Jordanhill, Glasgow, as soon as you can spare the cash to post it.

Grant'll be off tomorrow I suppose. Hope you're having better weather conditions and not finding going to the well, for the milk, etc. etc. too heavy for you. All my love.

P.S. I am haunted by an idea that there was something you wanted me to get you at Woolworth's or somewhere – or was it some hair stuff or something? Please let me know and I'll see to it immediately. Also if there are other odds and ends you want just tell me and I'll get them for you.

---

1. Mary Hughson was a teacher at Livister school, Whalsay, which Michael attended; she was married to Henry Grant Taylor.

20. *To Valda Grieve (NLS)*

c/o Grieve, 70 Grenville Drive, Cambuslang, Glasgow   20 February 1942

Dearest Hen-Bird

Was extremely glad this morning to get your letter, and J.M.'s, and other correspondence enclosed. Do hope the weather has abated now. I am extremely sorry you've been having such a terrible time and hope your trials and tribulations in snow-drifts etc. going for the milk and to the well have not affected your general health, and that your knee has healed nicely.

We've both been in the wars. I fell down a staircase on the ship in the pitch darkness and landed with a whack at the foot. I might have broken my neck, I suppose; fortunately I only skinned the knuckles of my left hand. Then last week I inadvertently stepped off a train before it came to a stop and had a lovely purler – went slithering across the platform on my tummy. Again, happily, escaped serious harm.

I wired you yesterday and sent some dough. I'd have sent more but had my out-of-pocket expenses to next payday to consider (about 6/- for bus and train charges and about the same for hot meal in works canteen at break half-way through shift). Also I had to pay back small loans – 5/- to Graham and 1/- to Morag. This means you'll get more once I get settled and know my way about better, as, of course, I spend rather more on trams, buses, and trains than I'll do when I have got the journeys properly taped. I'll be better next week when I'm on night-shift, as I'll be able to get about a bit in daylight and pick up my bearings, as well as see people, which I've had no opportunity to do yet. This week I've been on the worst shift from that point of view, not finishing shift till 10pm, after which I have to 'bus it into Glasgow and train out here, arriving just after 11pm, which doesn't allow me to see or do anything but just read a little and then pop off to bed.

Everything so far is going OK I am really greatly interested in the work and managing all right. I am working among hundreds of people from all over Scotland and they are a good and cheery lot. Getting about in the blackout becomes fairly easy once one has picked up one's bearings a little, and you'd be surprised how well I manage. Of course there is always a certain amount of tension in matters of this sort, and the work itself is tiring – particularly the standing which fairly wears out the feet and legs. The work is dirty – one's hands get all oil and metal-dust and paint, and one's throat full of metal dust too – but though tiring the work is not heavy and calls for more nervous than muscular strain. Taking precision readings on fine gauges is very sore on the eyes, especially in artificial light, but even so I manage well enough, though, just as a precaution, I intend to get a new frame for my specs this week-end – if such can be procured. Graham thinks I'll have to wait a while – nothing of that sort is easily got. The worst thing of all is matches. Can't get them for love or money. Cigarettes too are extremely difficult to get.

The things I thought I'd forgotten I found I had a note of in my little notebook. Not the dog-collar which I'll try to get this weekend, but henna, and the ounce of green yarn to mend socks. Henna does not seem procurable at all, but I'll see further into this question in a day or two. Morag thinks she has some wool which will do for the socks.

Thank Mike very much for his extremely nice letter. I'm so sorry he had a relapse of the abominable whooping cough. Do hope he's better now.

Be sure and let me know if there's anything I can get you. I'm going to see if I can pick up a few things this weekend and send you a little parcel.

Do not worry too much about me, darling. I'm really very fit, and much tougher than you'd imagine, and have managed to fit myself into this new sphere quite well. I'm not feeling in the least sorry for myself (apart from being separated from you and Mike) and am not exaggerating at all when I sound hopeful and promising. I honestly do think we've a real chance here and am determined to do the best I possibly can. And you need not fear I've got into trouble of any kind. I'll not go off the rails in any way at all.

I'm very comfortably fixed here at Graham's, of course; it's well worth the extra time and difficulty involved in travelling so far in and out from the Training Centre. I was over at the Scotts last Sunday – they are all in good form and send Mike and you their love (as do Graham, Morag and Angus, of course). I'll see more of them this weekend and next week. I'll probably see T.S. Eliot too; he's giving a lecture at Glasgow University. I've sent Miller a p.c. and arranged to see him early next week. Don't worry about the Central Library book – I have it all right – I'll write Cotton at Dunfermline tonight and put the matter right.

I do hope you are managing to keep good fires on and yourselves as warm and cosy as possible. I could get you a rubber hot water-bottle which might be a comfort? It's a good job there were a fair quantity of peats left at the corner of the house and in the dunnigan, for you won't have been able to get any from the hill.

Please excuse this very scrappy letter, darlings. I haven't time for a better or longer one just now but will write again in a day or so, and as I say try to send you a small parcel, plus, if possible, the dog-collar and a bicycle bell for Mike. Best regards to Mary Williamson, Mary Hughson and Babbie etc. and all my love and kisses to darling Michael and yourself. (Trust all well at Bude).

Yours, Christopher

21. *To Valda Grieve (NLS)*

70 Grenville Drive, Cambuslang   Sunday, 1 March 1942

My dearest Henbird

I have had a very strenuous week under adverse weather conditions – appallingly cold, with hard frosts varied with occasional showers of snow and more of sleet. I am sorry not to have been able to write you more frequently or more fully, but I think you will understand. This last week I have been on night-shift – beginning work at Thornliebank at 10pm and working to 6am. The work is not physically hard but of course demands concentrated attention and care all the time and reading precision instruments of measurement in the artificial light is very sore on inexperienced eyes. I have suffered too from having a very heavy cold. Nearly everybody has one and they are almost impossible to escape and very difficult to throw off quickly. While this made me more easily tired what I have felt most is the strain of having to stand for eight solid hours, and the other strain of travelling to and from work in the black-out, a journey which takes me about an hour each way and which also involves no little strain if one is to effect the necessary transitions from tramcar or motor 'bus to train and arrive, as one must, punctually to the minute. However I have managed all right, and got on quite nicely both with the work itself and with the crowds of other trainees from all over Scotland with whom I mix. Apart from the standing and the terrible noise the working conditions at Thornliebank are excellent and the instruction very lucid and intensive. With a full 6 months course no intelligent, physically fit person could fail to do well. The trouble now alas is that the course is being greatly cut down under the pressure of war-time exigencies and the whole thing speeded up tremendously, with the consequence that the whole scheme is now in the melting-pot, less than 25 per cent of the trainees are allowed to complete even the much shortened course, and the great majority are only given a week or two and then shoved out into jobs of one kind or another (not nearly so well paid, of course, as the kind of jobs they'd have got if they had been allowed to go through the whole course). However it's no use meeting troubles in advance; things may pan out all right; in any case however they pan out will be better than the hopeless position I'd got into at Whalsay, and you can be sure that whatever happens I'll do my very best and be glad of the chance and anxious to make the most of it.

Owing to the hours I've been working I haven't got about much or seen many people yet – or been free during the restricted hours the shops are open and hence unable yet to get the bicycle bell and dog-collar. I was disappointed not to be able to send you a better parcel. I had expected with Morag's assistance to be able to include some chocolate or sweets and some biscuits. But we couldn't get either, so I just sent what I could. This week I may be luckier; I begin work at 7am (which means leaving here about 6, and that involves rising just after 5) but I finish at 2.30pm and thus, getting into Glasgow about an hour later, I'll have an hour or two when the shops are still open.

The Scotts I have been at the last two Sundays, and am going again today. Douglas Young is also to be there. Morag and I went to the University the other day to hear T.S. Eliot lecture, but there was a tremendous crush, we had to stand in such a position that although we could hear we couldn't see the lecturer at all, and it was quite impossible to have a word with Eliot himself as I had hoped to do. I had sent him a note in advance to that effect but the crush made it quite impossible. Also Morag and I were to have met F.G. and Lovey but saw nothing of them as it happened, but I don't know whether they turned up or not. Last Sunday Scott and I went to a Fabian Society lecture in the Cosmo Picture-House. The lecture was by Wm Power and as it turned out a whole crowd of friends of mine happened to be there – Dr MacIntyre, Mrs Norrie Fraser, etc.[1] Apart from these activities the only other thing I have to record is that Morag and I have been twice to the pictures this week, once to one of the best cinemas in Glasgow and the other time to a cinema in one of the suburbs near Cambuslang. On both occasions we went specially to see exceptionally good films – in the one case Orson Welles's *Citizen Kane* and the other *Forty-Ninth Parallel*.[2] Both were splendid, and I only wished Mike and you could have been there with us too. The other items on the programmes – news reels, shorts, documentaries etc. – were also first-rate.

I do hope the weather is moderating in the Shetlands and that you are having a somewhat easier time and that your 'blue melts' are disappearing or at least ceasing to be painful. Also, that Mike has recovered from his relapse of whooping cough, and that you have good news from home too. Many thanks for the parcel of underclothing etc. (and the tobacco – but don't send me any more unless I ask for it, as I can get thick black here all right), and also for sending on the *Times Lits*, *New Statesmen*, etc. I was disappointed however that more letters hadn't come to hand, and surprised, amongst other things, that though I sent a year's sub. to *Indian New Writing* some time before I left Whalsay no acknowledgement and worse still no copies have yet come to hand. As to my *Autobio* and the poetry books in America it seems hopeless to expect any developments. Heaven only knows when they will appear now, if at all.

Be sure and let me know if there is anything I can get for you, and subject to the difficulty of the hours I work at, I'll do my best and quickest, you may be sure.

Tell Mike I'll try to get hold of some Westerns for him this week.

Every kind regard to Mary Shearer, Mary Hughson, Babbie, etc. – and to Miss Thule Grieve![3] And love and kisses to Mike and yourself.

Your loving, Christopher

---

1. Mrs Norrie Fraser, joint secretary of the London Scots Self-Government Committee.
2. A propaganda film by Michael Powell and Emeric Pressburger starring Laurence Olivier about a submarine-load of Nazis on the run through Canada.
3. Thule: Michael Grieve's dog.

22. *To Valda Grieve (NLS)*

Cambuslang   Sunday, 15 March 1942

My dearest Valda

You must be wondering again what has come over me and thinking I really could manage to write oftener. But really that isn't quite so easy as you might think. It was for one thing over a fortnight I had had no letter from you until I received yours – and with it those from Michael Roberts[1] and others – four days ago. I was beginning to be badly worried and on the point of wiring you. But I thought it was just due to the bad weather and probably interruption of steamer services. That in itself did not prevent my writing you oftener, of course, the main reasons for that being three – the utterly foul and extremely cold weather we've been having, the very awkward shift I've been on which has left me practically no time to myself at all, and the increasing claims of my literary and political interests.

I am getting more and more into the swim of affairs and meeting all sorts of people – Polish, Hungarian, and Austrian refugee writers etc. We had all sorts of things in common, not only politically but personally too, for some of these people knew friends of mine like Paul Potts and Sorabji etc. I am arranging to give all sorts of speeches to the Centre, and under the auspices of the Scottish Socialists etc. But it is very difficult developing activities of this kind under present conditions. For one thing, it is a different proposition altogether when one is also doing a full day's work, standing on one's feet and operating machines and using saws and files etc., to what it was when one's time was one's own and all one did was read and write. For another thing getting to and fro to different parts of Glasgow from Thornliebank and Cambuslang under black-out conditions is no joke. Altogether then I am leading a very strenuous life, and one that is likely to keep getting more strenuous as long as I can sustain it.

Apart from worrying about not hearing from you, I was all the more anxious as there was news in the papers here of some blitzing in the Shetlands and I was afraid lest that might be uncomfortably near you, with possibly the West as the enemy objective. Even when your letter did reach me at last I was annoyed too that you hadn't received the parcel. I can't understand why it should have taken so long. Tho' I had it in a tin I am afraid that when it does reach you now the chocolate cake will be old and stale and uneatable. Hard luck!

With regard to one of your commissions I have found where I can get Aladdin mantles all right here. The trouble is they have to know whether the lamp is a number 11 Aladdin or a number 12, as it appears that mantles for the one don't fit the other. However, I'll wire you tomorrow to find out and as soon as I hear from you I'll buy two or three and send them on packed in a tin box, so they should reach you all right and put matters safe in that connection for a while ahead. You must have had a dreadfully difficult time with no light or a mere candle.

I am awfully sorry too to hear about Aunt Jane and do wish you could go down there right away. But we'll try to arrange that as soon as we can now – a holiday beside me and then on to Cornwall for a little while. I do wish some money would come in, from America or somewhere. You ask about Methuen's and fear I have had bad news. But no news is supposed to be good news, and that is all I've had. All Mrs Watson had to suggest was that I should write Methuen's myself. I haven't done so yet. Apparently they've kept on promising her to get the book out but just failed to do so month after month. It's too bad. But the paper situation is becoming more and more hopeless and publishers are beset with that and all sorts of other difficulties. Of course they keep pouring out all sorts of books that aren't really worth a damn: but then these are the sort of books that command a big and ready sale and under present conditions the publishers naturally give these the preference. They simply have to.

Nor have I had any word at all from America, either from the Colt Press or New Directions.

I can't get much done myself either in the way of writing or reading – or even of keeping abreast of my correspondence. The work here, and the travelling out and in, takes far more out of me than I'd have imagined. However I'm in very good form – and very comfortable indeed at Graham's here, with plenty of hot baths etc., electric light, and all the rest of it. Morag of course is likely to be called up and what will happen then goodness only knows. Yes, Angus is at home, just finishing school, and likely to become an RAF officer shortly – he's in the ATC and will go automatically into the RAF soon, probably as an officer but perhaps not.

There are a few other points in your letter I should answer. 1/ Yes. I'll see and get myself a pair of strong serviceable shoes as soon as possible. 2/ You need not be afraid that going about and seeing so many people I am lapsing into my old ways. Contrary to your fears drink has no temptation for me at all now. Graham has both whisky and beer in the house but I have refused to touch either. And I have been absolutely TT outside too. So you can regard that matter definitely settled and know I won't be letting you down in that respect again.

I hope you were able to replenish your little stock of flour and oatmeal. Things are likely to become scarce and more difficult and I shudder to think what next winter may be like. I do hope I can get you out of the Shetlands and down beside me then. But there's no saying. It all depends how things go, and so far as engineering is concerned the outlook is not so good. This has nothing to do with the abilities a trainee may show at all, but simply the fact that the authorities are finding it more and more difficult to find jobs for men after they are trained – there are openings for six women for every opening for a man. And this is likely to continue and get worse. Besides for other reasons the authorities are cutting down the number of training centres and the period of training, shortening the training courses and so on. It is all very worrying and uncertain. But I'll do the best I can and hope for the best. Apart from that I'm keeping a close eye on the advertisements and in fact sent in applications this last week for two journalistic jobs. Here's hoping, darling!

The bundle of papers hasn't reached me yet, nor the two doctors' books

I asked you to send on. And now I want you also to send on as soon as possible the box of typescripts and manuscripts – parts of the *Autobiography* – which I arranged with you to send on when I gave the word. Please register it.

It was awfully good of Professor Knight to send me a copy of his book *The Starlit Dome*.[2] I'm writing him today. I enclose a few of the books. Tell Mike I haven't got the Westerns yet but will this next week without fail, as I'll be on night duty and will therefore have more time to myself during the day when the shops are open. The trouble about getting things is that this past fortnight I've never been free to get into Glasgow during the very restricted period in which the shops are open at all. I'm still hoping to get a bicycle bell, but the two or three shops I've been able to try yet hadn't any.

I do hope this finds both you darlings in good form and managing not too badly.

In the *New Writing* I enclose (*New Writing* No. 10) there is a very good article on Lawrence which you will find very interesting, I think.

One of the poets I met at the Centre, a Jew named Jack Singer, knows Charles Lahr and Phyllis very well and shared digs in London for a time with Paul Potts. He told me that after the Blitz, Esther[3] sold Charles's Blue Moon printing press for a pound – i.e. just gave it away at a scrap-iron price. What a damned shame!

Love to all friends and kisses to Mike and yourself. You must have got a horrible fright with these mines going off in the middle of the night. See and look after yourselves. I am greatly amused at what you tell me of the H.G. affairs under the ineffable Smith. Is there any word of Grant since he went back? I mean, is he still expecting or hoping to be stationed in the Shetlands?

See and look after yourselves as well as you can, my darlings, and do let me know if there is anything I can do or get for you.

Yours, Christopher.

---

1. Michael Roberts (1902–48), poet, critic, editor of anthologies including *New Signatures* (1932), *The Faber Book of Modern Verse* (1936).
2. G. Wilson Knight, *The Starlit Dome: Studies in the Poetry of Vision* (London: Oxford University Press, 1941).
2. Esther Lahr, née Archer, Charles Lahr's wife.

23. *To Valda Grieve (NLS)*

Cambuslang   Wednesday, 25 March 1942

Darling Valda

I was very glad indeed to get your wee note today but so sorry that when you wrote it you were still having such a bad time with snow and gales. Here the weather took a sudden change for the better three or four days ago and since then we have had brilliant sunshine and great warmth. I am so glad the New Directions cheque arrived. If the book comes to hand please send it on to me as quickly as possible; it will be the one with my 'Divided Bird' poem in it, I expect – not the selection of my own poems. I've had no word myself either from New Directions or the Colt Press, nor from Methuen's to whom I wrote a week ago or more.

Following up the good news I gave you in the letter I enclosed in my parcel of books about my being transferred to the Inspection work at last, and so having a much easier and more congenial time (though of course my hours are unchanged and I've still the same earlier rising etc., only no night-shifts) you will be glad to know not only that I am continuing to get on nicely but that I have still better news for you. Just after I'd been transferred to the Inspection section the clerk in the general office who has charge of placing trainees in jobs and is therefore called the Placing Officer – the same man who told me that they had had special instructions about me – asked me if I'd like to take on the job of Inspector at Hillingdon (in the Glasgow area). He said it was a staff job – that means that my insurance, compensation, etc. are seen to, but as a consequence the pay is somewhat smaller than it would be in other posts not staff jobs in that sense. I would start at almost £7.15/- per week. I said that would suit me admirably and that I'd like fine to be placed in the Glasgow area; but after some discussion of the outs-and-ins of the matter he advised me not to take it, remarking that by hanging on a little and gaining a little more knowledge and training and confidence in using them I'd probably do a good deal better financially and otherwise; and he finished the matter by saying that in any case I'd likely be in a job in almost a fortnight or so. It was very kind and helpful and I had no hesitation in taking his advice, as, of course, it is highly technical and very responsible work and I am anxious to be as well qualified as possible before I take on the responsibility. It is however jolly good news that there is every likelihood of my securing a well-paid job very soon now. You will understand of course the way income tax affects such earnings just now; for instance, if I'd taken the £7.15/- job, between £1 and 30/- a week would have had to come off that for income tax, and the returning £6 odds per week, while it would be perfectly all right as long as I am in digs with Graham as at present and would enable me to send you at least double what I've been doing would not be enough – or at any rate would be none too much – if I had Mike and you down here with me, as of course I want to have as soon as ever it is possible. Another point which has to be considered and which I may not have mentioned to you before is that the lodging allowance of £1.4.6 a week I get just now and pay to Graham ceases to be payable whenever you join me here, whereas, no matter how big the money I earn, it continues to be paid so long as I am away from home, maintaining you and Mike, but only on the condition that you do not come down and join me.

Besides, whatever else happens, I am anxious that Mike and you should have a good holiday as soon as the weather is really fine and settled, and if possible that you should go on to Cornwall for a while. You could come and see me here for a week or so first of course before going on to Cornwall; that would not affect the payment of the lodging money, so long as you were only on holiday and therefore only temporarily in the area in which I am employed. I hope you understand all this. It isn't very reasonable but just official red tape, of course; but we must watch ourselves in order to do the best we can financially, and there is no point in the meantime of forfeiting the lodging allowance until I get finally settled for the duration in a really well-paid job.

Meanwhile as I indicated in a previous letter I am very busy in my spare time, speaking all over the place and inundated with far more invitations than I can possibly accept, even with my abounding energy. Last night I spoke for over two hours to a packed house at David Archer's literary and artistic rendezvous, The Centre, and an animated debate followed. The meeting began at 8pm and it was midnight before I get back to Cambuslang. I enjoyed it immensely and so did the audience. It was a very lively crowd of literary and artistic people and keen Scottish Nationalists and Communists and I was at the very top of my form. Amongst those present were many friends of mine I hadn't seen for years, including David Archer himself., Harry Miller, J.D. Ferguson the artist and his wife Margaret Morris, the ballet dancer, Professor Boase, the Professor of French at Glasgow University, David Martin, a Hungarian Communist poet who fought with the International Brigade in Spain, etc. etc. All very well, but I am on the early shift this week and although it was midnight before I got home, and nearer 1am before I got to bed, I had to be up again at 4.45 to catch my bus and then a train to get to Thornliebank in time to clock in for the start at 7am. A strenuous life, my dear, but it is suiting me splendidly and everybody thinks they haven't seen me looking so well for years.

Amongst those present also was Margaret Black, looking extremely well, and asking most kindly after you and Mike. Rona is now a fine young lady of 17! I haven't seen Robin yet but will before the week is over.

Will write again to you – and to Mike before the end of the week. I hope his eye is all right again. I'm looking forward to seeing him down here ere very long and giving him a real good time on the 'buses etc. for a change. Paul Potts is due in Glasgow on 1st April.

Love and kisses to you both, my darlings, and kindest remembrances to all friends.

Yours, Christopher

24. *To Valda Grieve (NLS)*

Cambuslang   Sunday, 29 March 1941 [1942]

Dearest V.

    I enclose (at last! – but I hope you have not had to struggle along all this time without a lamp at nights; you did not say in your last letter how you were getting on in this respect, perhaps because you had given up hope and were too fed up to mention the matter) an Aladdin lamp mantle, which I do hope reaches you safe and sound. As I told you there is a serious shortage of these, and likely to get worse, and the shop is only allowed to sell one to a customer. However I think I'll manage through other people to pick up another two or three shortly. I'll certainly try to. This one cost 2/5½.

    I am also enclosing as you will see a very nice knife for Michael. You will see what I say about it in my letter to him and perhaps you will see that he does as I say and takes care of it, as it is a good one, and with proper usage and care should serve him very usefully for all sorts of purposes for years. The best thing will be for him either to keep it on a chain or a cord, attached to one of his trouser buttons and sufficiently long to enable him to use the knife without detaching it from the cord or chain.

    I have had no reply yet from Methuen's to the letter I sent them a week or ten days ago enquiring about my *Autobio*. Nor have I had any word at all from either New Directions or the Colt Press. I am hoping that following the receipt of the New Directions cheque you may have received a copy of the New Directions annual, and that if so you will send it on to me as quickly as possible, particularly if, as I imagine, the payment was for the 'Divided Bird' and that poem is in the book.

    Following the two or three really delightful sunny days a week ago of which I told you, we have had a very hard, bleak, cold spell again, and I do hope you are not in the throes of another bout of snow and gale-winds again.

    I spent an hour in Collett's bookshop yesterday, signing up copies of my *Golden Treasury* for them. It is a splendid bookshop, and I could have spent twenty or thirty pounds in it right off the reel on books I'd like to have. As it was, I spent nothing but the time required to sign my autographs. I have one or two other Penguins etc., which I will send on to you later, but in regard to buying any of the books must of course ca' canny. I noticed that one of the books I sent on to you with a recent parcel was the second volume of Laura Knight's *Autobiography*.[1] I'll pick up the first when I see it.

    Did I tell you that Johnnie Shearer's wife's sister is at the Thornliebank Centre? She is married but her husband is in the army. I wouldn't have known her of course but she knew me at once and when she was pointed out to me in the Canteen I went across and talked to her. I also met yesterday another Shetlander – Laurenceson, who was with me in the Faeroes. He is a chemist and has been working in Glasgow for the past 15 to 20 years.

Next week-end I am thinking of going through to Edinburgh to see Orr. I'll drop him a line today to see if he's to be at home all right and if it's convenient. I have a long week-end as we get the Easter Monday which is a general works holiday. I haven't heard again from Paul Potts, but expect he'll turn up about the middle of the week. Murray is expecting the young man to arrive for a week's holiday towards the end of next week.

One thing I've been meaning to mention is that I wonder if it wouldn't be a good thing to buy Michael a suit as long as they are to be had. I could get him a very nice Harris tweed one at reasonable cost. The opportunity may not recur for a year or two. Let me know and if you agree I'll set about it at once. I would require his measurements of course. The best plan would be for you to fill up the necessary particulars on one of these self-measurement forms and send it to me. If any additional money came in or I got a job I think it would be wise to buy a coat for you too as soon as possible. There are still plenty of nice ones to be had in the Glasgow shops, including some very nice camel-hair coloured ones. I am afraid if we cannot get hold of things of that sort just now while it is still possible that it may be a very long time before we have any other chance to do so, as things are likely to grow dearer and scarcer for a long time ahead and coupons less and less available.

This must do for just now, darling. I am off to a meeting in Glasgow in connection with the Scots Socialist Party. Kindest regards to all friends, and love and kisses to your dear self.

Yours, Christopher

---

1. Laura Knight, *Oil Paint and Grease Paint* (London: Nicholson & Watson, 1936; Penguin, 1941).

25. To Michael Grieve (NLS)

Cambuslang   Sunday [29 March 1942]

My darling Michael

I was very glad indeed to get your nice letter but so sorry to hear about your bad eye, which I hope is quite healed and all right again now.

You must think I have failed you badly, as I have been quite unable yet to get hold of a bicycle bell or even of some Westerns for you to read. But things are really very difficult and if I haven't managed to get these things yet it hasn't been for want of trying.

However I've now got something very nice for you and am enclosing it with this parcel. It is a very good knife indeed with all sorts of gadgets in addition to the ordinary blades. As you will see there is a ring at one end of it and the best plan is to fasten a chain or cord to that and the other end of the chain or cord to one of your trouser buttons. Then you can carry the knife in your trouser pocket and pull it out and use it whenever you want without undoing the chain or cord, which will thus make sure you don't lose it. It is well worth taking good care of, because it will be very useful to you for years.

I hope you are looking after Mummy nicely and seeing that she behaves herself, as, of course, while I am away you are the man of the house.

Love and kisses.

Write again like a good chap and tell me what you think of this knife.

Yours, Daddy

26. *To Michael Grieve (NLS)*

Cambuslang   1 April 1942

My dearest Michael

I was awfully glad to get your nice letter, and Mummy's, when I got back from work today. It was such a long time since I had heard from you, and I was worrying. I didn't know, of course, that the weather in Whalsay was continuing to be so rotten and that you had been a whole fortnight again without any mail boat. So when you wrote you hadn't got my various parcels of books, lamp mantle, and the knife for you. But you will have got them all now, I expect, and I will look forward to hearing how you like the knife. I am sure you will agree that it is a very nice one, and I hope you will be careful and not cut yourself with it. I am very sorry to have been so long in getting you the bicycle bell, tho' it wasn't my fault, but I have got it at last and enclose it now. Please tell Mummie I'll send her a comb as requested in a day or so. I am having a busy time. We have a holiday on Monday. I had meant to go through to Edinburgh for the weekend to see Dr Orr, but had to abandon that idea as I have a big open-air meeting to address on Sunday afternoon and another meeting to speak at on Sunday night. So I wrote to Orr and said if he was to be at home I'd try to run through just for the day on Monday. Graham, Angus, and Morag are going to Edinburgh on Saturday. But now I don't know that I'll manage after all, as Paul Potts turned up here today when I was away at work (I'm on the late shift and don't get back here at nights till 11 o'clock) and arranged with Graham that he'd come out for me tomorrow at 9am. So we'll have an hour or two together before I have to catch my 'bus at 1 o'clock to go to work.

Mummy tells me that you are having a great time on your bike, riding all around the island. But see and not overdo it and tire yourself too much, when you are not very well with that dreadful cold hanging about you still. I do hope that you can get rid of it soon and get some nice weather during your holiday and have a good time. The weather here is now very fine, mild and sunny, though showery, of course. I am hoping to get Mummy and you down here soon now, but I will write a long letter in a day or so and discuss the whole thing with Mummy and see what can be arranged. Please tell her anyhow that I'll write to Mrs MacArthur[1] as she suggests, and will let her know as soon as I hear what the chances are there – I think the idea is certainly a very good one.

I send all my love and kisses to Mummy and to yourself, and do hope you are looking after each other as well as you possibly can in the dreadful weather you are having.

Your loving, Daddy

Darling Valda

You will see what I say in this letter to Michael and I will write to you tomorrow or Friday, as otherwise I might not be able to manage it over the weekend, when I'll be very much taken up with Potts, and my various meetings, and meeting all sorts of people, even if I don't go through to Edinburgh on Monday (perhaps I will – Potts would probably come with me – but I won't know till I see him and learn what his arrangements are). I had a busy day last Sunday too, being the principal speaker at a meeting of all those connected with Miller's paper *The Scots Socialist*. It was a very successful meeting and I think I spoke as well as I have ever done anywhere. Afterwards I and Miller motored down to Paisley with Dr MacIntyre and spent a pleasant hour, and then MacIntyre motored me back to Cambuslang. It does seem funny to be leading such a very active and varied life again after the so very different course of my life all those years in Whalsay, but I am really in very good form and enjoying it all, tho' I'd enjoy it a hundred times better if you and Mike were here too and not having such a terrible time of it in that old cockpit of whirlwinds. My darling, do believe I love you all there is, too, and am every bit as eager as you possibly can be that we should get together again at the very earliest possible minute, and, also, that we should think well whatever we do and see that it is the wisest and surest thing for the benefit of all of us. Because things are very bad and I think likely to be a great deal worse, and whatever we do we must plan very carefully and see that whatever we try to do promises greater security and comfort for all of us through the very dark and difficult times which undoubtedly lie ahead and the end of which none of us can foresee.

At last Sunday's meeting I saw and talked to Robin Black and Margaret, and Rona who is now a tall and extremely good-looking and very well groomed young lady and sang a solo with a very nice voice and excellent platform confidence. To see and hear her made me feel about twice as old as Methuselah. All three – and many other friends – send their love and kindest remembrances to Michael and yourself, and are looking forward to seeing you when you come down.

Kisses, sweetheart, Yours, Christopher

1. Bessie J.B. MacArthur, Scottish poet. The suggestion was that Michael stay at MacArthur's house in the country along with her other evacuees, while the Grieves set up home in Glasgow.

27. *To Valda Grieve (NLS)*

Cambuslang   8 April 1942

Darling Valda

I received yours of 2nd today and was very sorry indeed to hear you were still having snow etc. and that poor little J.M. is afflicted with another dreadful sty. I hope the latter will clear up quickly and completely and not recur and that in the week that has now elapsed since you wrote the weather has really bucked up at long last and that you are having a pleasanter time.

I have been having a very busy and varied one indeed. On Sunday I spoke (very successfully) at a big open air meeting at which the other speakers were Oliver Brown, Arthur Donaldson, Alex Sloan MP (one of the best of the Scottish Socialist MPs). The occasion was the anniversary of the Declaration of Scottish Independence at Arbroath in 1620 [*sic*]. It was a very good meeting. I spoke mainly — and very strongly — about the deportation of Scottish women to munition works in England, and about the conscription of women generally, and the audience were with us all the way.

This whole question is causing such burning resentment throughout the whole Glasgow working class population that we are now organising a special big open air protest meeting for a week come Sunday, Sloan and another Socialist MP, Mrs Hardie, and myself will be the principal speakers. It will probably be a huge meeting.

Harry Miller was in the chair, and in the afternoon we had an indoors meeting in the Clarion Rooms on business about Miller's paper, the *Scots Socialist*.

Potts duly arrived and we had a great time together. He is a splendid fellow. On Tuesday night at the Centre he and I both spoke to a crowded house on Revolutionary Poetry, each of us reading a sheaf of our poems in illustration. Potts is a fascinating speaker with a perfectly original and most dramatic way of putting his stuff across. It was a brilliantly successful meeting with a long and most animated debate afterwards.

On Monday Potts, Archer, and I went to Edinburgh and spent a most enjoyable day with Dr Orr and Sidney Smith and his wife. Lizzie and Dr Orr send all their love to Mike and you. I enjoyed the break immensely. It was the Glasgow Spring holiday, all the works being closed. The weather in Edinburgh was splendid.

This week I have a somewhat quieter week. But on Thursday

(tomorrow) night I am to be one of the speakers at a big complimentary dinner given to R.E. Muirhead in appreciation of his lifelong services to the Scottish Cause.

Potts went back to Plymouth today after a most enjoyable leave, and asked me to send his warmest greetings to Michael and you. Coming up he had a parcel of papers and books for me from Charles, but fell asleep in the train and found on waking up that the parcel had got lost. Somebody had presumably stolen it. They'd get a surprise when they found it consisted mainly of little anarchist and radical publications; but I was disappointed as these are very difficult to get and I don't like missing them.

Did I tell you – or perhaps you saw in a paper – that Esmond Romilly (who was an officer in the American Flying Corps) was killed in action in Germany?[1]

Amongst other things I am busy writing a note for a little pamphlet of poems the Hungarian Communist poet, David Martin, is bringing out here shortly. He, and two Communist artists – one a Jew and the other a Pole, Janko Adler and Josef Hermon (both artists of European reputation; Adler fought in Spain too and Hermon has been in prisons all over Europe and escaped from the hands of the German Gestapo) – are great friends of mine of whom I am seeing a lot.[2]

You will understand that if I seem a little irregular re money, the reason is simply that I have other things to see to. I simply must get a strong pair of new shoes very soon; and also when in Rome one must do to some extent as the Romans do and this last week, in addition to my little jaunt to Edinburgh, I had to give birthday presents to Angus and to Graham. Angus is going in for wireless operating. Morag's young man arrives here on holiday next week. I like Morag very much. She has blossomed out into a very charming girl and is quite unusually brainy and extremely well-read. I gave Angus some tobacco and his father an anthology of nature poetry. They have been very busy gardening and I have given them a little assistance several times. You can scarcely credit it, I expect – me wielding a spade!

Orr is in great form and fatter than ever – quite a lot fatter. Lizzie is very homesick for Whalsay.

At the meeting at the Centre on Tuesday night I met again that very delightful little friend of mine, Sadie MacLellan, the stained glass artist. She is married now to an English artist living in Edinburgh, Pritchard by name,[3] and I'm going out to Milngavie at the weekend to the father's house where she is staying at the moment to have tea with her and see her baby daughter.

Willa Muir has been very dangerously ill and just escaped death by the skin of her teeth.

So you will see with all these activities I am having a very busy time indeed. I am still very busy at Thornliebank too, of course, but things are much easier for me now with the better weather and the summer time business has made a vast difference.

I will write you fully about the business of coming South, and about books I may want etc. in a day or two. I am hoping for news of a job any day now. We'll see. Here's hoping. But you can be very sure that I am extremely eager to see Michael and yourself again at the very earliest possible minute and hope we won't be separated again for another ten years at least.

I had thought you'd have received the parcels in which I sent Mike a knife and you an Aladdin mantel, and the other one in which I sent Mike a bicycle bell before the 2nd, the day for which your letter is dated, but you do not mention them, so it seems you haven't received them yet. I hope they arrive all safe and in good condition. I've tried to get another mantel for you, but failed so far: so I'm very glad you got one from Cornwall too. Poor darlings, you must have had a most dreadful and difficult time without a lamp.

I've no word from Methuen or America or anything yet.

Oh, yes. What I meant to say when I was referring above to the extra expenses responsible for the temporary irregularity of my sending moneys to you, is that I'm not going to let you suffer from this, of course. It's only that I've to do a little wangling at the time: but whenever I do as again this time I'll send more the following week and so even things out as well as I can and if you just have a little patience you'll find that I make it up to you over a week or two all right. You see things *are* very expensive and moving about means spending money at every turn, and I have all my tram and 'bus fares to Thornliebank, and into Glasgow etc. to meet – and I daren't run quite short of cash, also the little things I send you all cost, as does the wiring and the registration of the parcels etc. And Mike's knife made a hole in a pound note. I'll not tell you just how much I paid for it, or you'd be shocked, but it *is* a good one and I really felt the little fellow deserved a good one and I wanted to give it to him.

Yes, my dear, I got the raincoat all right: and also your two big registered parcels of underclothing and books and papers. Many thanks.

I hope your aunts are both well.

I have no more news at the moment, so draw to a close with fondest love and kisses to Michael and yourself; and kind remembrances to all friends. I am very sorry indeed if what you say is true of Mary H.

All the best, darlings. See and look after each other and may we be happily reunited very soon.

Yours, Christopher.

P.S. I'll send your brown papers, string etc. back one day very soon.

P.P.S. Re your torch battery query, I am OK as the battery I had in the torch when I left Whalsay is still giving as good a light as ever – Heaven only knows how; so I still have my spare battery unused. Besides tho' I have had to use the torch a great deal right up to now, I shall shortly not have any need of it for four or five months.

Your friend Struthers (who called on us in the Shetlands and to whom I gave the little cottage on the Atlantic side of the mainland) was in Barlinnie Prison as a CO but has been certified insane (quite wrongly, I think) and removed to Hawkhead Lunatic Asylum, Crookston; I am going out there if possible tomorrow to see him and intend to create as much of a row as I possibly can through the Glasgow MPs etc. about his wrongful certification.

---

1. Esmond Romilly, Winston Churchill's nephew, a Communist who also fought in the Spanish Civil War.
2. Jankel Adler (1895-1945) and Joseph Herman (1911-2000) were both Polish artists. Adler introduced the 'off set' monotype technique to Britain.
3. Walter Pritchard; see Appendix.

28. *To Valda Grieve (NLS)*

Cambuslang   Saturday, 11 April 1942

My dearest Valda

The first thing I have to tell you about in this letter is one in regard to which further and perhaps final developments may take place on Monday; and in that event I will add to this letter and not post if before I see what happens. The Manager of the Training Centre sent for me on Friday and suggested that if I cared he thought I might be placed in a factory as a progress man. The post and procedure of a progress man is a new one in industry and is a very important and responsible one. Briefly the duties of such an appointment are that the man in question moves freely through all the departments of the work, and must at every moment put himself in the position of knowing exactly what stage every part of the work on the various contracts the factory has in course of production is at, discussing every sort of difficulty that may arise either with the material or machines or the men themselves with all the foremen and charge hands etc., and see that everything that is slowing up or in any way spoiling the quality and quantity of the output is corrected as quickly and completely as possible, and that all the sections maintain the highest possible progressive programme and that no preventible cause of any kind is allowed to interfere with or impair the maximum output. To do this the man in question must elicit continually from all the departments precisely where they stand in relation to all the jobs that are going forward, find out exactly when those in charge of the various operations can complete their share – and see that they do it; and in order to do this three things are mainly necessary: 1/ the ability to circulate freely amongst all those concerned and ask the right sort of questions in the most tactful and encouraging, yet firm, manner, and enough knowledge of all the processes and types of machines involved to be able to check all the information so gleaned, to ensure that the timetable is adhered to all along the line, and the ability to keep all that information accurately co-ordinated from day to day, so that he will always have the whole business at his finger-ends and be able to answer any questions at any moment either about the progress of the work as a whole or any part of it. One of the advantages of such a key post is that the man who holds it is in constant consultation with the Directors and other head ones of the business and they depend upon his thorough diligence, accuracy, and judgment at every turn and rely upon him to remove all snags, anticipate and avert difficulties of all kinds, and, in short, keep all the wheels of the business well oiled in order to achieve the maximum results in the minimum time throughout the entire factory. II/ Such a man must have a knack of accurate note-taking, so that he can always have set down in his notebook in orderly and comprehensive fashion all the essentials of the information he gleans from day to day and hour to hour in his talks with the various chief engineers, firemen, charge-hands, etc., as well as directly from the General Office – all set down so clearly, and kept so continuously clear and complete and up to date that he can furnish instantly all the necessary information in regard to the position, progress and prospects of every piece of work in hand, and be able to do so, i.e. to assimilate and express all this information, in a clear and complete way whenever he is called into conference. The job therefore is mainly clerical and conversational; it is like a highly specialised kind of reporting – one goes about in the factory talking to everybody and finding everything out and keeping a continual clear record of it.

I need not tell you how extremely important such a post is or how fortunate I am to be put forward for it. It is indeed so enviable a job that I had to be warned not to say anything about it at the Training Centre itself since even the instructors on the staff (all of whom are first-class Chief Engineers) would prefer such an appointment if they could get it to their own posts, and in all the factories and engineering shops there is great competition and jealousy to secure such posts among the most experienced and highest-qualified workers themselves.

I said I would be glad to be put forward for such a post and the Manager said he expected to place me very quickly, in the Glasgow area, but that in the interval he would arrange that while I remained at Thornliebank I would be passed round all the instructors of the different sections in town and thus gain a quick insight into all the types of machinery and different processes of work. Accordingly I began this today, and for most of the time was in the Machine section, requiring a rapid familiarity with scores of different types of highly complicated modern machinery – capstan and turret lathes, grinders, milling machines etc. Also I have a great deal of technical reading to do to familiarise myself as quickly as possible with the whole run of the business.

I had expected that this intensive training through the different sections might take me a few weeks before the question of my securing an appointment would arise in final form. Instead of that, the General Office sent for me again today and I was told that a factory near Thornliebank wants a progress man and wants to interview me on Monday, but the Placing Officer says that factory will not be ready to start a progress man for a few weeks ago [sic], whereas our office are anxious to get me fixed up as quickly as possible. The Placing Officer added that he has several other things in mind which might be better than this and that he wanted to see me before I went to this Thornliebank factory on Monday, and would probably have other news for me then.

So, darling, that is the position at the moment and things look very promising indeed. These jobs are so important that during the whole time the Thornliebank Centre has been open they have only been able to place one other man in a similar post (of course, such posts only exist in the most fully equipped and most modern establishments).

I will, of course, wire you immediately anything final emerges, and otherwise keep you posted.

Yesterday (Friday) I had an exciting day of a different sort. F.G. phoned me to say that Willie Johnstone was to be in Glasgow and wanted to see me urgently. So as soon as I finished work at Thornliebank I went into Glasgow and on to Jordanhill. Johnstone had just arrived. What he wanted were 1/ doodles, 2/ sittings. Doodles as you will know are drawings (squiggles) made without exercise of any conscious control over the perfectly spontaneous directions your pencil may take, and are thus of high psychological interest and vitally related to modernist artistic developments. It is not easy to do as to sit down *deliberately* to produce something quite spontaneously involves a contradiction in terms. You know how difficult it is to sit down to a piece of paper without any idea of what you want to write and just splash down what comes into your mind, without regard to grammar, spelling, sense or anything else. Above all, you must not allow your conscious will to enter into the matter at all. In such a case it is even harder to draw than to write; and in the case of such a highly self-conscious person as myself it is especially difficult. I had a desperate struggle, but managed to cover four pages of a drawing-block with doodles, and signed them. They are to appear in a new and expensive (3/6 a copy) periodical of advanced art, called *Arson*, and I will send you a copy in due course.[1]

Item 2/ Johnstone is one of six leading British artists who are going to have a big show in London. Augustus John and Walter Sickert are two of the others.[2] For this Johnstone wanted a portrait of me, and as he had to return to London the following day, he had to get enough right on the spot to enable him to go ahead with the oil-painting without my giving him the usual long series of sittings. So he made drawings of my head and face from about a dozen different angles, and then tinted these drawings with water-colours. Some of them were extremely good. He will use these studies to build up the final portrait. For this purpose I had to strip naked to the waist and the whole job (he also made separate drawings of my hands etc.) took from about 6pm (when I arrived at Scott's) to 11pm when I left. Unfortunately I was just too late to catch the last train to Cambuslang. I only got a late car about a third of the way and had to walk the rest, arriving back here at 2 in the morning and having to knock up Graham who was, of course, in bed. Then I myself being on early shift had to be up again at 4.45, so now I am very tired and sleepy as you may imagine.

On Tuesday night we had the complimentary dinner and presentation at Muirhead. Maxton was there, so I met him at last. Also James Barr MP, Sir Hugh Roberton of the Orpheus Choir[3] and scores of other people many of them old acquaintances of mine I hadn't seen for years. It was a most enjoyable function. The principal speakers were Maxton, Barr, Oliver Brown, Dr James Dunlop, Sir Hugh Roberton and myself.

Tomorrow (Sunday) Harry Miller and I are going to have a day in the country. We are going down to Beith (near Kilmarnock) to see two friends of mine, David Murison[4] and his wife, and then on to Lugton (not far from Beith) to see Mr and Mrs Arthur Donaldson.

I hope Mike (and perhaps even yourself) likes the parcel of Western Cowboy books I sent him yesterday. I bought them at Robin Black's bookshop. Robin is also giving me a bicycle-pump for Mike, which I will send on with one of my next parcels. In the meantime I enclose one thriller for yourself.

Monday

I wired you today that I had got the job, i.e. that of Progress Manager for Messrs Henry Willett & Co Ltd, Thornliebank. I am to start on 5th May, but it may be before then, that is, starting on my real job, for which they can't start me just yet because they are still in the throes of building and equipping a big new factory. 5th May is three weeks ahead. Question is what I am to do during that time. Willett's were to settle that this afternoon with the Training Centre Office but I haven't heard yet. Either I'll just be kept on at the Centre, or Willett's will find some other temporary use for me in the meantime, until they are ready for me in my real capacity. I am of course enormously bucked about this. I am sure you will agree that to have pulled this off in some eight weeks, without any previous experience, is a feather in my cap and shows that I have put my back into the job all right. Willett's know all about me and were genuinely anxious to have me, going so far as to ask me, since they cannot start me for these three weeks as Progress Manager, not to accept anything else in the meantime but to reserve myself for them, as they really want me. Apart from that, I am very happy about it all because the firm (it is the Glasgow factory of a big English engineering firm specialising in aeronautical engineering) is one that is very well spoken of, as good employers, and as an exceptionally progressive and go-ahead firm employing all the newest machinery and most advanced up-to-date organisational methods.

So that's that, henbird. Thanks to your courage and patience we surmounted our very difficult psychological problems. And now, this time very largely through my initiative, I feel that we are at last on the way to solve our very difficult economic (financial) problems: and that soon I will have you and Michael with me again under conditions which will compensate you for the lean years of hardship and isolation in Whalsay and enable you to enjoy a full round of interests of all kinds, nice friends, and civilised circumstances generally, and also not only give Mike a happier time in these ways too, but also enable us to deal effectively with the problem of his proper education.

Finally, I understand that unless they are used soon the old clothing coupons (the Margarine ones) will become void, so if you have any of these you do not need for other purposes please send them on to me immediately and I will use them before they become void, to the mutual advantage of all three of us.

Cheerio, my darling. Yours, Christopher
P.S. I enclose a thriller, and two magazines.

---

1. *Arson: an ardent review: Part one of a surrealist manifestation*, ed. Toni del Renzio appeared in March 1942; no other issues survive and it is probable that no more were published.
2. Augustus John (1878–1961), Welsh painter; Walter Sickert (1860–1942), German-born British artist and critic who studied under Whistler.
3. Revd James Barr, Labour MP for Glasgow, Coatbridge, home ruler, Moderator of the United Free Church (1929–30); Sir Hugh Roberton (1874–1952), founder in 1906 and conductor of the Orpheus Choir.
4. David Murison (1913–97), Classics graduate of Aberdeen University (1933) and Cambridge (1936), Editor of the *Scottish National Dictionary*, 1946–76.

29. *To Valda Grieve (NLS)*

[Cambuslang]   Tuesday, 21 April 1942

Dearest Henbird

I was extremely glad to have your last letters and Michael's nice letter about the knife. He was, please tell him, right about the different blades; the one he didn't know about is used for a variety of purposes – e.g. paring horses' hoofs for shoeing, taking stones out of their pads etc.

This is only to be a short letter in order to avoid too long a gap. I have been plunged into the most intense form of armament work with a vengeance. As I told you the new Company – really it is the Mond Nickel Company, an affiliate of the ICI (International Chemical Industries) – were not ready to start me in the capacity of Progress Man for which they engaged me until at least 5th May. But they started me on Monday last in a stop-gap (mainly clerical) capacity until then, i.e. while the factory is being equipped and got into full running order. I will, I think, not get Progress Man's pay until I begin these duties; until then I shall, I believe (I am not sure of the exact position yet) only get a few shillings (about 7/6) more per week than I have had at Thornliebank Training Centre. But it is very difficult yet to ascertain exactly how things are to be; I am living in the centre of most intense activity and everything is still all sixes and sevens – fitting up machinery, inventoring vast supplies of tools and other equipment arriving constantly, and working also in a centre of absolutely appalling noise amongst many many hundreds of engineers and machine operatives. What I say above about the wages, however, applies only to my basic rate of pay. What payment for overtime I get in the meantime until things are regularised I can't find out yet; but I have begun and will continue to have to work incredible hours. Since I came to Glasgow I have been, as you know, having a very lively and interesting time meeting all sorts of people and speaking at all sorts of gatherings indoors and out of doors. Last Sunday I was at meetings continuously (and speaking continuously myself) from 2pm until 10.30pm – very good meetings they were, too, with really keen discussions. I was principal speaker at one of them, Douglas Young (whose trial as a conscientious objector takes place on Thursday) at the other: but all sorts of people I was glad to meet turned up at them, people I hadn't seen in some cases for years and from Aberdeen and Edinburgh as well as from the Glasgow area – amongst others Mary Ramsay,[1] Dr Orr, (who motored me back here to Cambuslang), George Campbell Hay (on leave) etc. etc.

But these stimulating meetings are apparently over for me and last weekend's activities must represent a last glorious burst of this kind of thing for a long time ahead. For at my new job I begin at 8am (which means rising at 5.30 and being out of the house and on my way not later than 6am) and work right on (with a short break for lunch in the canteen) until – most nights (including Saturdays and Sundays) – 9pm (which means that I don't get back to Cambuslang until between 10 and 11. And I believe that very soon in addition to all that I'll have to do my whack of either fire watching or Home Guard work (or, in lieu of that I may get ambulance and first aid work instead). In any case I'll be having an average day – seven days a week – of at least 14 hours. So, darling, please think of that when you feel the sorting of my papers and all your other preparations for coming South shortly pressing very hard on you. All the same I am very sorry indeed you are having such a hard time and only hope that you will not overdo it. Yes. Don't bother about the newspapers etc. in the other cottage – just give them to the salvage people. And I think you are right – sell the cottage. But use the money to fetch Mike and you down etc. – but not to pay our bigger debts (Hay's and Arthur's). These must wait until I can arrange a little later, as I hope to do. In any case these debts are not your concern but mine and if any question arises the parties in question must just be referred to me. So, to avoid trouble, I would if I were you go ahead with your arrangements as quietly as possible and say as little as possible about leaving till the day you do – and even then not tell people it is likely to be for good. And as to the money you get for the cottage if any question arises insist that it is *your* money (not *mine*) – and if need be later I will back you up in that claim.

As to sending on any stuff meanwhile send anything you want to – Morag can accommodate it here all right in the meantime until we are able to make other arrangements, but store what you can of the books etc. with Mary in the meantime.

As to Michael I have practically decided, subject to your approval, to send him to Kilquhanity School, of which I have spoken to you before. It is the only really good experimental school in Scotland – run somewhat on A.S. Neill[2] lines (and by a great friend of Neill's and of mine – John Aitkenhead), but without one of the principal drawbacks of Neill's school, namely, the high proportion of highly abnormal pupils which makes it dangerous to send normal bairns to it. It is located in lovely country in Wigtonshire and has beautiful grounds, gardens which grow all the necessary vegetables etc. for the school, a dairy which ensures plenty of fresh milk (as well as eggs etc.), a staff of ten teachers of the right sort in addition to the Headmaster, Aitkenhead, himself. And the school is not only run on lines which I feel certain Michael will enjoy immensely but which will be very good indeed for his development, but most of the pupils are about his own age, so that will be nice for him. And Aitkenhead is very keen to have him and will take a personal interest in him. I met Aitkenhead and his wife yesterday (Monday) night by appointment and had a long talk with them. They understand thoroughly just what sort of an education – or lack of one – Michael has had so far, and what must be done to overcome the leeway. I can think of no people I'd sooner entrust the boy to, and am sure they will do well by him. It is not too far away but that you – and, if free, I also – can go down for occasional weekends and see Michael; and, on the other hand, it is conveniently near to make his coming to us for holidays simple too. Normally of course it would be expensive out of all possibility for us: but Aitkenhead and his wife are anxious to have him; understand my position, and are ready and eager to make it possible by restricting the cost to the very minimum – and thus to a figure which we will certainly be able to afford if this new job of mine turns out all right. If Michael is to go to Kilquhanity it is desirable that you and he should come down as soon as ever you can now. I feel that this is a splendid opportunity and am very anxious to seize it. It will give Michael a thoroughly good – and at the same time most enjoyable – schooling of just the kind I have always coveted for him but up to now despaired of being able to secure.

All the other issues involved in your coming down and the arrangements we must make – as also of clothes and other things (including a little pocket money for Michael while at school) – I hope to touch on in my next letter by which time I hope – and will do my utmost to secure – the issues connected with my new job will be clarified and I will know much better just how I stand and what we will be able to do – or not do.

Now, darling, please understand that I am every bit as anxious to have you and Michael with me here as ever you can be, and am doing my very best in very difficult circumstances which I find it difficult to describe to you in adequate detail, at any rate in a letter of such a length as I can manage to write under present circumstances. I am of course extremely tired but otherwise in splendid form, and will adjust myself to circumstances once I've had a little time to get used to these very exacting new conditions.

Another point about Kilquhanity School is that if he goes there I think Michael will be able to keep Thule all right, and in that case it will be possible to bring the dog down and make temporary arrangements until the school is fixed up. In any case I am so glad Michael and Thule are now such good friends and am of course anxious not to part them if it can possibly be avoided. And I was also much touched by what Michael said of his just having to stay on in Whalsay with the dog by himself and not seeing me for a long long time perhaps. That must not be. I want to see him, complete with bike, dog, knife, and all the rest of it, as soon as possible; and his Mother with him.

Regards to all friends; and kisses and every loving thought to Mike and yourself.

Yours, Christopher

---

1. Mary Ramsay, leader of the United Scotland Movement.
2. A.S. Neill (1883–1973), author of *A Dominie's Log* (1916), started Summerhill School in 1927, a co-educational boarding school that sought to be without a hierarchy of authority between pupils and teachers. Kilquhanity was run by John Aitkenhead on a similar basis, classes being attended voluntarily.

30. *To Valda Grieve (NLS)*

c/o Scott, 44 Munro Rd, Jordanhill[1]   Monday, 15 June 1942

My dearest Valda

I have just received your telegram and of course quite understand how anxious you must be. My not writing you before now has been no lack of understanding of that, and no indifference, of course, but sheer inability to know what on earth to do for you, or myself, in the appallingly difficult circumstances in which I suddenly found myself, and in which I still remain. I was so looking forward to your coming down – so conscious of all it meant to you and to Mike, (and certainly no less to myself) and of the very hard time you have had not only during these years in the Shetlands as a whole but since I left you, with all the work of packing, sorting my papers, and all the other problems.

I have delayed writing for two reasons. I think you will believe that rather than write what I have to write and be the helpless agent in inflicting this terrible disappointment on you I would sooner my right hand withered off altogether.

Plunged in despair I have yet had no option but to try my utmost to solve the difficulty and have consequently kept hoping against hope that by waiting a little before writing again I could counterbalance my bad news with good news. For, of course, I have been desperately busy ever since the blow fell trying every possible way I could think of to secure something else that would save the situation and from day to day I have been hoping to be able to wire you to that effect.

The trouble is that I suddenly lost my job a fortnight ago. This had nothing whatever to do with any fault or failing found either in connection with my work or with myself (as you can speedily ascertain if you have the least doubt of it by writing to Mr Cromar, Production Manager, Mond Nickel MOS Factory, Thornliebank). I was simply dismissed owing to a change in the whole policy and organisation of the firm. I need scarcely tell you that war work is simply a vast racket under Monopoly Capitalism and that the training centres and other Government schemes are all keyed in to a cheap labour policy. That is what lies behind industrial conscription and in particular the conscription of women for war work. When I was engaged by the Mond Nickel it was as I told you made clear that the new factory was not yet (nor is it now) at a stage which could utilise me in the capacity for which I was engaged, but they started me in a stop-gap capacity pending the time when they would be ready to use me for that work. At the same time they engaged other men for diverse eventual posts in the new organisation – as inspectors, storekeepers, etc. These men like myself were suddenly dismissed, not because we had done anything wrong, not because we were incompetent, but simply and solely because in the interval the calling-up of women had led to a complete change of plan with regard to the new factory under which (for low wage reasons) at least 90 per cent of the personnel will be women, and consequently there would be no point in keeping us on at the high wages promised us when the jobs we were intended to fill could be taken up by women instead at very much smaller wages.

It will not require much imagination on your part, my dear, to understand how this sudden blow affected me. It came at the worst possible moment – just when you were about to come down and when I had made provisional arrangements about Mike's schooling. I fully understood what a devastating disappointment it must be to you and that wrung my heart. It was at least an equal disappointment to myself. All my hard work and seeming success had suddenly gone for nothing. Of all the blows sheer bad luck has ever dealt me this was by far the hardest. It would actually have been easier if I had been to blame in any way. But I wasn't and there was simply nothing I could do about it.

I set to work to find any other suitable job I could possibly do at a wage that would enable us to get together again and build a home. There is no string I can think of I have not pulled. So far without success. The only jobs I could get through the Labour Exchange would not yield enough to enable us to live together. Whatever they offered me I would have to take. They could and probably would send me to labourer's work in an English munitions factory. Where would we be then? So far therefore I have not gone to the Labour Exchange. I may not be able to help myself, but that must be the last recourse. In the meantime I – and many friends of mine – are doing our utmost to find something for me. I may have success to report at any moment now. (On the other hand, I may not.) Ex-Lord-Provost Sir P.J. Dollan has been specially anxious to help me and reassuring that he would be able to do so.[2] He thinks he can place me in a capacity like what I was to have had with the Mond Nickel Coy, at the big Rolls Royce factory at Hillingdon, South Glasgow, and I am to see him tomorrow again and he hopes to be able to arrange then for an interview for me with the Chief Labour Supervisor at Hillingdon. I hope to dear God this comes off and that I get the job. I will wire you at once if I do.

I need not try to go further into all the pros and cons of this most terribly torturing position. You will know, I hope, what my feelings are – for you and Mike and for myself. I will send you any money I possibly can the moment I can lay my hands on any. At the moment I am almost penniless. Even car-fares are nearly beyond me; tobacco is out of the question. Over a week ago I used a good deal of the last money I had in sending to America by clipper mail copies of poems to various likely periodicals there, also to New Directions (whom I asked, if they accepted them, to pay for at once and send the money to you). I also wrote the Colt Press asking them to send you at once the 25 dollars they owe me. And there is also 4 guineas to come to you from Faber and Faber for the two poems Walter de la Mare is including in his new anthology. You should also have heard by now from Macmillan, giving a statement of the sales of the *Golden Treasury* in this country and America, and I hope that may mean a fair-sized cheque. I also hope you get a decent fee from the BBC for the portion of the 'Birlinn'.

Through Black I am arranging now for the issue in pamphlet form of a lot of my new poems, at the rate of a 24 page pamphlet quarterly until all the main pieces in *Mature Art* and the Spain poem have been so issued.

I am extremely proud of Mike's success in again being first prize winner. Kiss him from me and tell him how glad I am and how anxious to see him and determined by hook or crook that he will have the chance he deserves.

I ask you no questions, my dear, about your own difficulties. I dare not. I love you and Mike, and am only anxious that we should be together again as soon as possible and that our hellish bad luck should cease a little at last and give us just half a chance.

I can say no more. If my heart were breakable I think this last blow would have smashed it to smithereens, but it must not break since it is necessary to fight and win through somehow yet, and in order to fight one must keep in good heart somehow no matter what blows one suffers, and in this I know that no matter how tired and disappointed you are too that you will never fail me.

Kisses to you both, my darlings. Your loving Christopher

---

1. CMG moved to F.G. Scott's house having been ordered out of his brother Andrew Graham Grieve's for drunkenly suggesting to AG's son, Angus, then home on leave, that he should consider carrying out seditious actions against the military authorities. See Alan Bold, *MacDiarmid Christopher Murray Grieve: A Critical Biography* (London: Paladin Grafton Books, 1990), p.435. In a letter to Valda, 21 May 1942, CMG wrote, 'I had a hell of a row with Graham – on politics: he is extremely reactionary and hates the working classes'.
2. Patrick Joseph Dollan (1885–1963), Lord Provost of Glasgow, 1938–41.

31. *To Valda Grieve (NLS)*

44 Munro Road, Jordanhill, Glasgow   1 July 1942

My dearest Henbird

I got your letter of 26th June today and my heart bled for you, though of course it was no news to me that you were in desperate straits and naturally felt like a rat in a trap. The trouble as you too well know was that I had been feeling like just such another rat myself. However, I have escaped and will very soon liberate you too. Reading your letter I was at least profoundly glad that in this interval between your writing this letter and my receiving it I had been able once again to send you good news. You obviously had not received either my last letter or my telegram when you wrote, but you would have them both mercifully by the time your letter reached me. I began my new job on Monday.[1] It is of course hard physical work – heavier than I expected indeed, and it will take me just a week or so to get tuned in to it again. The work goes on without a break –

except for meals – during the shift and one has to give one's whole mind and strength to it. The fitting section in which I work is happily comprised of very decent fellows and is a crack section – so much so that last week they set up a production record for Clydeside in turning out gun-shields. It is on these I am working – filing, fitting with bolts and nuts, drilling holes to receive the former, using the electric buffer to smooth the joins etc., etc. There will be a lot of overtime and we also get a bonus on production. It is in fact a well-paid section, but I don't come into bonus for the first two weeks and this first week I have not to work overtime. So it will be not Friday this week, but a week or perhaps even a fortnight come Friday before I receive my first good pay packet. On Friday first I expect I'll only get two days' pay – since that is the system; the pay week ends on Wednesdays – the books are made up from Wednesday to Wednesday, so of course on Wednesday noon I had only worked from the Monday to the Tuesday shift-ends, the Wednesday hours being carried over to the next week. However I'll send you whatever I possibly can, by wire if it's worth wiring; only I have to keep enough to buy meals for the ensuing week. I lunch in the works canteen and if and when I'm working overtime I'll have to get my tea there too. The food is good and cheaper of course than any café. Fortunately I can walk to my work from here – it only takes about 20 minutes; so I walk there – and walk back when I finish – and that saves 'bus and car fares. Next week when I have a full week's money to draw I'll not get less than £5 – once I come into bonus (probably the following week) I'll get, I understand, £8 or £9, and that is likely to be my average after that.

It is curious how one thing follows another. I have just heard from the Rolls Royce people since that they have a vacancy for the sort of job I am qualified to fulfil and they want to see me at my earliest convenience. But they stipulate it must be before 4.30pm. The only days I can go over to the Rolls Royce place before that time are Saturday afternoon and Sunday. I do not know whether these times will suit but I have written them to that effect; so we'll see. Probably the Rolls Royce job would be an easier and more suitable one. But I would not dream of changing over unless it was a much better and more highly paid job and likely to be also more secure, and even if I wanted to change over I couldn't do it unless the Ministry of Labour approve, so it is up to the Rolls Royce people to secure my transfer if they want me, once they tell me precisely what job they want me for and obtain my consent to being transferred to it if the Ministry approve. So we will see. I don't want to miss the chance of a more important and better paid job with a huge concern like the Rolls Royce people if I can help it, of course, but I'm not anxious to shift unless I know exactly what I'm going to and am sure I can do it satisfactorily and receive substantially higher wages. So you see, henbird, things are moving a little in our direction after all. I confess I was almost in despair, but despairing doesn't help, one has just to keep on trying, and while I hate like Hell the bad time you've had I am extremely glad that that'll soon be over and money a bit more plentiful than you and I have ever had it since we were married.

I'm not forgetting your birthday and Mike's this month and hope and expect – alas not this week! – to be able to give you little presents of some kind.

I'm fearfully worried about these damned sties of Mike's – he must be badly run down somehow. The change to Scotland soon may put him right and in any case we'll be able to have him properly seen to. Poor little fellow, he must have had a dreadful time, and we'll do our best ere very long now to make it up to him and give him a thoroughly good time riding on 'buses, going to the cinema, eating ice-cream slides, and so on.

F.G. and Lovey will be here for a week or two longer, but the boys have already cycled off to Taynuilt and Mrs Scott goes on Saturday. I'm to have this house while they are away. I'll simply use it for sleeping in of course, and have almost all my food at the canteen, except I'll make a cup of tea before I go out in the mornings and have a roll or so with it, and make my supper again before I go off to bed.

I have no other news yet either of Methuen's, Macmillan's, the American publishers, or in fact anything else.

I'm writing Ratter re the book which I sent back to Ipswich long ago. So don't worry about that.

As to your orange box of crockery that can be sent here; I'll see to it at this end – paying for it I mean when it comes. And in the same way anything else you want to send now can just be sent direct to me.

Love and kisses to you both, my darlings. May we be together very soon now. I'm longing to see you both and want you here while it is still summer weather. I'll write again at the weekend.

Yours, Christopher

---

1. In a letter to Valda, 27 June 1942, CMG wrote that he had a new job 'as an engineer in the big naval ordnance works of Messrs Meakin [Mechin] Ltd., Scotstoun, Glasgow'.

32. *To Valda Grieve (NLS)*

c/o Scott, 44 Munro Road,　　　　　　　　　　　Tuesday, 7 July 1942
Jordanhill, Glasgow

Darling Henbird

You would get my letter and 15/- posted on Saturday. I was extremely sorry to be unable to send you more, but I only got two days' pay – 27/9: and I cannot manage on less and retained from one payday to the next as

I have 1/2 a day to pay for my lunch at the Works Canteen, and if I am working late I have also to buy my tea, 4d. or 6d. To my disgust also this week a subscription list went round for a marriage present to one of the men, and I had to stump up 2/6 (which was what all the men were giving) which I really couldn't afford and had carefully banked on to see me through various little incidental expenses till next Friday. However, I'll have a better pay then (though I won't be in bonus for one week longer) and I'll hope to send you a decent telegraphic remittance then and thus end the horrible time you must have been having, as I know only too well.

Since I wrote last we have had a visit from the Welsh poet, Dylan Thomas and his wife, a daughter of Francis MacNamara, an Irish poet I once met and some of whose poetry I remember reading over 30 years ago! She is an extremely beautiful person. I liked Thomas immensely. They came out to Scott's and F.G. and I arranged a programme for them, F.G. playing and singing his settings of many of my lyrics and I reading them (so that they could get the right idea of the sound of the Scots language, and then translating them into English for them so that they could get the meaning). Thomas was on a trip up the West of Scotland for the Strand Films Coy Ltd for whom he works as a scenario writer.

The work has been going all right. I am getting used to it, though it is still a big physical effort and the long hours are very tiring. Last week I was attached to an experienced fitter and saw him doing – and helped him in doing – his jobs and he explained points that arose and gave me useful tips. But that came to an end on Monday and I was then put to doing the job on my own. The work is the fitting of side shields of gun armour. It involves all sorts of operations – filing, hammering, grinding with an electrical buff, boring holes, drawing them into line etc. etc. All the parts have to fit in perfectly even when all the bolts and nuts are in; and when one is finished it has to pass the inspection first of the shop foreman then of the Government inspectors. On Monday I did two of them unaided and they passed the inspectors O.K. I felt very bucked; you will understand why when I tell you that in a full day's work even a thoroughly expert fitter who has been doing this class of work for a long time can not do more than three. So I think I'll manage all right. The only thing is that the job involves a lot of very heavy lifting; also one gets one's hands hashed with handling the rough metal and gets them all cut with steel filings, as well as skinning bits at times, especially one's knuckles if the spanners slip when one is tightening the nuts, not to mention what an appalling mess they are always in with black oil and red paint. But there you are. Apart from such minor disagreeables, the consolations of work in Meechan's are very pleasant – I mean the chaps I am working with are all very decent fellows, the canteen food is quite good, and so on.

Also, I have begun to put in one evening's duty per week as a member of the works' Ambulance Squad. The first aid stuff will of course quickly come all back to me. If I had not taken this on I'd have had to do fire-watching or some other service of an ARP kind, and I not only preferred First Aid naturally, because of my extensive previous experience, but also because those who do it are exempt from all other such duties and get about 15/- a week extra pay for doing it (the amount depends upon the number of extra hours one puts in at First Aid practices etc.).

Friday 10/7/42
I had meant to have completed this letter and got it off to you before now, but have been too tired at nights to write again. Don't be alarmed by that statement. I don't get much time to myself. But I am in good form.

However, your letter came today (also the parcel of your laundry, etc.). So I can now answer a few of the points you raise, and get this off to you tomorrow morning. (Or perhaps tonight yet.)

First of all, I wired you £2.10/- today, so that will help to relieve the situation. I expect to be on bonus by next payday, and therefore to be able to send you more. Only I have to be careful this week to eke things out, as I have a holiday for a week from the 17th, so that pay will have to stretch out till I get back to work. (I intend just to have a quiet time reading and writing.) But after that things will be O.K. and you'll get more and get it regularly.

Yes, my dear, Angus collected the bag Grant brought down and I got it in due course and have it here. So that's all right. So about my receiving the Neugle etc.[1] I got them all right. I'm sorry I did not reassure you about this.

Re birthday presents, I'll get Mike the *Three Commanders* tomorrow if it's to be had here at all, and post it on to him.[2] As to yourself, the birthday present I have in view for you can't be cancelled – I'd meant to see if I couldn't send you a parcel of some nice eats and cigs for a change as well, but the main thing I am doing is having your *Cornish Heroic Song* produced in pamphlet form. You'll like that, won't you? There won't be a lot of them, but what there are you'll have to send to whom you like. Incidentally, I thought of this not only because it's something I always wanted to do, and felt you'd like, but because it puts a little printing job Robin Black's way, and I'm glad to do that.

I expect there are other things I should remember to say but can't just at the moment. However, I'll write again on Sunday. F.G. goes off on Monday; Lovey a week later. After that I'll be on my own here. But don't worry. I'll be O.K. I get my main meals at the Works Canteen, and require little apart from that – and that little (also whatever I need while on holiday or to tide me over Saturday afternoons to Monday lunch time), I can get from Robin's brother-in-law at his restaurant place – incidentally a very good place indeed for getting all sorts of things not easily got elsewhere.

As to laundry Mrs Scott has only done a few things for me, but I have a big pile of laundry now – mostly very dirty, as, of course, my work makes inevitable – and I'm making it all up into a parcel this weekend and sending it to a laundry.

I'll look after myself all right. Also you can now send to me here any parcels you want to; I'll add them to my collection until you arrive.

Love and kisses to Mike and yourself. And to the 2 Marys, and to Grant of whom I haven't had any word since he passed through Glasgow and left the bag.

Yes, sell the Aladdin etc. etc. Ever yours, Christopher

---

1. 'A Ride on a Neugle' was the last chapter of CMG's autobiography, *Lucky Poet* (1943).
2. William Henry Giles Kingston, *The Three Commanders: or active service afloat in modern days* (London: Griffitth, Farran, 1891).

33. *To Andrew Graham Grieve (EUL)*

44 Munro Road, Jordanhill, Glasgow   Thursday, 29 July 1942

Dear Graham

I have just received your characteristically silly postcard re the registered parcel lying for me at your home, also 'several lots of papers'. I do not know from your p.c. whether the latter arrived by post – or whether they are remnants inadvertently overlooked when the rest of my hoard chez vous was removed. In any case I must point out that you had no right to receive mail of mine if you did not intend to forward it to my new address at the earliest possible opportunity, and it is a serious offence to deliberately detain mail in this way, above all a registered package. I have no one I can send to collect these things, nor am I myself free at any practicable time to do it myself. You had better give them back to the postman, explain the circumstances, and say I will meet any redelivery charges exigible. Until I receive these things I cannot tell what harm your detention of them may have caused, but I will hold you strictly responsible. I have an idea what the registered package consists of, it is not as you presume from the gentleman you term 'S. Smith', and non-receipt of it by me weeks ago caused considerable difficulty to the sender, to myself, and to a firm of American publishers. I shall ascertain at the earliest now the date upon which it was delivered at your house, and take up the matter with the postal authorities. As to your 'advice' re redirection of my mail, I have already taken every possible step in this connection – but hundreds of people knew of your house as my temporary address (including many I do not know personally, and who do not know how to address me, and so may use 'Mr Grieve' simply, thus unfortunately prolonging a trickle of correspondence for me via Cambuslang) and even if I knew their addresses I could not advise them all of my change of abode. Your business is simply to see that nothing is accepted that is not for you or members of your household, and if anything is accepted by inadvertence which is for me to see that it is handed back to the postman *on his next call*.

Yours, C.M.G.[1]

---

1. In Andrew Graham Grieve's hand are notes on this letter to the effect that he did not 'receive' letters – they were put through his letterbox.

34. *To Andrew Graham Grieve (EUL)*

44 Munro Road, Jordanhill, Glasgow5 August 1942

Dear A

Your letter of 2nd Aug. contains three serious criminal libels for which I shall be glad to have your apology, together with complete and final retraction and guarantee of non-repetition in any shape or form.

The first of these in your reference to my 'paranoia'. Nothing whatever in my medical history warrants the use of this term; I could readily secure from competent specialists affidavits to this effect – and any competent lawyer will advise you of the seriously libellous nature of your attribution of this to me.

The second is the repetition of the statement, which so angered me the night I left your house, that I have made a 'convenience' of you. We have corresponded very infrequently during the past 29 years, – hardly more than annually – I have all the letters you have sent me during that period and the absence of any reference in all of these letters to any such solicitation for help or favours of any kind is significant enough. Even more clinching, however, is the fact that I have also copies of the letters I have sent you, since the end of the last War, and they too can be searched in vain for any cadging, let alone any acknowledgment of any assistance received. With two exceptions. One letter from the Gilgal Hospital when I asked for a loan owing to misunderstanding something you had said when you visited me there – and did not receive it. And the letter I wrote from the Shetlands asking if you could perhaps procure me a temporary clerkship and telling you something of the desperate straits in which this War was involving me. Here, again, as you know, I drew a blank. And I challenge you to offset these two instances with any on the other side of the account except once in Edinburgh – and once or twice in Cambuslang – very small temporary loans of cash, all repaid to the best of my knowledge and belief, and in any case extremely petty. During most of the past ten to twelve years I have been as is well-known in literary circles extremely hard-up and in fact practically destitute, not only have I said or written little or nothing to you about this at any time – and known better than to appeal to you of all people for any help – but it is devastatingly funny in the circumstances to have you pose as my great benefactor because I occasionally borrowed – and repaid – a bob or two. Other people have happily been proud and glad to help me from time to time, but to keep an indigent brother has never been in the character of that eminent Xian gentleman, yourself. So cut it out. You have never given me – nor with the above trivial exceptions spread over more than quarter of a century been asked to give, even as a loan – any assistance of any kind; and as to 'making a convenience' of you in any other way the extreme infrequency of our personal contacts or meetings of any [kind] with each other, the very rare occasions upon which I have ever been in your house, etc., give the lie to any such suggestion most effectively.

The third libel is your statement that I was drunk repeatedly in your house at Cambuslang. The fact is not only that I was never drunk there at all but very seldom had so much as 'drink taken'. The hours I was engaged at Thornliebank Training Centre and afterwards at the Mond Nickel are verifiable – and were such that I had extremely little opportunity to secure drink, being at work during public house hours. In the time I was free my notebook happily provides a complete list of the engagements, speaking and otherwise, and the people with whom I consorted during these times, and the nature of the activities I can prove myself to have engaged in, and the unanimous testimony of my audiences and other associates will, you will find, leave you an extremely small margin of time when I could possibly have secured liquor at all, let alone sufficient to inebriate me, and you will also find, in addition to the testimony of almost all my other associates during the period as to my practically complete sobriety (I could not have carried on my very arduous and unaccustomed work, let alone my multiplicity of other public activities, but for that), but you will find nowhere, no matter how assiduously you search, any independent witness – e.g. the 'bus and train conductors who must surely have observed my deplorable state if it had ever existed except in your cruel and cowardly imagination, the police who would have had a professional interest in the staggering phenomenon, etc. etc.

So far am I, as I have always been, from wishing to make a convenience of you, my dear brother, that you will find it not only difficult, but impossible, to reconcile any such suggestion with the alacrity and finality with which I now cease to have any relations whatever with you. And in that connection I must point out (since I am keeping a copy of this letter too) that despite all my (according to you) heinous offences it was I who took umbrage and forthwith left your house – not (as you will probably say, and no doubt probably already believe yourself) you who in self-righteous wrath ordered me out of it. And I got here all right – a remarkable achievement for a drunk!

As to the matter of the registered package, and papers, the letter to which my last letter was my reply was the only communication I have had from you since I left Cambuslang. I did not receive any such prior notification as you now say you sent to me here on the day of the receipt of the registered packet. And as to your not knowing my address, letters were redirected to me here, I wrote from here when I arranged with Morag to supply the Food Office with a note of my registered-for-rations shops at Cambuslang and again when I arranged about the carriers bringing my bags etc. here, and on several occasions Scott himself phoned up, mainly in connection with the latter matter, and you certainly had the telephone number through which he could be contacted.

Yours, Chris

P.S. Finally, as to making a 'convenience' of you when I came to Glasgow I intended to stay not with you but with Scott, and only went to Cambuslang instead because the Thornliebank GTC people advised me that Jordanhill was too far away and Cambuslang would be better. But I went to Cambuslang *on your invitation* – an invitation which would never have been extended if I had really been a person of the character you now seek to make out, but one who had no use of you except to sponge on you and bite the hand of smug generosity.[1]

---

1. This letter is also annotated by Andrew Graham Grieve, to the effect that CMG is lying throughout: 'He *has* chronic monomania' writes AGG, referring to his senses of persecution and self-importance; 'I didn't *say* it was due to his medical history but he himself told me in the Gilgal home in Perth ... that his illness there was due to *Syphilis*. What about *that* history?' 'He rarely saw me or wrote me without "cadging" money' '... he was frequently *very* drunk' '... I hoped the years would make a difference; but NO – the same Christopher.'

35. *To Valda Grieve (NLS)*

44 Munro Road, Jordanhill　　　　　　　　Wednesday, 12 [August 1942]

My dearest Valda

Many thanks for your birthday telegram which I got tonight when I returned from work. Also a big registered parcel of 'laundry' was safely received the other day. But I have had no letter for a fortnight and am wondering and worrying why.

I had not a very happy birthday. To begin with I celebrated the occasion by getting a 'fire' – a bit of hot steel – into my right eye. I had it taken off the eyeball with a pair of tweezers, and then went to the Ambulance Room where I washed the eye, and then the nurse put drops into it which soon soothed it all right. It was a pouring wet day too and very cold. It has been really a wretched summer again.

But I have more cause for depression alas! It seems we are never to get settled into any sort of security. I have just learned that Meechans will probably have to give notice to a lot of employees one of these days; and of course that means that those most recently taken on will be those who are dismissed. And that will include me. The reason is that contracts are hung up owing to material not coming in quickly enough from the iron foundries. That means that no overtime is being worked, and the regular hands object to that as it means they have only the basic wage and no overtime and no bonus, and they are accustomed to big wages. That also is why I have not been put on bonus by this time – none of them have been getting bonus since the holiday. By dismissing recent employees like me there will be more work, and possibly even overtime, for the regular hands, and the firm will also cut down overhead expenses. It is not a question at all of any dissatisfaction with my work. But it is infernally disappointing and I am very tired of the uncertainty and loneliness, in addition to the long hours and grinding hard work. Hope deferred makes the heart sick, and it seems that this is one of these things which always promise well but peter out before the big money is reached. I have no doubt I'll get another job quickly; but will it be any better? Will it last any longer? Will I just have another spell of hard drudgery and then find myself unemployed again just before I can get into the big money? And if this goes on how on earth am I to get you and Michael down, and help you here – and I am so longing to have you with me, and get poor little Mike to this school.

Also I know how difficult your own position is – not only if there is a week or two again with little or no money, but also with the cottage denuded and all your stuff parcelled up, and the bitter disappointment of delay and uncertainty again and the difficulty of making explanations to people. It looks so bad too, though it really and truly is due to no fault or failing of mine whatever but simply and solely to these truly infernal wartime conditions.

Above all, when you get this, darling, do not leap to the most doleful conclusions. If it really happens (it may not) and I am 'stood off' be sure I'll get on to the job of finding another billet right away and pull every wire I possibly can, and hope for the best. Also if I am 'stood off' I'll let you know as frequently as I can if there is anything else in view and wire you at once if I do get fixed up.

But at least you will understand that I am almost distracted with this recurring worry, and that this sort of thing (and the absence of all news of my books) is not conducive to a happy 50th birthday.

Amongst other things please tell Mike I had hoped he'd have been down here in time to have gone with me to Elderslie on 22nd inst, where the annual William Wallace memorial meeting is held. I am to be one of the speakers there this year.

I have no other news, but am most concerned about the absence of any letter from yourself, and do hope nothing amiss has happened at your end.

I'll add to this letter tomorrow (Thursday) if there are any further developments, and post it to you then.

Thursday
Darling: –
The blow fell as I expected – but with a quite unexpected sequel.
I was given a week's notice for the reasons stated: but almost at once I was called into the office and re-engaged, being, however, transferred to another department, the Stamping Shop, where they make copper belts for shells etc. My job there will be a responsible one but physically much lighter work, and the rates of pay are just the same both at present and in prospect, only I'll actually, I understand, begin to draw more right away as I'll have a good deal more overtime than we've had lately in the Fitters Section, and Sunday work as well.

What between the shock of dismissal and then the wonderful shock of instant re-engagement I'm a complete nervous wreck. God the relief, though. I'll write you again over the weekend. Blessings. Love to you and kisses. Yours, Christopher

36. *To Valda Grieve (NLS)*

c/o Black, 2 Park Terrace, Glasgow [August 1942]

My dear V.

Just a hasty note to say that I have sustained injuries at work today through a pile of copper plate falling on me. My injuries are extremely painful but I think not serious. I was I think very lucky. I might easily have had both legs and my left arm fractured, but actually I got off lightly considering the nature of the accident with a badly gashed right leg, a left leg put out of commission altogether with a muscular wrench which has swollen up greatly and which makes it impossible for me to walk, and a whole series of long slashing cuts on my left forearm. I went to the Western Infirmary and had my injuries dressed and my left leg with the bad knee X-rayed. And I am to report again on Friday and in the meantime lie up – at above address. I'll do my damnedest to collect my pay on Friday. Black's fortunately is not too far away from Scotstoun where I work, and if I do get it wire you £5 or so; and if I don't get it will do that as quickly as possible. Please don't worry any more than you can help. I'm in good hands – Robin and Margaret are extremely kind and helpful. Will write you fully as soon as I can. Best of love to Michael and yourself.

With kisses from Your loving Christopher

37. To Valda Grieve (NLS)

2 Park Terrace, Glasgow C.3   Wednesday, 9 September 1942

My dearest V.

I am going on all right. My left leg is still infernally painful, however, and quite useless. The injury is purely muscular; if the bone had fractured one would have known just how long it would have taken to get put right, but with a muscular injury there's no telling. However, the swelling is much reduced and you may be sure I won't be a moment longer off work than I can possibly help. My right leg is healing all right and my forearm is already O.K. but for a series of dry scars. I was jolly lucky. I'm not likely ever to have a narrower escape. I am very comfortable here and Robin and Margaret could not be kinder or more helpful.

Now about your last letter.

1/ You seem not to have received some letters of mine. You ask about why I didn't take the Rolls Royce job, for example. Well, I told you all about that. You can't just take a job these days. You must have the consent of the Ministry of Labour to change your job and tho' the Rolls Royce people specially applied to the Ministry to have me transferred to them the request was refused, on the ground that the Ministry had decided that all Progress Men's jobs, and other semi-secretarial and administrative jobs, were henceforth to be filled by women.

2/ In this connection I do not know what to do about your request that I should get a job ready for you to take up when you get here. In the first place, have you registered? If you have not – and it is found out – you will be in trouble over that. Secondly you can't just take anything you want. You have to go where the Ministry directs – or get the Ministry's approval before you can take up any job of which you may have the offer. I am very anxious about the whole thing but must leave it over till you arrive. You'll have no difficulty at all in getting a suitable job right away – if the Ministry will let you: but I'm not going to have you sent to some damned English munitions works or stuck into the ATS or anything of that sort, if I can possibly help it.

3/ I thought we had built up a thoroughly sound and lasting relationship during those happy years together at Whalsay. Apparently not. You do not trust me. In the absence of knowledge you fly to conjectures and speculations to my disadvantage. I quite understand your disappointment and the effect of the long delay and the fact that my work down here has not panned out as we hoped. (Do not forget that these things have affected me as much as they have affected you.) But it would have been wiser to have waited to make sure that I was really letting you down – that I, and not a complex of circumstances over which I have no control, have been to blame – before levelling your wild charges at me. You will understand once you are down here. Letter-writing is a pest – letters are so misleading and inadequate – half-an-hour's conversation could clear up the whole matter in a way that endless letters could not do. I am extremely fond of Mike and you and I am playing the game all right – but it is a hard game, and my luck has been out, and life down here under present conditions is no joke.

5/ My job is all right, waiting for me as soon as I am fit. In the meantime of course I do not get wages, but only about 30/- compensation money. However on Friday (or Saturday at latest) I'll wire you at least £2.

6/ We've had notification from the Railway Company of the arrival of your sea-chest. It's to be delivered tomorrow. I've given Robin the 10/5d which is payable on it at this end. I'll write again in a day or two and tell you in what condition we received it.

7/ I was frightfully worried to hear of Mike's bad turn and have been hoping for further news. I do hope he's been all right since. We must get him overhauled by a thoroughly good doctor as soon as he gets down here. And you too.

Now, darling, don't be vexed over what I say. You are all the world to me and I do not want any quarreling – besides I know what a hard time you've had – but all the same we must trust each other and it simply does no good when any snag crops up to fly to the worst conclusions and on a basis of pure conjecture level all sorts of accusations of neglect and selfishness against me.

Love and kisses to Mike and yourself.

Yours, Christopher

38. *To Valda Grieve (NLS)*

2 Park Terrace, Glasgow C.3   Saturday [19 September 1942]

Dearest Hen-Bird

Many thanks for your letter received today. I am going on all right and can hirple about the house quite quickly now, with a stick in one hand and a household broom, with its head under my armpit, in the other. My left leg, however, is still painful and very insecure; I can place no weight on it. I'm to try to go out a little this weekend, however, and if I can manage at all (which I don't guarantee) I'll do my damnedest to get back to work this incoming week.

I'll not really be fit for the hard physical work I was doing, but I could perhaps manage if they allowed me to do lighter jobs for a few days till my leg was really dependable again.

I thought I'd told you just how the accident happened. I was loading copper plates on to a lorry from a stack of these plates a little higher than myself. They are heavy – two being as many as I could possibly carry and throw up on to the lorry at once. I was taking two off the top of the stack, when the whole stack, which must have been insecurely built, collapsed on top of me. The weight was so great that of course if it had caught me the right way it would simply have crushed in my chest. As it was the bulk of the weight caught and pinned my legs. How these did not get broken is a miracle. As I said before I was extremely lucky to get off so lightly. Of course the pain was hellish and still is if I happen to give my left leg particularly a sudden turn or put any weight on it.

As I said in my last letter I had hoped to wire you a couple of pounds today again, but you will understand that I am only getting slightly over 30/- a week just now while I am off work (and no lodging allowance). Even so, I could have managed, but the arrival of two boxes at Robin's shop today made it impossible, for I had to pay 15/8d on them! It's a good job I had it, for Robin couldn't have paid it. Margaret says she has only had one pound from him since 1936. So, darling, just put that in your pipe and smoke it when you think you are ill-done to, and that I am a selfish skunk who neglects his wife and son!

I am glad to hear that your long hard task is practically over now and hope your permits to travel will come through O.K. and that you'll be here ere long. It'll be all right if I'm back at work as quickly as I hope to be.

I'll send you more cash just as soon as I can lay hands on any, but I enclose £1 in the meantime and am sure you'll understand that paying 15/8 on these boxes, 10/9 on your sea-chest, and the other unavoidable expenses in which this accident has involved me (for, amongst other things, I got the best doctor I could, as a private patient, instead of depending on a panel doctor at the Infirmary, since I wanted to be sure of first-class treatment and felt that would ensure my speedier return to work, and thus pay for itself) makes it impossible for me, with nothing but my sick pay, to send you more just at the moment.

Love and kisses to Michael and yourself but don't worry. I'll take every possible care, and write soon again.

Yours, Christopher

P.S. I'll enclose a letter to Hay's in my next to you.

39. *To Charles Lahr (NLS)*

c/o Donnelly, 35 Havelock St., Glasgow W   10 January 1943

My dear Charles

It is a very long time since I wrote you – and this is to be just a very brief note, as I have been working all day and am not in a mood for letter-writing, even to you – tho' I would dearly like to see you again and have a yarn. My purpose in the meantime is just to introduce a young friend of mine, Ian Finlay,[1] who is anxious to find a congenial job of some kind in London, – a job in a book-shop, or with some publishing firm, or in journalism. With the shortage of labour owing to the call-ups there are probably jobs of the kind offering all right if one knew where to find them. Perhaps you could help him, or give him introductions to people who could – my old friend, Charles Duff,[2] for example. I'll be very glad indeed if you can put him on to something. I hear you are very busy – and even seeing a little life now that you are just off Leicester Square. I certainly hope that some of the war-wealth is flowing into your coffers and that you personally are in good form. Heaven only knows when I'll see London again. As you probably know I've been working as an engineer in Glasgow for nearly a year now, and a month or two ago Valda and Michael joined me here. We are all in good shape. Writing is out of the question, of course, with the very long hours I work and the fact that I am doing very exacting physical labour. However, that doesn't matter much as I have heaps of stuff awaiting publication once paper ceases to be so infernally scarce. Things are moving at last, however, and Messrs Methuen are publishing very shortly now my huge *Autobiography* which has been hung up for over a couple of years. I hope you sell millions of it.

Love from us all and best wishes for 1943.

Yours, Chris

---

1. Ian Hamilton Finlay (b.1925), writer, artist and poet, famed for his concrete poetry and his garden at Little Sparta, Lanarkshire; the young Finlay was at Glasgow School of Art briefly around this period.
2. Charles Duff (1894–1966), English writer of travel guides, histories and a series of teach-yourself language books.

40. *To the Editor,* Tribune

[Glasgow] [March 1943]

Dear Sir,

Since my essay in *The New Scotland*[1] expressly disavowed any claim to being a comprehensive or even a summary account of contemporary Scottish literature, and confined itself to a few emerging tendencies which seem to me of prime significance and to the group of very young and little known writers who exemplify these tendencies, there is no valid point in Mrs Naomi Mitchison's complaint in her review of that publication in your issue of 12th March that I fail to mention Neil Gunn and 'James Bridie'. I equally fail to mention all other Scottish writers of established reputation, since I happen to be concerned solely with the younger writers. I only quote one poem of my own in a somewhat long essay, simply because it is extremely relevant and presents a point of view it would be difficult to express more concisely or effectively in prose. The quotations

I give from Somhairle Mac'Gille'Eathain's long unpublished Gaelic poem on the Cuillin of Skye are not, as Mrs Mitchson assumes, from an English translation of that great Marxist poem made by myself. Even if they were, I would be quite entitled to fill my essay with them, since, as I make clear, I regard this poem as one of the landmarks in recent Scottish literary development and, even if I am wrong in so regarding it, after all I am the author of the essay in question and, as such, am surely entitled to express and exemplify my own opinions in it in any way I choose, so that there is no legitimate ground whatever for Mrs Mitchison's curiously ill natured and (as it happens) factually erroneous objections either to what I do in that essay or to what she wrongly represents me as having done.

Yours sincerely, Hugh MacDiarmid

---

1. 'Scottish Arts and Letters: the Present Position and Post-War Prospects', in *The New Scotland: 17 Chapters on Scottish Re-Construction Highland and Industrial* (Glasgow: Civic Press and London: The London Scots Self-Government Committee, 1942), reprinted in Hugh MacDiarmid, *Selected Prose*, ed. Alan Riach (Manchester: Carcanet, 1992, pp.150–70).

41. *To Charles Nicoll (EUL)*

RN229, c/o FMO, Albert Harbour, Greenock   1 November 1944[1]

Dear Mr Nicol

Time is passing very quickly. It is incredible that so many weeks should have slipped away already since I left Mechans for the sea, without my getting a chance to drop you or Mr Ferguson a line. But you will understand that such a change-over needs a time to adjust oneself to it. Besides we have had an unusually busy spell, and less time to ourselves than is normally the case. On the whole, however, I think the change was a wise one. I am in excellent health, get on splendidly with the other members of the crew, and it is fine to be out in the open air all day and amongst the magnificent scenery of Loch Long, Gareloch, and Holy Loch. The weather, of course, so far has been extraordinarily considerate. We have had one or two very wet and stormy days, however, and it can be wild enough on these lochs all right. Winter conditions in their full rigour cannot be long delayed now, of course, but I do not think they will do me any harm, tho' I may feel them keenly enough until I get thoroughly hardened.

I hope Mrs Nicol and baby are well and you yourself. I'll take a run down to Scotstoun and see you again first chance I get. In the meantime I can only express again my warmest thanks to yourself – and to Mr Ferguson – for your great kindness to me while I was at Mechans. And perhaps you will be so kind as to tell old George and the girls in the Copper

Bands Department that I was asking for them. I hope all goes well there and that you are having a less worrying time than was the case when I left.

The skipper of my boat is very anxious to get some photos taken but even if you were willing to do this (and had the necessary films etc.) I am not sure how regulations stand – whether you could get a pass to come aboard in the first place, and in the second whether even if you did you would be allowed to bring in a camera and take photos. However I'll find out what the position is in those respects and let you know if the matter can be arranged.

I hope you are having success in marketing some of your photos through the agency: and also that at the London Salon etc. you carried off prizes all right.

Looking forward to seeing you again ere long.

Yours, C.M. Grieve

---

1. CMG had requested a transfer to the Merchant Service and was placed aboard the Norwegian ship *Gurli*, working, as he was to claim, as a deck-hand and then as a first engineer, or, as Robert Blair Wilkie claims (see Bold, *MacDiarmid*, p.445), as a postal officer to the Allied Fleets harboured at Greenock.

42. To Helen Burness Cruickshank (EUL)

c/o *Gurli* (RN229), MacIntyre's Slip,   23 January 1945
Port Bannatyne, Bute

My dear Helen

I was much distressed to hear from your letter to Valda that your health had for some time been so unsatisfactory that you had sent in your retiral earlier than the compulsory retiring age: but apart from the ill-health cause glad that you were freeing yourself from the Service after your long career in it. You speak of looking forward to just 'puttering about'. That certainly has its attractions: but I hope that with leisure, and restored good health, that there will be a good deal more to it than that and that you may have a good few years of happy retirement to devote profitably to the things nearest your heart – and by that I do not mean only gardening, delightful as that can be, but another rich crop of your Scots poems.

As you will know I am now in the Merchant Navy. Our ship broke down about a fortnight ago and we were sent down to go on the ship at Port Bannatyne for propeller shaft repairs: but when we got there found there was no vacant place on the ship for us, so we had to come round to Rothesay and have been lying here for 10 days and probably will continue to lie here for another 10 or so. Then round to Port Bannatyne where I expect we'll be for at least a month.

I am due – overdue 10 days' leave: but can't get it until we are running again. Which is a nuisance. As I can't finish my work on Soutar's *Collected Poems* till then. That task has been worrying me for a long time. It proved very much harder than I had anticipated – owing to the great mass of material; the as-yet-unpublished at least equaling the published, and much of it superior in quality too. I could not make headway with the task, with only broken bits of time to do it in – I needed a clear spell of a week or so to break the back of the job, and that I've never been able to get. This incidentally accounts for my terribly long retention of your Soutar books. But I'll return these to you now first time I get up to Glasgow.

In addition I have all sorts of things of my own in hand but these too must await a favourable break for completion and publication.

In the meantime I am in excellent health and greatly enjoying Bute – long tramps to Lochs Ascog and Fad, and so on; all new and delightful country to me – mostly in the company of Alex Orr (Dr Orr's brother) who is headmaster of the Public School here.

Compton Mackenzie is here on Wednesday to speak at a British Legion Burns' 'do'; and both he and I are proposing the Immortal Memory at different Burns's suppers in Greenock on Thursday, while he and I and David Kirkwood are addressing a big Ex-Servicemen's meeting in Partick on 29th. I wish I could subdivide myself into about 50; then I could possibly meet all the demands on me for speeches etc. But that can't be done and I simply do what I can. My hair is going noticeably grayer too but on the whole I retain my vitality pretty well.

Flos MacNeill sent us a card at Christmas. But we haven't her address and I don't know if Valda sent her a card via the SNP as I suggested. So if you see her please give her our kindest regards. Also Mary Ramsay, please. (I haven't heard or seen anything of her for a very long time now.) And remember us kindly to any other mutual friends you may be seeing.

I don't know when I'm likely to be in Edinr. again, but will try to see you then. In the meantime here's wishing you all the best in your well-earned rest from Michael (who is flourishing both physically and psychologically at Kilquhanity), Valda and myself.

Yours, Chris

43. *To the Editor,* The Scots Independent

27 Arundel Drive, Battlefield, Glasgow S.   30 May 1945

Dear Sir:-

May I crave a portion of your valuable space to express my deep concern and indignation at the dangerously reactionary decision of Caithness County Council to exclude from County Council and County Library appointments any who are not of the Protestant Faith, and, as a corollary to this decision, to dismiss Mr Fred Robertson, of Wick, from his post as County Librarian in view of his conversion to Roman Catholicism? I am sure that my protest will be supported by all in Scotland who really value freedom of opinion. That such an action can be taken in this country just when we have been engaged in a war on behalf of 'the four freedoms' is a sad commentary on the degree of reality or unreality appertaining to our Governmental and general public professions of zealous championship of liberty. I personally am neither a Protestant nor a Catholic, but a freedom-loving Scot, fully aware of the tremendous struggle throughout our history to develop a measure of freedom from religious intolerance and sectarian strife, and of the imminent danger of a widespread revival of these evils in our midst as part of the aftermath of this War. Reactionary religious elements of all denominations have been muscling in behind the smoke-screen of war-time requirements, and have already re-established an ominous hold in various departments of our public life from which they had been practically eliminated altogether. This is particularly true of the field of education. Are we to consent to have the hands of the clock put back in this way and compelled to fight all over again the hard battles which earned us the measure of freedom we enjoyed prior to the War? What makes the decision of the bigoted nonentities responsible for Mr Robertson's dismissal all the worse, of course, is that while they are all the veriest nobodies, clad in a 'little brief authority', Mr Robertson happens to be one of the ablest of our younger Scottish historians, and a man of a degree of education and culture all too rare in our midst. I am aware, of course, that the Caithness County Council's decision has still to be endorsed by the Secretary of State for Scotland. One wonders, however, what can be looked for in this respect from such a 'muckle hunk of gurry' as the Earl of Rosebery, whose appointment indeed is such an insult to Scottish intelligence that a man like Mr Robertson might well refuse to retain his post at the instance of such a creature, even if the latter did pronounce in his favour. However that may be, if effect is given to this monstrous piece of victimisation, I hope there will be a great rally of all Scots concerned with the maintenance and furtherance of our hardly-won civil liberties and that every possible action will be taken to secure the reversal of Caithness County Council's decision. May I suggest as a first step to this end that readers of the *Scots Independent* who realise the vital importance of preventing the thin end of this old wedge being re-inserted into our social structure should join with me in forming a special Committee to take whatever steps may be possible to protest against the Caithness County Council's action and compel its withdrawal.

Yours for Scotland, C.M. Grieve ('Hugh MacDiarmid')

44. To Compton Mackenzie (HRHRC)

27 Arundel Drive, Battlefield, Glasgow S   24 September 1945

My dear Compton Mackenzie

Very many thanks for your foreword to my poems, which I sent off at once to America.[1] While you are no doubt altogether too kind to my quality as a poet and as an influence in Scotland, I do value immensely what you say about the harmony of our personal relationship and our community of insight in regard to Scotland ever since we first came into contact.

I am sorry indeed to hear that amid all your pressure of work you have also been laid up and in pain: and trust that you are better again and swimming into easier waters. I too am fiendishly busy and constantly off to out-of-the-way places like Tighnabruaich, Tarbert (Loch Fyne), the Maidens (Ayrshire) etc. I'll be glad of a quieter spell for a while and a chance to concentrate and get some of my things finished.

Have you seen Gogarty? I've had several letters from him since his return from America; he seems in excellent form. But I'm sorry to hear he's going off to the States again – says he must, this incoming month.

Again, then, with my warmest thanks, and with every kind regard to yourself and to Miss Boyt and Miss MacSween.

Yours ever, C.M. Grieve

---

1. *Speaking for Scotland: Selected Poems of Hugh MacDiarmid* (Baltimore: Contemporary Poetry, 1946).

45. To Valda Grieve (NLS)

Carlisle   Friday [30 May 1947][1]

My dear V.

The very last thing in the world I want is to break with you. You must know that perfectly well. Any such break would finish me completely.

I have explained the horrible way things have turned out here financially – the hotel business, income tax etc. I am helpless in the matter. It simply means that I am working all week – and working jolly hard – just to pay my hotel: and sometimes my pay won't even do that. You may think I have been careless or not as diligent as I might be in trying to get digs or a place you could come to. That is not true. Either are extremely difficult to get either in Carlisle or anywhere near it. It is largely a matter of luck. So far I haven't had any.

I would have come up this weekend if it had been possible. But it is not. I am going to Chester tomorrow (Saturday) to do a football match. That is a long way and I'll have a full day of it from 8am to late at night.

You say you phoned me up again and I wasn't in. I am of course like most reporters far more out of the office than in – except on Press nights. Monday being Whit, we did not go to press as usual that night but the next – Tuesday night: and I finished at 2am on Wednesday. Then last night (Thursday) we were here till 1.30am this morning. And here I am back in the office again at 8.30.

The job suits me perfectly – if only I had digs or a home of my own. I have all sorts of things to do – City Council meetings, Divorce Courts, Cinemas, Theatre, Football and Boxing Matches etc. etc.

I am not 'whining' as you call it about money; I have simply explained again and again as briefly and clearly as I possibly can just what I am up against.

And as I say although I like the job perfectly – and it is what I have wanted so long – I would have chucked it up before now if I had anything else to go to: only I daren't chuck it up because if I did I couldn't even get the unemployment allowance.

Many thanks for the parcel received today.

It is all very well for Walter – but has he ever been up against it? And what else could he possibly do in the same circumstances but what I have done.

Yours, Chris

---

1. At the beginning of May 1947, CMG joined the staff of the *Carlisle Journal* at the invitation of its editor, Fred Sleath.

46. *To Sydney Goodsir Smith (NLS)*

32 Victoria Crescent Road, Glasgow W.2.,   15 June 1947
c/o *Carlisle Journal*, 60 English St, Carlisle

My dear Sydney

Many thanks indeed for yours of 11th inst. I was more than happy to meet you, and the others, again.

Re your Maclean suggestion I am in entire agreement: but as you perhaps know I am entrusted by Maclean's family with his official biography, and they have put all his private correspondence etc. at my disposal.

This in no way runs counter to your suggestion. But the position is this:
1/ Arrange the book
2/ Fix with publishers.
and I am willing to do myself [*sic*].

This is a very important book and I haven't the least doubt we can do it.

But you act as editor (and I'll send you my stuff by any date you fix); and the terms on which the matter is finally fixed up must be

1/ Whatever editorial fee you agree
2/ Not less than £1.1.0 per 1000 words for other prose contributions
3/ Not less than £2.2.0 per poem for verse.

I am writing in a hurry and trust this is O.K. by you: but let me know. I will certainly do all I can to help.

Please tell Marion I was extremely sorry not to have had an opportunity of seeing her again on my flying visit.

And apart from that, keep your nose clean (as I am sure you will), and here's to our next meeting.

Yours, Christopher

P.S. I can furnish Maclean's own writings – selected by me – up to 20,000 words for the book: and if you fix it up and let me know will send you typescripts by whatever date you fix.

Also, I can arrange for a good photo, or block, for frontispiece.

47. *To Valda Grieve (NLS)*

[Carlisle]   Friday [27 June 1947]

My dear V.

Enclosed photo of Benno's bust of me which is being shown at the opening of the Royal Scottish Academy in Edinburgh today.[1] Please keep it carefully: I may need it any time for press purposes.

The Dublin Celtic Congress is on 2nd July. I am trying Friday to see if I can get sailing permit all right.

Phone message yesterday when I was out from *Sunday Mail* wanting special article in hurry. I noted it last night, posted it this morning. *Sunday Mail* rang up again today and I was able to tell them article was on the way. Not bad going for a drunken sod!

Also letter today from Norrie Fraser, asking me to send article in reply to one of Professor John Orr's (French Professor: Edinburgh University). I'll do that today too.

No. Mike when I saw him in Carlisle was going back to Kilquhanity then: but he expected to be back again here the following weekend doing a little more hostelling in the Lake District. I haven't heard from him again.

1/ When is your birthday?
and
2/ When is Mike's?

I know they are both this month, but, of course, forget the dates.[2]

I don't think you need worry re this job; Carlisle will be your home I think quite all right – and it is certainly a fine place with a very beautiful district all round.

Will write again over the weekend. This is just a note in passing.

Love, Chris

1. Benno Schotz (1891–1984), Head of the Sculpture and Ceramics Department of the Glasgow School of Art, 1938–61.
2. Respectively, 1 July and 28 July.

48. *To Valda Grieve (NLS)*

Carlisle   Friday [11 July 1947]

My dear V.

I wonder what has happened to you; I looked forward to seeing you here on Tuesday or Wednesday. But no word.

You were wrong about the money question.[1] When I said I was going to send you a couple of pounds I was expecting money in for some dancing articles I had done. If they had appeared in the *Dancing Weekly* as was expected I'd have been paid: but it seems they have held them over for the monthly magazine instead. So that is still to come. Also payments for the first of a series of regular monthly leaders I am doing for a new Cumberland monthly.

As to last Friday's money that was damned bad luck on both of us. Carlisle Races were on, and three of us in the office here had a tip for a three-cross double. We got it from a bookie friend. But just before the race he came and told us he had just got another hot tip and advised us not to place the three-cross double bet but to back the other instead. We did – and lost: whereas if we had stuck to the 3–cross double we'd have won £80 for each 7/6 we had on. If that had only come off you would not have been blaming me. It was touch and go. And I would have so much liked to have wired you a good lump sum for the end of your holiday.

Besides I had meant to give you a portable wireless for your birthday. It is being reserved for me. You'll get it as soon as I can manage.

This is just a hurried scrawl. I wired you £3 to Glasgow yesterday not knowing whether you'd gone home or were still in London or Cornwall.

I have still no word of Mike at all.

Now I'm off to Whitehaven all day today. Am having a devilish busy time.

Do hope you are O.K. Love, Chris

P.S. Am getting a BBC cheque about end of next week I understand.

Sunday Mail cheque still to come in; I wrote them yesterday about it, also offering more articles.

---

1. In a letter to CMG of 29 July 1947, Valda wrote that she had heard enough excuses, that Michael's birthday had been missed, his coat was leaking and he could not return to school until £5 owed in fees was paid, and that unless CMG made amends she would write to the *Carlisle Journal* to request some of his pay went directly to her.

49. *To Valda Grieve (NLS)*

Carlisle   Friday [1 August 1947]

My dear V.

You are quite wrong. I was only stating a few facts – not making excuses at all; and I could not state all the facts. £7.10/- may seem a lot on the face of it: but it goes no distance at all if an effort is to be made to send £3 home and pay a hotel with the balance. Even if we had the balance. Income tax is still being deducted from me, and Journalists' Union fees.

The only effect of your writing to the proprietors of the *Carlisle Journal* would be to make my position here impossible. That would do neither of us any good. It would simply mean I'd resign at once – and have no job, and no dole either.

You think you understand. The fact is you have not the slightest understanding. If it was humanly possible for me to get work of my own done, over and above my day's work, I'd do it. I have been, and am, doing a great deal more than you think: but it is a terrible strain and I can neither keep on doing it long nor do what I may can I do a tithe of what I want to do.

You are quite wrong too when you say I could have had some cheques sent direct to you. That is precisely what I have arranged. You will receive £15.15/- or thereabouts from the BBC about 20th August.

There are cheques to come to you from Macmillan's and from *Contemporary Poetry* (America).

The Assistant Editor of *Picture Post* rang me up on Wednesday from London – wants an anti-Edinburgh article by next Wednesday morning. I'll do it this weekend and post it on Monday. *Picture Post* pay well: I am hoping to get about £21 for that article: and you will also receive in the course of the month £6.6/- from the *Sunday Mail*: and a little later £3.3/- from the *Scots Review*.

I am sorry these things could not come sooner. I have been very worried tho' you don't believe it both in regard to Mike's 1/ birthday 2/ clothes 3/ school: and in regard to what can possibly be done re my books and papers at 32 VCR – not to mention yourself and the rest of our goods and chattels. But what the H– can I possibly do that I have left undone. It's no fun for me either.

But as far as money is concerned just have patience a little longer and you will be all right. Don't jump to wrong conclusions. Apart from the things I have already mentioned coming in, – and there are several I haven't mentioned yet – I have nearly 30 speaking engagements between now and the end of the year at £2 or £3 a time and I have all these speeches and lectures to prepare.

Love, Chris

50. *To Seumus O'Sullivan (CUL)*

32 Victoria Crescent Road, Hillhead, Glasgow   26 August 1947

My dear Seumas O'Sullivan

    I was extremely disappointed not to get over to Dublin for the Celtic Congress. I was wrongly apprised of this opening date – 3rd July instead of 23rd – and booked a plane and made all the necessary arrangements. When I found out the right date I had to cancel these arrangements: but then it proved impossible to get either a plane or boat passage. I should have liked immensely to have seen Dublin – and you and other friends – again after all these years.

    This is a note to introduce two friends of mine, both distinguished Scottish artists – Mr and Mrs Walter Pritchard. Mr Pritchard is a painter and sculptor; Mrs Pritchard, under her maiden name of Sadie MacLellan, is our best stained glass artist, and she is a sister of Robert MacLellan, our best Scots dramatist.

    You will do me a great favour if you will introduce them to any writers and artists who happen to be in Dublin.

    I hope the years are very kind to you and that you are in good health and spirits.

    Please accept my compliments and every high regard.

    Yours, Hugh MacDiarmid

51. *To the Editor,* The New Alliance and The Scots Review[1]

32 Victoria Crescent Road, Glasgow W.2   15 September 1947

AUTHORSHIP IN SCOTLAND

Sir, –

    Mr J.M. Reid in his essay on 'Authorship in Scotland' in your September issue declares that my books 'are unread, except in a very narrow circle'. All literature is, and has always been, unread except in a very narrow circle relative to the total population of any country; but I think I have nothing to complain of in this connection. My books are in most of our libraries and are in constant demand. Some of my more recent books – e.g. *Lucky Poet, Golden Treasury of Scottish Poetry,* and *Selected Poems* have sold astonishingly well and I am constantly surprised at the out-of-the-way quarters to which they find themselves, not only in this country but all over the world. Mr Reid is probably confusing two things – the extent to which books sell, and the extent to which they are read. My readers are, I agree, out of all proportion to my purchasers.

    Apart from that point in regard to my own books, I have no sympathy at all with Mr Reid's argument. My attitude on the contrary may be gathered from the following passage from an essay on the contemporary Scottish literary position which appeared in *Voices* in Autumn, 1946, *viz*.:

'Dr Agnes Mure Mackenzie, Mr George Blake, and others have stressed the difficulty of making a living by authorship in a small country like Scotland, and especially in the case of writers who by reverting to Gaelic or to Scots cut themselves off from the great English-reading public. But it may be replied to them as Kirkegaard replied to advancers of a like argument in regard to Denmark: "Some of my contemporaries are of the opinion that to be an author in Denmark affords a poor livelihood. They do not merely mean that this is the case with such a questionable author as I am, who have not a single reader, and only a few who get so far as the middle of the book, and of whom therefore they are not thinking in passing this judgment; but they mean that it is the case even with distinguished authors. Now this land is only a little land. But in Greece was it so mean a position to be a magistrate even though it cost money to be one? Suppose it were so, suppose it were to continue to be so, and in the end it was the lot of an author in Denmark to pay a certain sum yearly for the labour of being an author. Well then, what if it were possible for foreigners to say, 'In Denmark it is a costly thing to be an author, hence, there are mighty few of them, but then again, they have not what we foreigners call catch-pennies, a thing so utterly unknown in the realm of Denmark that the language does not even possess an expression for it.'" That is the principle of integrity which is being regained by all the Scottish writers of any significance.'

Yours sincerely, Hugh MacDiarmid

---

1. Vol. 8, no. 6, October 1947.

52. *To Fred Sleath (NLS, DFF)*

[1947]

Dear Mr Sleath

You recognise, of course, that a man of my national and international reputation can not be dismissed as you dismissed me yesterday without repercussions.

I told you that I was – and intended to remain – a heavy drinker and that if my alcoholic habits interfered with my work you would be justified in dismissing me[,] Directors or anybody else. That is a principle for which I have always contended – and always will.

But I warn you now that if you or anybody else try to suggest that I was dismissed because of drunkenness you will be at once up against it.

I have had no trouble with the police or anybody else on that score. And I have plenty of friends of my own who would counter any assertions to the contrary.

In any case I was not confronted with any accusers and had no opportunity as you know of defending myself.

I did not attempt to argue the matter with you: but the fact remains that any reputation the *Carlisle Journal* may have is a fleabite to my own personal reputation.

And no matter what I do, or what happens, that remains untouchable. It will for centuries hence.

It does not matter one iota what you or they may think; my reputation stands high enough nationally and internationally to enable me to override such people and I promise you I will do it quite ruthlessly.

What I do in my spare time (and I have had little enough of that during the months I have been on the *Carlisle Journal*) is of no concern at all to you or anybody else.

But you also agreed yesterday & c[oul]d not but [have] done so [?] – that I had pulled my weight & done my work and you would not disclose just why I should be dismissed.

I can of course imagine I shall have a great deal more to say in national periodicals & elsewhere about the matter.

I am & have always been thoroughly competent. But I did not realise when I came to Carlisle these things: 1st that the *Journal* was run on such lines that I was obliged to put in up to 16 hours per day – thus having [?] no time to devote to my own literary work.

2/ that the directorate was of such a kind that I was bound sooner or later to expose the whole fit-up.

The latter I will of course do. I have no use whatever for such canting humbugs & hypocrites.

I could not care at all about that because almost everything the *Carlisle Journal* – or any other paper – is concerned about is beneath my contempt but I know that my personal reputation stands – and will stand – so high that I can discard anything of that sort with contempt.

You may have honestly meant to befriend me when I came to Carlisle and I am scarcely the man to be patronised by anybody – let alone by my professional and intellectual inferiors.

In writing this I have no idea whatever of asking you – or your Directors – to change your minds: but while I know that you gave me no warning, and that I have worked two or three times harder than I ought to have done because you believe in sweated labour and are grossly understaffed & by completely inefficient & underpaid youths at that, I do have in mind that I am not prepared for one moment to allow any unsupported statement to be made in any way reflecting either upon my professional efficiency or my personal character.

On the other hand I have not been blind while I have been in Carlisle, and through my contacts with the BBC and other bodies & you may be sure that I intend to blow these people sky-high.

I am not prepared to compromise in any way at all: but no suggestion against me while I have been in Carlisle can possibly be made to justify any dismissal but what I will at once instruct lawyers.

Without prejudice.

Yours sincerely[1]

---

1. This unsigned MS is almost entirely indecipherable in places, and where we have guessed at words or phrases we have inserted a question mark in square brackets. It is evidently a copy written at white heat and perhaps in a state of intoxication after CMG's dismissal from the *Carlisle Journal* towards the end of 1947 by the editor, Fred Sleath, who had apparently been friendly enough to invite CMG onto the staff in the first place.

53. *To Helen Burness Cruickshank (EUL)*

32 Victoria Crescent Road, Glasgow W.2   5 January 1948

My dear Helen

Trust the New Year is suiting you nicely.

This is just a very hurried note to ask if the Prophet's chamber is available. I have meetings in Edinburgh on 10th, 11th, and 13th inst. I would be out almost all day but must have somewhere to sleep o' nights. I'd try to be no more trouble than I could possibly help. Drop me a p.c. and let me know – failing the Prophet's Chamber I may be able to arrange with Dr Orr or Sydney Smith or Sorley Maclean.

Love from us all. Yours, Chris

54. *To the Editor,* The New Alliance and Scots Review[1]

32 Victoria Crescent Road, Glasgow W.2   9 January 1948

Sir, –

While I have not the necessary correspondence at my hand at the moment, I am fortunately in the habit of preserving all the letters I receive and I have piles of communications from most of those who took an active part in the formation of the 'National Party' including Mr T.H. Gibson himself, which amply attest the very active part I took in all the preliminaries to, as well as actual formation of, The Party. That I was 'largely responsible' for it might be putting the matter a little too high, but the fact remains that I did conduct a very active campaign to secure its formation, not only addressing many meetings to that end but writing innumerable articles for all sorts of local and national papers and periodicals and these are on file to prove the point. In addition to such activities there is the matter of direct personal influence and Mr Gibson would perhaps be surprised (or affect to be) if he could read the many letters I have preserved in which a high proportion of those who were most active in the formation of the Party and have since played a foremost part in the development of Scottish Nationalism attributed their 'conversion' to me. It is fortunate that I have preserved all these papers since so many of those with whom I was then associated have passed away in the interval – men like the late R.B. Cunninghame Graham, William Gillies,[2] and Angus Clark. Compton Mackenzie, the Hon. Ruaraidh Erskine of Marr, W.D. MacColl and others are happily still alive and can bear out all I say. Mr Gibson's statement that I had 'little or nothing to do with the formation of that Party and only associated myself with it when it was well on its way to be formed' is directly contrary to the facts and this is borne out, *inter alia*, by a photograph confronting me as I write which shows the speakers at the first public meeting held to signalise the formation of the Party, namely Mr R.B. Cunninghame Graham, Mr Compton Mackenzie, the Duke of Montrose, Mr J.M. McCormick, Dr James Valentine and myself.

Yours, etc.,

C.M. Grieve (Hugh MacDiarmid)

---

1. Vol. 8, no. 10, pp. 158–9, February 1948.
2. William Gillies (1865–1932), leader, with Erskine of Mar, of the Scottish National League (1920), founder and editor of *The Scots Independent*.

55. *To Michael Grieve (NLS)*

Glasgow   10 August 1948

My dear Michael

As you know I do not write any personal letters I can possibly avoid – having more than enough writing to do otherwise. And in any case I know your mother is writing and she keeps me informed. All the same I feel I should drop you a line now – if only because, as you will remember, I promised you a little belated birthday present. So to redeem that promise I now enclose £1 with my love and best wishes.

I do not know if Mummy has told you a long article about me has appeared in a Chicago magazine, and they also reproduced a photograph of the three of us. So, in addition to the note about you in *Our Time*, your photo has also now appeared in this American literary review. So you are getting on. The thin edge of the wedge has been inserted. It will be for you to bang it home.

The luncheon in Edinburgh at which a lot of the Scottish writers are going to present me with a painting of myself has now been fixed for 28th of this month. Mummy and I are going through for it. You were invited too, but unfortunately you will not be back in time. I would have liked you to be present. I think you would have found it very interesting. Besides it would have been a good opportunity to introduce you in a social way to a lot of friends of mine who could be very helpful to you later on. However, I have no doubt other opportunities will arise.

I had a talk last night to Bill McLellan[1] about *Scottish Arts and Letters* which I am going to edit in future. I will take good care that it appears quarterly in future – and not about once a year as it has been doing. You will be glad to hear, however, that the issue which is so long overdue containing the Kilquhanity material including your own poems is just on the point of coming out at long last. So that will be another little feather in your cap.

I am sorry the weather has not been good, but glad you are enjoying yourself and hope you are not being too much trouble to your aunts. Please give them my kindest regards. I hope they are both in good form. Mummie hasn't told me yet what your arrangements are about returning, but I'll be hearing in due course. You'll be needing some cash, of course, for the return journey. Despite the weather I hope you are managing to see a good deal of Cornwall, as it is a lovely and most interesting country and the chance of going over it may not come to you again for long enough.

Yours, Daddy

---

1. William MacLellan (1917–199?), Glasgow publisher of books and journals especially associated with the Scottish writers sympathetic to CMG in the 1940s and 50s. MacLellan was particularly advanced in publishing poetry by W.S. Graham, Sydney Goodsir Smith and Sorley MacLean, art criticism by J.D. Fergusson, and the periodical *Poetry Scotland*.

56. *To Barker Fairley (NLS)*

32 Victoria Crescent Road, Glasgow W.2   28 March 1949

Dear Barker Fairley

The occasion of this letter is seeing your name – and Mrs Fairley's – in print as having been arrested on your crossing over into the States to attend the Peace Congress in New York. I gather from the latest paragraph that you have been allowed to stay: but Mrs Fairley has had to go back to Canada. I hope neither of you had too trying a time – infernal nuisance as it must have been at the least. The witch hunt is on here too, but doesn't go to the same lengths. I am, of course, very active in the Scottish-USSR Society and am being more and more involved in all manner of associated near Communist, Peace, and Anti-Fascist bodies: but the authorities do not molest me directly, tho' of course it is taken out of me in all manner of other ways. That matters little, however; I am quite free and independent.

But I am running on without the necessary preliminaries. It is several years since I wrote you last and heard in return. I have no memory for dates, but so far as I can recollect the last time I heard from you was when I received your splendid new Goethe book.[1] I wrote you at considerable length, then – telling you all about my war experiences, how I was forced to leave the Shetlands, qualified as an engineer, served a year or so in a big munitions factory, transferred to the Merchant Service and spent the remainder of the war years on Norwegian vessels on British Admiralty charter. Since then I have been writing and speaking on my own – the Scottish Movement, cultural and political, has grown enormously, but tho' I suppose that my work in connection with it would constitute a full time job for anyone with less energy than I have (and that does not seem to be abating with advancing years), I am up to the neck in all manner of other activities – indeed I have had an average of two meetings and have delivered at least one speech per day every day since 1st January – with, I think, only three exceptions. The worst of this sort of thing is the amount of travelling it involves – Inverness, Oxford, Manchester, Edinburgh, Dumfries – all over the place: and I can't write – or even read – in 'buses or trains.

However I'm in good form generally and trust this finds Mrs Fairley and yourself in like case. Incidentally I think I met some mutual friends the other day – friends of yours I think in your Manchester days – Professor and Mrs A.J.P. Taylor. I stayed with them at Oxford where I was addressing the University Poetry Society. Taylor was of the Wroclaw Conference, but, of course, does not go nearly far enough to suit me. Dylan Thomas was there too and I thoroughly enjoyed myself. Dylan and I have seen a good deal of each other in the last year or two, and are great friends.

But what I was beginning to say was that after I wrote you re your Goethe book and did not hear from you again I wrote at least twice again; and then I wondered 1/ if for some reason my letters had not reached you; 2/ or if your replies had not reached me; 3/ or if you had left Toronto and I had lost touch with your whereabouts, or etc. etc. So I was at least glad to see from these current paragraphs that you are still in Canada (presumably at Toronto) and am therefore hastening to write in the hope that this epistle at any rate will reach you all right – and bring a reply which will bring me up to date with regard to you all.

I have done little poetry for the past year and more – owing to the tremendous pressure of other activities – but am getting down to it again now and hope to have another big productive period during the next twelve months if all goes well.

Please accept my kindest remembrances and best wishes to you all. I was wishing greatly when I was in Manchester the other week that you had been at Buxton still and that I might have seen you again.

Yours ever, C.M. Grieve

---

1. Barker Fairley, *A Study of Goethe* (Oxford: Clarendon Press, 1947)

57. To Walter Pritchard (NLS)

32 Victoria Crescent Road, Glasgow W.2　　　　　　　　13 July 1949

Dear Mr Pritchard

I am in receipt of your registered letter of 10th inst asking me to vacate this flat four weeks from that date.

As I told you verbally the other night we are as anxious to leave as you are to have us do so and if the matter had been under our own control would have done so, not when you first asked us to do so but somewhat earlier when Mrs Pritchard spoke so cruelly to my wife about her lying down so much through the day – which was urgently necessary for her and on doctor's orders.

However the housing position in Glasgow – and nearly everywhere else – is well-known and many thousands of people have been seeking incessantly and unsuccessfully for houses not for months like us but for years.

I note that you mention your 'legal rights'. Legal rights are a poor recourse in such a matter; all they mean is that you have more money than I have. May I say that I am sorry about all this for your sake more than for my own? You will be astonished no doubt to find how many people, fully aware of all the circumstances, have said to me: 'If anybody in Scotland deserves a house it is you.' We were grateful enough to you for accommodating us in our emergency: but to oust anyone from a home at the present time is an extremely serious matter and enough to cancel my sense of obligation. You have spoken to me frequently of spiritual matters. It is strange now to find you echoing 'Am I my brother's keeper?' and relying upon conventional bourgeois 'morality' and the idea that money should be the ruling standard. I can only in these circumstances remind you of the parable of Naboth's Vineyard.

Legally this house is yours but actually it will be always principally associated with me. I have done sufficient work of sufficient quality in it to ensure that. It is inevitable that the circumstances under which I have lived and worked here will be published in full detail – and the circumstances in which that work is now being interrupted. I am certain you will not be able to justify yourself on the score of relative value. Yet finally that alone will count – and not legal rights or money-power or any other conventional standard.

As I told you verbally we have done our utmost in the last few weeks to secure any alternative accommodation and are continuing to do so and hope we may be successful within the four weeks you now stipulate. But if we fail to do so you must just act on your legal rights then, and stand the consequences of the wide publicity that will then ensue. I have no doubt that all Philistia will be on your side and hope you may find that sufficient. For myself I am exclusively interested in other standards of value and have nothing to reproach myself with.

Yours sincerely, C.M. Grieve

PART FOUR

The 1950s

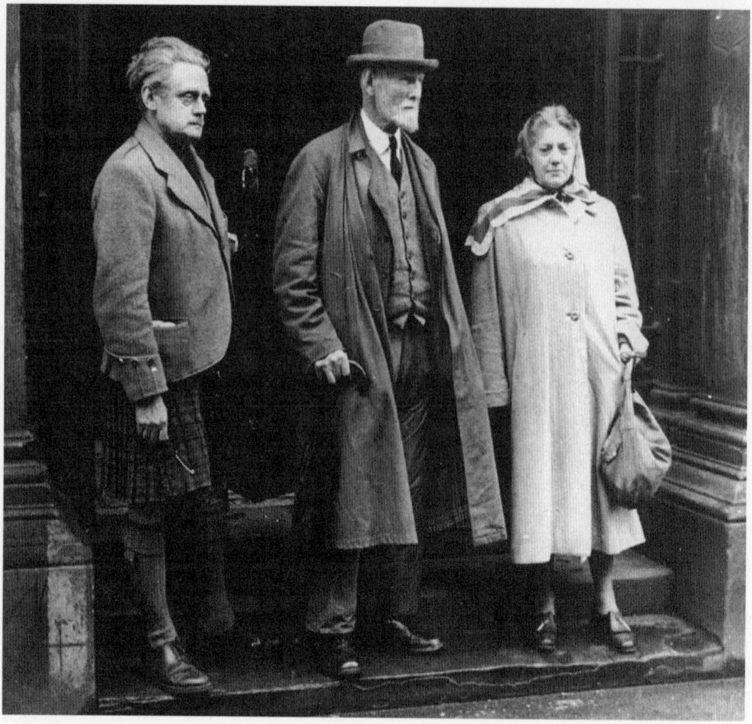

[CMG and Valda moved to Brownsbank Cottage, near Biggar, Lanarkshire, in January 1951. Most letters written thereafter are from this address. When travelling or writing from other locations, the address is noted.]

1. *To Michael Grieve (NLS)*

Dungavel						2 March 1950

Dear Mike

Many thanks to Margo and you – and to Morag and John[1] – for your telegrams of good wishes for the Election.[2] As you know now there was no chance – the whole thing was divided between the two big parties with their powerful political machines – and all the minority candidates practically were wiped out. This went not only for the Scottish Nationalists, but for the Welsh Nationalists, the Communists, the rebel Labourites, and almost all the Liberals. There will be another General Election soon and things may go differently then. We are preparing for it already.

It was of course a hectic campaign while it lasted. I must have addressed about 50 meetings, mostly open-air. Fortunately the weather was dry on the whole, if cold. We had a splendid loud speaker on one of our cars today and it went blaring through the streets all the time. I am enclosing a copy of my Election Address etc. We also had a splendid poster with a fine drawing of my head. I've asked Mummy to send you one of these.

She had a hard time of it – especially along with Ian (who was my Election Agent) at the counting of the votes in Kelvin Hall. The Hall was dead cold and they were not allowed out once they were in, of course – and the counting lasted over 8 hours. Ian too had a gruelling time with all the arrangements, and ended up like a dying duck in a thunderstorm.

I finished in good fettle myself, and am now preparing to go off to Wales – either Sunday or Monday – to address the Welsh students at Aberystwyth. I'll go by Birmingham and stay there a night or two and pick up my friend Delwyn Phillips who is going with me.

Mummy is in Glasgow today and I am going in there tomorrow to do some research in the Mitchell Library, and coming back here on Saturday.

Had a letter from Lida Moser from New York with a couple of stamps for you.[3] There are also a lot of stamps – some of them, I think, very good ones – from Dr Tom Robertson.

Everything is going here as usual but it has been devilish cold and today is pouring wet.

The address you want is: H.O.V. Hopkins, Esq. M.A. (Hons). / Scottish Organising Secretary, / Crusade for World Government, / Scottish Section, / 341 Bath St. / Glasgow C2.

I think you should write and join it as soon as possible. Several of its leading supporters are good friends of mine, which should be useful when the time comes.

You would see that Tom Driberg was re-elected all right as MP for Essex (Maldon). I had another letter from him.

Hope both Margo and yourself are OK. Will be glad to see you again whenever you get a chance to come up. Please give my kindest regards to Morag and John, and all at Kilquhanity.

With love, Yours, Daddy.

---

1. John Aitkenhead and Morag, his wife. Michael Grieve is now at Kilquhanity school.
2. CMG stood as an Independent Scottish Nationalist candidate for Glasgow Kelvingrove in the election of 23 February 1950. He lost his deposit. The poll was: Rt Hon Walter Elliot (Con) 15,197; J.L. Williams (Lab) 13,973; S.J. Ranger (Lib) 831; C.M. Grieve (Ind Scot Nat) 639.
3. Lida Moser, American artist and photographer. She visited Glasgow at the outset of her career in the 1940s, painting and photographing writers, artists and musicians of the period. The collection was purchased by the National Portrait Gallery.

2. *To the Editor,* The Nationalist, *(NLS)*

Dungavel, by Strathaven, Lanarkshire   25 May 1950

Sir: – A common line of criticism of the USSR is to contend that the Stalinist development is a distortion of Marxist Socialism. What is certain is that no less a distortion (albeit in a different direction) has been inflicted upon the British Labour and Socialist Movement. In a recent very able biographical sketch of Mr Herbert Morrison[1] the writer attributed this distortion to the line advocated by Mr Morrison which a little later became (and now is) the policy of the British Labour and Socialist Movement and our present Government, and added significantly that 'this is what makes the British Socialist movement so different from any other Socialist movement'. Personally I think the whole thing can be summed up by saying that the British Labour and Socialist Movement failed to learn the lessons implicit in the failure of the great Social-Democratic Movements in Germany, Austria, and Italy, and has now become corrupted in a similar way. This failure was always implicit in the difference between the tone and tendencies of English Socialism and Scottish Socialism, consciousness of which as a dangerous weakness was responsible for the way in which the differences between England and Scotland were carefully glossed over. If our intranational differences had been properly studied instead of the whole Movement being flooded by a phony non-dialectical internationalism, things might have been a great deal better today. As an old Socialist myself (my connection with the Movement dates back to 1908) and a personal friend and associate of Keir Hardie[2] and most of the other well-known Scottish Socialist pioneers, I have not only witnessed the great diminution of intellectual and cultural interest and the increasing concentration on mere grab which has overtaken our Movement in the last thirty years, but, addressing meetings all over Scotland as I have done in recent years, I have come into contact with a great number of old Socialists whose disillusionment is as great as my own, and I can assure Mr Morgan Thomson that in the vast majority of these cases the question of *Forward* cropped up in the course of conversation and unanimous regret was expressed at its increasingly low standards. If this is not true, how else does Mr Thomson account for the tremendous decline in *Forward*'s circulation and influence?

It is simply absurd to try to dissociate this from the increasing de-Scotisisation of *Forward*. In the days of Willie Stewart's essays a high proportion of them dealt with Scottish cultural matters. Almost everything that appears in *Forward* today is quite worthless in comparison with these essays. A passionate love of Scotland and Scotland's literature and distinctive traditions was indissolubly bound up with the Socialism of such men as Willie Stewart. To turn to another old *Forward* contributor, it is significant that Sir Patrick Dollan in his preface to *Songs of Liberty*, his selection of Burns's poems, says that Burns 'knew the value of understanding nationalism as a foundation for internationalism. Love of country was with him the gateway to world fraternity'.

The main purpose of Socialists must always be to make Socialists in their own country and achieve Socialism there. That is natural since their own country is the one whose conditions and needs they know (or should know) most thoroughly, and the advance of Socialism in other countries can best be left to those who are most familiar with and concerned in the very different conditions and needs of these countries. 'The eyes of the fool are in the ends of the earth', and the nemesis that has befallen, or is befalling, Scottish Socialists is the just and inevitable consequence of the fact that in the terms of the Parable of the Good Steward, they have not been 'faithful in little things' and have consequently no title to be set in charge of greater things.

The Scottish Movement has not only contributed little or nothing to the body of Socialist thought but has all along been infantilist and anti-intellectual – fatal faults which have been well displayed in *Forward*, but which seem to have reached bottom level in the past few years. It is in keeping with this that the Scottish Socialist and Labour Movement has contributed nothing of the slightest consequence to arts and letters, despite all its lip-service to culture. I have mentioned Willie Stewart's essays; there is scarcely anything else that can be mentioned – no novel, no play, no poem of more than mediocre merit. *Forward* as our leading Scottish Socialist organ, must bear a great deal of the blame for this sorry state of affairs.

Nowadays at all events, whatever it may have been in the past, it is destitute of any interest in literary or human quality; it has no distinctive character (and so apparently thinks Scotland can dispense with anything of that sort too); instead of encouraging writers in Scotland close to the facts and with something to say, it fills its columns with cheap syndicated material.

All these considerations are apart altogether from the great issues which lie at the root of the Scottish Nationalist Movement, and from these distinctive traditions which have given the Scot his great place in the world and which – though it fathered them in the first instance – Mr Thomson and most of Scotland's Socialist MPs and others prominent in the Scottish Socialist and Labour Movement are today busily exchanging for a mess of English pottage. But the failure of *Forward* to present these great issues fully and fearlessly, will undoubtedly be one of the most serious counts held against it and its editorship wherever in the future its influence comes to be considered, since that failure is a grave reflection on the intellectual integrity, editorial competence, and political nous of those responsible.

The fact of the matter is that what *Forward* promulgates is a species of Quislingism for which in the decline of its circulation and influence it has already paid dearly and which, if unchanged, will ere long encompass its extinction. It is also a peculiarly wrong-headed, futile, and indefensible policy at the very time when the Government it is supporting has given Home Rule to various other parts of the Commonwealth and loudly proclaimed its policy of raising the other elements to that level at which Home Rule can also be granted to them – all of them, that is, except Scotland! The reasons for that exception are bound up with the vile treachery of the whole development of that British Labour and Socialist policy in the past few years which has enforced (and is now extending) conscription in peace-time, engaging in a wild armaments race, and in every other connection standing for precisely the opposite of everything that Keir Hardie, John MacLean, and the other founders of the Scottish Labour and Socialist Movement worked for.

Yours etc., Hugh MacDiarmid

---

1. Herbert Stanley Morrison (1888–1965), Labour politician, Home Secretary in Churchill's coalition government, senior minister in the post-war Labour governments, whose model of nationalisation entailed control vested in bodies centred in London with committees in which token trade union officials were purported to represent workers' interests.
2. (James) Keir Hardie (1856–1915), one of the founders of the Labour party and its first candidate in 1888. CMG first met him in Wales in 1910.

3. *To Robert [Blair Wilkie] (NLS, DFF)*[1]

Dungavel, by Strathaven   Friday 6 July 1950

Dear Robert

    I am very sorry to hear you have been off colour again but trust that your day or two in the excellent company of John Morton will buck you up nicely.

    We have been a bit out of touch. I have been doing a great deal of work – and haven't been in Glasgow for quite a time. Partly because I wanted to get my decks clear before the PEN Congress time – partly because the furor scribenti got hold of me again. And over and above that because I know that my chances of getting on with solid work are unfortunately about to be interrupted again, since Dungavel Estate has been sold lock, stock, and barrel to the National Coal Board who with characteristic bureaucratic greed have grabbed all the cottages too, tho' they do not really need them, the big house being more than ample for all their reasonable requirements. Still there you are – it's public money, and so they can afford to do the whole thing in the most lavish way. That means we have to clear out by the end of August and are again in search of a house. It's an infernal nuisance and terrible worry.

    I do not quite know how to put the reference – i.e. to whom to address it M. Le Directeur or M. Le Chef d'école or how. But I have written out, and enclose a draft and if that is suitable, you can add the information as to how it should be addressed etc. and return it to me with any alterations or further suggestions you think fit and I'll embody these, make a fair copy and let you have it back again by return.

    Valda joins me in best wishes to Helen and yourself.

    Yours, Chris

---

1. The addressee is not fully named; we suspect it is Dr Robert Blair Wilkie; see Appendix.

4. *To Michael Grieve (NLS)*

Dungavel   Friday [July 1950]

Dear Michael

    Many thanks for your letter in reply at long last to mine of the previous term. I should have written you earlier again but have been very busy and am likely to continue to be so for a good while ahead. I am trying to complete several new books I have been planning, and have all the floor space in my room taken up with stacks of papers, notes etc.

    Mummy is having a high old time of it. She has got a fine new brown

Harris tweed overcoat, a very attractive richly coloured frock, and a pair of nice blue sandals. So she is all equipped for the Edinburgh Festival and PEN Congress in August.

I don't expect to be much away till then, but will be in Edinburgh on 19th inst I think to take part in a broadcast.

How is John? Is he still in hospital? I really should have written him. Please give him my kindest regards.

I do not know if you still have the same intention with regard to military service, but if you do still want to secure exemption, I notice that 'World Citizen' identity cards can now be obtained in Scotland at a centre established by the World Government Movement at 341 Bath St, Glasgow. So if you feel like it you can write them and get one. It might always help. All you need to say is: –

Kilquhanity House. (date).

The Secretary
World Government Movement
341 Bath St. Glasgow. C.

Dear Sir: –
I notice from the press that 'World Citizen' identity cards can now be obtained in Scotland from your office. I am in entire agreement with your Movement and anxious to know 1/ how to become a member, and 2/ how to procure a 'World Citizen' identity card. Will you please let me know, also what membership fees etc. are payable.

Thanking you in anticipation.

Yours sincerely,

Michael Grieve.

As Mummy has probably told you the question of the disposal of this estate is again to the fore and it is possible that we may not be able to retain this house much longer. I hope it does not come to that, not only because it would probably be extremely difficult to get another house but because this one suits us particularly well and I am anxious not to have to shift now when I have all my papers laid down and am getting on writing my new books. Besides just now it is very lovely round here.

However, it won't be long now till you are home again. We'll be glad to see you. Hope you are in good trim.

All the best to all of you. Yours, Daddy

5. *To Michael Grieve (NLS)*

Dungavel   Sunday [September 1950]

Dear Mike
As you know Mummy did not quite understand all you were telling

her on the 'phone, but she will be down to Kilquhanity on Friday or Saturday. She will let you know which. Will that be all right with John?

We have just had a visit today from Mr Dunlop and Mr Jamieson (of Mellis's), both of whom are on the outlook trying to get us fixed up with a house. They were both in good form and asking for you. Jamieson brought a nice bottle of Sherry, which made the party quite a jolly one.

Helen Cruickshank is coming here on Tuesday – just for a night or two.

I was down in Manchester last weekend at a Theatre Workshop meeting, and they too were all asking for you.[1] Things are in a very bad way with them just now financially, but we are hoping for some better developments shortly.

Mummy will give you all the news when she comes, of course, but in the meantime we are anxious to hear just what has been happening and hope everything pans out all right for John and the School.

Excuse this very short note in the meantime, as I have been up to eyes writing a 20,000 word essay on 'Aesthetics on Scotland' which is later to be published as a pamphlet by Glasgow Art Galleries[2] and which I am also to give as a public lecture. I have been having a strenuous spell of poetry-writing too.

Hope you are OK. Looking forward to seeing you ere long.

Love to all. Yours, Daddy.

P.S. I don't know just how one motors to Aberdeen. One can't go from Edinburgh across the Forth unless by ferry – and the charge for that for a motor car is about £1, I think, while to keep by road would involve a tremendous detour to get round the top of the Firth of Forth. It might be best to go via Glasgow, Stirling, Perth. But I don't know at all. You'll have to study the map and make sure of our route – and how long it will take at a reasonable rate, with due caution in built-up areas, and at corners etc., unless you want me reduced to such jitters that I'll be a gibbering idiot instead of an effective speaker by the time we get to Aberdeen. A good deal will depend on the weather too. The hurricane seems to have blown itself out at the moment, but according to the radio there has been extensive flooding in many parts and lots of rivers are 6 to 10 feet above their usual height and have burst their banks and flooded the adjacent countryside. The AA people will know what roads are under water and impassable. By Friday of course things may be much better in that way, but we'll have to see. All the best to you all. Daddy

---

1. Theatre Workshop was founded in 1945 and run by the actress Joan Littlewood and the folk-singer and playwright Ewan MacColl, with a commitment to producing socialist drama. CMG was director of the company.
2. This remained unpublished until Alan Bold prepared a copy published in 1984; it is collected in Hugh MacDiarmid, *Albyn: Shorter Books and Monographs*, ed. Alan Riach (Manchester: Carcanet, 1996).

6. *To Douglas Young (NLS)*

Dungavel, by Strathaven, Lanarkshire 4 October 1950

Dear Douglas

Many thanks for your note saying you had sent the kind of letter I solicited to Michael. I am sure it will be helpful. He has now quite a sheaf of such letters and Guy Aldred will speak for him when the thing comes up, while I understand that if it goes to Edinburgh Mr Muirhead has written offering to help and Michael has accepted.[1]

I am afraid I cannot be at the PEN AGM and Dinner. I am booked up for about 40 meetings between now and March, and besides that my house problem has not yet been solved. I have at last two choices – one of a bungalow near Strathaven and the other of a cottage at Balmacara, near Kyle of Lochalsh. Which I am to take will probably be decided tomorrow. While the former is near enough Glasgow to enable me to keep active in the various movements with which I am associated, and also to make our moving easy and inexpensive, the house is in some respects less suitable than the one in Wester Ross and I can have the latter on a long let of at least a year and probably several years whereas with the one near Strathaven I should probably be at the mercy of a cantankerous old farmer who might decide to chuck me out and install a farm-worker whenever he liked. We'll see. In any case I'll let you know my new address as soon as it is fixed.

I have been scanning the literary papers for news of your *Anthology*, but so far I haven't seen any reference to or advertisement of it as likely to be out soon.

With every kind regard to Mrs Young and yourself.

Yours, Chris

---

1. In December 1950, the Edinburgh Appelate Tribunal rejected Michael's application to be registered as a conscientious objector.

7. *To Michael Grieve (NLS)*

Dungavel Tuesday [October 1950]

Dear Mike

I was disappointed when I arrived home yesterday to learn you had been – and gone. Mummy had gone too – to a party at Wilkie's in Glasgow. She came back this evening, having had an excellent time. The Tannahills were there and Andrew asked her to send you his congratulations on the stand you are taking. Muirhead sent me a notice of a Scottish National Assembly meeting on 28th inst. I'll be away to Russia on 26th however, but Mummy will probably go to the meeting in my place and have a talk to him about your case. Unless it comes up before I get back, I'll be in court of course when your case comes up and if required will speak for you too. It seems that Muirhead agrees that Aldred is the best man to handle your case. But we'll see if in addition to that it would be useful to have me speak too when the time comes.

I had a very strenuous time all over Fifeshire – Kirkcaldy, Dunfermline, Buckhaven etc. etc. – and apart from doing some writing I have to I'm intending to have a quiet time between now and 26th inst if possible. That probably depends upon whether we get a house in the interval or not. I wish we could and have it all settled before I go. I have just written about another 4–roomed cottage for sale at Lanark. Here's hoping.

Hamish McIntosh sends his apologies to you and says he feels bad about it. It seems he was looking at you (and you at him) on the day of the Garden Party in Edinburgh, but though he thought he knew you he wasn't quite sure and consequently didn't speak to you.

May and Mabel were at Wilkie's party too. Mabel was just back from spending three months in Germany and was looking far more grown up and very pretty. Andrew had been wanting to write to you but every time he got to the point he felt that it was very inadequate merely to write when he didn't go through the same thing himself.

I enclose a packet of French stamps from M. Sully André Peyre.[1] Be sure and thank him for these.

Love to John and Morag and all at Kilquhanity. Yours, Daddy

---

1. M. Sully André Peyre (1890–1961), French poet, writing in Provençal and English.

8. *To Michael Grieve (NLS)*

Dungavel   Wednesday [15 November 1950]

Dear Mike

I got back here on Monday after my 12,000 mile trip to Russia, the autonomous republic of Georgia, and Czecho-Slovakia. We flew from Moscow to Tbilisi, the capital of Georgia, on the Black Sea, in a Dakota – 2,000 miles, but owing to weather conditions in the Caucasus Mountains had to return by train – three days and nights in the train. We came back by Prague, and flew the 1600 miles from Moscow to that city in 8 hours – i.e. at 2,000 miles an hour [*sic*]. From Prague we flew back to London via Frankfurt in the American zone of Germany, Brussels in Belgium, and Amsterdam in Holland. I cannot in a letter tell you much about the whole wonderful experience, but I'll be writing and speaking a lot about it all.

In London last Sunday I spoke at an immense meeting – to an audience of between 8000 and 9000 people.

Mummy will probably have told you I brought back a collection of Russian stamps, a few coins, and also a 10-rouble note with a fine engraved portrait of Lenin on it.

I was sorry to hear your case had been turned down – and sorrier still that it had taken place when I was not there to stand by you and perhaps speak for you.

I enclose one of the copies of the 'Cornish Garden' poem, with the mistakes marked. Will you please do me another, as carefully and clearly as you can? You need not do a duplicate, but it is essential that the copy I send in should be quite free of mistakes and typed as black and clear as possible. Please note that the front page giving the title, should not have my name and address on it, but simply 'Once In a Cornish Garden', by Pteleon.

I have not had time to go over the other poem yet, but will do so as soon as possible. When you do this new copy of the 'Cornish Garden' poem, please also return to me the copy I am now enclosing to you.

There is still no word of a house and we are of course very worried about that now.

Telegrams are already arriving asking me to address meetings in Newcastle-on-Tyne and elsewhere. As you will know the World Peace Congress at Sheffield had to be abandoned and was transferred to Warsaw. I should have flown right back there, but decided not to do so because of the number of writing commitments and speaking engagements piling up for me at home here and also because of the worry about getting a new house.

I am back in great form – Mummy was surprised how well I looked – but it has been far colder here since I came back then anything I experienced in Eastern Europe and I have now caught a cold in the head and a sore back.

Many thanks for typing the poems which I appreciate was a long and difficult job because of the very unfamiliar nature of the subject matter and the strange vocabulary I employed.

I hope to see you ere long. In any case it won't be long now to Christmas. Please give my kindest regards to Morag and John and all at Kilquhanity.

With love. Yours, Daddy

9. *To Michael Grieve (NLS)*

24 November 1950

Dear Mike

The Cornish Garden poem is OK. Many thanks and haven't managed to read through the typescript of the Vision of World languages poem yet, but I am off again tomorrow to Sheffield to address a big meeting there. I have a whole host of meetings looming up soon, including Burns Suppers in Glasgow and Edinburgh and Doune (Perthshire), as well as lectures for a week; and school probably in Dunfermline. Since I came back I have had a horrible cold in the head and a stye in the eye. However I've been able to do quite a lot, including a script for a broadcast on Burns, and an article for the British weekly on Scottish Poetry Today.

I am afraid I can't tell you more in a letter about my visit to the Soviet Union, Georgia, and Czecho-Slovakia. The Soviet Union is certainly going ahead at a tremendous rate. Nearly all the towns devastated during the war have been completely rebuilt already – and everywhere you go there are huge building projects, and jolly well-planned buildings with the modern conveniences there are. The people in the streets are all well-dressed (much better dressed than our own working class) and are quite evidently free of anxiety in regard to employment and wages, while the shops are crammed with excellent foodstuffs of all kinds at prices within everybody's reach. This evidence of ample food contrasts with conditions here. I am not going to set your teeth on edge by telling you of the gorgeous repasts we had, but you can imagine what breakfast is like when you begin with a glass of vodka, then have fish and slices of prime pork, and as if that isn't enough and you fancy an egg they don't bring you one, but four or five nicely fried, on a tin plate. It would take the whole of the rest of this page to describe one of the dinners we had – four or five courses with plenty of good red wine and ending with a sweet – say, a caramel pudding with a big glass of clotted cream to go with it, and finally a plate of ice-cream. And, of course, plenty of fruit – apples, tangerine oranges and pomegranates. Georgia of course is semi-tropical and we had brilliant sunshine and sat outside among the orange and fig-trees, drinking cognac, or wine, and quite regardless of the snow-clad peaks of the Caucasus Mountains towering up above us.

One thing is certain. The workers are in complete control of everything and are developing their productive resources and creative faculties at an enormous pace. The whole atmosphere is one of confidence and happiness and freedom – to an extent incredible to anyone who is familiar with the conditions here. All the Anti-Russian propaganda is simply a tissue of lies. I saw no sign of any iron curtain – nothing but friendliness and comradeship and a genuine desire for peace – and I did not see any sign at all of repression or fear until I came back when, touching down at Frankfurt in Germany, the American military were everywhere in evidence, swanking about in the most arrogant and offensive way; and it was the same at Northolt, the London airport – the Yankee gangsters were in control there too. So I have come back a more completely convinced Red than ever.

Prague is one of the most wonderful cities in Europe – full of beautiful old buildings, some of them dating back to the 9th century, and rich in art treasures of all kinds, including some of the most wonderful articles in gold and jewels in the world. I could well have spent a few weeks there just to take it all in; and there the people looked well and were full of gaiety and good fellowship.

That'll have to do for the time being. Anything else I'll tell you when you come home. This is just a hurried scrawl to go to you in along with Mummy's letter.

Love, Daddy

10. *To Michael Grieve (NLS)*

The Cottage, Brownsbank, Elsrickle, Skirling by Biggar   2 February 1951

Dear Michael

Your mother was in Edinburgh the other day and saw about your kilt material which they have promised to send by the end of this week. She also saw a very attractive russet cloth for a tunic which will go very well indeed with the ancient Tullibardine tartan.

I have been trying to find out about what facilities will be given you in prison for keeping up your shorthand and typing, and for reading and sending and receiving letters etc., and conditions generally. I have been in correspondence about it with Guy Aldred whose excellent issue of *The Word* you'll have received. I have also written to Sir Gordon Stott, K.C., who was himself a C.O., so I hope to know soon just how matters stand and how best to see that you get whatever privileges are to be had.

You will see from the *Radio Times* that a selection of my poems is to be broadcast on the Third Programme on Tuesday at 6.25 – and repeated on Saturday at 10.45. This is very important from my point of view – and should be financially beneficial too.

I have a debate in Paisley later this month on the Peace issue, but apart from that am now through with my programme of speeches etc. for a while and hoping to get a good deal of writing done.

Mummy is busy painting woodwork, stripping the old wall-paper from the kitchen, and so on; and the cottage is beginning to be very nice.

Hope you are in good form and all going well at Kilquhanity. Love to Morag and John and all of you.

Yours, Daddy

11. *To D.G. Bridson (LLIU)*

The Cottage, Brownsbank, by Biggar, Lanarkshire   6 February 1951

Dear Mr Bridson

Above is my new address. I am still hoping to see you in Scotland and if you do come up can meet you any time either in Glasgow or Edinburgh.

Preferably the latter, since there I could also arrange for one or two other poets to meet you.

I have been intending to write you again ever since I came back from Russia. But I have been extremely busy, addressing meetings all over the country, and finally flitting to this new place.

But I am writing you tonight not only to say what I have just said, but because I have just been listening to the recital of my poems on the Third Programme. It came across splendidly here, the readers were first-rate, and I was delighted with the choice of poems and with the points in regard to my work on which MacColl laid his emphasis. My warmest thanks therefore are due – and I now tender them – to you and to all those who took part in this most effective and helpful broadcast.

With every good wish. Yours sincerely, Hugh MacDiarmid

12. *To Peter Russell (SUNYB)*

22 February 1951

Dear Peter Russell

I am not in the least surprised to get the poem back. I felt it was too long to be suitable for *Nine* but I am glad you think sufficiently well of it to suggest you may be able to use it in a pamphlet later. It will be available if you do. There is no other periodical I know that would print a poem this length.

My Pound article has not appeared yet, but I will send you a copy as soon as it does.

Many thanks for the two new pamphlets.

I am busy amongst other things on a lot of new short poems and will send you some of these soon. But do not worry even if you like them about trying to arrange to publish them in *Nine*. Short poems I can always get published in various quarters here and in America. It is my long poems that are the difficulty: and the Cornish Garden one is only one – and the shortest – of some twenty I have had by me too long and would like to see printed.

However I think Bill MacLellan will publish most of them in a volume for me ere long.

I should have written in reply to your previous most interesting letter. But the question at issue is too complex to deal with in a letter. We must talk it out together sometime. Here I can only say that like many anti-Communists you seem to me to argue from *a priori* grounds. The use of the term 'the free world' is a case in point. So is the usual religious argument – viz. that unless a God is predicated, the world can't make sense. My reply is that I find more freedom in the USSR – the 'freedom' of the Western Democracies is mostly misused; the right to be ignorant, the right of stupid people to express what they call their opinions when they lack the means of forming any, the right to publish rubbish even when the effect is to sabotage that compulsory 'education' on which so much public money is spent etc. However you'll excuse my not going into all that just now.

I am much interested (and grateful to you) to hear about your recent public reading of my poems. Did you hear the Third Programme recital? It has brought me a spate of letters from all over the UK. Mostly very appreciative. The readers were James MacKechnie, Dermot Cathie, and Molly Weir, and on the whole they did very well. The selection was made and introduced by Ewan MacColl of Theatre Workshop, and I think he chose rightly when he gave, out of 11 poems used, 3 of my short lyrics and the other 8 of my later long poems.

We have had a strenuous time with snow and gales here but have now got settled in quite comfortably. Michael has been down with measles and his mother is down at his school for a week, so I am on my own, and trying to get a lot of work done.

The rise in production costs, shortage of paper etc. must be making it very hard going to keep *Nine* alive. And I am afraid things are going to be worse. If any way in which I can possibly help suggests itself to you please let me know. I'll be only too glad to do anything I can. There's some idea of my doing a Third Programme talk ere long. If that comes off I'll be in London and will of course get in touch with you.

All the best. Yours, C.M. Grieve

13. *To David Daiches, Cornell University (EUL)*

7 March 1951

Dear Professor Daiches

Very many thanks for your letter of 3rd inst.

I ought to have written you long ago to express my appreciation of your most understanding and helpful essay on my poetry which appeared in *Poetry Chicago*, but I always hesitate to write to people who say nice things about my work and in your case I hesitated too long and then heard you were to be in Edinburgh at the Festival time and hoped to meet you there. Please accept my very belated thanks now. I have had a very busy and distracting time this last year or so. I do far too much public speaking for all kinds of organisations. I was away in Czecho-Slovakia, Russia, and Georgia, and then I had to flit to this new address and most of my books, papers, etc. are still boxed up and inaccessible to me, which is a terrible nuisance. This is a nice quiet place and I hope to get a lot of work done here once I get properly settled in. In any case I have now more unpublished poems by me – to say nothing of other stuff – than all I have already printed. I have not seen your Burns book yet but have it on order and am looking forward to it very eagerly.

This place is quite handy for Edinburgh and I certainly hope that we can meet and have a good talk or two when you are over here this summer.

The copyright of the Shetland essay which appeared in *At the Sign of the Thistle* (London: Stanley Nott, 1934) is my own. The first portion of it originally appeared in *The New Age*, and the remainder in *The Scottish Educational Journal*, but there is no need to make acknowledgement to these sources. I think however – if you are republishing the whole thing as it appeared in the book – the date 1934 should be given at the end and a brief note appended, viz. 'Since the above essay was written, there has been, Mr MacDiarmid tells us, a considerable revival of local patriotism in the Shetland archipelago, carrying with it a fair amount of economic regeneration, including a marked development of the tourist industry and the provision of improved transport services, hotel and boarding-house accommodation, and other facilities for visitors, and the growth of a lively movement for the revival of the old Shetland language. Along with this a strong literary movement has manifested itself and *The New Shetlander* is a monthly organ of a numerous group of young Shetland writers whose work on the whole compares favourably with that of the writers of the Scottish Renaissance Movement on the mainland of Scotland. Many new books descriptive, scientific, and historical, dealing with Shetland have been published during the past few years.'

I need not say how pleased I am that you should wish to include this essay in such a collection.

With every kind regard. Yours sincerely, C.M. Grieve ('Hugh MacDiarmid')

14. *To the Editor,* The New Alliance & Scots Review

April 1951

PROTESTING POET

Sir, – I was surprised to read the paragraph in your current issue regarding the Third Programme recital of a selection of my poems. Unlike your commentator, I thought it was extremely well done. I could not have chosen anyone better qualified to introduce my work than Mr Ewan MacColl, the brilliant young Scots dramatist of Theatre Workshop, Ltd, and I was pleased that two of the three readers were Scots. Despite a few errors in pronunciation, I thought all three read excellently and did full justice not only to the texts but to the spirit of the poems. I am afraid that if any similar programme of my work had been arranged in Scotland the emphasis would have been on my early short lyrics; as it was, the stress was laid on my later longer poems and this accords not only with my own judgment but with the consensus of opinion of critics whose opinions I respect – everywhere except in Scotland.

I know nothing of what internal difference of opinion there may have been between those responsible for the Third Programme and the Scottish producer responsible for the James the First, Henryson, and Dunbar programmes in this series, but with the outcome so far as my work was concerned I was very well satisfied indeed, and that this is not merely my own view but was widely shared is borne out by many highly appreciative letters I have had from listeners all over Great Britain. I do, of course, agree with your commentator that Scotland has had nothing like its fair share on the Third Programme so far, but I understand this is now being remedied and that process is not likely to be encouraged by captious criticism like that in the paragraph in question.

Yours sincerely, Hugh MacDiarmid

15. *To the Editor,* The New Alliance & Scots Review

May, 1951

Behind the Curtain

Sir, – All I was concerned to do in my article on my tour of the USSR was to report accurately what I saw and the impressions made upon me, in so far as that was possible in about 1500 words.

As Mr Levack says, 'evil-disposed scandal-mongers say there are millions of labour-slaves living in sub-human conditions'. I am not in the habit of listening to what evil-disposed scandal-mongers say, but even if there were trustworthy reports to the same effect (and I have not seen any) it would hardly have been possible for me to ask to be allowed to visit these places during my fortnight in the USSR. Certainly I saw nothing of the kind in the great portion of the Soviet Union I covered, and I understand that most of the allegations are to the effect that these places are far away in Northern Siberia. I suspect they are still further away – namely, in Cuckoo-Cloudland.

There is no mystery about the prevalence of such allegations as those of Kravchenko and the others Mr Levack names. It is only necessary to remember that wherever established privilege has been threatened there have been plenty of people ready to prophecy red ruin if social change were encompassed; and as to sub-human conditions, I know that there are large numbers of wage-slaves badly enough circumstanced in this country and in America, and that all slums are neither more nor less than the slave-camps of Capitalist society. Nor is the preventible death-roll in such places a smaller proportion of those so enslaved than is alleged respecting the USSR even by the most fantastic of its enemies.

I know nothing of the circumstances in the two specific cases to which Mr Levack refers, but all governments, for various reasons, control the ingress and egress of people to and from their countries. Our own country has recently denied admission to many distinguished people from various countries who wished to attend a Peace Congress, and still more recently has similarly excluded a party of Chinese delegates. The USSR has far more cause than most countries to be careful who it admits, since there are no limits to the unscrupulous machinations of its enemies.

But I am sure Mr Levack knows perfectly well that the real reason so few can go to Russia is not the fault of the Russians, who would gladly revive the 'Intourist' agency and welcome as large an influx of visitors as possible, but simply that our own authorities will not grant would-be visitors to the USSR the necessary financial facilities, with the consequence that only those can go who are the guests of the USSR, since otherwise, they would be unable to pay for food, lodging, travel, and other requirements. In other words, in this, as in all other respects, the 'Iron Curtain' is imposed by our own authorities.

If it amuses Mr Levack to hear of Georgia successfully reviving its own ancient language, casting off the linguistic imperialism of an immensely larger and more powerful neighbour, and successfully fostering a renaissance in every department of its national life, who am I that I should question his perverted sense of fun? But to stigmatise one of the loveliest, most prosperous and happiest regions of the world I have ever seen in extensive travels of many lands throughout the past half-century as 'a vast charnel-house' is another matter, and all too typical of the venomous and unbridled opposition to which reactionaries have submitted every phase of the struggle of the workers against their class-enemies. No wonder I believe in the class-war.

Yours, etc., Hugh MacDiarmid[1]

---

1. This letter was followed by an editorial note: 'The *Scots Review* wishes to make plain that it published Mr MacDiarmid's article because he alleged that democratic organs were afraid to print pro-Communist opinion. From letters received, it is clear that readers no more regard Mr MacDiarmid's emotionalism as evidence of anything concrete relating either to Soviet Russia or to her intentions, than we do. This correspondence is now closed. – Ed.'

16. *To Michael Grieve (NLS)*

[1951]

Dear Mike

You ask about the challenge. Well, it was like this. In connection with the Festival of Britain there are separate prize competitions for poems in

Scotland and in England. But the conditions of the English competitions were announced long before the Scottish ones, so that English competitors have had far longer to write their entries.

I wrote a letter to *The Scotsman* protesting against this and also protesting against the panel of judges appointed to judge the Scottish poems.

The panel consisted of Sir Herbert Grierson, Sir Alexander Gray, Wm Power, and Douglas Young. Grierson and Gray are old men who have no sympathy with modern poetry, their own tastes having been formed on standards now generally discarded. Also they are both very poor poets themselves. Power also is an old man and a sentimentalist with no sound judgement of poetry. Young is also a poor poet and I have no great opinion of his critical ability so far as poetry is concerned.

Young was very annoyed at my letter and wrote to *The Scotsman* challenging me to name a panel of judges I would approve and send in poems to them. If they decided that my poems were better than the poems to which the prizes were awarded by the official judges, then he (Young) would 1/eat his blue bonnet, and 2/publish my poems at his own expense.

I accepted his challenge. Then Young began to hedge. He said that the judges I appointed must be Scottish and must themselves have published books in Lallans. I pointed out that there were not sufficient such Scots writers for whose judgement I had any respect and that in any case that stipulation was not in the terms of Young's challenge as originally stated by him and accepted by me. So I refused to accept this new condition.

The Scotsman then closed the correspondence.

I have not heard from Young himself and take it that the whole thing has now fallen through, which is a pity but not my blame. Anyhow I think I got decidedly the best of the controversy, so far as it went.

My tartan arrived today. Once my kilt is ready we'll make a great pair.

Hope you manage up this coming weekend.

Love to John and all at Kilquhanity. Yours, Daddy

P.S. Your mention of the Urr reminds me that in one of the poems in my book *Stony Limits*, there is the following verse:

> You remind me now of a sunset by the Urr and the Peaks of Screel
> When the tide-forsaken river was a winding ribbon of ebony
> Faintly washed with silver. With the passing of the splendour from
>   the heights
> The middle distance and foreground were suddenly lit up
> With a light (like that in which shingle lies under the sea-tide's
>   forefoot)
> Bursting from some hidden spring of the afterglow. All else
> Was darker save the quickened feeling – like the sense of a man
> Who returns from foreign scenes to the country of his blood and
>   birth.

The light melted from the water: mist curtained the hills,
But, breaking from the mist, the peaks again took shape
Dark and mysterious, yet clear and vivid, under the kindling
constellations.[1]

---

1. *Complete Poems*, vol. 1, p.471.

17. **To Michael Grieve (NLS)**

Saturday, 9 June 1951

Dear Mike

Glad to get your letter today. We keep worrying when a few days pass without word. Your collision with the 'bus explains why. It is a mercy it was not worse. The House of Commons as you say is a disillusioning place but nevertheless it is an interesting experience to go there. You do not say whether you met Emrys Hughes too.

Things are quiet here amid the garden coming on very nicely now. Mum and I are going up to Glasgow on Tuesday to the first night of Robert McLellan's new Queen Mary of Scots play at the Citizens. Today we have Mrs Wells coming from Edinburgh for a few hours. I have been very busy – have written a long political essay for the Oxford magazine, also a long essay on Soviet Writers for a book Andrew Rothstein is editing giving the experiences and impressions of all the delegation I was with in Russia. Mum would tell you I was down at Durham University lecturing on Scottish Literature.

Most hotels just now are suffering from labour shortage, so Mum has been worked in for rather more than she originally bargained for. But that's not too bad on the whole and she's enjoying the variety, I think.

If you see Angadi again tell him I thought over the question of trying to get a lectureship in India again and decided not to do anything about it for a while, as I have a lot of writing I want to complete first – including a commission from America that I hope will prove lucrative.

Mum suggested that I should try to place your account of the South Bank Exhibition with one of the Glasgow or Edinburgh evening papers but the paragraph in your letter about it, while graphic and interesting enough, was too short to be really useful. If you had expanded it into a short article of say 500 to 600 words ('A Scots Boy's Impressions of the South Bank Exhibition') I think we might have placed it easily enough with either the Glasgow *Evening Times* or the Edinburgh *Evening Dispatch*. You might think of that even yet if you have a chance – it would always be a guinea or so.

Charlie Lahr may know if the Welsh poet, Dylan Thomas, is in London and if so you could perhaps give him a call and my kindest regards.

Let us know as soon as you can how you manage to arrange things about getting a new bicycle.

Love to you and kind remembrances to all friends. Yours truly, Dad

18. *To the Editor*

From Mrs Valda Trevlyn Grieve, 7 June 1951[1]
Brownsbank by Biggar, Lanarkshire, Scotland

THE CORONATION STONE

As a Cornish woman married to a Scotsman, kindly grant me space to protest against the reference in your 'For Sunday afternoon' feature in your issue of 13th June, to 'some people covering themselves with ignominy by stealing the Coronation Stone in London'.

The facts are that the stone in question is one of the greatest Scottish historical treasures stolen from Scotland and that its return has been refused, despite the fact that this was solemnly promised centuries ago in a Treaty which like so many Treaties was entered into and never kept by the English. Other Scottish treasures similarly looted from Scotland by English armies and retained in England for long periods have been returned in recent years. Why not this one, the greatest of them all? Can anyone imagine England allowing one of the greatest symbols of its history to be kept in Scotland in this way?

Certainly not. Nor would any other nation in the world tolerate anything of the sort.

It is a mistake to imagine that only a few extremists, a 'lunatic fringe', favour the restoration of the Stone to Scotland. Even now over twenty MPs of all parties have signed a petition for its return and they have the support of many English and Welsh members too.

At the time of the so called 'theft', (a misnomer, since it is not theft to recover what is one's own) I had occasion to see a vast collection of press cuttings from all over the world dealing with the matter. It is a simple fact that the overwhelming majority of these supported the Scottish case for the return of the Stone. World opinion emphatically endorsed the action of the 'thieves' and renounced England for its retention of the Stone and persistent violation of Treaty obligations.

The Scottish Covenant Movement for justice in this and all other matters between Scotland and England has the signed support of over 2,000,000 Scots – a majority of the total Scottish Electorate. This Movement cannot finally fall.

(Mrs) Valda Trevelyn Grieve

---

1. Letter evidently written by CMG dated 17 June 1951.

19. *To Michael Grieve (NLS)*

Friday [1951]

Dear Mike

Enclosed letter from Mr R.E. Muirhead came for you today. I am dropping him a line to say I've sent on the letter to you but that I think you'll be away about a month. You should write him too, along the following lines: –

My father has sent on to me your letter inviting me on behalf of the Scottish National Congress to appear on the platform during your No-Conscription campaign. I do not expect to be back in Scotland until about (put in date), but if the meetings are still going on then I will of course be very willing to do what I can. With every good wish for the success of your effort, and best regards.

Yours for Scotland, Michael Grieve.

Hope you are going on OK and encountering decent weather and meeting some interesting folk in your travels.

Love, Daddy

20. *To Eoin O'Mahoney (NLS, DFF)*[1]

10 July 1951

Dear Friend

I heard you had been in Scotland some little time ago, and am sorry not to have seen you then. I do not know to what extent you are able to keep tab on current happenings in Scotland but you have always seemed to me virtually omniscient and thus it is more than likely that you already know a good deal about the matter which prompts this letter. My son, Michael, applied for recognition as a Conscientious Objector to military service but was turned down by the Tribunal and subsequently on appeal by the Appellate Tribunal. He is determined not to serve and if need be will rather go to gaol. He based his case largely on Scottish Nationalist grounds and the refusal to register him as a C.O. was largely prejudice against Scottish Nationalism and hatred of me personally. Since he was finally refused exemption, there have been several notices summoning him to attend for medical examination, but he has just ignored these and nothing else has happened yet. To pass the time until the matter was finally decided – since he could not get a job in the interval, being eligible for National Service and therefore precluded from obtaining employment – I sent him away on an extended holiday to London and elsewhere – a holiday he is still enjoying. Amongst other things this served the useful purpose of enabling him to see MPs like Tom Driberg and Emrys Hughes and others who are interested in his case. But Michael himself is very keen to get a start at what he is determined to be – namely, a journalist. He has his speed certificates for Shorthand (Pitman's) and Typing. I myself or other friends could easily get him a newspaper job – if he had done his National Service or if he had been exempted – but that is impossible in the circumstances, in this country at any rate. If he has to go to prison that will prevent him getting a start in journalism for a considerable time ahead – until, in fact, he will be of an age when it will be impossible for him to start on equal terms with younger men. It has been suggested to me that in these circumstances it might be possible for him to get a job in Eire and thus not only avoid going to prison but spend the time instead acquiring valuable experience. I wonder if you can do anything about this. All of us will be very grateful indeed if you can. I cannot remember whether you have met Michael or not but he is an intelligent boy (19 this month) and a good mixer which seems to make him popular in all sorts of company – and *that*, I take it, is an essential qualification of a good newspaper reporter. Added to his knowledge of stenography and typing (and also the fact that he has literary inclinations and has already written a short story or two and a few poems which have secured publication), he would seem qualified to do well in a junior reporter's post. I am sorry to trouble you with all this when I know you are busy enough yourself in all sorts of ways, but I would be very happy if you could pull a string or two on Michael's behalf in this way or write and tell me what you think of the idea and give me the benefit of your advice. I do not myself know so many people in Dublin nowadays; the only writers I can think of who might be able (as I am sure they'd be willing) to help are Austin Clarke, Frank O'Connor, and Desmond Ryan – all of whom are probably well known to you too.[2]

I hope you are fine and fit. Since we left Dungavel and came here some six months ago, the change seems to have benefitted both Valda and myself. This cottage on a hill-farm is really a bit too small for us, but it is set in a lovely countryside and while quite isolated yet handy enough for bus services either to Glasgow or Edinburgh; and I am finding it possible to get really a lot of work done here.

I had a letter the other day from Wilkie. He is remaining as lecturer Anglais at Clermont Ferrand for another year. His wife Helen was over on a flying visit some time ago and I saw her in Glasgow. As with us here, so with them as well, the move from Glasgow seems to have done them a lot of good.

My wife joins me in kindest regards and best wishes.

Yours sincerely, C.M. Grieve

---

1. Addressed to Eoin O'Mahoney, Esq. K.M., at Stephen's Green Club, Dublin, Eire.
2. Austin Clarke (1896–1974), Irish poet and dramatist; Frank O'Connor (1903–66), see Appendix; Desmond Ryan (1893–1964), Irish novelist and historian.

21. *To the Editor,* The Advertiser

[August 1951]

WOMAN EXPLAINS HER PROTEST AGAINST MINISTER

Sir,

As one of the two women members of the Scottish National Congress who protested against Mr Shinwell at the 'Pearlie' Wilson demonstration at Strathaven on Saturday, may I point out (1) that I am a Socialist and have always voted Labour; (2) that as a Socialist I am opposed to militarism and Imperialism; and (3) that I think it is a scandal that Mr Shinwell should occupy the post of Minister of Defence, since, although it is true that he was not a conscientious objector in the First World War, he undoubtedly escaped military service on specious grounds; the work of alleged 'national importance' he was doing could quite well have been done by an older man and Mr Shinwell released for military service.

In any case, Mr Shinwell may dispose by a verbal quibble of the allegation that he was a 'Conchie' but he cannot deny that at a sitting of the Lanarkshire Military Appeal Tribunal on September 17, 1917, he stated (note this first phrase) 'with regard to his conscientious grounds of appeal, that he thought it was not right to ask anyone to engage in a war, the merits of which he had not had the opportunity of considering and regarding which he had not been consulted'.

Now he is not only denying that principle by upholding conscription but refusing to modify the 'cat and mouse' treatment of objectors, and sending National Service youths to the war hells of Korea and Malaya.

As the mother of a boy of 18 refused recognition as a C.O. despite the testimony on his behalf of Mr Emrys Hughes, Mr Tom Driberg, Mr Guy Aldred and others, I have no apology to make for my action on Saturday.

I agree with Mr Strachey that there is a real danger of all true Socialism being taken out of the Labour Party and that its increasing Right Wing tendency is a menace to all the pioneers of Scottish Socialism stood for. This was strikingly exemplified by the brutality of the stewards at the Strathaven meeting which was more reminiscent of Mosleyite thuggery than anything one expects of Socialists. The youths who forced a sod into my mouth and eyes are scarcely creditable followers of Keir Hardie.

On leaving the Park, Mr Shinwell hardly set a good example in courtesy or the sort of behaviour one is entitled to expect of a Cabinet Minister when he told the other woman Nationalist concerned that she 'was potty and ought to have her head examined'.

The Labour and Socialist Movement was built up by men and women whom reactionaries regarded as 'potty'. It is an old gag. Was Mr Shinwell himself 'potty' when the police bludgeoned him in George Square? Perhaps a good deal more 'potty' then than he is now.

Valda Grieve

22. To A.D. Mackie (NLS)

18 December 1951

Dear Albert

Quite a long time ago I mentioned that my son, Michael, was anxious to become a journalist and you were good enough to say that when the time came you might perhaps be able to give him a start. He certainly couldn't begin under better auspices.

In the interval he has taken his certificates in Pitman's shorthand and in typing at a Glasgow Commercial College and since then has kept up and improved his speeds, and is now eager to get into the 'newspaper game'.

As I probably told you he has nascent literary abilities and has had two or three short stories and a few poems published, and I had given him various books on journalism etc. to read and guided his reading in other respects to some extent.

He won't be home till after Christmas – i.e. between Christmas and New Year – but could come through and see you at any time that would suit you then.

Every good wish for Christmas and the New Year to Mrs Mackie and yourself and your family.

Yours, Christopher Grieve

23. To His Excellency the Ambassador, U.S. Embassy, London (NLS, DFF)

[1951?]

May it please your Honour: –

We write to protest against the continued withholding of Paul Robeson's passport and to assure you that many thousands of Scottish people look back to Mr Robeson's last visit to this country as their greatest and most inspiring cultural experience. Like millions of other people all over the world, they regard Mr Robeson as America's greatest artistic contribution to the spiritual heritage of mankind and find the way in which they are now denied further opportunities of hearing his magnificent voice utterly at variance with the US Government's claim to stand for free democracy. The way in which Mr Robeson has been, and is still being treated is a very powerful cause of Anti-American feeling, and your Honour can render no greater service to your country or the cause for which it purports to stand than to make representations to your Government in this sense and add the weight of your influence to the world-wide demand for the cessation of this senseless injustice which is robbing great audiences everywhere of the services of one of the most superb voices in the world today.

We have the honour to be, Sir, yours sincerely. [Unsigned][1]

1. Paul Robeson (1898–1976), black American singer and actor who toured the world singing show songs and black spirituals, communist in sympathies but never a member of the CPUSA. In 1950, he attended a Civil Rights Congress rally to protest Truman's action in sending troops to Korea; subsequently his passport was made void under new national emergency laws, the authorities refusing to consider application for a new one unless he guaranteed he would make no speeches abroad. Under heavy foreign pressure, it was returned in 1958.

24. *To A.D. Mackie (NLS)*

10 January 1952

Dear Bert

I can't for the life of me remember whether I thanked you for your letter re my boy, Michael. There are reasons for my confusion of mind. My wife is in hospital and has to undergo an operation shortly. It is a heart case – not the worse kind of angina, but the other less serious sort – angina on effort, which means at least she'll have to be very careful henceforth not to overdo things.

But if I didn't write you, let me thank you now. I quite understand the difficulties of the present state of affairs, of course. I have written several others but they are all pretty much in the same position as yourself. I too know that a local paper is the best start, but I am not in touch with local papers now to the extent I used to be. However I'll keep trying, and I know that if anything should turn up to ease the situation so far as you are concerned you'll let me know.

My wife is in Law Hospital near Carluke and that is a rather difficult place to get to – and back from – on visiting days. But if that wasn't taking up so much of my time I think I would have succumbed to the temptation to run through to Edinburgh and see your play, of which I've read several excellent notices. Accept my warmest congratulations. And more power to your elbow. Now you've broken so successfully into this new field I hope you'll be able amidst all your other commitments to go on and give us more. I'll certainly hope to see this play yet – but anyhow, at the moment I hear the thing is packed out at every performance!

Every kind regard to Mrs Mackie and your family.

Yours, Chris

P.S. Thanks too for the *Broughton Magazine*. I'll write Mr Sinclair.

25. *To Miss Edith Trelease Aney (NLS, DFF)*[1]

7 February 1952

Dear Miss Aney

Many thanks for your extremely kind and interesting letter of 29th ult which reached me yesterday. I greatly appreciate your interest in my work and am of course anxious to help in any way I can. As you probably know quite a number of American scholars are interesting themselves in contemporary Scottish literature, and my work in particular. These include Professor David Daiches, lately of Cornell but now of Cambridge, England, with whose long essay on my poetry in *Poetry* (Chicago) of July 1948 you are probably familiar; Mr Kenneth Buthlay, who is now on a fellowship at Aberdeen University; and Geoffrey Wagner, 2310 Second Avenue, New York 35, N.Y.[2] The last-named would probably lend you *A Drunk Man Looks at the Thistle* if you wrote him, saying you did so at my suggestion. The book is out of print and I haven't a copy of it myself. It is, I think, undoubtedly my best long poem (or, rather, series of interconnected lyrics), and you will certainly require it. I have been trying for a long time to get hold of a copy for a friend, but without success. It never seems to crop up in the second-hand catalogues.

The 'Cornish Heroic Song' which you also star as one you particularly want is of course available in *A Kist o' Whistles* in which book it was reprinted. But perhaps you have been misled by my references elsewhere to an extremely long poem of this title. It was originally part of the latter which, however, I subsequently split up into a lot of parts which include the 'Cornish Heroic Song' as given in *A Kist o' Whistles*; *In Memoriam James Joyce* (a now separated portion of some 6000 lines, which will probably be published as a separate volume), and 'Once in a Cornish Garden', a piece of 3 to 400 lines which appears in the current issue of the Rome review *Botteghe Oscure*. Other portions of that now fragmented poem have been published in *The Voice of Scotland*, a now defunct quarterly which I edited, *Scottish Arts and Letters* (also defunct) and elsewhere.

Stony Limits (published by Messrs Victor Gollancz in 1934) is also I think important for your dissertation. Following this letter I will send you immediately a parcel of several things on loan, including my copy of the above which contains some of my best political poems.

Other points in your letter to which I may just reply seriatim are
1) William Stieg sent me a copy of his *Rejected Lovers*. Many thanks for your offer to do so if I hadn't seen it.[3]
2) As you probably know from my *Lucky Poet*, I am as much interested in the Irish, Welsh, and Cornish as I am in the Scots, and my wife is a Cornish woman.
3) There are several misprints in the portion of *This Generation* devoted to me. The book called *Rural Reform* was published by Messrs Constable for the Fabian Society in 1912, not 1922.
4) You ask if I have written political poetry not published in any of my volumes. I have – a great deal. This includes a 'Third Hymn to Lenin', and also a lot of poems dealing with the Spanish War and originally put together as a reply to Roy Campbell's pro-Franco *Flowering Rifle*. I hope

to send you some of these in parcel mentioned above. I haven't a copy of the long *In Memoriam James Joyce* but you will see what the late Miss Mary Baird Aitken says of it in her long essay on my poetry in *Scottish Arts and Letters* which I'll enclose in the parcel too; and T.S. Eliot said of it when he read it in my first draft several years ago:

(take in Eliot)[4]

5) With regard to whether there has been any change in my social or political views as represented by my poetry, since the 1930s, the answer is no (i.e. they remain essentially the same but have developed greatly). I have been for the most part writing the kind of poetry indicated in the 'Kind of Poetry I Want' section of *Lucky Poet* and have ceased almost altogether to write lyrical poems, or to write in Scots. This is not to be regarded as an abandonment of the lyric or of Scots, but as a necessary detour, from which I will return to write a new kind of lyric again in enriched Scots. I have a big programme of work of this sort in hand, but conditions have not been propitious. So in the meantime I am continuing to pour out long non-lyrical learned and argumentative pieces which may or may not be called poetry – that is a matter of definition.

I have as you will see made a number of additions etc. to your Bibliography, which I return herewith. These include a Centenary Study of R.B. Cunninghame Graham, which will be published shortly (I'll send you a copy): also my pamphlet on Charles Doughty (which I enclose), and two volumes of selections from the poems of the 15th Century Scots poet, William Dunbar.[5]

You ask about my relations with the CP. I joined the Communist Party of Great Britain in 1934 (there is no Scottish CP – that is one of the troubles) and was expelled in 1938 because of my Scottish Nationalism, but I exercised my right of appeal and was re-instated by the Comintern. Shortly afterwards I was expelled again by the same people responsible for my first expulsion, disgruntled at my re-instatement. I said then that I would never rejoin until the Party's official line in regard to Scotland was abreast of my own. It is virtually that now. Mr Wm Gallagher, our only Communist MP (until defeated at last election) and the Secretary of the Scottish Secretariat of the CPGB, William Laughlin, have both published statements on the Scottish issue I might equally well have written myself. But I have not rejoined, because it is felt that at this juncture I am much more useful to the CP as I am than I would be as a member. I speak for them, the *Daily Worker* gives me a good press, I generally take the chair for Russian and Chinese delegations visiting Scotland, and so on. I am most useful in relation to related organisations of all kinds. I am a Vice-President of the British Peace Committee, President of the Scottish Youth and Students Union, and a director of Theatre Workshop Ltd, a purely Communist body, probably the best experimental theatre group in Western Europe, which has been enormously successful in its tours of Scandinavia, Poland,

Czecho-Slovakia, East Germany etc. I am also a member of the National Council and Executive Committee of the Scottish-USSR Friendship Society.

In October-November 1950 I visited the Soviet Union and travelled over 25,000 miles in it. I met most of the leading Russian writers etc., and broadcast from Radio Moscow. I have written and spoken a great deal about my impressions which amply confirmed all my best hopes.

In the summer of last year (1951) I was a guest of honour at the World Youth Festival in East Berlin and broadcast about it from Radio Budapest and Radio Prague. I met most of the writers associated with that wonderful demonstration, Pablo Neruda, Nazim Hikmet, Anna Seghers, Johannes Becker etc. etc.[6]

For the past 30 years I have done a tremendous amount of public speaking on literary and political matters – not only in Scotland but in Wales and England, and have lectured at most of our universities – Edinburgh, Glasgow, St Andrews, Aberdeen, Aberystwyth, Manchester, Durham, and Oxford.

I have not used my poems much in my speeches, but I have given a lot of poetry readings, and my poems have been very frequently broadcast. Also it must be remembered that about 70 of my lyrics have been set to music by Francis George Scott, the greatest composer Scotland has ever had and undoubtedly one of the very best song-writers in Europe. These too are broadcast a lot and sung at all sorts of concerts.

You ask about the apparent incompatibility of some of my views with Communism, or at least with the line enforced in the USSR. I think 'apparent' is the operative word. As Engels pointed out he and Marx had only been able to do about a third of what they had planned. Amongst other things they failed to implement their philosophy with an aesthetic. Hence the confusion. But that great Communist critic, Professor Lukacs of Budapest (*vide* his *Studies in European Realism* etc.), such British fellow-travellers as the late Professor R.G. Collingwood (*vide* his *Autobiography*) and Professor Joseph Needham (*vide* his *Time the Refreshing River*) are substantially of the same mind as I am, which amounts to the claim that if the admittedly-incomplete body of Marx-Lenin-Stalinism is carried to its proper conclusions in regard to such matters this will be the agreed finding. This is subject in my case to the additional point that my mind in such matters is subtly differentiated from that of most of those who have occupied themselves with them, because of the extent to which I have been influenced by, and subscribe to, the Indian atheist philosophy of Sankhara instead of having the conventional Western derivation of most of the others.[7] In addition to the names mentioned above, there is also, of course, Berdyaev, to whom I am much nearer, who entirely approved the Soviet regime and had no political differences from it, but differed only in certain ultimate philosophical reaches.[8] He was exiled but continued to avow his approval of the USSR and to work for the Peace Movement.

I have had clashes at public meetings on some of these matters with Russian speakers, notably Pavlov (Molotov's Secretary, now Russian Ambassador in Paris), but these differences were only such as would occur at any time between a specialist on literary issues and a somewhat crassly dogmatic person with no special knowledge of, or interest in, such matters.

Another question you ask is about my most interesting employment. Most of my posts have been journalistic ones, generally on local papers, and as such purely routine, i.e. I could do them more or less mechanically – they took little or nothing out of me but left me fairly free to do my own work alongside them. The most interesting of these jobs was in 1911–12 when I ran a weekly paper for the South Wales Miners' Federation, because that brought me into close touch with the miners' leaders who at that time made South Wales the storm-centre of British working-class politics.

At Edinburgh University I took the Arts Course, but did not complete it owing to my father's death.[9] Few of my fellow-students then have made much of a name for themselves – most of the best of them were killed off in the 1914–18 War. But one exception is Professor Hyman Levy. I was at that time an active member of the Fabian Society and took part in forming the University Socialist Federation.

You also ask if I have taken an active part in public life. Yes. I have been a Town and a County and a Parish Councillor and a Justice of the Peace – I received the last-named appointment when our first Labour Government ruled that in future appointments to the Commission of the Peace each of the political parties should share more or less equally (prior to that, the Magistracy had been largely a preserve of the gentry). It is of course a life appointment, so I am still a magistrate.

I have said that I have had no trouble in recent years with the Party over my ideas. This is a matter that seems to cut both ways. Although I am regarded as a 'Red' and known in particular to be a Republican with a vitriolic hatred of the Monarchy, the late King awarded me a Civil List pension two or three years ago, and thus put me in a position to devote far more time than I could otherwise have done to Peace and Soviet Friendship work, and I must admit that I am well satisfied that these activities should be made possible at the public expense in this way.[10]

Finally you ask what poet has influenced me most. That is a difficult question to answer. I am not easily influenced. I have read enormously and known many great poets of many lands, but I think I have not been influenced directly very much, though of course I have learned technical devices and found myself impelled towards certain types of subject matter and forms of treatment by many very diverse poets, e.g. Yeats, Pound, Hopkins, Rilke, Rimbaud, Mayakovsky. Probably the best answer to your question is Doughty. You will see from my pamphlet (as also from what I say about him in *Lucky Poet*)

[MS ends]

---

1. The letter is addressed to Miss Aney at the University of Philadelphia, USA.
2. Kenneth Buthlay later worked in the Department of Scottish Literature at the University of Glasgow (the only university Department devoted to the subject), wrote an excellent introductory study of CMG and annotated *A Drunk Man Looks at the Thistle*. Geoffrey Atheling Wagner (b.1922), American poet novelist and critic, Professor of English at City College of New York from 1954.
3. William Steig (b.1907), American cartoonist and author of children's books. *The Rejected Lovers* (New York: Knopf, 1951) is an adult cartoon book; the rejected lovers are men and the form of rejection violent.
4. CMG quoted a letter from T.S. Eliot in a subscription prospectus for *In Memoriam James Joyce*: 'It is a very fine monument to Joyce... I not only enjoyed the poem but it has a great deal in it that has my sympathy and agreement as well as my admiration'.
5. Hugh MacDiarmid, *Cunninghame Graham: a centenary study*, with a forward by R.E. Muirhead (Glasgow: Caledonia Press, 1952). *Charles Doughty and the Need for Heroic Poetry* (St Andrews: The Modern Scot, 1936). Both are reprinted in Hugh MacDiarmid, *Albyn: Shorter Books and Monographs*, ed. Alan Riach (Manchester: Carcanet Press, 1996). *Selections from the Poems of William Dunbar*, edited with an introduction by Hugh MacDiarmid (Edinburgh: Oliver & Boyd, for the Saltire Society, 1952). *Selected Poems of William Dunbar*, edited and introduced by Hugh MacDiarmid (Glasgow: MacLellan, 1955); the book had been printed for the Crown Classics series of Grey Walls Press but the firm went out of business before publishing it. MacLellan took it over and published it under his imprint.
6. Pablo Neruda (1904–73), Chilean poet, member of the Chilean Communist Party, elected to the senate in 1945, winner of the Nobel Prize for Literature (1971). Nazim Hikmet (1902–63), Turkish radical poet and dramatist, Marxist and member of the Turkish Communist Party, imprisoned for his political activities (1938–51). Anna Seghers (b.1900), German socialist-realist novelist, member of the Communist Party (1929). Johannes Becher (1891–1958), German political Expressionist poet, novelist and critic.
7. Sankhara (788–820), Indian philosopher-monk who rejected dualism and held that absolute subjective consciousness is the only reality.
8. Nikolai Berdyaev (1874–1948), Russian religious philosopher who believed that individuals attain their existence to the extent that they realise their creative essence, which they might do in a society which embodies true community. He was opposed to the subordination of the individual to the community and was dismissed from a professorship in Moscow (1922) for his unorthodox views, settling eventually in Paris.
9. Although CMG does seem to have been active in peripheral University societies, he was not a matriculated student of Edinburgh University.
10. CMG accepted the pension of £150 per annum from the Attlee administration in March 1950.

26. To Frank Holliday (McMUL)

24 March 1952

Dear Mr Holliday

Mr F.G. Scott has written me – enclosing your letter to him – re the projected records of music by my friend Sorabji and I now write to say that like Mr Scott and Mr Chisholm you can count on me for £10 towards the cost. What that cost is likely to be I have no idea, but I imagine that £30 from Scott, Chisholm, and myself won't go far towards it. However I hope a lot of other friends will weigh in and make the thing possible. I haven't heard anything of Sorabji for a very long time, and am extremely sorry to learn that his financial position has again been whittled down by the present state of affairs. I realise of course that without a great deal of money there can be no question of the publication of any of the big post-*Opus Clavicembalisticum* works upon which he was engaged when he wrote me last. This must be terribly discouraging – to any artist but Sorabji himself, I fancy, it would put an end to all effort – but I hope that despite all adverse circumstances he has still sufficient confidence to keep creating – and that ultimately the world may have the benefit of all that work, on micro-strip scores or something of that sort – it seems impossible even to hope that a time will come again in our lives when publication in the magnificent fashion of *Opus Clavicembalisticum* will be possible. Anyhow I hope your appeal succeeds and that Sorabji himself agrees to the records being made. I will look forward eagerly to further news from you.

Please give my warmest greetings and every good wish to Sorabji if you are seeing him or writing him.

And accept for yourself my compliments and every high regard.

Yours sincerely, Christopher Grieve

27. To Lady Brooke (UDL)

19 April 1952

Dear Lady Brooke

In your very kind letter to me after the funeral of your uncle, the late Mr. R.B. Cunninghame Graham, you expressed the hope that I might write something about him. I have written the enclosed essay as a tribute for the occasion of the centenary of his birth next month. The copy I enclose for the favour of your acceptance is one of two I have had specially bound – the other I am sending to your brother, Admiral Cunninghame Graham. The ordinary edition, which will be bound in green cloth, will be published next week. As you probably know there is to be a gathering to mark the event at Ardoch, and also a public meeting in Glasgow at which I will speak as also will Mr R.E. Muirhead who provides the introduction to this little book.

With compliments and best wishes.

Yours sincerely, 'Hugh MacDiarmid' (Christopher Grieve)

28. *To F.G. Scott (EUL)*

2 June 1952

Dear F.G.

Many thanks for your letter received tonight. I did not know what songs Joan Alexander was to sing and am glad to have the list. I will simply be a formal Chairman at the Institute of Contemporary Arts Concert on Friday night and my introductory remarks will be brief and mainly concerned with the facts of the careers and output of yourself and Chisholm (whose Preludes and Pibroch Concerto Agnes Walker is playing). I do not think it will be necessary to explain the meaning of the words of the songs at all. The occasion is of course an important one. A bevy of leading critics (especially highbrow ones, like Edward Sackville West) will be there. So will the BBC Third Programme people. There is also a possibility that the British Council will arrange for us to repeat the programme in Paris. There will, of course, be no opportunity (even if I wished it) for me to be political on this occasion.

The following day I am going to Braziers' Park – College of Integrative Social Research, 18 miles from Oxford – to take part in a discussion on the Caledonian Antisyzygy.

And on the 8th I am addressing Oxford University Poetry Society on the differences between Scottish and English poetry.

On the 10th I am back in London at the Institute of Contemporary Arts giving a reading of my own poems, with G.S. Fraser in the chair. W.S. Graham is also to be there reading a selection of Scottish poems that appeal to him.

On the way back I am breaking my journey at Manchester to stay with Chiari, and incidentally to meet a group of young teachers who have a poetry study circle and are particularly interested in my work.

At Friday night's concert I understand Sorabji is to be present. I'll be very glad to see him again.

The long deferred second programme of my poems on the Third Programme is now scheduled for 23rd inst, with repeat on 27th.

Also, after 5 years' wait, my *Selected Poems* of Wm Dunbar, sponsored by the Saltire Society is about to be published by Oliver and Boyd. I'll send you a copy when I get them.

The other selection of Dunbar's *Poems* I did for publication by the Grey Wall Press is long overdue. I am now taking legal action. I instructed proceedings about three weeks ago, so the case should be up shortly. You do not refer to it in your letter so I hope you duly received the copy of my little book on Cunninghame Graham I sent you a week or so ago.

I was awfully sorry I did not see Mrs Scott at the Cunninghame Graham meeting in the MacLellan Galleries. Valda told me she was there, and she (Valda) was talking to her.

You would see from tonight's (Monday's) papers about Mike's case. He would of course refuse medical exam today, so will be up again tomorrow when I understand sentence will be pronounced – probably a year. It was impossible for lawyers on his behalf to intervene before that sentence is passed. Immediately it is we'll take the matter to a higher court, where he'll be represented by Stenhouse, Glasgow solicitor, and Hon David Watson, advocate, Edinburgh.

Please excuse this hurried scrawl. I've a lot to do yet in preparation for my London-Oxford and Manchester engagements. I was of course at the Court in Glasgow today but there was no point in my staying overnight and attending tomorrow's proceedings which will be purely formal and preliminary to the real fight later.

I hope you're all in good form.

Love. Yours, Chris

29. *To Compton Mackenzie (HRC)*

3 June 1952

Dear Compton Mackenzie

I was so sorry I failed to get to Inchmahome in time to see you. I went to the Dumbarton commemoration gathering where Moray MacLaren gave an excellent address. But the gathering was nearly ½ an hour late in starting. Even so I should have managed all right – if it had not been for a puncture. The consequent delay did not allow me to get to Inchmahome until just after you had left.

I gather from the *Radio Times* etc. that you may be still in Scotland and perhaps matters in connection with your Film Company's programme may keep you here for a while. If not, I wonder if you will be in London while I am there. I am taking the chair at a concert of the works of two contemporary Scottish composers – F.G. Scott and Erik Chisholm – in the Institute of Contemporary Arts in Dover St, W.1, on Friday 6th inst. Then I am addressing Oxford University Poetry Society on 8th inst and returning to London to give a poetry reading, with G.S. Fraser in the Chair and W.S. Graham also reading Scottish poems, in the Institute of Contemporary Arts on 10th inst.

In case you should be in Town and we could meet, my address while I am in London will be:– c/o Alex McCrindle, 17 Blomfield Road, London W.9.

With every good wish, Yours, C.M. Grieve

30. *To R.S. Silver (NLS)*

5 June 1952

Dear Silver
   I read your play with great interest and appreciation.[1] It does rise to some magnificent passages of poetic eloquence which in themselves are sufficient to carry the whole thing. The size of the cast should not be any bar to production. I note that Glasgow Citizens', Pitlochry, and the Festival have all turned it down, but these rejections should not be accepted as final. I am writing this hurriedly just as I am leaving for Oxford and London but I will take the first opportunity of seeing you and talking the matter over once I get back – about 12th or 14th inst. You would see Dr Honeyman's statement in the press the other day that the Citizens now intend to pursue a more Scottish policy. I do not know if you are personally acquainted with Honeyman, but I know him very well and we are good friends. I think pressure can be bought to bear on him. I do not think a Pitlochry production is likely. But the Festival is another matter. There again pressure can probably be brought to bear. Perhaps the likeliest avenue however is via Theatre Workshop. As you probably know they are producing at the Labour Festival in Edinburgh this year a John Knox play by a Kingussie man, and I am sure they would be quite willing to consider your play for next year. I am sorry there does not seem any chance of getting the thing done before then. Any re-approach to Honeyman or to the Festival Committee, as to Theatre Workshop, involves a wait, and arrangements for the current year are of course complete. I'll be seeing the Theatre Workshop people (I'm a director of it) in London and will broach the matter to them. The only other outlets in Scotland are the Perth Rep and the Dundee Rep. and the Byre Theatre, St Andrews. All these are less likely than Theatre Workshop or Citizens or Edinburgh Festival. I'm very sorry I can't make any more practical and immediate suggestion but we'll get together I hope as soon as I get back and see what can be done. The play's got to be produced somewhere and as soon as possible – that's certain.
   Do please excuse this rushed scribble. I'm desperately busy. But at least even this scrawl will convey my congratulations on a splendid bit of work, my confidence that we'll be able to force its production somehow, and every kind regard to your family and yourself.
   Yours, Chris

---

1. R.S. Silver, *The Bruce: Robert I King o' Scots* (Edinburgh: The Saltire Society, 1986), written 1948–51.

31. *To David Daiches (EUL)*

23 October 1952

Dear Professor Daiches
I have been away from home or would have thanked you for your postcard of 5th October long ere this. I am delighted that you are willing to write the Introduction to the new edition of *The Drunk Man*. It is exceedingly good of you and while I am very grateful I feel a certain compunction since I am sure to do this, and, as I suggested, do it quickly, must add to already heavy commitments – tho', of course, I know it is always the busiest man who can take on a little more. Please send the Introduction to me and I will pass it on to the Caledonian Press people.
With renewed thanks and every kind regard.
Yours sincerely, C.M. Grieve

32. *To Norman MacCaig (NLS)*

8 December 1952

Dear Norman
I have just written to McNeice to tell him that I too know of nothing of the kind he wants. I have consulted my own memory and what reference books I have here but can find nothing whatever that falls between the stipulated dates except Hogmanay – and that is nothing at all nowadays, tho' I remember when I was a boy that a rich enough traditional ceremony was gone through then and the play the children enacted, *The Galatians*, was a very ancient thing, handed down orally for centuries. This may not have been general throughout Scotland but it certainly held good for the Border counties. I do not suppose it is still gone through anywhere or that the children nowadays still act – or know – the old play at all. I have told McNeice this and expressed my regret that I cannot be more helpful.
Re Sidney's book I agree entirely with what you said in advance it would be.[1] In a word, damned little. A few goodish poems and the rest poor throw-offs unworthy of volume form. And Edith's foreword is just tripe. I am very sorry indeed about this. But I gather Sidney is home again and I trust greatly improved – and that he'll 'tak' a thocht and mend' in his poetic practice now.
The poem you had in the *Dispatch* the other night struck me.[2] I thought the germ of it was first rate but that it deserved less offhand treatment. You dealt with the idea too casually, I thought, and did not give it a form worthy of the end. You should reconsider it. The end calls for a different vehicle altogether.
What your final fling at me means I can't imagine at all. You must know that I am – or feel myself – more isolated than ever: feel, also, that the

whole Scottish movement is petering out from a paucity of those who have really the root of the matter in them and a hellish superfluity of copyists. And over and above that if you really think (which I don't believe) that I neither need your love or best wishes you utterly underestimate what the friendship of Isabel and yourself means to me and has meant this last year or so.

Michael is doing a part-time job in Glasgow pro tem and staying c/o Blytheman.[3] Amongst other things he is studying to take his university prelim. Valda and I are OK tho' I have just had a devilish dose of flu' which, however, I am now throwing off. We've been without our water supply for about a fortnight and had to carry pails from the farm etc.

All the best. Yours, Chris
P.S. I'll probably be coming to Edinr. this week some time to see Mike's counsel, Hon. David Watson.

---

1. Sydney Goodsir Smith, *So Late Into the Night: fifty lyrics* with a preface by Edith Sitwell (London: Peter Russell, 1952).
2. Norman MacCaig's poem, 'Slow Twilight Ended' appeared in the *Evening Dispatch*, 1–8 (5th) December 1952, p.10:

> Light ebbs away as though
>   Something has failed to be said.
>   Taking expectancy
> From troubled heart and head
> And leaving only darkness as
> Bedfellow till the night should pass.
>
> What was it hinted of
>   A revelation? What
>   Could it reveal? Did love
> Master my stiff thought
> And make my narrow bed so wide
> The world could sleep there at my side?

3. Morris Blytheman (1919–81), Marxist poet and songwriter, writing under the name Thurso Berwick (presumably to 'speak for' all of Scotland, from Thurso on the northernmost coast, to Berwick, on the borders), editor of the *Rebels Ceilidh Song Book*.

33. To Christine Macintosh

23 December 1952

Dear Christine

Many thanks for your kind letter received yesterday. C/o Caledonian Press, Glasgow gets me, but only after a time as a rule. In this case it was a week. I am seldom in Glasgow nowadays. It is a 3 hours 'bus run from here and I can seldom get back the same day. A good 'bus service runs me into Edinburgh in 40 minutes, so if we can meet as you suggest Edinburgh will suit me best if that's all right for you. But give me a day or so's notice, as I am a great deal away on speaking engagements etc. I am however fairly clear in January until 21st, when my usual round of Burns Suppers begins. I have no Edinburgh date until somewhere between 8th and 15th February [smudges on MS] (sorry! My pen isn't working properly) when I am broadcasting from the Edinburgh studio.

I am delighted to learn that my grandchildren are more numerous than I knew. My love and best wishes to them both.

And here's wishing you all a happy Christmas and a bright and prosperous New Year.

Yours, Christopher

34. *To the Editor (NLS, DFF)*
The Scotsman, North Bridge, Edinburgh
Forward, c/o Unity Publishing Coy, 308 Clyde Street, Glasgow.
Evening Dispatch, Edinburgh
Daily Record, Hope Street, Glasgow
Bulletin, Buchanan Street, Glasgow

2 March 1953

Sir: –

I enclose a letter signed by a number of well-known Scottish writers. The original, with the holograph signatures, is in my possession and may be seen at any time.

Yours sincerely.

Sir

One of the functions of a national PEN Centre is to afford public receptions to distinguished writers visiting the country in question. This duty is exercised by most of the European PEN Centres, as is only right, since at times of the annual International PEN Congress, the centre acting as host is largely dependent upon financial facilitations derived from public money. Why then does the Scottish PEN fail to recognise the occasional presence in our country of famous foreign writers? A case in point was the recent visit to Edinburgh of the great Irish dramatist Sean O'Casey. Mr O'Casey had not been in Scotland for over twenty years and since he is now 73 he may never come amongst us again. Surely this is an occasion which the Scottish PEN should have signalised by inviting him to be guest of honour at some function representative of the best in contemporary Scottish letters and allied cultural interests. There is no excuse for this

failure to do so.
   Yours sincerely, Hugh MacDiarmid[1]

---

1. The signatures are added of Sydney Goodsir Smith, Norman MacCaig and Hamish Henderson.

35. *To Edwin Morgan*

6 July 1953

Dear Mr Morgan
   Many thanks indeed for the copy of your translation of *Beowulf* which reached me this morning. I look forward to reading it, and have already given a first reading to your meaty introduction, many points in which I will wish to consider very carefully in subsequent re-readings.
   My son Michael when at home here a day or two ago told me that he had been approached to see if I would be willing to address the Literary Society early in November, and I told him to tell the students who had approached him that I would be very pleased to do so. Your letter says 'at the end of October'. That will suit me all right. Michael said he had been told that I could take any subject I cared to choose. In that event I think 'The Differences of English and Scottish Literature' (or as an alternative and perhaps a better title, 'A Scotsman looks at English literature') might be suitable. Please let me know. But if there is some other theme within the range of my special interests you would prefer me to take I will, of course, try to meet your wishes in the matter.
   With warmest thanks and best wishes,
   Yours sincerely, Hugh MacDiarmid

36. *To Honor and Alex McCrindle (EUL)*

21 July 1953

Dear Honor and Alex
   I am delighted to hear about the cottages at Kippen and will certainly look forward to visiting you there. We'd have been still better pleased of course if you'd been going to be nearer us. Still Kippen is not too difficult to get to. The idea of getting two or three cottages in a line and making them into one has always been in our own minds and we've seen several such that have been made into first-rate places. Just a few weeks ago I was at a friend's, who'd been lucky enough to pick up a row of three quite cheaply, and made an excellent job of turning them into one. But the initial cost of getting two or three cottages in that way has always been beyond Valda and I. But here's to Oxhill and to a really lucrative sale of your

London lease. I'm all for 'soaking the Yanks'.

It is very good of you to put Mike up overnight when I expect you are in a sufficient turmoil with your imminent 'flitting': but I understand it will be only for the one night – just till he contacts some of his own friends. He has stayed with divers of these in London before, but I think the position is that he isn't quite sure how some of them may be placed until he sees them. But there are sufficient of them to ensure that he can put up with one or other of them all right.

I haven't had any word about the position now of the Edinburgh People's Festival. I know that the Labour Party's ban shut them off from sources to which they could otherwise have looked to help them to meet their debts. But their total indebtedness was so great that in the circumstances the position seemed perfectly hopeless and I did not see how they could possibly reduce that debt sufficiently to carry on with any sort of programme this year. It is excellent news that your Ceilidh and other efforts have realised such a substantial sum. If a few other friends are being equally helpful they may be able to carry on after all. I certainly hope so. The 'other side' seem to be more powerful than ever in Scottish cultural circles. I personally seem to be out on a limb in this connection and am involved in more rows and personal enmities than ever.

Hamish H. is in Edinburgh still carrying on I think in the folk-song collecting business for the Scottish Studies Department of Edinburgh University, but I have seen very little of him this past year. Almost everybody I encounter who comes into contact with him loathes him. I am afraid if he hears (as he will) that you are at Kippen he'll turn up there. He is damnably persistent. I told him he was never to come here unless he wrote first in time to hear back from me (giving as an excuse – tho' it's true enough – that I'm so much away that if he came on chance he'd more than likely find nobody here (or, worse, only Valda). Yet the blighter did come without notice just the same. What the Devil can one make of such a fellow?

Excuse more at the moment. It was good to get your letters. Valda joins me in every kind regard to you all. Her own arrangements I think (they're not quite definite yet) preclude any staying over in London, but if she has a few hours she'll phone you – or if she finally wants to stay over a night (it'll only be one night in her case too) she'll be glad to accept your kind offer.

Yours, Chris

37. *To James D. Young (NLS)*

17 September 1953

Dear Comrade

In reply to your letter of 15th inst regarding Lewis Grassic Gibbon,

Gibbon's work has been the subject of extensive study by my friend Mr Geoffrey Wagner of New York University. He has now completed a book on the subject – a complete biographical and critical study – but this has not been published yet. He had the advantage of getting all the material we could give him from Gibbon's widow (Mrs Rhea Mitchell, 4 Attemore Road, Welwyn Garden City, Herts.), Miss H.B. Cruickshank, 4 Hillview Terrace, Corstorphine, Edinburgh, myself and other friends of Gibbon's. Pending the publication of his book, Mr Wagner has been doing a lot of writing about Gibbon in various quarters. I have the July 1953 issue of the quarterly journal, *Essays in Criticism*, which contains one of the best of Wagner's essays on Gibbon. I have also a copy of *Tribune* in which Wagner had another article on Gibbon. You probably know my own essay on Gibbon, which appeared originally in *Scottish Art and Letters* and subsequently in *Little Reviews Anthology* (1940). I can send you all these on loan and between them they contain the bulk of the material available. There is also as you probably know Mr Ivor Brown's introductory essay to the one-volume edition of Gibbon's trilogy published by Messrs Jarrolds. I can lend you this too if you haven't a copy.

The only other thing I can suggest is that you might write to Mrs Mitchell and Miss Cruickshank who might be able to put you in the way of supplementary material.

I regard Gibbon as the greatest Scots novelist since John Galt and as the only one who has shown real social awareness and faced up to the changes in Scottish life following on rural depopulation and the industrial revolution and brought his account of these changes right abreast of our contemporary situation.

With best wishes, Yours sincerely, C.M. Grieve

38. *To Christine Macintosh*

2 March 1954

Dear Christine

Sorry to have been so long in writing to thank you – and Alistair – for your kindness to me in Dundee. But I think seeing you again is responsible; in any case I found myself so stimulated that since then I have had one of the most productive periods for many years. I have really turned out an astonishing amount of stuff – poems, articles, radio scripts etc.

It occurred to me that you may have thought me strangely off-hand and unemotional. But I do not wear my heart on my sleeve and am not a demonstrative person. That, however, means that I am more, and not less, affected than people who find easier outlets for their feelings.

Suffice it to say, it was a great joy to me to see you and the children. I am sorry that I let Alistair and Dr Burnett in for what they must have thought a deplorable harangue at a type of meeting they would never have dreamt of attending in ordinary circumstances.

Love to you all. Yours, Christopher

39. *To Alex McCrindle (EUL)*

31 May 54

Dear Alec

Things went awry in Edinburgh and I never heard at all what you were thinking about the *Drunk Man* for Festival time. It was a pity we got involved in such a school. Peter Westwater is completely mad, and when he starts doubling up whiskies there's little chance of any rational talk.[1] I was sorry you didn't get back. Thanks incidentally for the telegram.

Valda's aunt died on Saturday, so she is going off to Cornwall tomorrow and will be away 2 or 3 weeks.

Michael turned up on Saturday complaining of a bad cold, but since he was running a temperature I called in the Doctor, who diagnosed tonsilitis, prescribed pencillin, and enjoined his remaining in bed till Thursday at earliest when he'll see him again. So I have my hands full.

Let me know if – and when – it'll be convenient for me to come to Kippen for a day or two. But if it is not convenient please just say so. I don't want you to put yourselves about in any way.

Love to you all. Yours, Chris

---

1. (Robert H) Peter Westwater (1905–62), artist, art critic of *The Scotsman*.

40. *To Christine Macintosh*

15 June 1954

Dear Christine

I saw the notice of Walter's marriage in yesterday's *Scotsman*. I would have liked to write and wish him and his bride good fortune and happiness. But I do not suppose he remembers me at all and such a reminder coming out of the blue after all these years might not please him. So though I would like him to know that I have never forgotten him I have decided not to write him, and can only console myself with the belief that my unexpressed blessing and good wishes cannot at any rate harm the young couple, and with the sense that if he does not know me or wish to that is because he has only heard at most one side of the story and circumstances have not allowed me to give my version.

While I know you are not keen on letter-writing and have enough to do in any event with your home and husband and the two children, I am sorry not to have heard from you again since I saw you. I think I wrote and said how afraid I was you'd been disappointed by my seeming casualness and inexpressiveness. It is a fear that has haunted me ever since.

With kindest regards and every good wish to Elspeth, Donald, Alistair and yourself.

Christopher

P.S. I promised you a copy of my big Joyce poem. It isn't published yet but is all set up and shouldn't be long now, I think.

41. *To Alistair Macintosh*[1]

18 June 1954

Dear Alistair

I cannot tell you how glad I was to see Christine again after so many years or how anxious to keep in touch with her. It was a great pleasure to me to meet you and the children in February. Since then I have written Christine several times, but have had no reply, and today my last letter which I enclose has been returned by the postal authorities. This is very worrying to me. I quite recognize that my desire to keep in touch may not be shared by Christine or yourself, but if so the simplest solution would simply be to say so. I certainly have no desire to make a nuisance of myself.

I would be grateful therefore if you will just let me know what the situation is.

Hoping you are all well, and with best wishes.

Yours, C.M. Grieve

---

1. The letter is addressed to Dr Alistair Macintosh, MB, ChB, MRCP, Mayfield Hospital, Dundee.

42. *To R. Crombie Saunders (EUL)*

6 July 1954

Dear Crombie

Owing to a family bereavement Valda was down in Cornwall for a month but returned a day or two ago. I had enough to do looking after myself and the cat – and occasionally at weekends Michael – or I'd have written sooner in response to your note and perhaps been able to send you something for the *S.J.* [*Scottish Journal*]. I'll try to do that soon now anyhow. I noted I'd been put on the mailing list – but, alas, only got one copy in that way, so am not up to date. But I hope all goes well with it and you.

Perhaps I'll see something of you at the end of this month and beginning of next when I'm to take over on the *Alloa Journal* during Peter Brodie's holiday.

This letter is prompted by something else. I wonder if you have a good snap of yourself – preferably an unconventional one, i.e. landing a whopping big trout. I do not want a 'studio portrait' or anything 'posed'. But it must be clear and sharply defined, i.e. capable of reproduction. This is for the next issue of the poetry magazine, *Lines*, for which I have undertaken to get a number of snaps of key people to form a sort of visual history (or 'Black Museum') of contemporary Scottish literature – the photos to be linked together with a minimum of (almost wholly merely factual) letterpress.

If you have such a snap – either of yourself alone or with one or more other people who also figure in contemporary Scottish literature (e.g. Norman McCaig) and can send it to me very soon, I'll be greatly obliged. Once the block is made the snap can be returned to you.

Kindest regards to your wife. I hope you all keep well.

Yours, Chris

43. *To Calum Macdonald (NLS)*

20 July 1954

Dear Calum.

Many thanks for your letter and copy of current issue of *Lines* and for your subsequent letter re Alan Riddell.[1] I was very sorry too to be unable to attend last meeting of Board.

I quite agree re postponement of photograph issue. I had sent out in good time all the necessary letters re photos but the response was most disappointing. Quite a number failed to reply at all and of those who did, despite the fact that I had emphasised that photos must be clearly defined and suitable for reproduction, most of those sent me were quite hopeless. So we must try to get a number of photos specially taken, and, as you say, probably the Festival time will give opportunities for getting group photos of some of right people. It is important, I think, not to have conventional studio photos, but informal ones of an interesting character and all the better if they show two or three writers together engaged in discussion.

As to Alan Riddell I for one entirely agree with you. I have not heard from Norman or Sydney about this and as you say they may have a somewhat different attitude from mine, but so far as I am concerned I am willing to do anything I possibly can, either as one of them if the editorship is to be the task of the Board, or, if it is agreed that I myself should act as editor with the same consultation with the Board as has obtained hitherto.

I am going off on Sunday to Alloa where I have agreed to edit the local paper for a fortnight while the editor is on holiday.

I had not forgotten about the essays, but have been unexpectedly very busy. However I'll send them to you in the course of the next day or two.

Hope all is well with you and with Mrs MacDonald and your family.

Yours, C.M. Grieve

---

1. Alan Riddell, then editor of *Lines Review*, poet.

44. *To Edwin Morgan*

9 October 1954

Dear Edwin Morgan

Your letter and Dialogue no. 1 reach me just as I am on the point of going off to London for a few days. So I have time for little more than the barest acknowledgments. You have, of course, my ready – and indeed flattered – permission. I enjoyed the Dialogue very much – and, seriously there are passages in it, in which a species of Scots (but I am thinking of the tone and movement rather than the vocabulary used) is employed in a way that shows that taken out of the context of the skit and worked up just a little you could challenge comparison with anybody as an important Lallans poet.

I'll certainly look forward keenly to the rest of the Whittrick Dialogues.[1]

I hope Alex Scott uses this one for the *Saltire Review*.[2]

It was great to meet you again at the USSR Society Conference – although I didn't recognise you at first (I am very bad at recognising people unless I've met them a good few times) and the occasion didn't let us have much talk together. We must rectify that in the near future.

With kindest regards to Mrs Morgan, Mr Drew, and yourself.[3]

Yours, C.M. Grieve

---

1. 'Dialogue 1' of Morgan's 'The Whittrick: A Poem in Eight Dialogues' was between Hugh MacDiarmid and James Joyce. See Morgan, *Collected Poems* (Manchester: Carcanet, 1990).
2. Alexander Scott (1920–89), poet, dramatist, then editor of the *Saltire Review*, first Chairman of the Department of Scottish Literature at Glasgow University.
3. CMG mistook Mrs Drew, wife of Philip Drew, one of Morgan's colleagues in the English Department at Glasgow University, for Mrs Morgan.

45. *To Calum Macdonald (NLS)*

Friday 6 August 1954

Dear Calum

Sydney sent me these poems. I should have returned them and written you sooner but have been desperately busy. In my opinion they are a poor lot. I think Iain Smith's 'Poem of Lewis' the best; and George Todd's 'Thochts In a Dry Closet' just misses being a great poem, because he lacks the imaginative lift to raise it from its essential sordidity. Garioch's 'A Wee Nicht-Music' while not up to his best form, is a *must*, I think: but friend of mine as he is Thurso Berwick's 'Tree of the Winds' is frankly unprintable rubbish. Of Crombie Saunders' three, while not of much worth, 'Song' and 'To a Don' are competent enough, but 'Echoes' is not good enough and is I think adequately characterised by its first phrase, 'Nothing of this is new'. ST's 'To JTG McL' is good enough of its kind – not a kind I have much use for – but compared with most of the others deserves its place. 'Blue Blazes' for me can go to blazes.

I am sorry to see in this lot nothing by Sydney or Norman and hope stuff of theirs is available. Also I note that my 'Millefiori in Clear Glass' is not here, but I gave Norman several other poems to pass on to you, which I hope you got all right.

We're going to Kippen tomorrow (Sat) and return home on Sunday or Monday. I've engagements on the following Friday and Saturday, but hope to see you during the Festival period. You will understand that this Alloa job has kept me from my own work but I have not forgotten about the essays I promised you and will send them as soon as possible now.

Kindest regards to Mrs MacDonald and your family and yourself.
Yours, C.M. Grieve

46. *To David Daiches (EUL)*

22 November 1954

Dear David Daiches

I enclose bibliography as promised. It is a complete list except for a few political pamphlets and a brochure of short stories, I think, but I haven't copies of these and can't give dates. You will see that I have been unable also to give dates for the two things I did for Benn's Augustan Poets Series.

You must have been very tired by the time you got home. I think the broadcast should go off fairly well if it is intelligently edited – but probably they'll cut out some of my Marxist and Scottish Separatist remarks. I thought Muir made a very poor showing.

Today I've been reading Kathleen Nott's *The Emperor's Clothes* and am struck by our identity of views in numerous matters. My Joyce poem in many of its passages – and indeed in its general argument – might well have been written immediately after I had read this book, instead of long before I'd seen it or, indeed, she had written it.

Every good wish to Mrs Daiches and yourself.

Yours, Christopher Grieve

P.S. Please excuse writing – I've got a wretchedly bad pen.

47. *To Edwin Morgan*

21 February 1955

Dear Edwin Morgan

Many thanks for your card and typescripts of poems. May I keep the latter by me for a time? I certainly want to use some of them but just which – and in what issue of the *V of S* – I cannot say at the moment. I would like to use 'From Cathkin Braes'; 'A View of Korea', and the Two Russian Poems, from Pushkin and Boris Pasternak, if possible in the next issue.

I wonder if I ever wrote to you about your Joyce poem. I certainly intended to, but cannot for the life of me remember if I did write. You said on your covering note with it that you thought it might be appearing in the *Saltire Review*: but it has not done so yet.

Ruth Pitter is an old friend of mine and will certainly not object to – or be surprised at – my guinea worm poem.

I will write you again as soon as I can make definite arrangements re the *V of S* etc.

With every kind regard. Yours, C.M. Grieve

48. *To Robert H. McGavin*

15 March 1955

Dear Sir: –

Many thanks for sending me your poem, ''Abram Crichton's Ghaist', which I have read with great appreciation, especially of your excellent handling of the Scots.

You would have heard from me sooner, only I have been almost continuously away from home this past month or so. But I regret the delay and any inconvenience it may have caused you.

Scottish Art and Letters, *The Scottish Journal* and other periodicals published by Messrs Maclellan with which I have been connected have discontinued publication for the time being: but you may know that I have resumed publication of my quarterly, *The Voice of Scotland*, published by M. MacDonald, 33 Marchmont Road, Edinburgh, who also publishes the quarterly Scottish poetry magazine, *Lines Review*. I edit the former, and the latter is edited by Mr Sydney Goodsir Smith.

The trouble with both of these periodicals is that they do not pay contributors. I do not know, however, of any other periodical that would publish (let alone pay for) a contribution of this length. But if you were agreeable I would either publish it in *The Voice of Scotland* or recommend my friend Smith to publish it in *Lines Review*.[1]

The Voice of Scotland is however full up for the next issue, due out next month, so that your poem could not appear in it before July. I do not know how Mr Smith is fixed in this respect, but I'll be seeing him tomorrow and I'll find out then.

Please let me know if you are agreeable to having your poem published in one of these two periodicals.

And let me thank you again for sending me such an excellent narrative poem. I hope you may send me other poems in the future. I am retaining this one until I hear from you again.

With best wishes. Yours, Hugh MacDiarmid

---

1. CMG published the poem in *The Voice of Scotland* vol. 6, no. 3 (October 1955), pp. 24–30.

49. *To Michael Grieve (NLS)*

[1955]

Dear Mike

Re Hugo – in case you see him on your way here – it is not about horror comics I want him to write: but about something much more horrible, viz. the Billy Graham campaign to engulf Scotland again in an even deeper fog of superstition.

I think Tonge has spoken to him about it: but in any case if you see him please remind him. I'm anxious to have it as soon as possible now.

You will understand it is not a couple of copies of the *Bulletin* your mother is talking about: but a couple of prints of the photograph.

Hope you get here all right on Saturday night. I know only too well what these infernal football matches are like. Your mother is quite right to urge you to go to them as well wrapped up as possible.

Love, Dad

50. *To Michael Grieve (NLS)*

Thursday [1955]

Dear Michael

We have just had Mr Suchanek, the first Secretary of the Czecho-Slovak Embassy in London, here, and he has asked your mother and I to go for a trip with him on Saturday and Sunday in his powerful big car. What he wants to do is for us to meet him in Edinburgh at 11am on Saturday. Then he'll motor via Stirling, Pitlochry, etc. to Inverness, and from Inverness via Dornoch etc. to Wick or Thurso – stay there overnight – and return by a different route (possibly West Coast via Ullapool etc.) the following day (Sunday). That will be a rare trip if the weather is half-decent. I do not know whether you can get off to come with us or not, but we will see you in Stirling on Saturday forenoon, and if you are free, it will be OK and you will see some of the finest parts of Scotland which you haven't seen yet. I hope you'll be able to manage.

Your mum and I had a nice time in Edin. last night with the Scottish Renaissance Society, in the Beehive Inn in the Grassmarket.

Love from us both. Yours, Dad

51. *To Edwin Morgan*

26 July 1955

Dear Edwin Morgan

Many thanks indeed for 'The Cape of Good Hope'. It is a splendid poem – with some resemblance to W.S. Graham's 'Night Fishing' but of course without the great fault of the latter which, as the *Times Literary Supplement* says, is 'the intellectual muddle of the poet when he tries to go beyond the appearance of the sea to an unknown meaning ... the poet has tried to say things about himself and life in general which are not worked out well either in language or experience'.

But I am not going to do more than thank you and congratulate you here on this fine poem, which, however, I will write about in the *Voice of Scotland*. Not alas in the forthcoming number which is already set up – and, I suspect, overset. But in the following one.

I am practically never in Glasgow nowadays or I would have sought you out to hear your impression of the USSR – as I'll hope to do yet, either from your lips or via your pen. I myself am just back from a splendid time in Czechoslovakia, where I not only was able to see far more of Prague and Brno and of the country generally than on my brief first visit 4 years ago, but had the pleasure also of seeing a great deal of all the leading Czech writers and also French (i.e. Tristan Tzara), South American (Nicholas Guillan, Jesualdo Portello etc.) and Indian poets.

Please excuse this short note. I am back of course to a great pile of things to do that had mounted up in my absence and I am trying to reduce that pile now as much as I can since I am going to Alloa on Sunday to take charge of a local paper there for two or three weeks.

Again with my warmest thanks and every good wish.

Yours, Hugh MacDiarmid

P.S. I've lost your address, so I'm sending this via Peter Russell.

52. To Michael Grieve *(NLS)*

Thursday [1955]

Dear Mike

Your mother has been thinking about the story re the 'phone and the iron and asked me if you should not keep back the woman's name until you know the story has been accepted – in case it is pinched and you are diddled out of the payment.

Well, my answer is that the woman's name doesn't necessarily mean anything, but her address does, and as a precaution you should certainly not include that in the story as you submit it: but rather send a covering note saying that you will supply the address (for verification purposes if need be) once the story has been accepted.

While I don't think it likely they'd try to pinch the story, still it is wise to take a little precaution.

Love. Yours, Dad

P.S. Many thanks for *Encounter*. Note what you say re *Saltire Review*. Don't bother more about it. Mum'll get it when she's in Edinburgh tomorrow. But it's queer – as it is reviewed in today's *Scotsman*. Mum says please don't forget her Diary.

53. To the Editor, The Glasgow Herald *(NLS, DFF)*

11 August 1955

Sir:– I am amused at the vindictiveness of your reviews of my books over a number of years and finally the ridiculous outburst against my *In Memoriam [James] Joyce* poem in your issue of today. I'll look them all out and base a little essay on them exposing your malignant stupidity. But, of course, the *Glasgow Herald*'s opinion on any literary matter is of no account, and happily very different estimates of the value of my books in question have appeared in all the really important literary organs not only in this country but in the USA and various European countries, all these books have sold – and are selling – well, and I can therefore treat your attacks with the contempt they deserve. They are only worth the bumf you print them on.

Yours etc., Hugh MacDiarmid[1]

---

1. The letter is addressed from Johnstone Arms Hotel, Alva, Clackmannan, where CMG was acting editor on a local newspaper (see next letter). The date is CMG's 63rd birthday.

54. To Kaikhosru Shapurji Sorabji (NLS)

19 August 1955

My dear Sorabji

It is a very great pleasure to hear from you again after all this time, and to have your words of appreciation, generous as ever, of my Joyce poem. I only received your letter two days ago, owing to my having been away from home in Clackmannanshire, where I was running a local newspaper for a fortnight as holiday relief for a chief reporter friend. I of course am entirely at one with you regarding English poetry which in the main I detest; and I owe a great deal to you, not only with regard to Ernest George White re Sinus Tone production, but in countless other ways.

You are very often in my mind, as the references in enclosed pamphlet will show you.[1] I wrote it for FG's birthday in the hope that it might bridge the chasm that has yawned between us in recent years. But, alas, he did not even acknowledge the copy I sent him. So there will be no reconciliation. He has tended for the past decade to sink into himself and resents my outgoing spirit and all such. It is a great pity but there is no help for it. Old age affects some people that way. My own disposition is wholly in the opposite direction.

Joyce was, of course, much preoccupied with musical matters. That is why (I hope not too incompetently – tho' I am very dubious as to what a man like you may think of some of my musical references in the poem). [*Sic*]

I trust you keep well and would be very glad to hear something about the works on which you are engaged. You will see in the pamphlet I quote a letter of yours – of how many years ago – mentioning several huge compositions on which you were then working. I hope these have been completed to your satisfaction (in so far as one is ever satisfied with one's works) long ago and that you are now actively concerned with subsequent compositions. How the devil you keep going on at all in this infernal state of affairs I cannot imagine. I know no parallel to your case in sheer lack of due recognition – in long-sustained exclusion, not so much from a fair measure of access for the 'few but fit', but from any possibility of even that minimum of appreciation from outside without which most of us could hardly carry on.

I need not tell you how you rank in my esteem, and how eager I would be to hear anything about you at any time – there are precious few who affect me in this way; and fewer still I'd give a great deal to see again.

With every high regard and affectionate esteem.

Yours as always, Christopher Grieve

---

1. Hugh MacDiarmid, *Francis George Scott: an essay on the occasion of his seventy-fifth birthday 25th January 1955* (Edinburgh: M. Macdonald, 1955), reprinted in *Albyn: Shorter Books and Monographs* (Manchester: Carcanet, 1996).

55. To David Daiches (EUL)

20 August 1955

Dear David Daiches

So far as I know the Joyce poem hasn't been reviewed anywhere, except – characteristically – as a compilation of worthless junk and I was ridiculed as a fallen Humpty Dumpty whose spilled contents had flooded all over him in a hell of a mess.

When one publishes such a book – and it meets with the sort of reception inevitable in most quarters, either the *Glasgow Herald* sort of thing or a lack of notice that makes one feel it has been still-born and probably a *lusus naturae* at that, it is reassuring to get a postcard like yours and to know you have written a review of it. I'll look forward to that. What I mean is that the general attitude – or lack of attitude – makes even a fellow like myself, and Heaven knows I've had plenty of experience, have doubts about his own work.

It isn't quite so bad as that. Yours isn't the only reassuring message I've had from people whose judgment I trust. Do you know Professor Richard M. Kain of Louisville University, Ky? He's publishing a book on the history of Joyce's reputation later this year and has several quotes and some very intelligent remarks to make about my poem. Kaikhosru Sorabji is another who hastened to reassure me in no uncertain fashion. So did Professor Barker Fairley of Toronto and Professor Dennis Saurat. So really I'm not without strong supports.

I am hoping to have a good winter and to clinch my whole problem then. I want to do two things in one big poem – push all I've been trying to do in the 'Joyce' and other poems of that sort to the Nth, *and do it in Scots*. And I think I've found a containing form for all that. Pray for me.

I hope Mrs Daiches and yourself are both well and have had a good holiday. I had a splendid three weeks in Czecho-Slovakia and then came home to find it necessary to run a local paper in Clackmannanshire as holiday relief for a chief reporter friend. My wife went with me and thoroughly enjoyed herself in the grand sunny weather in the small towns on the foothills of the Ochils – Menstrie, Alva, Tillicoultry, Dollar.

I'm busy meeting all sorts of interesting people – Rhine of the Extra-Sensory Perception business; Owen, the leader of the New Zealand Social Credit Party; and – on Thursday next – Thornton Wilder.[1] But I'll be glad when the Festival is over and I can settle down for several months seclusion here.

Again with my warmest thanks. Yours, Christopher Grieve
P.S. I am seeing the Buthlays here on Monday.
There are a few irritating mistakes in the Joyce poem. I list these on separate sheet for you.

p53   -   7th line from bottom should read: –

		Be <u>not</u> abashed not to have understood at once, as water
p71	–	11th line from bottom should read:
		<u>Meantime</u> handling a simple logarythmic progress not <u>meaning</u> etc.
p34	–	Footnote 19a refers to prose passage at foot of page, beginning
		'We have the privilege....'
		not to line 7 from top of page as given
p87	–	line 5 from top:
		<u>Genward</u> should be glossed false song
		and <u>gwawd</u> true song.

I don't know whether you get my *Voice of Scotland* but the next issue is due in a day or two – contains a longish supplementary poem I inadvertently omitted from the Joyce book: also two articles of an explanatory nature on that book – i.e. preliminary bits of a sort of *Exagmination round the Factification* ...!

---

1. Joseph Banks Rhine (1895–1980) American psychologist and pioneer of parapsychology, coined the term 'extrasensory perception'. Thornton Wilder (1879–1976), American best-selling novelist and playwright.

56. *To Mrs Mary Dott (NLS)*

1 September 1955

Dear Mary

I need not tell you how utterly ashamed I am of Wednesday's fiasco, and not only disgusted with myself, but extremely sorry at the way I must have disappointed and distressed you and spoiled the fine opportunity presented by so excellent an audience. I appreciate all the work that must have gone into organising the meeting and can only tender my very sincere apologies to all concerned. One thing is certain. I will take good care that nothing of the kind ever happens again.

   Yours, Chris

57. *To Michael Grieve (NLS)*

[1955]

Dear Mike

I enclose a letter which you should enclose along with your identity card and letter of application to Passport Office, London, applying for a passport. (I think you get a form of application to fill up at the Post Office.) It will be least complicated to try this first instead of waiting for birth certificate: but if they won't accept this then a birth certificate will have to be got. Your mother is sending for one anyhow now, so there won't be any avoidable delay either way.

If they don't accept the identity card and you have to send a birth certificate I don't think the fact the latter is in name Rowlands, not Grieve, will make any difficulty. You'll simply have to say in your covering letter that that is your mother's surname which you understand you are entitled to use provided you do so only for legitimate purposes.

Best of luck. Yours, Dad

P.S. Don't forget to write to George MacAlister of Scottish USSR Friendship Society, telling him 1/ who you are – i.e. my son 2/ when you expect to arrive in Vienna, and 3/ asking him to use his good offices on your behalf, if necessary with the USSR Embassy people in London, to expedite the visa you require.

58. *To Michael Grieve (NLS)*

Thursday [1955]

Dear Mike

It is a pity you are so bull-headed. The draft letter I enclosed to you was a much better way of going about the matter than phoning Glasgow branch passport office. However the whole business is very complex and difficult and I do not see how – in time for your purpose now – you are going to get a passport save in the name of Rowlands. I agree that that will create some difficulties for you. The only way now is to get your registered name changed to Grieve but that will take time and certainly can't be done quickly enough to serve your present purpose. The whole reason I wrote the letter I enclosed to you was so that you could send it to London as it is never any use dealing with branch offices – they never have any authority to deal with anything out of the ordinary run at all. The same thing happened to your Labour Card – but your mother went to the Head Office in Glasgow and the thing was OK, whereas you will remember that the local office originally would not accept your identity card in lieu of birth certificate. The same thing would probably have happened this time if you'd sent on my letter. That was the whole idea. The thing would have been set in motion and your birth certificate would have followed up, if they hadn't accepted the identity card in lieu. Your mother says for X sake use your head.

I got Mr Murray's cheque. It crossed my letter to him in the post.

Love, Yours, Dad

P.S. Have sent for birth certificate at same time as sent letter to you. It will come here but that will only delay it one post as we'll redirect it to you right away.

59. *To David Daiches (EUL)*

1 October 1955

Dear David Daiches

I should have written you sooner to express my appreciation of your article on the Joyce poem in *Lines*. But I was very late in seeing it and since then I have been inordinately busy with other things. So this is just a belated line to thank you and say how perceptive and helpful I found it.

I notice from the current *Times Literary Supplement* that the reviewer singles out your essay in a symposium on Whitman, and I look forward to seeing that in due course. I have always been interested in Whitman but have not read his poems for many years tho' I have read his prose several times. Randall Jarell's chapter on Whitman in *Poetry and the Age* has recently shown me how much – how much to my own purpose – I have missed and I now feel I must read him all through again.

You may have seen the extraordinary review of the Joyce poem in the *New Statesman* by G.S. Fraser. He declared that some of the Latin American terms I used were wrong. But another correspondent showed that on the contrary I was absolutely right and I have since had a letter from an Argentine using these terms precisely as I did. Fraser, tho' forced to apologise, was nothing daunted however and returned to the attack by citing my use of two bogus phrases attributed to Eliot and Spender and contended that these showed that I had no true idea of poetry or sound sense of language at all. I replied in a very brief letter saying that I used the phrases in question jokingly but knew they were bogus and that indeed I had derived them from the spoof writings of an Australian pamphleteer – and the same source as Fraser's own knowledge of them. But the *New Statesman* has not published that letter, preferring apparently to let Fraser get away with his false assertion.

Otherwise there have so far as I know been no notices of the poem anywhere. (I'm assuming you've seen the *Voice of Scotland* article, and the supplementary poem in it?)

Thanking you again and with best wishes.

Yours, C.M. Grieve

60. *To Hamish Henderson (EUL)*

7 October 1955

Dear Hamish

Many thanks for your letter. I replied to Fraser along the sort of line you suggest – i.e. I pointed out that the two phrases he cited were known to me from the same source as he mentioned – the only source they could be drawn from, and a source which made it perfectly clear that they were spoofs, as he knew and as I too could not but know. I also pointed out I'd used them jocularly as the reference to my own 'Eccelfechan Gongorism' in the same few lines would have shown any perceptive critic. Fraser knew that well enough of course. His letter was thoroughly dishonest, but to creatures like him without any integrity any stick is good enough to beat a fellow like me with. And they can rely on the press to let them get away with it. Though it was very short and simply factual – not more than three short sentences – the *New Statesman* didn't publish my letter. They also eliminated a key paragraph from the letter of mine they did publish before that. So the dice are loaded all the time. But what the Hell?

Longtime no see! Hope you are OK. Am looking forward to your broadcast. I thought your article in last *Lines* first-class. People in Prague etc. are interested and I'm sending them copies.

All the best. Yours, Chris[1]

---

1. This letter is in response to one by Hamish Henderson to CMG dated 5 October 1955 collected in *The Armstrong Nose: Selected Letters of Hamish Henderson*, edited by Alec Finlay (Edinburgh: Polygon, 1996, p.67). G.S. Fraser's review of *In Memoriam James Joyce* appeared in *The New Statesman and Nation*, 10 September 1955.

61. *To Gael Turnbull (NLS)*

8 December 1955

Dear Dr Gael Turnbull

Many thanks for your *The Knot In The Wood* and the excellent if too complimentary title poem dedicated to myself. I like many of these laconic but highly effective little poems. I note you are in England now – but wonder if you are coming North (since with your name you are surely Scottish) – and if so whether we may not meet. I am within easy reach of Edinburgh and if you are to be there, even if only passing through, and drop me a postcard, I'd be delighted to come and see you. I had a card regarding some new publications by your friends in Canada but have mislaid it. I meant to do something about it, but can't recall what not having the card to refer to.

I like the way in which your book is produced and hope you may have good luck with it. I'll have a note about it in the next issue of my quarterly, *The Voice of Scotland* and will send you a copy if the present address will find you.

With every good wish and renewed thanks.

Yours sincerely, Hugh MacDiarmid

62. *To Barbara Niven (NLS)*

Monday [1955]

Dear Barbara

Perhaps the *D.W.*[1] could find a place for the following:-

> Farewell Tribute to Churchill
>
> There can be no farewell
> Tribute to Churchill as good as
> Just burying him alive
> In the same grave as Judas.
>   Hugh MacDiarmid[2]

Your letter has just come. I will write you as soon as possible, and will also write to Lawrence Bradshaw[3] whose letter, sent you think to Dungavel, I certainly never received.

All the best to you all. Yours, Chris

---

1. The *Daily Worker*.
2. In 1955, Churchill retired to the back benches and his achievements were recognised by many tributes, honours and decorations. This was the occasion of the present 'tribute' (rather than his death).
3. Laurence Bradshaw, the sculptor of the Karl Marx monument in Highgate Cemetery, London. He made two busts of CMG in 1954.

63. *To Edwin Morgan*

17 May 1956

Dear Edwin Morgan

I do not think it would have cramped your style – but I'd probably have found it a shy-making occasion if I'd been able to be at your talk on my Joyce poem on 23rd inst, but, fortunately or otherwise, I can't. I'll look forward, however, to hearing about the points made.

I'm coming up to Glasgow on Sunday 20th inst to be one of the witnesses for the presentation in the Trial of one Will Shakespeare for exceeding the terms of his poetic licence and libelling his late Majesty, King Richard III. Whether you're to be at that I don't know, but it would be nice to see you again.

Many thanks for the poems which I'll be glad to use in due course. I think I'll be able to have the Gulliver in the next issue. The present one – of which I enclose a copy – is all prose. The poems you mention as having sent previously – but not yet used – must be with the publisher. I'll look into that. Do I have Dialogue (No 2)? If so, it is either with M. MacDonald the previous publisher – or with the Castlewynd Printers who publish the *Voice* now. I'd certainly like to use it either in next issue or the subsequent one.

The Scottish Home Service people have still not got anyone to review the Joyce book. Auden refused on the ground that before he could do it he'd need two or three months studying it.

All the best. Yours, Christopher Grieve

64. *To D.G. Bridson (LLIU)*

23 May 1956

Dear Geoffrey

Many thanks for yours of 18th inst. It is good news that passages of the Joyce poem are to be broadcast on 31st inst in the Third Programme and I am delighted that James McKechnie and Ewan McColl are to do the reading.

As to the talk by myself I haven't heard yet whether this has been arranged but the time is short now for it to be placed in the same week. Whether it would have meant my coming down to London I don't know but I'd certainly have welcomed the opportunity. Last time I was down was last July when en route to – and again returning from – Prague, but; was told you were away somewhere, and of course both going and coming my time in London was very brief.

I have however been listening with great interest to your Middle East programmes and also to the revival of your 1745 programme.

If I do manage to London any time I will of course hope to see you. Trust you are in good form.

With kindest regards. Yours, Christopher Grieve

65. *To D.G. Bridson (LLIU)*

7 July 1956

Dear Geoffrey

I am coming to London on 24th inst and will be in town until 28th at least. The occasion is a meeting of Theatre Workshop directors. If you are in town it would be nice to meet you again and perhaps we could talk about the discussion with MacKechnie and MacColl you suggested. As to the unpublished second volume of the huge poem of which *In Memoriam James Joyce* is the first volume, I am making good progress with this and will certainly be able to let you have the typescript in good time (i.e. before the end of September as you suggested).

While in London I'll be staying c/o Miss Barbara Niven, 11 Park Hill Rise, East Croydon, Surrey (Top Flat) – Ewan MacColl has his flat below Barbara's in the same house.

With kindest regards, Yours, Christopher Grieve

66. *To Edwin Morgan*

5 September 1956

Dear Mr Morgan

I have just read your article on my Joyce poem and write to thank you. That does not mean of course that I agree with some of your criticisms, but simply that I appreciate the article as a whole. It is one of those excellent articles the poem has evoked – the others being Hugh Gordon Porteus in *Nimbus* and Michel Habart in *Revue Critique* (Editions de Minuit). The poem is as you noticed part of a much longer work. (I originally called the whole thing *Mature Art*, that being not a claim of achievement but simply a statement of theme!) I have just had a desperately busy time putting the second volume (which is entitled *Impavidi Progrediamur*) into order, as the Third Programme people want to broadcast selections from it shortly. It is rather longer than the Joyce book I'm afraid.

I should have written you long ere this but have been away in London and elsewhere. I am using several translations of yours in the forthcoming *Voice of Scotland* but have been quite unable to lay my hand on the other poems about which you wrote me. I've hunted high and low for them. I thought perhaps they'd be left at MacDonald's printer's place when Kenneth Mackenzie moved to the Castlewynd Printers place in Ramsay Lane, Edinburgh, but there's no trace of them in either of these places. I do hope you retained copies all right; please accept my regrets and apologies for their having gone amissing so unaccountably.

Hope all goes well with your own literary activities.

With kindest regards, Yours, C.M. Grieve

67. *To Barbara Niven and Ern Brooks (NLS)*

5 November 1956

Dear Barbara & Ern

Many thanks, Barbara, for your letter. It means a great deal to have such an understanding appreciation of a poem like *Impavidi Progrediamur*. I thought you would perhaps find it, as it stands, not bearing out what I told you – i.e. that it is a completely Communist poem. But if so the reason is simply that it is still incomplete. The final section, of about 2000 lines, is still to come and that will, if I express myself successfully, pull the whole thing together and crown it – a regionalism seen under the conditions of universal poetry – since it is their innermost sense of the smallness of man which has made bourgeois thinking the mean and shabby thing it is. However I'm still struggling with that last section and only if I bring it off will the title be justified.

I had as you know expected the broadcast to have taken place before this – also to have been down to London for the talk which Bridson hoped to broadcast the same week. But I have had no further word, and the dates are evidently not fixed yet. I'll let you know of course as soon as I do hear.

Valda and I were disappointed you couldn't manage a night here while in Scotland but of course we quite understand your engagements made it impossible – just as it was impossible for us to get through to Motherwell to see you as we would have done had it been feasible.

I hope Ewan can send me back the typescript of the poem soon. I haven't another complete copy.

Excuse this very short scrawl. I am exceedingly busy and have just got back here after several days in the remote North West corner of Scotland – Kyle of Lochalsh, Plockton, Torridon etc. – magnificently savage country, seen however this time under the best weather we have had all this year – brilliant sunshine, hot as midsummer on my car windows.

Love to you both from Valda (who is off to Lanark today to buy apples) and myself.

Yours, Chris

Hope the Bandung material hasn't given you too much trouble to collect. I'll be glad to have it and hope to go right on with a poem based on it and other Afro-Asian material.

68. *To Misses Jessie B. and Mary S. Smeaton (EUL)*

25 March 1957

Dear Friends

How kind of you to write me apropos Edinburgh University's surprising decision to confer the LLD on me!

The Graduation Ceremonial will be on 5th July. I'll be back in time for that. But I have a series of lectures to give in South Wales in the beginning of April, and then I'm going to China. I'll be 4 weeks in China and 6 to 7 weeks out of Britain in all (flying via Brussels, Warsaw and Moscow).

I was very sorry my Edinburgh class had to be stopped this winter owing to inadequate attendance, but it was probably just as well, since I had to give lectures under Glasgow University Extra Mural scheme in Inverary and Campbeltown and then these South Wales lectures to prepare.

I hope you are both well.

With kindest regards, Yours sincerely, 'Hugh MacDiarmid'

69. *To Valda Grieve (NLS)*

Krasnagarsk, Siberia   Sunday, 28 April 1957

My dear Valda

Here I am within about 1500 miles from Pekin which I hope to reach tonight. We should have left from here earlier today but bad weather delayed our plane 4 hours. But all being well we should make the remaining distance by tonight in three hops. We had to stay overnight in Moscow on Friday owing to an error in the arrangements about our plane's timetable which was unfortunate as it meant we had to pay hotel expenses, meals, etc. and had great difficulty in making arrangements to go on. The flight to Brussels, and then to Prague was OK, and from Prague to Moscow we travelled by jet, at a great height and great speed. I was glad enough our jet did not go on from Moscow to Peking, as my sinuses troubled me a lot though I kept sucking sweets for all I was worth. However my ears and throat are all right today. We breakfasted off raw fish like what the Norwegians had; soda water, lemon tea, meat rissoles and potato chips. And at supper that night we had along with food a glass of vodka each which was very welcome as it is quite incredibly cold. In fact it has been snowing this morning. Siberia is desolate beyond imagination – literally just like an immense peat bog, with great rivers like the Volga and the Yenesei flowing through it.

I need not tell you I had a very nice time in London with Barbara and Ernest and Ewan and Jean MacColl.

I hope all's well with you. I got your p.c. in London all right.

I'll finish this letter tonight or tomorrow in Peking and post it then.

I'll certainly need to have my train fare and bus fare and a few shillings waiting for me at Barbara's when I get back.

I found out that Norman and Isabel will be in Edinburgh at Graduation Ceremonial time and are anxious that we should stay with them rather than at the Roxburgh, so I have written the enclosed letter to the University Secretary which please forward on receipt.

Monday.

No. Didn't get to Pekin last night. Have just arrived and attended first official reception. Have to go to another one tonight yet at the Ministry of Culture. Today's flight of about 1500 miles from Ikursk where we spent last night took us over the Gobi desert and we didn't get to Pekin until 5pm after leaving at 5am, flying for the most part at great heights and great speed. My ears are ringing yet.

Met the others here – Lord Chorley, Professor Lauterwys and Graham Greene, the novelist. All the party are extremely agreeable.[1]

All the guest houses we've stayed at have been scrupulously clean and each of us have had a self-contained flat – bedroom, bathroom, sitting room and all conveniences. Really hot water. Electric light. Telephone. We are now in Pekin's finest modern hotel with everything laid on. There was a vast crowd at the airport to meet us. Delegations are flocking in from all over the world for May Day which will be a super spectacle. Tomorrow I think we've an outing down the Yangtsekiang. Very warm here with brilliant sunshine.

Can't write more just now. Will write Michael as soon as possible but as you may imagine we're in for a desperately crowded time. Have already agreed to give a poetry reading (with Chinese translations of my poems following each as I read it) at a meeting to celebrate the anniversaries of William Blake and Henry Wordsworth Longfellow.

Love to you and your aunt, and all friends.

Yours, Christopher

P.S. I have just discovered that they do not give us money here, as the Secretary of the British-China Friendship Association said they would. In these circumstances I must have some more money. I hope you can send it. The Moscow business and delay in getting here cost me nearly half the money I had. So please send what you can by registered mail to C.M. Grieve, British Visitors, c/o Chinese Peoples' Association for Cultural Relations with Foreign Countries, 9 Tai Chi Chang, Peking, China.

You'll get it back, as I've just had a wire from the *Scottish Field* wanting my article by 19th May. And besides that I have discovered already that buying presents worth anything at all is a very costly business. Still I may pick up something as I'm going on a comprehensive fortnight's tour (mainly by air) to Shanghai, Hankow etc. and in fact a regular run through the provinces of this vast country.

---

1. Robert Samuel Theodore Chorley, first Baron, academic lawyer, Dean of the Faculty of Laws at the University of London, 1939–42; Professor Joseph Albert Lauwerys (1902–81), Professor of Comparative Education at the University of London, 1947–70.

70. *To Valda Grieve (NLS)*

Peking Hotel, Peking   Saturday, 4 May 1957

My dear Valda

My visit to Peking is still running its hectic course of receptions, discussions at the Writer's Club, outings to places of historic interest, visits to art shows, concerts, etc. The weather continues splendid and at times exceedingly hot. I am in excellent form and had a very lively discussion yesterday at the Writers' Club with Graham Greene and Margaret Lane (who is Lady Huntingdon).[1] On Tuesday the Huntingdons and I are flying to Sian in

N. West China and thence to Chungking, Hankow and other cities, where the H's will diverge and go on to Canton and Hongkong and ultimately to New Delhi, and I will go on alone to Shanghai for a day or two and then return to Pekin. Before Tuesday however I have discussions on literary matters to lead at Pekin University and at the Foreign Languages Institute. I hope to travel home by jet plane and thus avoid having to take the longer and slower way via Siberia. If I get travelling by jet then I'll be back in London by 3rd June or at latest 5th June.

First letters for some of our party arrived yesterday and I was disappointed there was nothing for me, but I shouldn't have been, because the letters which arrived had been posted the day after we left London and thus it takes 6 days for letters via air-mail to reach us.

The May Day celebrations were incredibly vast and colourful. President Voroshilov of Russia and Mao Tse-Tung of China were the two principal figures[2] but there were leading personalities from 46 foreign countries. There was a magnificent fireworks display at night and hundreds of thousands of people continued singing and dancing in the streets in the early hours of the morning.

On Wednesday we motored 25 miles out in the country, among the hills, and climbed a section of the Great Wall of China and subsequently visited the Tombs of the Ming Emperors. But I can't write about it all yet – and in any case my pen needs refilling with ink. I got off my article to the *Scottish Field* by air mail and also a letter to Michael. I expect you are still at Brownsbank but will be going off to Cornwall on Monday, so I'm addressing this letter to you at the latter address. I hope you are in good form. Dr Thomas phoned me when I was in London and I gave him the Bude address and he said he'd be sending on more of the vitamin tabloids to you and replying to points you asked about in your letter to him. The Thomases are coming up to Edinburgh for the Graduation Ceremonial. Ian Milner whom I met in Prague also hopes he may be able to come to Edinburgh for it.

Love and kisses. It seems very strange indeed to be so far away from you. My regards to your aunt and also to Janey and Judy.[3] I hope they – the latter two! – are behaving themselves.

Yours, Chris

P.S. How would you like to breakfast off 3 fried eggs and bacon, an apple, a Mandarin orange and a large tumblerful of China tea. That is my usual here. And lunch and dinner at night off fried rice, sliced chicken, bamboo shoots, cabbage soup, pork, fish etc. etc.

I also hope you remembered to send the parcel I left beside Encyclopaedia bookcase on to me c/o Barbara as I'll need it if I am to address the Geneva Club in London.

P.P.S. If you have a copy of the photo of Bradshaw's head of me you might please send it right away to the Editor, *The Scottish Field*, Mitchell

St, Glasgow

And write on back of it, Head of Hugh MacDiarmid, by Laurence Bradshaw, 1956. Photograph, Kaufman, London.

If you haven't one, please ask Mike to do this as I know he has a copy. I meant to ask him in my letter to him but forgot. The article is to appear in the July issue, and 'copy' had to be received by 20th May, so presumably photos must be had not later than then too, or perhaps photos may be needed earlier to get the blocks made.

---

1. Margaret Lane (b.1907), novelist, journalist and author of various literary biographies.
2. Klimenti Efremovich Voroshilov (1881–1961), Soviet commissar for defence at the time of Hitler's invasion and President of the Soviet Union from Stalin's death (1953) to 1960. Mao Tse-Tung (1893–1976), a founder member of the Chinese Communist Party in 1921, first Chairman of the People's Republic of China, 1949–59, remaining chairman of the politburo till his death and from that position launching the Cultural Revolution of 1966–9 against liberal, 'revisionist' forces, notably writers and academics.
3. Janey and Judy, pet dog and cat.

71. To Valda Grieve (NLS)

Sian, South China   10 May 1957

Dear Valda

We flew 4 hours flying time yesterday from Peking to Sian, the oldest – and surely one of the loveliest – cities in China. It was a wild flight in an old plane which gave us a good tossing as we flew over the mountains. In the afternoon we visited museums, art galleries, etc. here and at night I went to the local opera.

Food in Chinese restaurants in Britain is – or used to be – good, but gives no idea whatever of the extent and delicacy of the Chinese cuisine. I haven't been able to manage the chop-sticks at all, and have needed to use just knife, fork, and spoon. The night before we left Peking we had a farewell banquet (since the Huntingdons, who are here with me, are not returning to Peking but going on to Hongkong and India). There must have been 20 courses, including Mandarin fish and sliced chicken and roasted eels and pork etc. etc. together with red wine, yellow wine, beer, orange juice, and to finish up big yellow apples shaped like pears. What a feast!

You might think that in the provinces things would be on a less lavish scale. Not a bit of it. Here in this huge hotel I have again a suite to myself – sitting room, bedroom, bathroom etc. (and I've had hot baths twice!) In the sitting room I have three glass-topped occasional tables, a china cupboard for my decanter, glasses etc., and a big desk coupled with electric reading lamp, telephone etc. also a big thermos of China tea and a tea service, a bowl of fruit and a bonbonniere with caramels. And the view from the window right over the city to the distant hills is wonderful.

I went to the opera last night – the third Chinese opera I've been at – and enjoyed it immensely.

Before I left Peking I dictated to a Chinese editor an article on the current political and literary situation in Scotland: but whether I'll get paid for it or not I've no idea. There is an economy drive on in China. They are less free in handing out money and other gifts to guests. For instance they did not give us any pocket money and though I have been presented with lots of books that is the only kind of present I've had so far. So I got the wind up about money but I'm managing to scrape through. One of the troubles is that both here and in Moscow the exchange is very much against us, and what we get for a pound is less than half the value.

I had no letter up to time I left Peking and I won't be back there until 24th or 25th so I can't get any before that, which keeps me worrying. It seems a very long time. I hope everything is all right with you and that you got to London and Cornwall safely according to schedule and found your aunt in good form. I've written to Michael a couple of times.

I am sending the books in a parcel by book post, which is much the cheapest way of sending them. That means they go by sea and take 6 weeks or so. That costs about 1/- to 1/6 per lb. But to send them air mail would cost a fortune. And they are too heavy to take by plane along with my other stuff. Internal plane travelling only allows 30 lb weight of luggage by plane as against the 44 lb international flying allowance.

We're staying here today and then tomorrow we have another 4 hours' flight to Chungking. After that we go down the Yangtse by boat to Hankow and then on by plane again to Nanking and Shanghai and spend two or three days there before returning to Peking, for the last day or two before we are homeward bound.

I've sent postcards to Mrs Jackson, Helen Cruickshank, Norman & Isabel, David Orr etc.

With all my love, Yours, Christopher

P.S. I had a long talk the day before yesterday with Vellupillai, a Ceylon poet and member of the Ceylonese Parliament, and have agreed once I get back to write a preface for an anthology of English translations of poems by 36 Ceylonese poets.

I wish I'd arranged with Kenny to send on copies of the Spain poem if it is now published. What a pity Roy Campbell died before it appeared! That takes the kick out of it badly. David Crook, the head of the Foreign Languages Institute in Peking, who is a Canadian married to a woman with Peebles connections, fought in Spain and then with the army of liberation here right up to the establishment of People's China. He is also an old Party member. I had a long session with him and his staff and senior pupils – spoke for 1½ to 2 hours and then engaged in about 3 hours discussion. Had dinner with them too. But I cannot tell you in a letter all the interesting people I have met and the various activities in which I have engaged. Enough to say that while I am having a very strenuous time I am in capital form and enjoying myself up to the hilt, the only fly in the ointment being not hearing from you.

72. *To Valda Grieve (postcard) (NLS)*

10 May 1957

A typical scene in the wilder mountain country we flew over yesterday. South China through which I am now travelling is full of scenic beauty and the richness of the agriculture and the wealth of flowers – roses, huge lilies, and blossoming fruit trees is beyond description.

Love, Christopher

73. *To Valda Grieve (NLS)*

Chunkin, South China   11 May 1957

My dear Valda

After a 4-hour flight – sometimes at 4 to 5000 ft. above a range of mountains where we got quite a buffeting – we came into by far the most richly cultivated and fertile part of China we have yet seen: rich in ricefields, banana orange and bamboo groves, and after landing at the airport had an hour's motor run over a wonderfully precipitous and winding way, incredibly steep in places, into this ancient city and thence to by far the most amazing hotel we have ever seen. With pagoda roofs in blue red yellow and green tiles it stands on a mountain side and is about 4 times the size of the Princes Street Station Hotel in Edinburgh. Here again I have a suite to myself: and everything laid on – writing paper and envelopes, cigarettes, matches, a bowl of oranges for which this city is famous. And now we (the Huntingdons and I – the rest are elsewhere) have had I think the finest of all the fine lunches we've had – 10 different dishes, including one particularly hot one (about 100 times hotter than curry) for which Chungking is noted. We've a big programme for today and tomorrow and the day after tomorrow we go down the Yangstse by boat and then by air to Nanking and Shanghai. It is a strenuous life but everywhere we are treated as royalty is treated in Britain, and the scenic beauty is beyond description. Tonight one of our 'chores' is to go to a mountain top (by high-powered car) and see the view – of the landscape and of the two great rivers which meet here and the sea. It is terribly hot however – much hotter than Sian.

But then it is semi-tropical – as the palm trees, pandanus and other trees, shrubs, and flowers and fruit show. I do wish I'd got that linen suit. I had laundry done twice in Peking and have just sent off another bundle here, but one requires to change very frequently, and even with regular baths one sweats so much. I could only bring hand-luggage here too, and left my big bag in Peking. However I'll manage. I'm certainly in good form and brown as a berry.

I do hope this finds Michael and yourself OK and that the complete absence of letters does not mean anything wrong.

With all my love, Yours, Christopher

74. *To Valda Grieve (NLS)*

Hankow, China   16 May 1957

My dear Valda

I did not think I'd manage to write you again before I leave China as I'll be on the move constantly. However I have a spare hour now. We left Chungking at 4am this morning and motored up a winding mountain road and down the other side for about 30 miles to the airport and emplaned there. But we had to ground at Ichang about ⅔rds of the way to Hankow because of a storm. It was questionable whether we'd be able to go on or not, but finally word was radio'd allowing us to proceed, and proceed we did through a terrific barrage of thunder and lightning and got here about 1.30. Hankow is the centre of a conurbation with over 2 million of a population. After lunch we had a tour of the city and tonight we visited a playground. This is a building built round the four sides of a square courtyard. The building has 4 storeys and on each level there are balconies connected with stairways. Each balcony has tea rooms, sitting rooms, booths for sideshows like a shooting range, a coconut shy etc., and a theatre. There are more than 10 theatres in the place altogether. Each runs a different show. We looked in at three of them where different local operas were being performed. These are immensely popular and each of these three theatres was packed. In another of the theatres we saw a capital programme given by a troupe of Chinese acrobats. Then we climbed to the flat roof, which is a tea garden, and got a magnificent view of the whole expanse of the city and the great Yangtse river. Back to our hotel for dinner which included ducks' tongues and feet, frogs' legs, pork, chicken, rice, stuffed asparagus, meat pies (or noodles) apples and oranges. Now I've had a bath and am ready for bed and tomorrow's programme. Starting at 9am I am to make an inspection of the new bridge over the Yangtse – the biggest bridge in Asia. The people have wanted a bridge for ages but it wasn't possible to get it till they had a Communist Government. The parallel with Scotland is close in regard to the century-old demand for a Forth Bridge.

This Yangtse bridge which is nearing completion – the parts built from the opposite sides of the river were connected up in the centre only on May Day – is as follows

```
┌─────────────────────────────────┐
│                                 │
└─────────────────────────────────┘
```

Road bridge for vehicular traffic only

```
┌─────────────────────────────────┐
│                                 │
└─────────────────────────────────┘
```

Railway bridge with footpaths for pedestrians

And then after lunch I've to have a conference with the Hankow branch of the Writer's Union.

The following day I and my interpreter fly on to Nanking, and a day and a half later to Shanghai, where I'll spend a day or two, before flying back to Pekin.

This is a sub-tropical part of China and we arrived in blazing sunshine. It is a little cooler now (10pm) but not much.

The Huntingdons, with whom I've got on excellently, leave me tomorrow. They go on to Canton and thence to Hongkong, Cambodia, Burma, and India. The others of our party I won't meet again till I get back to Peking about 23rd or 24th.

I hope you've got all my letters and postcards. I've written Michael quite a few times too. Trust your aunt is keeping well. My kindest regards to you both. I do hope there'll be some word from you waiting for me in Peking.

With all my love. Yours, Christopher.

75. *To Valda Grieve (NLS)*

Hankow   17 May 1957

My dear Valda

Like wise people the Chinese keep the best things to the last. We are spending tonight (the last night before the Huntingdons and I part company and go our separate ways) in a wonderful place – a great lake, and on the shore a set of bungalows, equipped with every possible convenience. They belong to the Yuhan Province Writers' Union.

The cooking is admittedly the best even in China and you can have no idea how wonderful that is. I've spend today arguing with Chinese writers on various matters and I was terribly tired now owing to the tremendous heat when I arrived here but the gardens by the lakeside with magnolia, orchids, water lilies etc., the miraculous meal, and the whole arrangement have revived me. Hence this brief note. My dear girl, do you ever realise how much after ¼ of a century I love you, and how much despite all these foreign attractions I am glad to be back with you in the peace of Brownsbank.

They have just invited me to spend a year here. And with my wife. I'll accept it if I possibly can. That'll have to be approved by the Peking headquarters of the Chinese Society for Cultural Relations, of course, and we mustn't count our chickens before we get a formal letter of invitation. It is beyond description the best place I have ever seen. And tho' I have got on well with all the writers and University Professors in the other cities I have been in, I have got on better here with them, and they have asked me to contribute to their magazine, *Yangtse Literature* which is one of the very best in the whole of China and tho' it began as a provincial organ has now an all-China reputation and circulation.

Nanking
18/5/57

Flew here from Hankow. Have parted on very cordial terms with the Huntingdons who want to keep up friendship and have invited me to visit them in London. They live near Richmond Park when in Town.

Hankow was hot but Nanking is even hotter. I am simply boiling. We were met by Professor Chen Chia, head of the English Department of Nanking University. He says he and his senior students know of me but have been unable so far to get hold of my books, or Lewis Grassic Gibbon's. They know of me through Sean O'Casey's *Sunset and Evening Star*, Jack Lindsay's *After The Thirties*, and a Russian book on contemporary European literature which devotes a good bit of space to me. I have promised to read poems and talk about the present position of literature in Britain on Monday afternoon to the lecturers and students of Nanking University.

Then in the afternoon my interpreter (Fang Cheng Ping) and I fly on to Shanghai.

But we have a big programme tomorrow – to visit Sun-Yat-Sen's tomb,[1] go to Chinese opera, dine with some of the University Professors – and this afternoon I had a sail on a big lake and went to the cinema to see a fine film starring two of China's most famous stars.

All my love, Yours, Christopher

---

1. Sun Yat-sen (1866–1925) raised foreign support for the overthrow of imperial China, succeeding in the revolution of 1911. He was acknowledged by all factions as the father of the Chinese Republic.

76. *To Valda Grieve (NLS)*

Peace Hotel, Shanghai   21 May 1957

My dear Valda

Got to this enormous city of over 6 million inhabitants late last night after a six-hour train journey in blistering heat from Nanking where I had a very interesting time, indeed, and gave an hour's lecture to the senior students on the problems and possibilities of contemporary literature. The idea that I should go back there next year and deliver a regular course of lectures has now matured and been put forward officially to the Higher Education authority and the Chinese People's Society for Cultural Relations with Foreign Countries. If the former approve then the latter will write me officially making a definite offer. It is, of course, clearly understood that you would come with me and that it would be made financially well worth our while. But we'll go into the details when the final offer comes. But I certainly made some good friends – especially the head of the English Department (Professor Chen Ciao) and the Vice-Chancellor of the University (who incidentally knows Renwick of Edinburgh University and has entrusted me with a message to him).

While I have been enjoying all these contacts and admiring the lovely scenery, physically it has begun to get very tiring owing to the tremendous heat. It is the beginning of summer here and incredibly hot. Probably owing to the heat – or perhaps also the oil in which all Chinese food is cooked – I had bad diarrhoea yesterday and the day before and had to dose myself with sulphonamide tablets. I feel better today. Another nuisance has been some sort of inflammation of my lower gum which has made it very painful to wear my lower denture and to eat. I have just left my teeth out today but if it continues to trouble me I'll see a dentist. It may be a splinter of bone working up in the gum or a gumboil or an abcess.

Mrs Evelyn Brown of the British-China Friendship Society was here when I arrived. She had just come from Peking and told me there were no letters awaiting me there. I cannot understand this at all and it is terribly worrying. I do hope all's well with you and Michael and your aunt and everything.

I'm going back to Peking on 23rd and will be boarding the plane for home on 26th. But I cannot get by jet plane as I had hoped. So I do not know exactly when I'll get to London but I still expect to be there about 5th June.

All my love, Christopher

77. *To David Daiches (EUL)*

Shanghai   22 May 1957

Greetings from China, where I am just concluding a month's visit with a tour of the sub-tropical South. I hope you got my letter thanking you for your extremely kind response to my request re Bernie Landis and his application for a Fulbright Scholarship. I expect to be back in Scotland – via Moscow and Prague – about 5th June. If you are to be in Edinburgh hope to see you.

Yours, C.M. Grieve

78. *To Ian Milner (NLS)*

                                                                        26 May 1957
Dear Mr Milner

Your letter has just come. I'm sorry if I put Miss Semerakova about, and disappointed you, about staying off at Prague on my way home. I came a day or two earlier than I'd meant to because there was some doubt as to how many days later we'd have to stay if we didn't catch that particular plane, since an all-China TU Conference in Peking had caused a disruption of the internal air services and all planes were reserved for conference delegates. The consequence was that the plane we got from Peking to Moscow had no further connection there and it wasn't until we got to Moscow that we'd find whether it was possible to get on to Prague or not. I'd hoped to stay overnight in Prague but the upshot was I'd to stay in Moscow instead. Then the following day I got the jet plane to Prague but had only a very short wait at the airport before I got a plane for Brussels and thence on to London.

I had a wonderful time in China – met a lot of the writers – got pretty well all over that huge country – lectured in Peking and Nanking universities, and gave poetry readings in Peking, Chungking, Wuhan, Shanghai and elsewhere. The Nanking University people want me to go back in October for 6 months as a lecturer and have applied to the Higher Education Authority and the Chinese People's Association for Cultural Relations to that effect. If the invitation is approved and comes through officially I'll accept.

In the meantime I'm delighted at the prospect of seeing you about the end of August. August or September will be OK for me; in October I expect to be lecturing again in South Wales, and towards the end of that month will probably be going to Poland. The Central Council of Polish Writers have invited me.

This cottage of mine is about 40 minutes' bus run from Edinburgh. There is a bus every hour from the bus station in St Andrews' Square, Edinburgh. It is the Biggar bus, or Dumfries bus (via Biggar) you take and ask the conductress to put you off at Candymill. Our cottage is just a couple of minutes walk off the main road but if I know which bus you're coming by I'll be down to meet you, of course.

Or if that doesn't suit you, I can meet you any time in Edinburgh. The trouble with this cottage is that it is too small – just a but and ben – and we can't put anybody up overnight. Biggar is 4 miles further on. In any case please let me know when your arrangements are 'finalised' and we'll fix something up.

Yes, the Edinburgh Graduation business is on 5th July and a hectic time is entailed – an official dinner, a lunch with the Lord Rector, a Garden Party given by the Graduates Association, etc. etc. and then in the beginning of August there's a further series of functions apropos my 65th birthday, which is to be the occasion also of a special BBC programme to which all sorts of people are contributing their 2 or 3 minutes' say. What a life!

I'll be all agog for further word from you. In the meantime every kind regard to Jarmila[1] and yourself and any other friend you may be seeing.

Yours sincerely, Christopher Grieve

---

1. Ian Milner's wife.

79. *To Gael Turnbull (NLS)*

20 August 1957

Dear Dr Gael Turnbull

Since I got back from China I have been expecting to see you or hear from you, and hoping that your projected visit to Scotland had not taken place while I was out of the country.

So you can imagine how horrified I am to read in the *Daily Worker* that you have been ill and in Worcester Isolation Hospital with poliomyelitis, and not only you but also your wife and two children. The paper says you have all made a good recovery and are now home again. I do hope the paper is right and that you have all fully recovered and without disabling sequelae. Please accept my best wishes for your complete rehabilitation and better luck henceforward.

Yours sincerely, Hugh MacDiarmid

80. *To Edwin Morgan*

15 December 1957

Dear Edwin Morgan

Looking over the signatures of those who were at my birthday party in the Kenilworth I was astonished to find your name. I cannot imagine how

I failed to see and recognise you. True I knew almost everybody and had to have a word with as many as I possibly could, but I am sorry indeed to have missed the chance of holding converse with you, the more so since I wanted to tell you that there has been a change of management of the Castlewynd Printers and the position of the *Voice of Scotland* is at the moment obscure. I haven't any doubt it will go on all right but the hiatus in its appearance may be a little longer than usual.

I hope I may have better luck in meeting you when I come up to Glasgow in February to address the University Literary Society.

With every good wish for a happy Christmas and prosperous new year.
Yours, C.M. Grieve

81. *To Hugo Moore (EUL)*

19 December 1957

Dear Hugo Moore

Many thanks for the *Jazz Monthly* cutting re Kenneth Patchen. I'm delighted to hear of him again. I corresponded with him ages ago when I was in the Shetlands and have several of his volumes here. During the War he took seriously ill (T.B., I think) and T.S. Eliot issued an appeal for funds to help him to which I contributed. Another of the poets giving recitals of poetry-cum-jazz in Californian night-clubs – Kenneth Rexroth – is a particular friend of mine.[1]

Sorry I didn't see more of you at the Kenilworth, but you know how things were! Valda and I were touched by your kindness in toasting her.

As you say we'll look forward to seeing you again at the Congress affair.
Best wishes for a happy Christmas and good New Year.
From Valda & Christopher

---

1. Kenneth Patchen (1911–72) American poet, novelist and painter, influenced by European surrealists and often combining poetry and painting. Kenneth Rexroth (1905–82), American poet, essayist and translator, helped found the San Francisco Poetry Center, influenced the Beat poets though he did not consider himself to be one of them. Rexroth edited *The New British Poets: An Anthology* (Norfolk, Conn.: New Directions, 1949), including MacDiarmid.

82. *To The Editor,* The Scotsman *(NLS, DFF)*

22 March 1958

Sir: –

I regret that neither the Rev. Drs W.J. Morris or T.B. Stewart Thomson can help me over the legal question which was the real issue raised in my letter. But it really won't do for Dr Morris to suggest that I wished to abolish religious education since it does not ensure better behaviour or better citizens then since compulsory general education also fails in the same way I must wish to abolish it too. What I was concerned with was whether it is, or is not, the law that a father can be refused custody of his child if he refuses to send him or her to Church or Sunday School and to undertake to see that he or she receives regular religious education, an imposed obligation difficult to understand since statistics show that Church or Sunday School attenders and recipients of regular religious education are no better behaved and do not make better citizens in any respect than those who have not had the alleged benefits of such attendance and instruction. It is true that I would like to see religious education of any kind in schools under our compulsory educational system abolished for many reasons not mentioned in my letter, but that does not justify Dr Morris's initial sentence. His final paragraph is even less justifiable. My 'faith'[1] has won over nearly half the human race in a fortieth of the time it has taken Christianity to secure its present hold and if this rate of progress continues, as I believe it will, the issue with which I am concerned may well be finally settled before the end of the present century.

My query about the legal issue was mainly prompted by my doubt as to the sincerity of the claim that our legal and political systems, and the Christian churches in our midst, respect minority rights and the conscientious objections of individuals to legally-enforced practices.

As to Dr Stewart Thomson's statistics, I had in mind a General Assembly of the Church of Scotland statement a few years ago that fewer than a third of the population of Scotland had a church connection of any kind. But even if Dr Stewart Thomson's and Dr Highet's figures are correct, why should the beliefs of 60 per cent of our people be forced down the throats of the school-children comprised in the other 40 per cent? This business of 'catching them young' does not argue much confidence in their coming to the same belief of their own free will when they reach adulthood.

Another point concerns the relative growth of the Roman Catholic Church to Protestant Churches in Scotland, and the future prospects. I am sure most Scottish Protestants would find it intolerable that their children of school age should be subjected to Roman Catholic religious instruction as indeed they increasingly are via the BBC. Why then should they acquiesce in the children of people still further removed from their faith than they are from the Roman faith being subjected to such religious beliefs?

As to general education, I have, it is true, little regard for it and certainly do not think it is worth a tithe of the vast sum it costs, since it does not result in an educated people. But it does condition our boys and girls to qualify in at least a minimal way for the kind of jobs available to them under the existing economic system. I cannot discern any similar practical value in religious education, which seems, indeed, to take a base advantage of those otherwise least well, if at all, educated.

Yours etc., Hugh MacDiarmid

Finally, in reply to what Dr Morris says about the importance of a sense of spiritual values, may I say that in my extensive experience of religious people of many faiths in many lands I find that Church membership or adherence is almost always used to absolve people from religious thinking or any preoccupation with spiritual matters? Toeing the line becomes all there is to it. So long as people join the Church they are taken to be Christians. Very few of them are; nominal membership is an alibi which exempts them from undergoing any spiritual experience.

---

1. CMG applied to the Communist Party of Great Britain in 1956 at the time of the Soviet invasion of Hungary, rejoining in 1957.

83. *To W.R. Aitken (NLS)*

10 April 1958

Dear Bill

Many thanks for informative letter just received. I hope Betty[1] and you aren't worried about what I said re Kemp. I want to be at all the functions, of course – only I refuse to be brought into contact with Kemp in any way at all. As long as I am just an ordinary member of the audience, OK, but I won't be actively associated with him in any way – i.e. as one of any platform party or anything of that sort. I do hope this won't embarrass you in any way. There need be no unpleasantness. My feeling is not due at all to thinking I ought to have been asked to speak rather than Kemp – tho' I deny that he has any title at all. Certainly I knew Soutar longer and better than almost any other Scottish writer, but I'd not have felt it out of place if Alex Reid[2] or Alex Scott or Douglas Young had been chosen. My attitude to Kemp is simply one of complete hostility to all he is and stands for. The term 'creeping Jesus' is the description I apply to him. I regard him as an assiduous but irredeemable mediocrity, furthering his own petty ambitions quite unscrupulously at the expense of his betters, a man with nothing to say worth saying and yet tending to monopolise the microphone whenever he can and usurping a place in the public eye for which he has no qualifications at all. I needn't go on. You'll appreciate my point of view.

But I'm delighted Helen Cruickshank is to speak. She was with us at Carnoustie at Mike's wedding.

I'll certainly be very interested to hear what the miserable circumstances (relating to the selection of Soutar's poems) to which you refer so cryptically were.

Valda wonders if your dog and ours will be OK together. We've nobody we can leave Janey with over the weekend, so propose bringing her. I hope that will be all right.

Looking forward to seeing you all.

Love, Chris

---

1. In fact, Betsy, Bill Aitken's wife.
2. Alexander Reid (1914–82), Scottish dramatist and poet.

84. *To Valda Grieve (NLS)*

Balkan Hotel, Sofia, Bulgaria   15 July 1958

My dear Valda

Just a few lines to let you know Ewan and I arrived all right in Sofia after a splendid flight. The weather here is incredibly good. I've seen more sun during the past three to four days than in Scotland for the last quarter of a century. We have been having a series of motor runs to the mountains and conferences with Bulgarian writers etc. and tomorrow (Wednesday) we are flying to the resorts on the Black Sea in the extreme East of Bulgaria.

Sofia is a very lovely city – by far the cleanest I've ever been in. Christine and her husband and children left for Britain yesterday. They are to be in Glasgow for several weeks and I gave them Michael's address and said you or I or both of us would try to meet them there. But there [they] are to be in London and Cornwall before that, so I gave them your Bude address too.

Ewan's radio Ballad of John Axon has won the Italia Prize of £1800 and he has to go to Italy for the presentation. We will leave together and go to Prague. Ewan will go on to Paris and then to Italy, while I will spend a few hours in Prague (and contact Milner if possible) and then return to London myself via Brussels.

You'll be glad to know that I am OK financially – quite wealthy in fact. Brigita – Barbara's friend who is a Bulgarian girl married to a young English poet, Peter Tempest, is taking me shopping today.

So far as my health goes I am all right, but being careful so far as spirits are concerned and keeping to beer. I've spoken about the Yoghourt bacillus and am told to get it on the morning of the day I leave and buy a thermos to bring it in.

I hope Janey and you had not too tiring a journey and found your Aunt not too bad.

I have already taken on the sun and expect by the end of the week to be tanned a nice monkey colour.

I'll try to write Michael today also.
All my love, Yours, Christopher

85. *To Valda Grieve (NLS)*

54 Trinity Church Square, Southwark,   Saturday, 26 July 1958
London S.E.

My dear Valda

I arrived back here early yesterday evening after a splendid flight, leaving Sofia about 6am and with touches down at Belgrade, and Vienna, while we also flew over Budapest. So that was Bulgaria, Yugloslavia, Hungary and Austria all in one day. The delegation man here met me at London Airport and motored me in to Barbara's, and Barbara, Ewan and I had a happy little quiet evening together last night. Both my arms are healing nicely now but that means of course that the top skin is peeling off and I leave a little snow-storm of skin fragments wherever I go. Apart from this sun-burning business I am in splendid form and have had no black-outs or other trouble of any kind and have in fact thoroughly enjoyed myself.

I am anxious to get back to work now of course and the first thing I have to do is to work out a list of my speaking engagements. Also I am anxious to know what mail awaits me at Michael's. I will go there on Monday and am writing Michael now to that effect.

Glad to have your letter when I got here and to know that Janey had behaved so well and proved so adjustable. It is a pity the weather at Bude hasn't been too good, and I am sorry you have found your Aunt so much failed. All in all you must have had a pretty thin time yourself but I hope that you have not been working too hard and that your health is OK. I'll give you all the details about Bulgaria when I see you. This is just a quick letter to let you know I've got back to England safe and sound.

All my love. Wearying to see you. Yours, Chris

86. *To Valda Grieve (NLS)*

Brownsbank   Wednesday, 30 July 1958

My dear Valda

I got back here yesterday. I travelled up to Edinburgh on Monday and caught a train to Glasgow immediately. I stayed overnight with Mike and Deirdre and was in time for a big birthday party they had that night. I had brought Mike and Deirdre presents from Bulgaria so that was all right.

Mrs Jackson[1] tells me she had your letter and so she was expecting me and had a fire on and bottles in my bed. There has been terrific rains in Scotland and as I travelled up there were signs of very extensive flooding

– hayricks floating in lakes of water. It has been heavy rain here most of today.

Everything seems OK with the house, but, as usual, the garden is a bit overgrown.

There was nothing of any consequence in my accumulated mail. Mike tells me he sent on a cheque to you but couldn't remember who it was from. There was, of course, no word from Bill McLellan.

I've been having a busy day answering some of my letters.

It was quite strange arriving here and no you – and no Janey. But the cat was glad to see me. Mrs J. says she has seen very little of it. But it has evidently been lonely, seeing the fuss it has been making of me – or rather the fuss it has been insisting I should make of it.

I had thought I'd have had a letter from you. Perhaps there will be one tomorrow.

I was very tired by the time I got to Glasgow, but am rested now and quite OK.

Trust you are ditto.

The only visitor here seems to have been the Rev W.J.B. Martin who called, returning some books of mine I had loaned him, as he was just leaving for New York.

Let me know if there's anything you want me to do before your return.

Mike is coming down for a few hours on Friday. I left my big trunk with him to bring down in his car, as that was easier than bringing it myself on the bus.

Kindest regards to your aunt. And all my love to you, Christopher

---

1. Mrs Jackson was the Grieves' neighbour at Brownsbank.

87. *To Ian Milner (NLS)*

1 September 1958

Dear Mr Milner

I was glad to get your letter just before I left for Bulgaria and hope all is going well with you – academically and in your private life.

I had a wonderful time in Bulgaria – writing articles, broadcasting, travelling all over the country. And what a wonderful country it is – so fertile, so rich in history, so full of song and dance. Unlike the so-called summer in Britain – and I believe over most of Europe – we really had a super-summer there; blazing sunshine all the time. I am not a sun-bather but at Varna on the Black Sea the sands were covered with hundreds of honey (or chocolate) coloured people nude or next to, and because I felt so odd fully clothed one day I took off my jacket – and sustained second degree burns in both forearms. These were extremely painful and I had to go to hospital and have them attended to. Certainly Bulgaria is the visit of which I'll always have happiest recollections – more so even than China. I had long talks with many of the Bulgarian writers, and now have a lot of writing and translating to do. Amongst other things a Burns bi-centenary article for their literary gazette. Also I've just done one for Budapest and am also doing a Burns programme for Radio Budapest.

I've a Burns book coming out before the end of the year and will send you a copy. My best news is that Macmillans America are bringing out my *Collected Poems* – a book of over 400 pages uniform with their *Collected Yeats*.[1]

So much for good news. Now for bad. I had a postcard from Vlasta Semerakova saying she was to be in Edinburgh for three or four days' stay ending on 27th Aug, and hoping to get in touch with me. She gave me the name of her hotel. Alas! it was indecipherable. Nothing I – or Valda – or other friends could make of it corresponded to the names of any Edinburgh hotel. Finally I concluded that perhaps she had only heard the name of a hotel and tried on the p.c. to reproduce it as it had sounded to her.

Anyhow I got the Festival Society, the Scottish Tourist Board, the Edinburgh Hoteliers Association and several people in Edinburgh likely to know of Czech visitors – e.g. Jessie Kocsmanova's[2] father, Tom Murray (former Secretary of the Scottish-USSR Society) etc. – to do what they could to try to find her. All in vain alas! I am very sorry indeed about this. If she had only wired me from Edinburgh I'd have gone on the next bus. Now I don't know her Prague address. Are you still in touch with her? And if so will you be so kind as to transmit this explanation to her and say how extremely sorry I am to have been unable to contact her. As it happened, too, I was free and could have taken her about and shown her a good deal of Scotland – if she had the time. Of course I don't know but that she may have been there on some official business. Anyhow I hope she enjoyed her brief visit, and send her my love.

Valda joins me in every kind regard to yourself – and to (I'm never sure if I spell this rightly – and I can't refer to her save by the nearest approximation I can make to her Christian name, not knowing her surname) – Jagmilla?

Yours, Christopher Grieve

---

1. Hugh MacDiarmid, *Collected Poems* (New York: The Macmillan Company, 1962).
2. Jessie Kocmanova, Scottish literary critic and translator, Professor at Brno University.

88. *To Valda Grieve (NLS)*

Hotel Duna, Budapest   6 February 1959

My dear Valda

Just arrived in Budapest after a delightful journey by air from Prague.

Have already met numerous friends here, including Charlie Coutts,[1] Josef Szili who is translating my poems, and Professor Lutter, who is Professor of International Literature at the University and whose students I will be addressing tomorrow.

I trust all goes well with you and your Aunt – and, of course, Janey. I had hoped there would be some mail for me, especially from Macmillans, America. But so far I have had nothing at all since I left London. If there is anything urgent, my address is Room 116, Hotel Duna, Budapest, Hungary.

I expect to be here for a fortnight and then to fly back to London.

All my love, Yours, Christopher

---

1. Charlie Coutts, British communist, worked at Radio Budapest from 1953.

89. *To Valda Grieve (NLS)*

Hotel Duna, Budapest   10 March 1959

My dear Valda

I am very disappointed and worried about not having any mail since I left London.

I am having a perfectly splendid time here and am extremely busy with Radio and TV programmes, interviews with newspapers, and lectures.

As I told you I have signed a contract with the Corvina publishing house here for which I'll receive an initial payment of 4000 forints (over £100). Also I have come to a similar arrangement with the Sandor Petofi Literary Museum. And my radio fees will amount to at least another 2000 forints.

I hope you have received my previous letters and p.c.s all right.

I sent p.c.s to Mrs Jackson, Mrs Tweedie,[1] Helen Cruickshank, Barbara Niven, David Orr, Norman McCaig etc.

In every way this has been a most rewarding visit and while I have had a very strenuous time I think it has all been very much worth while.

I'll be flying back to London on 19th inst and will if possible wire Mike my time of arrival at London Airport.

Ian Milner & Charlie Coutts ask to be remembered to you.

I have arranged to open a banking account here and will deposit this money (probably at least £200) so that if you and I come here we can have that to draw on.

That doesn't mean I am short of spending money, and I will certainly bring you some nice presents.

You must please excuse a short letter as I have so many people to see and my programme till I leave now is absolutely crammed full. I am going for a whole day on Thursday to Debrecken about 200 miles away to talk to the writers there and get information about the Cooperative Movement.

I do hope you have not had too terrible a time and that you are keeping well. And tho' it is perhaps too much to hope for that you are longing as much to see me again as I am to see you.

Love and kisses, Yours, Christopher

---

1. The Tweedies were farmers who let Brownsbank Cottage to CMG rent-free.

90. *To Valda Grieve (NLS)*

34 Redcliffe Gardens, London S.W.10   Friday 20 March 1959

My dear Valda

I got your second letter on my arrival here last night, and your letter-card this morning. Either Wednesday or Thursday will be quite convenient if you feel able to come then, but please write or wire what train you are coming by so that we can meet you.

I got in to London Airport about 9pm last night. I knew Mike couldn't meet me. In any case I'd wired him from Budapest I'd arrive about 6, but my plane was derouted from Prague to Amsterdam instead of Brussels, hence I was three hours later in arriving than I'd expected, and very tired. So I just took a taxi, which swallowed up my remaining cash.

However I had a most successful time, especially in Hungary – far better than any of my previous European tours so far as personal prestige is concerned. Actually I had a far busier time than I had in January with the Burns Suppers. An endless succession of lectures, talks, interviews, broadcasts and long journeys all over Hungary. I'm taking it easy today and making up my correspondence, so I'll not go into details now but tell you all the main items when I see you. Incidentally it was all very profitable. I have £100 banked in Budapest, and that is after having to pay all my hotel meals, laundry, postages, and cigarettes, tobacco, and other expenses. Also I've entered into a firm contract with Corvina Publishing House, and Europa Publishing House are to put out a selection of my poems in Hungarian next Spring. The letter from Macmillans New York is very satisfactory indeed. I was worrying badly over the long delay. However all's well that ends well.

I haven't heard again from Bulgaria but that is because I haven't written Stoyanoff yet, but I'll do that now. I will be OK, and it will be easy to spend some time in Budapest too and use the £100 I've banked. An American woman who is the head of English Broadcasts of Hungarian Radio has a big house and told me any time we came to Budapest we could stay there and thus save hotel expenses which are very heavy.

Altogether I had a perfectly wonderful time with Radio Budapest announcing every morning what my programme was for that day, and consequently I was bombarded everywhere with journalists wanting interviews, photographs etc.

Now I have a devil of a lot of hard work to do. Despite his resignation from *The People*, Mike is doing all right – getting plenty of free-lance work from *Sunday Pictorial*, and of course also his full salary from *The People* until the end of April. So he is for the time being better off than ever.

I don't want to stay in London any longer than I can help, but get home and clear up my papers etc.

Deirdre is going to Carnoustie for an extended weekend over Good Friday and the following three or four days.

I am not going to comment about your Aunt. The whole thing is damnable. But you must not reproach yourself at all. You had no alternative in the circumstances. I do hope your visit to Truro will find her reconciled and not too unhappy. You must be completely worn-out with it all, and must certainly have a good rest here.

All my love, darling: and an extra pat or two for Janey.

Yours, Christopher

91. *To Michael Grieve (NLS)*

Hotel Tintyaro, 122, Sunny Coast, Nessebur, Bulgaria   16 July 1959

Dear Michael

I got your letter dated 1st July today together with other letters, including at long last one from Macmillans New York. On final costing they found they could not publish my book under 9 dollars or more – a prohibitive price if they are to reach, as they wish, a large public. So we are going effect certain cuts to reduce the size of the book to allow a reasonable publishing price.

Re the Civil Pension warrants, as you may have noticed, not only a magistrate but a clergyman, banker, etc. can sign the forms attesting that I am still alive. But Mum told you to send them on unsigned by anyone except where you sign my own name to her bank in Biggar. She arranged before leaving they would be accepted there, signed by the bank agent, and the amount (£103 odds) credited to her account.

Saw *Daily Worker* and *Times* of 9th and 10th inst but they were normal size, whereas your letter said papers were down to half-size and might shut down altogether in a day or two. So I don't know whether the strike is going on or not. I only hope 1/ it does not affect your job 2/ that Deirdre may get a post nonetheless, and 3/ that the strike remains 100 per cent effective and destroys half the British Press for good.

We are just ending our holiday here. It has indeed been a wonderful one. I have a rich brick-red countenance and with my white moustache and whitening head of hair look like an Indian army colonel. Your mother is browning now but has been worried at 'catching the sun' so slowly.

I return to Sofia tomorrow (Friday). Your mother will remain here until Sunday and then rejoin me in Sofia. I don't know returning date yet but think about middle of September.

Wish Deirdre and you had been here. Hope you are both OK.

Love, Yours, Dad

P.S. Stoyanoff's visa came through all right last Wednesday and he'll be flying to London on Tuesday or Wednesday. I'm sending this letter with him as that will reach you as soon – or sooner – as post would. I think the whole trouble re his visa was that in my letter to you I called him Boris Stoyanoff, mixing up his Christian name with that of other friends of mine, whereas his name is Istavan (pronounced Sve-tan). However all's well that ends well and we are grateful for the trouble you took.

92. *To Michael Grieve (NLS)*

Room 169, Hotel Bulgaria, Sofia   21 July 1959

Dear Mike

This is just a line supplementary to my last two letters to warn you not to accede to any requests Stoyanoff may make for loans additional to the £15. He seems to be a regular borrower with no intention of repaying. If he really needs money in London he can get it from Mrs Peter Tempest (Brigitta). There have been further red-tape difficulties about his journey and he may have to travel by train now instead of plane and in that case, if he leaves on Saturday, may not reach London till Wednesday next week – ie 28th.

Still no mail. I had hoped to have had the papers you said in your letter of 7th that you'd be sending later that week.

However I've been able now to buy *Daily Workers* here up to 17th inst. See Roy Thomson has brought over the Kemsley interests. Hope strike and other developments not jeopardising you, and that Deirdre's job may soon be available.

Mum and I are OK but beginning to weary for home.

Love from both of us to both of you, Yours, Dad

P.S. Can you please type out the poem in *Lucky Poet* which I call 'Song of the Seraphim' and which begins something like 'Poverty is an outworn convention – nothing can bring it forward creatively now – the urge is towards blossoming – the primordial power today demands nothing less'.

Also the poem I call 'Reflections In a Slum' which you will find in the PEN Anthology, *New Poems 1958* – if you haven't this please ask Norman to send you a copy of it.

And send these two to David Wright, *X Quarterly Review*, c/o Messrs Barrie and Rockliff Ltd., 15 New Row, St Martins Lane, London, W.C.2 with a covering note saying you do so during my absence in Bulgaria.

Wright needs these immediately for first issue of above quarterly.

Head the typescript
'Two Poems' by Hugh MacDiarmid
1/ Song of the Seraphim
2/ Reflections In a Slum.

93. *To Michael Grieve (NLS)*

Room 169, Hotel Bulgaria, Sofia, Bulgaria   22 July 1959

Dear Michael

Your mother is writing you in the hope that you'll receive her letter in time for your birthday. So here's a line from me too to wish you an enjoyable anniversary and many happy returns. I'm not posting you any parcel but will bring you a box of matches or something when I return to England. Your last letter to reach me was dated 7th inst and said you would be sending me some papers in a day or two thereafter. These have not yet come to hand. But today's post hasn't arrived yet.

I am now accumulating material for my Botev[1] translations here, and have had further correspondence with Corvina Publishers, Budapest, and expect a further parcel of typescript from them for revision by any post now. *The New York Nation* has also written me again wanting an article so I'll have to do that. But the heat is too great to engender any working mood.

I expect Mum and I will be going down to Varna soon for a couple of nights to meet my friend Ian Milner, the Australian who conducts the English Seminar in Prague. A motor run to an interesting old village in the hills is also scheduled, and certainly it will be good to get up out of the closeness and humidity of Sofia which lies in a hollow surrounded by mountains.

Mum has taken to the life here like a duck to water and jabbers essential Bulgarian names and phrases to the waiters quite successfully. My deafness prevents my catching vocabulary accurately and so my laziness excuses me for not trying.

It must have been gruelling for you to have had such intense heat in London.

I'll drink an extra iced beer or a slivovitz to you on your birthday forenoon and wish you were here to see me do it and perhaps have a little lemonade yourself.

Love to Deirdre and yourself and the little Fiona and other friends.

Yours, Dad

---

1. Hristo Botev (1848–76). Although the main intention of the Bulgarian government in funding CMG's trip was that he translate the work of their national poet, he did not finish the job and the translations were not published. However, two curious legacies of this visit should be noted. Two young left-wing New Zealand authors, Maurice Shadbolt and Kevin Ireland, met CMG and Valda in Bulgaria at this time. Shadbolt recounts an episode in his memoir *One of Ben's*, cited by Angus Calder in *The Raucle Tongue*, vol. III (Manchester: Carcanet Press, 1997), in which CMG was rescued from assault at an alcohol-enhanced literary soirée for declaring that Botev was not a great poet but merely a national monument. The same anecdote is recounted in Ireland's memoir, *Forwards to Backwards* (Auckland, New Zealand: Vintage/Random House, 2002). At moments of threatened violence, Ireland interposed infectious general toasts to Scottish-Bulgarian literary relations and Bulgarian-New Zealand friendship, saving CMG from certain pummeling. Ireland went on to translate Botev himself: see *Hristo Botev Poems* (Sofia, Bulgaria: Sofia Press Productions, 1974). There is, moreover, a curious short story entitled 'Cultural Relations' in Kevin Ireland's book *Sleeping with the Angels* (Auckland, New Zealand: Penguin Books, 1955), which features characters unmistakably similar to CMG and Valda.

94. *To Michael Grieve (NLS)*

Room 169, Hotel Bulgaria, Sofia, Bulgaria   31 July 1959

Dear Michael

The sun is overpowering and not conducive to work. Nevertheless I have not been, as you think, just gallivanting about. My primary job is translating the great Bulgarian patriot poet Hristo Botev. He fell at an early age in the fight for Bulgarian National Independence and his work consists of only some 23 poems. I have to make translations of about 15 of them. I have managed to get literal-prose translations of most of them, also notes on the metrics of the originals. He is a very difficult poet to translate – and not the kind of poetry for which I have much – if any – use. Rather like Burns at his worst, i.e. without the song qualities that redeem Burns. His utterance is very plain and direct – not to say platitudinous, and the poetic value of his work depends largely on the words. In other words the value of his work lies largely in the manipulation of the language, and the effects he so secures are virtually untranslatable into any other language.

However I'll do my best but won't really work on the versification until I get home. In the meantime I have familiarised myself with his background and historical significance, and I have visited his birthplace and other places associated with his life.

This has meant a lot of travelling and Mum and I have now been virtually all over Bulgaria. Tomorrow we are flying to Varna on the Black Sea for the weekend, the reason being that my friend from Prague, Ian Milner, (an Australian who is head of the English Seminar in Prague) is holidaying there with his wife and step-daughter and as he and a friend of his are translating a number of my poems for a Czech periodical the title of which, translated, is *Foreign Literature*. I want to discuss these with him.

Today with the interpreter who has taken Svetan's place, Paul Zlatarev, and a young poet, Stefan Izanev (who writes over the name of Stefan Dorba) I have to read and explain some of my poems which they have to translate for a Bulgarian periodical.

In the meantime the group of London dancers specialising in Bulgarian dances has arrived here, and one of them is Mrs Barbara Morris, who was with me in Bulgaria last year. Her husband, Max Morris, who is a well-known English educationist, is also here on a commission investigating Bulgarian schools etc.

I and Mum are very sorry indeed – not to say alarmed – at the halving of your income and hope this sorry situation will soon be over and Deirdre and you back in the money again. Also you must be badly needing a holiday after working in such torrid weather.

Your letter with papers etc. has not reached me yet although you said it had been posted before your last letter. Two things I have been wondering about – 1/ did you manage to type and send off all right the poems to Europa Publishers in Budapest; 2/ also the poems to J. Callan for Alan Bush, the composer. I have had no letter from either source acknowledging these.

Yes, the Macmillan USA letter came direct to me here and I replied to it at once – also I have replied to all the other letters I received.

I am beginning to be anxious to get back and settled down again to my usual routine, and I think Mum also has just about had enough of it, tho' she has enjoyed it immensely. After a while the incessant sun gets one down. However we have both had – and are still having – a good rest and we should reap the benefit later.

Mum has attended hospital here and had the lot – electrocardiagraphs, X-rays, blood count etc., and the findings are very good on the whole. The principal trouble has been a sore back deriving from the time when she crossed her lumbar muscles. The Biggar doctor of course did not bother to have her properly examined at all but just told her that of course after such a wrench a little rheumatism was apt to lodge in the injured part. Nonsense! What had actually happened it now transpires is that there was some displacement of two of the vertebral bones with the result that the flanges of these were rubbing on each other thus causing a constant gnawing pain not unlike toothache. When we return from Varna on Monday she is to begin a 20 days' course of treatment, with applications of mud and infra-red ray therapy. So she should be much better. She does not need to go into hospital but simply to attend about 20 minutes or so daily, and she will have first-class specialist attention and not just the perfunctory rule-of-thumb service of a small town GP.

I have no other news, but if you have any *Times Lits.* covering the period I've been abroad please keep these for me – and don't let them be thrown out – as Mum unfortunately cancelled my order for this, as for our other papers, and I like not to miss them and can always read back issues with advantage.

All the best to Fiona and other friends, and love and best wishes to Deirdre and yourself.

Love, Yours, Dad

P.S. Stung to the quick by your suggestion that I am simply enjoying myself I must also point out that I have a great pile of typescripts to read, revise, and advise upon for Corvina Press, Budapest. Also a smaller batch to treat likewise for the Petofi Museum, Budapest, Also that as with the Bulgarian poet Botev, I am perpending – to finalise when I get home – translations of the Hungarian poet Joseph Attila, and the Rumanian poet Arghezi.[1] So!

---

1. Attila József (1905–37), Hungarian poet, predominantly concerned with working-class, suburban life, expelled from the Communist Party for his divergence from Party doctrine. Committed suicide. Tudor Arghezi (1880–1967), Romanian poet and journalist, responsible for many breakthroughs both of form and subject matter in Romanian poetry. Always controversial, he came to be regarded as the greatest Romanian poet after Eminescu.

95. *To Michael Grieve (NLS)*

Room 169, Hotel Bulgaria, Sofia   14 August 1959

Dear Mike

Many thanks to Deirdre and you for telegram, also for letter received today.

My birthday was duly celebrated. Got big sheaf of white gladioli also bottle of Slivovitz and can of crystallised fruits from Bulgarian Writers' Union. Also carved wooden hip-flask, and sheep's horn carved in form of seal etc.

Had very good birthday party at Hungarian Restaurant where Valda drank champagne, cognac etc.

Observer article very disappointing & bad. However will hope to rectify that on my return.

Had intended returning 1st week Sept, but 9th Sept is great national demonstration for start of Communist uprising so will wait for that, & get earliest plane thereafter.

Should be in London 11th or 12th Sept, but will wire you if possible time of arrival.

Hope now strike is over all's well with Deirdre, Fiona and yourself. Love, Yours, Dad[1]

---

1. The handwriting of this letter suggests that it was written in the immediate aftermath of the party mentioned.

96. *To Michael Grieve (NLS)*

Hotel Bulgaria, Sofia, Bulgaria   30 August 1959

Dear Michael

Glad to get your letter of 25th inst today. Also letters from Judy in Budapest, Income Tax, and George MacFarlane about his father's death. His father, latterly a very active Scottish Nationalist, was a friend of mine over thirty years. He succeeded me in 1929 as the only Socialist member of Montrose Town Council.

While these letters came, there is still no sign of the *Times Lits.* etc. you sent off at same time as your previous letter.

Please do not forward – but just retain for me – any further mail, as I am afraid it may not now arrive here before we leave and go amissing. In particular do not forward any letter from the Ministry of Pensions and National Insurance but keep it safely for me. I'll need it as soon as I get back in order to claim my accumulated Old Age Pension.

After [*sic* – presumably, Apart] from an occasional little stomach upset due to the rich Bulgarian food and/or Bulgarian drink Mum and I are quite OK. I note what you say about my writing in one letter, but that was because we'd had a rather complete binge the night before in the Hungarian Restaurant [added in Valda's hand: ' – Not me']. Your mother has put on 14 lbs weight at least, and I suspect I have too.

The weather is becoming autumn-like now but up to today we have mostly still had brilliant sunshine and great heat. We are now beginning to put things in order for our return to Blighty. The books – at least the paperbacks – were for Deirdre and you. There is another one still here but Mum was reading it and she'll bring it. If the parcels contained any Bulgarian or Rumanian books these are of course just to be kept for me.

Glad Deirdre now has a couple of things lined up. That will be a blessed relief to her. You don't say if Fiona has found a job again. I hope so. I'll try to advise you in time about the number of our flight. We expect to arrive at London Airport about 4pm on Saturday 12th Sept. Have quite a strenuous programme before then and of course 9th Sept is a great National Holiday to celebrate Bulgaria's Liberation and there will be tremendous processions and junkettings of all kinds.

Love to you all. Yours truly, Dad

97. *To Michael Grieve (NLS)*

Tuesday 29 September 1959

Dear Mike

Sorry to have been considerably longer in writing you than I meant to be, but I have been bothered a lot with my head-and-throat cold, and, secondly, as you may imagine with accumulated arrears of correspondence and other work.

Yesterday Mum and I were in Edinburgh, where, *inter alia*, I
1/ got myself measured for a posh new suit
2/ ditto for a new kilt, tunic, etc. which a lady friend of mine is presenting to me
– all this in preparation for the TV business in week commencing 19th Oct.

In addition to that, and to the progress at last being made by Macmillans, New York, with my *Collected Poems*, you'll be interested to hear that the BBC have *bought* the head of me done by Benno Schotz on TV.

Yesterday the Abbot was full of people – Alex, Honor, and Jean McCrindle, R.B. Wilkie, R.R. Robertson, Hamish Henderson, John Tonge etc.

Now I don't want to bother you unnecessarily but I'd be glad if you could
1/ send me the short stories you were to type
2/ let me know if you've been able to find out from the man upstairs about my brother.

Maisie Graham and Miss La Rue are coming out here on Wednesday. David Orr and Marjorie have been out twice and are soon going off to Orkney for a holiday. Will be glad to see Deirdre and you – both or separately – if you can get a holiday soon.

Hope all going well with both of you – and the little Fiona.

All the best. Yours, Dad

98. *To Michael Grieve (NLS)*

13 October 1959

Dear Michael

Many thanks for typescripts and sporran. I couldn't get old Murray tartan but got a fine saxony Red Murray.

We'll be glad to see you whenever you can manage. Hard lines you couldn't come up with Ron Christie. As you know I have TV crew and team of broadcasters here all next week.

I think there can be little doubt it is your uncle who has died. His initials were A.G. (i.e. Andrew Graham) and he was born 7th April 1894. He had been in the Customs & Excise since he was 16. Poor beggar! He didn't get enjoying his retirement long. I haven't heard from or of him or his son and daughter (Angus and Morag) for over 15 years. I expect Morag is married and will now be a Mrs Entwyck. If your friend upstairs can find out I'd like to know where he is buried.[1]

We've now received the advance from Macmillans NY, and your mother will be sending on the balance of the payment as promised in due course.

Mum and I were in Glasgow on Sunday – at a China Friendship Society Concert – and went out in the afternoon and spent an hour or so with Mrs F.G. Scott and Lovey.

All the best to Deirdre and yourself. Dad

---

1. Andrew Graham Grieve did not, in fact, die, until 1972.

99. *To Edwin Morgan*

24 November 1959

Dear Mr Morgan

Many thanks for your postcard. I enclose the booklet of Italian translations of Attila Jozsef's poems, and am very grateful indeed for your willingness to help me in this matter.

I will look forward in due course to your visit here.

I have not (I am glad to say) seen copies of the *Glasgow Herald* more than a couple of times for several years past, and consequently did not see the review there of *Honour'd Shade*.[1] But I am not surprised that your Mayakovsky translation (which I like very much) displeased the *G.H.* reviewer.

The anthology evoked a very unfavourable review in the *Scotsman* – of the usual anti-modernist and pro-conventional-mediocrity kind. I replied to it defending the anthology; today the reviewer returns to the attack and is backed up by Douglas Young. Well, well! – What a life!

It was good to see you again. I wish we could meet more frequently.

With kindest regards. Yours, Christopher Grieve

---

1. *Honour'd Shade: An Anthology of New Scottish Poetry to Mark the Bicentenary of the Birth of Robert Burns*, ed. Norman MacCaig (Edinburgh: Chambers, 1959).

100. *To Ronald Stevenson (NLS)*

27 November 1959

Dear Ronald Stevenson

Many thanks for your letter, and cuttings which I return but have read with much interest. We'll certainly be delighted to meet Mr Ogdon and hear (if he'll be so good as play part of it) some *Opus Clavecambalisticum*. I feel a bit compunctious about not getting in touch with you for so long, but I have really had a terrific year (Czechoslovakia, Hungary, Rumania and finally – for three months – Bulgaria) and since we returned in September I've been simply desperately busy.

Tuesday will suit us better than Wednesday and we can come any time convenient to you. It'll be nice to meet the Gordons again too.

Looking forward to seeing you then, and with every kind regard to Mrs Stevenson and yourself.

Yours, Christopher

P.S. We'll talk about the Bill McLellan business.

101. *To Edwin Morgan*

29 December 1959

Dear Edwin Morgan

Many thanks for the Montale volume – excellently printed and produced – which I have read (and will read and reread) with great interest and appreciation.[1]

Please excuse a very short note. All the seasonal doings on top of too much work-in-hand anyhow, leave me no margin of time or energy. I told you I think I have undertaken the English translation of the Swedish poet Harry Martinson's epic scientific poem, *Aniara* – 29 cantos comprising 123 interlinked poems. I'm struggling under an avalanche of writing, about it by the author and various Swedish critics.[2]

I hope to see you ere long but I don't think I'll be in Glasgow before 13th Feb. when I'm giving a lunch-time talk on 'Marxism & Literature' (1.15 to 2.30) to the University Communist Club.

Again with my congratulations and warmest thanks and every good wish for the New Year.

Yours, Christopher Grieve

P.S. May see you, of course, in Edinburgh if you're to be there for the *Honour'd Shade* filmings in the BBC studios on Tuesday, 5th Jan.

---

1. *Poems from Eugenio Montale*, translated by Edwin Morgan (Reading: Reading University School of Art, 1959).
2. Harry Martinson, *Aniara: A Review of Man in Space and Time*, adapted from the Swedish by Hugh MacDiarmid and Elspeth Harley Schubert (London: Hutchinson, 1963).

PART FIVE

The 1960s

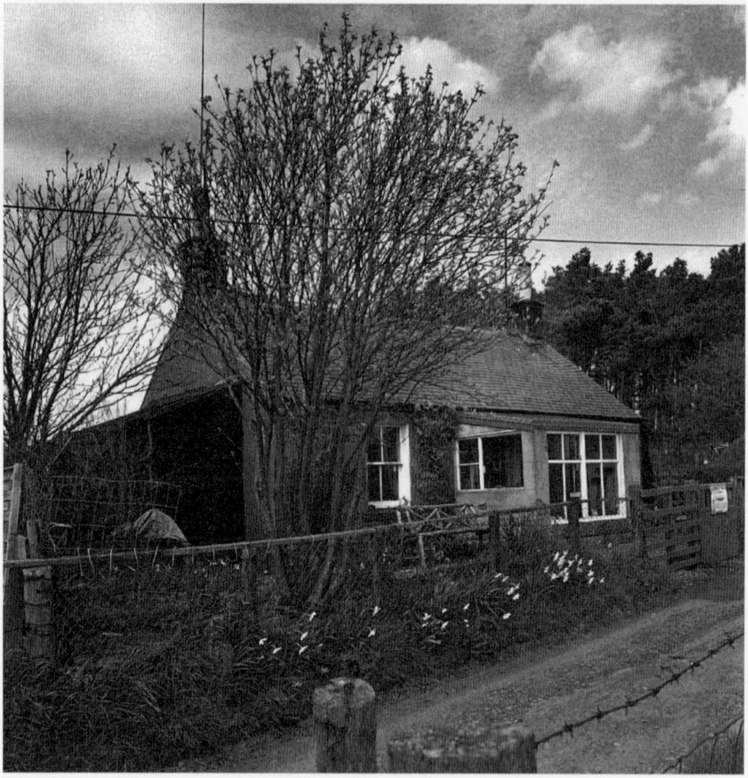

1. *To Michael Grieve (NLS)*

12 February 1960

Dear Mike

Glad all's well with Deirdre and you, note the new MG car, and will be very pleased to go for runs in this whenever time permits – of course, with Janey driving!

I've had a very busy spell. The Bo'ness Burns Club affair was sensationalised by the Press. Great banner headlines in many papers – Scots Poet in Burns Club Scuffle. This was all nonsense. There were no fisticuffs; we were not put out of the pub; the police were there at the end only as a routine call since the Special licence ended at 1am – and the whole thing happened just on 1am. Charles McCrorie, the Edinburgh journalist, proposing the Toast of the lassies, made a belittling reference to the conscription of Scots girls during the war and said he'd been in England at the time and had met many of the girls and they were perfectly happy. I took immediate and violent exception to this. So did Tom Scott and Sydney Smith. There was a tremendous racket, but that was largely due to Morris Blythman and some of his friends from Glasgow who wouldn't obey the chair but persisted in singing American folk songs to guitar accompaniment. I am enclosing some of the cuttings. Let me have them back. You'll see I added fuel to the flames again on Tuesday when I addressed the Scottish Neutrality League in Edinburgh.

In addition to this I've been in the wars since there has been a long and acrimonious correspondence in *The Scotsman* apropos McCaig's anthology;[1] and another similar correspondence sparked off by an attack on me by Alex McMillan, Hon President of the Burns Federation, speaking at a Dumfries Burns Supper.

I got off to BBC the other day a 40 minute script re Lewis Grassic Gibbon which is to be broadcast on Scottish Home Service in last week of this month.

Monitor TV hasn't been released yet, but can't be long now, and all is set for two Third Programme readings by me of my poems and talks about them. Also I've supplied the material for another long Third Programme reading of *The Kind of Poetry I Want* drawn from *Lucky Poet* and *A Kist of Whistles*.

My other Burns Clubs went off OK. St Andrews was particularly good. Then at Bowhill Norman was the principal speaker and did splendidly and both Abe Moffat of the Scottish Miners and I also spoke.[2] A Students Burns Supper in Imperial Hotel, Leith Walk, was also very good.

I've been having articles in *Forward Scotland* (National Congress paper) also in *Context* (Edinburgh University magazine). My translations from German of Rilke have now appeared in an Anthology published in Anchor Books paperback in America – a really first class anthology.

I have an article to write now in a hurry for a literary symposium to appear in a Hungarian periodical – also the first two of my articles for *Sunday Mail* over heading *Scots Rebel* – controversial stuff on Scottish political, cultural, and general issues in an autobiographical framework. I'm lunching with the Editor again on Tuesday and handing over the stuff. I expect also to fix up with him a regular weekly feature – 'Something I want to say' – on current topics.

I got off a long essay on John Davidson for a volume of his poems to be published by Hutchinson's – T.S. Eliot is also contributing an essay to that.[3]

The big Swedish science-fiction epic translation job has not been finalised yet. My collaborator and I are sticking out for bigger pay, also I want to go to Sweden and take Valda – at the publishers' expense. There is no further word – no sign of proofs or anything – not even a reply to my letter asking what the position is – from Macmillans, New York. This is very puzzling.

Kulgin Duval's Scottish Renaissance Catalogue will be out any day now. It is a splendid production with many fine illustrations. *Inter alia*, Duval has had several of my books specially – and most beautifully – bound. The prices will be high, but he sold over 70 per cent of his Irish catalogue and should do equally well with this Scottish one. I hope you can see some of these bindings – they are extremely fine.

Re speeches I'm getting into the clear now – only have the Edinburgh University Cosmopolitan Club shortly, and Brechin Arts Centre lecture on Contemporary Scottish Literature for the Arts Council in the beginning of March – at an appropriate fee of course.

As to my correspondence that is more overwhelming than ever. Heaven only knows when I'll get level with it all again.

We've had heavy frosts lately, and last night quite a bit of snow. Mum is off to Lanark today to see Inspector of Taxes re certain income tax points.

Various friends always asking for you – Charles Reid, David Young, and of course the regulars like Norman, Sydney, Orr, etc.

Going to Walston tomorrow night for supper with the Grays at Schoolhouse.

What has happened to my new pipe you took away to be re-shanked?

Love to you both, and to Fiona.

Yours truly, Dad

The new (2nd) issue of *X Quarterly* should be out. I have an article in it.
Sunday – P.S. I've contracted another nasty head cold and bad cough, which is an infernal nuisance as I am unable to get on with a big programme of work which I had hoped to do today and must somehow or other get done by tomorrow night. Amongst other things this has prevented me hunting out the cuttings about Bo'ness rumpus and other things I'd meant to enclose with this letter. I'll send them on as soon as I can. I'm enclosing some now, however, which Mum had kept.

You'd hear or read about the big fine of *Daily Record* and of Johnston, the assistant editor. It seemed to me a borderline case of 'contempt' which should not have been punished so severely but Lord Clyde is a tyrannical lawyer out to show his authority to the utmost.

---

1. The correspondence had begun with CMG defending *Honour'd Shade* against accusations that it only represented one branch of Scottish poetry, the 'Rose Street' group of poets that centred on MacDiarmid, MacCaig and Sydney Goodsir Smith.
2. Abe Moffat (1896–1975), president of the National Union of Miners, 1942–61.
3. *John Davidson: A Selection of his Poems*, ed. Maurice Lindsay (London: Hutchinson, 1961).

2. *To Michael Grieve (NLS)*

Friday night, 4 March 1960

Dear Mike

Mum and I got back from hospital today – both with various scars and bruises but on the whole much better than we could reasonably have expected from an accident that might well have been fatal – indeed, it's almost a miracle it wasn't.

Mum has a split nose that is healing very well. Also her face is black blue & yellow in various places and has a certain distorted look. The worst thing is that she has a very sore right side – internal injury – so she'll have to take things very easy for a while – no lifting, no hard work.

My worst thing is that my dentures were smashed in my mouth. So my gums are torn and until they heal up I can't get new dentures.

We both were extremely well treated in the Law Hospital – had 60 or so letters of sympathy and enquiry – and numerous visitors.

Just been listening to my first 3rd Programme broadcast. It came over excellently. Geoffrey Bridson did a first-class linking job.

Hope Deirdre and you haven't been unduly worried. Dr Brooks was undoubtedly going far too fast and ran into telegraph pole. Fortunately it was a temporary pole not fixed in with iron stanchions in a concrete bed. So it snapped. If it hadn't we would almost certainly have been killed. The car was a complete wreck – seats torn out etc. Janie escaped unhurt and made her way home and up to the farm.

I've had to cancel various speaking engagements. But that isn't a pity, as I have enough other things to do to keep me busy enough.

Is there no word at all of *X Quarterly*? Can you 'phone David Wright and find out what has happened?

This is just a brief note at the earliest to let you know we're home and not too bad, tho' battered a bit and feeling as if we'd been 'knocked about in the Old Kent Road' as the music hall song says.

Love to Deirdre and yourself, and Fiona and all other friends, from Mum.

Yours, Dad

P.S. Next 3rd programme broadcast on 9th, and the third one on 14th.

3. *To Jean White (EUL)*

7 March 1960

Dear Jean

Many thanks for your kind letter. I got a huge batch of letters from all over, not to mention telegrams and phone calls, but a letter from Langholm is such a welcome novelty that it deserves priority of reply.

Valda and I certainly had a close call. The telegraph pole was fortunately a temporary one – not a permanent one, grouted with a concrete base and fortified with iron supporters. So it yielded. Otherwise we must almost certainly have been killed. As it was I came worst off, sustaining multiple head injuries and a bad right knee. The worst was that my dentures were smashed in my mouth and the fragments gashed my gums and the roof of my mouth. So it'll be a little time before I can get new ones fitted. Already I've had to cancel several lecturing engagements which is a nuisance.

Valda had a split nose and a very sore side due to internal injury. But we both got out of hospital on Friday and are glad to be home again – and convalescing. I would like fine to have come down to Langholm for a holiday, but I seem able to get almost anywhere else much more easily. I was abroad most of last year in Czechoslovakia, Hungary, Rumania, and finally, for 3 months, in Bulgaria where Valda flew out and joined me. And now I expect to go to Sweden in April. What a life!

I am glad to hear your mother is holding her own against the inexorable march of time. I can never think of her except as a slim young woman, of whom I was very fond, singing in her drawing room in Parliament Square, when she and your father were courting. John and Janet are indeed wonderful. Please give my love to them all, and to Jim and Bill and their families, and accept same yourself.

Yours, Chris

4. *To Valda Grieve (NLS)*

Tuesday 21 June 1960

My dearest Valda

I had hoped to hear from you by today, as I have been worrying about your tummy trouble since Isabel McCaig wrote that you had been having a bad time again with it, and Mrs Jackson was also speaking about it. The sooner you have a complete overhaul the better. I do hope you are not having too trying a time now, and that Aunt Jane is enjoying her visit, and is in as good form as one can expect.

I had Deirdre and Mike here for the weekend. In Glasgow I visited their new house in Park Terrace. It is a magnificent flat, with a tremendous view over Glasgow. But it was in a bad state of neglect and disrepair. That is now being put right but that will certainly cost a packet, tho' Mike says they got the house for so much less than expected (£600) that the cost of renovation etc. can be set against that.

As I told you in my last letter, I had a wonderful time at Reading, and since I came back I've written my article for the *Daily Express* and hope to finish one today for the *Saltire Review*.

There is no word yet about the *Sunday Mail* articles, but Mike thinks they are OK.

A huge mail was awaiting me here but it boiled down to little of any importance, and – worst of all – there was nothing whatever from America – neither Macmillans nor anything else.

I did a huge recording for Yale University in London – reading poems continuously one day from 11am till 6pm.

The weather here is extremely hot with blinding sunshine. I hope you are having it equally good and managing to soak in a good deal of it.

Now I'm going to settle down to write a lot of other articles, and then think about my speech for Jedburgh.

I'll write you again in a day or so.

All's well here but a cow got into the front garden – I think on Saturday afternoon when Mike, Deirdre, and I were out, and broke down some of the surrounding planks, and also lay down on and crushed a lot of the flowers. This was a great pity as the garden was looking really lovely with a mass of peony roses, great trusses of canterbury bells, and two fine clumps of tiger lilies.

I'm not forgetting to water the pot-plants – the cyclamens are flowering nicely.

Love to Aunt Jane, and to yourself, and Janey.

Yours, Christopher

5. *To Valda Grieve (NLS)*

Thursday 23 June 1960

Dearest Valda

Glad to get your letter-card, but very sorry you are having a difficult time, and trust your aunt is better reconciled now she has been back home for a while. The whole thing is a very horrible but inevitable situation, and it is a great pity you should have to undergo it when you are not really well enough. The weather here remains glorious, and I suppose it does in Bude too – if only you can get out as much as possible and enjoy it.

Mike and Deirdre came down late last night and have just tootled off to Glasgow again. I am going into Edinburgh tomorrow 1) to have my hair cut, 2) to see Norman before he goes off to the wilds of Achmelvich. But I'll only be there a couple of hours and then I'm going to Glasgow and will stay with Mike and Deirdre till Sunday evening when Mike'll run me back. The reason is that they can't come down here this weekend but must get things ready to leave their present flat and migrate into their new home in a day or two. I've arranged to send your divan up with Hogg the carrier on Monday as they need a bed. Of course they'll just be camping out in one of the rooms in the meantime. I'll also send the two bookcases – the glass fronted one in the shed, and the one in Norman's cottage.

Nobody been out here.

Mail almost non-existent – as usual in mid-summer. But I wish to God I could hear from America at last. I've brought my own correspondence almost up to date this last day or two – written and posted over 20 letters. Have also done my article on McCance for the *Saltire Review*, and hope to do the second two articles for Webster of the *Sunday Mail* at Mike's on Saturday and Sunday.

The Jacksons are off today to the Royal Highland Show in Edinburgh. Think the Tweedies must be away there too.

Glad Adela is coming down all right to keep you company and help in putting the house free. Kindest regards to Dorothy and all my love to you, and to Janey.

Yours, Christopher

Kulgin and Edward Nairn are apparently still holidaying in Northern Ireland.

6. *To D.G. Bridson (LLIU)*

24 August 1960

Dear Geoffrey

I am afraid I am incurably antipathetic to Robert Graves, and for that reason only enjoyed your two programmes, as one enjoys the famous parson's egg – in bits! But I hope you enjoyed your trip to Majorca.

I don't know if you welcome suggestions for programmes. But I think you could have a very interesting interview with the veteran Scottish artist, John Duncan Fergusson. J.D., who is a very lively octogenarian, was friendly with all the modernist artists – Matisse, Cezanne, etc. – and played an active part in the Fauvist movement, editing a magazine *Rhythm*, devoted to that phase, along with Estelle Rice and Othon Friesz. He is busy writing his autobiography. At present he is in France and will be there to the end of September. Then he will be in London where his wife, Margaret Morris, has to rehearse her ballet for two weeks prior to a London premiere.

J.D.'s present address is:– Dr J.D. Fergusson, chez Madame Ardisson, Villa La Follette, Rue de l'Orangerie, Antibes, (Alpes Maritimes), France.

And his home address is 4 Clouston Street / Glasgow W.

With every kind regard from Valda and myself.

Yours, Chris

7. *To Michael Grieve (NLS)*

Monday 3 October 1960

My dear Mike

Mum and I were very sorry to see the state you were in yesterday. We are not kill-joys and have no wish to preach at you. On the contrary we want you to have a good time and are happy occasionally to share it. We always look forward eagerly to your visits here. You have done very well so far and we are proud of you. But you are young yet and have a long way to go and may well rise a lot. That's what we want you to do. But there are always more ready to pull you down (and edge themselves in at your expense) than help you up, and these include many apparent friends. Beware of them and don't play into their hands. You lay yourself open to them unless you are always on your guard. Drinking too much is one thing and can at times be bad enough, but to get into trouble through using foul language is quite another thing. If you get into rows because of that it is frightfully ignominious. You should really cut that out altogether. It is not worthy of you and quite unnecessary. Also there is no point in high jinks that go so far as wrecking the happy home. Smashing things up is poor fun. Anyhow at this juncture you have more than enough serious responsibilities and need to keep a level head. If you do that you can establish yourself securely and have a good home, no worries over debts, no lack of domestic amenities, and the respect, goodwill and help of all who are fond of you and wish you well. You may be sure that Mum and I will always do anything we possibly can to help you. The best way after all to beat your enemies is to keep your ambitions high and make good. And there is nothing to prevent you doing that if you just keep within bounds and never lose your self-respect. You may think I'm not a very fit person to say all this. I have my faults, but on the whole I do keep things going and I certainly avoid bad language and any resort to mere physical force. But I am fairly choosey about who I associate with. So, dear boy, haul up and put first things first – and to hell with all the hangers-on, no-gooders, and mere mediocrities of all sorts. With love and every good wish to Deirdre and yourself.

Yours, Dad

8. *To Alex McCrindle (EUL)*

18 November 1960

Dear Alex

Hope you are OK after our busy time in old Aberdeen. I enjoyed it all immensely. But I came home to find police stationed at the bottom of the lane and the whole farm subject to control owing to an outbreak of Foot and Mouth Disease. All 500 sheep and 135 cattle (including two heifers born this morning) have had to be destroyed and buried in a huge 15-feet-deep pit. And of course the farm will not be free of control for six weeks to come.

This involves a big loss – and an element of personal tragedy – for the farm people. So for a little while I cannot go any further with them into the matter of this house. But as I told you he (the farmer) is willing to use his name in application for grant, and, as to security of tenure, to give us a life-rent of the cottage.

Kindest regards to you all, and again many thanks for your help in Aberdeen.

Yours, Chris

9. *To Christine and Alastair Macintosh*

10 January 1961

Dear Christine & Alasdair

Nothing could have been a happier surprise than your popping in here. Both Valda and I were delighted. It was a pity it was so brief. Deirdre and Michael greatly enjoyed your visit too.

I should have written you sooner but have been – and remain – quite desperately busy. Partly because of arrears incurred owing to the after-effects of the motor smash: and partly because my commitments seem to increase continually. Just now my *Collected Poems* are about to appear in New York; I have a long new poem due out shortly, and am part author of another book which is to be published shortly;[1] worst of all I am wrestling with a verse-translation of an enormous Swedish epic (29 cantos and over 200 interspersed lyrics); and I am busy too with a libretto for an opera due to be performed in London at Easter. Then towards the end of the month I have my usual quota of Burns Suppers.

On top of all that Christmas and New Year meant all sorts of junketings – in Glasgow where Valda and I spent a day or two, seeing the new little Christopher Grieve;[2] then in Edinburgh at various social functions; and of course all sorts of visitors, first-footers etc., here. I hope you all had a good time too, and that when you got back you found the children all in the best of fettle.

Many thanks for your Christmas card. I'd have sent you one too, but found to my dismay that I'd stupidly omitted to get your address and only discovered when it was too late that Michael had it. Hence this belated letter, which carries with it nevertheless our best wishes to you all for 1961 (and every subsequent year for the matter of that).

In lieu of a Christmas card I'm enclosing for your amusement a cutting of some illustrations from a recent catalogue of Scottish books. The camera is not supposed to lie: but my experience is that photos, portraits, sculptures etc. of a person are apt to vary so much as to be scarcely recognisable as appertaining to the same person.

Looking forward to your next visit (and that of any of the children), and with love and best wishes.

Yours, Christopher

P.S. And please try to warn us in advance next time. Valda hasn't yet ceased to lament that you came at a time when owing to the Foot and Mouth disease business you found, like Mother Hubbard's dog, the cupboard bare!

It was very kind of you to send the rompers for your nephew, Christine. Michael and Deirdre were very pleased.

---

1. Hugh MacDiarmid, *The Kind of Poetry I Want* (Edinburgh: K.D. Duval, 1961). Limited to 300 copies.
2. Christopher Murray Trevlyn Grieve, CMG's grandson; see Appendix.

10. *To Edwin Morgan*

7 April 1961

Dear Edwin Morgan

I have just received – and had a first run-through of – your splendid *Sovpoems*. I need not tell you how much I appreciate your introduction. I tremendously admire – not without an element of envy – your great range as a translator. But in this connection I wonder if you know the worth of the leading living Swedish poet, Harry Martinson. I am just in the last stages of translating his immense science-fiction epic, *Aniara* – over 100 cantos. As you may know (if you heard the opera based on it at the Edinburgh Festival two years ago) it deals with the evacuation of the earth (due to radiation poisoning) and the subsequent adventures of the mass space travels of humans freed to emigrate to other planets. Martinson is a near-Communist, and an out-and-out materialist. It is a very various work, including songs in Swedish slang. I'll hope to be able later to send you a copy. It is to be published simultaneously by Hutchinson in Britain, Bonniers in Sweden, and Knopf in America.

I note from the accompanying sheet of info. that you and I have another link – namely, your service in the RAMC. I had over 8 years in the same corps – but, Private Morgan, not as a private but as a QMS!

Hope to see you again ere very long. Many thanks indeed for the book. Every good wish.

Yours, Christopher Grieve

Have mislaid your Rutherglen address. Hence sending this c/o Migrant.

11. *To D.G. Bridson (LLIU)*

7 April 1961

Dear Geoffrey

Haven't heard a cheep about you for a long time. Of course you may be in Tibet or Patagonia!

I've just had another street accident – not as bad as that over a year ago, but it seems to have shaken me more. I gashed my head and hurt the base of my spine and one of my shoulders. Damn it! Just when I am specially busy too. I'm on the point of completing translation of the great epic poem *Aniara* by Harry Martinson, the leading living Swedish poet. A huge thing – over 100 cantos.

It is in this connection (tho' I don't know if you are the person to approach – and certainly I do not wish to presume on our friendship) I am writing. I'd like to do a talk (with readings of some of his poems) on Martinson. What I'd really like to do, however, are talks on three poets (some of them adequately known in the English speaking world but all of them, in my submission, important poets who ought to be much better known) – viz. Harry Martinson (Sweden), József Attila (Hungary) and J.D. Arghezi (Rumania). I'd be pleased to send in scripts right away if there is a chance of such talks (say 20 minutes each).

Tho' I haven't seen your name lately in *Radio Times* or elsewhere I hope all's well with you, and your wife. Valda joins me in kindest regards.

Yours, Christopher Grieve

12. *To Edwin Morgan*

17 July 1961

Dear Edwin Morgan

Many thanks for your letter. I certainly hope to do something about Attila József some time – but when? if ever. I am indeed desperately busy and likely to remain in that deplorable condition for long enough ahead. So I do hope you will go ahead with verse translations of some of his poems. I had hoped to restart the *Voice of Scotland* ere this and intended in that case to importune you again for contributions: but the restart is still delayed. So far as I am concerned my interest meanwhile is limited to getting hold of all the material of, and about, József I can.

In this connection I wonder if you've seen the two issues of *The New Hungarian Quarterly*. Vol. II No. 1 (January 1961) contains a long essay 'A Portrait of Attila József The Poet' by László Pödör, in English, with various poems of József's in French translations by Jean Rousselot, and Guillevic, and in German versions by Franz Fühmann. And Vol. II No. 2 (April-June 1961) has 7 poems of József's (including two longish ones) in English renderings by J.C.W. Horne.

If you haven't seen these I'm coming up to Glasgow on Friday 21st inst to the Polish Consulate Reception, & can lend them to you. Hope all goes well with you. With warmest regards.

Yours, Christopher Grieve

13. *To Helen Burness Cruickshank (EUL)*

14 August 1961

Dear H.B.C.

Many thanks for your birthday greetings and the little volume of engravings of H.M. The Queen – it was far too good of you to bother sending me that. [Added in H.B. Cruickshank's hand: 'A 5/- book of stamps!']

This is just a line to say that Valda and I expect to be present, duly equipped with the instruments of (gustatory) War on Sunday 27th inst.

I don't know whether I'll see you tomorrow (Tuesday) night at the *New Saltire* reception in Gladstone's Land. So – in case you're not there – I'm posting this.

We're having a very busy time here too – 13 visitors yesterday (Sunday) – and everything still higgledy piggledy with the alterations and extensions. Then too a whole flock of my chickens are coming in to roost now and I've been up to my eyelids in proofs etc., with 4 books and a pamphlet coming out shortly now. After all, of course, I'm only 69! Love from Valda and I.

Yours, Chris

14. *To Ronald Stevenson (NLS)*

15 August 1961

Dear Ronald

Yes. I have been – and am – desperately busy or I would have been over to see you ere this. Today I've to go in to Edinburgh to a reception in connection with the launching of the *New Saltire* and tomorrow I've to go to a wedding.

I must write the two chapters I promised re Sorabji within the next few days, or Heaven only knows when – or if – I'll be able to.

And the problem is not made less by Ogdon's essay. How the devil I'm going to conjure up anything that can stand alongside it I simply can't imagine! It is a magnificent bit of work – profound in its implications and absolutely just in its applicability to Sorabji's genius.

I used to have S.'s *Round About Music* but someone borrowed it and failed to return it long ago. So I will be glad to borrow yours. Also I haven't a copy by me of my pamphlet on F.G. Scott, and I'd be glad to have that too. Can you please send them to me?

Heartiest congratulations on your own great burst of creativity – I'll look forward eagerly to hearing these compositions in due course. I'll return the American magazine for which too many thanks. Love to Marjorie and yourself.

Yours, Chris

15. *To Edwin Morgan*

5 January 1962

Dear Edwin Morgan

Many thanks for your letter. The line you ask about in my poem on Charles Doughty is difficult and probably grammatically indefensible, but what 'where you lie needs tells' means just as you suggest 'where you lie (no other sign is needed to tell)' or 'necessarily' for 'needs'. Petavius, Langrenus and Arzachel are all placenames in the landscape of the moon. Hope this makes things clear.

Here's wishing you a good creative New Year. My own has begun in style, with the appearance of my *Collected Poems* (Macmillans, New York), and *The Kind of Poetry I Want* (K. Duval, Edinburgh).

Yours sincerely, Christopher Grieve

16. *To John Laidlaw (EUL)*

10 January 1962

Dear John

Yes, it's time I was writing you. I meant to do so long ere this. But the reconstruction of our house here, just at a time too when I was exceptionally busy, upset all my work and especially my correspondence. I have always difficulty in keeping up with the latter anyway as I have many hundreds of correspondents all over the world. But I meant particularly to let you know how sorry I was not to see you (and Janet too) at the Common Riding. Michael was covering it for his paper (*The Scottish Daily Express*) and had to see as much of the carry-on as he could in the short time and I had to keep beside him to tell him things. Also he had a very strict deadline to meet. So we just had no time to spare by the time he got his article written and phoned through to Glasgow. You probably saw what a mess some incompetent sub-editor made of it too. Michael was naturally furious.

Another reason I delayed writing you was that I expected my *Collected*

Poems and wanted to send you a copy. The publishers (in New York) have taken nearly four years to produce it. But I understood I'd get copies by the end of October or early November, and therefore would have them to send to friends for Christmas. However they didn't arrive. Only this morning I got one advance copy. The others can't be long now and I'll send you one as soon as they arrive. It is a big book of course and will keep you reading for long enough – if you can be bothered with the stuff.

Another book of mine has just appeared. Printed in Italy by the most famous press in Europe – handset on hand-made paper and beautifully bound in vellum – it is a collector's piece. The edition is limited to 300 copies numbered and autographed by me – and of course the price is correspondingly high. Six guineas!

But I have been really busy. I have translated into English verse a huge epic on the nuclear menace by the leading Swedish poet, Harry Martinson, and this is to be published simultaneously in London, Stockholm, and New York. I have also made a selection of Burns' love songs for Vista Books Ltd, and have two pamphlets coming out on David Hume the philosopher.[1]

And now I'm on the verge of my usual January rush. I have five Burns Clubs to address – beginning with Greenock Burns Club (the mother club) and then the Scottish Arts Club in Edinburgh. And on Friday I've to be in Brechin addressing the Arts Guild there on behalf of the Arts Council.

Valda and I are both well, but like you have been having trouble with [MS ends]

---

1. Robert Burns, *Love Songs*, selected by Hugh MacDiarmid (London: Vista Books, 1962); *David Hume: Scotland's Greatest Son* (Edinburgh: The Paperback Booksellers, 1962); *The Man of (Almost) Independent Mind* (Edinburgh: Giles Gordon, 1962).

17. *To Jean White (EUL)*

10 March 1962

Dear Jean

Valda and I were in Glasgow yesterday. I was one of the speakers at an important memorial gathering for a Scottish artist who died recently – an engagement I could not have cancelled. I got back here in the early hours of this morning to find your letter among my mail the postman had left in the porch in our absence. But I had seen the notice of your mother's death in *The Scotsman*. I was not surprised, but hoped only that she had passed away peacefully and painlessly, as your letter tells me she did. I would, of course, have come down if that had been possible. You will understand how glad I am in the circumstances that I was able to see her again recently – and that she knew me. When one has known, and been fond of, someone for sixty years, it is a sad wrench to know that one will not see her again. Please give my love to John and Janet. I am glad Jim and Bill and their wives were able to be with you.

With all sympathy and affection from Valda and I.

Yours, Chris

18. *To Alex Neish (UDL)*

22 March 1962

Dear Alex Neish

Yes, I intend to be present at all the sessions of the Writers' Conference. Somebody (Jim Haines or Colin Hamilton, I think) advised me that I was expected to speak on Scottish Writing Today on the second day (21st August) and I understood that that was to be a full address, to be followed by discussion – in other words that I was to be the speaker.[1] I agreed to do this. But your letter today says 'a brief outline of my attitude'. I am wondering therefore what precisely the arrangement is, and in particular whether there are to be other speakers apart from people merely asking questions or taking part in the discussion. If I am to be just one of several speakers my final agreement will depend entirely on who the others are; also, of course, if I am to prepare an address I'll need to know about how long I'm expected to speak. I note you say you'll forward me final details later. I'll look forward to these, but I must make it clear right away that there are certain people I am not willing to share a platform with.

All the best. Yours, C.M. Grieve

---

1. Jim Haynes (b.1933), American founder of The Paperback Bookshop, Edinburgh (1959) and the Traverse Theatre (1963), organizer, with John Calder and Sonia Orwell, of the first Edinburgh International Writers' Conference (1962), a precursor to the Book Festival.

19. *To Ian Milner (NLS)*

14 April 1962

Dear Ian Milner,

It must have been a failure in coordination between Macmillans New York and their London branch that led you to receive two copies of my *Collected Poems*. In any case you – and Jessie and other friends in various countries – were luckier than I was. For up to the time I got your letter I hadn't myself received my author's copies. However I've had them since. By all means present the extra copy to the English Seminar.

Unfortunately as you'll have seen there are a terrible lot of printers' errors. One of the worst is with the poem to Charles Doughty entitled

'Stony Limits', where the last three verses should not come at the end but go in after the first verse on the previous page. This infernal transposition of course makes nonsense of the whole poem.

However such things were, I suppose, inevitable in a long-distance business. Effect was simply not given to many errors duly corrected on the galley proofs, and I did not receive revised proofs. I'm depositing a copy with all the mistakes marked in the Scottish National Library. And I hope that when Oliver and Boyd issue the United Kingdom edition in August they'll have an erratum slip inserted.

My life continues to be more hectic than I could wish. The Granada TV interview with Malcolm Muggeridge went off all right.[1] One can't see these programmes in Scotland – only in London and in the Manchester area. But all concerned were very pleased with it. I didn't stay in London any longer than I could help – and didn't see anybody. I should add that the interview was not concerned at all with my poetry or literary matters, but solely with my politics. An extension in a way of a sort of witch-hunt to which I've been subjected in various quarters recently. Happily I am invulnerably circumstanced.

You'll know perhaps that the official programme of the forthcoming Edinburgh International Festival includes a writers' conference – mainly concerned with the position and future of the novel. Novelists from all over Europe are to be there. I'm to speak on the second day (21st August) on 'Scottish Writing Today', with Professor David Daiches in the chair.

Everything is now with the printers for a huge *Festschrift* to be published for my 70th birthday in August: 14 or 15 essays by various writers.[2] I've only seen one – an excellent one on my early lyrics by David Daiches.

Also Professor Kenneth Buthlay has written a monograph on me for Oliver & Boyd's excellent Writers and Critics Series.[3] Buthlay is now in the Chair of English Lit. at Sao Paulo University in Brazil. This, however, is not to be published till March.

I'll have a copy of the translation of *Aniara* sent to you when it is published – but have no word yet when that'll be. It shouldn't be long, I think.

Otherwise things are OK here – except that Valda is laid up with flu'. There's been a regular epidemic of it. I had a dose of it a few weeks ago but managed to throw it off pretty quickly. Also, it has been the longest and most severe winter we've had for 15 to 20 years and it is still bitterly cold weather save for an hour or so of sunshine in the early afternoons. The lambing time testifies to the hardship. There is scarcely a green blade of grass to be seen, so a great dearth of feeding, and the ewes are just dropping the lambs and walking on and leaving them – having no milk to give them.

Hope all's well with Jarmila, Linda, and yourself.

Every kind regard from Valda and I.

Yours, Christopher Grieve

1. Malcolm Muggeridge (1903–1990), English journalist and television interviewer; his own series included *Appointment With ...* (1960–1) and *Let Me Speak* (1964–5).
2. *Hugh MacDiarmid: A Festschrift*, ed. K.D. Duval and Sydney Goodsir Smith (Edinburgh: K.D. Duval, 1962).
3. Kenneth Buthlay, *Hugh MacDiarmid (CM Grieve)* (Edinburgh: Oliver and Boyd, 1964).

20. *To John Montague (SUNYB)*

14 April 1962

Dear John Montague

Very many thanks for your letter, and your book. I like these poems of yours very much. It was good of you to chip in with your excellent letter in the *Guardian*. But that was just a preliminary skirmish to a sort of witch-hunt against me which has since developed in all sorts of quarters. I am not surprised and fortunately I am invulnerably circumstanced. Another instance, stemming directly from the *Guardian* affair, was a Granada TV interview I did with Malcolm Muggeridge. His questions did not involve my poetry or literary matters at all – but solely my politics. I think there will be a lot more of this sort of thing, since I have a 70th birthday in August and all sorts of preparations are being made for it. The Communist Party is giving me dinners in Glasgow, Edinburgh and London, my portrait is to be painted for the Scottish National Portrait Gallery and a huge *Festschrift* is to be published with essays on my work by 14 or 15 contributors. All this is just asking for it, and I have no doubt I'll get it hot and strong. My *Collected Poems* (published in America about 6 weeks ago) are to appear in a United Kingdom edition in August, and I fancy a lot of the reviewers will seize the opportunity to emulate John Wain.[1]

I'll hope to do a review of your book in *The New Saltire*, and will certainly review it in my own quarterly *The Voice of Scotland* which I expect to revive (after a couple of years hiatus) in the Autumn.

I agree with what you say about Lewis Grassic Gibbon's work (yes! I know Carleton's stories, too). Gibbon was a great friend of mine. We did a book together *Scottish Scene* (1934, I think). You mention Francis Scarfe[2] too, and I know him also. I too just had a very interesting letter from Ewart Milne about Dublin literati of today. All the older writers I knew – Yeats, A.E., Gogarty, 'Seumas O'Sullivan' etc. (except Sean O'Casey) are dead, but I hope to go over to Dublin in the Autumn and meet Milne, and Patrick Kavanagh, and a few others perhaps. No: there is one older writer I've known for 30 to 40 years – Austin Clarke.

I hope to meet you sometime too. I haven't been in France for 40 years – but I do get about a lot (Russia, Hungary, Czechoslovakia, and elsewhere) and I may pop up in Paris – not that I know anyone there now, except Tristan Tzara. But we have a writers' conference as part of the programme of the Edinburgh International Festival this year and there are to be a lot of French writers there — Beckett isn't coming, but Sartre, Sarraute, Butor etc. are.

Again with warmest thanks for your poems (which have given me real joy in the presence of so overwhelmingly much that is phoney) and with every good wish for your further work in poetry and prose.

Yours, Hugh MacDiarmid

---

1. In response to an article by CMG in *The Guardian* ('MacDiarmid on MacDiarmid', 22 February 1962), John Wain had written a letter attacking CMG for rejoining the Communist Party in the wake of the Hungarian invasion and calling him a 'flunkey of international communism'.
2. Francis Scarfe, translator and author of books on Baudelaire and Auden.

21. *To Jean White (EUL)*

1 May 1962

Dear Jean

I am very sorry indeed to hear of Janet's death. I gather it was very sudden and hope that means that she passed without suffering. I am very sorry I did not manage to see her the last time I was down. I knew she hadn't been well but John said in a recent letter that she was perking up again. I would have come down for the funeral tomorrow but have an engagement in Edinburgh which I cannot break. Also the rest of the week is an extremely busy one for me. I have to be here on Friday as the Russian poet, Ivgeny Yevuskenko [*sic*] is visiting me here by arrangement with the British Council.[1] Then I have to go to Glasgow on Saturday and give a lecture at the University there on Sunday. Michael unfortunately is away on a sailing holiday in the Hebrides. I'll write John in a day or two but perhaps you can show him this letter and that will explain things to him. Otherwise I would certainly have wanted to stand side by side with him. I am sorry he is feeling unwell too. It has been a very sad and trying time for him and for you with your father and mother and now Janet all dying. I hope you are managing to bear up in your loneliness. Valda joins me in deepest sympathy and all love to John and yourself and of course to Jim and Bill and their families.

Yours, Chris

---

1. Yevgeny Aleksandrovich Yevtushenko (b. 1933), Russian poet, popular with the post-Stalinist generation in Russia, travelled widely from 1960 gaining international celebrity.

22. *To James Burns Singer (NLS)*

2 June 1962

Dear James

I am very glad to get your letter. Only the other day I was asking Norman McCaig if he had any word of you, since I had seen no new book of yours announced nor any contribution by you in any of the periodicals I see. Of course I knew that quite probably you were doing reviews or other work for the *Times Literary Supplement* or other papers who do not publish the names of their contributors. However it is good to know you are alive and presumably active.

It is also very good that the *Observer* should have asked you to write the Profile. Your *Encounter* article on me remains, I think, the best written about my work so far.[1] This approaching 70th birthday is going to be signalised by a host of articles. Duval, Edinburgh, is publishing a huge book with essays on my work by over 12 authors. It will also be copiously illustrated and will be published early in August (my birthday is 11th August). The August issue of *The Scottish Field* will have five articles about me (by Neil Gunn, Norman McCaig, Sydney Smith, David Daiches and Maurice Lindsay), also a photograph in technicolour etc. Kenneth Buthlay (Professor of English in Sao Paulo University, Brazil) has written a study of my work for Oliver and Boyd's paperback Writers and Critics Series, but this will not be published till the following March. And another man, Duncan Glen, has written a book about me which Messrs Chambers are considering.[2]

I'm desperately full of engagements in July and August but this month (June) is free apart from the fact that I'm obliged to be away one day, and sometimes two days, per week giving sittings to a painter[3] who is 'doing me' for the Scottish National Portrait Gallery.

So I think it best if you would come out here rather than that we should meet in Edinburgh. There is an excellent hourly 'bus service (either Biggar 'bus or Dumfries 'bus) from the St Andrew's Square 'bus station in Edinburgh. The conductresses of the 'bus all know where I live, so you ask to be put off at Candymill (4 miles on the Edinburgh side of Biggar) and it's only a couple of minutes walk up a farm road to my house. But if possible let me know in advance which day you are coming and approximately when (i.e. forenoon or afternoon, so I'll be sure to be here).

Looking forward then to seeing you any day you care to fix between today's date and the end of June.

And with every kind regard to your wife and yourself.

Yours, Christopher

---

1. Burns Singer, 'Scarlet Eminence: A Study of the Poetry of Hugh MacDiarmid', *Encounter*, March 1957.

2. Duncan Glen, *Hugh MacDiarmid and the Scottish Renaissance* (Edinburgh and London: Chambers, 1964).
3. R.H. Westwater.

23. *To Tom MacDonald (Fionn Mac Colla) (NLS)*

13 June 1962

Dear Tom

I am delighted to hear you've found a publisher to re-publish *The Albannach* and will, of course, be very agreeable to write an Introduction, and can do so in the first week of July – provided you can lend me a copy. My own disappeared from my shelves years ago, but I succeeded in getting another about a couple of years ago and find that that has now vanished too.

Please excuse a very brief reply. I am desperately busy just now. It was good to see you again, if too briefly, in Glasgow. Best wishes to Mamie and yourself, and all your family.

You'll be sorry to know that Peggy died on 8th inst after a very brief illness.

All the best. Yours, Chris

24. *To Henry Rago, Editor,* Poetry Chicago *(LLIU)*

20 June 1962

Dear Sir: –

Mr Emile Capouya of the Macmillan Company, New York, has forwarded me your letter of 11th inst. I regard it as a very great honour to be invited to contribute to your Golden Anniversary number. First of all, however, let me congratulate all concerned on this jubilee and express my warmest appreciation of the very great service *Poetry* has rendered to literature in these fifty years, and along with that my hope that it may go on into its second half-century with every encouragement and success.

Having said that, I have pleasure in enclosing three poems.

(1) In Memoriam Dylan Thomas
(2) Speech, My Beloved (specially inscribed to *Poetry* for this occasion)
(3) Love and Death

in order that you may have a choice and in the hope that one of them may appeal to you.[1]

With heartiest congratulations and best wishes.

Yours sincerely, Hugh MacDiarmid

---

1. 'Speech, My Beloved' appeared in *Poetry*, October-November 1962.

25. To Barbara Niven (NLS)

6 July 1962

Dear Barbara

Very many thanks for the typescript of your article. You could not fail to be perceptive – and clear in the expression of it – if you tried, but as you yourself say, this is not the quintessential statement of which you – almost alone – are capable. How should it be, having regard to the conditions under which you did it? These things take time, concentration, peace in which to mature. But there is something more. I know myself how much more difficult, almost impossible, it is to express what is closest to one's heart than to write on a subject in which one is less involved. I have been quite unable to do any sort of justice to him and to myself on F.G. Scott, for example, and quite recently for another very old and close friend I found a way out. We had collected essays on the composer Sorabji for a *Festschrift* for him, and finally Ronald Stevenson (another composer), John Ogdon the great pianist who recently won the Tchaikowsky Prize in Moscow, and I got together and simply had a three-cornered talk which we tape-recorded. This was quite spontaneous. We wanted it as a final chapter for the book if it turned out all right. It did. You would hardly believe how well. We were all in good form and spoke fully and freely – and our respective contributions to the talk fitted in wonderfully. I believe in the same way if instead of writing it you had just talked about my work, with someone else to ask a question occasionally and draw you out the result would have surprised you – as this Sorabji one surprised Stevenson, Ogdon, and I. However as I say there are things in this essay of yours which could only have come from you and I am very appreciative of your understanding and our community of insight.

I have just been reading page-proofs of all the dozen or more essays in the *Festschrift* for myself. Some of them are very good. But there is one by Dr David Craig on my Marxism which he finds not altogether satisfactory. He complains it is too abstract – and, as reflected in my poetry, lacks the pressure of actual social life. Also it is contradictory. As to that of course I'd be sorry if it weren't – a lack of contradictions, changes of opinion, etc. in half-a-century would simply mean an absence of mental activity and development. But why do fellows like that fail to give credence to what one says oneself. All the points he makes against my Marxism are completely covered by what I said long ago in *Lucky Poet*, viz. 'As a Socialist, of course, I am, it should be obvious, interested only in a very subordinate way in the politics of Socialism as a political theory; my real concern with Socialism is as an artist's organised approach to the interdependencies of life'.

Valda tells me she has just written you in reply to your query re evening dress. Well I just don't know. I have been told that the CP, the PEN Club, and others will be giving me parties – but not one of them yet has advised me of the date of any party. And how they expect to fit them in at the last moment I simply can't imagine. It is a perfectly absurd – and very worrying state of affairs. I think the actual presentation of the portrait is to be on the 11th of August (my actual birthday), and that will be the main function. However I wouldn't worry about it – Ern and you will be OK at any thing that's going no matter in what garb you present yourselves. I'm doing my damnedest to get all sorts of things finished now to leave me as free as possible: but demands keep pouring in – latest for an article comparing Mayakovsky and Yevtushenko. I've just got from the Polish PEN a volume of tributes to Mickiewicz by writers from most European countries. Britain is represented by C.V. Wedgwood, Storm Jamieson, Jack Lindsay, and myself.[1] I say nothing of the articles: but photos of the contributors are in the book – and I defy you to deny that I'm the best looking of the lot. So there!

Love. Yours, Chris

---

1. 'MacDiarmid' in *Pisarze Swiata Mickiewiczowi: glosy wspólczesnych pisarzy zaproszonych przez* PEN Club Polski zebral i wstepem proprzedil Jan Parandowski (Warszawa: Czytelnik, 1962).

26. *To Hugo Moore (EUL)*

26 July 1962

Dear Hugo

I should of course have written you long ago (I am horrified to see just how long ago) and you probably feel you've had a raw deal. But then you can't have any idea just how infernally busy I've been – and remain. This next month is going to be an absolute crusher – so much so that I've decided if I survive it never to have a 70th birthday again.

Even so I could have sent you a line – if I hadn't mislaid your typescript and accompanying letter and consequently hadn't your address. This was due to the upset here caused by the reconstruction process and installation of mod. cons. – a job I was told would take 3 weeks, but has actually taken eleven months. It's finished now but even so I can't find all sorts of books and papers. Your article was, I thought, and think, absolutely first-rate – certainly a good deal better than several of those actually included in the *Festschrift*. But Kulgin thought it 'didn't fit in' and I was not in a position to override his decision. He did say however that if you were agreeable he'd publish it as a separate pamphlet. I told him I was strongly in favour of this. Whether he suggested that to you I don't know. Anyhow he probably hasn't been able to do it so far, because with the cost of publishing the *Festschrift* and other things he is lying [*sic*] out of a devil of lot of money now and his resources must be at a low ebb.

The *Festschrift* itself will be an excellent book. The photographs have come up splendidly and the book should be out in a few days' time now.

Other things are developing. I'm addressing the Writers' Conference at Edinburgh Festival on 21st August, and Ian Finlay, Jessie McGuffie, and their friends have got police permission to have a protest march from the Mound to the McEwan Hall, where they hope to stage an anti-MacDiarmid demonstration.[1]

Hope things are going OK with you. I've been unable to find anyone who could tell me how you're faring.

Valda joins me in every kind regard.

Yours, Chris

---

1. Jessie McGuffie and Ian Hamilton Finlay were co-founders of the Wild Hawthorn Press and the anti-establishment poetry broadsheet *Poor, Old, Tired, Horse* (1961–70). McGuffie had said that CMG's poetry was hopelessly provincial and out of touch with contemporary life and Finlay that everyone he knew under the age of forty was bored stiff by MacDiarmid. CMG responded in a pamphlet, *the ugly birds without wings* (Edinburgh: Allan Donaldson, 1962), collected in *Albyn: Shorter Books and Monographs*, ed. Alan Riach (Manchester: Carcanet, 1996).

27. *To James Burns Singer (NLS)*

18 September 1962

Dear Jimmie

Sorry to have been so long in writing to thank you for the *Observer* profile and your review of my poems in the *Listener*. But you'll understand I've been submerged for weeks under the avalanche of cards, letters, and telegrams my birthday evoked, and then the Edinburgh Festival, Writers' Conference, and radio, TV, and miscellaneous speaking engagements resulted in a monstrous piling-up of arrears in replying to correspondence. However I thank you now, also for the information re the killer whale (I'll correct that poem when I can). Michael Peto has given me your Cambridge address. I hope all goes well with you, and with your wife.

Valda joins me in every kind regard.

Yours, Christopher Grieve

28. *To Oliver Brown (NLS)*

30 October 1962

Dear Oliver

What you say of Frenssen's book and *Sunset Song* is a fair puzzle.[1] I am pretty sure Gibbon didn't read German and the idea that he plagiarised from Frenssen is certainly inconsistent with his statement (and his wife supports it) that *Sunset Song* was the product of an upsurge of memory so overwhelming that he could hardly keep pace with it and get it written down. His widow – Mrs Ray Mitchell – went to New Zealand some months ago and I don't know if she is back yet. Her address is 34 Attemore Road, Welwyn Garden City, Herts. The German translation of *Scots Quhair* [sic] is on the way but I don't think it has been published yet. I should have thought the publishers' editorial staff (i.e. the German publishers) would have spotted the likeness you mention to Frenssen's work.

Yes, I read German and will be very interested to see the MSS. While I have survived all the incredible hullaballoo of my 70th birthday, I am still terribly busy, with meetings in next week or thereby in Edinburgh, Glasgow, Duns, Durham – and all sorts of writing commitments too.

Hope Margaret and you are OK and your family too. Love to you all.
Yours, Chris

---

1. Gustav Frenssen (1863–1945). The novel refered to is *Jorn Uhl* (1901).

29. *To Sorley MacLean (NLS)*

4 December 1962

Dear Sorley,

It is a long time (far too long!) since I was in touch with you. I hope this note finds Renée and yourself, and the children (hardly children now – they must be well grown up) in the best of health.

The occasion for my writing is this. An Irish friend of mine, resident in Barcelona, (his name is Pearse Hutchinson) has just written me a long letter in the course of which he says: 'You may or may not have seen a 1956 number of the *London Magazine* with three poems I translated from the Catalan of Salvador Espriu. One of them. "Assaig de Càntic en el Temple", has become, here and elsewhere, his best-known poem. Partly because it's about the only one he's written that isn't in any way at all obscure. And partly because it says one of the last words possible about loving and hating a country. I believe it's a great poem, as I believe, with a growing number of people, both here and in other places, that Espriu is the best Spanish poet alive – or, certainly, in Spain. His last book, *La Pell de Brau* (i.e. *The Bull's Hide*) 1961, which is a 54–poem sequence, and which I've just finished translating – we're now negotiating with the only decent publishers in Ireland, the Dolmen Press, to see will they handle it – is not only almost beyond dispute the finest poetry written in Spain since the Civil War, but has quickly become a rallying-point, a home, a hope, for every young or red creature here with life and spirit left or in sight. It's a very angry poem and a very disciplined one. I read six poems from it at the British Institute here in March. The Catalans and the Irish came in force, but the Director (he's an "educationist") couldn't come to meet the poets; he was taking some visiting doctors golfing! ... Now, the point is: a young publisher, called Santiago Albertó, is bringing out, as soon as possible, the *Collected Poems* of Espriu – all, including his last book, are out of print. And as a kind of appendix he's doing some twelve or so versions, each in a different language of the "Assaig de Càntic" – including my English one and an Irish one I printed in "Comhar" in 1958. (Espriu, by the way, said he didn't give a toss about being turned into English, but into Irish warmed his heart). And Alberti asked could I rustle up some other tongues. So I at once thought of you to put Lallans on it. And Somhairle MacGill-Eain for Scots Gaelic ...?'

Hutchinson goes on to say: 'The thing has only been sanctioned at the last minute and Alberti wants to get it out for Christmas if possible.'[1]

So the matter is urgent. I hope to do the Lallans version tomorrow or by Thursday at latest, and send it off to Hutchinson by air-mail.

I hope you will make a Scottish Gaelic rendering. Short and lucid tho' the poem is, translating from a language one doesn't know is a very chancy and questionable business, but as a help I enclose three other versions (in addition to Hutchinson's English one), viz. Castilian by José Augustín Goytisolo, French by Jordi Sarsanedas, and Espriu's Catalan original.

Pearse Hutchinson's address is En Casa de Sra. Soques, Nilo Fabra 12–2–2, Barcelona 12, Spain.

All the best. Yours, Chris

---

1. Salvador Espriu, *Obra Poetica* (Barcelone: S Alberti, 1963).

30. *To Charles Nicoll (EUL)*

5 December 1962

Dear Mr Nicol

I had meant to write you months ago to say how pleased I was with the reproduction in *Festschrift* of your photographs. But the circumstances attending my 70th birthday in August were absolutely overwhelming. I got hundreds of telegrams, letters, and cards from all over the world, numerous radio and TV engagements, journalistic commissions, and (in addition to the essays in *Festschrift*) there were articles in all sorts of papers and periodicals at home and abroad. Besides all that, there were birthday parties and speaking engagements. Fortunately I was in good form, but you may well imagine that I had cause to compare all this frantic hullaballoo with the comparative peace of Mechan's. How time goes! It is incredible that it is already so long ago since I was busy with copper shell bands under your kindly supervision.

As you have probably seen from the papers, in the interval since I last saw you and Mrs Nicol in Buchanan Street I have been all over the place – Russia, Siberia, China, Bulgaria, Rumania, Hungary, Czechoslovakia. And of course there has had to be a steady output of books, pamphlets, poems and articles. It is a busy life – indeed I have been busier since I retired than I ever was in the preceding 65 years!

I am very seldom in Glasgow – and then briefly, just to address some meeting, and get the next bus home. Both Valda and I are in good fettle: and in August I had all my seven grandchildren here.

I wonder how you, and Mrs Nicol, and your family have been keeping – and whether you are still working, or retired too?

Hoping to see you again some time, and with every good wish to you and yours.

Gratefully yours, Christopher Grieve

31. *To John Laidlaw (EUL)*

6 December 1962

Dear Cousin John

Many thanks for your long letter received today. I quite understood the trouble it causes you to indite such an epistle. I have a huge mail myself and try as far as possible to reply by return, but every now and again some letter calls for a lengthy and carefully considered answer and sometimes it is not convenient to write that immediately. As a result, it occasionally happens that time slips by in the annoying way time has and I find that I have failed to reply for too long. I have not your excuse – but on the other hand my correspondence is not only very extensive and international in character but often concerns intricate and difficult matters which just can't be disposed of in a hurry. As a rule, however, I don't manage too badly, but the tremendous influx of letters etc. last August did beat me, and I have a considerable backlog to answer yet – if ever!

I am very sorry indeed to hear of your various mishaps and attendant difficulties but glad you have made a fair recovery from the worst of these and hope you may long continue to do so.

I am grateful to you for the two photographs. The little one with me as an infant is one I particularly wanted. My mother had a copy of it of course but when she died my brother collared all her effects and I have not been in touch with him for many years now. I heard indirectly from someone who knows him that he had recently had a thrombosis. He is about 18 months younger than I am, and is, of course, retired now from the Customs & Excise. He lives somewhere in the South of England I think.

On the bigger photograph I recognised all but a few of the group without the aid of your key, and to see their faces again conjured up a host of memories.

I'll write Jean White one of these days. She must have had a busy time too, with the tradesman doing up the house, and her shop etc. Please give her our love.

As to the books if I hadn't sent them to you, you wouldn't have been able to get them now. The *Collected Poems* (with the American and the United Kingdom editions) and the *Festschrift* are sold out: The *Collected Poems* will of course be reprinted but it may be some time before it is on the market again.

As you probably saw, five programmes of selections from my translation of a big Swedish poem were broadcast recently on the Third Programme. This translation hasn't been published yet but will be in the beginning of February.

Valda and I are both well tho' we had a tough time during the recent snow-storm when we were completely blocked up for several days. No buses were able to get through even in the main road and telephone communication was broken out, which was a nuisance as I should have been at a couple of meetings in Glasgow and couldn't even inform the organisers so that they could get a substitute speaker.

Speaking is one of my main occupations. I had several days recently in Berwickshire – at Gifford, Hoddington, Duns etc. – lecturing for the Extra Mural Department of Edinburgh University. Next Wednesday (12th December) I am addressing the Publicity Club of Edinburgh, and I have all sorts of other engagements looming up – and, of course, the usual crop of Burns Suppers in January. But I like that sort of thing and it helps to keep me going.

Michael and Deirdre continue to do well on the Scottish *Daily Express* and little Christopher (now 2) is in fine fettle.

I'll seize the first chance I can to come down to Langholm and see you – but that won't be now till after the end of January.

In the meantime, thanks again for your letter and the photos. Valda joins me in warmest regards and best wishes.

Yours, Chris

32. *To David Daiches (EUL)*

17 December 1962

Dear David Daiches

Many thanks for your letter. I consider myself very fortunate in that friends of the calibre of Robin Lorimer[1] and yourself are willing to explore the possibilities, and if it can be arranged undertake, a complete edition of my poems. The Macmillan Oliver & Boyd book is really shockingly full of errors of all kinds. Incidentally it has sold out both here and in America. The *Festschrift* has sold well too – between 700 and 800 copies to date.

Yes. I was very sorry Mrs Daiches and yourself and the children didn't manage out here, but of course I understood how busy you were. I haven't recovered yet from the birthday celebrations – articles continue to appear in all sorts of quarters, and I am still choc-a-bloc with speaking engagements.

Incidentally I haven't had time since August but I hope after January to be able to get down to writing a lot more poetry. I've had the ideas in my mind for a long time now. Poems in Lallans, I mean. So I hope to add another big section to the eventual labours of the editors of my Works.

I hope this finds you all fine and flourishing, and that all good fortune may be yours in 1963.

Yours, Christopher Grieve

---

1. Robin Lorimer, director of the Edinburgh publishing company Oliver and Boyd.

33. *To Edwin Morgan*

8 January 1963

Dear Mr Morgan

I'd have written you sooner but I had heard you'd moved to a new address. Kulgin Duval promised to send me that address some weeks ago, but I have only this morning received it. So, belatedly, I send you my best wishes for 1963.

What I meant to write you about was to thank you for your articles about my poetry in *Festschrift* and elsewhere. These were certainly among the very best evoked by my birthday. Particularly I think the one on my later poetry. I had heard too about your article in the *Glasgow Herald*, but did not manage to receive a copy of it until recently. It, too, was, I thought, excellent and certainly most encouraging. But I haven't had time yet to read systematically through all the articles published at home and abroad – over 30 of them, and they are still coming in.

I have been looking for (or news about) your *Anthology*, which I had thought would be published long ere this, not that I am unfamiliar with publishers' delays. Only it seems an inordinately long time since I first heard about this.[1]

I hope all's well with you. We've been for the last week or two – and still are – snow-blocked here and I've been unable, owing to transport difficulties (impossibilities, rather) to fulfil various speaking engagements, and now on the verge of the annual Burns Suppers I'm hoping things may clear away and let me get about.

With kindest regards, Yours, Christopher Grieve

---

1. *Collins Albatross Book of Longer Poems: English and American Poems from the Fourteenth Century to the Present Day*, ed. Edwin Morgan (London: Collins, 1963).

34. To Ronald Stevenson (NLS)

12 March 1963

Dear Ronald

Long time no' see! As you'd know we had a terrible time here with snow etc. – no water in house still since 12th January; boiling snow for washing water etc. I'd have been over to see you or in touch anyhow ere this but I've been and remain incredibly busy. Valda and I go to London tomorrow for the Foyle Poetry Prize presentation and will be there till 18th–19th inst. I'll be on BBC TV in *Tonight* programme on 14th. Then back to Carlisle for Border TV interview on 19th, and then to Hamilton to address Scottish Library Assocn. Today we're going into Edinburgh where a Dominican priest, Father Anthony Ross, is lecturing on my poetry.[1]

Michael has recovered well from his motor smash. He was virtually scalped but his head wounds have healed up nicely, as have the gashes on both his legs. His right arm is still in plaster of Paris, however, owing to fractured wrist.

Hope all has been well with Marjorie and yourself and the children. What developments re South Africa? Don't go away without seeing us. You'd see that I agreed when Lord Harewood wrote me to take part (by way of reading the text of my lyrics set by F.G.) in concert in Leith Town Hall on last day of Festival.[2] It was to be mainly an F.G. programme. But since then I've learned Kenneth McKellar and others, including Robin Hall, Jimmie McGregor, Jimmy Shand and his band are taking part. What chances will my lyrics or F.G.'s settings have in that milieu? The *Sunday Express* gave a column to the thing, with the photos of principal participants alongside, and the whole under the appropriate heading, 'Introducin' Hoochin' for the Festival'. Nothing was further from my mind, of course, and I've written to Harewood protesting – but haven't heard from him again yet. God! I feel like emigrating to Africa too – Scotland is just too bloody awful for words.

I wonder if you see Ian Nicol if you could drop a word to him saying I'd like the books I lent him in August back. They include Leavis, Pound, Rosenthal.

All the best. Yours, Chris

Hope you've managed to finish the Ben Dorain to your satisfaction.

---

1. Father Anthony Ross (b.1917), Roman Catholic scholar and social reformer, superior in the Dominican Chaplaincy in Edinburgh, 1959–77.
2. George Henry Hubert Lascelles Harewood, Seventh Earl (b.1923), English patron of the arts, artistic director of the Edinburgh International Festival, 1960–5.

35. *To John Laidlaw (EUL)*

18 March 1963

Dear Cousin John

I had meant to write you before this, but we've been blocked up here by snow-drifts, without water for five or six weeks, and obliged to boil snow for washing water — while for drinkable water we've had to carry buckets-full from a nearby farm in so far as we could get to and from that in knee-deep snow. And of course all this had played Old Harry with all sorts of speaking and other engagements. Still, despite difficulties and lack of transport etc. I've managed to get about quite a lot.

I wonder how this severe winter has affected you. I hope you've been keeping as well as possible, and not been wholly confined to the house.

I don't know whether my letter in reply to the remarks made by the Provost, Town Clerk, etc. about John Ritchie's proposal that I should be given the Freedom of Langholm appeared in the E & L [*Eskdale & Liddesdale Advertiser*] or not, but if it did — and if there was any other stuff about it in the paper — I'd be very glad if you could send me copies.

As matters stand, honours continue to be showered upon me and I have just had word that the Foyle Poetry Prize of £250 is to be awarded to me at a luncheon in London on 14th March. Valda and I are going to fly down for that.

I should have written Jean before this too, but continue to be quite incredibly busy.

Still, later on, I hope I'll be able to give myself the Freedom of Langholm and come down and see you again.

With best wishes. Yours affectionately, Chris

P.S. You may have seen in the papers or heard about Michael's serious accident on 9th inst. He — and another journalist, features editor of the Glasgow *Record* — had been at a Burns Supper in Leith at which I was speaking — and were motoring back to Glasgow. They had got to the outskirts of the city when the car skidded on ice, smashed into a lamp-post, and burst into flames. Fortunately they were ejected through the doors, and a police patrol was close-by. So the police dragged them clear and got them into an ambulance and into Glasgow Royal Infirmary as speedily as possible. Both had multiple injuries. Michael was virtually scalped, the top of his head just hanging like a flap. Also he had his right wrist broken, his teeth smashed out, and leg injuries. He is out of hospital now less I think because he should be than because of the shortage of beds. Still if he has a good convalescence he should be all right. The other fellow had a depression of the skull, pressing on the brain, and did not recover consciousness for nearly a week, and is still very confused and foolish. It was a hairsbreadth escape for both. Chris

36. *To Jean White (EUL)*

23 March 1963

Dear Jean

Many thanks for your fine long letter. Valda and I just got back from London a couple of days ago. We had a really splendid time – but a very exhausting one, as, in addition to the Presentation and Luncheon, and private engagements, I had a couple of sound radio interviews and a TV one in London, had to get back to Carlisle for a TV interview there, and then to Hamilton to address a Scottish Library Association Conference.

I am very sorry indeed John Laidlaw isn't so chipper. I must get down to see him as soon as possible, but can't say yet just when I'll be able to. I continue extremely busy. Amongst other things I had to write no fewer than 21 articles for a *Spanish Encyclopaedia of World Literature*, and these have to be received by the editors in Barcelona within the next three weeks. Even if I had only these to do it would take me all my time. So I am afraid I can't manage down until about the end of April or even the beginning of May. But I'll let you know as soon as the way is clear. Michael has made an excellent recovery from his many injuries (tho' his right arm is still in plaster of paris) but he is back at work. He flew over to Spain for 4 days investigating the whisky distillery business there; perhaps you saw the three articles about it he had in the Scottish *Daily Express*. He arrived back at London Airport while we were there and met us down town and spent a few hours with us.

It is very good of you to invite us down and you may be sure that sleeping under an unpainted ceiling won't disturb us in the least. We've slept in some queer places in the course of the last thirty years.

Please give my love to John and say we hope to see him ere long.

Re the *E & L*'s for which many thanks, I was amused to read the letters re the Freedom. In any case you may be sure I'll keep my own freedom: but I don't intend to write any more in reply – just let the thing fizzle out.

Kindest regards to Jim and Willy and their wives, and to yourself from Valda and I.

Yours affectionately, Chris

37. *To Jean White (EUL)*

17 April 1963

Dear Jean

I see from the paper today that you are again standing as a candidate for the Council. Here's wishing you the best of luck.

As you probably know rather than allow the Council to reject the proposal that I should be given the Freedom of the Burgh I wrote to the Town Clerk saying that if it were offered to me I would refuse it. I understand the Council accepted my refusal.

The weather is still very patchy. Cold and wet. I have to go to Aberdeen on 6th May for a TV programme. But if it is convenient to you Valda and I would like to come down to Langholm for a day or two, either later that week or the following week.

Hope all's well with you and with Cousin John. Our visit to Langholm need not of course prevent you bringing John up here. I have engagements in Edinburgh on 19th and 20th of this month and a BBC recording session here on 23rd and another Edinburgh engagement on 4th May and again on 12th May.

With kindest regards, Yours affectionately, Chris

38. *To Jean White (EUL)*

18 April 1963

Dear Jean

Postscript to letter I posted this morning. The *Daily Express* people want to do a pictorial feature of me in my native town, so we'll probably be down on Monday, arriving between midday and 1pm. The matter is not definitely certain yet but almost arranged. And amongst other things they'd like to take a photo of Cousin John along with me. I don't know if he'll be willing and fit but I hope so. So this is just a hurried note so that you can tell him to be ready and looking his prettiest. And of course the same applies to you too.

All the best from Valda and I.

Affectionately, Chris

39. *To Jean White (EUL)*

27 May 1963

Dear Jean

I hope you have recovered from the upset to your way of life as a consequence of our invasion of Eldon. I should have written you sooner, but there is little need, I hope, to say how grateful Valda and I – and Janey – are to you and how much we enjoyed our holiday with you and the excursions to Eskdalemiur, Tarras, Crowdieknowe, New Abbey etc. No sooner was she back here than Valda plunged into an elaborate spring-cleaning, which, to my disgust, is not quite finished yet. As for myself I resumed my usual carry-on, with piles of correspondence to tackle, and then, on Saturday, I took part in the big Anti-Polaris demonstration at Holy Loch. I stayed the night with Michael in Glasgow. He tells me, to our disappointment, that the photos he took of John Laidlaw and me did not come out well at all. The light, as we remarked at the time, was bad. Deirdre is in Switzerland, on an *Express* assignment with one of the staff photographers. They are not expected back until Wednesday at earliest. I'll be writing John ere long. I hope he was none the worse of the excitement of my visit.

The weather is still pretty broken and uncertain, but today here is sunny and warm.

I notice in one of the Edinburgh papers that the office bearers of the Langholm branch of the SNP have been appointed and that you are Vice-Chairman. Good. I hope the membership swells and that you are able to make yourself felt in the counsels of the Party.

With renewed thanks and every kind regard from Valda and myself.

Yours affectionately, Chris

40. *To Cousin Ann (EUL)*

29 May 1963

Dear Cousin Ann

It was nice to revisit Laurie's Close the other week and see Dave, Ad, and you after all these years. I was sorry Dave was not so well and suffering with his back. I saw Waddy too in Langholm. I had meant to come out to Laurie's Close again but I was hard pressed for time. My son Michael, and his wife, and little son came to Langholm but Michael hadn't his own car – he had had to put it in for repairs. However we did run out to Crowdieknowe one day in Jean White's car and took some photos. We'd meant to call in on you, but I had an engagement to keep in Langholm with some American writers and time didn't permit. However Valda and I hope to be down again at Langholm Common-Riding time and we'll hope to be able to see you then. The same goes for Wat at New Abbey. All the best to you all.

Yours, Chris

41. *To John Laidlaw (EUL)*

17 July 1963

Dear John Laidlaw

This is going to be only a very short note. I believe you have your 90th birthday tomorrow (18th) and Valda and I send you our congratulations and best wishes. I know you smoke and I believe this is the kind of tobacco to which like myself you are addicted, but when I was asked what sort of pipe you used I hadn't any idea, so the enclosed 'cheek-warmer' is the one with which Valda returned from her shopping expedition. I hope it serves the purpose.

With love from us both and looking forward to seeing you again at Common-Riding.

Yours, Chris

42. To Jean White (EUL)

1 August 1963

Dear Jean

Michael and I enjoyed our trip to the Common-Riding very much and got back safe and sound, calling in on my cousins at Laurie's Close on the way, and also on another old friend I hadn't seen for about 60 years.

I hope John was none the worse of his sojourn in the Market Place and posing for the camera. I haven't seen Michael since we got back, so don't know yet how the photos turned out.

I was particularly pleased to see Jim and Betty again, both of them looking so well.

On 14th Valda and I are going down to Newcastle-on-Tyne for a few days to attend an exhibition of paintings by a friend of mine. Today Valda is in Biggar at the annual Agricultural Show. Most years since we came here show day has been pouring wet. Today is an exception, with brilliant sunshine. She went off about 10am and won't be back before 8pm at earliest. She enjoys these things and won't leave till she has savoured all the fun of the fair – merry-go-rounds, coconut shies, and all the rest of it.

Apart from thanking you for your kindness again, the purpose of this note is that there was something I think I forgot to mention to you – that I have not had any word at all from Beattie's about the cleaning and re-lettering of the gravestone.

Love from Valda and I. Yours, Chris

43. To Duncan Glen (EUL)

2 August 1963

Dear Mr Glen

I was very pleased to get your letter this morning. I would have written you long ere now but I could not find your Glasgow address and I was not sure what the position might be with Messrs Gibson. I had heard they had removed to a new address and also that there had been some sort of take-over or amalgamation with some bigger firm. So I am glad to gather that my fears for your security have been unfounded. I can well imagine that you will be glad to get a house of your own again.

I am not surprised that 'Poetry like the Hawthorn' has gone so well – and without advertising. The same thing happened with the *Festschrift*, also with *The Kind of Poetry I Want*, despite the high cost of the latter. And of course Macmillans New York and Oliver & Boyd in this country completely underestimated the demand. They could have sold twice or thrice the number they made available. Yes. I hope they will issue a second edition soon now. I keep getting letters from people unable to get copies and as a last resource invoking my aid.

The last people in the world whose opinion I'd ask on any publishing proposition are Messrs Menzies. They are incredibly mean and myopic. But I am surprised that Penguin Books' advice re the American sales prospects of your projected anthology was so discouraging. My advices are all to the contrary. I have a large number of American contacts and they all speak of the large and unsatisfied demand for my work – and Scottish literature generally – in USA. This last week or so I've had three American professors here. Well implemented with funds for the purpose they all made back purchases of Scottish books for their University libraries. Perhaps you've seen the first issue of the *Studies in Scottish Literature* quarterly edited by Professor Ross Roy, who was one of my visitors. Other publishers seem to have been advised differently. I know the Oxford University Press have commissioned Tom Scott and a man McQueen, a lecturer at Edinburgh University, to prepare a comprehensive anthology of the whole range of Scottish poetry in Scots, Gaelic, and English from the beginning up to the present day. That involves a big capital investment, but I have no doubt whatever it will amply justify itself.

I am delighted that Chambers are going ahead with your book – albeit in somewhat reduced form. I hope they make up for lost time yet and get it out before Kenneth Buthlay's study in Oliver and Boyd's paperback series. This has been delayed. It was originally intended to have it out in the Spring, but now it is scheduled for publication in March. Louis Simpson, the American poet (whose study of James Hogg, the Ettrick Shepherd was published recently by Oliver & Boyd) is at work on a critical study of my poetry but this will not be ready for two or even three years.

One of the things I wanted to write you about is the Claude Henry thesis. Can you please send this back to me? I realise of course that in the course of 'flitting' and not yet being settled with a home of your own you may not yet be wholly unpacked and it may be difficult for you to lay your hands on this in the meantime. In that case please don't worry, but if it is convenient I'll be glad to have it back.

I need say no more than I have said before about your generosity, but simply thank you for your cheque.

Re the two poems you think of republishing, which you say appeared in *Poetry Review* in the 40s, I am afraid I don't remember just what they were. But of course I'll be very pleased if you reissue them in the form you describe.[1]

With warmest regards and good wishes to you all.

Yours, Christopher Grieve

---

1. Hugh MacDiarmid, *Poetry Like the Hawthorn. From In Memoriam James Joyce* (Hemel Hempstead: Duncan Glen, 1962). Limited to 150 copies. *Two Poems: The Terrible Crystal; A Vision of Scotland* (Skelmorlie: Duncan Glen, 1964). Limited to 55 copies.

44. To Alan Bold (NLS)

23 August 1963

Dear Alan Bold

Many thanks for your letter and the excellent essay on the paintings by Moffat and Bellany. I expect to be in Edinburgh this incoming week, and see them and a few other things. As you know I'm reading poems at the Concert in Leith Town Hall on 7th Sept. Also in the Regent Halls on 30th August. Meantime like yourself I've had to become art critic too. I wrote a longish essay for the catalogue of a one-man show by William Johnstone given in the Stone Gallery, Newcastle-on-Tyne. Unfortunately I haven't a copy to send you, but if you see K.D. Duval (who was there too), I think he'd give you one. Also for Tyneside & Tees BBC TV Johnstone and I walked round the paintings and I talked about them. An American poetess for whom I have a high regard and with whom I have corresponded for over 20 years but had not met before was there too; her name is Muriel Rukeyser.[1]

I certainly enjoyed the wedding reception. Please give my greetings to your wife (and to your mother), and once again I wish you both all happiness.

Please excuse this short note but I am as usual desperately busy. I never got M.L. Rosenthal's book back but I think Ian Nicol is bringing it out on Saturday. I hope so. I want to have another look at it before Rosenthal arrives – about 8th September I think.[2]

Yours, Christopher Grieve

---

1. Muriel Rukeyser (1913–80), politically active American poet, often doing extensive personal research into the areas of neglect and injustice which informed her poetry.
2. Macha Louis Rosenthal (1917–96), Professor of English at New York University, 1961–87, prolific critic of modernist poetry, friend to CMG and instrumental in arranging his reading at the New York Poetry Center (1967).

45. To John Ogdon (EUL)

23 August 1963

Dear Mr Ogdon

How kind of you to write me. I would like very much to be able to attend Mrs Ogdon's recital on 22nd Sept, but I am afraid it is impossible. I have a very busy time in prospect, especially in October and November, and I must devote the second half of September to preparing lectures etc. I am consoled however by the hope of hearing you both at the Chamber Concert in Leith Town Hall on 5th September. I am myself reading poems there on 7th September; the programme is one mainly of Francis George

Scott's settings of lyrics by Burns and by myself.

I haven't heard from Ronald since he went to South Africa and miss him. Also, I have been anxious to know if he has made any progress with the book about Sorabji.[1] I hope you are right and that now he may indeed receive the appreciation he ought to have. When I saw him last he was busy on a setting of my translation of the Gaelic poet, Duncan Ban MacIntyre's poem on Ben Dorain. I'd like to know how he has got on with that. But of course he'll have been very busy settling into his new job, and new home.

Best wishes for your trip to the USSR again.

My wife joins me in kindest regards to Mrs Ogdon and yourself.

Yours sincerely, Christopher Grieve

---

1. This book was not published.

46. *To Christine Macintosh*

3 September 1963

My dear Christine

I was very glad to have your letter-card, and, later, Elspeth's. But sorry to hear of Alistair's virus infection. I hope he is OK again by the time you get this. I'll write to Elspeth shortly, but am as usual extremely busy. I've taken part in one poetry reading at the Edinburgh Festival and have to figure in another on 7th inst. Valda and her friend Maisie Graham from the North-West Territory in Canada, used up all my tickets between them, while my share of the on-goings was mainly to welcome all sorts of visitors here, mainly American and Canadian Professors. Also Valda and I were at a one-man show of the paintings of a friend of mine at Newcastle-on-Tyne, and there I met an American poetess with whom I'd corresponded for some thirty years but hadn't met before. Muriel Rukeyser, she and her son were here on Saturday, as were Walter and Ann. Michael looked in too and met Walter for the first time. He and Deirdre and Christopher are just off to Andorra for a three weeks holiday.

One of the visitors too was my old friend Professor Barker Fairley of Toronto who was lamenting that you hadn't called on him and asked me to assure you that he and Mrs Fairley are very decent people who would give you a genuine welcome.

So all in all my 71st birthday has been almost as busy a time as my 70th. I think I'll just have to stop having birthdays. Amongst other things Mrs Rukeyser, and another friend here recently, also a poet, Professor Louis Simpson (who is writing a big critical study of my work – which he estimates will take him two years)[1] are determined to get me over to America and busy pulling all kinds of strings to that end. So I may look you up in

Georgetown yet. Last year we had a Novelist's Conference in Edinburgh, this year it's a Drama Conference, but next year it's to be a Poetry Conference in which I'm expected to take a prominent part, so I must see if an American trip is on that I keep the Festival period clear – i.e. the second half of August and first week of September.

I still hope to see Alistair and you here later this year. But in the meantime here's hoping Alistair has now fully recovered, that you are OK yourself, and with love to you all. Splendid showing on the part of the children. Yes, the genes may work that way. As I said in my *Autobiography* the literary strain which has culminated (so far) in me had been working in a smaller way in several generations of my folk, so it may well come to a fine and fuller development yet in one of your bairns.

Valda joins me in best wishes and kindest regards to you all.

Yours, Christopher

---

1. No large study by Louis Simpson appeared.

47. *To Christine Macintosh*

1 January 1964

Dear Christine

Apart altogether from your kind invitation your letter which reached me yesterday morning was the best Hogmanay gift I could possibly have had. I am glad Alistair is keeping better and hope he can find some way of shedding his work load a little. As to coming to Canada there's nothing we'd like better. Poets are impecunious people and it was the financial aspect which made me think that if the American trip came off I could visit you then too. But I've not heard any more yet about that. I couldn't do two separate trips of course – and since the people who are trying to arrange it for me have a lot of influence I must wait till I hear from them. Anyhow some time must elapse. I've had a bad spell with flu' these past two to three weeks and my work is consequently in arrears. Then I have contracted to translate a German play and the contract has a time/penalty clause, so I'd have to do that translation before I could leave. That applies also to a poem the Arts Council of Great Britain have commissioned me to write for Shakespeare's 400th Anniversary.[1] So April would be the earliest we could travel. Would that be all right for you? I do not like your paying half our airfares and am sure you have enough to do anyhow with your four children. If the German play translation came off – i.e. would duly [be] produced in both Britain and America – I'd make a lot of money, but that may be a year or two yet. The initial payment for the translation isn't much; real money only comes in the form of royalties if and when the play is produced. And if we are to come to Canada it had better be as soon as possible now. I'm not getting any younger. What you say about the life-span of Alistair's parents reminds me that my folk on both sides have been very long-lived – one grandfather 96, the other about 90. A cousin of mine who was (as a boy of 16) best man at my father and mother's wedding is 93. The exception was my father who died at 47, but that was not necessary – it was due to a doctor who was OK for wealthy and upper-class patients but had no use for working class ones. My father had never had an illness of any kind before he caught pneumonia at a funeral, was given morphine, and his heart gave out. On the whole at 72 I'm well enough, and like Alistair best when I'm almost overwhelmed with work. Amongst other things I'm addressing Nottingham University students in March and Walter is going to pick me up after the meeting (and after a subsequent sing-song and poetry-reading in a pub) and run me out to his home at Stourbridge. Valda too if she is with me but that depends on how things go – all sorts of things can happen in a couple of months, so it's impossible to make definite arrangements so far ahead. You'll know their little Angela had had a serious bout of pneumonia, but has I understand made an excellent recovery.

Visitors will be coming in shortly now and I'll be toasting you in (tell Alistair – I wish he were here to share it) Glenfiddich and if that runs out there's a whole bottle of Laphroaig in reserve.

Glad you had a nice visit with the Fairleys. He is really a tip-topper. Several of his books, especially on Goethe, are among the profoundest studies of a poet I know. I owe a lot to them.

Love to you all from Valda and I. We'll certainly be hoping to see you ere long.

Yours, Christopher

P.S. There's a friend of mine, George Emmerson, who returned to Canada a year or two ago. I've just had a Christmas card from him from London, Ontario, but he doesn't give me any address. He's a lecturer I think either at a university or some other higher educational establishment, but he's sure to be on the phone. I've no idea how far London may be from Georgetown but if your phone directory covers it I'd be very grateful if you could look it up and let me know so that I could write him. I am sure he's either a teacher of science or has a good post with some atomic energy establishment or something of that sort.

---

1. 'Virgilium Vidi Tantum' in *15 Poems for William Shakespeare*, ed. Eric W. White (Stratford-upon-Avon: Trustees and Guardians of Shakespeare's Birthplace, 1964).

48. To Paul Potts (UDL)

20 January 1964

Dear Paul

Glad to hear from you and hope 1964 is going to prove a good year for you.

I am very sorry if I omitted to answer a previous query of yours regarding Civil List Pensions.

I had nothing whatever to do with procuring mine and in fact did not know the matter was afoot until I received the letter from the Prime Minister's Office offering it to me.

There is certainly no such thing as applying for one. What has to be done is that some well-known people must recommend H.M. the Queen to grant one to such and such a person on the ground of the good work done by that person in Literature or Art or Music etc.

In my case my special sponsors were George Bernard Shaw, James Bridie (the playwright) and Compton Mackenzie. As a rule I think the letter has to be drawn up in proper form by a lawyer. That was certainly done in my case. Then I think the letter has to be sent to the Queen's Remembrancer at the Exchequer Office, tho' I think sending it to the Prime Minister's Office would serve just as well. Awards are notified in the London *Gazette* as part of the Honours List. The award is a life appointment and in recent years the amount given is increased to accord with the current cost of living.

I hope things are well with you. I haven't been in London for a long time but expect to be in the latter part of March when I've to give a lecture in Downing College, Cambridge University, I might have a day or two then in London, but not longer.

Valda and Michael join me in every kind regard.

Yours, Chris

49. To Edwin Morgan

24 February 1964

Dear Mr Morgan[1]

Can you please help me with the enclosed? i.e. tell me what it's all about, who it's from etc. It has just reached me by registered mail, so for anything I know it may call for a quick reply.

I am delighted to see your translations from Attila József in *Outcry*. I was very sorry to be unable to get to the Bowhill People's Burns Supper after all, and hope you had a good time there. With best wishes.

Yours sincerely, Christopher Grieve

---

1. The letter is addressed to Edwin Morgan, Esq., Lecturer in English Literature, The University, Glasgow.

50. *To Edwin Morgan*

3 March 1964

Dear Edwin Morgan,

I am compunctious at having let you in for such a task, but very grateful for the particulars about the letter from School No. 109, Kuibyshev (Volga). This will enable me to send in return an appropriate message but whether I can lay my hands on a photograph, let alone copies of one or more of my books, is another matter. I get a lot of demands of this kind but am chary of complying too much, save by simple acknowledgement. I really don't think activities of this kind are worth-while, any more than collecting autographs or Burns Supper menus signed up by the people at the Top Table.

With renewed thanks and best wishes.

Yours, Christopher Grieve

51. *To Barbara Niven (NLS)*

30 April 1964

Dear Barbara

As time passed, and no word, I was worrying in case you were ill or something. I knew of course you are always busy. However it's good to hear from you, and to know your 2 days off has now taken effect. Once you get used to this relief I've not the slightest doubt you'll be able to make good use of it.

I agree with you about the Buthlay book. I knew of course he was all in favour of my early lyrics and had little or no regard for my later work. But his book will serve as a useful introduction for many people unable to go deeply into anything.

The other book – *Hugh McD and The Scottish Renaissance* – is at least seven times bigger, and is packed with detail. The author has read I think everything I ever wrote – including letters to Editors, unsigned articles in local papers etc. etc. It won't be out till Autumn. You'll get a copy in due course.

I wish I'd been able to get to you in London or get you here. The publishers are very anxious to get a drawing of me for frontispiece – one of me as I am now (a doddering septuagenarian) and one that has not appeared anywhere before. They ruled out your drawing of me because it was of me as I was years ago, and also because it had appeared in various magazines etc. I think Willie Johnstone will draw one specially for this purpose – but he'll have to do it within the next day or two.

What you say of the rarity of dialectical understanding came home to me very much the other night. For some time I and others have been having a tremendous controversy in *The Scotsman* about folk-song. My main opponents were Hamish Henderson and David Craig. Finally a public debate was arranged in the Traverse Theatre Club in Edinburgh. I did not take it lightly but *thoroughly* prepared my speech. The general view is that it was probably the best speech I ever made. But I had paid Henderson and Craig the compliment of not underrating them. Well, they made an incredible poor showing. They had obviously completely underrated me, and simply hadn't a leg to stand on. I simply ridiculed them and left them completely exposed and defenceless. It was recorded and the BBC (Scottish Home Service – and Third Programme) are I believe going to broadcast a programme.

Canada is to be a real holiday. Both Valda and I need one badly – we are both suffering just now from post-vaccination malaise. Christine has arranged picnics to the Canadian lakes etc. I've only agreed to do two public engagements – one a lecture on Scottish Poetry in the University, Toronto, and the other to address a Peace meeting. I don't intend to take on any more, tho' I'll probably have TV and/or Sound Radio things to do.

All love to Ern and you.
Yours, Chris

52. *To Alexander Trocchi (HRHRC)*

8 June 1964

Dear Alexander Trocchi

I was in Canada for a month and only got back here on Saturday – to find your letter of 17th inst among my accumulated mail.

I cordially reciprocate all you say in your letter, and share your hope that next time you are in Scotland we can meet and discuss things. I do not know at the moment what the position is regarding the proposed 'unofficial conference' but I'll be in Edinburgh one day this week and hope to see Jim Haynes then and find out just what's afoot. I'll certainly help such a Conference in any way I can, and I'll be available personally, as I expect to be here – or in Edinburgh – all summer.

With best wishes to yourself.
Yours, Hugh MacDiarmid

P.S. The typescript of *Sigma* is with your letter, but I got an enormous bundle of held-over correspondence, not half of which I've digested yet. I'll read *Sigma* tonight or tomorrow, and if it calls for comment from me that won't wait till we meet, I'll write you again.[1]

---

1. 'Sigma, a Tactical Blueprint' was printed in *City Lights Journal*, no. 2, 1964. Sigma was Trocchi's project to create a worldwide network of intellectuals and artists designed to outflank traditional media outlets and 'evolve the technique of acting together to raise the whole tenor of daily living beyond the level of stock response'.

53. To Christine and Alastair Macintosh

16 June 1964

Dear Christine and Alastair

We got back all right and Michael met us at Prestwick with one of the *Daily Express* cars (his own being in dock at Motherwell with a cracked petrol pump). We went first to Glasgow, then on to Motherwell to collect his car – but one trouble followed another; his car wasn't ready – a new petrol pump was on the way; a half-hour or so had to be waited – then en route for Brownsbank he ran out of petrol. We were dead tired by the time we got here, and the next few days were mainly spent resting. Hence my delay in writing you – I hope you haven't worried at not hearing from us sooner.

When I left you at Toronto air-port, I said we'd never be able to thank you enough for all your kindness. I can't even now try to thank you enough. Suffice it to say that we had the most wonderful holiday of our lives and are tremendously grateful to you – and to all your circle of friends who were so kind to us – Esme and Ernest Ball, the Alcocks, the Farrars, Mabel, Mrs Crichton etc. Above all we appreciate the sacrifice Alasdair made in giving up so much of his time to us when he was so busy. I'll be writing the Fairleys, Professor Milner, and others now. But in addition to being terribly tired, my return here presented me with a host of problems with which I am just starting to cope. There was a monstrous accumulation of mail, including requests for lectures by Glasgow University Extra-Mural Department, Glasgow Secularist Society, Edinburgh Fabian Society etc. etc. – a plan for a fully-professional ½ hour film of me by Scottish Film Associates Ltd which includes in its directorate several of the best cinema people in Britain – and, of course, the inevitable demands for articles of various kinds. And now before the Edinburgh International Festival starts – and the influx of visitors from various countries that entails for us – I've to complete and get off a new translation of Brecht's *Threepenny Opera* and various other things.

I am not forgetting the things I promised to send you. The big book about me won't be ready till September. I was in Edinburgh the other day and finally approved the frontispiece – a very surrealistic drawing of me by William Johnstone. I have asked the publisher to send me a copy of *In Memoriam James Joyce* and will post this to you as soon as it comes to hand. And I've not forgotten the Saltire Flag for the motor-boat.

A curious reflection arises out of my contact with you two, and the children. It is generally believed that parental love is important and that parents should have a say in the development of their children. I have always doubted this, nevertheless nothing ever hurt me, or could have hurt me, so much as being kept out of touch all these years with you and Walter and denied the right to guide or keep you in any way. But what my visit to you has shown is that all my agony and worry over this was misplaced.

It is very questionable indeed if we hadn't been separated that my influence would have been good for you – as it has turned out without my influence you have grown up just what I could have hoped. And found yourself just the sort of husband I could have wished for you. In short the conclusion is the not very profound one – that 'all's well that ends well'!

In the mass of mail awaiting me there was no word from Walter. I hope all's well there. I'll try to write him now too.

Deirdre, Michael and Christopher were here for a couple of days until yesterday. Both the parents OK, but Christopher very difficult and demanding. A hundred Rorys would have been easier to deal with.

Please forgive this hurried and inadequate letter.

With renewed thanks and love to you all from Valda and Christopher

54. *To Ronald and Marjorie Stevenson (NLS)*

27 June 1964

Dear Ronald and Marjorie

Many thanks for your letter. I am very sorry indeed to hear of your resignation – but not surprised. When I said I thought you should go to S. Africa what I had in mind was your insecurity at Broughton and Walker's witch-hunting activities; also I thought that a spell there would improve your chances later of a University post and for that you might well succeed Chisholm as Professor (I thought he was due for early retirement – but apparently he has had an extension of his time). But as you know I also feared you'd have trouble with Chisholm. When I didn't hear from you (tho' I didn't expect to for a considerable time, since I knew you'd be busy enough settling in in your new sphere – and also busy enough with your own real work, e.g. your success at the concert), I began to fear that the reason might well be that being in contact with me might exacerbate your relations with Chisholm, since he had written me a shoal of letters suggesting I write libretti for him, give him songs of mine to set, etc., etc. – a host of suggestions that seemed to imply that I had no purposes of my own and would naturally be free to devote myself to collaboration with him. So I just did not reply to his letters at all. I had one from Lilias too – but did not reply to that either. I am very sorry to hear she has marital troubles – sorry for Mrs Scott's sake too – but then I did not think that marriage should ever have taken place; it was enough to make F.G. turn in his grave – and meant to me a repudiation by his widow and daughter of all he had stood for.

You may be sure I'll mention nothing to Bill McLellan, whom I never see nowadays anyhow. He and Chisholm are birds of a feather – destitute of spiritual integrity or any concern for or insight into the creative process.

I am as you requested returning the duplicate of your letter to Alan Bush[1] and can only hope that some suitable and worthwhile opening will turn up for you soon. I know of course how few and far between such openings are. And alas! Scotland has none. I'd have been glad if you'd been coming back to Scotland. We have missed you a great deal.

Valda and I were over in Canada for a month and had a splendid time – spending a good deal of it on the Muskoka complex of lakes where my son-in-law has a summer chalet and a motor-boat. It was purely a holiday and I refused various invitations to lecture, limiting myself to one lecture on Scottish Poetry at Toronto University, and one address at the Peace Centre in Toronto. But I met a host of friends and thoroughly enjoyed myself.

You will know that J.G. Sinclair of Broughton School has died. I think Thms Allan has succeeded him as head of the English Dept. and Deputy Head Master.

Things go on here much as usual. I'm still trying to read with the monstrous accumulation of mail I found awaiting my return here: and have a crowded programme of writing, speaking etc. now until the end of September, including of course the fact that all sorts of friends will be in Edinburgh over the Festival period – tho' the Festival Committee blue noses and the Moral Rearmament people managed to squash any idea of our running a Poet's Conference.

Keep in touch and let me know what your plans (and whereabouts) are.

With love and best wishes to both of you and the children, from Valda and I.

Yours, Christopher Grieve

---

1. Alan Bush (1900–95), Marxist Communist British composer. A poetry text entitled 'Cantata 1917–1977' by Hugh MacDiarmid and Alan Bush was published in the Marxist periodical *artery*, no.13 (Autumn-Winter 1977), pp.17–19, with parts for 'Solo singer and Choir', 'Man Speaker' and 'Woman Speaker'. It begins: 'The whole world is thrilling from pole to pole / With the first clear ray / Of the starry life of the earth that at last / Transfigures its clay…' and ends '…Oh, this is the time for all mankind / To rejoice without a doubt – / And break the neck of the bottle / If the cork will not come out!'

55. *To Alexander Trocchi (HRHRC)*

26 August 1964

Dear Mr Trocchi

Just got your telegram. I was at the Poet's Conference in the Traverse Theatre on Monday. I was also in Edinburgh yesterday on a BBC/TV job, but could get no word about you. I wrote Jim Haynes in the end of last week asking what the arrangements were but Jim, who is of course desperately busy, did not reply. Now alas I have shot my bolt and cannot get in to Edinburgh again. I've a job of writing to finish and then I have to go to London and will be there for several days. I am sorry about this mix-up which has prevented us meeting.

With best wishes. Yours sincerely, C.M. Grieve

56. *To D.G. Bridson (LLIU)*

9 September 1964

Dear Geoffrey

I am making one of my rare visits to London this weekend. I'll be there from Friday to Monday. On Saturday I may be tied up most of the day but should be free in the evening. On Sunday I'm one of the speakers at a Rally of Communist candidates in Hyde Park. I don't know whether you are in town or not, of course – you're more likely to be in Outer Mongolia or Brazil – but if you are available we might meet somewhere for a drink on Saturday evening. You could perhaps phone me and leave a message for me (I'll not likely be there myself) at Temple Bar 2151–5. Anyhow I hope Mrs Bridson and you are both OK and Valda joins me in every kind regard.

Yours, Christopher Grieve

57. *To Jean White (EUL)*

4 October 1964

Dear Jean

Home for the day to write some more speeches and make up – few arrears of correspondence, then back tomorrow to my vast constituency (second biggest in country – 8000 square miles, with only 4 people to square mile – incredibly feudal), but an area of incomparable scenery in this splendid weather.[1] I've a tremendous week before me, not only with indoor and outdoor speeches, but interviews with French and Belgian TV. There is no chance of denting Sir Alec's 10,000 majority, but I've been concentrating on denting his image and laying a foundation for future developments.

Hope things are going well for Gair. Best wishes to him.

Valda joins me in love to yourself, Yours, Chris

---

1. CMG contested Kinross and West Perthshire in the election of 15 October 1964 against the-then Prime Minister, Alec Douglas-Home. The poll was: Sir Alec Douglas-Home (Conservative) 16,659; A. Forrester (Labour) 4687; A. Donaldson (Scottish Nationalist) 3522; Dr C.M. Grieve (Communist) 127.

58. *To Mrs Mary K. Peddie, Miss Christian Mackay
and Miss A. Katherine Mackay (NLS)*

6 October 1964[1]

Dear Mesdames

Thank you for your letter of yesterday's date.

I cannot pledge myself to support legislation totally prohibiting the use of live animals in experiments involving pain. Scientific progress essential to human welfare may require some such experiments but these should be as few as possible and properly controlled, while the question of pain is one on which there is still a need for research into this 1/ to ascertain if and when pain does exist, and 2/ to avoid and/or minimise this wherever possible.

I am in favour of the redirection of Medical Research Council funds along the line indicated where alternative methods of research are regarded by competent authorities as likely to be equally or more valuable scientifically.

I will certainly if elected take an interest in all legislation pertaining to animal welfare, particularly the elimination of avoidable cruelty in exporting live animals, but in regard to factory farming I think there should be research into whether in fact this does involve cruelty, and secondly whether the product of the process is in fact better or a great deal worse than that secured by 'natural' means.

I agree that better control is necessary in the use of pesticides.

Yours sincerely, Christopher Grieve

---

1. Letter addressed from Strathearn Institute, Crieff

59. *Alex Clark (NLS)*

18 October 1964

Dear Alex

I'm suffering from reaction – expect you are too, but hope it's only that – we overworked you badly, I know.

I'm not sure what I owe you but enclose £3. Let me know if that's OK or not.

I had three phone calls yesterday from Tass (the Soviet news agency), but couldn't make out precisely what they wanted, so I wired them and am now expecting a return telegram tomorrow. All I know is that it's some article they want me to write for the *Moscow Literary Gazette*. Denis Ogden also wants a short human interest article about the Kinross and West Perth campaign.

But there's no peace here. A couple of wizards turned up late last night and I've had three other visitors so far today – and am still half expecting [MS is cut off]

All the best to Jessie, Kathy, Sandy and yourself.

Yours, Chris

60. *To Barbara Niven (NLS)*

22 October 1964

Dear Barbara

The campaign in Kinross and West Perthshire was most exhilarating and we got more votes than we expected. But of course that was not the object of the exercise – which was, to secure maximum world publicity, and that we did to an unprecedented degree: no other candidate got anything like it – and that of course accrues to the prestige and influence of the CPGB.

Also we'll get a good branch of the Party there: and I want to have a meeting now and again to hold our friends together and develop an organisation for next time.

I was OK after it all, but since have developed an excruciatingly bad back and can only move with agony. Which is a damned nuisance. Since I'm entering on a still busier time, from now till the end of January.

Amongst other things I'm leading in a debate in the Oxford Union on 3rd Dec. on 'Extremism in defence of liberty is no vice – moderation in pursuit of justice is no virtue'. My seconder is Professor Isaiah Berlin,[1] and my opponent Humphrey Berkely MP whose seconder I don't know yet. I hope to come to London on 2nd Dec. and stay overnight (with you, if possible) and go down to Oxford the following day.

I do get into some queer places. On 1st Nov. I have the dinner of the Speculative Society in Edinburgh at which I am to be formally introduced – in an eulogy in Latin which will be presented to me. This is a very exclusive 200 year old Society of which the membership consists mainly of Senators of the College of Justice, Chancellors of Universities etc. Membership is limited to 30. Sir Alec Douglas Home and I were recently elected. It is all done with the height of formality – i.e. I've to have tails and white tie tho' members (other than the new one) can wear dinner jackets.

Other looming events are at Aberystwyth, St Andrews, Glasgow – and I have a class in Scottish Literature every Friday night at East Kilbride.

I'm expecting Mike today and will ask him about the copy of *Express* interview for you.

No post-poll-declaration celebration in Edinburgh – but J.R.C. & Alex Clark and I did not so badly in Perth and when Alec and I got back to Glasgow there was a party at Bill Cowe's with Gordon McLennan, Bill Lauchlan etc. etc. which also we had to tear ourselves away from prematurely in order to motor from here to restore me to the bosom of my family.

We had Valda (Janey too – very well behaved at meetings!) up in Kinross for a couple of days which she greatly enjoyed; Mike was there too, briefly, on business; also the Belgian TV team who interviewed me and televised several of our meetings – as did French National TV and a Mrs Doane, for some American journals.

Gollan[2] told me definitely that an action was to be started to unseat Sir Alec for breach of representation of the People Act: and I told Press Association and other reprinters. Injunction? No. But action, yes!

Hope you soon get effective assistant, and much needed spare time.

Love from Valda and I to Ern and you.

Yours, Chris

P.S. Have you – or Ern – seen Willie Johnstone's show in Reid Gallery (14th Oct to 7th Nov.)?

---

1. Sir Isaiah Berlin (1912–97), Russian-born British philosopher, Professor of Social and Political Theory at Oxford University.
2. John Gollan, former General Secretary of the Communist Party of Great Britain.

61. *To Alex Clark (NLS)*

28 October 1964

Dear Alex

I agreed with you re the invitations to me from Newton of Aberdeen Central Branch that such requests should be made to the Scottish Office of the Party in order to enable them to allocate my services to the best advantage. So I am writing now to tell you Leeds University Communist Society (branch secretary, Jeremy Hawthorn) have written asking me to give them a meeting on 12th Nov. I have replied that other engagements prevent my doing so on that date but that I would be pleased to accept if they propose a later date when I am free to accept. I think I am likely to get other such requests and that it would be well to have the matter regularised so that in future these things can be arranged through the proper Party channel.

All the best to all of you.

Yours fraternally, Chris.

62. *To Ronald Stevenson (NLS)*

28 November 1964

Dear Ronald

Glad to have your letter. Afraid Scotland has given you (weatherwise at least) a chilly welcome back. Valda saw your next door neighbour in

Biggar the other day and sent a message to Marjorie per her, just hoping she was OK after the journey, ditto with the children. I had a very reproachful and sentimental letter from Mrs Chisholm and have replied in a non-commital and none too cordial fashion.

This is just a hasty note to say of course I must see you as soon as possible, but I go off on Tuesday to deal at Oxford with (as Shakespeare calls him) 'the blasted Heath'[1] and don't expect to be back here till Friday night or even Saturday. But Sunday 6th, or the following Monday to Wednesday any time if you can come over we'd be delighted to see you. Hope you too are in good fettle after the journey — and change of climate. Also that you have, if not anything already netted, at least some good prospect.

Please excuse this scrawl. I'm appallingly busy. Love to you all from Valda and I.

Yours, Chris

---

1. Edward Heath (b.1916), Secretary of State for Industry and President of the Board of Trade in the Douglas-Home administration, elected opposition leader of the Conservative Party, 1965; Prime Minister of Great Britain, 1970–74.

63. *To Duncan Glen (EUL)*

1 December 1964

Dear Duncan Glen

Many thanks for letter and copy of 'Ministry of Water'.[1] Have sent off the copy to Copyright people, duly signed. The pamphlet looks very nice indeed. I had meant to tell you the drawing you thought of having as a frontispiece stumped me; I knew one I wanted — but couldn't find it. I think I forgot to mention this when I wrote you.

Reviews are always slow but there have been some good ones — and I'm sure will be more. Once the leaflets are out and the libraries circularised sales are sure to jump up, and besides there should be an American demand.

I hope I behaved myself not too badly at the party. I had had to meet a couple of American journalists who wanted to interview and photograph me in the pubs we writers frequent for a feature in some Yankee magazine, so I'd had rather too much to drink just before the party.

Every kind regard to Mrs Glen and yourself.

Yours, Christopher Grieve

---

1. Hugh MacDiarmid, *The Ministry of Water: Two Poems* (Glasgow: Duncan Glen, 1964).

64. To Jean White (EUL)

16 December 1964

Dear Jean

We were glad to get your letter today. As time went on I began to think something really serious had happened to you – like going off and getting married!

The election certainly took a lot out of me. It is such an enormous constituency, and apart from my own meetings I had also to speak for Communist candidates in Glasgow, Clydebank, and West Fife. Recently I have had to cancel a lot of engagements and will have to cut down my activities henceforward. I find it very difficult to realise that I haven't the same energy as I had 20 or 30 years ago, but there it is.

However I still get round quite a lot. Before the Oxford Union debate, I had a couple of days at Aberystwyth at a students' Art Festival, and I've still got Durham University and Bangor University College to do. We get a wrong impression from our press of Malcolm X – as a sort of wild fascist-type, but actually he is a splendid chap, a Left Winger, but very reasonable and pleasant to deal with, and a first-class speaker. The Tories against us were painful – Lord Stoneham and Humphrey Berkeley. But then most University students are Tories and quite incredibly callow; all they want on such occasions is plenty of giggles.

Michael was with me at Oxford. Like myself he and Deirdre have had dreadful bouts of flu'. I don't know if you knew they've had a second son, Lucien. I've just had a long session with Maurice Lindsay and a number of his staff, and they're doing a comprehensive film interview with me here tomorrow.

I'm hoping my cold will ease up and that I'll be in better fettle by Monday for the Home case.[1] I'll be in the witness box for 20 minutes to ½ an hour. We have first-class counsel and solicitors and believe we have a very good case. But as Lord Migdale remarked the other day the case is one of very great public interest and may have very far-reaching consequences. That is why I'm afraid the Judges may be even more than usually cautious. Because if we won there would be a very considerable upset – about 30 other seats would be voided (including Harold Wilson's). I see the Postmaster General has just declined to meet deputations from the SNP and Plaid Cymru, or to give time for more political broadcasts to these parties. He will probably be forced to change his mind. Damn him!

Yes, a few days in Langholm later on would be most welcome. And of course we'll be glad to see you here anytime. Anyhow here's best wishes for Christmas and the New Year from Valda and I.

Yours affectionately, Chris

P.S. Hope Jim and Willie and their wives are all OK. Kindest regards to them all from Valda and I.

1. Before the election CMG had said that if Douglas-Home appeared in any political broadcast, whether as Prime Minister or as candidate for Kinross and West Perthshire, he would request similar representation from the broadcasting authorities and, if refused, would seek that the election be annulled. CMG's contention that Douglas-Home's actions were in breach of election law, the costs of party political broadcasts not being included in his return of election expenses, was not upheld and he was ordered to pay costs.

65. *To Noel Stock (HRHRC)*

3 January 1965

Dear Mr. Stock

Many thanks for your letter of 20th ult. This is just a note to say that I'll be delighted to contribute to the book of tributes etc. you are editing for Ezra Pound's 80th birthday; and will see that my contribution is in your hands by not later than the middle of next month.[1] As you know Pound had greatly influenced my own work, and he and I share many ideas – particularly our detestation of usury and belief in the Social Credit proposals of the late Major C.H. Douglas.

With my compliments and best wishes for this New Year.

Yours sincerely, Hugh MacDiarmid

---

1. *Ezra Pound: Perspectives: Essays in Honour of His Eightieth Birthday*, ed. with an introduction by Noel Stock (Chicago: H. Regnery, 1965). The essay, 'The Return of the Long Poem', is reprinted in Hugh MacDiarmid, *Selected Prose*, ed. Alan Riach (Manchester: Carcanet, 1992), pp. 254–67.

66. *To Barbara Niven (NLS)*

20 February 1965

Dear Barbara

Many thanks for your letter. I knew you'd understand. The little men are always looking for any slip – it's an expression of their envy and their only chance of getting into the limelight. I am not worried. We are all plagiarists or nothing. Language is a social thing as Dr Johnson said when somebody complained of a writer having recourse to too many quotations from other writers: That only shows a due sense of his social obligations. Those who do not use quotations are doing nothing else but quote all the time. The law of copyright is nonsensical – as is shown by the fact that it only subsists for 50 years. In other words it is OK to steal from the dead – you mustn't steal from the living – because money is involved. It is a matter of business. I have never disguised that I live, write, and have my being in a 'strong solution of books' – and I'm not in the least ashamed of it. Honi soit qui mal y pense!

I am as usual (or more than usual) desperately busy. Speaking at Newcastle University on Tuesday, Durham University on Wednesday, Manchester University on Thursday – all students Marxist societies or branches of CP.

The real purpose of this hasty scribble however is just to forewarn you that I am about to descend upon you again. I'm due to address Cambridge University Marxist Society on 6th March – will travel to London 5th and if possible spend the night with you. The affair is Poets Reading, discussion etc. – I'm supposed to keep going till midnight! What a life.

You'll probably have seen or heard of my article in this week's *New Statesman* on Burns' bawdy poems. I should have another in tomorrow's *Sunday Times*. Also in this week's *Listener* I have an article on Charles Murray, the Aberdeenshire dialect poet. And I've just heard from Italy that a long essay of mine is to be included in a volume of appreciations of Ezra Pound on the occasion (in June) of his 80th birthday, and now I must try to write another long essay putting the Marxist case in regard to recent social and psychological changes and trends in Britain (Scotland in my case) for a forthcoming issue of *Twentieth Century*; the whole number will be devoted to that, by various writers: I'm the only Marxist among them apparently.

Love to Ernest and you from Valda and Chris

67. *To Ronald Stevenson (NLS)*

Monday 26 April 1965

Dear Ronald

I have completed my translation of Brecht's *Threepenny Opera* – all but the songs. And the trouble with the latter is that they must be singable to Kurt Weill's music. To ensure this I need someone who can give me a notation – longs and shorts – so that I can make the words of my translations conform to that. I know you are very busy but I wonder if you could spare an hour or two to help me in this. I could come over to you on Saturday or Sunday – or you could come here if you prefer. I have a complete set of LP records and we could get the notation for the songs from that. I'd be very grateful. But the trouble is it must be soon – the London people are waiting impatiently for these songs now: they have already all the rest of the thing and are highly pleased with it – and I am going away to East Germany on 12th May. I haven't had final word about Cuba yet but expect to know by any post now. If the Cuba dates clash with the East German ones, I'll cancel – or cut short – the latter.

Hope all goes well with your own work. Duval told me he'd been to see you. I was very annoyed that he got hung up in the Gordon Arms, and as a result I didn't see Hilda Albery, whom I particularly wanted to see!

All the best to Marjorie and the children and yourself.

Yours, Chris

68. *To Ronald Stevenson (NLS)*

11 May 1965

Dear Ronald

I ought to have written you long ere this to thank you for the Brecht song notations. I had not realised they'd involve you in so much work. It was cheek on my part really to ask this of you. But they are exactly what I needed.

I am off to Germany on Friday. I had hoped the Cuba visit would run in sequence but so far I've no final details yet, so presumably I'll have to come back and start afresh instead of, as I'd have preferred, going right on from Germany.

One of the items on the German programme is a reception given by Helene Wiegall-Brecht.[1] I'd also a nice letter from Brecht's son, Stefan Brecht, in America.

Hope all goes well with you. I couldn't get to Manfred Gordon's inaugural lecture but see a summary report in today's *Scotsman*.

Love to you all, and renewed thanks.

Yours, Chris

---

1. Brecht's second wife, Helene Weigel.

69. *To Ian Milner (NLS)*

1 June 1965

Dear Ian Milner

I had an extremely good time in the GDR and liked your Australian friends immensely – especially Judah Waten, a great guy. Also Frank Hardy, with whom, as with John Berger, I discovered a (largely alcoholic) affinity. I had to sing for my supper, of course, and not only addressed the manifestation (or general assembly) of the Congress, but also had the hardihood to speak at a meeting of the Editorial Board of *Sinn und Form*, surely a better magazine than any in the English-speaking world and equal to the best anywhere in Europe. I also spoke at a Berliner Ensemble reception and talked to – and kissed – the red battle-axe herself, Frau Weigall-Brecht. The *Sinn und Form* people want to publish in it some translations of poems of mine – and I think the translator will be Arno Reinfrank of whom I saw a good deal at the Congress and who has followed my work for years.[1] Also the GDR state publishing people want to publish a volume of translations of my poems, and I think the people who will see to it are Ruth Werner-Buerton (she is married to an Englishman) and Jack Mitchell, a Scot who is a lecturer at the Humboldt University.[2] I was glad to strengthen some of my American ties – with Walter Lowenfels[3] and others, and have agreed to be one of the sponsors of, and to contribute to, the new periodical, *American Dialog*, by the first numbers of which I was favourably impressed. Now I am busy trying to digest my myriad impressions, and finish off some chores, before going to Cuba – tho' I haven't heard yet the date on which I'm to go.

I had indeed hoped I might call in by Prague, but it was out of the question. So many delegates wanted alterations of one kind or another on their itineraries.

The Australian delegation was a numerous one, and in addition to Waten (and James Alridge, whom I'd met before) included Clem Christiansen, Frank Hardy, Flexmore Hudson, and about a dozen others i.e. Geoffrey Dutton, Dorothy Hewett, Max Harris, John Manifold (another old friend of mine) Alan Marshall, John Morrison, F.B. Vickers, Bill Wannau (not counting womenfolk and children). We went from E. Berlin to Weimar, Dresden, Buchenwald etc.

I'm glad Linda liked the brooch and that it arrived timeously for her birthday – on which our belated but very sincere felicitations and good wishes.

In haste, with every kind regard to Jarmila and yourself, from Valda and I.

Yours, Christopher

---

1. *Sinn und Form*, vol. 18, no. 1 (1966).
2. Hugh MacDiarmid, *Ein Wind Sprang Auf*, tr. Heinz Kahlau and Gunter Kunert (Berlin: Verlag Volk und Welt, 1968).
3. Walter Lowenfels (1897–1976), American avant-garde, expatriate poet of the 1920s; Communist Party organiser and editor of the *Daily Worker*, Pennsylvania, in America during the 1950s.

70. *To Khaikhosru Shapurji Sorabji (McMUL)*

27 June 1965

My dear Mr Sorabji,

It was a real thrill for me to receive your letter the other day – and such a characteristic letter (tho' far too kind for my remarks in the Symposium!) The Symposium was quite extempore, without any preparation, and I do not know whether Ronald Stevenson sent you a copy of my essay on your work as a critic, which is referred to by Stevenson & Ogdon in the Symposium.[1] I thought that essay perhaps did more justice to you – and to myself. I was very sorry Stevenson failed to find a publisher for the book, but that, as you know, is very difficult.

The trouble (or one of the troubles) with men like Stevenson and Ogdon is, it seems to me, that they have no background – they just express whatever happens at the time to pop into their heads – in other words they remind me when they tackle any subject just of a rabbit or a caterpillar nibbling at the fringe of a cabbage leaf. The effortless way in which a well-stocked mind like yours can produce references to the Saints, to Cardinal Consalvi and Tallyrand, etc., etc., is quite beyond them. In other words again, they have no depth to their minds.

I am glad to conclude from the spirit of your letter that you are in good form. I wish I could see you again. I was really extremely disappointed when there was word a year or two ago that you might visit us here – and that didn't transpire. For myself I seem to get everywhere and meet everybody except the few places and people I really should. Recently I had an extremely interesting time in Germany (Berlin, Dresden, Weimar) at an International Writers' Conference, with representatives of 51 countries. And now I expect to go any day to Cuba. I'll be there a full fortnight but must, to fulfil other engagements, be back here by the first week of August. However I too keep well.

With every high regard. Yours as ever, Christopher Grieve
P.S. – You'd see in the press of Erik Chisholm's death in South Africa. He married F.G. Scott's younger daughter. De mortuis – etc., but alas, I felt about him, even more than about Stevenson and Ogdon, what I have said above about mere rabbit – or – caterpillar nibbling.

---

1. Symposium on Sorabji in *Gambit*.

71. *To W.R. Aitken (NLS)*

19 August 1965

Dear Bill

Excuse just the briefest note to enclose three letters of introduction which may be useful to Christine in Moscow. I hope I have remembered correctly that it is next month she is going to Russia – and that I am not too late in implementing my promise to furnish these.

Is Betty home again? Hope all's well with all of you. Kindest regards from Valda and I.

Yours in haste, Christopher Grieve

Konstantin Fedin[1]
c/o *Soviet Literature*, 9/11 Dobrolyubov St, Moscow

Dear Comrade

I was delighted to see you at the International Writers' meeting in the German Democratic Republic, but did not have an opportunity of speaking to you. If I had done so I would have recalled my meeting with you, and Mr Tvardowski in Ayr. We were joined at lunch on that occasion by a friend of mine Dr. W.R. Aitken, who is now President of the Scottish Library Association and Editor of *The Library Review*. I am writing to you now to solicit your friendly interest on behalf of Dr Aitken's daughter, Miss Christine Aitken, a graduate of St Andrews University, who is coming to Moscow next month (September) to continue her studies there. Any kindness you can show her, to help her to feel at home in Moscow and enjoy her stay there, will be very greatly appreciated by your friends in Scotland.

With every expression of my high regards and best wishes.

Yours fraternally,

Hugh MacDiarmid

Boris Polevoi, Esq.
c/o *Soviet Literature*, 9/11 Dobrolyubov St, Moscow, USSR

Dear Friend

I hope this finds you fine and flourishing as it leaves me.

This is just a short note to introduce you to a friend of mine – Miss Christine Aitken, a graduate of St Andrews University, who is coming to Moscow next month (September) to continue her studies there.

She is the daughter of Dr. W.R. Aitken, who is President of the Scottish Library Association and Editor of *The Library Review*.

I will appreciate it greatly if you can show her kindness and enable her to make herself at home in Moscow and enjoy herself there.

It is too long ago now since you were in Scotland. I hope we may see you here again ere long. I am an older man than you and have not yet ceased my travels. I was in the German Democratic Republic recently and am going to Cuba soon.

With every expression of my warmest regards and best wishes.

Yours fraternally,

Hugh MacDiarmid

G.Feldman
Secretary, Burns and Pushkin Friendship Club, c/o Professor S.A. Urlov, Head of Department of Western Literature, Gorky State University, Moscow

Dear Friend

As an Honorary Member of your Club I write to ask you to extend your kindness to a young Scottish student, Miss Christine Aitken, who is to come to Moscow next month (September) to continue her studies there. She is a graduate of St Andrews University in Scotland, and comes from Burns' own town of Ayr. Miss Aitken's father – Dr. W.R. Aitken – is President of the Scottish Library Association and Editor of *The*

Library Review. I am sure that with your kind help Miss Aitken will find good friends in your Club.

In conclusion may I express the hope that the Club is in a most flourishing condition.

With best wishes.
Yours fraternally,
Hugh MacDiarmid

---

1. Konstantin Aleksandrovich Fedin (1892–?), Russian novelist, First Secretary of the Union of Soviet Writers, 1959. Boris Polevoi was another Russian novelist.

72. *To Alexander Trocchi (WUL)*

31 August 1965

Dear Alex. Trocchi

When I got your note at the Traverse yesterday I told Pete Brown[1] I thought I could manage to get to Cardiff. But I hadn't my engagement book with me, and I see now it's quite impossible. I'm very sorry about this. But I have four or five engagements this next fortnight in Edinburgh and Glasgow, and in addition have a hell of a lot of writing to do to meet dead line of 1st Oct. subject to penalty clause. So I must remain 'eyeless at the mill in Gaza with the slaves'. Please tell Harps – and accept for yourself – I am very sorry indeed. Had thought I might see you at the Traverse. Believe my wife did. Hope all's well with you.

Yours, Hugh MacDiarmid

---

1. Pete Brown, poet who had been part of Trocchi's 1965 Albert Hall poetry reading; lyricist for the rock group Cream.

73. *To Camille R. Honig (NLS)*

1 September 1965

Dear Sir:-

Many thanks for your very kind letter. Nothing would give me greater pleasure than to be able to accept your invitation to attend the In Memoriam Martin Buber Symposium on 23rd inst, but, alas, it just cannot be done. I am exceptionally busy and have a deadline to meet to deliver a big new book to the publishers by 1st October, and I am going to have the utmost difficulty in fulfilling that contract.

I have not only read, but written about, a great deal of Buber's work but I had the pleasure of meeting him and talking with him in Glasgow a few years ago.[1] I then found that he had read my autobiography *Lucky Poet* in which I have poems about him; and that he knew, and appreciated, my work.

I would be very pleased to send you books of mine as you suggest. Alas, they are all out of print. I do not even possess copies of some of them myself. I will see what I can do, but I am afraid I cannot hold out any hope.

I will look forward with great interest to any reports of the Albert Hall Symposium. Sir Herbert Read, one of your Vice-Presidents, is of course an old friend of mine.[2]

I am afraid there is little or no likelihood of Lukács being able to come, but I will write to him today.[3] Your letter has just reached me and I will have to think who might possibly be willing, and able, to come from the Communist countries, but I will think about it and do whatever I can.

With compliments and best wishes, Yours sincerely, Hugh MacDiarmid

---

1. Martin Buber (1878–1965), Austrian Jewish theologian and philosopher.
2. Herbert Read (1863–1068), English art historian, critic and poet, championed Modern art movements in Britain.
3. Georg Szegedy von Lukács (1885–1971), Hungarian critic and philosopher, early Marxist literary theorist, minister of culture in the revolutionary government of 1956.

74. *To John Gawsworth (UDL)*

21 October 1965

Dear John

Just a brief line, since I appreciate the urgency called for in complying with your request. Valda and I are terribly sorry to hear the tale of your distresses, and hope that these may be alleviated shortly. Above all, the Royal Literary Fund must surely respond to your application. I am not sure in what form my support to the application should be couched. But I do trust it is effective.

With best wishes. Yours, Chris

75. *To Kenneth Campbell (UDL)*

21 November 1965

Dear Mr Campbell

Many thanks for your interesting letter of 17th inst. I am very glad to hear about the intention of setting up a society to disseminate ideas about the Arts, and so counterbalance the dangers of an excessive emphasis on technological matters. I regard it as an honour to be asked to deliver a lecture as guest speaker at the inaugural meeting of such a society, and I would certainly be glad to agree – if a convenient date can be arranged. At the moment I am hopelessly tied up, and January is always a busy month for me, with Burns Suppers, poetry readings etc. In February however I am free, except on 6th February. If you decide to delay your inaugural till February any date that month except 6th will suit me. Your suggestions as to subject of lecture is all right and I will think along these lines until I hear from you again, and by then I should be in a position to give you a brief summary of what I would propose to say.

With best wishes. Yours sincerely, C.M. Grieve

76. *To Ronald Stevenson (NLS)*

29 November 1965

Dear Ronald

Glad to hear from you. I've been away again but I'll certainly write to *The Scotsman* re the Festival of (alleged) Scottish (alleged) music of the BBC and the criminal neglect of F.G. Scott and yourself in favour of young composers who haven't won their spurs yet – or any ability to ride – simply because, in several cases, they are BBC employees. I'm sick to death of all this preference for promise rather than achievement – and the detection of 'promise' by people without any ability to discern anything worth noting.

I knew of course you were very busy. You do not say whether you have been able to secure a publisher for the Busoni book. I hope so. It is a big undertaking, and with costs as they are now – and still rising – publishers are not easy to find for serious work on a big scale.

I too have been – and remain tho' I have broken the backs of all my contracted jobs – extremely busy. But I have now completed not only my autobiographical *Scottish Poet And His Friends* (100,000 words), which however won't be out till Autumn 1966; also the *Threepenny Opera*. A new edition of my *Collected Poems*, with necessary corrections and a really thorough glossary, is to appear in USA, and perhaps also a paperback edition. The publication by Volk und Welt of a selection of my poems in German translation will not be published until 1968 – because the publishing house in question has a backlog of stuff already which must have priority in publication.

And now, if I can get a breathing space, I want to write a batch of new poems. I need to, for I have none in hand not already published.

I am greatly bucked to know you've done 17 poems of mine and are still working on the Ben Dorain.

Christmas and New Year are approaching – perhaps we'll meet over the Festive Season (tho' for Christmas we'll be in Glasgow). Anyhow in advance best wishes to Marjorie and yourself and the children for a happy and prosperous time. I hope you are all well.

Love from Valda and I.

Yours, Chris

77. To Edward Lucie-Smith (HRHRC)

29 November 1965

Dear Mr Lucie-Smith,

How kind of you to write me. The trouble is that I have no – or almost no – unpublished poems now and tho' I have hope of writing a new lot, heaven only knows if – and when – I'll get time. I have been, and still am, desperately busy with other things. I've just finished a big autobiographical book, and a new translation of Brecht's *Threepenny Opera*. Macmillans New York, are putting out a new edition of my *Collected Poems*, with necessary corrections and, at last, a really thorough glossary. But if – as I will try to do – I manage to get a chance to write the new poems I have in mind I'll be very happy to send Turret Books what I hope may be a suitable batch. Anyhow I wish the enterprise well. As you say I have another publisher of limited editions – two other publishers actually – and I have things in hand for both of them – but not things, of course, that will in any way conflict with what I hope to send Turret.

I will write you again when I see how things develop. (But of course, being a Scotsman, that means not until after New Year!) Your own work is of course known to me and highly appreciated. Perhaps we may meet if I am in London – which, however, I do not visit frequently, regarding it, as I do, as the enemy capital.

Anyhow, thanks again for your letter, and with best wishes for a happy Christmas and prosperous New Year.

Yours sincerely, Christopher Grieve

78. To Ian Milner (NLS)

19 December 1965

Dear Ian Milner

I wonder if I may ask you to do something for me. If it would embarrass you – or for any reason you feel you don't want to do it – please don't bother with it. I have a friend, a composer, Ronald Stevenson, who for some time has been composing a symphonic setting of my translation of Duncan Bàn McIntyre's *Ben Dorain*. At one point he wants to introduce an 'echo' or 'suggestion' or some reminiscence of bagpipe music, and the problem is the orchestration of the Pibroch mode, i.e. of microtonal music. He wrote to a great authority on that matter – Alois Haba, Professor of Music at Prague Conservatoire – seeking his advice on this abstruse matter. It is known that Professor Haba received Stevenson's letter (or letters) and has said he would write Stevenson. The trouble is that he hasn't written yet – after about 6 months – and Stevenson urgently needs the information he sought. Professor Haba may be an old man, and/or he may be ill, or there may be some other reason for his delay, but I wonder if it would be possible for you to contact him and tell him that your friends in Scotland are very urgently awaiting the favour of his advice on the matter about which Stevenson has written him? We would be grateful if you feel you can do this, without too much trouble to yourself.

Valda joins me in all seasonal greetings for a happy Christmas and prosperous New Year to Jarmila, Linda, and yourself.

Yours, Christopher Grieve

79. *To Ronald Stevenson (NLS)*

10 December 1965

Dear Ronald

It is very desirable that the facts about BBC in Scotland in its dealings with artists should be exposed, of course. But that can only be done if individuals affected take action in the knowledge that if they do they will almost certainly be blacklisted. As you may have noted, I have had no broadcasting myself since I headed a CP delegation protesting about the political broadcasting time, and I expect my taking action against Sir Alec Douglas Home has made an ineradicable black mark against me. However facts are chiels that winna ding and the pressure to have them realised must be maintained somehow or other.

I thought Cedric Thorpe Davie's letter very bad.[1] His impudence in his references to Sorabji, and in his final sentence praying Heaven to save F.G. from such 'friends', told me all I ever want to know about Thorpe Davie. However I have replied. We'll see if *The Scotsman* prints my letter.

Barbara Niven was asking for you in a letter received today, and asked me to pass on to you her regards and good wishes.

Yours, Christopher

P.S. I have just seen my letter in today's (Friday's) *Scotsman*. They have mauled it badly and there are a lot of misprints e.g. comparisons for compositions. They have left in the sentence in which I said the public could judge for themselves – but cut out the preceding part in which I gave the facts in question, i.e. the names of the 3 BBC producers and the fact that one of them is Watson Forbes's son. Also, alas, they left out my final paragraph in which I asked, (apropos Thorpe Davie's remark that he has been exhilarated & excited for many years by Sorabji's compositions), where, when, he had heard these played and precisely which of S's works he had heard.

---

1. Cedric Thorpe Davie (1913–83), Scottish composer, Professor of Music at St Andrews University.

80. *To Ronald Stevenson (NLS)*

25 January 1966

Dear Ronald

I hope you got my last letter enclosing Ian Milner's re Haba, and I write to ask you please to return Milner's letter as I must write to him.

Barbara Niven tells me you are playing? or lecturing? or something on Busoni in London on Saturday, and she is looking forward to seeing you then.

I hope things are going well with you now, and especially with the Busoni book.

As to myself, I have been off with a bad dose of flu', and, tho' still shaky, am now embarking on a marathon of Burns Suppers.

As you many know one of the *Kaleidoscope* programmes, sponsored by 5 smaller TV companies – Border, Grampian, STV, Tees & Tyneside, and Welsh – is devoting one of its series shortly to me – a full film.

I think it might be possible a little later to induce them to put on a programme of your settings of M'Diarmid poems, if you think that a good idea. It would all depend, I suppose, on getting a suitable singer.

I hope Marjorie and the children are all in good form and that we may see you again sometime ere too long.

Yours, Chris

81. *To Kenneth Campbell (UDL)*

2 February 1966

Dear Mr Campbell

Many thanks for your p.c. re Arts Group meeting on 10th inst, which I have owing to absence from home since 27th ult just received. I am to be with a joint SNP and Poetry Society meeting in Aberdeen on 8th inst and will stay c/o Ian S. Munro, Braeside, Catterline, in Stonehaven (Tel. Catterline 272) and come on to Dundee from there, so I should arrive all right before 7pm on 10th, and will be very pleased to join you and your friends for a meal before the lecture as you so kindly suggest. Many thanks too for booking me a room in the Queen's Hotel.[1]

I'll write or wire you again from Aberdeen or Stonehaven saying when I'll get to Dundee.

With best wishes, Yours sincerely, C.M. Grieve

---

1. Ian S. Munro was a lecturer in the Department of English at the Aberdeen College of Education and the biographer of Lewis Grassic Gibbon: *Leslie Mitchell* (Edinburgh: Oliver & Boyd, 1966). From 1950, Catterline was the favoured place of the artist Joan Eardley (1921–63). In the event, CMG was unable to go to Dundee.

82. *To William Johnstone (NLS)*

10 February 1966

Dear William

Sorry you had to 'phone up to find out what had happened to me not replying to your last letter. Valda told you I'd been having flu'. I caught a second dose of it and had to cancel engagements in Aberdeen and Dundee. Fortunately I'd completed all my major undertakings – autobiography, translation of Brecht's *Threepenny Opera*, essays for Ezra Pound's 80th birthday, etc. And most recently a new long poem about the Borders which will be read shortly on BBC TV, with illustrations by photos specially taken for it by Alan Daiches. Border TV in association with four other small TV companies in Scotland, England, and Wales will be showing soon a complete film interview with me in their fortnightly magazine of the arts, *Kaleidoscope*.

Normally I'd have joined in the correspondence in *The Scotsman* re subsidisation of the Arts. I quite agree with you that these can do nothing for the arts as such, but Benno Schotz was right too in pointing out that it is the interpreters – not the creators – who benefit, and I object to that. However I was too busy with other things to chip in and the opportunity passed.

I like very much the big portrait of me by the Canadian artist, Aba Bayefsky, which was presented to me at the 200 Burns Club Supper. It is a very dynamic bit of work. His portrait of Valda (also presented) is not nearly so good. It brutalises her to the point of caricature – the only good thing is that it strongly emphasises what I've had to put up with all these years.

Valda tells me you'll be at Satchells till mid-March. By that time this extra dose of winter should be over. We've had quite a fall of snow, and the wind today is bitterly cold.

Hope you are all well. Love to all three of you from Valda and I.

Yours, Christopher

83. *To James D. Young*
(Text published in Cencrastus.*)*

14 May 1966

Dear Mr Young

I haven't seen Ian Munro's biography of Grassic Gibbon yet. Gibbon (James Leslie Mitchell) never met Maclean and was a sentimental socialist with little knowledge of, or interest in, Marxism. Towards the end of his life he became better equipped and entitled to call himself a Communist, albeit with ineradicable Trotskyist leanings. I do not think he ever appreciated the vast gulf between John Maclean and Jimmy Maxton. In so far as they went Gibbon's Left-Wing views were consistent enough throughout his adult life, until towards the end, as I say, he began to appreciate the Scottish issue *vis-à-vis* English Imperialism, expressed himself as an out-and-out Republican, and on the whole I think had come to agree with what I said about Maclean and the Scottish separatist line in my book *Lucky Poet* published by Methuen's in 1934 [*sic*]. *Grey Granite*, the weakest of the novels in *A Scots Quhair* [*sic*] – when it should, of course have been the strongest – suffered from Gibbon's inadequate knowledge of urban industrial life and lack of Marxist understanding. The earlier novels were feats of memory, full of nostalgia and reflecting his boyhood experiences in the Mearns. Gibbon died too young; he was just finding himself as a Socialist writer. The weaknesses of *Grey Granite* were obvious enough, but the incomprehension of aesthetic activity, the hatred, indeed, of the creative faculty, common to all Socialists, and particularly to Scottish Socialists, were mainly responsible for the critical attacks of many Socialists on *Grey Granite*. They carried off an objection against the earlier two novels as 'muck-raking', as insufficiently laudatory of the working-class, and applied it to the third novel too, to which it was less applicable.

After all Gibbon was not the only Socialist who misunderstood John Maclean and the Scottish Question. Those who do are not numerous even yet – though the Scottish CP's 'Policy for Scotland' (issued at the 1964 election) should have cleared matters up for them. As you probably know John L. Broom has now completed a full-scale biography of John Maclean. He has done the job splendidly, I think, but, alas, has not found a publisher yet.

I'll look forward to your reviews in the *Political Quarterly*.

With best wishes. Yours fraternally, Hugh MacDiarmid

84. *To Ronald Stevenson (NLS)*

2 July 1966

Dear Ronald

Many thanks for your note. Glad you are back and had a successful and enjoyable time. I've been away too in Nottingham and other places, and not being like you a well-organised and orderly person am in a perfect chaos of commitments of various kinds.

I saw in the *Daily Telegraph* a long (and I thought excellent) article about your Passacaglia – and rejoice generally at what seems to be the general break-through you are now having.[1]

As to the *Golden Treasury* this is, *mirabile dictu*, not only still selling steadily after all these years, but is increasingly being used as a textbook, e.g. in Glasgow University, and in various secondary schools.

We'll put West Linton and Candymill on the map yet – the only trouble is that they're so far apart. But we'll perhaps be able to bridge that gulf ere too long.

All the best to Marjorie and yourself and the children from Valda and I.

Yours, Chris

---

1. Ronald Stevenson's *Passacaglia on DSCH for Dmitry Shostakovich* for solo piano was premiered at the Aldeburgh Festival in 1966.

85. *To John Broom (NLS)*

14 October 1966

Dear John

I have just had a letter from Ronald Lewin, of Messrs Hutchinson & Co. (Publishers) Ltd, 178–202 Great Portland Street, London W.C.1 in which he says: 'I shall look forward in due course to receiving the manuscript of Mr Broom's biography of John MacLean'. So I hope you can send it to him and that you will have luck at last.[1]

I told Lewin how highly I thought of it and that the great name of John Maclean was still a potent one in Scotland and a biography of him 43 years after his death still one of the main desiderata in the documentation of Scottish politics. Also that your book was an invaluable and indispensable complement to the book they published by Middlemiss on the Glasgow 'Reds'.

All the best. Yours, Chris

Send a covering note with the MSS saying you send it at my suggestion in previous correspondence.

---

1. The biography appeared with an introduction by Hugh MacDiarmid: John Broom, *John Maclean* (Loanhead: Macdonald Publishers, 1973).

86. *To Tom Scott (NLS)*

19 December 1966

Dear Tom

Many thanks for your letter. I enjoyed the cocktail party and meeting so many friends again. I appreciate what you say of Janet Adam Smith's remarks on the anthology.[1] I have no use personally for the niggling technical editorial points made by Lorimer and David Daiches: but I did agree with Rillie in the *Glasgow Herald* that there had been a division of counsel or anyhow that the claim made in the preface had not been borne out fully. You won't have seen yet my short review in *Akros*, but I think you'll understand (tho' not agree) that I could well have dispensed with Edwin Muir, R.L. Stevenson, and several others, and, indeed, would have kept the English element out altogether. As to my own longer poems balance I think required that if earlier poets were to be represented by longer poems so should living poets. Of course the Wheel section of my *Drunk Man* is long enough, but it is neither so good a poem, nor does it employ the full resources of the auld leid to anything like the same extent as 'Water Music', 'Wauchopeside' and 'Whuchulls' – all three of which are I believe among my very best work. I am, of course, not complaining – generous enough space was given to me – and opinions naturally differ. But the poems of mine included are not I think representative of my achievement. By and large however the fact remains that it is the best anthology of Scottish verse yet made. I hope it is going well. I have no doubt it will – even if not immediately.

Apart from myself, so far as Lallans goes, I'd fain have had more of Garioch, and a good deal more of T.S. Law.

I hope all goes well with your various projects.

Since were are on the verge of the Festive Season, Valda joins me in wishing your wife and children and yourself a happy Christmas, and all health and good fortune in 1967.

Yours, Chris

P.S. You'd see my 'Dunbar' review in *Agenda* – disfigured alas by many printers' errors.

---

1. *The Oxford Book of Scottish Verse*, ed. John MacQueen and Tom Scott (Oxford University Press, 1966).

87. *To Alex Clark (NLS)*

26 February 1967

Dear Alex[1]

Yes. Honor McCrindle was out here the other day and showed me a list of her proposals for celebrating my 75th birthday in August. I do not know whether the Party has approved all these and has decided to go ahead with the whole programme – including the Usher Hall affair which struck me as extremely ambitious and perhaps not altogether practicable. However I said that of course I would do anything I could to help.

I'll be available all right. I'm going to Sweden on 7th and returning on 9th March: then to USA and Canada on 20th April and expect to be back by end of May. I must be in London from 6th to 12th July. So East Germany and Hungary can come after August.

All the best. Yours, Chris

---

1. The letter is addressed to Alex Clark, Treasurer, Scottish Committee of CP.

88. *To John Montague (SUNYB)*

2 March 1967

Dear John Montague
 Many thanks for your letter. I have wondered where you were and how you are faring. I'd have written you if I'd known, apropos that incredibly vicious review of our tribute for Austin Clarke in the *Times Lit.*[1]
 I have wished again and again in recent years to revisit Ireland, but it has not proved possible. Your suggestion re the proposed Festival of Poetry would have been extremely welcome – at any other time. Alas! I am going to Sweden on 7th inst; to USA and Canada on 20th April, returning end of May; I am to be at the International Poetry Festival in London 6th to 12th July,[2] and have other July and early August dates at functions in Edinburgh and elsewhere to mark my 75th birthday, and the (dates not yet finalised) I've to go to East Germany and to Hungary. That does not, of course, absolutely rule out any chance of my coming to Ireland in June and I'd do it if I possibly could. As to finance, airfare and hotel exes are the main thing, and if I could make a few guineas on the side via radio etc. that would be OK. Please let me know the precise arrangements in due course. And accept my best wishes for the success of this occasion, whether I am there or not.
 Amongst the many (mostly university) engagements I have in America, there is to be a poetry reading at the Poetry Center in New York, and I am told that Austin Clarke will probably be in New York too at that time and may share the platform and poetry reading with me, I'll be very glad if this is so.
 With every high regard and good wish to you and Liam Miller and all concerned with *Poetry Ireland*.
 Yours sincerely, Hugh MacDiarmid

---

1. *A Tribute to Austin Clarke on His Seventieth Birthday, 9 May 1966*, ed. John Montague and Liam Miller (Dublin: Dolmen Press, 1966). Liam Miller was the founder of the Dolmen Press in 1951.
2. See Donald Davie, 'Go Home, Octavio Paz', in *Trying to Explain* (Manchester: Carcanet, 1980; 1986), pp. 49–51.

89. *To Valda Grieve (NLS)*

Hotel Sutton East   21 April 1967
330 East 56th Street, New York 22, N.Y.

My dear Valda

We had a lovely flight and got to the John F. Kennedy airport here a little earlier than scheduled time. Martin Tucker (who once visited us at Brownsbank) met us and motored us into the city. It is a long way and we had a good view of the incredible streams of traffic and the towering skyscrapers. After we had booked in here, Galen Williams of the Poetry Center came round. She brought me a copy of the New Edition of my *Collected Poems*. Wait till you see it! It is a magnificent volume. She also brought me two prints of Leonard Baskin's drawing of me, with 'The Eemis Stane' beautifully printed under it. She also brought me engagements to do a Radio Interview and a TV one. We are going today to Newhaven to spend the next couple of days there with a friend of Norman's before we plunge into the real business of our visit. The weather is variable, dry, a little chilly at night, but yesterday was very warm and brilliantly sunny for the most part.

In the evening we went to the flat of Bill Cole, who makes his living by editing anthologies and edited, amongst others, the big anthology of *Erotic Poetry* which I have. He has a really wonderful collection of books including *Lucky Poet* and other books of mine.

I'm feeling OK. Had a good night's rest and am now shaved and dressed and all ready for Norman to come for me. His room is four stories above mine. But I wish he'd come – I'm longing for some breakfast. My watch stopped and I don't know what time it is.

Hope you got home all right and not too tired. See and look after yourself. I'll write Mike in a day or two.

All my love; and best wishes to Clootie.

Yours, Christopher

90. *To Christine Macintosh*

New York   30 April 1967

Dear Christine

Just a line to say I'll be flying to Toronto (International Airport) at the time I stated but on 6th May instead of 7th May as originally stated. I couldn't get my visa extended so had to have my air reservation altered from 7th to 6th. Norman McCaig will be coming with me but he will be met by, and staying with, a friend of his own in Toronto.

We have been having a splendid time, mainly at Amherst (Massachusetts University) – poetry reading, lecturing etc., and meeting all sorts of people.

We came back to New York yesterday and have a terrifically crowded programme all this next week – Poetry readings, television and radio engagements, press interviews, and private parties. The weather of course is glorious and we have been about quite a lot – in the Holyoke hills, the promenade at Brooklyn, the Bowery, Chinatown, Greenwich Village etc. etc. We had snow one day at Amherst, and Valda told me in a letter she'd been having snow at Brownsbank also.

Looking forward immensely to seeing you all again.

Love, Christopher

91. *To Michael Grieve (NLS)*

New York   4 May 1967

Dear Mike,

I am not sure Mum is at Brownsbank – she may be in Langholm, or St Monance, or Torr. But just in case she is running short of cash I am enclosing herewith a cheque for 150 dollars, which please cash and give her the money as soon as you can.

Macmillans' party for me last night was really a gala occasion and we vastly enjoyed ourselves. Both Norman and I are in excellent form but beginning to be a little tired. We have had a very busy time. The poetry readings at Amherst, at Long Island University, and several other places all went off splendidly and today I have a big programme at the Poetry Center, at New York University, as well as a radio interview in Long Island. I had an hour's TV programme and a couple of radio interviews.

On Saturday both Norman and I fly to Toronto.

Love to you all, Dad

Tell Mum this 150 dollars is in addition to the £160 I'll be repaying her.

92. *To Valda Grieve (NLS)*

10 McIntyre Crescent,   8 May 1967
Georgetown, Ontario

Dearest Valda

Glad to get your airmail letter-card today. Norman and I arrived in Toronto on Saturday. Christine, Alasdair, and all the children met me at the airport, and George McAskill met Norman. The weather here is very mixed, as with you. We had snow yesterday. Today is dull but much milder tho' the Spring is very retarded – scarcely any leaves on the trees yet.

Norman and I had a very busy but very successful time in New York. My Poetry Center reading went off extremely well – also my TV appearance. At Poetry Center I met Bob Curran (whose mother was sorry she couldn't come to the reading, having fallen and broken a hip-bone), Elspeth and Maurius Blum, A.E.'s granddaughter, and Marshak's niece – also lots of people I'd corresponded with over the years whose names wouldn't mean anything to you. But the big hall was packed and I received a standing ovation.

Mack Rosenthal and the Westons (Jack and Judy) and Prof. Martin Tucker – all of whom have been at Brownsbank) sent their love to you. Yesterday at dinner here Esme and Ernest were asking about you too and deploring your absence. I am glad the McGibbon & Kee proofs came and also the *Glasgow Herald* cheque. You should have had the Ludovic Kennedy STV cheque also and McGibbon & Kee ought to have sent the £150 advance.

I sent Mike a 150 dollar cheque for you: and you should also have received a bigger one (200 or 300 dollars) which the TV people in New York arranged to send direct to you, for an hour's programme I did for them. I don't know my Canadian arrangements yet but am seeing Barker Fairley and Humphrey Milnes tomorrow. Love from all here, darling, and of course mine.

Christopher

93. *To Valda Grieve (NLS)*

Georgetown   Monday 15 May 1967

My dear Valda

I was glad to get your letter-card and know you'd had an enjoyable run-round many of the places in Scotland you hadn't seen before, and hope you are still having a good rest and an enjoyable time either at Langholm or elsewhere. I've been taking it easy here for over a week now, but have a busy week in prospect. I'm going off tomorrow by plane to Ottawa, returning the following day, when there's a sort of gathering of friends at his daughter Joan's house to celebrate Barker Fairley's 80th birthday. Mrs Fairley is still the same – there's no hope there, alas – it's just a question of time. Alasdair, Christine, and I are also going in to Toronto on Saturday 20th inst. to a 'do' at the University Faculty Club where you'll remember we were entertained to food and drinks after my poetry reading last time we were here. Barker and Humphrey Milnes were out here, both in good form. Also I've had dinner at the Terra Cotta Inn, where both the Farrars were asking after you. On Saturday night, after the University Club affair, we're going up to Muskoka Lake. The weather has been very uncertain – fine and sunny one day, dull and cold the next.

You do not say whether you got the Channel 13 TV cheque or not. It should have been at least 200 or even 300 dollars. Also you ought to have received ere this the cheque for my STV interview with Ludovic Kennedy and also the advance from McGibbon & Kee. To lighten my luggage I sent most of the books I had with me back by parcel post and there should also be a parcel from the publishers of copies of the new edition of my *Collected Poems*.

Aileen and family left Terra Cotta Inn in March and Farrars didn't know their present address, so I haven't been able to get in touch with them.

We are all OK here. Donald was home from school yesterday and Elspeth will be next weekend. Alistair and I have been out in the woods several times digging up young cedar trees and bringing them back to form a screen round the lawn here.

Love to Clootie. Glad she's behaving herself.

And all love and kisses to you. It won't be so long now till I'm back.

Yours, Christopher

P.S. I was very angry about Norman getting Mike to phone up Alasdair to say I was carrying too much money around. I am quite capable of looking after myself and do not require supervision of this kind. I had made up my mind to be on my best behaviour in the United States – and I was. But Norman evidently thought he was in charge of me – and often he wasn't too tactful about it. He humiliated me several times in company by his over-zeal which was quite unnecessary. He is in some respects an abominable fuss-pot and like all teachers apt to be very dictatorial.

94. *To James Crichton (EUL)*

1 June 1967

Dear Jimmy

I have just returned from a busy lecturing and poetry-reading tour in the United States and Canada. I hope you are now fully recovered. I understand Davy Orr is doing a locum in Aberdeen.

I do not know whether there are still any copies of *A Drunk Man Looks at the Thistle* available, but if so I am anxious to have half-a-dozen copies as soon as possible. There is, it seems, a wave of interest in my work in Australia and I need these copies to serve the purposes of Australian friends.

With best wishes, Yours sincerely, Christopher Grieve

95. *To D.G. Bridson, BBC (LLIU)*

17 August 1967

Dear Geoffrey

Alas, unless I take some of it with me for the purpose (and I'm not familiar enough with customs regulations to risk that) I won't be able to toast your birthday on 21st inst in malt, since Valda and I will be in Budapest then. Still we'll toast it in whatever is available – Mastika or Peach Brandy or Rocky Cellar (Pilsener Type beer). And anyhow I'll toast you in malt tonight. My birthday has bought me a great supply of Glenfiddich, Morangie, and other superb distillations.

Seriously I do hope you make a complete recovery. In most of these cases it seems rest and an avoidance of sudden and unnecessary exertions is what is needed. Valda needs to be more careful than she sometimes is for the same reason. Personally I think that whisky is a sure recipe – it keeps the arteries from hardening. I am apparently a proof of its efficacy. Before going to America in May I consulted an Edinburgh specialist and he assured me that I was OK in every respect and that my condition would do credit to a man half my age. I thanked him and pointed out that he'd just given me carte-blanche to continue my excesses for another half-century. Later in Canada I underwent another thorough examination in the hospital to which my doctor son-in-law is attached, with the same result!!

At the moment, however, I'm thoroughly exhausted. This has been a terrific year for me – and the tremendous hullabaloo over my birthday has put the peter on it. I'd fain just rest instead of going off to Hungary, but Valda and a lady friend are eager to enjoy the amenities of Lake Balaton – and can't go unless I go along too to 'justify' the journey by giving a lecture or two.

I'm not sure if I'll be in London more than an hour or so on the way back. If I am I'll try to contact you, but it's unlikely – anyhow I haven't worked it out but you'll probably be still in Venice. It was certainly a great disappointment that I couldn't see Joyce and you when I was down for the International Poetry Festival. I had a short list of four or five things I wanted to do – but I'd no sooner arrived in London than the thing escalated and I found myself with a list of engagements resembling an old-style railway timetable, while the clerk at the hotel desk was kept busy taking down phoned messages for me and there was always a sheaf of these waiting for me if I was out of the hotel for an hour or two. The whole experience was utterly fantastic and I won't readily subject myself to it again. I'll just come incognito – and see nobody but Joyce and you.

In the meantime every good wish for your (if I can count) 57th anniversary and love to both Joyce and you. I don't know at the moment if Valda, busy packing, will be able to enclose a note for Joyce in my envelope. I've no doubt she will if she can. Your letters greatly bucked her – and she needed a bit of a hoist up, poor girl – it's hard work enduring somebody else's sudden access of international celebrity.

Yours, Chris

96. *To Alan Bold (NLS)*

14 November 1967

Dear Alan,

I am sorry to have been so long in thanking you for the copy of your new volume of poems which I was delighted to receive.[1] But as you probably know I have been repeatedly away from home and up to my eyebrows in work of all kinds (I have, for example, commissions for no fewer than seven new books which I must complete within the next 4 years!) The older I get the more my commitments seem to increase and my correspondence is necessarily the main casualty. In fact I've never recovered from the terrific avalanche of telegrams and letters etc. which descended upon my hapless pow last August.

I am sorry to see that most of the reviews I've seen haven't been favourable. Most of them accuse you of banality etc. And I certainly think that without in any way abating the didactic or polemical character of most of your poems you would be well advised to give more scope to sensuous elements. After all, the public — and above all the reviewers — need to have a good deal of jam with it if they are to swallow the medicine, and plenty of jam doesn't affect the potency of the essential dose.

I'll be looking out in due course for announcements of your novel etc. I hope all goes well with you, and with your wife and family.

Again with my best thanks, Yours, Christopher Grieve

---

1. Alan Bold, *To Find the New* (London: Chatto & Windus, 1967).

97. *To Christine Macintosh*

14 November 1967

Dear Christine

I can't remember when I wrote you last. A long time ago I fancy. But I have not yet got out from under the avalanche of telegrams, letters, etc. occasioned by my 75th birthday; and since then, instead of easing off, I seem to have been busier than ever. And must, apparently, keep on that way, since I have now signed contracts for seven new books which I must deliver to the publishers within the next 4 years. We heard from Mrs Galloway — they had been having a very difficult time, financially and otherwise. I don't think Valda has written to her yet, tho' I have reminded her several times of the need to do so.

As I think you know Valda and I had a very pleasant holiday in Hungary. She was with me too for a week in London where I was taking part in an International Poetry Festival. Since then I've had another Poetry Festival at Doncaster and am going for yet another to Dublin in the beginning of December. I was at Aberdeen talking to the students the other weekend and had a very enjoyable time, and then Valda and I were down in Kirkcudbrightshire and Dumfriesshire (Langholm) for a week. Now we'll have to settle down and have a quiet week or so here before the Christmas, New Year, and Burns Supper rush starts. So it's probably as well Alastair gave up the idea of having a yachting tour of the Hebrides. I couldn't have gone with them, as I've been far too busy – and I'd have worried myself stiff if they had gone without me. I hope the idea will materialise some other time while I'm still fit enough to superintend the operation. Incidentally I've been hoping to hear how Alistair's course panned out. Triumphantly I hope.

While 'seas divide' I keep getting references to you in the most unexpected quarters. I went a week or two ago to get measured for a new suit (Langholm tweed – advertised as the dearest in the world – and not sold generally at all but only to a select list of private customers). The tailor was Main in St Enoch Square in Glasgow. I'd never been there before. The business while retaining the old name of Main is run by a man called Mitchell, and the first thing he said to me was that he had been at Aberdeen University with my son-in-law, and also knew my daughter! So there you are. It's a small world.

I've had no word of Fairlie and am wondering how he is keeping. Months ago I did have a letter from Humphrey Milnes in which he said Fairlie had taken Joan's death very badly.

I see Bayevsky is having a show of his paintings. I'll drop him a line wishing him good business. He seems to have recovered from his illness. I hope you are all in good fettle. Has Elspeth begun her University career? I presume she settled on a Canadian University after all. I had a couple of professors from near Georgetown here the other week – Professors McIntyre and Duncan, from Guelph University; they are planning to start a School of Scottish Studies there.

I'm enclosing this with a copy of a volume of poems addressed to me by various poets. One of the curiosities of my birthday business is that this book sold out completely right away tho' it was published at the absurd price of 73/6.

Please remember us to Mabel, to the Balls and to the folk at the Terra Cotta.

With love to you all from Valda and I.

Yours, Christopher

P.S. We haven't seen Mike for weeks. He was busy all the time with the Hamilton Bye-Election which as you'll have seen was won by a Scottish Nationalist who turned a huge Labour Majority of over 18,000 into the first Scottish Nationalist win with a majority of 2000.[1] She is going to London tomorrow – and special trains and buses loaded with supporters, Pipe Band etc. are going down to see her take her seat. Both Michael and my cousin Jean White will be among the happy throng.

---

1. Winnie Ewing.

98. *To Sydney Goodsir Smith (NLS)*

21 November 1967

Dear Sydney,
    I was distressed to hear about your eye operation. It is one thing – and a good thing – to have one's eye on the ball. But not to have the full ocular equipment is of course all balls!
    I do hope the whole business wasn't too painful and otherwise troublesome. It is too long ago now since we met. I hope you have joined the 1320 Club, and may be at the Press Conference held Tuesday in Lucky McLucker's Lounge. All being well I intend to be there. But of course as you know I have Valda to contend with. She was at the Soviet thing yesterday and having sipped the Vodka when it is disarmingly like water would persist in interrupting my few well-chosen remarks. Wish you'd been there. You'd have appreciated better I think the difficulties under which I labour. However I did manage myself to absorb a sufficiency of the Russian spirit – – –
    All the best. I hope to see you ere long.
    Yours, Chris

99. *To Hugo Moore (EUL)*

4 February 1968

Dear Hugo
    Many thanks for your excellent essay in *Agenda*.[1] The issue was of course a great compliment and several of the essays were quite good tho' they did also contain some wild writing. Incidentally yours had a few errors. Who, for example, was Richard Haldane who you say was instrumental in obtaining the Civil List Pension for me? I have always understood I owed it to James Bridie, George Bernard Shaw, Walter Elliot, and Sir John Boyd.[2] Also, of course, I did not found the Scottish Home Rule Assocn. – I joined it in 1920 but it had been in existence decades before that. Nor did I form the Scottish National League – it was formed by the Hon. Ruaraidh Erskine of Mar, Angus Clark, and William Gillies – all friends of mine and all dead now.
    I'm sending this c/o Bauermeister because I don't know your own whereabouts. I expect you've left that firm now and hope things are OK with you. Penicillin seems to have cleared away the flu which sent me into hospital and had apparently (so the x-rays showed) affected both my lungs and I'm all right – only I've had to promise the doctors not to undertake any engagements I can possibly avoid for a month or two. Hospital in any case has left me unusually lazy and tho' I have heaps of work awaiting my attention I can't bring myself to do anything very much yet.
    All the best from Valda and I.
    Yours, Chris

1. *Agenda*, 5–6 (1967–8) was a Hugh MacDiarmid Special Issue.
2. Walter Elliot (1888–1958), Conservative MP for Lanark, 1918–23; Glasgow, Kelvingrove, 1924–45; Scottish Universities, 1946–49; Secretary of State for Scotland, 1936–38. John Boyd Orr, first Baron (1880–1971), biologist and Nobel Peace Prize winner in 1949 for his efforts as Director of the UN Food and Agriculture Organization.

100. *To Christine Macintosh*

4 February 1968

Dear Christine

There seems to be a conspiracy to turn me into a dandy in my old age. Your splendid pair of gloves are the last of a series which includes a suit in what advertises itself as the dearest twist cloth in the world and is only sold privately to an exclusive list of customers; a fine pink shirt to go with it; and several new ties and boxes of handkerchiefs. Perhaps I did need all these new habiliments to back me up. I had two or three weeks in hospital in Edinburgh with so-called Asian flu! X-rays showed it had affected both of my lungs, but penicillin seems to have cleared that away all right. I'd have been home more quickly but couldn't get – all the roads hereabouts were blocked with fallen trees. Our kitchenette windows were smashed in, and we'd no electricity, and no 'phone. Valda had quite a time carrying on. It was certainly the worst gale in Scotland in my lifetime. Glasgow suffered most – many deaths, property damage of nearly £9 million, and damage throughout Scotland to forestry another £8 million or so. I'm OK again but unaccountably lazy – due I think to the really appalling pile of work I should be tackling. I've had to promise my doctors to accept no engagements I can possibly avoid for a month or two yet. Anyhow I was reading a thriller when the gloves arrived, and it incidentally said gloves were usually worn by doctors, undertakers, bankers, burglars and aristocrats. I'm not sure which category I fall into now. Love to you all.

Christopher

101. *To William Johnstone (NLS)*

26 March 1968

Dear William,

Many thanks for your letter and the newspaper cutting which I return. You are of course absolutely right. The trouble is just that the truth is unbelievable – in all the arts Scotland is just nowhere, the practitioners Scotland has are almost without exception not worth a damn. It is difficult to see how we can ram this fact home, and how we can instigate any improvement, if indeed any improvement is possible at all and the Scots are not just a horde of morons.

I haven't quite recovered my wonted energy, and indeed am obeying my doctors' injunctions to do nothing I can possibly avoid. Ironically this state of affairs is accompanied by an increased demand for my services from all sorts of quarters. I think I'll follow the example of the Beatles and go off to the Himalayas to meditate.

While I am refusing all sorts of requests for speeches and poetry readings etc. there are some I can't avoid. I've just been down for a day or two at the University of Lancaster. I have Birmingham in the offing. And next week I have a couple of things in Glasgow.

However my stock seems to be rising in many countries. The German *Sonntag* devoted a whole page to a write-up about me and translations of several of my poems. Two Hungarian magazines have also just had translations of poems of mine and also in one of them a long essay on my work. And today I've had a new periodical from Denmark with a translation of a long poem of mine, and also a paperback book on Modern Poetry which is the best comprehensive account of poetry today all over the world, and devotes half-a-dozen pages to an excellent critical account and also reproduces a photograph of me in company with the sort of people I am glad to be associated – the Russians Mayakovsky and Pasternak, the German Brecht, etc. And apart from a brief and unflattering reference to Edwin Muir no other damned Scot at all!

As you'll know our proposed excursion to Tushielaw was cancelled – owing to the weather, since the chief promoter of the outing would have had to bring his wife and a young baby with him – and the weather was too wild for that. Valda 'phoned through to Mrs McLarty to explain but got a bad line and only, she thought, a young girl at the other end, and isn't sure that the message saying we weren't coming after all and thanking her for the willingness to give my cousin Jean a bed overnight was properly received.

I hope all goes well with all of you. This is I believe lambing time and what that entails in the sort of weather we've been having lately moves me to compassion.

Every kind regard to Mary, Sarah, and yourself.
Yours, Chris

102. *To Brian Lambie, Biggar (BMT)*

25 May 1968

Dear Mr Lambie

I was glad the Museum opening passed off so nicely and attracted such a good audience. They gave me a very attentive hearing and I can only hope my remarks were appropriate to the occasion and not too long.

I am going to Glasgow tomorrow and will be there until Thursday or Friday next week when my wife returns from Ireland. I will make a copy of my speech and send it to you. But I feel I must write you at once to say you were far too generous and to thank you for the bottle of Glenfiddich and the gift token you gave me. It was far too much for a small service I was only too pleased to perform.

With best wishes, Yours sincerely, Christopher Grieve

103. *To Oliver Brown (NLS)*

6 July 1968

Dear Oliver

Many thanks for your letter and the cutting of your article on my poetry. This, I see, is from a periodical called *The Declaration* but where does this appear and who puts it out?

Please give my heartiest congratulations to Catriona on her 1st Prize in Alex Scott's class. News of her enthusiasm for my poetry is very encouraging. You and I have been long in the Scottish field, political and cultural, but it is inevitable and right that the young people are now taking over. As you with Catriona, so I with Michael. He grew up of course in an atmosphere of poetry and literature but I did not press him into acceptance of my own attitudes in any way. Nevertheless he has come round off his own bat to share my views in large measure both as a Socialist and a Scottish Nationalist, and I am very pleased with his work alike in his *Daily Record* Voice of Scotland column and his editorship of the *Scots Independent*.

Catriona will be put to it if she tries to keep up with my output, *The Uncanny Scot*, a selection of my short stories and essays (MacGibbon & Kee) and *Celtic Nationalism* (Routledge and Kegan Paul) will be published in August. A selection of my poems in German translation is being published, also my last book of verse, *A Lap of Honour*, is being translated into Italian for early issue.[1]

I've been trying to cut down my public engagements and have refused many invitations but I am going to the Cheltenham Arts Festival in October and to Birmingham University and Cambridge a little later, while towards the end of the present month Valda and I will [be] at Langholm for the Common-Riding. I've hardly been in Edinburgh or Glasgow at all this year and while I'd be happy to see you at any time I can't at the moment say when I'm likely to be in Glasgow next. If anything opens up to take me there I'll let you know at once in the hope that we can arrange to meet. Failing that we'd be glad to see you here anytime, of course, but if you think of that please phone just to make sure we're at home. (Phone – Skirling-Biggar 55).

Love to Margaret and your daughters and yourself.

Yours, Chris

P.S. Best wishes for success with the doctoral thesis on Franco-Scottish relations.

1. Hugh MacDiarmid, *The Uncanny Scot: A Selection of Prose*, ed. Kenneth Buthlay (London: MacGibbon & Kee, 1968); Owen Dudley Edwards, Gwynfor Evans and Ioan Rhys, Hugh MacDiarmid, *Celtic Nationalism* (London: Routedge & Kegan Paul, 1968); Hugh MacDiarmid, *A Lap of Honour* (London: MacGibbon & Kee, 1967).

104. *To Jean White (EUL)*

17 August 1968

Dear Jean

You said you might attend one of the Poetry Readings in Lucky McLuker's Lounge, so this is a note to let you know alas! that they won't take place. It has been discovered at the last moment that the room there does not conform to some bye-law regarding places where such events can be held, so the Corporation has refused permission. It will be impossible to find an alternative hall now. Edinburgh is choc-a-bloc – more so apparently than at any previous festival.

It was nice seeing you and your friend the other night, and far too good of you to give me the splendid Japanese angle-poise reading lamp. It will be most useful in a few weeks' time when I settle down to heavy writing in my Garden Studio.

Hope however to see you again soon. All the best.

Yours, Chris

105. *To Duncan Glen (EUL)*

24 September 1968

Dear Duncan Glen

I am very glad to have your long letter this morning. I should have written you ere this, but all my correspondence is sadly in arrears and I have more work to get done somehow or other than I can possibly do. I've been trying to cut down outside engagements, but though I have refused all sorts of things I now feel like the man who suddenly to his horror realised that he belonged to 58 different organisations but after he'd resigned from as many as possible was pleased to find he now belonged only to 76!

I go to Cheltenham Festival of Literature on Monday, give an address on changes in Scottish Literature in the 20th Century to Glasgow Univ. Extra Mural on 8th Oct, and chair and speak at a Symposium on legal aspects of Scottish Independence run by the 1320 Club in Edinburgh on 12th Oct. In November I'm lecturing to St Andrews students on 8th and going, with Valda, to Dublin on the 10th to, *inter alia*, record the whole of *The Drunk Man* for Claddagh Records. But to my regret I've had to decline an invitation from the Oxford Union to take part in debating on

31st Oct. the following motion, which I would have been very happy to support viz: 'That, in Britain, violent demonstrations are a legitimate instrument in politics'. If I'd been able to go I would, of course, have argued along precisely the line you indicate in your letter.

I've told Cape I have two or three essays I can send them to choose one or two if they so desire as replacements for 'The Dour Drinkers' and 'McD on McD'. I don't think the latter is any loss, and feel the former is much more suitably included in *The Uncanny Scot* – of which I think McGibbon & Kee have made an excellent job. But I will suggest they might use the Arthur Leslie essay, with a footnote by you along the lines you indicate, so if you have it by you you might please send it to Cape now. (If you haven't a copy of it, let me know and I'll send one to them myself).[1]

Re the book of translations you are of course very welcome to include the Blok and Rilke (if Macmillan's agree), and also the two from the Gaelic of George Campbell Hay.

If you get a team of essayists by Scottish intellectuals, I'd certainly contribute an essay. I think Dr Geo. Davie would be willing too (tho' he is badly handicapped by eye trouble) and also Murison of the Scottish National Dictionary. My son Michael would too – he is as you know editor of *The Scots Independent*: but he has developed quite remarkably well both as a speaker and as a writer and has all the available information at his finger ends.

Let me know about these various propositions again – say about the middle of October – and I'll weigh in as well as I can.

As to the flattering idea of a photographic study, I think a day could be arranged towards the end of October – any day between 21st and 27th – but if that won't do, any day in November from 18th to 24th. If either of these suggestions is suitable, please let me know as soon as you can which day so that I can keep it free.

I am sending you on by separate parcel post a collection of the verse of Willie Neill, who writes in *Catalyst* and *Sgian Dubh* over the pseudonym of Will O'Gallowa, both in Scots and Gaelic. It is not high poetry, but good Scottish Nationalist popular verse, and I think would go well among the Scots Nats. I know of course that you are probably committed up to the hilt and book production is a costly business. But I think if you can see your way to publish that a guarantee against loss can be arranged by myself and others.

I don't know when Routledge and Kegan Paul are going to publish *Celtic Nationalism*. I had hoped it would be out long before this. If they don't hurry events will make a lot of the text out of date.

With every kind regard to Mrs Glen and the children, the Penrises, and others.

All the best. Yours, Christopher Grieve

1. Hugh MacDiarmid, *Selected Essays*, edited with an introduction by Duncan Glen (London: Cape, 1969). Arthur Leslie (one of CMG's pseudonyms), 'The Politics and Poetry of Hugh MacDiarmid' was reprinted from *The National Weekly* (Glasgow: Caledonian Press, 1952) and is also in Hugh MacDiarmid, *Selected Prose*, ed. Alan Riach (Manchester: Carcanet, 1992), pp. 201–19.

106. *To Kulgin Duval*

3 March 1969

Dear Kulgin,

Many thanks for specimen page of Bodoni *Drunk Man* and one of Masereel's illustrations.[1] It is a typical example of his work. As I think I told you in a previous letter I had the good fortune to see a lot of Masereel woodcuts when I was at Josef Herman's place, and the one you sent certainly shows that the old man's hand has not lost its cunning.

Yes, I think we should just wait until Mardersteig, if he is willing, cuts the italic – tho' I personally do not see (not being a perfectionist) why he cannot use the italic of the present type, inserting it where necessary (there isn't so much of it anyhow) in the very dark type.

I'm sorry I retained Douglas Sealy's letter and *Drunk Man* so long. He has been [*sic*] a lot of work into regularising the orthography etc. and it is a pity this cannot be used at present. But I have no doubt it will be required for some later issue. In any case I am very grateful to him.

Gareth has never sent me back my copy of the Major/Minor Records contract.

Hope Colin and you are OK.

I'm off to Durham University tomorrow (Tuesday).

All the best. Yours, Chris

---

1. Hugh MacDiarmid, *A Drunk Man Looks at the Thistle*, illustrated with eight woodcuts by Franz Masereel (Falkland: Kulgin Duval & Colin Hamilton, 1969); 160 copies printed in Dante type by Giovanni Mardersteig on the hand-press of the Officina Bodoni in Verona. The woodcuts were reproduced in *Edinburgh Review*, 86 (1990), pp.131–47.

107. *To Christine Macintosh*

27 March 1969

My dear Christine

Sorry to have been so long in writing you. As usual I've been extremely busy and much away – at Durham, Birmingham etc. This weekend is typical. I'm chairing a Conference at Berwick on Saturday, addressing the Scottish section of the Guild of Editors at Peebles on Sunday, and on

Monday Valda and I are flying to London and then by a Polish plane to East Germany where we'll be a fortnight.

I'll be over for the wedding all right – unless something unforeseeable comes in the way. But I don't think Valda will. She hasn't been – and isn't – well. The trouble is diverticulitis – inflammation of the diverticulum with, it seems, adhesions.

The doctors thought they could put things right by medical means, and certainly she seems a good deal better and has at any rate less pain. But she's still attending hospital. Her idea of a holiday is just a quiet time somewhere on her own, and I think that is certainly what she needs.

It was extremely kind of you to suggest having one of Michael's boys over, and I said I'd be pleased to take Lucian over with me. But Deirdre feels he is too young. It's a pity. Such a holiday in Canada would be splendid for him.

I've just heard from Barker Fairley and am writing him today.

Love to you all. Yours, Christopher

108. *To Kulgin Duval*

11 May 1969

Dear Kulgin,

I am sorry you feel disappointed at first sight with Masereel's woodcuts. After all it is virtually impossible to illustrate a poem – a complex poem anyhow – nor is that the function required of the artist. That is not to illustrate the poem but to decorate the book; and in this case Masereel's reputation must add to the value of the book, at any rate as a Collectors' piece. Apart from that as you know I had the opportunity of seeing a lot of Masereel's work when I was at Josef Herman's, and these pictures for the *Drunk Man* are quite characteristic of his work, and have the same force and economy as of old which shows that even at his advanced age (and with all the difficulty of not knowing the poem save in an indifferent translation) his hand has not lost its old cunning. As you rightly say of course when they are in their proper place along with Mardersteig's typography they will produce a different, and more favourable, impression.

I hope you will convey to Masereel through Mardersteig that I am pleased with him and regard it as a great compliment to have had him make these pictures for the *Drunk Man*, and give him my warmest thanks and kindest regards.

I am glad to learn from your letters that the trouble with the type-face has been overcome and I will look forward now to the book. I suppose you haven't any idea yet when it will be ready. I still hope to go to Verona on a flying visit to celebrate the occasion.

Valda has just had your 'phone call saying you hope to come here on Tuesday. So I'll cut off this letter – Yours, Christopher

109. To Ruth McQuillan (NLS)

24 May 1969

Dear Miss McQuillan

Many thanks for your letter. It reinforces my conviction that I have been singularly fortunate in having you write a dissertation on my work. I say this because a lot of students in half-a-dozen different countries have done theses on my *oeuvre*, and I am not similarly impressed by any of them. I am particularly struck by your angle of approach, and the fact that you have hit on my explanation of the form of *Clann Albainn*. I remember it, of course, but I must look at it again (I haven't seen it for quarter of a century at least) and I may be moved to take it up again and do the job.

With regard to Langholm I suppose you know the Langholm stories (especially the Waterside one) in *The Uncanny Scot*. That, and the 'Wauchopeside' and 'Whuchulls' poems in *A Lap of Honour* are, I think, the best things I have written about Langholm (especially 'Whuchulls' which I think is the best statement I've managed of my particularism). I don't know if you saw an article of mine [in] *The Listener* a year or two ago on 'Growing up in Langholm'. That is being published shortly in a book edited by Karl Miller (the editor of *The Listener*), as is also a piece entitled 'Satori in Scotland' (Satori = sudden revelation) dealing with how I came to write my early Scots lyrics. I don't know what this book is going to be titled: Faber and Faber are publishing it.[1]

It also occurs to me that an essay on *The Drunk Man*, by Professor Weston of the University of Massachusetts at Amherst might be worth your glancing at. It hasn't been published yet, but will be, probably in *The Massachusetts Review*. I think it is better than the essays on the same poem by David Daiches and Crichton Smith. Please return in due course.[2]

Anyhow here's hoping your thesis is accepted all right and that you come out of the examination on modern poetry in Britain, France, and America with flying colours, and are enabled in due course to write the much longer thesis you contemplate. I'm sorry you've lost Dr Holloway as your supervisor. I haven't heard of Dr Rathmell but hope he is of like calibre.

I'll look forward to the two separate essays you mention as well. The Pergamon Press are publishing a book comparing Dunbar and myself.[3]

I hope your July job is an agreeable one.

Yes, Valda and I did thoroughly enjoy East Germany, tho' I was worked rather too hard. We were both pretty well fagged out when we got back here, but have recovered now.

I expect to go to Canada about 16th or 17th June. Italy won't be till September I think and Wales and Ireland that month too.

I'll pass on your regards to McCaig. He and the Irish historian, Owen Dudley Edwards, are coming out here on Monday.

All the best from Valda and I.
Yours, Christopher Grieve

---

1. *Memoirs of a Modern Scotland*, ed. Karl Miller (London: Faber, 1970).
2. John C. Weston, *Hugh MacDiarmid's A Drunk Man Looks at the Thistle* (Preston: Akros, 1970).
3. This study was not published.

110. *To Christine Macintosh*

27 May 1969

Dear Christine

    I am hoping to get a plane to Toronto on 16th June and will let you know flight number etc. as soon as I am definitely booked. Valda alas won't be able to come. She is a gay old girl and hates missing the celebrations – all the more so now, when in addition to the wedding, there is Elspeth's engagement. This came as no surprise, since you'd told me before that she had a boy-friend. I note what you say about their ages, but they are not really marrying (when they do) young as things go nowadays. Over here a high percentage marry at 16 or 17.
    The invitation cards have just arrived. Church weddings are not much in my line; I remember when Deirdre and Mike married, Deirdre's parents were very upset when I, and Mike himself, decided to attend in our kilts. They felt it would spoil the whole thing and that morning dress, top hats, gloves etc. were *de rigueur*. So on this occasion if I am odd man out among a company of elegant gentlemen in the conventional attire you must excuse me if, in the Biblical words, I find myself 'without a wedding garment' and turn up in the 'garb of old Gaul'.
    That apart I will try to behave myself and not disgrace the party.
    As to Elspeth I am enclosing a separate note to her.
    Looking forward immensely to seeing you all again.
    With love to you all from Valda and I. Yours, Christopher

111. *To Christine and Alastair Macintosh*

[13 July 1969]

Dear Christine and Alastair

    I got home all right, by wheel-chair, plane, and finally Mike's car – he met me at Prestwick and drove me straight home. I was about all in. Despite the comfort of the seats you got for us on the plane, neither Mr Smith nor I slept at all on the flight. Since then I have spent most of my time in bed. Tomorrow (Monday) I am going into Chalmers' Hospital in Edinburgh for X-ray etc., and Dr Davidson (who got Alistair's letter) hopes I'll stay in for a week or so. I probably will. I certainly won't be able to do any of my work for a while. I need not repeat how sorry I am to have been such a trouble – or how grateful to Alistair for his care of me. Yet I was pleased to see you all again and enjoyed what I could share of all the ongoings. Valda is OK but suffering from the continued bad weather here – very dull and much rain. I hope you are all fine and fit after all the fun and games. I'm writing to Barker Fairley and to Ina as well. Love from us both to you all.

Yours, Christopher

112. *To Barbara Niven (NLS)*

7 August 1969

Dear Barbara

It is a long time since I wrote you, but that, alas, has been unavoidable. I went to Canada in June to attend my son-in-law's sister's wedding and after the first day or two caught a virus infection. At first I only felt seedy. I went and stayed a few days with Barker Fairley in Toronto and by the end of these few days the virus had really got to work. It attacked my internal organs one after the other. I went back to my daughter's home in Georgetown and by that time I was seriously ill. My son-in-law is a doctor and he took good care of me. But I had to spend most of my remaining time in Canada in bed. The virus by then had given me a bad dose of pneumonia. On the assumption that the trouble was bacillar I was given a lot of penicillin, but while that is effective when bacilli are the cause of the trouble, it is not so with virus, so I was switched on to tetra-mycin. I was taken on the plane for home in a wheel-chair!!! On getting home I went into a hospital in Edinburgh. X-ray showed I'd still pneumonia on my right lung. That cleared up in a week or so, and I then went, with Valda, to convalesce in Langholm, hoping my native air would rehabilitate me. I think it has done and that with care I should go on all right now. But I am still weak (as a consequence of the heavy drugging) and not only lazy and disinclined to work but actually obliged to cancel all sorts of engagements. Certainly I'll now need for an indefinite time ahead to reduce my activities.

The worst of it is that my obligations to publishers, editors, etc. are multiplying all the time. I have a book of my *Selected Essays* due out any day and am part-author of two other books due out soon. But editions of the *Drunk Man* are coming out 1/ through the Bodoni Press, Italy and 2/ through the Massachusetts University Press in America, and the Swallow Press, Chicago, are to publish American editions of the three books of mine Messrs MacGibbon & Kee have published – a copy of the latest which, just out, I enclose. Also I am contracted [for] five other books which ought to have been done by this time but are still hopelessly in arrears. One of these is a study of Communists & Poetry, dealing with Mayakowski, Brecht, Aragon, Eluard, Alberti, Hikmet and others.[1] Then Bertrand Russell's former Secretary, Ralph Schoenmann is starting a new magazine in America – *Socialist America* – for which I have just promised a long essay on Aesthetics and the Future of Mankind or The Masses of Mankind and the Future of Poetry. I'm not neglecting the fact that I'm a card-carrying Communist – tho' I am completely opposed to the CPGB with regard to the 'invasion' of Czecho-Slovakia and my attitude thereto has been published all over Europe.[2] Also I've written a long article on my impressions of the GDR for *Neues Deutschland* which will be printed in September as one of a series apropos the 20th Anniversary, and I've congratulated the Ulbricht regime in broadcasts on Bremer Radio and on International Radio, Berlin.[3] So there's life in the old dog yet.

Valda is in fair fettle – but the garden was a wilderness of weeds on our return from Langholm, so she is working too hard. She was at a show today where our Border Terrier, Clootie, won a 3rd prize.

If you haven't had news from me for too long, I also have not had news of you. So let me have it soon. I trust you are both well and have been able to enjoy the summer.

Love to all friends from Valda and Yours, Christopher

---

1. John Manson has suggested that this book may have been commissioned by Nathaniel Tarn of Cape and that perhaps as a result of Tarn leaving Cape, the book was never published. Louis Aragon (1897–1982), French poet, novelist and journalist, whose early work was much involved with surrealism but turned to more traditional patterns after a visit to Russia in 1930; Paul Éluard (1895–1952), French poet, prominent in the surrealist movement, also moved away from surrealism in 1930, joined the Communist Party in 1942; Rafael Alberti (1902–1999), Spanish poet, best remembered for his 'crisis' poems concerning the emptiness of twentieth-century life, joined the Communist Party in 1931.
2. The CPGB position was in favour of the de-Stalinisation programme of Dubcek's Prague Spring and against the subsequent invasion by the Warsaw Pact countries.
3. Walter Ulbricht (1893–1973), the East German communist politician responsible in large part for the creation of a one-party state, the 'sovietisation' of East Germany and the building of the Berlin Wall (1961).

113. *To the Editor,* The Scotsman

25 August 1969 [published 30 August]

Sir – Whoever was responsible for giving Malcolm Muggeridge the freedom of the pulpit of the High Kirk of Edinburgh did a notable disservice to the Edinburgh Festival. Why was he invited? Because it seems of a desire on the part of those responsible to cash in on the notoriety he has acquired by his manipulation of the great mass media in the interests of a propaganda that would not be out-rivalled by the worst of the Bible-thumping excesses of America's Bible Belt. In any case it was 'cauld kail het again' – simply a repeat of the monstrous slander Mr Muggeridge vented on the student body of Edinburgh University.[1]

Not limiting himself on this occasion to the student body, he now vilified the whole range of contemporary literature and the arts.

His Sermon was in fact simply an 'Epistle to the Philistines' and as such not only uncanonical but a preposterous and utterly unwelcome addition to the *Apocrypha*. In its violence and lack of discrimination there was a sorry echo of John Knox's outburst against the 'Monstrous Regiment of Women'. No one perusing it can fail to mark its sad lack of Christian charity. Mr Muggeridge may have an eunuch-like immunity from the sins of the flesh and their mental counterparts (if indeed even eunuchs are so immune), but it beggars belief that at a time when all the world's authors, artists and composers are united in reproducing in our midst the horrors of Sodom and Gomorrah Mr Muggeridge alone has been vouchsafed the honour of preserving his virginal innocence.

He quoted, 'and God said let there be light – and there was light'. I have said in one of my poems, 'God said let there be light and there was a little'. It is too bad that Mr Muggeridge should have a monopoly of it.

Particularly atrocious and unforgivable were Mr Muggeridge's remarks on the Minister of the Arts, Miss Jennie Lee, at a time when she was honouring the city with Government support of the Fringe Society. Mr Muggeridge should have been there in the Chaplaincy Centre. He might have compared his own unbridled hysteria with the gentle and modest helpfulness of Miss Lee's.

There is a lunatic fringe in Literature and the arts as well as in religiosity and rancorous moralism, but Mr Muggeridge is quite wrong when he throws his blanket denunciations so widely. Ninety per cent of the enormous output of literature and the arts today is entirely free of the vices to which Mr Muggeridge refers.

When he refers to naked actors scampering about a stage at a 'happening' he is elevating one exceptional case into an allegation of typicality and giving undue prominence and publicity to what is only a grenz-situation. That is more likely to exacerbate the trouble than to eliminate it, and, indeed, it is most likely that Mr Muggeridge's sensation mongering attracts the attention it does just because it also feeds the appetites responsible for the phenomena he denounces.

In any case he has no qualification whatever as a critic of literature and the arts. He has himself no substantive work to his credit and to all appearances a complete lack both of judgement and creative ability. It is highly probable that in the last analysis the burden of his disgraceful harangue is attributable to an inferiority complex and to jealousy of the mandarins, authors and artists endowed with the abilities he envies, and for which he has found a very transient and disreputable substitute given to him by the left hand of exactly the same forces busy dispensing with the right hand the phenomena he stigmatises.

I am etc., Hugh MacDiarmid

---

1. Muggeridge was Rector of Edinburgh University 1967-8 and had resigned the post over alleged student liberalism and promiscuity.

114. *To Arno Reinfrank (EUL)*

9 September 1969

Dear Arno Reinfrank

I have just received your letter of 7th inst.

I knew of course that my correspondence is hopelessly in arrears and has been so for months now and is likely to remain in that condition for an indefinite period to come. But I am appalled to think that I have not written you since before I went to Canada. That was a disaster. I caught a virus infection immediately I landed in Canada. It assailed all my internal organs in turn and finished by leaving me with a bad dose of pneumonia. It was really touch and go. Fortunately I was in good hands. My son-in-law is a highly qualified doctor. But I had to spend most of my time in Canada in bed, and when I enplaned for home I had to be taken in a wheelchair from the observation gallery in Toronto airport, down to and across the tar-mac and on to the plane, as I was too weak to walk. On getting home I went into hospital in Edinburgh. X-ray showed I'd still pneumonia on my right lung. This cleared up in a few days and then I went on convalescence to my native town in Dumfriesshire, hoping the air there would rehabilitate me. It did. But I am still very weak and unable to do much work. Also, of course, I had had to cancel all sorts of outside engagements. So I wasn't able to go to the Celtic Conference in Cardiff after all – much to my disappointment. I particularly regretted being unable to meet John Montague again.

This curtailment of travelling, lecturing and giving poetry readings must continue. I'll have to cut out all kinds of activities for a long time yet. And needless to say I am still unable to get on with various books which should have been in the publisher's hands before now. However leading a quiet and careful life I think I'll be all right again in a few months' time.

I am very pleased to hear of the West German arrangement to publish your translation of 'On a Raised Beach' and will look forward to this in due course.

I hope you have a good time in Stockholm, and later, at Düsseldorf –

West Berlin – Frankfurt.

I am very sorry to hear about Helen's trouble but glad your own work is doing well enough to keep you from undue worry. Please give Helen my best wishes for her speedy and complete recovery. So much wonderful progress has been made in the last few years in cardiac matters that one can hope that the sort of thing that has been afflicting Helen can be rectified. My own wife has had heart trouble too; also recurrent inflammation of the diverticulum, but is better again at present.

While I have been quite unable to make headway with the various books I am under contract to produce, things are going ahead in other directions. Massachusetts University Press are issuing an edition of my *Drunk Man* shortly, and the de luxe edition of the same poem by the Bodoni Press, Verona, Italy, and illustrated by the veteran Belgian artist Franz Masereel will be out soon. Also the Penguin edition of my *Selected Poems* is on the way.[1]

All the best to Helen and you. I am indeed very sorry to have been so long in writing you, but you will understand.

Yours, Christopher Grieve

---

1. Hugh MacDiarmid, *Selected Poems*, ed. David Craig and John Manson (Harmondsworth: Penguin Books, 1970).

115. *To Ronald Stevenson (NLS)*

10 October 1969

Dear Ronald

No hard feelings? If I haven't replied to your last two notes, you also were a devil of a long time out of touch with me. But we are both busy men – excessively busy perhaps. Anyhow I'm looking forward to the 60–mile cross country run, delighted with your article in today's *Listener* on the *Passacaglia on DSCH*, and very interested in what the *Radio Times* says about the song-cycle commissioned by Peter Pears.

As you may have heard I've had a bad time. I caught a virus infection in Canada which upset all my internal organs in turn and then gave me double pneumonia. On my return I went into hospital in Edinburgh, X-rays showing I'd still pneumonia on my lungs. This cleared up and I convalesced in my native town of Langholm hoping my native air would rehabilitate me. It did. And I should be OK now – with care.

I've had to cancel many engagements, my correspondence is in a state of chaos, and several books, contracted for and due for delivery to publishers, I haven't been able to begin yet. I'm afraid this reduction of my activities must be permanent – after all, not to be wondered at, as I'm over 77 now.

I hope despite your load of work that your own health is all right.
I wrote to Martin Dalby.
Valda joins me in best wishes to you, and to Marjorie and the children.
Yours, Christopher Grieve

116. *To Michael Grieve (NLS)*

Xmas Eve, 24 December 1969

Dear Michael

Sorry not to be with you this Xmas but I must attend to the zoo here. However love to you all, and to Harry and Mina, and hope you have a good time.

You never sent me the *Glasgow Herald* notice of my *Selected Essays*. I am anxious to have it. So please send it. In one of his new publications Duncan Glen has a good deal to say about it, and I am anxious to read exactly what it said – and determined to get my own back whenever opportunity offers. It is far too late in the day for malicious attacks of that kind, by some anonymous journalist not fit to tie the latchets of my shoes.

Hope you are being very careful in your movements, and that the stitches are out and have taken the pain away with them.

Love, Yours, Dad

117. *To Tom Pickard (UDL)*

[1969?]

Dear Mr Pickard

Many thanks for your letter of 27th ult inviting me to give a reading in the Morden Tower Book room, Newcastle-upon-Tyne, on 22nd February. I have pleasure in accepting. It is very good of Mr Bunting to have me stay with him and I'll be very happy to do so.[1] I was delighted to meet him some time ago at a show of paintings in the Stone Gallery but I lost my note of his address and phone number and could not communicate further with him. So I am particularly pleased to have this opportunity of renewing and extending our acquaintance. Congratulations on the scope of your readings during the 7 to 8 months past and the present plans for the Newcastle Festival, to which I wish all success.

Yours, Christopher Grieve ('Hugh MacDiarmid')

Nota Bene

A Scottish writer need not be
A left-winger to be frozen out,
Denied a livelihood, condemned
By every mindless popularity-tout.

All he needs to do indeed
Is to approach reality and write
Anything any intelligent person can read.
Few this ferocious fate invite!

The Highlanders Are Not A Sensitive People.

The Highlanders are not a sensitive people.
But exactly the opposite. I am all
For the de-Tibetanisation of the Hebrides.
It is perfect humbug to imagine
There's a reservation there for fine forms of consciousness
Where the natives cultivate rare soul-states
And hand-fed principles and choice spiritualities
Much as the Sassanach tenants of the deer forests, grouse moors, and
                                                                               lochs
Rear and tend the young stock of their sports.

Yet, my dear, as who upon the Cornish moors
Breaks apart a piece of rock will find it
Impregnated through and through with the smell of honey
So lies the Gaelic tradition in the lives
Of our dourest, most unconscious and denying Scots.
It is there, although it is unnoted
And exerts its secret potent influence.
That a spiritual ideal of life
May revive among us is largely due
To its subtle emanation.[2]

---

[1]. Basil Bunting (1900–85), English poet, disciple of Ezra Pound.
[2]. 'The Highlanders Are Not A Sensitive People': Hugh MacDiarmid, *Complete Poems*, vol. 2, p. 1417 (dated 1963). 'Nota Bene' seems hitherto uncollected.

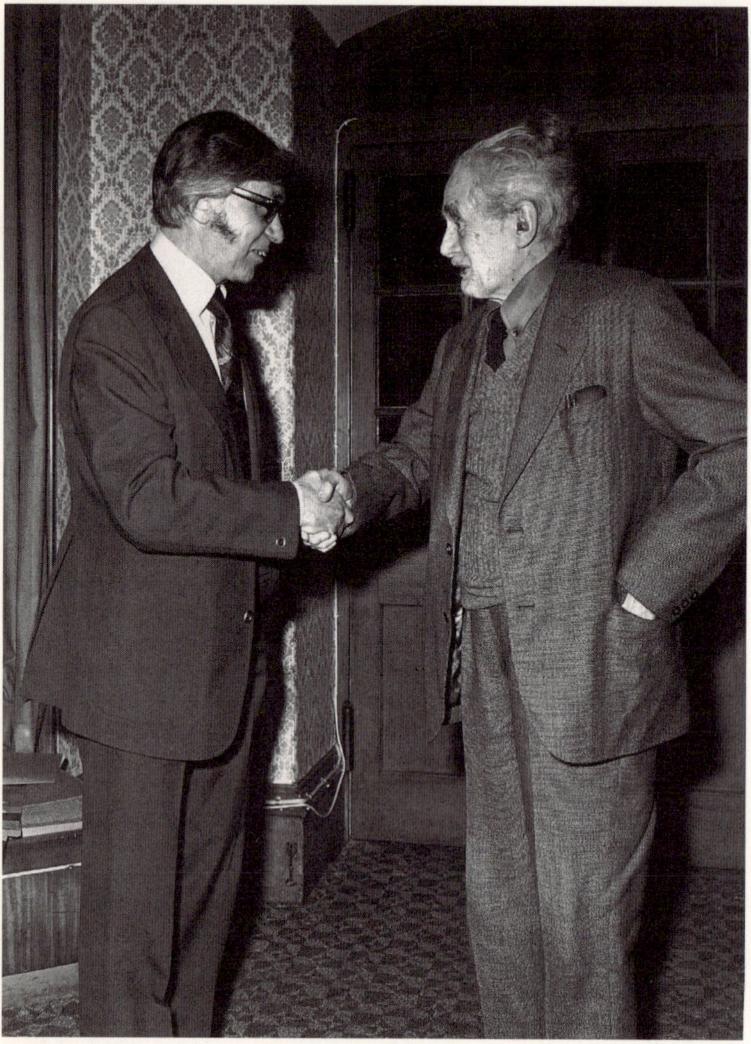

PART SIX

The 1970s

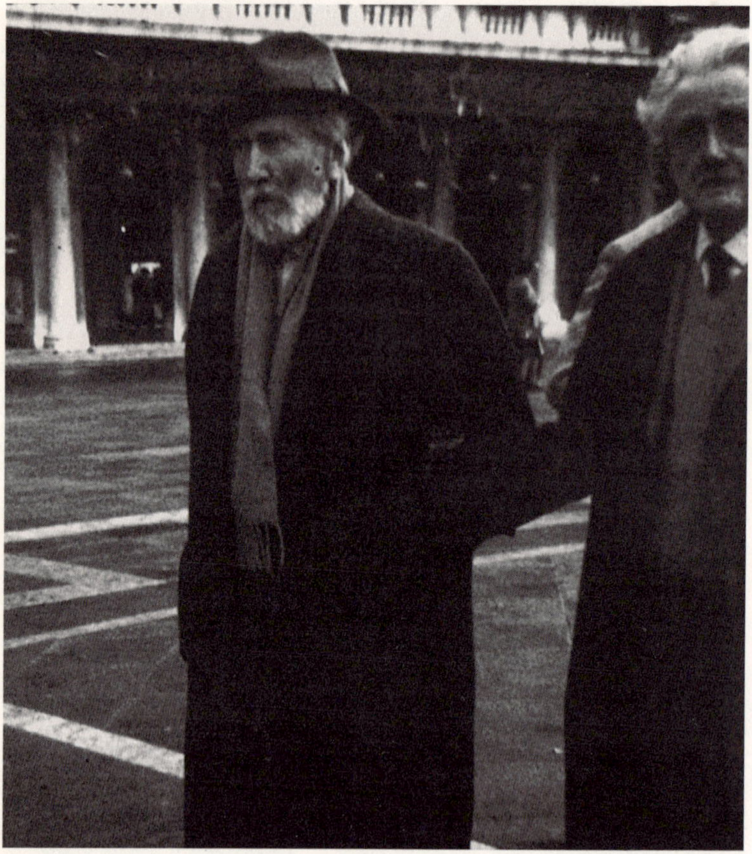

1. *To Alan Bold (NLS)*

10 February 1970

Dear Alan Bold,

I won't be able to take part in the Lyceum poetry reading. Since my recent illness I have been obliged to cut down my commitments for lectures, poetry readings etc. to a minimum, and I am afraid this state of affairs must be permanent. In any case I make it a rule not to take part unless the other participants are approved by me in advance. I saw your recent interview in the *Sunday Times* in which you said you were not a communist, wanted a big mass public and were opposed to the literary and aesthetic. I am a Communist. Poetry is a branch of literature so the more 'literary' the better, and the higher the aesthetic level the better. I think there has always been – and likely to continue to be – a very small public for any poetry worth the name. What appeals to a big public is rubbish, and I am utterly opposed to playing down to that public, though I know it can be lucrative. In any case I am not prepared to share a platform with 'concrete poets', 'beat poets' and the like.

Even if I were – and even if the other participants were acceptable to me – I couldn't take part at the Lyceum, because I am gong to Ireland on Saturday, then to Italy, then to Canada – and I have already more writing I must do and more engagements to fulfil than the time above travels will leave me.

All the best. Yours, Chris

2. *To William Johnstone (NLS)*

22 February 1970

Dear William,

I should have written you sooner to thank you for your congratulations re the Arts Council award which was totally unexpected but will no doubt come in useful to Valda if not to me.

I was sorry to hear you were not keeping too well. As I've told you before there is only one good medicine – whisky.

I hope the arrangements for your Retrospective are going ahead all right.

You'll be interested to know that I've agreed to open the Heartfield Collection of Photomontage which the 67 Gallery are putting on in Edinburgh at the Festival time. I know little about it yet but it will at least give me an opportunity of denouncing the safety-first and Philistine attitude of the Festival Committee to experimental Art. The Arts Council had it on in London and my friend, the German poet Erich Fried gave a splendid speech when he opened it there.[1] So for Scotland's credit I must try to say something equally good on this occasion. I don't know the date yet – probably about time Festival starts.

I just got back from Ireland on Wednesday. I had a very strenuous and rewarding time there.

Now I'm trying to clear my decks prior to going to Italy and then to Canada. I'm slowly making up the arrears of work I incurred during my illness and certainly so far as books are concerned I'm making headway – one coming out in Italy, one out in America and another about to appear, and the Penguin edition of my *Selected Poems* due to be published at end of May or first week in June, with first edition of 20,000. Not bad for a lazy old septuagenarian.

I hope all's well with Mary, Sarah, and yourself.

Here I'm the centrepiece of a gradually diminishing menagerie. Valda has now sold 3 of her 6 Border Terrier pups but the remaining 3 are noisy enough to be an infernal nuisance.

All the best. Hope to see you again ere long.

Yours, Christopher

---

1. Erich Fried (1921–88), Austrian poet, living in London from 1938 and working for the BBC.

3. *To Alan Bold (NLS)*

8 March 1969 [1970]

Dear Alan Bold

Alas, not even the change of date to May 4th will enable me to join in the Poetry Reading at the Lyceum. I'm going to East Germany, then to Italy, and finally to Canada, and as I do not intend to return to Scotland between these trips that means I'll be away from the beginning of April until June.

I'll look forward to the *Penguin Book of Socialist Verse*.[1] I'm writing a book on Communist Poetry, with chapters on Neruda, Hikmet, József Attila, Mayakovsky, Brecht, etc. – not quite so wide a range as your Penguin, as I won't have space to deal with (tho' I may refer briefly to) Vallejo, Faiz, Iqbal.[2] But I don't know when it will appear yet. My many other engagements are slowing up my productivity.

I'll look forward to the *Perpetual Motion Machine*.

All the best to you and your wife and family.

Yours, Christopher Grieve

---

1. *The Penguin Book of Socialist Verse*, ed. Alan Bold (Harmondsworth: Penguin, 1970).
2. Sir Muhammad Iqbal (1873–1938), Muslim Indian poet, writing in Urdu and Persian, national poet of Pakistan. He wrote much on the need for social harmony

and although sympathetic to Marxist ideas, his ideology was based on Islam. Faiz Ahmad Faiz (1911–84), Pakistani poet with communist sympathies, awarded Lenin Peace Prize (1963). César Vallejo (1892–1938), Peruvian poet, always left-wing and active politically, he joined the Spanish Communist Party in 1931.

4. *To the Editor,* Times Literary Supplement

4 June 1970

SUMMITS AND SPOIL-HEAPS

Sir, – I am accustomed in *TLS* and like periodicals to an alternation of articles praising my work in the highest terms and raising all manner of niggling and irrelevant points against it. A typical example is the review, in your issue of May 14, which I have just seen, having been in Canada since the middle of April.[1]

I make nowhere any claim to be an expert bibliographer or good editor, and my lack of qualifications in these respects does not seem to me relevant to my status as a poet. What does your reviewer think ought to have been done in view of the fact that my *Collected Poems* (Macmillan, New York, 1962) was a misnomer and excluded a great deal of my work? Any complaint on this score should have been directed not against me but against the editor and publishers of that book, but surely it is only reasonable that the remainder of my work should be brought together when and as practicable to make up for the omissions in *Collected Poems*. I consider myself fortunate that Messrs MacGibbon and Kee should have undertaken this work and already issued three volumes of my verse (including poems written since *Collected Poems* was published). Your reviewer's hope that subsequent *Clyack Sheafs* and *Still More Collected Poems* are not in the offing is likely to be disappointed, and will certainly not be shared by many hundreds of readers at home and abroad who have bought up the three supplementary volumes in question and are calling for more. Your reviewer, himself, indeed suggests various poems not yet collected but which he thinks ought to have been. I have no apology to make for the absence of sources and dates, but Mr Duncan Glen, who is severely criticized by your reviewer, has done a very great deal to provide these and to recover many poems I'd lost sight of and forgotten I'd written.

There is a cleavage between my lyrics written in the early 1920s and the kind of poetry I have written in the past forty years, and lovers of the former frequently dislike the latter. I do not agree with them, however, and find it significant that though your reviewer stresses the need to distinguish between 'the achieved and integrated poetry, and that which is too inert stylistically' he himself exemplifies the confusion as ludicrously as any, as when, for instance, he quotes a passage from my 'Ode to All Rebels' and suggests that by no criterion could this be excluded from the canon of my work. Quite simply, I do not agree with him, and however essential he and a few others may regard the clearing up of sources and dates and the final achievement of a complete works comparable to the Vaniorum Yeats, I am not willing while still alive and writing to allow editors or publishers to reach and base editions of my work on such 'rational decisions' as apparently I am unable to stand back and reach myself. Failing that, however, Messrs MacGibbon and Kee have undoubtedly come to the rescue of my work as effectively as I am prepared to allow anyone to do in the meantime. The books are beautifully printed and produced and have met with a ready acceptance in many quarters at home and abroad including the publication of American editions of all of them.

  Hugh MacDiarmid

[Our reviewer writes: The point of my review was that a remarkable body of poetry has been sadly mangled by years of erratic editing and publishing. Mr MacDiarmid's way of 'denying everything' and meeting detailed critical points with simple rebuttals in effect endorses this state of affairs. If he thinks it 'niggling and irrelevant' to object that a fine lyric of the 1930s, 'From "The War with England"' has been arbitrarily and silently robbed of its clinching couplet and one of its three verses, I can only marvel that he cares so little for the integrity of his own poems. It is because I care for his integrity that I want no more scrappy gleaning of late sheaves but instead (a) the reprinting for the first time for nearly fifty years of his first good poems in Scots, the lyrics from before *Sangschaw*; (b) a *Collected Poems* that is complete and properly arranged by dates of writing: and (c) selected volumes that are clear about sources and that abridge only sparingly and on explicit principles.]

---

1. *A Lap of Honour*, *A Clyack Sheaf* and *More Collected Poems* (London: MacGibbon and Kee, 1967, 1969 and 1970, respectively) were all published as supplements to the Macmillan *Collected Poems* (1962, 1967).

5. *To Duncan Glen (EUL)*

15 June 1970

Dear Duncan Glen

  I wrote out the stuff I'd planned as promised and would have posted it to you a few days ago – but when I re-read and reconsidered what I'd written I realised it wouldn't do. Whither Scotland is going will not be clear in many respects until after Thursday's declaration of the polls. There have been during the election meetings – and the candidates' addresses and newspaper leaders and special articles – all sorts of declarations as to what Scotland needs and wants: and this material is difficult to digest and boil down to definite statements. That is what I'm trying to do now. What I achieve I'll post to you tomorrow (Tuesday). I know it is long overdue and must have upset your arrangements badly. But things are moving fast and in so many different directions, or rather on so many different levels, that it is damnably difficult, or even impossible, to see the wood for the trees. But on the other hand anything that does not take account of these things (straws tho' they may be, yet showing the way the wind is blowing) may quite easily be falsified by what Thursday discloses. And that seems to me a risk not worth taking. There is no point in sending you something that will be out of date before it reaches you. I am extremely sorry about this delay. If I am too late now just cancel my engagement to write this part of the book. I will quite understand. But I have just been unable to help myself. Even since my last letter to you little of my time has been my own. I had six visitors yesterday, five the day before. And all sorts of other things — and more visitors — are pressing on me.

One of yesterday's visitors was Jack Weston. We had a long session — there were so many questions he had to ask and information I had to give him. And tomorrow or Wednesday I must go into Edinburgh and have another session with him. And so it goes on. I have no doubt you are equally worried and subject to all manner of pressures. But two blacks don't make a white.

The Bodoni edition de luxe of *The Drunk Man* is now out. It is a very handsome book, but so it should be at £40 a copy!! And I'm waiting now for the Penguin of my *Selected Poems*. Tom Scott's *Penguin Book of Scottish Verse* seems to me a splendid job — the best Scottish anthology to date — and his preface covers the whole field of our independent tradition of Scots poetry succinctly and admirably. I have seen no reviews of it yet, and fear it will be black-balled in several quarters. Indeed it has already been the victim of some of our inveterate internecine feuds and the Inter-Universities Committee on Scottish Literature has decided not to adopt it as a textbook for our schools and universities. A monstrous decision since it is by far the best thing in the field and at 10/- at a price students and school pupils can afford.

Blessings on you and again my sincere apologies and regrets.

Yours, Christopher Grieve

6. *To Kulgin Duval*

17 June 1970

Dear Kulgin,

Valda told me today after Colin and you left that you'd been upset by what Jack Weston said about my not having been paid for doing the English translation of the *Drunk Man*.

It was Norman MacCaig who asked about this and I told him I'd been adequately paid – not specifically for the translation, but for the whole job.

Norman is very secretive about his own affairs. He is always very anxious to know what I am doing, who I am seeing etc. etc. But he never reciprocates by telling me anything about his own affairs. I do not trust him, and in particular I detest his attitude of being afraid anyone is making anything out of him. So long as he gets a fair price he has nothing to do with what is subsequently made by re-sale. It is a mean and jealous attitude. You will agree that I have never asked you what you sell anything for. It is not my business and I certainly do not grudge you anything you make.

In any case, as I have often told you, Valda and I regard Colin and you as good friends, who have always given us a fair deal and on top of that been very generous to us in other ways.

I am very sorry you have been upset by these unwarranted imputations. We must be very careful not to give any information whatever to people like Norman – and there are plenty of them – who are simply greedy and envious.

As I said I'll let you know dates as soon as I get things fixed up, and Valda and I will certainly be looking forward to Falkland, Balcarres, Italy, etc. in a month or so.

I am not forgetting that I owe you a holograph copy of the *Drunk Man* and will let you have this as soon as I can. But that is just another instance when the boot is on the other foot and you have paid me for something I haven't yet done.

With warmest regards to you both.

Yours, Christopher Grieve

7. *To the Editor,* The Irish Times

10 November 1970

Sir,

I read with great regret Mary Leland's article in your issue of Saturday October 31st, about 'the Poignant death rattle of Midleton whisky'. I have been a whisky drinker for over 60 years and have a thorough knowledge of all the Scottish malt whiskies in particular. But it was a red letter day for me when I encountered Midleton whisky two or three years ago.

I had never heard of it before, but recognised it at once as one of the – if not the – finest whiskies in the world. I was amazed such a treasure was not better known, and remain sure that if it had been properly advertised it would have appealed to connoisseurs all over the world. Even now I cannot understand how such an undoubted 'world-beater' has been allowed to go by the board.

We all know the enormities of which Big Business is capable, but this is a particularly gross example. It is as if it had been agreed to destroy a priceless Titian, El Greco, or Velasquez. Just because they were less appreciated by the mass of people than some crude photographs. I agree entirely with the remarks of a publican printed in the final paragraphs of Miss Leland's article and in particular with the final two or three sentences.

After I came on Midleton's, I wrote to friends of mine, Professor David Daiches and others, who have written very knowledgeably about whisky and found no reference to Midleton in their books on the subject. I hope they took steps to sample it before it was done away with, and that in subsequent editions in their books proper tribute may at last – if, alas, too late – be paid to this incomparable whisky.

I mourn it as one might mourn the wanton slaughter of a lovely woman.
Yours etc., Hugh MacDiarmid

8. *To Morag Enticknap*

27 November 1970

Dear Morag

I was surprised, and delighted, to receive your letter of 11th inst. But I only got it yesterday. I was away doing a poetry reading at Bristol University, then a colour TV interview at Newcastle-on-Tyne for Tyneside and Teeside TV. Prior to that my wife and I were away in France and Italy. She didn't come back with me when I flew back from Milan, but went onto Austria and motored back to Hamburg, then sailed to Hull and so home.

For nearly – or just over – quarter of a century I haven't known your – or your father's – whereabouts. Your address in Canonbury Park South is a part of London well-known to me and indeed friends of mine – a good poet, and the widow of a former Swedish diplomat to the Court of St James live there and when I'm in London I generally visit them.

Some months ago I was speaking at a dinner near there and my table neighbour was a Mr Forsyth (or Fordyce – I am very deaf and don't catch names well) told me he had worked with the Customs and Excise along with your father, and that your father had remarried – but that his wife had had serious malignant tumour trouble. I hope she recovered and that they are both well and happy.

He also told me you were married and had a family, but not how long you had been in that felicitous condition. I hope Mr Enticknap and you are happy. He is the only man into whose shoes I ever stepped – briefly and unsuccessfully – an escapade for which I hope he may have long ago forgiven me.[1]

You do not say how many children you have. We are a prolific breed. My son Michael, a Journalist and Public Relations Officer in Glasgow, has two sons. My son Walter, a mining engineer at Stoke-on-Trent, has three daughters. And my daughter Christine married to a medical consultant in

Ontario, Canada, has 2 sons and 2 daughters. The eldest of the latter has married last year to a brilliant Ukraninan astro-physicist. My wife and I were at the wedding – I have been in Canada five or six times, and indeed have been a great traveller in the past ten years – in the USSR, China, Bulgaria, Rumania, Czecho-Slovakia, and the German Democratic Republic.

I am pleased to hear of Alasdair's concern with my poetry and will be glad if I can help him in any way.[1] I have published over 50 books (prose and poetry) now. The best is a long poem called *A Drunk Man Looks at the Thistle*. This has gone with many editions. The Bodoni Press, Verona, Italy – the finest hand press in the world – recently published a beautifully printed and broad limited edition, illustrated with woodcuts by the Belgian artist, Franz Masereel, at £40 a copy – and sold out before publication. Another edition, excellently edited and fully glossed, is due shortly both in hard back and paperback forms from the University of Massachusetts Press.[2] Easier for Alasdair to get hold of is a Penguin paperback at 5/- – *Selected Poems of Hugh MacDiarmid*. This should be readily available in London bookshops.

But if Alasdair cares to write and tell me just what aspects of my work interest him, and what books he would like to borrow I'll be happy to send them – if I have them. I add that last phrase because as a rule when a book comes out the author gets about six copies – not nearly enough to give one to all the friends who expect one, with the consequence that I generally have to buy supplementary copies to give away and often find myself left without one. However I can certainly lend him a number of books, including my *Collected Poems*, published eight years ago by the Macmillan Company of New York. It is misnamed – it only includes about a fifth of my verse (though it is a whacking big tome) and is really not a *Collected Poems* but just a big selection.

Perhaps your father in refusing to lend Alasdair my books wasn't altogether acting in a dog-in-the-manger way, but feared that my work – or some of it – is too subversive and might have a bad influence on your son.

I don't know who the Professor of English Literature at Kings College is now, but it used to be a friend of mine, Professor Jack Isaacs, who wrote and broadcast very intelligently on modern poetry.

But just you or Alasdair let me know and I'll send you a parcel of books.

Valda and I are both well enough but exhausted after our travels – and we join in sending our best wishes to you and your husband and your sons.

Yours, Chris

---

1. See Appendix.
2. Hugh MacDiarmid, *A Drunk Man Looks at the Thistle*, ed. John C. Weston (Amherst, Mass.: University of Massachussetts Press, 1971).

9. *To Kulgin Duval and Colin Hamilton*

27 November 1970

Dear Kulgin and Colin,

I hope you are both fit and fine after your travels. Valda and I are both very tired but we enjoyed ourselves immensely and are extremely appreciative and grateful for all [y]our kindness and generosity.

Since I got back I've been very busy indeed. I went to London, then up to Bristol where we had a very successful poetry reading, and then on to Newcastle-on-Tyne, where I did a colour TV interview for Tyneside and Teeside TV. I did another long interview on Lewis Grassic Gibbon in Glasgow. Now we're all set for Solsgirth on Monday. George Bruce will motor us over.

Michael, or Valda, should not have said anything about the wedding. For certain reasons the fact that it has taken place must be kept a strict secret – in the meantime, anyhow.

When I was with Garech and Tiger in Glasgow the Australian photographer Jeffrey Craig took a lot of photos of me posed against the glass conservatories of the Botanic Gardens, and these I'm told have come out splendidly and all concerned are delighted with them.[1]

Many thanks for typescripts and Massey College pamphlet. I've sent all these in today with Valda to Miss Wakeman and she promises to let me have the typescript next.

I haven't had time or energy yet to write Dr and Mrs Mandersteig or to our friends at Aix or to Ezra and Mrs Pound, but hope to do so soon. They were all extremely kind.

With renewed thanks and best wishes to you both.

Christopher

---

1. Hon. Garech de Brun, member of the Guiness family, founder of Claddagh Records and his partner Lady Tiger Cowley. On one occasion, after a long lunch, CMG declared he was a Justice of the Peace and as such was able to marry them, which he proceeded to do, observing throughout what might have been correct legal process, had the power to marry not passed from JPs some time before.

10. *To Ruth McQuillan (NLS)*

7 December 1970

Dear Miss McQuillan

Many thanks for your charming letter to Valda and for returning the Karl Miller book, for which we were in no hurry.

We had a splendid time in Provence and Italy. Valda and two friends went on into Austria, after I returned by air from Milan. Then they motored back through Holland and sailed from Hamburg.

Yes. I had a great meeting with Ezra Pound. The old man has trouble with his speech but otherwise was very alert. He and his wife gave us a great welcome and we had lunch with them, then crossed the canal by Vaporetta and went to St Mark's Square and had coffee in the famous Café Florian there.

Since I came back I have had a poetry reading at Bristol University, done a colour TV interview at Newcastle-on-Tyne etc., and am due in London on 10th inst to speak on behalf of the Irish detainees.

Weston's edition of the *Drunk Man* has been delayed and won't be out until, I think, March, when it will appear both in hardback and paperback forms.

Louis Simpson is a splendid person. I wasn't surprised some of Valda's outbursts rubbed him the wrong way.

We'll be delighted to see you either about New Year time or later in the Spring. The McCaigs will be at home too over the Festive Season. Isabel was out here this weekend.

Yes. I too remember that occasion of the first meeting of McCaig and I very well. Sorley McLean and his sister were there too.

Hope all goes well with you, and with best wishes for a happy Christmas and good New Year, from Valda and I.

Yours, Christopher Grieve

P.S. The photos taken at the Common-Riding by David Wright's photographer who promised to send me prints have never reached me. Wright told me they'd come out splendidly.

11. *To D.G. Bridson (LLIU)*

5 January 1970 [1971]

Dear Geoffrey and Joyce

We could not have had a more welcome present this Festive Season than the copy of Geoffrey's splendid book.[1] It is immensely readable and full of interesting material of divers kinds. Geoffrey must have what I have always lacked – a card-index mind. How otherwise could he have remembered so much in such exact detail? As an unsuccessful autobiographer myself, my trouble has always been that though down the years I have know innumerable interesting people, I have never known much about them – the facts, I mean. All I have known is what they stood for – the quality (or otherwise) of their minds, the ideas they had, the movements in which they were involved. Not the sort of thing prescribable for good autobiographic material. And certainly not for anything like the human interest, the personal friendship element, in which Geoffrey moves so freely.

That said (enviously) I should at least acknowledge the many kind references to myself, and especially perhaps (since I am an unforgiving character) the excellent way in Mr Hugh Wheldon is ticked off and given his deserts.[2]

Tho' we have met so seldom (however memorable these few occasions are) in the flesh, it is curious how the book gives me all through the sense that Geoffrey and I have for many years been describing circles round about each other without these circles actually cutting into each other at all. This is because such a large percentage of the people he writes about were (or are) friends — or at least acquaintances — of mine too.

We will look forward eagerly to your book on Wyndham Lewis and to the verse play you have in mind to write and wish you well with both of these — and any other projects — you have in view.

But your letter of 20th ult concludes by saying: 'To show you that I'm beginning to limber up again, I enclose a translation I did recently which I hope you like' — alas! the translation wasn't there. Limber up that little more please, and send it on.

Valda joins me in all good wishes to you both for this New Year.

Yours, Christopher

---

1. *Prospero and Ariel: The Rise and Fall of Radio, A Personal Recollection* (London: Gollancz, 1971).
2. Sir Huw Wheldon (1916–86), Controller of Programmes for BBC television, 1965–8; Managing Director of BBC Television, 1968–75.

12. To Duncan Glen (EUL)

20 May 1971

Dear Duncan Glen

Many thanks for your letter just received, and copy of new book of poems. I'll write you about these at weekend. I'm having to rush off now to Lanark to address a meeting. Glad you got Michel Habart's permission.

What I'm concerned about in a hurry at the moment is a different matter altogether. I presume you have a copy of the 200 Burns Club edition of *The Drunk Man*. The curriculum of the newly-established Department of Scottish Literature at Glasgow University prescribed it as a text-book for the students. Stirling University has just done ditto. I have no doubt Edinburgh, Aberdeen, Strathclyde and St Andrews will follow suit. The trouble is they can't get copies — the 200 Burns Club edition is exhausted — and there is no other edition at a price students can pay. Stirling wants 200 copies at once; Glasgow ditto. What I wonder is if you could rush out an edition quickly — to sell at 10/- if possible and not more than 15/- anyhow. Apart from the immediate sale of upwards of 400 copies the thing can be a 'dripping roast', as it will continue in demand as a text-book for several years. I know you have enough on your plate and do not wish to increase your burden in any way. But if you can do this I think it will pay

you and thus facilitate your other plans too. Please let me know.
   In haste, with warmest regards to you all from Valda and I.
   Yours, Chris
P.S. I'll let you know about *Collected Poems* shortly. I expect to see Jack Weston in a few days' time.

13. *To Tom Murray (NLS, DFF)*

5 July 1971

Dear Tom Murray,
   Many thanks for copies of *Vanguard* and pamphlets etc.
I am horribly hard-pressed and in arrears with all sorts of things. Besides which I have engagements in this month and August in Langholm, Harrogate, Hereford, and Haddington, and then (if I get a visa – which is still doubtful) I am off to talk about and read poetry at various American Universities (in Pittsburgh, New York, Amherst, Kansas City etc.) and then in Canada at Ottawa, Toronto, Sudbury, etc.
   Literature is an immense subject, and I could not comment usefully on 'To Trumpet Bourgeois Literature is to restore Capitalism' in short space. It would need several thousand words. The title of the pamphlet is absurd. There has never yet been any literature and very little art that is not bourgeois (or earlier, aristocratic and religious) and I have no sympathy at all with the Bogdanov heresy of a purely proletarian art.[1] It does not exist, and to write as if it does is to hopelessly simplify and falsify what is really the most crucial problem. Stupidity and ignorance are the two greatest millstones round mankind's neck, and to bring cultural discussions down to the level of the illiterate and plantigrade is a betrayal of all the best potentialities of mankind. However at the moment at least, I cannot, as I'd like, go into the matter, and to do that would require a long essay.
   Kind regards and best wishes to you and your associates.
   Yours, Christopher Grieve

---

1. Aleksandr Alexandrovich Bogdanov (1873–1928), Bolshevik philosopher and idealist, who held that art was purely functional and its function was to serve the people. His ideas were condemned by Lenin as a revisionist heresy.

14. *To John Montague (SUNYB)*

14 September 1971

Dear John Montague
   Forgive a very short reply to your kind letter of 9th inst. It's only so I can reply immediately – or perhaps in the near future. As you may have heard I have been in hospital and undergone a major operation – not just

a routine one of its kind but more severe and difficult. However I was in the hands of a really first-class surgeon and I made a very rapid recovery and got back home (probably too early) a fortnight ago. I am still very weak and unable to get about freely and safely.

The thing flared up very suddenly – on 11th August when I was preparing to celebrate my 79th birthday. My daughter, son-in-law, various grandchildren were all here and we were going out to celebrate. Instead I was rushed into an Edinburgh hospital. So I'm not counting that birthday – my next is not my 80th but still my 79th.

The surgeon (and my son-in-law who is a consultant physician in Canada) both insisted that there was no need for me to cancel the arrangements I was making to go to USA and Canada about 25th October – to about 11th November. They said I was fitter to go now than I'd have been before being operated on. The trouble is my visa application is still delayed – for political reasons no doubt – but various powerful organisations in USA (viz. the American Centre of PEN, the National Council of the Arts, etc.) are pressing the authorities to grant me a visa.

We'll see but all being well I'll fly to USA about 25th Oct and do talks and poetry readings at Yale, Columbia, the International Poetry Forum in Pittsburg, the University of Missouri at Kansas City, the Poetry Centre in New York, Pembroke State University in North Carolina, and Massachusetts University at Amherst. Then I'll cross into Canada and fulfil similar engagements at Carleton College, Ottawa, the Laurentian University at Sudbury, and Toronto University.

Alas, one of the after effects of hospitalisation is that I've developed a tremendous allergy to paper and ink. All my contracted work for various publishers is hopelessly in arrears. Heaven only knows how I'm to make up any – let alone any substantial part – of this infernal backlog. It would not take me more than an odd half-hour to write you such a brief recommendation as you desire – but that is not the way I work, and I am apt to make heavy going of even the most seemingly simple job.

However I am honoured and delighted you've asked me to do this – and I will with great pleasure. The problem is *when*! Send me a postcard just saying the date by which you want it – and I'll see that it's written and sent to you straight away.

I do hope that your affairs find a satisfactory settlement soon – in some American College. Scotland would be splendid – if it were practicable, but a modus vivendi is not so easily found here.

Yes. I have most of your work. I'm delighted that Dolmen Press are busy with the first version of your long poem on Ulster[1] – and glad you're contemplating another long poem. You'll appreciate this is just a very hasty reply and leaves out many things I should, and wish, to say.

In the meantime best of luck to you, kind remembrances to Evelyn, and my regards to Serge Fauchereau.[2]

Yours, Christopher

P.S.: The best 'crack' my illness evoked was from another doctor friend, who said: 'Unpleasant and painful as these genito-urological operations are, at least you have the consolation of being spared the cultural horrors outside!' (i.e. the events of the current Edinburgh International Festival).

---

1. John Montague, *The Rough Field* (Dublin: The Dolmen Press, 1972).
2. Serge Fauchereau, art historian specialising in twentieth-century art and surrealism.

15. *To Gordon Wright (EUL)*

19 September 1971

Dear Gordon

I've been wondering how things were going with you. I'd heard about Helen's *Collected Poems* but had no further news of your publishing programme. So I am delighted to have your letter and the excellent photograph of myself you propose using in the projected issue of authors' photographs – a good idea which I hope is very successful. I'll certainly be very pleased to co-operate as you suggest.

I am more than pleased to know you are republishing Fionn MacColla's *Albannach*. This is long overdue. I was glad to see he's at last getting an innings with the radio production of *And the Cock Crew*. But I still think the *Albannach* is his best work.

With every good wish. Yours, Christopher Grieve

16. *To Barbara Niven (NLS)*

8 November 1971

Dear Barbara

I am OK again, except for an antipathy to any avoidable physical activity. My convalescence was unduly prolonged, and precarious, owing to certain distressing post-operation troubles. But these cleared away suddenly a fortnight ago and now I am perfectly all right. Doctors assure me that after these operations men often acquire a new lease of life, and one medico told me that there is no reason now why I shouldn't live to 100. You should have seen the disgusted look on Valda's face when she heard this.

Anyhow I am making progress now making up the arrears of writing built up while I was in hospital. And already various American Universities are renewing their invitations to me for next Summer or Autumn, and these I will hope to accept and carry through all right – including a revisit of course to Ontario.

I hope you are in good fettle. Also Nan and Sherry. Valda joins me in every kind regard to you.
    Yours, Christopher

17. *To Brian Lambie (BMT)*

23 November 1971

Dear Mr Lambie
    Many thanks for the surprise bottle of Glenfiddich!
    This was indeed far too good of you, but it served to signalise my first venture out since my return from hospital. And Glenfiddich is, of course, my favourite malt whisky.
    With renewed thanks and best wishes.
    Yours sincerely, Christopher Grieve

18. *To Richard Demarco (LLIU)*

24 November 1971

Dear Mr Demarco
    I am delighted you are putting on an exhibition of the work of my friend for over 40 years, the late William McCance. This is long overdue. It must have been a great disappointment to him when he came back to Scotland (which spiritually he never left, of course) to find so little recognition amongst his compatriots. The reason is just that it is wrong to write of him as 'the late', when, in fact, he was always immeasurably ahead not only of the mass of his fellow Scots but of practically the whole body of his (saving the mark) fellow artists. A fuller exhibition than has been possible on this occasion would demonstrate conclusively that he is (I insist upon the present tense) one of the very few Scottish artists of any conceivable interest to anyone fully abreast of the whole range of modernist developments in the Arts (in *all* the Arts), not only because he was fully *au fait* with all these developments, but because – if not always in his practice, certainly in his understanding and sympathies – he actually anticipated many of them.
    The accepted image of the Scot is a dour, barely-articulate, cautious person but throughout our history among the most distinguished of our breed a very different type has constantly appeared. Highly intellectual, completely free of all the Philistine inhibitions and prejudices of the majority, brilliant conversationalists, men of great personal charm, ceaselessly adventurous in spirit, thoroughly international in their sensibility, interdisciplinary and versatile. It is to this minority that McCance belongs – and he has had to pay the customary penalty for being so far in advance of his time and so opposed in all his ideas to the mindless majority.
    Forty years ago I wrote that one was handicapped in writing about

McCance by the fact that probably none of one's readers had seen any of it. Exception might perhaps be made of McCance's portrait of Mr William Brewer and of the fifty-foot panel he painted for the *Daily News*, which has been described as one of the best examples of progressive unity in modern painting. He is a highly productive artist – concerned exclusively, and this is the measure of his artistic integrity – with the basic problems with which progressive artists everywhere are today preoccupied, and not with the commercial application of established, that is to say, effete techniques. And he is necessarily approaching these problems, and resolving them, as a Scot. The traditions of what is called 'Scottish Art' mean nothing to him – but in so far as these are not the products of acquired techniques incapable of relating Scottish psychology to art products in a specifically effective fashion correspondences will be discernible in retrospect. In the meantime, his work is probably unintelligible to the great mass of those who look to find a 'likeness' in a portrait (and are at sea with a psychological criticism expressing itself in terms of the interrelationships of planes) or who demand of a picture that it reproduces a recognisable place or embodies a pleasing conception or 'points a moral or adorns a tale'… The whole course of modern art in all its amazing and absorbing developments is a sealed book to all but a mere handful of the population of Scotland. And as a consequence to speak or write of art in Scotland today is almost inevitably to find oneself in a position similar to that so well described by Lord Dewar when, as he says, 'I, once, during an after dinner speech, used the word Lipton when I was treating of Milton, but soon found that my audience were with me in spirit.'

McCance in all his work ruthlessly traverses the prevailing conceptions of Art in Scotland, and nowhere more so that when he declared: 'So far there has been too great a cleavage between Engineering and Art … let us no longer alienate our engineers from Art. Let us advise our sentimentalists in Art to migrate to "spiritualism" or let us equip an expedition for them to explore the possibilities of Celtic Twilight in some remote corner of the world where they will not disturb us in our work. Let them give up cumbersome paint and canvas and take to photographing fairies on uninhabited islands. Anything. Anyhow now is the time for a real Scottish culture!!'

This clarion call has been little heeded, but in time to come it will be and McCance will be recognised as one of the precursors in Scotland of an art 'fully alive in its own time'. As a lecturer and art critic for *The Spectator* and University teacher of typography, and book-production, and in his own work in oils and pencil drawings, portrait heads and figure drawings in charcoal, wood engravings for the Gregynog Press, including initial letters for Aesop's *Fables* and some of the books, Cartoons for *The Free Man* in 1932–3, sculpture, bronzes and fireclays, he stood by his guns and accomplished a wonderful variety of work despite lack of public recognition. His 'Another Window in Thrums' was well calculated to make Sir J.M. Barrie turn in his grave. It is a splendid example of McCance's wit and intellectual penetration.

It is to be hoped that a full retrospective Exhibition may yet be mounted, but the present selection, mainly of his earlier work (of the pre-1940 period) should surely create a demand for that from all the really discerning in our midst. In the meantime, you are to be heartily congratulated on your enterprise in thus bringing together and putting on show this splendid sample of the word [sic] of one who was, and is still, before his time but must, if there is any hope at all for the Arts in Scotland, come into his own yet. May it be soon! The need is great, and the success of this Exhibition will mark the point we have reached in discarding the worthless past and achieving a future-looking stance.

Yours, with every high regard and good wish, Hugh MacDiarmid

19. *To Provost Grieve, Langholm (NLS, DFF)*

1 January 1972

Sir: –

You were of course perfectly entitled to refuse the granting of the Freedom of Langholm to me. But you have not allowed the matter to rest there. Though I had published the fact that even if it were offered to me I would refuse it, and any other official recognition Langholm might offer me, you have gone outside of your province and carried on a campaign of denigration. In other words when, as Provost of Langholm, you could have claimed privilege, you can no longer do so since you have yourself stated that the matter has never come before the Council officially. So your attitude now can only be one of sheer personal spite and a determination to belittle my reputation. In other words, to ridicule and vilify me in any way you can. Well of course I have a remedy at law for that, and I have taken counsel's opinion and now intend to force you into the open, since you have no ground at all for acting as you have done.

If you have any intelligence at all you must know that people all over the world have asked what you have against me and naturally inferred that there must be some fault in my character in record that has forced you to act as you have done.

In your latest outburst, as reported in the Glasgow *Daily Record*, when pressed to recognise that I am a very distinguished poet with a national and international celebrity you said 'that is a matter of opinion'.

Whose opinion? Certainly not yours. Any pretension on your part to literary judgment or aesthetic appreciation could not be sustained for a second in any cross examination. That there is no question at all of my reputation is amply borne out by the fact that HM the Queen's advisers granted me a Civil List Pension for my services to Scottish Literature. The University of Edinburgh gave me a Doctorate of Laws on the same ground.

The Speculative Society of Edinburgh and the American Association of Modern Languages, elected me as an Hon. Fellow, and so the list can go on. I can produce testimonials from Institutions and scholars of many nations for the same effect. Who are you to question this? And why? – except on the ground of personal hatred.

You are Provost of Langholm, but I also have given public service as a Town Councillor, Magistrate, JP, and in other capacities. I had arranged to donate a large and valuable collection of books to Langholm Library and to establish a Lectureship in Scottish Literature when a distinguished Speaker would annually give a lecture in Langholm in memory of my father who had unfortunately the same name as you have disgraced, but who tho' he died young had a record of public service and general respect to which you have never been able to claim. I have now decided – and instructed my lawyers and my heirs accordingly – that effect to these arrangements will not be given until after you are dead and forgotten. As you will be. Centuries after that Scottish school pupils and students of Scottish universities will be studying my poems.

It is absurd of you to claim any knowledge or understanding of my work. But literary reflections do not depend on public opinion but only on this verdict of the few who know and appreciate such things. I do not write for morons like you, and while your senseless prejudices have acted against me in this matter I know that many of the citizens of Langholm do not agree with you. They have approached me and told me so. So it would be wrong to penalise Langholm people for the ignorance and stupidity of you and a few other members of the Town Council.

But you will not be able to continue to vent your denigrations, which are demonstrably unjustified and calculated to bring me and my work into contempt and ridicule. Whether you like it or not I am by far the most celebrated writer Langholm has ever produced and I do not intend that fact to be besmirched by a brainless nothing like you.

With scorn and contempt. Yours etc., Christopher Grieve.

20. *To Morven Cameron (NLS)*

1 February 1972

Dear Morven

I have been trying for days to get time to reply to your letter, but I am incredibly crowded out with letters etc. I must write. I was very sorry I could not keep my promise to 'phone you from Michael's, but I was never near Michael's or anywhere other than where the Johnnie Walker reception was held. They laid on a car and we came back home in it as soon as we could disentangle ourselves from the function which, however, both Valda and I enjoyed much more than we'd expected to. You probably saw the prize-winning poems in the *Glasgow Herald*! They were of course terrible.[1]

But talking about poems, the new editor of *Poetry Review*, Mr Eric Mottram, who has just enthusiastically accepted a longish poem of mine which he invited, asked me if I knew of any other Scottish poets with unpublished poems I thought good.[2] So I took the liberty of giving him your name and address, and you will probably hear from him. I hope so. They don't pay much. *Poetry Review* has been up to now a very fuddy-duddy affair but Mottram is out to give it a new image.

As to Communism you seem to have just the ideas about it the anti-Communist West has been so assiduously formulating. But I have been in all the Communist countries except Albania and I have a very different view. You may find it impossible to believe that I hold that Communism is the only guarantee of individuality in the world today. But I cannot go into the matter in a letter – I would be glad to discuss the whole thing fully with you on some suitable occasion.

I was very sorry to hear about your tummy upset, and trust that rebellious member has long since been reconciled and that you are OK again.

With every kind regard and good wish to you and to your father, from Valda and I.

Yours, Christopher Grieve

---

1. CMG was judge. See *The Glasgow Herald*, 1 February 1972.
2. 'At James Joyce's Deathbed', *Poetry Review*, vol. 63, no. 2 (Summer 1972).

21. *To Edwin Morgan*

23 February 1972

Dear Mr Morgan

Many thanks indeed for *Wi the Haill Voice*.[1] I was saying on TV apropos my new version of Brecht's *Threepenny Opera* that there are elements in Brecht with which modern English can't deal – for which it is far too refined. These elements are nearer elements in Scots, e.g. in Dunbar and Burns.

This is the same claim you make with regard to Mayakovsky, but you not only make the claim but prove it in your translations. One has only to compare them with the translations into English by Marshall, Reavy, and others. Congratulations, and additional thanks for your brilliant introduction.

Our paths don't seem to cross but we may meet each other again yet. In the meantime renewed thanks and every good wish.

Yours, Christopher Grieve

---

1. *Wi the Haill Voice: 25 Poems by Vladimir Mayakovsky*, translated into Scots by Edwin Morgan (Carcanet, 1972).

22. To Morven Cameron (NLS)

6 March 1972

Dear Morven

It is absolutely shocking that I haven't been able to write you since Hartree – but I am hopelessly tied up. Today the man in overall charge of the film, and a photographer came *two hours later*! than they arranged. What on earth can I do with such people? I am far too busy.

On Friday a film unit (i.e. photographer and two – or three – assistants) are to arrive, followed by Bryan Eadie (the overall man), Norman McCaig and Michael, to do the job. Amongst other items there is to be recorded a very frank – no punches pulled – quiz of me by Norman and Mike.

But if I hadn't enough on my plate apart altogether from this sort of thing, I am having trouble with the Brecht play. A lot of money is involved. I have a 20 per cent overall agreement. But one fellow tinkered with some of the lyrics. I agreed to give him 2½ per cent of my percentage on ten lyrics. Now he won't get it. The appetite feeds on what it gets. He's been well enough paid already – *without reference to me.*[1]

But the play continues to draw excellent business despite the fact of the unlit traffic signals and other troubles in congested London which don't help to induce people to leave their suburban homes and telly screens. If I'm not careful I'll end up as a royalty millionaire.

If I hadn't a wife – and that wife Valda! – she went into Edinburgh the other day, and bought a new suit, which outside on the pavement, she promptly lost. So she toddled back into the quite expensive boutique and bought another. Today she learned that her lost suit had been found. So she got two. I don't believe a word of it. It was all carefully planned in advance!

I hate these panel things on BBC or TV. Nobody really gets a chance to talk out an argument. You did better than most. I can't get away with it so easily – they just censor me the moment I want to say anything I think really important.

However my ideas really must not be boundless. All authorities issued agree to that. I'm not democratic at all – I believe in selection – not in favour of those who can pay. But in favour with the old Scottish tradition of the 'Lad o' Pairts'. I am utterly opposed to the few brilliant children being held back to the level of the others. And indeed I am opposed to all compulsory education. Because it doesn't educate. It only multiplies those who are minimally literate!

But you could have looked more vivacious on the screen – your little sketch of yourself was, alas, too accurate.

And now I've yattered on without coming to the point. The trouble is that Saturday is no good. I've the Film Unit, Norman, Mike etc. on Friday – and on Saturday Valda has a party at West Linton, and I'm told it wouldn't do to have you here without somebody to chaperon us! What about

Sunday? That would be OK. As to further ahead, Saturday 18th I have to be at a 1320 Club Symposium in the David Hume Tower in Edinburgh. On Monday 20th I'm talking to the pupils of St Modan's High School in Stirling, and on Saturday 1st April Valda and I have a dinner engagement in Penicuik.

Too bad altogether – and I'm refusing or cancelling everything I possibly can – but even so I see just no hope of getting time and place to do the things I really should be doing, i.e. writing poetry.

All the best to you and your father and Marguerite.

Yours, Christopher

---

1. Who this man is remains unknown. He was probably at least the fourth person to aid CMG with the translation, the others being Ronald Stevenson, Deirdre Grieve and Norman MacCaig. Surprisingly, perhaps, given his evident awareness of rhythm, CMG seemed unable to 'hear' how to fit the metre of his translation to Weill's melodies.

23. *To Barker Fairley (NLS)*

8 March 1972

Dear Barker

I was delighted to receive the excellently produced volume of your poems of the Twenties. It is well worth while and serves to round out, up to now, your literary output, and presents another facet of your talent, a facet many of your friends must have been conscious was lacking up to now. For it must have been clear to all who know your work on Goethe, Doughty, etc. that you are really a poet who for some reason just hadn't (so it seemed) written poetry.

My Brecht *Threepenny Opera* continues to do well. Valda and I finally went to London for the first night. A packed house! And the theatre was fully booked up from then until the middle of this month. Barbara Niven and Ern were with us at the opening. And Lotte Lenya[1] and others of the Berliner Ensemble came over specially for it.

Now I'm trammelled with film units, photographers, tape recorders etc. etc., for the Arts Council has set aside £3000 to do a film of me to be ready for my 80th birthday in August.

I've just had an air-letter from Christine, holidaying at ski-resorts in Austria with Alison and Rory.

Hope this finds you in the best of fettle. Love to Nan and Sherry, and Humphrey Milnes.

Yours, Christopher

1. Lotte Lenya, the pseudonym of Karoline Wilhelmine Blamauer (1898–1981), Austrian actress who appeared in the original production of *The Threepenny Opera* (1928), Kurt Weill's wife.

24. *To Jean White (EUL)*

11 March 1972

Dear Jean

Many thanks for your letter.

Valda and I will be hoping all day that you succeed in handing over the Lunar Tartan without getting entangled in its folds.[1]

A prophet is not without honour save in his own place, and while Langholm has refused to recognise me my further coming 80th birthday is not going unmarked.

Edinburgh University are giving a select dinner party on a date between 24th and 26th May at which Valda and I are to be the guests. The following day the symposium is to be held in the University at which various speakers British and foreign, will discuss my work.

The Scottish Books Council have set aside £3,000 to have a film of me done by the Films of Scotland organisation. And yesterday we had the film unit here, so the thing is under way.

Also the Arts Council are running a Poetry Competition for Poets anywhere in the world to send in poems addressed to me on approaching my 80th birthday for prizes of £75 etc. And I am to write one of these poems on the same subject for which I'll be presented with £100.

John Elliot (Puffle) sent me a couple of old photographs, in one which I appear aged I think about 18 – in return for a copy of *A Drunk Man Looks at the Thistle* I promised him long ago.

My version of Brecht's *Threepenny Opera* is doing well at the Prince of Wales Theatre in London. Valda and I thoroughly enjoyed our trip down there for the opening performance.

Hope to see you again before long.

With love from Valda and I. Yours, Chris

---

1. The Freedom of Langholm was conferred on Neil Armstrong, Armstrong being a common Borders name, and a specially commissioned tartan commemorating the moon-landing was presented to him at the event.

25. *To Ronald Stevenson (NLS)*

29 March 1972

Dear Ronald

I've just been having a good time listening to the Radio 3 broadcast of your *Border Boyhood* song cycle and Peter Pears' singing, Your preliminary talk on how you did it was fascinating and illuminating; and the song-cycle itself was a splendid achievement. Evidently the audience at Aldeburgh thought so too judging by the prolonged applause.

I've been meaning to reply to your last note. The conflation of the *Beggars' Opera*, Brecht's *Threepenny Opera*, and Burns' *Jolly Beggars* has been in my mind for years. Whether I ever manage to do it I can't tell – certainly it won't be this year. I've far too much in hand – and while OK physically am still allergic to work. But if I do there will certainly be songs for which your collaboration would be very welcome indeed. The Brecht has had a very successful run at the Prince of Wales Theatre and is transferring on 10th April to the Piccadilly Theatre. The main trouble with it was Kurt Weill's song settings i.e. to get versions in English singable to Weill's music which is extremely tricky. But the general opinion of all with whom I've discussed it (including Lotte Lenya, Weill's widow) is that the renderings in my version of the Opera are surprisingly successful.

Hope all goes well with you and that you have better word of Gerda. Your friend, Marjorie Clark, had arranged to come here the other night, but something came in the way she 'phoned to say. But she'll arrange another date.

Love to you all. Yours, Christopher Grieve

26. *To Ian Milner (NLS)*

8 May 1972

Dear Ian Milner

I am glad to get your letter of 29th April. I did get the note you sent me from New Zealand, telling me you were returning to Prague, and I wrote shortly after receiving it, addressing my letter to you at Na Dulinach 3, but since I didn't know whether you'd be returning to that address, I put on my envelope the alternative c/o English Seminar, Charles University. It seems that despite this precaution you have not received that letter.

Yes. I had a difficult year. Last August just as my daughter, son, and grandchildren were assembled here to go out to a nearby hotel to celebrate my 79th birthday, I took seriously ill and had to be rushed into hospital and operated on immediately. It was a prostate operation and I came through it splendidly and was very quickly discharged from hospital. However various after-effects developed and I had a protracted and precarious convalescence. I have had to reduce speaking, poetry reading, and other public engagements to a minimum. Just before hospitalisation I had arranged a splendid series of readings in American and Canadian universities (Harvard, Yale, Columbia etc. etc.), but had to cancel the lot.

Now things are building up for my 80th birthday. Edinburgh University is giving a small dinner party in my honour and the following day there is a symposium of which speakers home and foreign will discuss aspects of my work. David Daiches is the only speaker whose name I know yet, but I know they wanted Auden, but I vetoed that and now they are trying to get Pablo Neruda.

You probably know there has been a tremendous escalation of the Lallans Movement. The Association for Scottish Literary Studies has drawn together all five Scottish Universities and the other day we had a Conference in Glasgow at which the speakers included Professors, Lecturers, and an HM Inspector of Schools. Now a non-academic but probably popular Lallans Society has been formed and is to have a symposium in Stirling University in June at which I'll speak about the Makars (DV and WP). Apart from functions in Scotland the only two engagements I've accepted are to speak for Scotland in a debate in Cambridge Union on the urgent need for Scotland and Wales to have self-government, and a reading of my poems at the Mermaid Theatre in London. There are a lot of books due to be published by or before August on my work, including a big selection of my poems edited by my son Michael and Alex Scott of Glasgow University (through Routledge and Kegan Paul); a new edition of *Lucky Poet* (Cape); and *Selected Poems of Robert Henryson*, edited and introduced by me (Penguin). Also two de luxe editions through Bodoni Press, Verona.[1]

Valda and I will be delighted of course if you can come up and see us. I hope both Jarmila and you are in the best of fettle. I am glad to hear you've seen Jessie; I've been worrying about her but hope more or less needlessly.

You'll know that my version of Brecht's *Threepenny Opera* was splendidly produced at the Prince of Wales Theatre in London, and has since been transferred to the Piccadilly Theatre.

Valda joins me in warmest regards to you both.

Yours, Christopher Grieve

P.S. I was glad to receive – and in the letter you haven't received acknowledged with thanks the copies of your Penguins of Holub etc.[2] I'll reciprocate when some of the forthcoming publications mentioned above come to hand.

---

1. *Direadh I, II and III* (Frenich, Foss: Kulgin Duval & Colin Hamilton, 1974). Limited to 200 copies. An edition of *In Memoriam James Joyce* was also planned but it was not published.
2. Miroslav Holub (1923–98), Czech poet and scientist, whose career in medicine often informed his poems. Penguin Books published Miroslav Holub, *Selected Poems*, translated by Ian Milner and George Theiner (1967) and also the Czech Vladimir Holan's *Selected Poems*, translated by Jarmila and Ian Milner (1971).

27. *To Janet Caird (NLS)*

11 May 1972

Dear Mrs Caird

It is very kind of you to give me this inscribed copy of 'The Loch'. James told me he thought it one of your best. I am an inveterate thriller reader, but the producers of readable thrillers, detective stories etc. are too unproductive for me. Their output doesn't keep pace with my appetite. Fortunately there are a few new ones I like immensely – Len Deighton, Hilary Waugh, Emma Lathen, Desmond Bagley.

My son Michael reviews all the new paperbacks for the *Daily Record* and gets a copy or two every week as they come out. He has thousands of them in his Glasgow house. They don't all fall into the categories of detective, thriller, mystery etc., of course, but of those that do only a small percentage meet my requirements. And if I may say so few of these are by women. So you are a genuine 'find'. I have greatly enjoyed 'The Loch' and liked 'Murder Scholastic' too. Please keep on doing it. I'll be on the look-out.

It was good seeing your husband again and he gave an excellent address. When he comes South on some of these occasions he should bring you with him – although not if that interferes with your output. Thanks again and all the best to you and your daughters.

from Christopher Grieve

P.S. I've mislaid your note, and so haven't your address. So I'm addressing this to J.B. Caird, HMI, Inverness. I hope it gets to you all right.

28. *To Morag Enticknap*

14 June 1972

Dear Morag

I am very sorry to hear of Graham's death. It is one of the effects of Scottish individualism that members of the same family so often have little or nothing in common and can't get on with each other. It was hereditary too in my family. My father and one of his brothers lived in the same small town – and never visited or even spoke to each other.

I can't remember when I wrote to you last or whether I told you I had a serious abdominal operation last August. I came through it all right but after-effects entailed a frustrated and somewhat precarious convalescence. And though I am OK again I have to ca' canny and am obliged to restrict my public appearances to a minimum.

However I have two engagements towards the end of November – one to engage in a political debate in Cambridge University Union, and the following day to give a reading of my poems in the Mermaid Theatre, London.

As you may know my translation of Brecht's *Threepenny Opera* had a successful run at the Prince of Wales Theatre, and then transferred to the

Piccadilly Theatre where it is still attracting good houses. But I think it will be taken off soon now.

I am very busy with events of all kinds in celebration of my impending (August) 80th birthday. There have been functions in Edinburgh and Stirling Universities, a film has been made of me and will be shown in August, and there will be MacDiarmid Exhibitions in Glasgow and Aberdeen.

I hope all your sons are well and doing well. The younger generation seem to be brainier than Graham or I. My eldest daughter, who married a Ukranian astrophysicist, has just graduated BSc and been awarded the University of Western Ontario Gold Medal in bio-chemistry.[1]

With kindest regards to your husband and yourself and all of you from Valda and I.

Your uncle Chris

P.S. I am afraid I may have misspelled your married name. I have just tried to spell it from memory.

---

1. CMG means his eldest grand-daugher, Elspeth Macintosh, who married Ukrainian astrophysicist Danny Kushnir.

29. *To Hamish Henderson (EUL)*

30 June 1972

Dear Hamish

Many thanks for sending on the *Golden Treasury*. McKechnie must have borrowed it over 20 years ago – when I was living in Victoria Crescent Road. I haven't seen or heard from him since then, and did not know he was dead. Please thank Freddie Anderson on my behalf. A lot of books of mine, and Valda's, must be in all sorts of hands. I loaned them pretty freely and did not keep a record, but I can think of at least twenty books missing from my shelves which I'd gladly – but do not expect to – have back.

Thanks also for the two copies of *Tocher*.[1] Full of interesting stuff.

I thought the Symposium went off very well. I did not attend, of course, because I am too deaf to hear. I only heard bits of David Daiches' lecture tho' I sat as near his lectern as I could.

Several friends have told me that Garioch's remarks were obviously derogatory. He apparently said some things about Grant Taylor and I am told suggested I owed Taylor a great deal. That is absolute nonsense. Taylor – even if he had the necessary knowledge – was in no condition to do more to help me than simply type my stuff. I do not know what mare's nest Garioch was harrying, but his intention was apparently malicious.

Hope all goes well with you and yours.

I'll be glad when my 80th birthday is over. Exhibitions in Edinburgh, Glasgow and Aberdeen – two films – Tom Fleming's reading of *The Drunk*

Man on Radio 4 etc. etc. I have made up my mind never to have another 80th birthday!

Glad HBC is still able to get about and do a little gardening.

Yours, Chris

---

1. A periodical from the School of Scottish Studies, University of Edinburgh, devoted to oral traditions.

30. *To Jean White (EUL)*

30 June 1972

Dear Jean

You may have seen from *The Scotsman*, if you watch the Death notices – that my brother Andrew died on 10th June and there was a private cremation on 14th. I can't remember if you ever knew him, but others – like Joan Wilson – always asked about him when I came to Langholm. He would be 78. I understand the cause was some kidney disease.

As usual I am up to my neck in all sorts of things. MacDiarmid Exhibitions in Edinburgh, Glasgow, and Aberdeen. And all sorts of other engagements for my 80th birthday. I'll be glad when it's all over.

In the meantime am looking forward to a brief respite at the Common-Riding. Hope you are OK.

All the best from Valda and I. Yours, Chris

31. *To Alan Bold (NLS)*

4 September 1972

Dear Alan

Many thanks for your letter of 2nd inst.

My own view is that my best poems in English are 'On a Raised Beach', 'The Impossible Song', 'Bracken Hills in Autumn', 'The Kind of Poetry I Want', 'Dìreadh III', 'The Glen of Silence', 'The Glass of Pure Water', 'Reflections In a Slum', and 'In Memoriam Charles Doughty'.

'Bracken Hills in Autumn' was published as a pamphlet, now very difficult to obtain – I haven't a copy of it myself.

By 'The Kind of Poetry I Want' I do not mean the book published under that title but the poem as given 1/ in *Lucky Poet* and 2/ as republished in my *Collected Poems*, pp.333 to 344.

'The Glass of Pure Water' was first published in *The Canadian Forum*.

As to detachable parts of long poems, I would like to choose 'At James Joyce's Deathbed' as given in *The Poetry Review* Vol. 63 No. 2. I enclose my copy of this, which please return as it is the only one I have.

I'll be very pleased – and prompt – to give you reasons for my choice (once I know the ones you decide on – I know of course that the titles I indicate would occupy much more space than you can possibly allocate to me.) But there is a lot of critical opinion on 'On A Raised Beach' as my best poem in English; 'A Glass of Pure Water' has been much admired, and so also the poem to 'Charles Doughty' (which unaccountably is not in my *Collected Poems*!).

Another poem I'd enclose if space permitted is 'In The Fall' given on p.400 of my *Collected Poems*.

With regard despite my political and linguistic propensities to my latterly writing so much in English, this has been due to a shift in my fundamental intellectual interests. More and more I have been concerned with scientific matters, and I found it impossible to express these at any rate, with the necessary precision even in my aggrandized Scots – even English does not have anything like an adequate scientific vocabulary – one must use all sorts of *ad hoc* neologisms, and that is one of the reasons why I have had to eke out my English with all sorts of words and phrases from other languages – of course that is the very way English itself has been built up.

In answer to your other question, I think my best *lyrics* are all in Scots; but like Heine I felt I had to cease writing lyrics and import into my work all sorts of (conventionally considered) unpoetic material. So I am specially proud of my few successes in this endeavour, e.g., for Doughty poem, the 'At James Joyce's Deathbed' etc.

No I wouldn't think I was given directions by any other English-Language poets other than those you mention (Doughty, Pound, Milton, Blake) save only – and very influentially – Walt Whitman.

I'm sorry I cannot at this moment reply more fully to your letter. I'm still having a hell of a time and hardly know whether I'm standing on my feet or my head.

Every kind regard to Alice and your family and yourself – and the best success with this Cambridge Book 1939–72.[1] I'm going to Cambridge at the end of November to take part in a Union debate on Scottish and Welsh Nationalism and also to give a poetry reading.

Yours, Chris Grieve

---

1. *The Cambridge Book of English Verse 1939–1975*, ed. Alan Bold (Cambridge University Press, 1976).

32. *To Meic Stephens (EUL)*[1]

29 September 1972

Dear Mr Stephens

I have been away from home or I would have received and replied to your letter of 23rd inst sooner.

There is no writer in the world today I hold in higher esteem and greater respect than Saunders Lewis. I regard it as an honour to be asked to contribute my view of him to the forthcoming volume you mention.[2]

I will have this typed tomorrow and should receive it back from the lady who does my typing, in time to post it to you by the first post on Tuesday, and trust this will be in time for your deadline (and trust too you will find it suitable for your purpose).

Please excuse this very hurried note. As you probably know I am taking part in a debate in Cambridge University Union on 26th Nov. when I hope to express some of the ideas Saunders Lewis and I hold in common – in contradistinction to those held by one of the other speakers in the debate, Mr Gwynfor Evans.[3]

I would dearly have loved to see you in Edinburgh on 4th Nov, but, following an operation last year I am obliged to conserve my energies and avoid all the engagements I can. I have in any case seen these Scottish Arts Council films of Neil Gunn, myself etc.

It will be another great honour to have an article by you on myself and Mr Lewis in *Taliesin*.

With grateful acknowledgment of your congratulations and good wishes on my 80th birthday.

And every high regard from my wife and myself.

Yours sincerely, Christopher Grieve

---

1. The letter is addressed to Meic Stephens, Assistant Director, Cyngor Celfyddydau Cymru, (Welsh Arts Council).
2. A *festschrift* for Saunders Lewis did appear in 1975 but CMG was not a contributor.
3. Gwynfor Evans (b.1912), first Plaid Cymru MP, 1966–70.

33. *To Alex McCrindle (EUL)*

15 November 1972

Dear Alex

I heard your excellent account of the Tashkent Conference on Radio 3 (thanks to your p.c.) and agreed heartily. You must have had a most interesting and useful trip.

We were delighted to have Honor and Joan Lingard out here. Honor was looking well, but of course appearances are deceptive and we can only hope that the outward look reflected the inner position. It must have taken her great courage to undertake the journey. Please give her our love and best wishes.

We liked Joan Lingard very much too. We'd a note from her yesterday promising to come again.

Valda and I go to Cambridge on Saturday 25th. I've a reading in the

Mermaid Theatre on 26th and another reading in Cambridge on 27th. Pioneer Theatres Ltd are hoping to have a director's meeting and if they can have it on the 28th we stay over for it and come back here the following day.

    Kindest regards to Honor & you, and to Catherine and Jessica.

    Yours, Chris

34. *To Christine Macintosh*

1 January 1973

Dear Christine

    It seems a very long time since we heard from you. Incredible as it may appear the celebrations of my 80th birthday have been going on in one way or another ever since you were here. I got very tired of it all – and am glad it is now over. The final event was a very acceptable one. A lot of people in Langholm angry about the Town Council's refusal to give me the Freedom of the burgh met in convivial conditions to present me with a Parker-Knoll armchair. This is extremely comfortable and a welcome replacement for the old one I had which was falling to pieces. No wonder. It was a second-hand one Valda bought about a dozen years ago for 14/-. The new one cost £120!

    Valda and I were in London and Cambridge. In London I gave a tremendously successful poetry reading in the Mermaid Theatre. In Cambridge University I took part in a broadcast political debate, and also gave a poetry reading under the auspices of the English Faculty.

    I am hoping to restrict my public engagements to a minimum this year and by staying at home as much as possible get a lot more writing done.

    You may wonder why I want to do this. I've done enough already – and in some ways too much. One satisfaction as I look back over 1972 is that I almost completed the big programme of authorship I had planned. You know about the new edition of *Lucky Poet* and about the *Hugh MacDiarmid Anthology* Michael and Alex Scott edited, also about the Pibroch to me by Alastair Crampsey [Campsie]. But in addition to these there was an American edition of my *Scottish Eccentrics*. There are five more books to come. One of these, very elegantly printed and produced, is a volume of essays by various writers in a critical survey of my work. I had hoped to send you this for Xmas, but it will be a belated present now, though I'll probably have it in a day or two.

    The other books not yet to hand are *Selected Poems of Robert Henryson* in the Penguin paperbacks; my translation of Brecht's *Threepenny Opera* which Methuen are publishing and two de luxe books from the Italian Bodoni Press, one volume containing my three *Dìreadh* poems, and the other being a republication of my *In Memoriam James Joyce*.

    Valda and I spent the Xmas weekend with Michael and Deirdre in

Glasgow, and they come to us tomorrow. Charles Smith was out here two or three days ago. I had a Xmas card from Walter, but did not see him when he was in Glasgow recently and stayed with Mike.

It is difficult to write a long letter when one has no news. It is ages since I heard from or of Barker Fairley though I met his niece in Cambridge. But we had a letter from Vincent Thomas, urging Valda to come out to Canada again soon as his wife, Susan, needed help and advice with a litter of puppies her bitch is expected to produce any day now.

We also heard from Mabel and from the Farrars.

Hope you are all well and have had a good time on the ski runs. We've had a very open winter, practically no snow at all.

We heard from Fergus and Carolyn too, but no word of or about Ina.

I'd have written to Elspeth too but didn't have an address to write to. But I expect they are on vacation now and probably with you. Please give them – and Alison, Donald, and Rory – our love and best wishes for a happy New Year. And of course the same goes with our love to Alastair and yourself.

Yours, Christopher

35. *To Christine Macintosh*

1 February 1973

My dear Christine

We are greatly relieved to get your letter yesterday. As time went on, and there was no word from you, we guessed that something was seriously amiss. It is splendid to know that the lump was benign. But you must all have had a very worrying and difficult time. And then on top of that Rory's need to have the fenestration operation. Hope all of you, these alarms over, are now back in your usual comfortable groove.

Barker Fairley evidently did not know what has happening. I had a letter from him simply saying in reply to my query that he hadn't seen Alistair or you for some time.

I've been trying to cut things down, but as in a quicksand the more you struggle to get out of it the more hopelessly you become involved. I have imminent engagements in Oxford, Leeds, London, Newcastle-on-Tyne, Cardiff, Norwich, and Belfast – to say nothing of local things in Edinburgh and Glasgow.

But I am wonderfully well. So is Valda. Michael is far too busy, and Deirdre is of course nearing her time but in excellent spirits.

As to getting to Canada this year, it is too early to say, but I doubt it, unless late in the year.

With love to you all and hoping all goes well with you now. Regards to Mabel too.

Yours, Christopher

36. *To Morven Cameron (NLS)*

7 June 1973

Dear Morven

I am sorry to hear your Father has not been well again and wish him a speedy recovery.

Valda tells me you may come to the Clyde Fair poetry reading in the McLellan Galleries (8 pm) on Sunday. I am not looking forward to it. The other readers on the programme are Liz Lochhead and Bryden Murdoch and their kind of verse is much more likely to appeal to the audience than mine – viz. emotion without intellect, fancy without imagination, and a careful withdrawal of all the crucial problems of life today in the interests of reducing Poetry to the level of mere entertainment.

I'll be faced with the same thing to some extent in Holland too, where too many of the poets taking part (e.g. Allen Ginsberg) are pop purveyors.

However I'll hope to see you. I'm coming up on the Saturday as I have an appointment at 5pm with Stephens Orr, the photographer.

I've not heard yet whether Gillie had any luck with the School of Scottish Studies.

Hope you're not having too bad a time.

With love, Yours, Christopher

37. *To William Johnstone (NLS)*

9 October 1973

Dear William,

Many thanks for your letter. I hope you are fine and fit after your holiday in the South of France. I didn't know you were away, of course, until Bob Muir told me. And I was very sorry indeed to miss seeing the film and also the exhibition – but I have not only been dreadfully busy, but afflicted by a severe dose of flu' from which I have just recovered.

And tomorrow I am off again – to Newcastle-Upon-Tyne to take part in the Festival there. I'll be away 4 or 5 days, and I'll no sooner be back here than I'll be off again to London to do a poetry reading in the Mermaid Theatre and other things. And later on I have engagements in Dublin and Swansea. But I keep astonishingly well despite my intemperate habits! Perhaps that's the secret.

I've just had a long letter from a lady whom you met recently – Tamara Kirkorian – and she is full of the wonder of meeting you and convinced that you are one of the greatest characters in the world today. She agrees entirely of course with what you say about the incredibly large percentage in the population of Scotland today not only of hopeless and aggressive mediocrities but of positive morons and vicious nitwits.

But of course despite a handful of perspicuous people like Miss Kirkorian and myself, you cannot really hope to compete with people like your near neighbour Willie Turnbull,[1] whose genius was celebrated on Monday in the *Scope* program by that ineffable idiot, W. Gordon Smith.

Hoping to see you again ere long and with every kind regard and good wish to you – and to Mary and Sarah.

Yours, Christopher Grieve
In which sentiments of course Valda joins me.

---

1. William Turnbull (b.1922) artist and sculptor, employing purely abstract, geometric shapes in his work since the 1960s.

38. *To Jarmila and Ian Milner (NLS)*

9 October 1973

Dear Jarmila and Ian Milner

I was delighted to receive your postcard from Jugoslavia, since I had come to fear I'd lost touch with you altogether. I think the last time was when you so kindly sent us a tablecloth on my 80th birthday – a year past August. I wrote thanking you but addressed my letter to the old New Dolinach address. After some weeks I wrote again to English Seminar, Charles University. I did not know of course whether either of these letters reached you. I knew you had a cottage somewhere outside Prague but could not find the address of it. Correspondence with friends in Europe continues to be very chancy. I have given up hope of hearing from Jessie Kocmanova altogether. Valda and I were in Holland this year at an International Poetry Festival in Rotterdam, and subsequently spent a few days with friends in Amsterdam – about 50 years to the day since my previous visit to that city. Then I took part in Poetry International '73 in London.

I keep trying to cut down my engagements – especially when they involve travelling far. But I don't succeed, and now I am off tomorrow to Newcastle-upon-Tyne Festival and will spend several days there, come home, and almost immediately be off again this time to London. I am in fact choc-a-bloc till the end of the year, with engagements in Dublin, Swansea, etc.

As you will gather from the above I keep wonderfully well – considering my intemperate habits. So does Valda with better reason, but she does too much and doesn't take the care of herself she should seeing she has a 'dicky' heart.

Apart from absences from here, there is still a continual influx of writers. We had recently an interesting Swedish poet, Ivan Malinowski, two journalists from Amsterdam, a French scholar from the Ivory Coast, and a very nice team of technicians from West Germany doing a TV interview of me.

I do not know if you see the poetry magazine *Stand* but I had a long poem in the last issue fully exemplifying my concurrence with David Hume in 'praying for the re-enthronement of the great God, Difficulty'.[1] If you haven't seen that, please let me know and I'll have a copy sent to you.

You would know we'd been in Italy and had a long meeting with Ezra Pound, and at the London International mentioned above I had a long talk with W.H. Auden. Both of these men are dead now, and so, alas, is Neruda whom I met in East Germany.

I wonder how things are with you. You certainly put Holub on the map – his name and kind of work seems to be very well known now. I haven't seen any notice of any subsequent translating or other work by you, and as you will appreciate can form no idea of how things are now in the literary scene in Czecho-Slovakia. In Rotterdam I was greatly taken by a young woman (Baranova, I think) who knew of you but did not know you personally. One of the things we were doing (a group of Irish, Welsh, Breton, and other poets) was translating poems from various languages, and this young Czech was certainly an adept at it and rapidly furnished translations which had a concision, wit, and punch resembling the best of Emily Dickinson.

Jugoslavia is one of the few European countries I don't know. The Embassy invited me several times, but that was when they were having differences of opinion from Moscow, and I had to refuse.

Yugoslavia is a sort of Mediterranean Scotland, but it is not really better than the original, and we'll hope to see you over here again where if we can't give you as much sunshine we can at least give you a good equivalent in bottled form.

Valda joins me in every kind regard to both of you – and to Linda of whose circumstance (i.e. married or not?) and whereabouts (I have a vague idea she went to the United States) we have no knowledge now.

Yours aye, Christopher Grieve

---

1. 'The Divided Bird', *Stand*, 9 October 1973.

39. *To Ronald MacDonald Douglas (EUL)*

1 November 1973

Dear Ronald

I am sorry to have been so long in acknowledging and replying to your letter re my article on Boothby's giving up *Skian Dubh*. I have been busier than usual even, with a constant succession of time-consuming visitors from Sweden, Holland, France, etc.

I am not good perhaps at explaining myself. But I am essentially a 'loner' and I always do things first off my own bat, without consulting anybody.

The trouble is that I am so absolutely certain of my own integrity in relation to all matters Scottish.

You will know that for many years I have made a principle in my agitation for a psychological and political revolution in Scotland of what is called 'The Scottish Antisyzygy', i.e. the refusal to be channelled into a single course and the belief that contrariety rather than consensus is a good thing.

Apply this to Boothby. I will not have any truck with mere personalities. His attacks on you – his absurd references to Duck – are beneath contempt. I have told him so. They are even far beneath the general level of his writing. And nothing I said in my article is at variance with that view of the matter.

I brushed all such consideration aside and endeavoured to appraise *Skian Dubh* as it might *in toto* be considered by a historian of the Scottish Cause some time in the future – i.e. objectively.

It certainly always contained a lot of information I was pleased to have and could not have obtained elsewhere at any rate so easily.

You say I – and Valda and Michael – know Boothby is a police informer. I don't. I may have – or have had – my suspicions. But I have never been able to secure any proof. But what if he is, or has been? Better a known police informer than any of the host of unconscious servants of the status quo. I do not think there is much rectitude anywhere – and certainly I can think of several prominent Scottish Nationalists whom I'd better reason to suspect of being hand-in-glove with the police – and some of these are still held in high esteem in SNP quarters – and even in the 1320 Club.

My main point is that it doesn't matter much, since there is so little alas! to inform the authorities about.

Boothby may be a trouble maker but that is precisely what we want. Anything rather than respectable conformism, belonging to the 'silent majority'.

After all I for one have always agreed that there is sound sense in the dictum: 'The worse it is the better'. And from that standpoint one Boothby (whether a wolf in disguise or not) is infinitely better than a flock of sheep. But, of course, you have always known I regard the population of Scotland as one of about 90 degrees morons. I rejoiced recently when somebody expressed the opinion that the majority of the Scottish clergy were mentally diseased.

I am aware of course that in pursuing the antinomian line I do that I fall foul of respectable opinion, honest stupidity and all the rest of it, but I run that risk unrepentantly. Intellectual integrity is perhaps the rarest quality in the human make-up, and if Boothby lacks it he need not be singled out for that deficiency since almost everybody is deficient in that respect.

Whatever mistakes or follies or even crimes he has made, at least he has done what he could to keep the pot of Scottish Nationalism on the boil and that is a great thing. It conforms to what the old Aberdeen wife said of maligners of her son: 'Speak ill o' my son or speak weel o' my son – but aye be speaking'.

There is political value in unsubstantiated rumours, out and out lies even – and I for one am not disposed to make moral judgments.

Kindest regards to Roisin, Margery and yourself, from Valda and I.

Yours, Christopher

40. *To John Montague (SUNYB)*

4 December 1973

Dear John Montague

Valda and I will be coming to Eire on Monday 10th inst, by plane leaving Glasgow at 10.30 and due to arrive at Dublin Airport at 11.15.

Colm Tóibín says he and Seumas Heaney will meet us. Our meeting for English Literature Society is on 12th.

I cannot fly direct from Glasgow to Cork, but after we get to Dublin Airport I'll be able to find out if there is a local flight to Cork or express train.

We've both had an exhausting time in London, Ewell (Surrey) and Oxford University, and this past weekend I had to address two political meetings in Glasgow.

Travelling was made more difficult by heavy snowfalls but on Sunday and yesterday a thaw cleared all the snow and ice away. So we hope travelling conditions will remain easier, and that the strikes in Britain and the energy crisis will not affect the flights from Glasgow.

With love to Oonagh, Evelyn and yourself from Valda and I.

Yours, Christopher

41. *To D.G. Bridson (LLIU)*

4 December 1973

Dear Geoffrey

Valda and I are delighted to have your letter of 27th ult. Our visit to London was a very rushed affair, I not only had the Mermaid Theatre reading, but another reading at Ewell (Surrey), then back to London to record for the Dial-a-Poem service and then on to Oxford where I read and talked about Scottish Literature for the Union Society. Valda was with me – in fact I need her nowadays to get about safely; I just cannot cope with city traffic, travel arrangements etc. Once back here I had to go to Glasgow to address a couple of meetings commemorative of the Fiftieth Anniversary of the death of the great Scottish revolutionary Marxist and Republican, John Maclean. And in a few days time Valda and I are going to Ireland where I have engagements in Dublin and Cork.

Yes. It was splendid that Olga Rudge was able to come over for the Mermaid reading and I was glad also to meet Omar Pound and Walter de Rachewiltz.[1]

It is splendid news that you are about to do a film on Ezra. That will indeed be something to look forward to. It is good, too, that the Australians are putting on your *Aaron's Fall-out Shelter* and I hope New Zealand follows suit.

I'll hope – no; we'll hope – to see you when we're next in the London area, which I think will be in March when I've readings to do in Greenwich and some other borough for the London Poetry Secretariat.

Christmas will be here by the time we get back from Eire, so please accept best wishes to Joyce and you for a happy Christmas and a good New Year.

With love from Valda and I. Yours, Christopher

---

1. Olga Rudge (1895–1996), American violinist, partner and friend to Ezra Pound. Omar Pound (b.1926), Pound's son by his wife Dorothy Shakespear. Walter de Rachewiltz (b.1947), Pound's grandson, son of his daughter by Olga Rudge.

42. To Meic Stephens (EUL)

17 December 1973

Dear Mr Stephens

If I seem to have delayed in replying to your letter of 7th inst, transmitting to me the invitation of Yr Academi Gymreig to be the Academi's guests at Lampeter from April 6th to 8th, that's because I've been in Ireland and only got home here last night.

I regard the invitation as a great honour and appreciate the added kindness of asking my wife as well. I am free over the weekend in question and while at my age it is risky to accept engagements for some time ahead, I have great pleasure in accepting for my wife and myself. It will be a great privilege to address the Academi on one of the evenings as suggested.

Will you please convey to the Secretary and Chairman of Yr Academi Gymreig my gratitude and every high regard?

Also my wife and I wish Mrs Stephens and yourself a happy Christmas and bright and prosperous New Year – and our good wishes go too to all the Welsh Arts Council and in general to all organisations concerned with the Welsh language and literature, and Welsh affairs.

Yours sincerely, Christopher Grieve

43. To John Montague (SUNYB)

19 December 1973

Dear John

Valda and I enjoyed our visit to Cork immensely and are grateful for all your kindness. The audience at the poetry reading, in addition to being unexpectedly large, was I think the most responsive I've ever had anywhere. Tho' the studio audience at the Late Night TV show in Dublin was also surprisingly enthusiastic.

We hope the anxieties you were suffering from have now been relieved and that all is now, or will soon be, well.

And this brief note is just to wish you and Evie and Oonagh all the best for Christmas and New Year.

With renewed thanks and every kind regard.

Yours, Christopher Grieve

44. To Barker Fairley (NLS)

28 December 1973

Dear Barker

I ought, and had intended, to have written you long ere this. I can't remember when I wrote last. If I did perhaps I told you I'd been having a particularly busy time. Valda and I were in Holland for Poetry International '73. Then I had various engagements in London. More recently I did another poetry reading in the Mermaid Theatre – telephoned poems on the Greater London Arts Association's 'Dial a Poem' scheme – and spoke and read poems at Oxford for the Union Society. Then Valda and I went to Ireland where I gave poetry readings in Dublin and Cork, two lectures on Scottish Literature, and Radio and TV items as well. And over Christmas we were as usual in Glasgow with Michael and his family who come to us over New Year's day.

I ought at my age to cut down a lot of these engagements, but I just can't, and I am fully booked up now till the end of March. London and Oxford again, then Swansea where I'm taking part in a Dylan Thomas commemoration week, and Wales again a little later when Valda and I will be guests for a weekend at Lampeter College, Cardiganshire.

With it all both Valda and I are in good form. But nowadays I cannot cope with the exigencies of travel and particularly with the traffic problems and general noise and congestion of city life, so Valda has to go with me.

I hope this finds you and Nan in the best of fettle, and that you have had a pleasant Christmas. That goes too for Tom, Lorraine, and family and your other kin, and also for Vincent Thomas of whom I retain vivid recollections.

I haven't heard from Christine or Alastair or any of their children this

Christmas, but they are very infrequent correspondents at any time.

With every kind regard and good wish for the New Year from Valda and I.

Yours, Christopher

P.S. We had a visit here a month or so ago from Oliver Edwards, with whom I participated at Queens Belfast, a little earlier in an Ezra Pound commemoration.

45. *To Meic Stephens (EUL)*

23 April 1974

Dear Meic Stephens

I should have written you sooner, but since our return to Scotland I have been whirling in a worse vortex even than usual of engagements of all kinds. So my correspondence is badly in arrears.

I do not need to tell you how greatly Valda and I enjoyed our visit to Lampeter and later to Aberystwyth and Cardiff, and how grateful we are to all concerned – the Academy, Professor Caerwyn Williams, Sir Goronwy Daniels and many others and above all to you and Mrs Stephens.

We were especially lucky in the weather, and I will always be particularly glad to have met again, and had a talk with, Mr Saunders Lewis.

I have been reading the books the Academy so generously presented to me – and particularly Sir Ifor Williams' essays on the beginnings of Welsh Poetry, which I have found so fascinating that I think if I were about half-a-century younger I'd devote myself to learning Welsh!

Valda joins me in gratitude and warmest regards to Mrs Stephens and yourself, and your three delightful daughters.

Yours sincerely, Hugh MacDiarmid

46. *To Jean White (EUL)*

15 May 1974

Dear Jean

Valda told me about what you said on the phone yesterday about *The Library*. I haven't heard from Ruth McQuillan since the article in the *Scotsman* about the Library, but I am glad to hear she has been so active in the matter. As I told you when we first discussed it, I thought it might be worth seeing if the following societies would help, viz.

The Scottish Arts Council
The Civic Trust
Scottish Television
The Thomson Organisation
The Gulbenkian Foundation

I still think they might be worth writing to. (I understand you – or Ruth

– have already written to the Civic Trust.)

I do not quite gather from Valda what the position is with Langholm Town Council. Have they now agreed to take over, and run, the Library? In any case surely this could only be a temporary solution since Langholm Town Council will cease to exist in a year's time.

The point about the Thomson Organisation of course is simply Lord Thomson's association with Westerkirk.

The other societies I had in mind were the Scottish PEN, the Saltire Society, the Lallans Society, and the Association for Scottish Literary Studies. But I question if any of these would have money to spare.

I was sorry to hear you had been unsuccessful for the election for the Eskdale District Council. I did not know you were standing. And it is no consolation to know that Provost Grieve was successful.

Walter's eldest daughter Judith is to be married in Rochdale on 31st August and we are expecting to go down for it, as also are Michael and Deirdre. It is almost certain some of the Canadian folk – Christine and Alistair, or some of their family – will be coming over for it, but we've had no word yet to that effect.

Hope you are in good fettle.

Valda and I were up at Ochtertyre, near Crieff, where Sir William Keith Murray has a theatre and I gave a poetry reading. Hope to see you soon.

Yours, Chris

47. *To Jonathan Williams (SUNYB)*

10 June 1974

Dear Jonathan Williams

Many thanks for your greetings and leaflet re Jargon 66 and proposed *festschrift* to Basil Bunting.

It is a long time since I heard from you or you visited me here. I hope all goes well with you and the Jargon Society.

Here then is my Salutation to Basil on this occasion: –

★ Slainte curumath! May the skin of your bottom never cover a banjo.

Yours sincerely, Hugh MacDiarmid

★ Scottish Gaelic means 'a very important toast'.

48. *To Ian Campbell*

19 August 1974

Dear Dr Campbell

I am delighted to know that your labours of Thos. Carlyle are coming to publication and I am looking forward eagerly to your biography of Carlyle due out in September. The sample in *The Weekend Scotsman* is most appetising. I knew Joyce Wilson and Dr J.L. Halliday,[1] but as you know I too am a Dumfriesshire man born not so many miles from Ecclefechan. I may have told you I walked there once when a boy and went to the Carlyle House and tried on the great man's hat. It was too small for my head. What effect this has had on my subsequent development I'm hardly prepared to speculate.

I do not know if I ever thanked you for a letter in which *inter alia* you invited me to your house. If I neglected to do so I am sorry, but I'd certainly have been very pleased to accept if opportunity had offered. I have an enormous correspondence and great difficulty at times in coping with it.

With congratulations on the completion of your book and with kindest regards and best wishes.

Yours sincerely, Christopher Grieve

---

1. James Lorimer Halliday (b.1897), author of *Carlyle, My Patient* (1949).

49. To Desmond O'Grady

12 September 1974

Dear Desmond O'Grady

My son Michael has passed over to me the copy of your *Reading the Gododdin* which I have read with great interest and appreciation. Your foreword covers the field excellently – most of the literature you refer to is known to me and I have of course a particular interest in the subject matter since these classics of early Welsh poetry were written in Scotland.

That you should have followed to some extent the method Ezra Pound adopted in his 'Homage to Propertius' is a splendid idea, and your 'reading' abundantly justifies it.

It is very kind of you to give me this copy, and I will look forward to its eventual publication and probably find it possible to review it in certain periodicals.

In the meantime please accept my congratulations and best wishes.

Yours sincerely, 'Hugh MacDiarmid'

50. To Charles Nicoll (EUL)

24 February 1975

Dear Mr Nicol

At least you should have no difficulty – as many retired people have – in knowing how to fill up your time. I didn't know you were a painter as well as a photographer. It is very kind of you to send me the transparency of your portrait of me, based on the *Scottish Field*'s colour photograph. But you should have roughed me up a great deal more. The *S.F.* photograph was quite unnaturally neat and refined-looking and I have never had so trim and tidy a coiffure. At 83 I am shaggier than ever and not in the slightest danger of going bald. I hope you are successful in having the portrait hung in the Civic Art Association's exhibition. My wife has an album or filing system of such transparencies and has pleasure in adding this one to her collection. I do not know if on the one occasion you came here you noticed that there were about a dozen paintings (to say nothing of photographs) on the walls of our living room – a sort of shrine to my vanity! I still get photographed, painted, and sculpted – there are about a dozen busts of me in various art galleries and other establishments now. I cannot take all that as a tribute to my personal beauty, but it is interesting to see how very differently various artists have seen and painted me.

I hope some day I may see some of your landscape paintings too, but I am very seldom and then as briefly as possible in Glasgow. And now I am reducing all my public appearances to a minimum, especially if they involve travel. Even so the pressures on me remain heavy enough. Both Valda and I caught bad doses of flu' about Christmas time and are only now recovering from some of the after-effects. To make matters worse the type of flu' we caught has been called 'the Tartan virus' and is thought to be indigenous to Scotland. I should have been immune to that surely!

You will be interested to know that in April I have to receive the Freedom of the Burgh of Cumbernauld!

I hope this finds Mrs Nicol and yourself in good health and the same applies to your daughter. With warmest thanks for the portrait.

Yours, Christopher Grieve

51. *To Ronald MacDonald Douglas (EUL)*

7 March 1975

Dear Ronald

Many thanks for your letter and the 1320 Club news-sheet.

It so happens I've to be in Stirling giving a poetry reading at a Conference in the Studio Theatre at the University on 4th April. So I'll simply stay over and be available to accept the Executive Committee's kind offer to my wife and I to be guests at the luncheon on 5th April. But I do hope too much will not be made of my presence – and that I will not be expected to make 'an important speech'. I'm just not feeling like taking any very active part in anything at the moment. Both Valda and I caught bad doses of flu' at Christmas, and have been – and still are – suffering from the after effects.

We'd heard about the raid on Boothby's house, but not about John Stewart being up on a very serious charge. Also I see in the current *Scots Independent* Oliver Brown mentions one of his pamphlets in which he says he names three agents provocateurs. I must have missed that pamphlet but I am curious to know just who he named, so I am writing to him – I want to see if the names he gives coincide with those I've suspected.

It will be good to see you and Marjorie and Roisin again. I hope you are all in good form. I am sorry Marjorie is giving up the Treasureship and that you will not stand again for re-election. You have both done a splendid – but alas, thankless – job and I am not surprised that you feel you've had enough of it.

Every kind regard to you all. Yours, Christopher Grieve

52. *To Oliver Brown (NLS)*

7 March 1975

Dear Oliver

I note from current *Scots Independent* what you say about a pamphlet of yours in which you name three agents provocateurs. I have never seen that pamphlet and wonder if you have a spare copy. I am anxious to know if the three you name coincide with those I suspect.

Things are hotting up. Derek Boothby's house has been searched – by local police and not Special Branch. Inquiries are being made about others, including I am told, my son Michael. As a model of discretion I am apparently immune. Trust you are too. Police searches are an intolerable nuisance.

Kindest regards from Valda and I to Margaret and you.

Yours, Christopher Grieve

53. *To Major F.A.C. Boothby (NLS, DFF)*

13 April 1975

Dear Derek

I need not tell you how shocked I was to learn of your arrest.[1] That condition has not abated since I am very apprehensive of what will come at your trial. The authorities are, I am sure, out to make the most of the occasion. The farce of State Trials is not confined to the USSR, and the exemplary sentences already passed show that the authorities are determined by hook and crook to stamp out any signs of Scottish insurgence. Not what anyone has said or done – but the possibility of a Scottish uprising – is what the authorities are concerned about. It is the future – and anything already done or advocated – they are fearful of, and in Lord Wheateley they have an admirable 'hanging judge'. It is the ridiculous nemesis of the Reformation that such power in Scotland today should be in the hands of a Roman Catholic.

Rosalie, Jennifer, and her two boys, were here on Saturday and told us how you are and of some of the many dehumanising atrocities of the Barlinnie regime. Also I was angry – but not surprised – to hear that so few 'friends' had written Rosalie or tried to help in any way. The trouble of course is that there is so little any of us can do. If there is anything we can do, or send you, Valda and I will be only too pleased. In the meantime we can only keep our fingers crossed and hope against hope.

Sursum corda – but I have no need to tell you that. I can only hope that your physical condition is as strong as your courage.

With warmest regards and good wishes. Yours, Chris

---

1. Major Boothby was arrested on 29 March 1975 for conspiracy to import explosives for the purpose of damaging property in connection with the Army of the Provisional Government of Scotland. The jury, specifically exonerating him from any intent to endanger life, found him guilty of one of the eight charges facing him and he was sentenced to three years, serving thirteen months.

54. *To Ruth McQuillan (NLS)*

12 May 1975

Dear Ruth

The Cumbernauld Freedom ceremony went off splendidly. They certainly did me proud. I think Jean enjoyed the affair but I don't know what has happened to reports, photos, etc. They promised to send me copies of the local weekly, a representative of which tape-recorded the speeches, but that has not been received. Apart from the paragraph in *The Scotsman* I do not think there was anything in any of the other papers.

Alas! I have just had to cancel my visit to the Socratic Society. I have been cited as a Defence witness in the Scottish Provisional Government trial, which is expected to last several weeks. I am obliged to hold myself available at any time, and the Defence lawyers are sending someone out here one of these days to 'brief' me. I've written to Michael Farthing, Secretary of the Socratic Society, and Valda phoned Timothy Cribb at Churchill College, explaining and tendering my very sincere regrets. I am really sorry tho' I was dreading the journey – but I had hoped to see you and the Knights and others.

I remember David Mitchell. I never saw much of his work but thought what I did see 'promising'. I have no idea what has happened to him since.

I am not surprised at what you say about Donald Campbell and Walter Perrie. Campbell can be amusing company and an admirable compere at gatherings of Lallans Society etc. but neither are worth anything as poets – and in that resemble I think the whole of the 'monstrous regiment' Duncan Glen advertises. Apart from Norman McCaig and Sorley Maclean I've refused to take part in Poetry readings etc. with any other Scots versifiers. The audacity of poetasters like these putting themselves forward as spokesmen of Scottish Literature appalls me.

Valda joins me in every kind regard.

Yours, Christopher Grieve

55. To Gavin Muir (NLS)

23 June 1975

Dear Gavin,

It was a great pleasure to meet you in Milnes – the first occasion for a long time I've been in there. I hope we may meet again ere long under conditions that will permit us a better opportunity to talk with each other. My friend Douglas Muir had taken me out for a pub-crawl, but in each of the three pubs we visited I met so many old friends that he and I scarcely had a word together.

Many thanks for the volume of your father's *Selected Letters*.[1] It is full of good things, of course, but every now and again I had fresh cause to realise how opposed our opinions were on vital matters and – as I think you may agree – on the whole in most of these cases I think time has proved me right and your father wrong.

However, it was good of you to give me this book. Douglas Muir sent his daughter out in the car to bring it to me.

While I hope to see you ere long again [added in margin: Our 'phone number here is Skirling 255], in the immediate future I am afraid it will be impossible. I have a couple of important engagements away from home early in July, and later this month (June) am flying to the Shetlands and will be away for 4 or 5 days.

With renewed thanks and best wishes.

Yours sincerely, Christopher Grieve

---

1. Edwin Muir, *Selected Letters*, ed. P.H. Butter (London: Hogarth, 1974).

56. To T.D. MacDonald (Fionn Mac Colla) (NLS)

25 June 1975

Dear Tom,

I am very sorry indeed to hear today that you are ill and in Edinburgh Royal Infirmary and hope it is not serious and that you will make a speedy and complete recovery.

It is a long time since I saw you but I have been very seldom in Edinburgh in the last 2 or 3 years, and when I am it is just to fulfill some engagement and get back here as quickly as possible again.

But I was at the Lady Antonia Fraser party the other week and had the pleasure of meeting your wife – the first time, I think, since shortly after your marriage.

Our ideas may be far apart in many ways but I have always wished you well and, while knowing all the difficulties, hoped you'd find a way through them and get your books published.

I was glad when David Morrison published the brochure of essays about you and had hoped that that and earlier the film of you – marked your emergence into something like your due.

Be sure I'll be hoping to hear good news of you soon.

Yours, Christopher Grieve

57. *To Christopher Grieve*

[1975]

Dear Christopher

My answers to the questions are as follows – in the order of the questions, which I return also now, in case you have not a copy. [Questions from Christopher Grieve, CMG's grandson, were asked for the magazine committee of the *Hillhead High School Magazine*, and are printed in italics below, followed by CMG's responses to them.]

1. *You are known to have strong political views. How would you describe these?*

I am a Marxist-Leninist, and as such a member of the Communist Party of Great Britain.

2. *Is it possible for a state to exist which would satisfy you completely? Can you describe such a state?*

No Communist would claim that either the Soviet Union or any of the other Communist Countries has yet achieved a perfectly satisfactory state – but we do claim that the USSR has solved, or is solving, many of the greatest problems of any modern country and has evolved a state, whatever its imperfections, which is very much better than any country has achieved under Capitalism.

3. *What do you think of the views expressed by Solzhenitzen on television recently (i.e. we have lost many of our freedoms and also Russia is not sincere about détente)?*

I think Solzhenitzen is a malignant enemy of the Soviet system, exploiting purely personal grievances, and deliberately playing into the hands of the enemies of the USSR.[1] He tremendously overstates whatever case he has, and is not a writer of any real quality. Naturally he has been boosted by the anti-communist forces as a great literary genius and the equal of Tolstoy. He is not, he is simply a sensational reporter and if he had attacked the United States of America, or France, or Germany in terms similar to his attack on the Soviet System he would have been sentenced to a long term of imprisonment and treated very much in the same way as he alleges he was treated in Russia. He is a purely temporary phenomenon and of no lasting importance at all.

4. *You have a strong interest in Scotland. How would you describe yourself – patriot, nationalist, chauvinist?*

I am a Scottish Nationalist and Internationalist. The two things go together and I would not be one without the other.

5. *Can you reconcile nationalism with international socialism?*

You cannot have internationalism without nationalisms to be inter with. There is no question of the strong nationalist feelings in the Soviet Union – and in China. Both have encouraged the languages and cultures of the minority elements in their populations, as the English Government for example has utterly failed to do. I have been in Russia and China and seen how the national minorities are treated, and only wish the Scots and the Welsh and the Cornish, to say nothing of the Irish, were treated in the same way. The Communist Party is on the side of the national liberation movements.

6. *Would you like to see an independent Scotland? If not, how far would you like to see devolution go?*

I have no use for any measure of devolution. I want complete independence and the complete disjunction of Scotland from England. The Westminster Government can never give us independence. Independence is not given but taken.

7. *Do you think there is a Scottish culture? Do you agree with L.G. Gibbon's claim that almost all the writing done by Scots is in the English language and tradition?*

Lord Acton, the historian, has said that no small nation in the history of the world has had a greater impact on mankind at large as the Scots have had. That influence flowed from the national character which is utterly different from the English. To analyse that national character is to discover the factors comprising our Scottish culture. L.G. Gibbon was taking too short a view when he declared that almost all the writing done by Scots had been in the English language and tradition. This has only been true since the Union with England and the suppression of the Scots and Scottish Gaelic languages by English Imperialism. But no Scottish writer, writing in English, has succeeded in achieving first, second or even third degrees of importance or contributed significantly to the mainstream of English literature. English literature has had no good influence on Scottish writers and while English literature has owed a great deal to Scottish practice – in, for example, descriptive writing and in ballads and song lyrics – Scottish literature has no similar debt to English literature. It is precisely in the things that English literature is most conspicuously lacking that Scottish literature, alike in Scots and in Scottish Gaelic, has excelled.

8. *Is, say a poem about Scotland, written by a Scot, in a Scottish dialect, Scottish or English literature?*

Anything written in English is a contribution to English literature, speaking in the broadest sense, but is unlikely as our literary history shows, to be able to compare favourably in quality with the genuine article, i.e. with writing by someone whose native language is English.

9. *Do you still stand by your statement in 'Hymn to Lenin' 'What matters it wha we kill?'*

Yes, I still stand by the statement. Progress demands that recalcitrant or reactionary elements must be swept away. This has always happened throughout history. The USSR, under Stalin, is no exception and indeed in sacrifice of life compares favourably with USA or UK.

10. Do you wish to be remembered for your short lyric poems or for the longer ones where you formulate ideas?

Whatever the value of my early lyrics I think my later concern with long poems was necessary. Two great European poets – Heine in Germany and Pasternak in Russia – both masters of the lyric were agreed that life has today been far too complicated and full of change to be adequately reflected in the form of short lyrics and that much longer poems, i.e. epic, are called for the modern world.

---

1. Aleksandr Isayevich Solzenitsyn (b.1918). The Russian writer was imprisoned from 1945 to 1953 for his criticism of Stalin's conduct of the war. Rehabilitated in 1956, he enjoyed success in Russia and the West until his denunciation of Soviet censorship in 1967 led to his books being banned there. In 1974 he was deported to West Germany.

58. *To Olive M. Squair (EUL)*

13 August 1975

Dear Miss Squair

I am delighted to hear about your forthcoming history of Scotland in Europe and will look forward to it in due course.[1] I'll be very pleased to write an introduction as you invite me to do, but of course I will need to see the manuscript before I can do so – or at least galley proofs.

I hope this finds you well and that in these days of increasing difficulties in the publishing world no snag develops in the smooth issue of this 3-volume work. I am however a bit apprehensive because of the publisher. I knew his bankruptcy was over, but I have never found him very reliable and I know several friends of mine whose books he has published who were very badly treated by him. I do hope you have not a similar experience.

Please excuse this short and hurried letter. I am just trying to emerge from the overwhelming mail, letters, telegrams, etc., which has signalised my 83rd birthday.

With every kind regard and good wish.

Yours, Christopher Grieve

---

1. Olive M. Squair, *Scotland in Europe: A Study in Race Relations* (Inverness: Graphis Publications, 1976).

59. *To Maurice Lindsay (NLS)*

21 August 1975

Dear Maurice,

Many thanks for your letter. The fee you suggest for the re-use of the poems in your anthology's new issue is of course OK so far as I am concerned and is, I think, very generous. I'll look forward to the book in due course.[1]

Glad to hear that Joyce and you had a good holiday in Poland. That is one of the very few European countries I don't know. I have only passed through it. Nor do I know anything of the poet Rydla. I hope you'll tell us more about him in an article in the *Scottish Field* or somewhere.

I believe you had a wedding (the first) in your family recently. Please accept our best wishes for the happiness of the young couple.

Valda goes off to the Medit. for some sunshine shortly. Why I can't imagine, as we have had plenty of sunshine at home recently.

I'll be in Glasgow at Mike's for a day or two, and then further north for a week or so while she's away.

With every kind regard to Joyce and you.

Yours, Christopher Grieve

---

1. *Modern Scottish Poetry: An Anthology of the Scottish Renaissance*, ed. Maurice Lindsay (Manchester: Carcanet, 1976). The proposed fee was £40.

60. *To William Johnstone (NLS)*

12 October 1975

Dear William,

I am due at Ormiston Hall, Melrose, at 7.30 on 21st inst. The Secretary of the Literary Society there, Mr John Angus, is coming here for me and will motor me to Melrose.

I expect to be able to keep this appointment, but it has been a question whether I could. I had a nasty accident, falling down an awkward stair in Michael's house in Glasgow. I had a sore toe and must have put pressure on it causing me to miss a step. So I hurtled down the whole stair, sustaining scalp wounds and a badly wrenched back. At my age one doesn't recover quickly from such a shake-up, and I'm still hors de combat. I was lucky not to break any bones, but I was unlucky in being sober, since with drink taken I'd have fallen more lightly.

I hope Mary has recovered completely now from her far worse accident. And that all's well with you.

Yours, Christopher Grieve

61. *To William Johnstone (NLS)*

2 November 1975

Dear William,

I have to go into the Eye Department of Edinburgh Royal Infirmary on Thursday 6th inst for an operation. I am assured I'll get home the same night, but of course with any operation one never knows. Then if possible I've to go to Glasgow on 8th inst to meet the Russian poet, Yevtushenko, either on the 9th or 10th. So if I am to come down to you it'll have to be after that. I am sorry indeed to delay completing my sitting.

I thoroughly enjoyed my visit to Palace and am very grateful to Mary, Sarah, and yourself.

Yours, Christopher.

P.S. Perhaps you can 'phone and say which day will suit you best.

62. *To Rosalie Boothby (NLS, DFF)*

18 November 1975

Dear Rosalie,

Just a line to go with Valda's to say how sorry I am to hear of your troubles. I haven't written to Derek again but I am sure he'll understand that with my accident and eye operation I've had enough to do. Anyhow I really envy him, since it would be better in some ways to be in prison and away from all the horrible shilly-shallying of the Assembly Debate. I never expected anything worthwhile for Scotland from Westminster but the determination of all three older parties to make the Assembly utterly powerless and in the meantime to ensure that no real advantage accrued to Scotland from the North Sea Oil has not surprised me in the least.

Give my love to Derek when you see him again, and accept some for yourself.

Yours, Christopher

63. *To Major F.A.C. Boothby (NLS, DFF)*

3 December 1975

Dear Derek,

I have recovered all right from the effects of my accident and my subsequent eye-operation. I do not know what news percolates into your establishment but as you probably know the SNP scored great victories in the local government by-elections in Bo'ness and Bishopbriggs at the expense of Labour. These represent the first test of the effect on public opinion of the Devolution White Paper. It seems highly likely now that if a General Election is not long off the SNP will sweep into first place and greatly reduce the Labour hold on Scottish electorates. The White Paper has been roundly condemned almost everywhere as a disaster, a gross insult to Scotland, and there have been innumerable articles, letters to Editors etc. I'd fain have been able to discuss with you. The general view is that the upshot must favour what are called 'the extremists'. Certainly the general public are not likely now to be fobbed off with less than a great deal more than any of the Westminster parties are so far prepared to give.

We've had – and are having – a damnably cold spell and I shudder to think what conditions must be like chez vous. I do hope you are managing to keep reasonably fit. Valda is in touch with Rosalie who is having a very bad time of it. We are hoping to see her soon, but transport is the difficulty for her, of course.

George Reid has shown conclusively that he is head and shoulders above all the other SNP MPs and he has made numerous excellent TV appearances.[1] That is a medium for which unlike the others he has the technical expertise.

I hate to think that you will still be in your present quarters over the coming Christmas and New Year but we will at least put something aside in order that we may celebrate properly when we have the pleasure of seeing you again. We won't lack matters to talk about. But be assured things are moving very rapidly and substantially in the direction we want.

All the best to you. You are in our thoughts all the time.

Yours, Christopher Grieve

---

1. George Reid (b.1939), Head of News and Current Affairs at STV in 1969, SNP MP for East Stirlingshire and Clackmannan 1974–9.

64. *To Alex Clark (NLS)*

12 January 1976

Dear Alex

You know how absent minded I am in practical matters – largely due so far as the CP is concerned to my isolated position here. But I think I should have had my 1976 card by this time, also a note of dues outstanding.

I know you no longer hold the same position in the Scottish section of the Party, but on previous occasions you have stamped up a card for me and told me what I owe, which I have then had the pleasure of sending. Can you please do this for me again?

Best wishes to Jessie and you and the other members of your family for 1976.

It hasn't opened well for me. Following my fall down Michael's stair in Glasgow, I had two eye operations, and then to top things up I contracted a very bad flu' which is still hanging over me.

Trust you are all well. I had a card from Alex, Catherine and Jessica the other day. He expects to be in Scotland shortly and I am hoping to see him then.

All the best. Yours, Chris

65. To Ronald MacDonald Douglas (EUL)

13 January 1976

Dear Ronald

Alas I missed your piece on Radio today but Valda heard you and said you were very good indeed. I am sure of that and would not have expected anything else.

I was also very pleased to read the *Scotsman* report today of the 1320 Club warning to Westminister that if Scotland did not get a measure of real Home Rule civil uprising would follow. I am sure we are heading in that direction. And welcome it.

The 'great Debate' on Devolution has been the unholy farce we were sure it would be, like the Barweans the English are ineducable. They learn nothing – and forget everything worth remembering.

I am sorry to have been so long in writing to wish Roisin, Margery, and you. All the best in this New Year. So far as I am concerned it has begun badly. I wrenched my back badly in a fall down a stair in Glasgow, then I had two eye-operations, and now on top of that I've had – and still am – the worst flu' type cold I've ever had.

So all my work is at standstill. I haven't the energy to write or even read. But I am if slowly recovering from these set-backs, and hope to be soon fine and fit again. The way things are moving those of us who have the root of the matter in us will need to be.

I hope all three of you are in good form.

Love to you all. Yours for Scotland, Christopher Grieve

66. To Olive M. Squair (EUL)

14 January 1976

Dear Miss Squair

I quite understand how anxious you must be at the delay, and it is kind of you to express concern lest a worsening of my eye condition may be the cause. But no! Troubles do not come singly and I was just recovering from my back injury and the eye-operations and addressing myself to the mounting arrears of my work when I contracted a particularly virulent flu'-type cold and that has quite frustrated me.

I do hope the delay has not caused any delay in the printing and that Mr McLellan can keep to his time schedule.

I could not in the space condescend on details regarding even the main points in your book but I felt it better just to write in general terms. That's all I'm qualified to do anyhow. I hope you like this introduction. Your suggestion that you might use my letter in the preface would have been accepted by me but I had already started to write the present introduction. I haven't a copy of the letter but if you care to use parts of it and incorporate these at suitable points in my introduction that will be all right, of course.

You refer to the postage rate. As you see, I have just enclosed the material in the envelope you provided and I trust the postage you then affixed is adequate tho' the bulk of matter enclosed is greater.

With every good wish. Yours, Christopher Grieve

67. To Alan Bold (NLS)

30 January 1976

Dear Alan

I've just received – and read – the CUP anthology and hasten to congratulate you most heartily. It is a really excellent production. The notes on the various poets are blessedly succinct and free of reviewers' clichés and blah-blah generally and the extensive notes on the poems are wonderfully informative and helpful.

Personally I (but this is no criticism – only the sort of thing all anthologies invoke) I'd have included David Jones. I have little use for Philip Larkin.[1] I am, however, delighted to have such a good selection of Empson with whom, and Basil Bunting and George MacBeth, I am doing a poetry reading at the University of Warwick shortly.

I hope Pergamon are going ahead with your anthology of Peace Poems. I can think of nobody who'd do it better, or as well.

You have certainly added to your Laurels with this CUP one. Bless you. One triumph like this completely outweighs any alleged faults of yours.

Every kind regard to Alice and Valentina and to your good self.

Yours truly, Chris

---

1. David Jones (1895–1974) Anglo-Welsh poet and artist, author of epic poems *In Parenthesis* (evoking the First World War), *The Anathemata* and *The Sleeping Lord* (on the Arthurian legend), with stylistic affinities to Pound's *Cantos*. CMG's antipathy towards Larkin was reciprocated. While editing *The Oxford Book of Twentieth Century English Verse*, Larkin was ultimately persuaded to include some poems by MacDiarmid, writing to Dan Davin in a letter dated 2 April 1971, 'if you like I will make another effort to find some stretch of his verbiage that seems to me less arid, pretentious, morally repugnant and aestheticaly null than the rest'.

68. To Christine Macintosh

21 March 1976

My dear Christine

I need not tell you how desperately sorry I am – for you. One infidelity of this kind is bad enough but to have the same thing happen again is crucial and almost necessarily terminal. I am simply appalled at Alastair's selfishness and insensitivity.

Valda and Michael kept the secret until a couple of days ago when they gave me your letter. But that letter was dated 4th March; and I wonder what has happened since then. Presumably Alastair is back in Georgetown, whether he has got on your track I don't know.

I assume that unlike the last time twelve years ago his career is not in jeopardy. I shouldn't imagine the woman is still a patient of his so he should be free of professional discipline.

Charles Smith came out a day or so ago and showed me your letter to him. In it you said you were seeking divorce. Charles wondered if you had considered the alternative of judicial separation, which he thought would safeguard your interests and the interest of the children better than divorce. I agree with him but said I thought your lawyer would have gone into that with you.

You may be sure that you – and your children – are never out of my mind, and that all my love and anxiety is yours. After all these years and just when the children are all doing so well and the older ones entering on their own careers, you were well entitled to expect to rest on your laurels and enjoy a period of happiness, peace, and security – a blaze of sunshine after bearing the heat and burden of the day. It is monstrous that you should be cheated of this. And our hearts go out to you in this sad state of affairs. If there is anything I can do to help in any way just let me know. In any case please keep me informed.

Donald's wedding must be badly affected. I feel that to attend it under the circumstances will be a very awkward and painful thing. But I won't decide whether to come to it or not until I hear what you think. I will be very sorry indeed if I have to miss it. I'll write Donald in any case and hope he will not be too badly affected. I see that the children all feel much as I do – and it must be some help and comfort to you – that they have all rallied to you.

Valda joins me in love and every good wish, and we'll both be very anxious indeed to hear how things turn out for you.

Love to you all. Yours, Christopher

Love to Mabel too – she must be a great standby to you in this terrible predicament.

69. To Alan Bold (NLS)

23 March 1976

Dear Alan Bold,

Your reply to Toynbee in the *Observer* said effectively enough all that needed to be said. He is an old enemy of mine, of course. But I'll bide my time and have a real go at him when occasion presents itself.

Alec McCrindle is taking part tomorrow in London at a memorial gathering in honour of Paul Robeson and *inter alia* he is reading from the 'Third Hymn to Lenin' from your anthology. In a letter from him today he says 'Incidentally Alan Bold seems to have done a better job for Scotland than we used to think him capable of'. I don't know who that 'we' means but it certainly doesn't include me.

I'd have written you ere this re your invitation to come to Balbirnie. But nowadays I have literally no time for social visits. However I'm to be in Fife again giving a reading in the Beveridge Suite, Adam Smith Centre, Kirkcaldy in the evening of Thursday 22nd April, and on the afternoon of the same day I'm giving a reading to senior Fife pupils in Cowdenbeath.

Hope all's well with you and Alice and Valentina. You'll have heard of the terrible mugging of Norman McCaig. As he was walking home from Dolina MacLellan's he was set up by a number of youths who came up behind him and kicked him at the back of his knees. Once they had him on the ground they put the boot in. His face was dreadfully cut up and one of his eyes was badly damaged. The doctors say that if the kick had been a little higher he'd have had his skull fractured. Then they rubbed his face in the ground. It was sheer wanton brutality. Norman had money on him and a gold watch, but the brutes did not steal anything.

With regards for you all. Yours, Chris

70. To Christine Macintosh

15 April 1976

My dear Christine

Very glad to get your two air-mail letters – the second arriving several days before the first. You have been having a devil of a time. I never thought there was any need for you to go to a psychiatrist – no matter how hurt and worried you were I had no fear of your essential balance and rationality. But it seems that it is rather Alastair who needed – and still needs – the services of a psychiatrist! You – and all the children – are constantly in our thoughts and we continue to hope that the ultimate outcome in terms of your, and their, happiness may be much better than at present seems likely.

It was a pity your minister had just left when you 'phoned and we only knew he was going to Stirling but had no address at which we could contact him. He is a splendid chap and we were very pleased to have his visit.

Yes. I think I'll be able to come for the wedding all right but will let you know my travelling arrangements nearer the time – also whether Valda is coming too.

Very many thanks for the photos – the single one – not the group – is OK for the future.

With love to you all. Yours, Christopher
P.S. Valda will write you separately.

71. *To Olive M. Squair (EUL)*

31 May 1976

Dear Miss Squair

Many thanks for proof of preface. It is, as you say, set up very cleanly. I've only been able, as you will see from the galleys I return herewith, to spot one or two small errors, due I've no doubt to my own bad handwriting.

Yes I'm very glad you've found a more reliable printer for the book. MacLellan is really a menace. He turned up here the other day but I would not allow him in or speak to him. He knew that would be my attitude but he persists in turning up from time to time.

I'll be looking out for the book in due course. My wife and I are going off to Canada for the wedding of one of my grandsons. We fly out on 12th July and are due back here on 3rd August.

I've had pleasure in autographing the book you sent me.

With every kind regard. Yours, Christopher Grieve

72. *To Christine Macintosh*

7 June 1976

Dear Christine

They say no news is good news, but I had my doubts about that as time went on – though, of course, I knew you'd plenty to do without writing. But we are very glad to hear from you. I cannot comment on what you say as I don't know enough and as you recognise Alastair's attitude is incomprehensible and inexplicable. The position may be clearer by the time we see you.

We are travelling on 12th July from Prestwick by British Airways Flight No. BA 411, and are due to return Toronto to Prestwick on 3rd August BA 410.

I had a card from Nan and Barker saying you'd agreed to share me with them, which is OK with me. Valda will probably prefer a different arrangement.

I cannot tell you how much I am looking forward to seeing you all.

Love, Christopher

[Added in Valda's hand:]
Dear Christine

Just a footnote – I realise the house will be quite bursting at the seams – with Walter & Ann & others of the family – so if you wish to 'farm' me out – I don't mind – but think Christopher would be happier with you – he's not so adaptable – now we've got everything settled – we are looking forward to our visit immensely.

Valda

73. *To Roderick Watson (NLS)*

8 August 1976

Dear Rory Watson,

I have just received from Graham Martin in a reply of the course on my poetry prepared by you. I do not know if copies can be purchased but I have written to Graham Martin asking since they would be extremely useful to other scholars in France, Italy, and USA and Canada – and incidentally save me the enormous difficulty of having to try to explain myself and my work to these people. Even as I write you I have just had a visit from a Japanese Professor – an extremely intelligent and charming man, who is well on the way to completing a translation of the whole of the *Drunk Man* into Japanese.

Your work is of course by far the best exposition of my work available anywhere.[1] And (save for occasional paragraphs in essays by Eddie Morgan or David Daiches) indeed the only real exposition at all, all the rest of their animadversions being like the Barber's Cat, just 'wind and piss'.

You know me well enough to know that on many points I do not agree with you, while tremendously impressed by the acuity of your insights. Especially I do not find my withers wrung by your dismissal of much of my later long poems as 'prose'.

I think this is adequately answered in my preface to *In Memoriam James Joyce*. And in the relentlessness of my philosophy, I am struck by its concurrence with what George Steiner says in his *In Bluebeard's Castle* – viz. 'There is Freud's stoic acquiescence, his grimly held supposition that life was a cancerous anomaly, a detour between vast stages of organic repose, and there is the Nietzschian gaiety in the face of the inhuman, the tensed ironic perception that we are, that we always have been, precarious guests in an indifferent, frequently murderous, but always fascinating world … Both attitudes have their logic and direction of conduct. One chooses or alternates between them for uncertain reasons of private feeling, of authentic or imagined personal circumstances. Personally, I feel most drawn to the *gaia scienza*, to the conviction, irrational, even tactless as it may be, that it is enormously interesting to be alive at this cruel, late stage in Western affairs. If a dur desir de durer was the mainspring of classic culture, it may well be that our post-culture will be marked by a readiness not to endure rather than curtail the risks of thought. To be able to envisage possibilities of self-destruction yet press home the debate with the unknown, is no mean thing.'

Anyhow I am enormously indebted to you. This script of yours is full of brilliant aperçus illuminating in many ways to the poet himself – and of how few studies of any poet is this the case!

Every kind regard to you, and to Celia and your children.

Yours, Christopher Grieve

---

1. Roderick Watson, *Hugh MacDiarmid* (Milton Keynes: The Open University Press, 1976). The 'Japanese Professor' was Maseru Victor Otake, who was driven to Brownsbank by Douglas Gifford, and whose translation of *A Drunk Man* into Japanese, with an introduction by Cairns Craig, was published in 1980.

74. *To Angus MacIntrye, Editor,* Scottish Educational Journal

10 August 1976

Dear Angus

Very many thanks for the copies of paperback *Contemporary Scottish Studies*. It is splendidly laid out and produced. I hope it goes well. I'll need more copies of course but not just yet.

Already things are building up for my birthday tomorrow. We have two Dutch journalist friends here and yesterday had a Japanese Professor and a Polish student. As if I were not busy enough without such visitors just now!

But for the incredible amount of work confronting me since our return from Canada and the appalling engagements of various kinds lying just ahead, I'd have written you sooner expressing again our great gratitude to you for meeting us at Prestwick and bringing us home.

We hope to be in Edinburgh on 26th inst for the exhibition of the Galloway Winslow at 5.30pm at the Royal Repository, 137 George St. and Paris on Saturday 4th September to meet under 1320 Club auspices the Breton nationalist Oliver Mordrell at the Scotia Hotel, at 2.30; and then attend the Edinburgh Festival reading of *The Drunk Man* by Tom Fleming.

I am glad you got the Open University book of Roderick Watson's course on my poetry which I think is by far the best critical work so far devoted to me. I'm retaining your copy as I understand you may be coming out one of these days. If not I'll return it to the *S.E.S.* office. I've got a copy myself and have written to the Open University to find if it is on general sale and if so asking them to send me half-a-dozen additional copies.

With all the best from Valda and I.

Yours, Christopher Grieve

75. To Christine Macintosh

17 August 1976

Dear Christine

I am sorry to have been so long in writing you. But both Valda and I arrived back here completely worn out. A heap of work was awaiting me but I just haven't been able to tackle it yet. The plane back was jammed full and through some confusion Valda and I were separated and had seats in different parts of the plane.

One thing I was glad about was that (apart from half of the monstrous sandwich) I did not eat the meal at the airport. We were told that there would be no meals on the plane, but there were and I (not Valda) ate with relish and also drank the free whisky provided – Valda had to pay for her drink.

My birthday went off as usual with scores of cards and telegrams. We had two Dutch visitors here for several days and then a Japanese Professor and a delightful Scots-Polish student came. The Professor is busy translating *The Drunk Man* into Japanese.

I'll be writing you again in a day or two, with the document about the books, etc.

We are both so glad that the latest examination did not reveal any malignancy. A stay at Muskoka should give you a much-needed respite.

I had a nice letter from Dorothy Livesay who incidentally expressed her thanks for your hospitality.[1]

I cannot, of course, make head or tail of the situation. Alistair seemed pretty much as usual in his attitude to me. Of course I saw little of him and there was no possibility of discussing matters with him. You yourself bore up wonderfully. Tough you may be, but we'll remain extremely anxious till the whole thing is settled.

Love to you all. Yours, Christopher and Valda

---

1. Dorothy Livesay (1909–96), Canadian poet and University professor.

76. To Morag Enticknap

5 September 1976

Dear Morag,

It was a great surprise and pleasure when your son Nicholas and a friend called here today. I am afraid we were in disarray, as we have been at a solo reading of the whole of *The Drunk Man Looks at the Thistle* given by a distinguished Scottish actor, Tom Fleming, before a packed audience to mark the jubilee of its original publication in 1926. So we were very late in getting home and consequently lay in longer than usual this morning.

I had thought I'd never get in touch with you again. When I got your long letter saying you had left your husband, I wrote you at once. Unfortunately you had given no address on your letter, so I addressed my reply to your marital home in London, and some time later had it returned via the Dead letter office marked 'not known here'.

So I had no means of getting in touch with you, but I have always wanted to do so, and hoped you were all right.

Valda and I returned in the beginning of August for several weeks in Canada, and since then we've both been badly out of sorts. Whether this was due to the jet lag or just old age we don't know, but certainly the Canadian trip took a lot more out of us than we could afford. We are daft to forget that we are not so young as we used to be and should realise that long journeys are out of the question for us now. After all I had my 84th birthday on 11th August, so I have had to curtail my activities very considerably. I do not get down to London often now, and had to cancel two engagements there – one to open Collet's new bookshop in Charing Cross Road, and the other to attend the production at Saddler's Wells of my translation of Brecht's *Threepenny Opera*. However I have to be down on the 23rd of this month at the Poetry Society's place in Earl's Court Road. I have just been elected President of the Poetry Society, and must keep this engagement if I possibly can. Valda won't be with me, as she is going off on holiday in Italy on 12th inst.

So if you are in London we can perhaps meet then. I will not be staying more than one night in London, I think, as I have a lot of things on here.

Nicholas and his friend were en route for Mallaig from which they intend to go to the Island of Rum. Nicholas, as you must know, has a very soft voice, and I am very deaf, even with a hearing aid, so I couldn't glean much information from him. Not that I could have asked him many questions anyhow. He might well have resented that.

So I can only hope that this finds you in good health and circumstances. Not receiving my letter you must have thought I just didn't care. That would be very far from the truth. I have thought of you ever since and wondered how you were fixed. And also how your sons all were.

Valda joins me in kindest regards and best wishes.

Your affectionate uncle, Chris

77. *To Maurice Lindsay (NLS)*

7 October 1976

Dear Maurice,

I was delighted to get your *Modern Scottish Poetry* and agree that in this revised edition you have greatly strengthened the anthology and made it thoroughly representative of the period in question.

But I was amazed – and hurt – at the ascription to Compton Mackenzie of my 'Little White Rose of Scotland'. I cannot understand why you took it upon yourself to do this. As is widely known there have been allegations of plagiary about this poem. I have purposely refrained from doing more than denying of these. But I have always had an ace in the hole.

Compton Mackenzie was aware of the allegation too and wrote me a letter acquitting me of the charge and saying that he thought it very likely that the borrowing was not mine but his – probably he thought from some article of mine in *The Pictish Review* or *The Voice of Scotland* or whatever.[1]

He would also have agreed that he had never written a poem as good, though he versified for many years.

Plagiary is a ticklish subject. Another poem I was charged with plagiarising was 'Perfect'. I was alleged to have versified a passage in a short story by a Welsh writer Gwyn Jones. But his short stories were in Welsh which I don't know, and have never been translated. I saw Gwyn Jones in Cardiff and he agreed that it was impossible for me to have taken the words from his story.[2] Not only so, but he thought his story could only reach a very small public whereas the poem was known to a far greater readership and highly esteemed, and he was very grateful and we parted on – and remain on – cordial terms.

The letter in question from Compton Mackenzie will be included in my archive which I have promised the National Library of Scotland. But that consists of many thousands of letters, and other documents, and I just haven't been able yet to sort them out and give them to the National Library, or, some of them, to the Edinburgh University Library, though both these libraries keep pressing me for them.

Your assumption that the charge of plagiary was justified does not accord with the tribute you may use elsewhere in your preface. A poet with as many good poems to his credit as I does not need to take another man's words and his record should entitle him to respect. Also the poem is very much in my vein and quite unlike anything else Mackenzie wrote.

I believe Michael wrote you an indignant letter. He did not do this with my knowledge or approval.

I say no more, just now but am certain the charge cannot be substantiated and the publishers have certainly made an expensive error.

Yours, Christopher Grieve

---

1. The letter to which CMG refers has not come to light, however in Mackenzie's autobiography, *My Life and Times Octave Seven* (1968), he says that this 'lyric has been perhaps the best loved of all he [CMG] wrote'.
2. Whatever CMG understood, it seems extremely unlikely that Gwyn Jones made any such agreement. Jones's story did appear, in English, in *The Blue Bed and Other Stories* (London: Cape, 1937) and in 1965 CMG admitted the words of 'Perfect' had come, circuitously, from that volume. The poem was printed without acknowledgement to Jones, something to which he had not agreed, in the *Complete Poems* (1978). This was rectified in the Penguin edition (1985) where the poem appears with an acknowledgement approved by Jones.

78. *To Carcanet New Press, Ltd (NLS)*

19 October 1976

Dear Sirs: –

Thank you for the cheque of £40 in respect of copyright fees for Mr Lindsay's book *Scottish Modern Poetry 1925–1975*. In the circumstances I cannot accept this and now return the cheque to you – since you will know that legal proceedings are likely to ensue.

Apart from that I have never been offered such low fees for the total of 15 poems plus 3 translations from the Gaelic. In addition I understand that Mr Maurice Lindsay is proposing to carry the matter further, by publishing an article purporting to contain the results of his research into the circumstances surrounding the poem, 'The Little White Rose of Scotland'.

I have never read a more feeble explanation for the transference of my poem to another writer. Mr Lindsay insists in the original proof the poem was ascribed to me, but he substituted Sir Compton McKenzie's name for mine – on the advice of Mr Alex Scott head of the Scottish Literature Dept Glasgow Uni. This Mr Scott denies.

Sincerely, Valda Grieve[1]

---

1. Evidently dictated by CMG to Valda.

79. *To Maurice Lindsay (NLS)*

22 October 1976

Dear Mr Lindsay,

Since I'm unable to write I have to get my wife to do it for me. [The MS is in Valda's hand.]

I am concerned I have forgotten to deal with your proposed footnote and Explanation re 'The Little White Rose of Scotland'. So I must now make it completely clear that I cannot agree to any such proposal and nothing at all will be acceptable to me except the restoration of my name as author without any explanation of any kind.

Either that or the exclusion of the poem from the anthology all together.

Sincerely, Hugh MacDiarmid

80. *To ? (NLS, DFF)*

[1976?]

Sir:-

Like most of the main public bodies in Scotland – and I am sure the great majority of the consumers of alcoholic beverages – I regard the proposals of the Clayson Committee as a big step forward in the main. In particular the proposals for longer pub hours and that pubs should open on Sundays meet with my hearty approval as long overdue reforms.

On the other hand I regard the plans for more civilised or Continental type drinking – and the attempt, to ensure that pubs are in future places to which men can take their wives and children, and not simply go to meet and drink with other men, as only the latest step in the effort that has been made in all connections for over two and a half centuries to assimilate Scottish social habits to English standards. And that is something which must, I think, be resisted at all costs.

Tarting-up pubs, till they resemble English lower middle class parlours is something that is objectionable in itself and no solution to the problems. A pointer to the defect of the proposals lies in the fact that the Committee consists of upper class and totally unrepresentative professional people who certainly do not represent the desires of the bulk of the Scottish working-class.

Much is made in certain quarters of the amount of drinking associated with the rowdiness at football matches and the wrecking of railway carriages and other forms of wanton vandalism. But in so far as drinking is responsible for these deplorable misdeeds, it is not whisky but beer and cheap wine that is consumed by those responsible. Whisky drinkers have been victimised by successive Governments in a totally unjustified way. These Governments have always known they dare not tax beer to anything like the extent imposed on whisky.

I think it would be a good thing for Scotland if whisky was made much cheaper and beer doubled in price.

As for social drinking the tarting-up of pubs and the introduction of TV sets and singing and the rest of it must lead to a reaction. Personally I would never enter such 'refined establishments', and this does not mean I would drink less. It simply means that I would do my drinking in places more congenial to me and certainly where I would not be lumbered with women and children. After all, the old-fashioned pub was the working-man's club and the upper-classes have clubs where they can get away from their wives and families and enjoy themselves in the company of fellow-members.

Yours sincerely, Hugh MacDiarmid

81. *To Ruth McQuillan (NLS)*

12 January 1977

Dear Ruth,

I am delighted to get your letter today and despite your injunction not to, must of course reply. I cannot tell you how absolutely horrified I was that you didn't get the research fellowship and it went to someone working on – of all things – Evelyn Waugh. If I'd known there was such an entrant on such a subject I'd have known, of course, that you hadn't an earthly. I need hardly tell you that I agree entirely with you about Arts Council help, yet they have the money and if you don't get some of it – or refuse to take it – then it'll simply be wasted on someone who'd never be subsidised the extent of a brass farthing in any sane society. If you can get any of it grab it with both hands – so long as there are no strings attached to accepting it.

In the meantime I am glad you are contriving to get some sort of modus vivendi. Alas, I cannot help in putting any work in your way. I myself am busy refusing all sorts of jobs. I have a contract to do a pre-view article for *Radio Times* once every six weeks. There is a team of us who write it and our turn comes in six weeks. I wanted to make sure my stuff was sent in when I was in hospital so that I shouldn't lose the job so I asked Michael's wife to do it for me. Alas, she devoted most of the column to praise of the Orpheus Choir, which I detested and satirised repeatedly in earlier writings, and its conductor, the late Sir Hugh Roberton, whom Deirdre described as 'my old friend' – whereas he was a man I hated like hell. He was in business in Glasgow as an undertaker, and I said he should stick to that role and eschew any other kind of undertaking, anything musical especially! Readers cognisant of my much publicised dislike of Roberton and all his works must have been astounded at the lavish praise devoted to him under my name in Deirdre's article! It is things of this sort that have given [me] such a reputation for contradicting myself.

I have had an extremely lazy time since I came out of hospital. I keep making lists of things I should do and letters I should write – but that is as far as I go. I never get around to doing any of them. A lot of quite lucrative poetry readings involving travel to London or Loughborough or what not, which I have had to turn down, have gone instead to Norman McCaig, so all's not lost that a friend gets. St Andrews Festival is the latest I've had to cancel. I am afraid I'll be doing a lot of such refusing or cancelling henceforward. My travelling days are over.

I don't know how long I'll be in hospital this time, but I am pretty sure I'll need another abdominal (i.e. abominable) operation, since the condition necessitating it, is apt at my age to be chronic and redevelops after an operation of acid cauterisation.

In the meantime, I am suffering a little apprehension at the relentless approach of my 85th birthday next August. All sorts of things are being planned for it, and I am gong to be subjected, *inter alia*, to a rally here of my children and grandchildren from Canada and elsewhere. It'll be a real ordeal. Good luck to you. I hope something turns up to ease your way. Your letter today came along with another very nice one from [indecipherable words] so for once I'm feeling very bobbish and if my pen hadn't suddenly run out (note the second line above [i.e. the indecipherable words]), there's no knowing what length this epistle would run to.

Yours, Christopher

82. To Edwin Morgan

18 January 1977

Dear Eddie Morgan

I have just been reading (several times) the galleys of your essay on my work which Longmans are publishing for the British Council in their 'Writers and Their Work' series – an admirable series on the whole in which it is an honour to be included. And I do not know anyone to whom the job could have been entrusted who would have done it better than yourself. You have written a good deal about me, and here you have surveyed the whole of my work in a way that splendidly measures up to what has been said of previous issues in this series, very 'helpful but not condescending, intelligent but not intricate, and valuable therefore as introductions', or 'sensitive and perceptive criticism'.

A lot of things will be appearing this year. Yours will remain among the best, and though I do not agree with you in all particulars, I am very appreciative and grateful indeed. It occurs to me that you will be interested in what a correspondent wrote to me the other day: he says: 'you will remember that we spoke about the title of your poem "Esplumeoir" and I mentioned that I had found the word in John Cowper Powys's long novel *A Glastonbury Romance* where it is referred to as a "mystical word" and as a "mysterious word used in one of the Grail books about his (Merlin's) final disappearance". Powys interprets it as some "Great Good Place", some mystic Fourth Dimension or Nirvanic apotheosis, into which the magician deliberately sank or rose", and speaks of the "occult escape ... so strangely handed down from far-off centuries in these thaumaturgic syllables, the escape offered by this runic clue from all the pain of the world". This meaning chimes well with the thought of the poem.'

My correspondent goes on: 'Now David Murison tells me something more about the word. He writes: "It seems to have been used only in the Perceval romance in reference to the haunt, habitation, or cage of the enchanter Merlin ... the context in the Perceval makes it quite clear that it means the home of Merlin. The problem is to determine precisely what it was, and the answer depends on etymological speculation. One theory is that it is a corruption of some Celtic word but no-one can say what. So they fall back on analysing it as a normal French-Latin derivative: In this direction the suggested explanation is explumere, to take the feathers off, though a middle French form esplamer, which also means metaphorically (like to pluck) to cheat, swindle, hoard, deceive; so esplumeoir would mean a deceiver, hoaxer, enchanter, magician like Merlin; or the place where he does his magic, his cell or whatever."'

And he reminds me that when I 'published part of this poem in the *Scots Review* in May 1951 the title you gave it was "The Resurrection".'

You have, amongst so much else, a wonderful knack for lighting on and evaluating poems that have hitherto attracted no attention – e.g. *The*

Battle Continues, 'On the Ocean Floor' etc.
With renewed thanks and best wishes,
Yours sincerely, Christopher Grieve

83. *To D.G. Bridson (LLIU)*

28 January 1977

Dear Joyce and Geoffrey

Delighted, Geoffrey, to get your letter today and to know you are safe home after all your travels. I am afraid my travelling days are over. We were in Canada earlier last year for the wedding of one of my grandsons and were both utterly exhausted by the time we got back here. Ill-advisedly I was in London a few months ago – to open Collet's new International Bookshop in Charing Cross Road, and to address the Poetry Society of which I am now President. That visit about scuppered me. It took far more out of me than I could afford to give. I'll not be repeating it, I think. Of course I can't refuse all requests for poetry readings, speeches etc., but I refuse far more than I accept (and those I accept I do so on the clear understanding that fulfilment all depends on my state of health when the time comes – and frequently that means cancelling them!).

Yes, I had a slight stroke which affected my right side and paralysed my right hand so I couldn't write at all. Happily that condition responded well to physiotherapy and I can write again – but only a little. If I write more than a couple of letters I get infernally tired. Valda did all our Christmas mail. We were both delighted by Joyce's note inside her Christmas card.

It wasn't the stroke only. When I got into hospital examination showed I had a rectal ulcer which had to be removed – by cauterisation with acid. This seemed quite successful, but it is a condition that requires careful monitoring even after the operation, as it is apt to be chronic. So I was supposed to go into hospital again on 15th ult. However we were then snow-bound and all roads blocked, so I couldn't get. Now the road is clear and I'm going into hospital tomorrow (29th) and expect to undergo another operation on Monday.

Valda is fairly well but plagued by angina and for the past couple of months she has had to do all the outside chores I normally do, and she is very tired.

August sees my 85th birthday and already all sorts of celebrations are being planned. For one thing my daughter from Canada and my four grandchildren (and the partners of two of them who are married) are descending on me here. My own inclination is to go to some hideaway on a remote island and stay there till all the fuss is over. But of course I can't.

All my work is hopelessly – and I am afraid permanently in arrears. But I really shouldn't care. I've done too much already. Do you know (leaving out of account contributions to multi-author books and to anthologies – not to mention an enormous quantity of journalism) I have up to now published 137 books and pamphlets! But I have more to come shortly. My *Complete Poems*, in two volumes, is being printed by the Stamporia Valdoneza in Verona and will be published by Brian, Martin, and O'Keefe, Museum St, W.C. My two longish Cornish poems are being published by the Lodonek Press, Padstow, as a sort of present for Valda who is an enthusiastic Cornish Nationalist.[1]

But what I can't do myself others are doing for me. An illustrated biography of me, published by Gordon Wright, of Edinburgh, is due out very soon. And in the 'Writers and Their Work' series published by Longman's for the British Council, Professor Edwin Morgan has written a comprehensive survey of my work. The Ramsay Head Press in Edinburgh recently initiated a series of small books on Great Scots (to which series I contributed an essay on John Knox) and now they are including me in this series – who is writing this brochure I don't know yet.[2]

Then Granada are doing an Omnibus TV programme on me (I understand they were prepared [to pay] a great deal more for this than the BBC were).

So there you are. The caravan goes on and all manner of dogs are yelping behind it.

Glad you both liked Valda's 'Grey Ghost'. She should write more but it is difficult for her to find time and enough spare energy. I must be content then just to read – and reread – that wonderful poem of Neruda's on Macchu Picchu (which I've read in several translations), and also the poems about the same country by Ernesto Cardenal in his *Homage to the American Indians*. He is a disciple of Pound's and one of his poems against usury and the money monopoly is better I think than even Pound's best on the same subject.

Valda joins me in love to you both and I must close now my hand is too tired.

Yours, Christopher

---

1. *Cornish Heroic Song for Valda Trevlyn* and *Once in a Cornish Garden*, with illustrations by Lorgan (Padstow, Cornwall: Lodenek Press, 1977).
2. Hugh MacDiarmid, Campbell Maclean, Anthony Ross, *John Knox* (Edinburgh: Ramsay Head Press, 1976). The volume on CMG was never published.

84. *To Ronald Stevenson (NLS)*

20 February 1977

Dear Ronald

I have just listened to your excellent talk on F.G. Scott and the rendering of several of his songs. And I look forward to the programme on Friday.

As you probably know I had to go into hospital again and had a second operation. This seems to have been entirely successful. But it has left me very easily tired and, despite arrears of work and correspondence, utterly disinclined to do anything.

I have read and re-read the Ernesto Cardenal poems with much appreciation. He is to me a real 'find'. A friend of mine who has just been at Macchu Picchu hadn't read Cardenal but will now.

I'll return the book to you first opportunity – or earlier if you want it. But I haven't been out-of-doors since I got out of hospital.

Love to you all.

Yours, Christopher Grieve

85. *To Deirdre Grieve (NLS, DFF)*

18 April 1977

Dear Deirdre

I had meant to write you a wee note of thanks before this. But I am still incredibly lazy. I mustn't let it go any longer, however, just to say how delighted I was with your piece in the *Radio Times*. It was not only much better written than I could have done, but nothing in it in any way traversed my own views. Indeed I'll have to be very wary of you in the future, since you seem to know my mind at least as well as I do myself.

I hope all goes well with you and that the Dray report is a favourable one.

We had a happy hour or two last night with Garech Browne and his new love – Princess Maya of Morvi (India): a very charming person indeed. Garech certainly knows how to pick them![1]

With renewed thanks and best wishes.

Yours, Christopher

---

1. Garech Browne is Garech de Brun. See note to letter 9 (27 November 1970) above.

86. *To Nancy Gish*

7 May 1977

Dear Professor Gish

Many thanks for your letter of April 30th. I am very sorry I have been unable to reply sooner. I have been in and out of hospital several times since December and have undergone three operations. I was to have gone into hospital again on Thursday of next week but this has been altered to Saturday – a week today. I think I will be detained for several days – not,

I hope, longer. But I expect to have another operation on Monday which the surgeon thinks will be the last and finally dispose of the trouble which has necessitated the series. I have however had several very bad turns this week and as you will see from the atrocious writing of this letter I have not yet recovered from the effects of a stroke which affected my right side and all correspondence are hopelessly in arrears.

Meanwhile all sorts of things are building up for the celebration of my 85th birthday on August 11th – publication of several books, a conference lasting on 3 days in Edinburgh under the auspices of the Scottish International Institute at which a number of speakers will discuss aspects of my work, a 75 minute film of my life and personality by Granada TV, etc., etc. Also I expect my sons, daughter and 12 grandchildren here from Canada and elsewhere.

I would certainly wish to talk with you. I think sometime in July will be best. My phone number is Biggar 255 and we could fix the best days. I'll be here, but I am afraid my wife will be away. She generally holidays in Europe. I don't go. But sometime in June or July if possible I want to spend a few days at Frenich, Loch Tummel, Perthshire.

Looking forward to seeing you,
With my compliments and best wishes,
Yours sincerely, Christopher Grieve

87. *To Christine Macintosh*

12 May 1977

My dear Christine

All my correspondence is hopelessly in arrears. Donald and Ann in particular must think me a skunk. But I have no energy left. We will certainly be happy to see you in June-July. But so many things are being arranged to mark the occasion that I would fain go away to some desert island till it's all over.

I had a very bad seizure a few days ago. Valda thought my end had come and phoned Mike who in turn got in touch with Dr Enshor and Mr Thompson at Chalmers Hospital, who phoned instructions. I recovered but am extremely weak.

I go into hospital again on Saturday (14th) and expect another operation on Monday.

Lucky Rory! Lakefield is a splendid place. I hope Ina looks after him and is not too preoccupied with His Royal Highness.[1] Love to her and to you all, and to Barker and Nan who also must think I've forgotten them.

Until the end of June then. Yours, Dad

---

1. Prince Andrew, later the Duke of York, also attended Lakefield College School, Ontario.

88. To Kaikhosru Shapurji Sorabji (McMUL)

12 June 1977

My dear Sorabji

I watched the Television with great delight. I thought it was an excellent exposition of your work and was glad that after so many years of your interdict on performances of your music you had found such a worthy exponent as Yonty Solomon and such a promising young disciple as Mr Hinton. As you know I thoroughly approved of your action in banning all performances but I am glad you have found it possible to release that now.

It was good to see you in the programme. You looked – and I hope you are – well. We are about the same age and although for almost all my life I have enjoyed good health I have had a bad time recently. I have had four abdominal operations since Christmas and have to go into hospital again in early August and expect another operation then.

All sorts of public and private functions are being arranged to celebrate my 85th birthday, but I do not approve of most of them and so far as I am concerned they will have to be held *in absentia*. I have to lie low nowadays and must do as little in the way of public affairs as possible and especially anything that entails travelling.

I would fain avoid the coming fuss altogether and hie me away to some remote hideaway if that were possible. Your home in Dorset is the sort of place I envy, but I am unlikely now ever to see it.

You are never out of my mind however and I had a visit the other day from Norman Peterkin who has come to see me about twice a year now for the past 8 or 9 years.[1] I get news of you from him. I am also in touch with Sacheverell Sitwell and was glad to see him on the TV programme.

With congratulations and every good wish.

Yours as always, Christopher Grieve

---

1. Norman Peterkin (1816–1982), British composer.

89. To Alan Bold (NLS)

15 September 1977

Dear Alan,

Many thanks for your letter of 13th inst. I had seen somewhere that you were to edit an anthology of erotic verse, and I am of course pleased to give you permission to include the two poems you mention.[1] For 'O she was fu' o' lovin' fuss' the acknowledgement should be to me, but for the 'O wha's the bride' from *A Drunk Man*, the acknowledgement should be to me, and, as publishers, Kulgin Duval and Colin Hamilton.

I did not attend any of my birthday celebrations except one concert. I have been having a very bad time from after-effects of the operations I've had, and I am due back in hospital on 12th Nov.

Much of my earlier Scots poetry is in ballad measure, but I do not think I was otherwise influenced. The exclusion of any concern with Scottish Literature in our school extended to the ballads. I do not think I knew – or knew of – more than a couple of them until after I was demobbed in 1920.

I'll think over the matter of sending you a sentence or two about the impact the ballads (however belatedly) had on my poetic development, and try to send you something along these lines shortly –

Glad to hear of your own new collection and I'll certainly look forward to it.

Hope all's well with you and Alice and the bairns.

Yours, Chris

---

1. *Making Love*, ed. Alan Bold (London: Picador, 1978).

90. *To Charles Nicoll (EUL)*

20 October 1977

Dear Mr Nicol

Many thanks for your letter of 11th inst. If I have been slow in acknowledging it that is just because I have been having a bad time. I go into hospital on 12th Nov. for another operation – my 6th this year.

I was delighted to hear that Granada TV had not forgotten to pay you the fee for use of the photograph. This of course was stipulated at the start, and I supplied your address for that purpose.

After all these small payments are a very tiny percentage of the costs. Granada TV got the contract because they were willing to finance the plan to the extent of £30,000 whereas the BBC would not go beyond £10,000.

Hope you and Mrs Nicol are well.

With warmest regards. Yours, Christopher Grieve

91. *To Alan Riach (EUL)*

23 November 1977

Dear Alan Riach,

Sorry to have been longer in implementing my promise to send you a poem or two for the journal you are editing.[1] But instead of improving my condition is much worse and when I had my 6th operation ten days ago it was found on examination that there had been a great deterioration in my trouble in the interval between that 6th operation and the preceding 5th one. So much so that the surgeon told my wife my life-expectancy was now only 6 months. So it was agreed that some more drastic treatment was needed and it was agreed that I should have a course of radio therapy – not the old X-ray therapy which has grave drawbacks but the new neutron therapy. This course will begin early in January.

I hope you have a most enjoyable time with Sorley MacLean and Robert Garioch.[2]

Many thanks for Cribb's Nigerian address.[3]

With my best wishes. Yours, Christopher Grieve[4]

---

1. *Gallimafray* (Cambridge, 1978), edited by Alan Riach and David Richards. One issue was produced.
2. Riach and a fellow-student, Christopher Larsen, organised a poetry reading at Churchill College, given by MacLean and Garioch in 1978.
3. T.J. Cribb, Riach's English tutor at Churchill College, Cambridge, was on sabbatical leave in Nigeria; CMG had asked for his address.
4. Enclosed: Two poems by Hugh MacDiarmid, 'Under The Hallior Moon' and 'My Sailor Son Comes Home (After the German of Stefan George)'.

92. *To Jean White (EUL)*

21 November 1977

Dear Jean

I am sorry to have been so long in writing you. I was upset when I heard about you crawling like a tortoise on your hands and knees downstairs and through the house. If it had been me the cause would have been put down at once as alcoholism, but of course that does not apply in your case. I should have written then to express my anxiety, but I couldn't. All my correspondence is similarly or even worse in arrears, and now likely to remain so.

There has been a drastic turn for the worse in my condition. Several weeks ago the chief surgeon told Valda I had perhaps six months to live. A week ago today I was in Chalmers Hospital again and underwent another operation – my sixth this year. Alas, these operations have not been successful. Examination showed that my condition has badly deteriorated in the interval between this last stay in hospital and the previous one. So that phase of my illness is over and something much more serious has to be tried. I am to have radio therapy at the Western General Hospital – not the old X-ray therapy which had certain grave drawbacks, but the new neutron therapy sponsored by Dr Arnot of Glasgow and others which is a major break-through in radio therapy and avoids the drawbacks of the old X-ray method.

This of course is a kill or cure treatment. I expect it to begin in the first week of January – Dr Arnot himself will administer the treatment to me.

Consequently I have now finally abandoned any hope of going to

Canada in February for the Celtic Consciousness Symposium. This is a great pity as it is an extremely important occasion.

I had hoped to give you another 50 or 60 books for Langholm library if you'd been up. But that must wait now. Michael will see to it once he goes through all my stuff.

As perhaps you know a very beautiful limited edition of my lyrics was privately printed as a birthday present for me by the Bodoni Press at Verona in Italy.[1] Not only is the Bodoni Press the most famous in the world, but added importance is given to this book by the fact that it will almost certainly be the last publication over that famous imprint, since the printer who runs it, Dr Mardersteig, is dying of cancer. He did it specially for me. The book is of course valuable and will become increasingly so. I am giving you a copy but I have just signed it but not inscribed it to you personally since you can either have it as your own property or give it to Langholm Library. I cannot alas manage two copies – one for you and one for the Library.

Much as I'd like to I am afraid I won't be able to come to Langholm. While it would be all right if a small deputation came here, we have not the accommodation or other facilities here for coping with people. So I'll just have to leave it to you to make what arrangements you can.

As you will understand I am now very busy making final arrangements for the settlement of all my affairs. Everything I leave will go to Valda and Michael.

Our friendship in recent years – and your kindness at Common-Ridings etc. – has been a great joy to me, and I am very grateful. I hope this finds you well and returned to modes of locomotion of a more approved character than crawling about.

Valda joins in love and best wishes.

Yours, Chris

---

1. Hugh MacDiarmid, *Selected Poems*, ed. Duval and Hamilton (Frenich, Foss: Kulgin D. Duval and Colin H. Hamilton, 1977).

93. *To John Montague (SUNYB)*

12 December 1977

Dear John Montague

I could not have had a more enheartening letter on the eve of going into hospital again than your most interesting (tho' far too kind) epistle just to hand.

When I had my 6th operation recently it was found that in the interval between that and the preceding operation my condition had deteriorated very seriously. So some more radical treatment was called for, and I am to go into hospital again tomorrow for a course of radio-therapy: not the old X-ray treatment (which has grave disadvantages) but the new neutron method (which has not these disadvantages, but represents a real breakthrough in deep heat therapy and has already had splendid results with old people).

I expect, if all goes well, to be in hospital now for 3 weeks or more. Ward 3, Radio Therapy.

I have had to cancel my intended presence at the Celtic Consciousness Symposium in Toronto. And indeed I have cancelled or refused all other commitments, and my correspondence and literary work is all hopelessly in arrears.

I like Crotty very much and think if he can hold to his course that he will do very well.

Valda is not too well but owing to my total inability to help in any way has had this past year had to do far too much.

She joins me in every kind regard to Evelyn and yourself, plus of course best wishes for a Happy Christmas and good New Year.

Yours, Christopher Grieve

P.S. I only met Berryman once and did not know that he knew or was interested in my *Drunk Man*.[1]

---

1. John Berryman (1914–72), American poet and academic, Regents Professor of Humanities at the University of Minnesota, 1955–72. See 'The Long Way to MacDiarmid', *Poetry*, vol. 88, no. 1 (April 1956), a review of Hugh MacDiarmid, *Selected Poems*.

94. To Janet Caird (NLS)

18 January 1978

Dear Mrs Caird

I ought to have written you immediately I received my copy of your poems.[1] Norman Wilson of the Ramsay Head Press wrote to me when he received my order that he had let you know and you'd been thrilled. Why you should be I don't know. It is I who was thrilled. Edwin Muir somewhere refers to very slight verbal effects which have the power to release significances out of all proportion to their size and apparent capacity. So it is with your little poems. They are all worth acres of more ambitious efforts.

I hope you are keeping better and that your husband is in good form. As you know I have been very ill. After my 6th operation examination revealed that in the short interval between that operation and the preceding one my condition had deteriorated seriously and a different treatment was obviously required. This took the form of a course of radio therapy (not the old X-ray business but the new Neutron treatment). This has probably helped me but it is several weeks before one knows. In the meantime all I know is that it has left me with a very nasty radio burn.

So your wonderful title for your elegant little book is very much to the point and I am afraid not only that I have written far too much but inexcusably forgotten that the broad road leadeth to destruction.

With all my kindest regards to Mr Caird and yourself.

Yours, Christopher Grieve

---

1. Janet Caird, *Some Walk a Narrow Path* (Edinburgh: Ramsay Head Press, 1977).

95. *To Alex McCrindle (EUL)*

3 March 1978

Dear Alex

The title of the book of tributes to Lenin on his centenary – it's a big book – is Bes-sme-r-t-l-e (all one word) and it is published by Progress Publishers Moscow.

I got Professor Henry of the Chair of Slavonic Studies at Glasgow University to read the translation of the 'Third Hymn to Lenin'. He went to great trouble and enlisted the help of his Honours students. His report on the whole was favourable – the essence of the poem had been memorably conveyed – and here and there the translator had modified expressions in accordance with the Party line, and in a few cases he had just omitted phrases.

The name of the translator is I. Berlin.

Hope all goes well with you. I am having a pretty hard time again and will be glad when I get into Chalmers Hospital again on 13 inst. I don't know yet if I'll be kept in or simply have a check-up.

All the best. Yours, Christopher

96. *To Sorley MacLean (NLS)*

27 March 1978

Dear Sorley,

Many thanks for your letter of 21st. I am sorry you had difficulty in trying to 'phone us. I only got out of hospital on Saturday after two very trying and painful operations. These are supposed to have put an end to the main source of my trouble. I certainly hope so. I have no vitality left and am near the end of my tether.

I was very sorry indeed to miss the Toronto Symposium. I heard it degenerated into a battle-royal between Conor Cruse O'Brien and Sean MacBride[1] and an old friend – Professor Barker Fairley – regretted my absence as he was sure if I'd been there I'd have shifted the debate on to other lines.

I do hope I may see you when you are next in Edinburgh. You'll have heard Dublin University are giving me the Litt.D. on 6th July. I'll do my utmost to be there as they do not confer Hon. Degrees *in absentia*.

Every kind regard to Renée and your good self, and your family, from Valda and I.

Yours, Christopher Grieve

---

1. Sean MacBride (1904–88), son of Maud Gonne, a founder member of Amnesty International, winner of the Nobel Peace Prize (1974).

97. *To Walter Grieve*

28 March 1978

Dear Walter

I believe your 50th birthday falls in a few day's time. I have not been an indulgent father – as I would have wished to be. But I write to offer you my congratulations and best wishes on reaching the half-way stage.

Michael has some idea of running down to you on that great occasion and wants me to go too. I will if I can but I am in a very poor state. I only got out of hospital and home two days ago after two very exhausting and painful operations. They are believed to have settled the basic cause of my trouble. Certainly they have rid me of the pain of that, but then they were so painful in themselves that no other pain could coexist alongside theirs.

Whether or not I am still in great pain. I am of course housebound and have been ever since New Year. The only engagement I am determined to keep if physically possible is to go to Dublin on July 6 when the University of Dublin is going to confer a D.Litt. on me. But they do not confer honorary degrees *in absentia* so I must be there.

I am glad to hear from Michael that the virus trouble which afflicted you here has cleared away all right, I hope this is so.

I thought Judith would have had her baby by now. But I have had no word. I am looking forward to my first great-grandchild.[1]

Love to Anne and all the rest of your family, and to you from Valda and I.

Yours, Dad

---

1. Michael Behagg was born on 26 August 1978.

98. *To Anne and Donald Macintosh*

28 March 1978

Dear Anne & Donald

I was delighted to receive your letters and am sorry I have been unable to reply sooner. I only got out of my latest spell in hospital two days ago after two very exhausting and painful operations. I am far from out of the wood yet and am due to return to hospital in a fortnight's time or thereabout. You will understand I am completely exhausted.

I was very pleased to hear of Donald's appointment and trust you, Anne, will get a permanent teaching post shortly.

I'll write you a decent letter as soon as I can, but for the time being this must suffice. I owe letters also to Elspeth & Danny, and to Rory.

Yours with love and best wishes, from Grandad & Valda

99. *To Alistair Macintosh*

25 April 1978

Dear Alistair

I am very pleased to have your letter unexpected as it is and so far as I am concerned undeserved. I was very sorry indeed to be unable to reply to the letter you sent me on my 85th birthday. But all my correspondence and other writing is hopelessly in arrears. As you know I underwent some cauterization operations and firstly a course of Neutron radio-therapy. The last-mentioned left me with severe 'radiation burns' which have rendered it virtually impossible and exceedingly painful to perform any natural functions, excretary and urinary. And of course the pain I have renders it impossible for me to have any spare energy. I just can't concentrate to read, write, or even watch TV.

But on the credit side I think the radio-therapy has done its job. The tumour in my rectum has been brought under control and is now unlikely to develop further. But it has left me with a problem of ulceration. What the doctors and surgeons will do now I cannot guess. I am for the time being housebound. I haven't been out of doors since New Year's day.

It was a very great pleasure to have Christine here and to find her so well. She has evidently found a modus vivendi at Lakeview that suits her. And there was good news of all the children – to all of whom I also owe letters which I am not likely to be able to write in the near future.

All my effort now is to try to be able to go to Dublin on 6th July to receive the D.Litt. I am very tottery on my feet and certainly could not stand for more than a few seconds to be 'capped'.

It would be a great pleasure to see Aidan Kennedy there. But quite a number of my friends intend to be present. In normal circumstances there would of course be a great binge, but as matters are I'll have to be extremely careful in every way if I am to get through the ceremony at all.

I was very sorry indeed not to get to the Celtic Consciousness Symposium but I do hope I can get to Canada again – especially to have a few quiet days at Muskoka.

I hope all goes well with you and as I said you'll be welcome here any time. It is impossible for any outsider to judge between a man and his wife. It is not his business anyway. And I am certainly not going to attempt to judge between Christine and you. I can only hope all will turn out as well as possible for all of you.

If Mabel is still looking after you please give her my warmest regards and best wishes.

I'll not try to write any more. The effort takes more out of me than I have to give and as you can see my handwriting has deteriorated terribly and I hesitate to inflict illegible scrawls on my friends.

Valda joins me in kindest regards to you.

Yours, Christopher

100. *To Nancy Gish*

5 May 1978

Dear Professor Gish

Many thanks for your letter of 21st April. I am still very far from well and expect to go into hospital again shortly for further operations. As matters stand I am housebound and haven't been out of doors since New Year's Day.

So this is just a brief letter to say that of course I will do my best to answer any specific questions about my work you care to send me.

If I am well enough I hope to go to Dublin on 5th July where the University of Dublin are to confer a doctorate in letters (D.litt) on me, *honoris causa*.

With my best wishes.

Yours sincerely, Christopher Grieve

P.S. I am of course extremely interested in what you say of the interest of the students in your graduate course on my poetry. I have just had similar information from Australia and from Egypt (both Cairo and Alexandria Universities).

101. *To Morris Blythman (NLS)*

16 May 1978

Dear Morris Blythman

As Valda told you on the phone I received an advance copy of my *Socialist Poems* with the statement that the date of publication hadn't been fixed yet but I'd get the rest of my copies as soon as that was decided. I have since had a letter stating that publication date has now been scheduled for 15th June.

The book is splendidly printed and produced and as far as I can see completely free of errors of any kind. So I am immensely indebted to Tom Law and you.

I haven't heard yet when the *Complete Poems* is going to be published, but I expect it about 10th June.

You'd see the article by Neal Ascherson in the *Sunday Times* Magazine. This was meant to coincide with the publication of the *Socialist Poems*.[1] It is a pity the latter was not ready but the article should do the book a lot of good.

I've been having a bad time again and going back into Chalmer's Hospital on 7th June for a cauterisation operation the following day.

Hope this finds Marina and you in good fettle.

Sorry the portrait by Morris Grassie was spoiled by the smoothing out of all the lines and wrinkles. The result babyfied me. I never in fact looked so innocent.

With best wishes, Yours, Chris

---

1. *The Socialist Poems of Hugh MacDiarmid*, ed. T.S. Law and Thurso Berwick (London: Routledge and Kegan Paul, 1978).

102. *To Miss Smeaton (EUL)*

12 June 1978

Dear Miss Smeaton

I write to thank you for your many enquiries as to how I was keeping and your repeated assurances to my wife that I am the greatest – a flattery that, of course, I cannot accept. But I'd have written to you long ago if I had had your address.

It is, I am afraid, too late now to suggest that we might meet somewhere in Edinburgh, or even that you might care to visit me here.

For the past 18 months I have been in and out of hospitals and undergoing successive operations and finally a course of Neutron Ray Therapy. Last week I had two operations. The first of these confirmed what I had suspected but did not know. My wife and son had known for 6 months but did not tell me. Namely that my main trouble is a rectal cancer.

So I must be near the end of my tether. I cannot say I am sorry. I have had a long and interesting life, but I feel that I have done the work I was sent to do, and that I can hardly hope to add to that if I were granted a few more years.

All I want to do now is to go to Dublin on July 6th when the University of Dublin are to confer an honorary doctorate in literature on me.

Please accept my thanks for your support and with it my compliments and best wishes.

Yours sincerely, Christopher Grieve ('Hugh MacDiarmid')

103. *To Michael Grieve (NLS)*

12 June 1978

Dear Michael

Since the first of the two operations I had in Chalmers Hospital last week – namely fulguration of rectal carcinoma – confirmed what I had hoped might not be the case, it is necessary now to put my affairs in order. This holograph letter should therefore be accepted as a death-bed statement. It is in any case my last will and testament and cancels and supersedes any previous documents I may have signed.

I wish everything I possess to go to your mother, my wife Valda, and to yourself, and am sure you will agree to any division that may be necessary.

I want you to have all my works and papers, except those valuable works I gave Valda and which she has deposited in her bank in Biggar.

I want my cousin Jean White, Langholm, to have 30 to 40 books either for Langholm Library or herself if she wants any of them. The books I want you to give to Jean must be books of some value (not paperbacks).

All the rest are to be yours.

As to my correspondence there are many letters from other well-known writers or on literary matters or concerning my conferment of LLD from Edinburgh University, my election as a Fellow of the Modern Language Association and of Edinburgh Speculative Society. I wish a selection of these to go to the National Library of Scotland and a small selection to Edinburgh University Library. Apart from hunting out and sending these to the two institutions in question I want you to do as you care with all the rest. This also applies to books given to me and so signed by their authors.

It also applies to any manuscripts (other than those I have already given to your mother), and/or typescripts or printers' proofs, including recent correspondence with the University of Dublin re the D.Litt degree *honoris causa* they are giving me.

If I should die before the publication of *The Socialist Poems of Hugh MacDiarmid* (Routledge and Kegan Paul) or the two volumes of my *Complete Poems* (Brian, Martin, and O'Keefe, Museum St, London) I wish copies of these to be given, with a note thanking them for their kindness to me, to

Sister MacGillivray, Surgical Dept, Chalmers Hospital, Edinburgh and Mr. J.W.W. Thomson of same address, at which he is consultant surgeon.

Finally I want to say how grateful I am to your mother for all the half-century of happiness she has given me, and to you for being all that a son can be.

With love to Deirdre and your three boys, and to Christine and Walter, and their families.

Your father, Christopher Murray Grieve

P.S. Postscript to letter.
I should say I hereby appoint you, acting where possible in conjunction with your mother, as my Literary Executor, and hope in this you may have the help of Dr W.R. Aitken and Norman McCaig.

In the event of my death you should write to
Messrs Routledge & Kegan Paul,
Miss Margory Vesper, of International Copyright Bureau (whose address you'll find among my correspondence)
Messrs Macmillan, Administration, Basingstoke
and ask them for a final accounting of any monies due to me.

Yours, Dad

104. *To Alex Clark (NLS)*

13 June 1978

Dear Alex Clark

I have emerged from hospital again after two major operations – one of which, alas, confirmed what I had suspected nobody told me and Valda and Michael knew at least 6 months ago – namely that my basic trouble is a cancer of the rectum.

In these circumstances I am trying now to put my affairs in some order. I may not be able to see you again. This does not mean that I am about to die. I am a tough old customer with an astonishingly strong constitution and may last for years yet. I still hope to go to Dublin for the ceremony on July 6th.

But I would like to thank Jessie and you for your friendship throughout the years and wish you – and your family – well.

Many thanks for Jimmy Callan's address. I have written to him.

With fraternal greetings and best wishes.

Yours, Christopher Grieve

105. *To Cousin Betty McEwen*

14 June 1978

Dear Cousin Betty (McEwen)

Many thanks for your long and interesting letter just received. I am afraid you have contacted me at a bad time so far as my replying is concerned. My life this past 18 months has been a matter of being in and out of hospitals and undergoing all sorts of operations.

I only came out of hospital again two days ago, after two major operations. One of these showed that the main cause of my troubles is a rectal cancer, which I had suspected but did not know. Both my wife and son were told some months ago but did not tell me. The doctors warned them then that I'd probably have about 6 months to live. Doctors can be wrong. I have a very strong constitution and may live for years yet. But I'll be 86 in August and have no particular desire to live longer. I have had a long and very interesting life, but I feel I have done the work I was born to do and am unlikely now to be able to add to that.

It is a hazardous business writing to a relative you don't know. I did not write again to my cousin Julia Grieve Johnson because I felt we had nothing in common.[1] She ended her letter to me with a sort of religious exhortation but I am an atheist and a card-carrying member of the Communist Party, well known in the Soviet Union, China, and all the Eastern European countries, in all of which I have travelled.

You mention my visit to Amherst (Massachusetts University) but though I have had many invitations from American Universities and learned Societies the American authorities won't grant me a visa. And now it is too late. I won't be able to do much more travelling.

The difficulty of writing to a stranger (even if related) is illustrated by your poem of which you enclosed a typescript. It is a good set of verses. But all over the world in the past half-century there has been a fierce conflict between what is popularly regarded as poetry and I belong to the extremist wing of modernist poetry. I have written a great deal. I have published to date 137 books and pamphlets and many books have been published about me, including an illustrated biography with many Langholm illustrations.

I have been married twice. My present wife and I (married in 1932) have one son, a journalist in Glasgow, working mainly for Scottish Television. He is married and has three sons. Christopher, Lucian, and Dorian. By my first wife I had a son and a daughter. The son Walter is a mining engineer and has a family of 4 daughters. My daughter Christine is married to a Scottish doctor (from whom she has just separated), and lives in Ontario, where I have visited her five or six times. She has two sons and two daughters.

My wife and I go to Langholm every year if we can – to the Common-Riding. But I'm afraid we won't manage this year, as I have to go to Dublin where I am to receive an honorary doctorate in literature on July 6, and intend to go if I possibly can but I am now very weak and it may not be possible.

I never saw my Uncle Henry, but I remember Uncle Archie. I am afraid we Scots in Scotland are much less concerned about or interested in family connections than you in America are. But I see a good deal of my second cousin, Jean White, and she will know how to answer many of your questions better than I can. Uncle Tom was my father's brother but died a year or two ago, and both his sons, Henry and Jimmy, died in the First World War. Annie Grieve (Barnfather) died last year, not long after her husband Johnny Barnfather; they had several children who, however, I do not know. But a married sister of Annie's, Chrissie, still lives in Langholm. Her married name is Elliot and I see her occasionally when in Langholm.

Uncle Tom's wife, Bella, was a Charlton, but the Scots are a quarrelsome lot, and Uncle Tom and Aunt Bella were not on speaking terms with my father and nephew. My father died in 1911, and as you say with proper medical attention such as is now available would not have died. It was a case of sheer neglect. My mother was a Graham, from near Waterbeck. She died in the late '30s in her seventies. I had one brother Graham who died a year or two ago. He was married 3 times and had quite a number of children. His daughter Morag, married a Dutch doctor attached to a London Hospital, and had 4 sons – all of whom have done well in University etc. I have only met one of them. Morag and her husband separated a few years ago. My brother also had a son Angus, who is married with a family and lives in High Wycombe in Buckinghamshire.

When I was a student in Edinburgh – 1908–9–10 – I used to cycle from Edinburgh to Langholm and generally called in to see my Uncle Bob and Aunt Liza in Hawick. They are both dead now.

Maggie Laidlaw White and her sister Janet (who was Mrs Adam Beattie), and their parents are all dead too.

I'll ask Jean White about Bacca's third wife, and any children by her but I certainly never heard of her.[2] My father was 47 when he died in 1911, so he must have been born in 1864.

I am very sorry I do not know more to answer your questions properly, but once I've seen Jean White again and shown her your letter, we may be able to fill the gaps. So I'll write you again. Meanwhile, with kindest regards and best wishes to all our relatives in USA.

Yours, Christopher Murray Grieve

---

1. Julia Grieve Johnson (b.1897), born in Steamboat Rock, Iowa, had written in 1967 requesting details for a family tree she was compiling.
2. Bacca, the nickname of John Grieve (1824–97), a Langholm woollen weaver, CMG's grandfather.

106. *To the Editor,* The Scotsman

14 June 1978

Sir, – It is all too typical of Scotland still of course, despite the escalation of nationalist feeling in recent years, that plans to mark the centenary of Francis George Scott should have (in the words of your contributor, William Chisholm) 'received a decidedly cool reception in his native town of Hawick' (though the 'Teries' sing the Common Riding song which Scott wrote as a teenager lustily enough!).

I am not surprised at all that a number of members of Roxburgh District Council do not seem to have heard of Scott. I imagine that is not the only gap in their knowledge of anything pertaining to Scottish arts and letters.

I am horrified to know that Mr Maurice Lindsay is heading the centenary committee. Mr Lindsay has no competence whatever and it is typical that this (apparently self-appointed committee) contains no musician of standing, except one English professor who admits he knows nothing of Scottish music and does not want to.

As to the gap between the £1700 offered by the Scottish Arts Council and the actual cost of the proposed record (£2300) I understand that an Edinburgh lady who is administrix of funds designed to help the Scottish arts has now come to the rescue and offered to make good the deficiency.

As one of Scott's oldest friends and the provider of most of the lyrics to which he gave such wonderful settings, I personally will have nothing to do with this matter as long as Mr Lindsay is on the committee.

It is far too much to say that Scott's works are performed by most of Scotland's serious singers. They used to be by vocalists of the calibre of Sydney McEwen, Joan Alexander, William Noble, and 'F.G.'s' wife, the late Burges Scott. But they are difficult and have been seldom sung in recent years.

Hugh MacDiarmid (Christopher Grieve)

107. *To Christine Macintosh*

20 July 1978

My dear Christine

I am sorry to have been so long in writing you, but I am sure you understand that I just couldn't help it. I continue to have a great deal of pain which monopolises all my attention and prevents me doing anything else.

But by a great effort of determination I did go to Dublin. Valda and Michael were with me. I had to take things very quietly, of course, and hardly left my hotel room at all and resisted all temptation to 'celebrate'.

So far as the graduation ceremony itself went I was grateful to the University authorities for their understanding and care. They knew in advance of course just what my condition was and during the actual 'capping' posted a stalwart 6 foot graduate at my side ready to grab me if I seemed about to fall, and to give me a strong right arm whenever I had to move a foot or two.

So the whole thing went off beautifully and I looked very braw (as we say in Scots) or brave (as the Cornish put it) in my heavy blue and scarlet robes. We came back to Scotland the following day.

Characteristically none of the Scottish papers mentioned the matter but the Dublin papers give it a good show with photographers.

I've been lying low since but have managed to bring a lot of my correspondence up to date, though I am still unable to write longer things as I am longing to do.

We were sorry you didn't manage to Dublin but look forward to seeing you shortly at my birthday.

We had a couple of visits from Peter Barrow and Carol. Hope you are still in the wonderful form you had when last here, and have good news of all the family. I haven't written to Barker Fairley either but may manage today or tomorrow – or some time!

Love to you all from Valda and Yours, Dad

108. *To William Johnstone (NLS)*

8 August 1978

Dear William,

Sorry I've been so long in writing to you. Valda tells me you think of a volume of F.G.'s compositions, which Mrs Hope Scott might finance, and which would include poems of mine F.G. set. I entirely approve of this but what I meant last time you were here is that I am winding up my affairs as well as I can, and so anything to do with permissions for copyright material must now be referred not to me but to Michael, who understands the whole position. His address is 7 Hamilton Drive, Glasgow. He would need to get consent from Messrs Routledge and Kegan Paul, and from Timothy O'Keefe for some of the poems, but he knows all about that and will do whatever is necessary.

I've been having a very bad time again, with far too much pain, so I can't get on with my work and it is piling up on me.

I hope you are well and that everything is going well.

I notice you are being represented in a big Exhibition being organised by Alex Moffat but I am a bit surprised by the statement that his portrait of me is being included. I haven't seen it, but some time ago he came out here and did some drawings of me which did *not* impress me in the least. They had no discernible likeness to me at all. Of course perhaps he has used them as notes on which he has based the portrait he is now going to show. But I have no confidence at all in his turning out what can legitimately be called a portrait of me at all.

Every kind regard to Mary and Sarah – also to Bob Muir.
Valda goes to Spain on 10th September. I'll be in Glasgow at Michael's.
Yours, Chris

109. *To Jean White (EUL)*
13 August 1978
My dear Jean

When Valda and you arrived back from your mammoth shopping in Biggar, having evidently bought up the entire stock of several shops, I suspected you'd have been foolish enough to get me a birthday present, and I was relieved when nothing was handed over to me. I thought you'd got some sense at last. I might have known better. Valda did not hand over your gifts till Friday. I can only thank you – but you really shouldn't. I get too much – a lot of boxes of chocolate, several bottles of whisky, several books, a 7 lb tub of honey etc. etc. And a host of cards, letters, and telegrams I'll never be able to acknowledge.

The Dutch turned up braded with gifts. Christine wired she couldn't come – no stand-by plane available. But Mike, Deirdre and family were all here, Henk and Jeanine from Holland etc.

I've been having – and am still having – a very bad time, lot of pain.

You've probably seen the horrible portrait of me in the Weekend *Scotsman*.

There are a lot of things I hoped to do, but I have just had to abandon the idea and realise that I must not attempt anything at all in the meantime, or possibly ever.

Valda is run off her feet and has had trouble again with her angina pains. She goes to Spain on 10th September. I'll go to Mike's in Glasgow and then I hope for a couple of days to Loch Tummel.

Hope you are behaving yourself (tho' I don't believe it) and are none the worse of your jaunting about. I'll have a load of books for you next time, so keep the back of your car vacant.

Renewed thanks & love.
Yours, Chris

Appendix:
Biographical List of Recipients

Biographies are followed by index references to letters, arranged chronologically by decade and number.

ADVERTISER, The Editor of.
   1950s: 21.

AITKEN, William Russell (1913–98). Bibliographer, librarian and university teacher. Assistant Librarian in the Scottish Central Library 1936–40. RAF 1941–6. County Librarian for Clackmannanshire 1946–9, for Perth and Kinross 1949–58, for Ayr 1958–62. Became Lecturer in Librarianship at the University of Strathclyde, being promoted Senior Lecturer and Reader and retiring in 1978. President of the Scottish Library Association in 1965, and editor of the Library *Review* 1964–76. MacDiarmid's chief bibliographer. Edited the *Complete Poems* with Michael Grieve. First made friends with CMG in the 1930s while still a student, visiting the family in Whalsay in 1937. He also edited William Soutar and wrote *A History of the Public Library Movement in Scotland* (1971) and *Scottish Literature in English and Scots: a bibliographical guide* (1982). He and his wife Betsy retired to Dunblane.
   1930s: 25, 81, 82, 95, 99, 104, 106, 107, 108, 109, 112, 116. 1950s: 83. 1960s: 71.

ALDRED, Guy (1886–1963). Independent Communist. Served many sentences of imprisonment for opposing conscription, imperialist war, etc. Stood against John Wheatley in Glasgow Shettleston in 1919. Became involved in complicated action taken against him by Tom Johnston's paper *Forward*, when Aldred was established as the anti-parliamentary Communist Federation at Bakunin House in Glasgow. Aldred also ran the Bakunin Press, issuing many pamphlets. CMG did not take sides on the *Forward* row but helped raise money to save Aldred from bankruptcy in 1927–8, with aid from R.E. Muirhead. Sir Walter Strickland died in 1938 on the worst of terms with his family and the heir to his baronetcy which he exemplified by making Aldred his heir in all else: Aldred, now of the United Socialist Movement, founded the Strickland Press in Glasgow whence he published his journal *The Word*. Aldred stood again as parliamentary candidate after the Second World War for the United Socialist Movement and finally contested a by-election in Glasgow Woodside, the year before his death. When Michael Grieve was faced with imprisonment for nationalist resistance to conscription, Aldred was very helpful with advice as to his own precedent.
   1930s: 115.

ANEY, Edith Trelease. American student, teacher and critic-historian of MacDiarmid, Ph.D. (University of Pennsylvania, 1954) on 'British Poetry of Social Protest in the 1930s: The Problem of Belief in the Poetry of W.H. Auden, C. Day Lewis, Hugh MacDiarmid, Louis MacNeice and Stephen Spender'.
1950s: 25.

BARNFATHER, née Grieve, Ann (c.1899–1977). Cousin to CMG, born in Langholm and life-long resident there, the fourth of eight siblings. Married John Barnfather in 1922, four children.
1960s: 40.

BLYTHMAN, Morris (1919–81). Poet and editor, writing under the pseudonym Thurso Berwick, presumably thereby signalling a desire to speak for all of Scotland, from Thurso on the north coast to Berwick on the border with England. With John Kincaid, George Todd and F.J. Anderson, his poetry appeared in *Fowrsom Reel* (1949), introduced by MacD. With T.S. Law, edited *The Socialist Poems of Hugh MacDiarmid* (1978).
1970s: 101.

BOLD, Alan (1943–99). Poet, critic, MacDiarmid biographer and editor. Born Edinburgh, educated at Broughton High School and the University. First met CMG 1962. Prolific poet and anthologiser. Edited *The Penguin Book of Socialist Verse*, anthologies of erotic poetry and drinking poems, and produced critical studies on *George Mackay Brown* (1979) and *Muriel Spark* (1986). His own books of poetry include *To Find the New* (1968), *This Fine Day* (1979) and *In This Corner: Selected Poems 1963–83* (1983). Worked tirelessly to promote and publish MacDiarmid's work, editing the *Letters* (1984) and writing *MacDiarmid: Christopher Murray Grieve: A Critical Biography* (1988).
1960s: 44, 96. 1970s: 1, 3, 31, 67, 69, 89.

BOOTHBY, Major Frederick Alexander Colquhoun, former officer in the British Army, cousin of Conservative MP Bob Boothby. Lived in Broughton, published *Sgian Dubh*, a 'newsletter of the National movement' (1963–76). Founder-member of the 1320 Club (1967) of which CMG was President. Alleged leader of a Nationalist direct action group dubbed the 'Tartan Army' by the press. Husband of the artist Rosalie Loveday who painted several portraits of CMG.
1970s: 53, 63.

BOOTHBY, Rosalie Loveday. See BOOTHBY, Major Frederick Alexander Colquhoun.
1970s: 62.

BRIDSON, D.G. (1910–80). Broadcaster. Born Manchester. In 1934 contributed radio criticism to the *New English Weekly*. Became a producer for the BBC and wrote an important memoir of his career, *Prospero and Ariel – The Rise and Fall of Radio: A Personal Recollection* (1971). Obtained radio production for 'a comprehensive selection of the work of Hugh MacDiarmid' in 1956. Made a TV film of CMG in 1959, later remarking, 'Only the Scots – or, to share the blame, the British – would cheerfully leave their greatest living poet to write his work in a two-room cottage – then without the benefit of either lighting or plumbing', where Valda had to go for water 'from a tap in the cabbage-patch'. (See McCrindle, Alex.) BBC mogul Huw Wheldon axed the film because of CMG's Communism and Scottish Nationalism and 'nobody' (i.e. Wheldon) had heard of him. Bridson later used some of the sound footage for radio programmes.

1950s: 11, 64, 65. 1960s: 6, 11, 56, 95. 1970s: 11, 41, 83.

BROOKE, Lady Olave, niece of R.B. Cunninghame Graham and wife to Treasurer of Queen Elizabeth (Queen Mother). Cunninghame Graham (1852–1936) had no children. Admiral Sir Angus Cunninghame Graham (1893–1981) being his uncle's heir but initially leaving some immediate duties to his sister, wife of Rear-Admiral Sir Basil Vernon Brooke (1876–1945).

1950s: 27.

BROOM, John. Librarian. Friendly with Scottish poets such as Sydney Goodsir Smith and George Mackay Brown, author of *John Maclean* (1973), the first full biography of Maclean, completed as early as 1963 and published in the same year as that of Maclean's daughter, Nan Milton.

1960s: 85.

BROWN, W. Oliver (1903–76). Scottish educator and nationalist. Born in Paisley, graduated from Glasgow in Latin and French. Schoolmaster. BBC broadcaster. Edited *Selected Poems* of HMacD (1954). Published a large range of polemics in book, pamphlet and column form including *Scotland: Nation or Desert?* (1943), *Scotlandshire – England's Worst-Governed Province* (1944). Brought to a fine art the Scots tradition of teaching by epigram captured most notably in the anthology *Witdom* (1968) introduced by HMacD. His column in the SNP periodical *Scots Independent* was delivered on time to the very week of his death.

1940s: 15. 1960s: 28, 103. 1970s: 52.

BULLETIN, The Editor of.

1950s: 34.

CAIRD, James Bowman (1913–90), critic of Scottish literature and educationist. Born West Linton, educated Edinburgh University, active for Scottish literature, publishing on Lewis Grassic Gibbon in the student English Literature Society's *Essays in Literature* (1936). Studied at the Sorbonne and became an English teacher at Wick High School, then Trinity Academy, Edinburgh, until war service in 1940. Principal teacher of English at Peebles High School; became H.M. Inspector of Schools, 1947–74. Published criticism on Neil Gunn and Fionn Mac Colla as well as MacDiarmid.

1930s: 29.

CAIRD, née Kirkwood, Janet Hinshaw (1913–92). Scots poet and detective novelist. Born Nyasaland, now Malawi; educated Scotland, to which her parents, its natives, returned. Married J.B. Caird and in the 1960s began a series of mordant, moderately satirical Scottish mystery thrillers, including *Murder Scholastic* (1967), *The Loch*, *The Umbrella-Maker's Daughter* (1980). The latter uses Scots language dialogue. Also wrote for children (*Angus the Tartan Parton*) and three slim volumes

of verse, *Some Walk a Narrow Path*, *A Distant Urn* and *John Donne, You Were Wrong*.
1970s: 27, 94.

CAMERON, Morven. Teacher. Friend to a number of Scottish poets. Head of English at the Girls High School, Glasgow (later Cleveden Secondary School), 1969–76. Produced with Maurice Lindsay *Voices of Our Kind: An Anthology of Contemporary Scottish Verse*, 2nd edtn., 1975.
1970s: 20, 22, 36.

CAMPBELL, Ian (b.1942). Professor of Scottish and Victorian literature in the English Department, University of Edinburgh. Wrote *Thomas Carlyle* (1970), *The Kailyard* (1981) and *Lewis Grassic Gibbon* (1985). Assistant editor of the *Letters of Thomas and Jane Carlyle*.
1970s: 48.

CAMPBELL, Kenneth. Unidentified.
1960s: 75, 81.

CARCANET. Poetry imprint, founded in Oxford, 1970, by Peter Jones and Michael Schmidt; moved to Manchester in 1972. Early publications include work by Edwin Morgan. Foremost British publisher of modern poetry.
1970s: 78.

CLARK, Alex (b.1922). Working miner, resident in Douglas Water near Brownsbank. Scottish Organiser for the CPGB (1955–7), continuing to handle CMG's subscriptions thereafter in spite of leaving the post, Glasgow Secretary (1957–62), Assistant Secretary (1962–9), election agent for CMG's 1964 Kinross and West Perthshire campaign. Organiser for Equity until 1984. First Arts Officer for STUC. Retired to the Isle of Arran.
1960s: 59, 61, 87. 1970s: 64, 104.

CORNISH GORSEDD, The. The Gorseth, a Bardic Assembly, was in fact strongly under Welsh influence, having had its first meeting in Wales in 1928. It was a conscientious and highly respectable body, which had 140 Bards by 1936, somewhat impeded by the extinction of the Cornish language.
1930s: 105.

COUSIN ANN, see BARNFATHER, Ann.

CRICHTON, James. Founder, with CMG and Dr David Orr, of the 200 Burns Club (1959). The Club published an edition of *A Drunk Man Looks at the Thistle* in 1962.
1960s: 94.

CRITERION, The Editor of. See ELIOT, Thomas Stearns.

CRUICKSHANK, Helen Burness (1886–1975), Angus-born poet, joined the Civil Service in 1903, retiring after WWII, resident in Edinburgh from 1912, briefly joined the British Socialist party; sent CMG poetry for *Northern Numbers*. A feminist, she felt after suffrage that she 'needed another cause for which to work and found it in Scotland itself'. Took over from CMG as Secretary to Scottish PEN, 1929–34. CMG often stayed with her when visiting Edinburgh, sleeping in the attic bedroom, referred to as 'the Prophet's Chamber'. Cruickshank was an essential figure in the Scottish Renaissance, helping CMG throughout his middle-age both in financial terms and in securing him various grants and jobs, including her position in the Civil Service to divert him from being sent to do war work on the roads. Her volumes of poetry were: *Up the Noran Water* (1934), *Sea Buckthorn* (1954), *The Ponnage Pool* (1968). Her *Collected Poems* came out in 1971, her *Octobiography* in 1976, and *More Collected Poems* in 1978.

1940s: 42, 53. 1960s: 13.

DAICHES, David (b.1912). Historian and critic of Scottish and English Literature. Daiches is the author of over a hundred books, some of them deserving immortality. Professor of English at Cornell University, USA, 1946–51. Wrote a multi-volume *Critical History of English Literature* and major studies of Stevenson, Burns, Scott and Fletcher of Saltoun. Wrote many critical assessments of MacDiarmid from 1948 on, including 'Hugh MacDiarmid and Scottish Poetry', *Poetry* (Chicago) vol.72, no.4 and the introduction to the second edition of *A Drunk Man* (1953). Daiches came back to Britain in 1951 to teach at Cambridge and was first Professor of English at Sussex University, 1961–77, after which he was Director of the Institute for Advanced Studies at Edinburgh.

1950s: 13, 31, 46, 55, 59, 77. 1960s: 32.

DAILY RECORD, The Editor of.

1930s: 77. 1950s: 34.

DAWSON, Elizabeth. See GRIEVE, Elizabeth.

DEMARCO, Richard (b.1930). Artist, teacher, impresario, cultural philosopher. Born in Edinburgh. Studied at the Edinburgh College of Art, 1949–53. A dynamic figure in the promotion of modern art and theatre in Edinburgh. Co-founder of the Traverse Theatre; relentless advocate of Scottish cultural internationalism. Headed the Richard Demarco Gallery since 1966, functioning at a variety of locations, and bringing major work from Italy, Poland, Ireland, India, Canada, the USA, the Netherlands and elsewhere.

1970s: 18.

DOTT, Mary. Lifelong Scottish nationalist and SNP member. The occasion referred to in CMG's letter to Mary Dott was in fact not the first. See Father Anthony Ross's autobiography *The Root of the Matter* (1989), p.155, which recounts an event held under the auspices of the Scottish Literature Society in the late 1930s which Mary Dott was attending: 'a most disappointing evening, when Hugh MacDiarmid came to talk ... eyes focussing with some effort' – an 'aggressive character who subjected us ... to a rambling tirade': 'he was going through...one of the most deeply unhappy periods of his life ... It was a sad evening, but the most memorable in the society's experience.'

1950s: 36.

DOUGLAS, Ronald MacDonald (1896–1984). Scottish nationalist and short-story writer. Early life obscure. Author of *Stranger Come Home* (1935) and *The Sword of Freedom – a Romance of Lord James of Douglas and Scotland's War of Independence* (1936); edited *The Scots Book* (1935) and *The Irish Book* (1936). Founded and financed Inverness Little Theatre from 1937 but abandoned it rather than play 'God Save the King' after performances instead of his own choice, 'Scots Wha Hae'. Visited Deputy Fuhrer Rudolf Hess at Nazi HQ Munich, 1938. Raised band of Nationalist 'activists', was threatened with prosecution and on legal advice left UK for the duration of World War II to avoid internment. Lived in Ireland until 1945 then in post-war France for a time. Published further fiction collected posthumously as *Gizzageak* (1988), with racial and sado-masochist content. Edited *Catalyst* for 1320 Club whose first President was CMG. Douglas lived with Marjorie Brock and Roisin Napier, the ménage lasting for over forty years.

1970s: 39, 51, 65.

DUVAL, Kulgin D. and Colin H. Hamilton. Bibliophiles and rare and antiquarian book-sellers. Duval published a limited edition of *The Kind of Poetry I Want* (1961), printed by Giovanni Mardersteig on the hand-press of the Officina Bodoni, Verona on hand-made paper by Fratelli Magnani, Pescia; and in 1962, *Hugh MacDiarmid: a Festschrift*, edited by himself and Sydney Goodsir Smith, which was the first volume dedicated entirely to the study of MacDiarmid. Hamilton discovered a lost MS of 'Bracken Hills in Autumn' which he published in 1962. Thereafter they published special editions of *A Drunk Man Looks at the Thistle* (1969), the three *Dìreadh* poems (1974), and a *Selected Lyrics* (1977) for CMG's eighty-fifth birthday. They took CMG and Valda to Venice in 1970 where he met Ezra Pound. Built the MacDiarmid archive now housed in the NLS and material housed in the EUL, helping CMG and Valda financially.

1960s: 106, 108. 1970s: 6, 9.

ELIOT, Thomas Stearns (1888–1965). Poet. Worked in Lloyd's Bank. Founded and edited the *Criterion*, a quarterly review (1922–39). Director of Faber & Gwyer from 1925, afterwards Faber & Faber. CMG first wrote to Eliot as Editor of the *Criterion* on 9 December 1930 offering 'English Ascendancy in British Literature' which Eliot published in July 1931. They met for lunch at the Royal Societies Club near the end of 1930. The *Criterion* published 'Second Hymn to Lenin' in July 1932, and 'Cornish Heroic Song for Valda Trevlyn' appeared in its last number.

1930s: 103.

ENTICKNAP, née Grieve, Morag (b.1922). Daughter of Andrew Graham Grieve and Chryssie, academic career curtailed on Chryssie's death when she acted as house-keeper to her father, also, in 1942, to CMG with whom she shared a close friendship. Married Dr John Brandon Enticknap in 1944, three children Nicholas (1947), Jonathan (1948) and Alasdair (1950); divorced in 1972. When John Enticknap was Morag's fiancé in 1942, he visited her in Glasgow at her father's house, where CMG was staying; John found himself confined to the house for a day as CMG had gone out wearing his only pair of shoes. 'Well,' said CMG, 'it was wet, and mine were letting in water.' Ever after, John referred to the event as evidence of CMG's truly communistic spirit. See Morag Enticknap, 'A Memoir', in *Hugh MacDiarmid: Man and Poet*, ed. Nancy Gish (Edinburgh University Press,

1992), pp.29–37.
1970s: 8, 28, 76.

EVENING DISPATCH, The Editor of.
1950s: 34.

FORWARD, The Editor of.
1950s: 34.

FAIRLEY, Barker (1887–1986). German scholar. Lecturer in German, University of Alberta, Edmondton, Canada, 1910–15. Professor of German, University of Toronto 1915–32, then Professor of German, Victoria University of Manchester 1932–6, then University of Toronto, 1936–57. Published *Charles M. Doughty* (1927), and selections from Doughty's epic *The Dawn in Britain* (1935) asserting Doughty's ideas on language and prosody. Wrote books on *Goethe* (1932), *Heine* (1954), translated *Faust* (1970).

1940s: 56. 1970s: 23, 44.

GAWSWORTH, John (1912–70). Anthologist, literary critic, publishers' editor, poet. Born Terrence Ian Fytton Armstrong, in Kensington. Published his own *Poems 1930–32* (with fresh instalments 1938, 1939, 1943, 1948). Gave lodging to CMG in London, 1934. CMG dedicated 'The Little White Rose' to him. Gawsworth included four stories by CMG in an anthology *Thirty New Tales of Horror Fiction*. Gawsworth rose to obscurity via three marriages, the Freedom of the City of London and lectureship to the Royal Asiatic Society at Bengal in 1945, succession to Kingship of Redonda, British West-Indies, 1947 (abdication for reasons of health, 1967) and the editorship of the *Poetry Review*, 1948–52.

1960s: 74.

GIBBON, Lewis Grassic. See MITCHELL, James Leslie.

GISH, Nancy K. (b.1943). MacDiarmid scholar. Assistant Professor in the Department of English at the University of Pennsylvania, conducted an interview with CMG in July 1977 (see *The Raucle Tongue*, vol.3). Became Professor at University of Southern Maine and, along with studies of T.S. Eliot's poetry, wrote *Hugh MacDiarmid: The Man and his Work* (1984) and edited *Hugh MacDiarmid: Man and Poet* (1992).

1970s: 86, 100.

GLASGOW HERALD, The Editor of.
1950s: 53.

GLEN, Duncan (b.1933). Poet, publisher and critic. Author of ground-breaking *Hugh MacDiarmid (Christopher Murray Grieve) and the Scottish Renaissance* (1964) and shorter essays on CMG. Published *The MacDiarmids – A Conversation* (1970) and edited MacDiarmid's *Selected Essays* (1969), the collection *Whither Scotland?* (1970) and *Hugh MacDiarmid: A Critical Survey* (1972). He has been described as 'a MacDiarmid industry in himself' but there are also numerous books of his own poetry and prose, including *Selected Scottish & Other Essays* (1999). Edited fifty-one issues of the influential literary periodical *Akros*, founded in 1965, and directed

Akros publications, specialising in small print runs of beautifully-produced items. Wrote memoir, *Hugh MacDiarmid: out of Langholm and into the world* (1982).

1960s: 43, 63, 105. 1970s: 5, 12.

GRIEVE, Andrew Graham (1894–1973), brother of CMG. Born 7 April, in the house in Arkinholm Terrace, Langholm, Dumfriesshire where his brother was born twenty months earlier. There were no more siblings. Worked as boy clerk, Inland Revenue, in Burton-on-Trent, Staffordshire, whence he moved to its offices in Cupar, Fife, alerting CMG to vacancy in the local Innes group of newspapers and possibly helping him get the job (as a result of which CMG met his first wife). Enlisted 1917, serving in France. Demobilised 1919. First Clerk in 4th Inland Revenue Division, Edinburgh, and custodian of CMG's early poems. Contributed two poems to CMG's *Northern Numbers*, First Series (1920). Told by CMG of identity of Hugh MacDiarmid, June 1923. Declined to lend CMG money to buy his way into literary advisership to the Unicorn Press, 1931, but was generous with small sums when needed. Co-dedicatee (with wife Chryssie, née Christian Kinnear) of MacDiarmid's 'In the Caledonian Forest', 1933. Moved by I.R.S. to Woking, Surrey. Widowed there, 1940. Two children by his second marriage, Angus and Morag. Moved to Cambuslang, near Glasgow, where CMG lived with him until they separated forever after a major row, July-August 1942. Married fellow-taxperson Irene Abbott. Promoted to London office 1945 and thence to Llandudno.

1920s: 1, 2, 3, 4, 5, 10, 15. 1930s: 2, 3, 16, 17, 22, 24, 30, 32, 33, 38, 42, 45, 50, 53, 56, 60, 61, 64, 67, 80, 118, 119. 1940s: 1, 2, 4, 17, 18, 33, 34.

GRIEVE, Christine Elizabeth Margaret. Born 4 September 1924 to Margaret Cunningham Thomson Grieve, née Skinner, and CMG in Montrose. When her parents' divorce was pronounced in Edinburgh on 16 January 1932, Christine and her brother Walter were placed in their mother's custody without paternal access, and CMG saw neither for over twenty years. Christine attended school in Ottawa 1939–43 then became a nurse in Dundee, marrying Dr Alistair Macintosh (b.1921). Renewed relations with CMG in 1953, defying her mother's demand (respected by Walter) that the children refuse to see CMG until after her own death in 1962. Emigrated to Georgetown, Ontario, Canada, 1955, where she was matron of Lakeside School. Four children, Elspeth (b.1949), Donald (b.1952), Alison (b.1960), Roderick (Rory, b.1962). CMG visited them in 1964, staying in chalet at Muskoka Lakes and reading poems at the University of Toronto. He visited them again. Christine saw CMG in 1975 when his imminent death from terminal cancer had become known, though not to him.

1930s: 98. 1950s: 33, 38, 40. 1960s: 9, 46, 47, 53, 90, 97, 100, 107, 110, 111. 1970s: 34, 35, 68, 70, 72, 75, 87, 107.

GRIEVE, Christopher. See GRIEVE, Michael.

1970s: 57.

GRIEVE, Deirdre. See GRIEVE, Michael.

1970s: 85.

GRIEVE, Elizabeth (1856–1934). Mother of CMG. Born Kirtleton Lodge, Kirtleton Farm, near Waterbeck, ten miles southwest of Langholm, to Isabella

Graham nee Carruthers) and Andrew Graham, molecatcher. Married (15 October 1891) to Langholm postman James Grieve (1864–1911) before Church of Scotland minister at Middlebie, Rev. James Monilaws. Her parents buried in Crowdieknowe churchyard, Middlebie. Moved from Arkinholm Terrace to Henry Street, Langholm, 1896, thence to Library Buildings, Parliament Square, 1899, she becoming caretaker to Langholm Library. Wrote verse. A devout Presbyterian. Brother a gamekeeper, Dingwall, where boys sent on visits and encountered his wife's Gaelic. Widowed, 3 February 1911. Supported Christopher between Tredegar and Clydebank jobs, 1912. Married a widower, James Dawson, forester, of Lammermuir Lodge, Whittingame, East Lothian, 1 June 1918, CMG witness (thirteen days before he married Margaret Skinner). Widowed by Dawson's death, 15 September 1932. Died of stomach cancer at Laurie's Close, Waterbeck, 11 April 1934.

1920s: 14. 1930s: 4, 6, 10.

GRIEVE, James, the last Provost of Langholm.
1970s: 19.

GRIEVE, James Michael Trevlyn (1932–95). CMG's son by Valda Trevlyn Rowland. Born Sussex, 28 July 1932. Parents settled in Whalsay, Shetlands, in June 1933, where he remained, apart from a six-month sojourn with mother's family in Cornwall, 1934. Attended Kilquhanity boarding school, near Castle Douglas, Kirkcudbrightshire. Registered as a conscientious objector on Scottish nationalist grounds in 1950, serving six-month prison sentence. Journalist, beginning on *Alloa Journal*. Moved to Glasgow to the *Daily Record* where he met Deirdre Chapman, then a feature-writer on the *Evening News*, whom he married in 1958. Moved to London to the *Sunday People* and thence to Glasgow, to the *Daily Express*, becoming a feature-writer. Edited the SNP *Scots Independent* in the late 1960s, making the best of the somewhat proprietorial control exercised by the party President, Dr Robert McIntyre (1913–98). SNP Vice-Chairman for Publicity for several years, and stood for the SNP in Glasgow Govan in 1970 fertilising the ground for Margo MacDonald's election victory. Arts producer on STV in the early 1970s. Edited HMacD's *Complete Poems* with W. R. Aitken. He developed cancer of the larynx, bore the loss of his voice with characteristic fortitude and grim humour, and died among his family, Deirdre and his three sons Christopher (b.1960), Lucien (b.1964) and Dorian (b.1973).

1940s: 25, 26, 55. 1950s: 1, 4, 5, 7, 8, 9, 10, 16, 17, 19, 49, 50, 52, 57, 58, 91, 92, 93, 94, 95, 96, 97, 98. 1960s: 1, 2, 7, 91, 116. 1970s: 103.

GRIEVE, née Skinner, Peggy (Margaret) Cunningham Thomson (1897–1962). CMG's first wife. Born in Cupar, she worked as secretary to the Colonel of the Black Watch, Perth, in the Women's Auxiliary Army Corps during WWI. Married CMG 13 June 1918. After their move to London, she found secretarial work including typing the MS to Edwin Muir's *The Three Brothers*. Split with CMG 1931, divorced January 1932. Became partner to William McElroy, working in London as secretary and then director of his business. Lived in Scotland 1938–9. Worked at the Ministry of Fuel and Power during World War II. Emigrated to Canada 1956, later marrying Harry Piller.

1930s: 65, 72, 83, 84, 97, 117.

GRIEVE, Valda Trevlyn (Rowland) (1906–89). Born Bude, Cornwall, brought up by her mother, Florence Ann Rowland, and an aunt. Cornish nationalist. Dissatisfied with opportunities in Cornwall, she left in 1928, worked as a shop assistant in Bristol, moving to London in 1930. Met CMG 1931 and married him 12 September 1934. In Whalsay she supplemented their income by Fair Isle knitting and their diet by gathering gulls' eggs. Worked in Lyons' book department from 1943 and John Smith's bookshop in 1946. Occasionally known to cast Cornish curses on those who displeased her, effectively. Several poems, inspired by her native Cornwall, were published in the 1970s. Actively outrageous in any social context, particularly at public events, in later life she dyed her hair orange with a mixture of Nescafé and henna.

1930s: 18, 19, 20, 21, 23, 31, 34, 35, 36, 37, 39, 40, 55, 57, 58, 59, 62, 63, 69, 71, 73, 74, 75, 76, 90, 91, 92, 93, 94. 1940s: 19, 20, 21, 22, 23, 24, 27, 28, 29, 30, 31, 32, 35, 36, 37, 38, 45, 47, 48, 49. 1950s: 69, 70, 71, 72, 73, 74, 75, 76, 84, 85, 86, 88, 89, 90. 1960s: 4, 5, 89, 92, 93.

GRIEVE, Walter Ross. Son of CMG and Peggy. Born Montrose, 5 April 1928 and baptised in the Scottish Episcopal Church, Montrose, with Compton Mackenzie and Neil Gunn as godfathers, on Sunday 13 May. Lived with his mother in 1932 in London and Surrey. Unlike his sister Christine, Walter accepted his mother's demand that he not see his father again until she was dead. Took a B.Sc. degree from Durham, at King's College, Newcastle. Became a mining engineer, worked for the National Coal Board for twenty-five years, and was living in Rochdale when, in 1963, he saw CMG once more. Married Ann Newman; four daughters, Judith (b.1955), Angela (b.1959), Jane (b.1964) and Kate (b.1971). Became Managing Director of a Research company. Visited his father at Biggar, notably in 1975 when CMG's illness was terminal. In 1981, became a consultant engineer in Cincinnati, Ohio.

1970s: 97.

HENDERSON, Hamish (b.1919). Folklorist, teacher, composer, poet, polemicist. Born in Blairgowrie, Perthshire. Served in the eastern Mediterranean in World War II whence he produced *Elegies for the Dead in Cyrenaica* (1948). Henderson promulgated the ideas of Antonio Gramsci, introducing CMG to them and thus infiltrating *In Memoriam James Joyce* with them. He translated Gramsci's *Prison Letters*. Henderson's other great songs included the non-militarist Scottish Left's choice of national anthem, 'Freedom Come All Ye', born of protest against apartheid. CMG and MacCaig dismissed Henderson's evangelisation of the folksong renaissance, but it was the product of his superb research, conservation, and teaching at the Edinburgh School of Scottish Studies.

1950s: 60. 1970s: 29.

HENDRY, J.F. (b.1912). Poet. Born Glasgow, studied modern languages at the University, serving in Intelligence Corps during World War II and working afterwards as a translator for the United Nations. Central figure in the New Apocalypse movement, editing that movement's three anthologies, reacting against political literalism of the Auden-Spender-Day-Lewis group. Wrote a memorable novel of memories of a west-coast of Scotland childhood, *Fernie Brae* (1947), poetry collected in *A World Alien* (1980) and a critical biography of Rilke, *The Sacred*

Threshold (1982).
1930s: 102.

HOLLIDAY, Frank (d.1997). Close friend and admirer of the composer Sorabji. In the 1960s, Sorabji allowed Holliday to make audio tape recordings of him playing his own compositions.
1950s: 26.

HONIG, Camille. Organiser of Martin Buber symposium.
1960s: 73.

IRISH TIMES, The Editor of.
1970s: 7.

JOHNSTON, Thomas. County Assessor, resident in Lerwick, sometimes referred to by Shetlanders as the 'County Aggressor'.
1930s: 114.

JOHNSTON, Thomas (1881–1965). Scottish socialist and cabinet minister. Founded socialist weekly *Forward* with R.E. Muirhead, attracting contributors such as James Connolly and John Maclean. Author of *The Case for Women's Suffrage* (1907), *The Railway Difficulty and How to Solve It* (i.e. nationalisation), *Our Scots Noble Families* ('Time and again they have sold our land to the invader', 1909), *The History of the Scottish Working Classes* (1923) and *Memories* (repudiating earlier vehemence, 1952). Under-secretary of State for Scotland in second Ramsay Macdonald government 1929–31. Ceased editing *Forward* 1931. Secretary of State for Scotland, Churchill wartime coalition, 1941. Became Chairman of Hydro-Electric Board, Head of Scottish Forestry Commission 1945–8, Chairman of Broadcasting Council for Scotland 1955.
1940s: 11.

JOHNSTONE, William (1897–1981). Hawick-born artist, studied in Edinburgh and, in the 1920s, in Paris under André L'Hôte, where he was influenced by the Cubist and Surrealist movements. Married to American sculptor, Flora Macdonald (1927), and later to Mary. Introduced to CMG by his cousin, F.G. Scott. Employed in a series of teaching posts in London from the early 1930s; Principal of the Central School of Arts and Crafts, 1947–60. His publications include: *Creative Art in England* (1936), *Child Art to Man Art* (1941) and an autobiography, *Points in Time* (1980). Painted many portraits of CMG. They collaborated on two books: *Poems to Paintings by William Johnstone* (1963) and *Twenty Poems by Hugh MacDiarmid With Twenty Lithographs by William Johnstone* (1977).
1960s: 82, 101. 1970s: 2, 37, 60, 61, 108.

KERRIGAN, Peter (1899–1977). Scottish Communist leader. Born Glasgow, Gorbals. Boxing champion. Joined the CPGB in 1921, was a member of its Executive Committee from 1927 to 1929, and again from 1931 to his retirement in 1965. Lifelong member of the Amalgamated Engineering Union and had hopes of 100,000 engineering workers coming out to swell the General Strike in 1926. 'But they entered the battle, so to speak, just as their power was already being flung away by the TUC leaders.' He had never anticipated such 'betrayal' and had envisioned Glasgow as 'the Leningrad of British Socialist Revolution'. He and his fiancée, later wife, Rose, would cycle out with food for the miners still holding out, but psychologically Kerrigan never seems to have recovered from the strike leaders' capitulation, or so he implies in his apocalyptic memoir contributed to Jeffrey Skelley ed., *The General Strike* (Lawrence & Wishart, 1976). Rose in the CPGB. Attacked MacDiarmid's identification of Scottish nationalism with Communism (*New Scotland*, 26 October 1935, see also Bold, ed., *Letters*, pp.773–7, and *The Raucle Tongue*, vol.2, pp.543–6). CMG was expelled from CPGB in November 1936 and readmitted in May 1937. This may have arisen from Kerrigan's hostility to Scottish nationalism in the ILP which he deemed Trotskyite, all the more when in 1937 John McGovern, ILP MP for Glasgow Shettleston, denounced Communist repression of non-Stalinist Marxism in Catalonia (as did Orwell). Kerrigan was Political Commissar for the International Brigade in Spain and therefore implicated in the witch-hunt. Back in Scotland, his *Scotland's March to Peace and Progress* (1939), formally blessed by Harry Pollitt, strictly limited Scottish Communism's national identity to quotations from Burns's Bannockburn march ('By oppression's woes and pains' etc) and 'Scotland marching shoulder to shoulder with the rest of Britain for peace in a fuller, freer life'. CMG was expelled from the CPGB for a second time at almost exactly this period, in February 1939. He rejoined CPGB after the Hungarian revolt in 1956 but he might have joined several years before had it not been for apparatchik hostility for which Kerrigan is the prime suspect.

1940s: 40.

LAHR, Karl (afterwards Charles: 1885–1971). Anarchist bookseller of German peasant birth, eldest of fifteen, Wendelsheim, Rhineland Palatinate. Apprenticed at thirteen to chemist uncle. Became Buddhist, then anarchist. Emigrated to London to avoid conscription in German army. Worked in bakery. Frequented Anarchist Club, Hampstead. Inseparable companion of Guy Aldred then, in Union of Direct Actionists, translating for *Herald of Revolt*, breaking with Aldred to join British Section of IWW. Razor-grinder. Interned in Alexandra Palace 1915–19. Appears in Bonar Thompson, *Hyde Park Orator* and R.M. Fox, *Smoky Crusade*. Founder-member of CPGB 1920, left 1921. Established Progressive Bookshop, Holborn. Married his comrade Esther Archer 1922. Published *The New Coterie* and various fugitive pieces including D.H. Lawrence, *Sun and Pansies*. Discovered Rhys Davies, George Woodcock. CMG, who first met him 1929–30 when he ran Blue Moon Press and shop, said of him, 'Charlie had an infectious love of life, an irresponsible gaiety, and a deep rooting in a sardonic contempt for all conventions and values, all "received" opinions'.

1940s: 39.

LAIDLAW, John (1873–1964). Langholm printer, cousin to CMG who took lifelong pride in the Laidlaw link, taking Alister K. Laidlaw as one of his earliest pseudonyms from 1911. John wrote occasional articles for the *Eskdale and Liddesdale Advertiser* under the pseudonym A.T. Wauchope. Laidlaw's brother Bob (1882–1949) taught CMG shorthand, encouraged his literary and poetic interests, lending him books and papers. Bob Laidlaw's wife Alice was sister-in-law to Rev. Thomas Scott Cairncross (1872–1961), under whom CMG was a thirteen-year-old Sunday School teacher at Langholm South United Free Church. CMG resumed correspondence with John Laidlaw with a letter of sympathy on Bob's death.

1920s: 6, 7. 1960s: 16, 31, 35, 41.

LAMBIE, Brian. Bailie of Biggar. Set up the Biggar Museum in 1968, inviting CMG to open it, which he did with a long inaugural speech.

1960s: 102. 1970s: 17.

LINDSAY, Maurice (b.1918). Broadcaster, journalist, editor, conservationist, poet. Author or editor of over seventy books. Glaswegian. Trained as violinist but injury aborted musical career. War service in military intelligence in London as a Captain in the Cameronians. Edited periodical *Poetry Scotland*, 1943–6. Began writing heavily under the influence of MacDiarmid, who introduced *Hurlygush: Poems in Scots* (1946). Edited *Modern Scottish Poetry: An Anthology of the Scottish Renaissance 1920–1945*, published by Faber & Faber in 1946, bringing Scottish poets to a wider readership. William Maclellan published *A Pocket Guide to Scottish Culture* in 1947. Lindsay later worked for the BBC and vigorously dissociated himself from CMG's extremist politics and polemics. Lindsay produced a *Robert Burns Encyclopedia*, a valuable anthology of poetry by John Davidson introduced by T.S. Eliot and MacD, and numerous collections of his own, including *Comings and Goings* (1971), *Collected Poems 1940–1990* (1990) and *Requiem For a Sexual Athlete* (1991), as well as the memoir *Thank You for Having Me* (1983). Programme Controller of Border Television and its chief interviewer, 1961–7; Director of the Scottish Civic Trust, 1967–83; presenter of BBC radio arts programmes. Author of the only book-length study of the composer F.G. SCOTT (1980).

1970s: 59, 77, 79.

LORD CHANCELLOR, The. Sir John Allsebrook Simon, first Viscount Simon (1873–1954), English politician. A Mancunian son of Congregational minister. Educated at Fettes College in Edinburgh and Wadham College, Oxford. Barrister. Liberal MP supporting MacDonald National government 1931 as Liberal National. Home Secretary 1915–16, resigning on issue of conscription. Served in France as Major, Royal Flying Corps. Foreign Secretary 1931–5. First cabinet minister to visit Hitler, 1930. Home Secretary, 1935–7, Chancellor of the Exchequer, 1937–40, Lord Chancellor in the Churchill coalition government 1940–5. Lloyd George said of him: 'Simon has sat on the fence so long that the iron has entered into his soul'.

1940s: 12.

LUCIE-SMITH, Edward (b.1933). Poet, art historian, anthologist. Born Jamaica, settled in Britain 1946. *Movements in Art since 1945* (1969). *Symbolist Art* (1972); *British Poetry since 1945* (1970).

1960s: 77.

MacCAIG, Norman (1910–96). Poet, teacher. Father a chemist in Edinburgh; mother a Gaelic-speaker from the Outer Hebrides. Edinburgh-born and educated at Royal High School and University. Classicist. After World War II, when he was imprisoned as a conscientious objector, MacCaig became CMG's best friend and remained so for the rest of his life. MacCaig was a primary school teacher for almost forty years, dividing his time between work in the city and summers in the north-west, by Lochinver in the Highlands. See 'Norman MacCaig in Conversation', *PN Review*, 120 (vol.24, no.4, March-April 1998), pp.19–27. His 'A Note on the Author' reprinted in MacDiarmid's *Scottish Eccentrics* is seminal. Early poetry influenced by the New Apocalypse movement and later rejected by MacCaig himself. Later poetry characterised by exceptionally objective precision possessed of sophistication derisive of pretension.

1950s: 32.

McCANCE, William (1894–1970). Artist, art-critic, conscientious objector, Scottish nationalist. Born Cambuslang, Lanarkshire. Trained at Glasgow School of Art and finished teacher training, 1916, but refusal to serve in armed forces prevented his obtaining teaching post. Moved to London, 1919–30. Art-critic, *Spectator* 1923–6. Modernist printmaker. Vorticist, in association with Percy Wyndham Lewis and David Bomberg. CMG championed his paintings in *Contemporary Scottish Studies* series for *Scottish Educational Journal* 1926–7, at which time CMG and he worked on Scottish Ballets. Exhibited at James Whyte's Gallery, St Andrews, and, like CMG, wrote for Whyte's *The Modern Scot*. Cartoonist for *The Free Man*. Controller of Gregynog private printing press, Newton, Montgomeryshire, Wales, for which his first wife Agnes Miller Parker (1895–1980) made wood engravings. Lecturer in typography and book production, Reading University, 1944–59. Married Dr Margaret Chislett, 1963, living and painting in Girvan, Ayrshire. CMG hailed McCance's work as 'passionately Scottish' in opening Reading Museum and Art Gallery's Retrospective exhibition which opened 11 June 1960.

1920s: 16, 17.

Mac COLLA, Fionn. See MacDONALD, Tom.

MacCORMICK, John MacDonald (1904–61). Scottish nationalist leader. Born Glasgow, prominent Glasgow University student politician first in the Independent Labour Party and then in the National Party of Scotland. Competition with the more right-wing and less separatist Scottish Party led MacCormick to favour merger (realised in the Scottish National Party 1934) with consequent repudiation of 'extremists' such as CMG. MacCormick, now a Glasgow lawyer, remained Chairman of the SNP until 1942 when Douglas Young became Chairman, committed to opposition to war service save in an independent Scotland. MacCormick now left the SNP (which Grieve now joined) and founded an all-party Scottish Union (later Scottish Convention), organised a National Covenant demanding a Scottish Parliament in the UK framework: it won half a million votes in three months after launch in October 1949 and rapidly rose to two million, but politicians ignored it. Wrote a memoir *The Flag in the Wind* (1955). 'King John' was certainly the great driving force behind the birth of constitutional Scottish nationalism, and Grieve had happily campaigned for him in 1929–31. Their sons Iain and Neil MacCormick and Michael Grieve were colleagues in the SNP in its rebirth in the 1960s and 1970s.

1930s: 15.

McCREATH, Mr. Unidentified.

1920s: 19.

McCRINDLE, Alex. Actor. One of CMG's close friends, sharing political and cultural commitments to socialism, Theatre Workshop and the People's Festival (launched in Edinburgh in 1952 as an alternative to the official Festival). McCrindle's wife wrote children's fiction and Marxist criticism under the name Honor Arundel and was prominent in Scottish literary circles. She died of cancer in 1973. McCrindle read MacDiarmid's poems alongside John Laurie and Norman MacCaig on 'The Lallans Makars', a programme produced by Ewan MacColl and broadcast on the BBC Third Programme on 23 June 1952. In 1960, McCrindle wrote to prominent Scottish writers (including Compton Mackenzie and Naomi Mitchison) asking for contributions of £50 to enable some improvements to be made to the Grieves' home at Brownsbank. According to CMG, along with a group of Edinburgh University students, members of the Young Communist League and other friends, digging and draining the property, McCrindle was crucial in seeing to it that the cottage was installed with kitchenette, bathroom, hot and cold running water, flush lavatory, electric light 'and other gadgets'. As Philip French pointed out in the *Observer*, 23 March 1997, McCrindle is familiar to later generations for another reason, as the actor who played General Dodonna in *Star Wars*, the 1977 film so loved by US President Ronald Reagan that he drew on it for the name of his outer space defence system and for his description of the Soviet Union as 'the Evil Empire'. Did he know that Alex McCrindle, who is the first person to utter the words, 'May the Force be with you' as he sends the rebel pilots to destroy the Empire, was a life-long member of the Communist Party?

1950s: 36, 39. 1960s: 8. 1970s: 33, 95.

MacDONALD, Callum. Essential post-WWII 'small publisher' of the Scottish Renaissance, printer and publisher of the literary journal *Lines Review*.

1950s: 43, 45.

MacDONALD, Tom (Fionn Mac Colla) (1906–75). Novelist. Born Montrose, educated as a Plymouth Brother. Worked as a teacher in Wester Ross and Palestine. Studied Gaelic and became a Headmaster at various schools in the north-west of Scotland. Joined SNP. Went to London with the Grieves in 1929. Returned to Scotland to finish writing novel, leaving CMG suspicious that he may have been Peggy's lover. *The Albannach* (1932) is set in the contemporary Highlands and Islands; *And the Cock Crew* (1945) is a novel of the Clearances, with a great central debate between a minister and an old poet. CMG stayed with the MacDonalds in Edinburgh, in 1936 and 1937. MacDonald typed much of *Lucky Poet*. CMG wrote enthusiastically about MacDonald's novels. MacDonald embraced Catholicism, abhorred the Reformation and denounced Communism. Passionate concerns about Scottish and international cultural and historical change are gathered in *At the Sign of the Clenched Fist* (1967) and his autobiographical essay *Too Long in This Condition* (1975).

1960s: 23. 1970s: 56.

McELROY, William. Rich coal-merchant over twenty years Peggy's senior when they met in 1929. Made his fortune from the sale of slag abandoned around the coal-mines closed in the General Strike of 1926. Lived in grand fashion with servants, Rolls-Royce and racing stables, promoting his cultural interests, for example, by funding the transfer of plays by Sean O'Casey (*Juno and the Paycock* and *The Plough and the Stars*) from Dublin to London. McElroy figures as Cyril Poges in O'Casey's 1940 play *Purple Dust*. Poges's young mistress in the play, Souhaun, may have been modelled on Peggy.

1930s: 78, 85.

McEWAN, née Leader, Betty. CMG's first cousin, once removed, born 1921 in Tacoma, Washington, author of a thirteen page family-tree of the progeny of John Grieve (1824–97).

1970s: 105.

McGAVIN, Robert H. Poet.

1950s: 48.

MACINTOSH, Alistair. See GRIEVE, Christine Elizabeth Margaret.

1970s: 99.

MACINTOSH, Anne and Donald. See GRIEVE, Christine Elizabeth Margaret.

1970s: 98.

MACINTOSH, Christine. See GRIEVE, Christine Elizabeth Margaret.

MacINTYRE, Angus. Editor of the *Scottish Educational Journal*. CMG wrote a wickedly controversial and iconoclastic series of essays for the *SEJ* in the 1920s, collected as *Contemporary Scottish Studies*. Angus MacIntyre reissued them in book form in 1976, along with the correspondence they elicited, as part of the celebrations of the journal's bicentenary. See *Contemporary Scottish Studies*, ed. Riach (Carcanet, 1996).

1970s: 74.

MACKAY, Miss Christian and Miss A. Katherine. See PEDDIE, Mrs Mary K.

1960s: 58.

MACKAY, Eneas. Stirling bookseller and publisher in a small way for roughly the first half of the twentieth century. His list was largely Highland, Gaelic, topographical, and faintly Jacobite, plus much Burnsiana. Published Hugh MacDiarmid, Scots Unbound and other Poems (1932) at 10 shillings and sixpence limited to 350 signed copies.

1930s: 9, 11, 14.

MACKENZIE, Sir Edward Montague Compton (1883–1972), Scottish novelist and nationalist, born into theatre family (sister Fay Compton), West Hartlepool, Durham, England, added final name asserting his Scottish ancestry. Educated St Paul's, London and Magdalen, Oxford, career of incessant novel-writing with *Carnival* (1912), followed by *Sinister Street* (1913) a masterly study of adolescent masculinity which would influence Scott Fitzgerald. His six-volume autobiographical *The Four Winds of Love* (1937–45) is of major Scottish intellectual significance and his *My Life and Times* (10 vols., 1963–71) is historically perceptive if apt to justify Norman MacCaig (who timed him) in the belief that he transformed any conversation into one about himself in two minutes flat. His hilarious, affectionate and shrewd novels of the Highlands and Islands from *The Monarch of the Glen* to *Rockets Galore* do not disguise the cold anger in the last against Whitehall readiness to eradicate an Island way of life and thus document a crucial origin of modern Scottish nationalism. Mackenzie served in the secret service in World War I and was prosecuted for writing about it. He had converted to Roman Catholicism when he met CMG while establishing the National Party of Scotland.

1920s: 20, 21, 22, 23, 24. 1930s: 1, 12, 13. 1940s: 44. 1950s: 29.

MACKIE, Albert David (1904–85). Journalist, poet and playwright, pupil at Broughton School, edited the *Broughton Magazine* (1922–3) and the Edinburgh *Evening News* (1946–54). CMG admired his Scots poems in *Poems in Two Tongues* (1928) and included 'Molecatcher' in *The Golden Treasury of Scottish Poetry* (1940).

1940s: 9. 1950s: 22, 24.

MacLEAN, Sorley ('Sam'), Somhairle MacGILL-EAIN (1911–96). Gaelic poet, English teacher. Born on the island of Raasay, near Skye, Gaelic his sole language until 6. Studied English Literature at Edinburgh University, 1929–33 (where he was profoundly influenced by MacD's poetry.) In mid-May 1934 he was introduced to CMG by his fellow-student the future nationalist philosopher of education George Elder Davie in Rutherford's Bar (formerly beloved of Stevenson and Conan Doyle). CMG became fascinated by Gaelic and built it into his evolving cultural nationalism, drawing heavily on MacLean for source material and translation, later aid in translation. MacLean was the poet closest politically to CMG, nationalist but Labour-voting (as was CMG in his last years). MacLean worked on *Dain Do Eimhir (Poems for Emer)* published in 1943 after he had returned, wounded, from El Alamein where he served in the Signal Corps. Became Headmaster of Plockton secondary school. Retired in 1972 and brought out *Reothairt is Contraigh (Spring Tide and Neap Tide)* in 1977. *O Choille gu Bearradh/From Wood to Ridge: Collected Poems in Gaelic and English* (1989).

1930s: 43, 44, 54, 66, 70, 79, 96, 100, 101. 1940s: 3, 10. 1960s: 29. 1970s: 96.

McQUILLAN, Ruth. MacDiarmid scholar. Began work on MacDiarmid in late 1960s, winning a Ph.D. from Cambridge for her thesis on him. A local organiser of SNP, South Edinburgh Constituency Association, Morningside and Inch-Gilmerton branches, in later 1970s, and prominent in the Eastern Orthodox Church, Edinburgh. Wrote 'Langholm Library', *Akros* (August 1974), 'Hugh MacDiarmid, "On a Raised Beach"', *Akros* (1977) and 'MacDiarmid's Other Dictionary', *Lines Review* (September 1978) and, with Agnes Shearer of Whalasay, *In Line with the Ramna Stacks* (1980), a study of MacDiarmid's fishing poems. A major review of MacDiarmid's *Complete Poems* appeared in *Studies in Scottish Literature* vol.18 (1983) and *Hugh MacDiarmid – The Patrimony* was published by Akros in 1992. Edited *The Galliard Book of Shorter Scottish Poems* (1991).

1960s: 109. 1970s: 10, 54, 81.

MARWICK, Ernest Walker (1915–77). A local Orkney writer, historian and folklorist, editor of *An Anthology of Orkney Verse* (1949). Born Fursan, Evie. Self-taught, he left parish school at ten, after which he worked on the land. First wrote CMG, 1935. Moved to Kirkwall to become a bookseller 1941 and then a journalist for the *Orcadian* and the *Orkney Herald*. Founder and Chairman, Orkney Heritage

Society. Author of *The Folklore of Orkney and Shetland* (1975). Killed in a road accident.

1930s: 51.

MILLER (Wheeler), James Harrison. Editor, *Scots Socialist*.

1940s: 13.

MILNER, Ian (1911–91). New Zealand academic and Czechoslovak sympathiser, son of famous New Zealand headmaster Frank Milner of Waitaki Boys' High School. Educated also at Canterbury University College from 1930, MA 1933. Reared in devotion to 'home' i.e. respectable Englishness. Rhodes Scholar, New College Oxford 1934–7. Civil servant, New Zealand Department of Education from 1939. Later in N.Z. Department of Foreign Affairs, also United Nations. Subsequently reputed, not necessarily accurately, to have been KGB agent. Visited Czechoslovakia 1950. Lecturer, Charles University, Prague, from 1951. Divorced from first wife who had accompanied him to Prague and married former American student, Jarmila Finhaufiva, 1958. Died Prague. Unfinished memoirs posthumously published as *Intersecting Lines* (1993).

1950s: 78, 87. 1960s: 19, 69, 78. 1970s: 26, 38.

MITCHELL, James Leslie (Lewis Grassic Gibbon) (1901–35). Major novelist of the Scottish Renaissance. Born at Hillhead of Segget farm, Auchterless, Aberdeenshire, educated at Arbuthnott Village School and Mackie Academy in Stonehaven. Joined CPGB on news of October Revolution 1917. Junior Reporter aged 16 on *Aberdeen Journal* then to Glasgow as a journalist for *Scottish Farmer*. Became a socialist and joined the Communist Party; was dismissed from his job. Enlisted in the Royal Army Service Corps, spending the First World War in the Middle East, Mesopotamia, Palestine and Egypt. Joined the Royal Air Force, serving until 1929. Published under his own name and his pseudonym over a dozen books in the last decade of his life, including the trilogy *A Scots Quair*. Collaborated with CMG on *Scottish Scene; or The Intelligent Man's Guide to Scotland* (1934). Died very suddenly of peritonitis.

1930s: 41.

MONTAGUE, John Patrick (b.1929). Irish poet, born Brooklyn, N.Y., childhood partly in Co. Tyrone (where he descended from Catholic republican antecedents). Educated Armagh, and University College Dublin, lived Paris, taught University College and Cork State University at Albany NY. His celebration of identification with the Northern Ireland Catholic minority was expressed in poems and stories published in various volumes. Of Montague's major work *The Rough Field* (1972, 1984) HMacD said in *Agenda* (Spring-Summer 1973) 'How far we are here from anything savouring of the Celtic Twilight!'

1960s: 20, 88. 1970s: 14, 40, 43, 93.

MOORE, Hugo. Resident in Paisley, a man around the Edinburgh arts scene, accompanied Michael Grieve on a trip to Vienna in the 1950s.

1950s: 81. 1960s: 26, 99.

MOORE, Thomas Sturge (1870–1944), English-born minor poet and memorabilist for the 1890s. Correspondent of W. B. Yeats.

1930s: 5.

MORGAN, Edwin (b.1920). Poet and university teacher. Glasgow-born, served with the RAMC in World War II, mostly in the Middle East. Educated at the University of Glasgow where he was appointed as lecturer becoming titular Professor of English in 1975 before retiring in 1980. Since the 1960s, Morgan has written a major body of work, with an inimitable range of poems: lyrical, science-fiction, explicitly political, concrete, sound-poetry, translations, love poems, dialogues, libretti, poem-sequences such as *Demon* (1999) and plays, including the controversial *A.D.: A Life of Christ* (2000). Morgan's plenum matches MacDiarmid's in variety, substance and quantity. A popular reader and performer of his own work and well-known, respected and loved as an encourager and inspiration to others. Awarded the Queen's Gold Medal for Poetry and the Poet Laureateship of Glasgow. *Collected Poems* (1990) and *Crossing the Border: Essays on Scottish Literature* (1990).

1950s: 35, 44, 47, 51, 63, 66, 80, 99, 101. 1960s: 10, 12, 15, 33, 49, 50. 1970s: 21, 82.

MUIR, Gavin. Son of Edwin and Willa Muir.

1970s: 55.

MUIRHEAD, Roland Eugene (1868–1964), Scottish nationalist and philanthropist, inherited fortune from family tannery, Bridge-on-Weir. Co-founder with Tom Johnston (1881–1965: Secretary of State for Scotland 1941–5) of Scottish weekly journal *Forward*. Re-founded Scottish Home Rule Association 1918, transforming it from its previous Gladstonian Liberal identity 1886–1914: Secretary until 1929 when he resigned and it evaporated. Established and financed the Scottish Secretariat for Home Rule and Scottish propaganda mostly written by CMG anonymously or as Mountboy, essentially as front for SHRA and NPS, and later for SNP. Chairman of NPS until merger with SNP. Published *Scots Independent* from 1926 until SNP took it over, making it official party paper. President, SNP. Founded Scottish Congress 1950, publishing *National Weekly* and supporting Michael Grieve in his ideological refusal to be conscripted. CMG presented him with the Andrew Fletcher Award, 11 September 1956: 'In any other country in the world he would have been recognized as a Grand Old Man of his people'.

1920s: 8, 9, 11, 12, 13.

MURRAY, Tom (1900–90). Active member successively of the SHRA, ILP, CPGB and, as a principal founder (1966), The Workers Party of Scotland, a Marxist-Leninist group of 35 members dissatisfied with the CP's increasingly parliamentary line; edited the *Workers Vanguard*, founder of the John Maclean Society in 1968.

1970s: 13.

NATIONALIST, The Editor of.

1950s: 2.

NEISH, Alex. Edited a short-lived continuation of the Edinburgh University

Liberal Club's *Jabberwock*, *Sidewalk*, 'Scotland's quarterly review' (1960). Owner of a large collection of pewter.
1960s: 18.

NEW ALLIANCE & SCOTS REVIEW, The Editor of.
1940s: 51, 54. 1950s: 14, 15.

NEW ENGLISH WEEKLY, The Editor of. See ORAGE, Alfred Richard.
1930s: 86.

NEW SCOTLAND (ALBA NUADH), The Editor of.
1930s: 68.

NICOLL, Charles. Born Glasgow 1906. Skilled engineer and Foreman of the Copper Shell Band Section, Mechan's Engineering Company, Scotstoun, in the early 1940s. Amateur poet, accomplished photographer, member of the SNP.
1940s: 41. 1960s: 30. 1970s: 50, 90.

NIVEN, Barbara (1896–1972). Artist and Communist Party member, studied mathematics at Cambridge and painting and sculpture at the Manchester School of Art. Chief fund-raiser for the *Daily Worker* for many years. Married to fellow-artist Ern Brooks. Niven was involved in raising support for the Spanish Republicans and arranging for Picasso's 'Guernica' to be exhibited in London and Manchester in 1938. The two spent the summer of 1938 with the Grieves on Whalsay. She painted several portraits of CMG, most notably a Vorticist portrait, 'Hugh MacDiarmid – 1935', presented to CMG as part of the Andrew Fletcher Award for 'Service to Scotland' (1958).
1950s: 62, 67. 1960s: 25, 51, 60, 66, 112. 1970s: 16.

NOTT, Charles Stanley. Publisher, disciple of Gurdjieff, flits evasively around the perimeter of CMG's London life in the early 1930s. Links with A.R. Orage, publishing ventures, Social Credit, but was not as dependable as CMG was hoping. Nott became his partner in the Unicorn Press, apparently agreeing to put up share capital, then defaulting on it as a result of which CMG and Nott were both thrown out of the firm by J.F. Moore and L.N. Cooper. Nott now set up as a publisher, Stanley Nott, which printed CMG's essays *At the Sign of the Thistle* in 1934 and produced a second edition of *Second Hymn to Lenin* (1935). In the 1960s Nott wrote two memoirs of Gurdjieff which are bland about CMG and uninformative about finance. Charles Stanley Nott must be carefully distinguished from Stanley Charles Nott, who wrote about jade and dedicated the results to Queen Mary, with no known links to CMG. Also, see SECKER, Martin.
1930s: 26, 27, 47.

O'CONNOR, Frank (real name Michael O'Donovan) (1903–66). Irish short story writer, Gaelic poetry translator, anthologist, critic and biographer. Born in Cork city. Grew up under the influence of Daniel Corkery and the Irish language revival. Fought under Michael Collins against the British, and later under de Valera against Collins and his pro-Treaty heirs in government. See *An Only Child* (1961). His first stories, *Guests of the Nation* (1931) were fine realistic primitive work, deeply compassionate and sensitive to human drama working its contrary way amid patriotic war. O'Donovan supported himself working as a librarian, published in the *Irish Statesman* under George Russell (the poet 'AE'), and was brought on the Abbey Theatre Board by Yeats in the 1930s. The Irish Censorship Board banned four volumes of his work. In 1951 he emigrated to the United States, teaching in several universities. Social ostracism as well as official stringency dictated the move. But he had returned to Ireland and to his childhood Catholicism when he died.

1930s: 111.

O'GRADY, Desmond James Bernard (b.1935) Irish poet. His first book of poems, *Chords and Orchestrations* (1956) was peddled around Dublin by youthful acolytes such as the future Professor T. Augustine Martin. Moved to Rome whence his major poetic volume *Reilly* (1961). Master's degree, Celtic Studies (Harvard, 1964). Senior English master Overseas School, Rome; friend and secretary to Ezra Pound until his death in 1972. Taught from mid-1970s in American University (Cairo), University of Tabriz (Iran), University of Alexandria. Ph.D. (Harvard, 1982). Translated poetry from Irish-Gaelic, Welsh, Greek, Armenian, Arabic: see his collection *Trawling Tradition* (1994). An elected member of the leading Irish official writers' body, Aosdana.

1970s: 49.

O'MAHONY, Eoin (1904–70), Irish exotically biographical anecdotalist popularly known as 'The Pope O'Mahon'; unsuccessful barrister and politician, loyalties ranging from Parnell to de Valera. Born Cork. Nomadic be-suited umbrella-ed hitch-hiker, won fame as genealogist broadcaster on Radio Eireann (host of 'Meet the Clans') early 1960s. Visiting Professor University of Southern Illinois, 1966–8, annotating its Irish collections. Knight of Malta. His destitute status would not necessarily have prevented his aiding Michael Grieve towards an opening in Dublin journalism, any more than it inhibited his membership of Dublin's most fashionable club.

1950s: 20.

O'SULLIVAN, Seumus (1879–1958). Irish poet and founder-editor of the *Dublin Magazine* from 1923. Born James Sullivan Starkey in Dublin. Protegé of the poet George Russell ('AE'). Elegist for Thomas MacDonagh (poet-martyr of Easter Rising, 1916), friend of Arthur Griffith of Sinn Fein, his *Dublin Magazine* published 'prentice work of Austin Clarke, F.R. Higgins, Liam O'Flaherty, Samuel Beckett, Patrick Kavanagh, Mary Lavin, R.S. Thomas, Paul Valéry, S.S. Koteliansky, Gordon Bottomley, but his own work (Celtic twilight and Dublin street lyricism) was subordinated to the encouragement of others. Died in Dublin.

1930s: 7, 8. 1940s: 50.

OGDON, John Andrew Howard (1937–89), virtuoso pianist and composer, joint winner of the Moscow Tchaikovsky Competion (1962), performed Sorabji's *Opus Clavicimbalisticum* in 1988.

1960s: 45.

ORAGE, Alfred Richard (1873–1934), editor. Member of the Independent Labour Party. A schoolteacher from 1893, he became the centre of a Nietzschean circle in

Leeds including his future journalistic colleague Holbrook Jackson. Edited the *New Age* 1907–22, initially famous as battle-ground for Shaw, Wells, Chesterton, etc., but quickly became an outlet for pre-war avant-garde poetic modernists such as Ezra Pound. It published (20 July 1911) his earliest known prose work 'The New Astrology' (see *The Raucle Tongue*, vol.1). CMG became acting literary editor for a short time. Founded the *New English Weekly* in 1932. CMG revered him as a hard, scientific critic, hostile to the flab and favour-trading current in literary circles, masking ignorance and want of reading. Orage died suddenly after broadcasting on Social Credit. The *New English Weekly* was taken over by his assistant, Philip Mairet.

1930s: 86.

PAPE, Captain Alfred Garbutt (1888–?). Racial theorist. Member, Royal Societies Club, London. Living in Edinburgh in the 1920s, publicising ideas about the evolution of humanity into a new and superior race, which he seems to have preached with no racial hatred of any kind although with assumption as to non-Aryan races being earlier stages of evolution emanating from Atlantis and its predecessor Lemuria. Fellow of the Royal Anthropological Institute of Great Britain and Ireland. Author of *Is There a New Race Type?* and *The Politics of the Aryan Road* (1928); *The Alternative to Communism* (1932); *A Cure for Poverty and War* (1937). Although initially non-democratic, believing inequality the first law of nature, worked on fringe of National Party of Scotland 1928, organising a preliminary draft memorandum for its educational policy (preaching voluntary self-elimination etc). Sought to win MP support to use national resources to eliminate poverty.

1920s: 25, 26.

PATERSON, A.J.B. Sales manager of Routledge Publishers.

1930s: 46, 48, 49, 52.

PEDDIE, Mrs Mary K., Miss Christian Mackay and Miss A. Katherine Mackay. Constituents of Kinross and West Perthshire at the time of the General Election of 1964.

1960s: 58.

PICKARD, Tom (b.1946). Newcastle poet who, with his wife, Connie, set up and ran the Morden Tower poetry readings in 1964; among those who read there were many who had been previously neglected in Britain such as Basil Bunting, Robert Creeley and Adrian Henri. His own work includes *High on the Walls* (1967) and a novel, *Guttersnipe* (1972).

1960s: 117.

POTTS, Paul. Anarchist poet. British Columbian. Served in 12th Commando during World War II and the Army of Israel during Israel's War of Independence. MacD contributed a 'Foreword' to *A Poet's Testament* (1940). *Dante Called You Beatrice* (1961) includes a personal memoir and tribute to MacD.

1960s: 48.

PRITCHARD, Walter. English artist, medievalist, teacher at the Glasgow School of Art, painted the 'seven poets' mural formerly on view at the Curlers pub, Byres

Road, Glasgow. Married to Sadie McLellan who was a teacher at the Edinburgh College of Art. The Grieves stayed in their basement flat at Victoria Crescent Road, Glasgow, from 1946 to 1949.

1940s: 57.

RAGO, Henry Anthony (1915–69). American poet, Assistant Professor of Humanities at the University of Chicago (1947–54), assistant editor of *Poetry* (Chicago) under Karl Jay Shapiro (1954–5), becoming editor from 1955 till his death in 1969.

1960s: 24.

REINFRANK, Arno (b.1934). Poet and translator. Born in Mannheim, Germany. Translated several MacDiarmid poems including 'On a Raised Beach', published as *Die hohe Felsenkünste*.

1960s: 114.

RIACH, Alan (b.1957). Poet, critic, academic. Author of *Hugh MacDiarmid's Epic Poetry* (1990); poetry collected in *This Folding Map* (1990), *First and Last Songs* (1995) and *Clearances* (2001). General editor of Hugh MacDiarmid's *Collected Works*, 16 vols., Carcanet Press. Taught at the University of Waikato, New Zealand, 1986–2000. Returned to Scotland 2001. Head of the Department of Scottish Literature, University of Glasgow.

1970s: 91.

RICHARDS PRESS, The. See SECKER, Martin.

1930s: 87, 88.

RUSSELL, (Irwin) Peter (b.1921). Poet and translator, editor of the magazine *Nine* (1949–54, irregularly thereafter), championed Ezra Pound in Britain, among other things editing *Ezra Pound: a collection of essays; to be presented to Ezra Pound on his 65th birthday* (1950).

1950s: 12.

SAUNDERS, Robert Crombie (b.1914). Poet, schoolmaster, edited *Selected Poems* of Hugh MacDiarmid (1944), and the magazines *Scottish Art and Letters* (1944–8), with J.D. Fergusson as art editor, and *Forward* (1951–6). His own first volume of poetry was *XXI Poems* (1955).

1950s: 42.

SCHLAPP, Otto (1859–1939). German scholar. Educated at Jena, Edinburgh, Berlin, Leipzig, Strassburg. Associate of Robert Fitzroy Bell in invention of Students' Representative Council at Edinburgh (and hence UK) on lines of Jena self-policing by students mid-1880s. Taught German in Edinburgh schools 1887–1894. Lecturer in German, University of Edinburgh 1894–1920, Reader 1920–6, Professor 1926–9. Published *Modern Languages in Scottish Schools and Universities: thier present position and prospects* (1899), and *Kant's Lehre vom Genie* (1907). A philosopher and aesthete, deeply interested in music, painting and sculpture.

1930s: 28.

SCOTS INDEPENDENT, The Editor of.
   1940s: 43.

SCOTSMAN, The Editor of.
   1950s: 34, 82,. 1960s: 113. 1970s: 106.

SCOTT, F.G. (1880–1958). Composer, largely of song-settings of poems by MacDiarmid, Burns, William Soutar and other Scottish poets. Teacher at Langholm Academy, he became a friend and mentor to CMG, helping him arrange the lyrics of *A Drunk Man Looks at the Thistle* into a coherent shape; the poem is dedicated to him. His songs are the equal of his contemporaries in the European avant-garde, including Bartok and Schoenberg. Born in Hawick, his cousin was the artist William JOHNSTONE and at one point they imagined themselves along with CMG effecting a triumvirate Scottish Renaissance in music, art and literature. Lecturer in music at Jordanhill Training College for teachers, 1925–46. Fell out with CMG in later years, CMG alleging that Scott was anti-semitic, but continuing to champion him as a composer, writing a small book in tribute to him on the occasion of Scott's 75th birthday in 1955 (reprinted in *Albyn: Shorter Books and Monographs*).
   1940s: 6, 7, 8. 1950s: 28.

SCOTT, Tom (1918–95). Poet. Born Glasgow, educated there and at St Andrews, then Newbattle Abbey College and Edinburgh University. Author of *The Ship and Ither Poems* (1963) and *The Tree* (1977). Edited *The Penguin Book of Scottish Poetry*.
   1960s: 86.

SHETLAND NEWS, The Editor of.
   1940s: 16.

SHETLAND TIMES, The Editor of.
   1930s: 113.

SECKER, Martin (1882–1978). Publisher. Founded Martin Secker 1910. Within a few years Secker's authors included Compton Mackenzie, Norman Douglas, Edward Thomas, Arthur Ransome. He published all the work of D.H. Lawrence's last ten years. CMG's anonymous translation of Ramon Maria de Tenreiro, *The Handmaid of the Lord* published by Secker (1930). In the early 1930s the firm ran into difficulties and it was enlarged and remodelled as Secker and Warburg but by 1937 Secker had severed his connection with it and started out again with the old firm the Richards Press. In the late 1930s it was publishing a series of pamphlets of selections of poets, some very obscure. Became proprietor of the Unicorn Press, of which CMG had briefly been a director and which he left after bitter recrimination, early in 1932. CMG's alienated partners, L.N. Cooper and J.F. Moore, became its Managing Director and Secretary when Captain Michael John Hunter (1891–1951), Tory MP for Brigg Division, Lincolnshire, became Chairman, later in 1932. Cooper was out in 1934 and the firm was moribund by 1936. Secker specialised in material relating to the 1890s in both Richards and Unicorn Presses.
   1930s: 87, 88.

SILVER, R.S. (1913–199?). Scientist, nationalist and playwright. Born Montrose, studied at Glasgow University and became a research physicist at ICI and Head of Research at G. and J. Weir, Glasgow, during World War II. Contemplating the fate of Europe during Nazi rule led him to study the conquest of Scotland under Edward I of England and the growth of Scottish resistance, culminating in a large play *The Hert o Scotland*, published as *The Bruce* (1986) and staged in abbreviated form in Edinburgh by Theatre Alba in the 1990s. Silver was Professor of Mechanical Engineering at Heriot-Watt University; awarded CBE 1967; published *An Introduction to Thermodynamics* (1971); honoured by UNESCO for his achievement in desalanisation. Member of the SNP. Wrote 'Student Culture in the 1930s and Acquaintance with C.M. Grieve', *Edinburgh Review* 74 (1986), pp.63–75.

1950s: 30.

SINGER, James Burns, pseudonym of James Hyman Singer (1928–64). Poet, journalist and marine biologist, born in America to a Scottish mother and Polish-Jewish father, moving to Glasgow in 1932. *Still and All* (1957) was the only volume of his poems published during his life; CMG prefaced his *Collected Poems* (1970). Also wrote *Living Silver*, a prose work on the fishing industry, edited and translated an anthology of Polish poetry, and the pioneering article on MacDiarmid, 'Scarlet Eminence', published in *Encounter* (March 1957).

1960s: 22, 27.

SLEATH, Fred. Editor of the *Carlisle Journal*.

1940s: 52.

SMEATON, Misses Jessie B. and Mary S. Students from an adult education class taught by CMG.

1950s: 68. 1970s: 102.

SMITH, Sydney Goodsir (1915–75). Poet. Born New Zealand, arrived in Edinburgh 1927 and educated there and at Oxford. Writing includes major sequence of love poems, *Under the Eildon Tree* and the Joycean prose extravaganza *Carotid Cornucopius*. Friend and drinking companion of CMG, Norman MacCAIG and others in the amber mile of Rose Street, Edinburgh, in the 1950s and 1960s. *Collected Poems 1941–1975* (1975) was introduced by MacD.

1940s: 46. 1960s: 98.

SORABJI, Kaikhosru Shapurji (1892–1988). Composer. Son of a Spanish-Sicilian mother and Parsi father. Financially independent. Reviewed for the *New Age* and the *New English Weekly*. CMG met him in the early 1920s. A masterly pianist, giving recitals in London, Paris, Vienna and Glasgow, but disliked performing and abandoned concerts. Composed *Opus Clavicembalisticum*, the longest non-repetitious published piano piece. Sorabji performed the work in public once, in Glasgow on 1 December 1930. He dedicated it 'To My Two Friends (E Duobus Unum): Hugh MacDiarmid and C. M. Grieve Likewise to the Everlasting Glory of Those Few Men Blessed And Sanctified In The Curses and Execrations Of Those Many Whose Praise is Eternal Damnation'. Sorabji banned all performance of his works as unsuitable under 'present or foreseeable conditions' in 1940, lifting the ban in 1976. CMG's second chapter of *The Company I've Kept*, devoted to Sorabji, begins, '... merely to think of him, let alone see him, still gives me the same thrill I experienced when we first met' which had been in Chingford, in the home of the poet George Reston Malloch (1875–1953).

1920s: 18. 1950s: 54. 1960s: 70. 1970s: 88.

SQUAIR, Olive M. *Scotland in Europe: A Study in Race Relations* was published in 1977 with an introduction by MacD in which he calls Miss Squair's book 'a landmark in Scottish historiography'. Reprinted in *The Raucle Tongue*, vol.3. MacD wrote the 'Foreword' to Squair's *The Quest of Ailsa Macrae* (1931).

1970s: 58, 66, 71.

STEPHENS, Meic (b.1938). Welsh cultural historian. Founded the Triskel Press and edited *Poetry Wales*, quarterly, 1965–73. Took particular pride in the discovery of new Welsh poets writing in English, seeing the 1960s as a 'second flowering' of Anglo-Welsh poetry. Appointed Literature Director for the Welsh Arts Council, 1966. Wrote *Linguistic Minorities in Western Europe* (1976) and edited the *Oxford Companion to the Literature of Wales* (1986) and the *New Companion* (1998). His dismissal from Welsh Arts Council elicited an overwhelming storm of indignation in the 1990s. Author and editor of a large number of invaluable works on Welsh culture.

1970s: 32, 42, 45.

STEVENSON, Ronald (b.1928). Composer, pianist, writer on music. Born in Blackburn, Lancashire, England. Studied at Royal Manchester College of Music. Married Marjorie Spedding, 1952. Taught in Broughton High School, Edinburgh. Became Senior Lecturer in Composition at the University of Cape Town, South Africa, 1963–5. Returned and settled in Scotland as freelance composer and pianist. Author of *Western Music: An Introduction* (1971). Among many works, he has composed a selection of songs for voice and piano based poems by Hugh MacDiarmid. Composed the large-scale *Passacaglia on DSCH* for piano. Like CMG, an enthusiast for the work of Sorabji and that of F.G. Scott.

1950s: 100. 1960s: 14, 34, 54, 62, 67, 68, 76, 79, 80, 84, 115. 1970s: 25, 84.

STEWART, Douglas (1913–88). Scottish journalist and nationalist. Educated at the University of Edinburgh. Wore a kilt all his life. Edited the *Straits Settlement Times* for several years after the Second World War and subsequently was in the public relations department of the BBC. So outstanding was his work that he was recalled to service after his retirement. Among his duties was the provision of data for the preview columnists commenting on the week's programmes in the *Radio Times*, among whom was MacD. Stewart was also the inspirational editor of the *Scots Independent* in the 1970s in succession to Michael Grieve.

1940s: 14.

STOCK, Noel (b.1929), Australian writer and translator, published unsigned articles by Ezra Pound sent from the Chestnut Ward of St Elizabeth's mental hospital in the mid-fifties. Moved to Europe, 1958, met Pound in 1959, edited a volume of his essays, *Impact: Essays on Ignorance and the Decline of American Civilisation* (1960), catalogued Pound collection at Brunnenburg, Italy and went on to write a biography of Pound (1970).

1960s: 65.

TIMES LITERARY SUPPLEMENT, The Editor of.
1970s: 4.

TREVLYN, Valda. See GRIEVE, Valda.

TRIBUNE. See Kerrigan, Peter.
1940s: 40.

TROCCHI, Alexander (1925–84). Glasgow-born novelist, translator and internationalist, associated with 1950s avant-garde and the American 'beat' writers, resident in Paris (1951–6), New York (1956–61) and London thenceforth, edited a literary magazine, *Merlin*, (1952–5) with Christopher Logue, its small publishing wing bringing out the first English language editions of Beckett's *Molloy* and *Watt*. His works include several pornographic novels, such as *Thongs* (1955) and *White Thighs* (1955). *Young Adam* (1954, UK 1961) and *Cain's Book* (1960, UK 1963) remain influential. His famed encounter with CMG at the Edinburgh Writers' Conference (1962) is described in *A Life in Pieces: Reflections on Alexander Trocchi* (1997); the debate, at which Trocchi described CMG as 'an old fossil', was polarised by CMG, who chose to view Trocchi as pro-American and obsessed with homosexuality and lesbianism, his adversarial approach being nonetheless rewarded by huge publicity for the event and its participants. See also Edwin Morgan, 'The Fold-In Conference', *Edinburgh Review* 97 (Spring 1997), pp.94–102.
1960s: 52, 55, 72.

TURNBULL, Gael (b.1928). Poet. Edinburgh-born, grew up in England and Canada 1940–4; studied Natural Sciences at Cambridge and qualified in medicine at the University of Pennsylvania, Philadelphia, 1947–51. Worked as a general practitioner and anaesthetist in Canada, California, London and Worcestershire. Founded Migrant Press, 1957. *A Gathering of Poems 1950–1980* (1983), *From the Language of the Heart* (1985), *For Whose Delight* (1995), *A Rattle of Scree* (1997). After corresponding for some time, CMG was astonished when he was finally introduced to GT, gasping, '*You're* Gael Turnbull? – But I thought ye were a lassie!'
1950s: 61, 79.

WATSON, Roderick (b.1943). Poet, critic, academic. Professor of Scottish Literature at the University of Stirling. Author of *Hugh MacDiarmid*, a study-guide for the Open University (1976), *The Literature of Scotland* (1984) and editor of *The Poetry of Scotland: Gaelic, Scots and English* (1995).
1970s: 73.

WELSH NATIONALIST MEETING.
1930s: 89.

WHITE, Jean (1912–94). Cousin of CMG. SNP councillor. Ran jeweller's shop in Langholm.
1960s: 3, 17, 21, 36, 37, 38, 39, 42, 57, 64, 104. 1970s: 24, 30, 46, 92, 109.

WHITE, William. It is uncertain exactly who William White was. The typed letter

to him is addressed to a number in 'Craigcrook Road, Blackhall, Edinburgh'.
1930s: 110.

WILKIE, Robert Blair, editor of the *Scots Independent*, a member of the National Council of the SNP, later expelled for extremism and forming the Scottish Renaissance Committee (which became the Scottish National Congress) under whose aegis CMG stood in the 1950 General Election.
1950s: 3.

WILLIAMS, Jonathan (b.1929). American poet and critic. Studied at Black Mountain College, North Carolina, associated with Charles Olson, Robert Creeley and Edward Dorn. Author of numerous books of poems including *Mahler* (1969), a sequence of forty-four poems written in response to the forty-four movements of Mahler's ten symphonies, as well as *The Magpie's Bagpipe: Selected Essays* (1982).
1970s: 47.

WRIGHT, Gordon. Photographer, publisher, rare books dealer. Born in Edinburgh. Started publishing under the the imprint Reprographia, 1969. Author of *MacDiarmid: An Illustrated Biography* (1977). A major exhibition of Wright's photographic studies of writers was held at the National Library of Scotland in Summer 2001.
1970s: 15.

YOUNG, Douglas (1913–73), Scottish nationalist and classicist. Believed conscription for Scots illegal under Treaty of Union. Prosecuted for refusal to be conscripted and served eight months, CMG vociferous in welcoming crowd on release. Married 1943. Chairman SNP 1942. Won 42% of vote in Kelvingrove by election 1943. Imprisoned for three months 1944 (refusing labour conscription). H. MacD introduced his Lallans verses *Auntran Blads* (1943); translated Aristophanes plays into Lallans, *The Puddocks* (1957), *The Burdies* (1959). Taught University of Dundee 1947–68, Professor of Greek University of North Carolina 1969–73.
1940s: 5. 1950s: 6.

YOUNG, James D. (b.1931). Historian and socialist. Left school 1945 aged fourteen, working as a labourer in a sawmill for eight years. Studied at Newbattle Abbey College from 1953, under Edwin Muir, then at Ruskin College, Oxford, under G.D.H. Cole. Lecturer then Reader in History at Stirling University. Published *The Rousing of the Scottish Working Classes*, *Women and Popular Struggles: A History of Scottish and English Working-Class Women 1560–1984* and the standard historical biography of John Maclean (revised edition 1996). Chairperson of the John Maclean society 1981–5. Wrote personal memoir *Making Trouble*.
1950s: 37. 1960s: 83.

Index

Acton, Lord, 495
Adams, Francis, 81
Adler, Jankel, 217
Aesop, 464
Aitken, Betsy, 167, 168, 336
Aitken, Betty, 409
Aitken, Christine, 409, 410, 411
Aitken, James M., 132
Aitken, Jenny, 24
Aitken, Mary Baird, 289
Aitken, William R., 64, 112, 130, 131, 146, 151, 155, 157, 158, 159, 160, 163, 167, 336, 409, 410, 529
Aitkenhead, John, 225, 263, 264, 268, 269, 271, 272, 274, 280
Aitkenhead, Morag, 225, 263, 264, 271, 272, 274
Albert, L., 146
Alberti, Rafael, 440
Albertó, Santiago, 378
Albery, Hilda, 406
Aldred, Guy, 166, 270, 271, 274, 285
Alexander, Joan, 294, 532
Allan, Thomas, 398
Allenby, General E.H.H., 110
Alridge, James, 408
Anderson, Freddie, 474
Anderson, G.K., 171
Anderson, John, 61, 73, 75
Andrew, Prince, 517
Aney, Edith Trelease, 287, 292
Angus, John, 497
Angus, Marion, 87
Annand, J.K., xx
Aragon, Ferdinand of, xxiii
Aragon, Louis, 440
Archer, David, 211, 216
Archer, William, xvii
Arghezi, Tudor, 348, 364
Arlen, Michael ('Dikran Kouyoumjian'), 85
Armstrong, Neil, 470

Arnold, Matthew, 187
Arthur, Harriet, 73, 109, 111, 114, 122, 124, 125
Arthur, Hugh, 74, 225
Arthur, James, 97
Ascherson, Neal, 527
Attlee, Clement, 292
Auden, W.H., 166, 319, 371, 472, 482
Augustín, José, 378
Ayrton, Michael, 114

Bagley, Desmond, 473
Bain, Robert, 163
Baldwin, Stanley, xxvii, 64
Balfour, Earl Arthur James, 24, 30
Ball, Arthur, 87
Ball, Ernest, 396, 424, 428
Ball, Esme, 396, 424, 428
Barnfather, Ann, née Grieve, 69, 386, 531
Barnfather, Johnny, 531
Barr, Rev. James, 222
Barrie, J.M., 64, 112, 464
Barrow, Carol and Peter, 533
Baskin, Leonard, 422
Baudelaire, Charles, 371
Bayefsky, Aba, 417, 428
Beattie, Janet, née Laidlaw, 358, 366, 371, 531
Becher, Johannes, 290
Beckett, Samuel, 371
Behagg, Judith, see also Grieve, Judith, 524
Behagg, Michael, 524
Bellany, John, 389
Berdyaev, Nikolai, 290
Berger, John, 407
Berkely, Sir Humphrey, 401, 404
Berlin, Sir Isaiah, 401, 523
Berryman, John, 522
Bevin, Ernest, 189
Bialik, Chaim, 173
Bithell, Jethro, 4
Black, Margaret, 211, 215, 239, 240, 242
Black, R.M., 47, 69, 77, 84, 97, 211, 215, 222, 229, 233, 239, 240, 241, 242

Black, Rona, 211, 215
Blake, George, 254
Blake, William, 187, 323, 476
Blamauer, Karoline, see Lenya, Lotte
Bligh, E.W., 131
Blok, Aleksandr Aleksandrovich, 434
Blum, Elspeth, 424
Blum, Maurius, 424
Blunden, Edmund, 190
Blythman, Morris ('Thurso Berwick'), 298, 307, 355, 526, 527
Boase, Alan, 211
Bogdanov, Aleksandr Aleksandrovich, 460
Bold, Alan, ix–xi, xiv, xix, xx, 229, 245, 269, 389, 426, 427, 449, 450, 475, 476, 501, 503, 518, 519
Bold, Alice, 389, 427, 476, 501, 503, 519
Bold, Valentina, 501, 503
Boothby, Major F.A.C. ('Derek'), 482, 483, 490, 491, 498
Boothby, Rosalie, 491, 498, 499
Botev, Hristo, 345, 348
Bottomley, Gordon, 47
Boyd Orr, Sir John, 429
Boyd, William, 91
Boyt, Nellie, 49, 248
Bradshaw, Lawrence, 318, 324, 325
Brecht, Bertolt, 396, 406, 407, 414, 417, 431, 440, 450, 467, 468, 469, 470, 471, 472, 473, 478, 508
Brecht, Stefan, 407
Bressler, Margaret, 81
Bridie, James (Mavor, Osborne Henry), 243, 429
Bridson, D. Geoffrey, 274,

319, 321, 357, 360, 364, 399, 425, 458, 484, 514
Bridson, Joyce, 399, 426, 485, 514
Brock, Margery, 484, 491, 500
Brodie, Peter, 159, 305
Brooke, Lady, *née* Cunningham Graham, 109, 110, 121, 293
Brooks, Edwin, 357
Brooks, Ernest, 164, 167, 320, 322, 375, 395, 402, 406, 469
Broom, John L., 418, 419
Brough, John, 164
Brown, Alec, 92
Brown, Evelyn, 331
Brown, Ivor, 302
Brown, Margaret, 491
Brown, Oliver, 196, 216, 222, 376, 432, 490, 491
Brown, Pete, 411
Bruce of Whalsay, Mrs, 111
Bruce, George, 457
Bruce, Michael, 183
Bryce, James, 4
Buber, Martin, 411
Buchan, Col. John, xv, 3, 5, 6, 21, 23, 24, 64
Buchanan, George, 132, 157, 160, 164
Bulloch, Brodrick, 132
Bunting, Basil, 444, 488, 501
Burke, Edmund, xxx
Burns, John, 114
Burns, Robert, xxiii, xxv, xxvii, 89, 158, 160, 246, 265, 273, 276, 299, 340, 342, 346, 351, 355, 362, 367, 380, 381, 383, 390, 393, 394, 406, 410, 413, 416, 417, 427, 459, 467, 471
Burt, William, 26, 183
Bush, Alan, 347, 397
Busoni, Ferruccio, 413, 416
Buthlay, Kenneth, 159, 288, 313, 369, 372, 388, 394, 433
Butor, Michel, 371
Butter, P.H., 493
Byron, Lord George Gordon, xi, xiii, xxxi

Caimbeul, Aonghas, 80, 96
Caird, James B., 68, 473, 523

Caird, Janet, 473, 522, 523
Cairncross, Thomas Scott, xv, 3, 5, 6
Calder, Angus, 346
Calder, John, 368
Callan, Jimmy, 347, 529
Cameron, Margerite, 469
Cameron, Morven, 466, 468, 480
Campbell, Donald, 492
Campbell, Ian, 488
Campbell, Kenneth, 412, 416
Campbell, Roy, 73, 161, 288, 326
Campbell, Sheriff MacMaster, 80
Campsie, Alistair, 478
Canton, William, 4
Čapek, Karel, 41, 83, 157, 160, 173
Capouya, Emile, 373
Cardenal, Ernesto, 515, 516
Carleton, William, 370
Carlyle, Thomas, 488, 489
Carroll, Lewis, xi
Carswell, Catherine Roxburgh, *née* Macfarlane, 75, 89, 94, 111, 146, 157
Carswell, Donald, 90, 178
Cathie, Dermot, 276
Cattell, Raymond B., 155
Caudwell, Christopher, 151
Cautley, J. Cargill, 16
Cézanne, Paul, 360
Chambers, Walter Duncanson, 96, 97, 99, 103, 104
Chapman, Harry, 444
Chapman, Mina, 444
Chen Chia, 330, 331
Chiari, Joseph, 294
Chisholm, Erik, 185, 293, 294, 295, 397, 409
Chisholm, Mrs E., 403
Chisholm, William, 532
Chopin, Frédéric, 83
Chorley, Lord Robert, 322
Christianson, Clem, 408
Christie, Ron, 351
Churchill, Sir Winston, xv, 64, 191, 219, 266, 318
Clark, Alex, 400, 401, 402, 420, 499, 529
Clark, Angus, 257, 429
Clark, Marjorie, 471
Clarke, Austin, 42, 163, 284, 370, 421
Clyde, Lord, 357

Coia, Emilio, 114
Collingwood, R.G., 290
Corkery, Daniel, 44, 45
Corneille, Pierre, 160
Cornish, Vaughan, 164
Coutts, Charlie, 341
Cowe, Bill, 401
Cowley, Lady Tiger, 457
Craig, David,·374, 394, 395, 443
Craig, Jeffrey, 457
Cribb, Timothy J., 492, 520
Crichton, James, 425
Cromwell, Oliver, 196
Crook, David, 326
Croskey, Betty, 74, 75, 114, 119, 122, 124, 126, 153
Crotty, Patrick, 522
Cruikshank, Helen Burness, 47, 53, 57, 66, 75, 99, 126, 166, 245, 256, 269, 302, 326, 336, 341, 365, 462, 475
Cunningham Graham, Admiral, 293
Cunningham Graham, Robert Bontine, xxvi, xxvii, 30, 31, 33, 89, 109, 110, 114, 117, 119, 122, 158, 257, 289, 293, 295
Curran, Bob, 423
Cuthbert, Lt Colonel Thomas, 133

Daiches, Alan, 417
Daiches, David, 276, 297, 288, 307, 313, 316, 332, 369, 372, 380, 419, 437, 455, 472, 474, 505
Daiches, Mrs D., 308, 313, 380
Dalby, Martin, 444
Daniels, Sir Goronwy, 487
David, Donald, 421
Davidson, John, 356
Davie, Cedric Thorpe, 415
Davie, George Elder, 110, 112, 124, 126, 131, 132, 146, 147, 151, 153, 163, 180, 434
Davies, Moya Llewelyn, 84
Davin, Dan, 501
Dawson, Elizabeth, *see also* Grieve, Elizabeth, 41, 43, 46, 69, 71, 173, 379
Dawson, James, xx
De Brun, Hon. Garech,

457, 516
De Gaulle, General Charles, 184
De la Mare, Walter, 228
De Valera, Éamon, xxvi
Deighton, Len, 473
Demarco, Richard, 463
Deutsch, Babette, 128
Dewar, Lord, 464
Dickinson, Emily, 482
Dimitrov, Georgi Mikhailovich, 108
Dollan, Sir Patrick Joseph, 228, 265
Donaldson, Arthur, 189, 192, 196, 197, 216, 222, 399
Dott, Mary, 314
Doughty, Charles M., 131, 289, 291, 366, 368, 469, 475, 476
Douglas, Lord Alfred, xv
Douglas, Major C.H., xxvii, 48, 405
Douglas, Norman, xxvi, 89
Douglas, Ronald MacDonald, 482, 490, 500
Douglas, Sir George, 4
Douglas-Home, Sir Alec, 399, 401, 402, 404, 415
Dowson, Ernest, xi
Drew, Mrs P., 306
Drew, Philip, 306
Driberg, Tom, 264, 283, 285
Ducasse, Roger, 83
Duff, A. McN., 99
Duff, Charles, 243
Dunbar, William, 278, 289, 294, 437, 467
Duncan, Joseph, 91
Dunlop, James, 222, 269
Dutt, Rajani Palme, 196
Dutton, Geoffrey, 408
Duval, Kulgin, 356, 360, 363, 366, 370, 372, 375, 381, 389, 406, 435, 436, 453, 457, 472, 518, 521

Eadie, Bryan, 468
Eardley, Joan, 416
Edwards, John, 133
Edwards, Oliver, 487
Edwards, Owen Dudley, 433, 437
Eimhir, 179
Eliot, T.S., xvii, xxviii, 156, 187, 204, 205, 289, 316, 334, 356

Elizabeth II, 365, 393, 465
Elliot, Chrissie, 531
Elliot, John ('Puffle'), 470
Elliot, Rt. Hon. Walter, 264, 429
Éluard, Paul, 440
Eminescu, Mihail, 364
Emmerson, George, 392
Empson, Sir William, 501
Engels, Friedrich, 290
Enticknap, Alisdair, 456
Enticknap, Graham, 455, 473, 474
Enticknap, John, 199
Enticknap, Morag, see also Grieve, Morag, 351, 455, 473, 507, 531
Enticknap, Nicholas, 507, 508
Erskine, Hon. Ruaraidh Stuart, xxvi, 18, 22, 32, 33, 34, 257, 429
Espriu, Salvador, 377, 378
Evans, Gwynfor, 433, 477
Ewing, Winnie, 428

Fairley, Barker, 94, 258, 259, 313, 390, 392, 396, 424, 428, 436, 439, 469, 479, 486, 504, 517, 523, 533
Fairley, Joan, 424, 428
Fairley, Nan, 258, 259, 390, 392, 396, 424, 504, 517
Faiz, Ahmad, 450
Falconer, Agnes, 12
Fang Cheng Ping, 330
Farthing, Michael, 492
Fauchereau, Serge, 461
Fedin, Konstantin Aleksandrovich, 409
Feldman, G., 410
Ferguson, J.D., 211, 258, 361
Ferguson, John Alexander, 3, 5, 6
Finlay, Alec, 317
Finlay, Ian Hamilton, 243, 376
Fitzgerald, Desmond, xxvi
Fitzgerald, Garrett, xxvi
Fleming, Tom, 474, 506, 507
Forbes, Watson, 415
Forrester, A., 399
Foulis, Timothy N., xv, 3, 6, 7, 11
Fraser, G.S., 158, 294, 295, 316, 317
Fraser, Lady Antonia, 493

Fraser, Norrie, 206, 250
Frenssen, Gustav, 376, 377
Freud, Sigmund, xi, 505
Fried, Erich, 449
Friesz, Othon, 360
Fühmann, Franz, 365
Fullerton, John, 112

Gallacher, William, 166, 289
Galt, John, 302
Garioch, Robert, see Sutherland, Robert Garioch
Gawsworth, John, 57, 141, 412
Geddes, Patrick, 173
George, Stefan, 100, 520
Gibb, Andrew Dewar, 48, 91, 160
Gibbon, Lewis Grassic, see also Mitchell, James Leslie, 57, 65, 69, 75, 78, 81, 82, 87, 93, 301, 302, 330, 355, 370, 376, 416, 417, 418, 457, 495
Gibson, T.H., 256, 257
Gillies, William, 257, 429
Ginsberg, Allen, 480
Gish, Nancy, 516, 526
Glass, Douglas, 140
Glen, Duncan, 372, 387, 388, 403, 433, 435, 444, 451, 452, 459, 492
Glen, Margaret, 403, 434
Glenconner, Lady, xv
Glibie, Johnny Jnr., 121
Goethe, Johann Wolfgang von, 259, 392, 469
Gogarty, Oliver St John, xxvi, xxvii, 34, 44, 117, 134, 248, 370
Goldie, Ian ('John'), 263
Gollan, John, 402
Gollancz, Victor, 57, 71, 125, 161, 177, 180, 288
Gonne, Maud, 524
Gordon, Manfred, 407
Gould, John, 4
Graham, Andrew, 392
Graham, Billy, 309
Graham, Laurence, 166
Graham, Masie, 350, 390
Graham, W.S., 258, 294, 295, 310
Grassie, Morris, 527
Graves, Robert, 360
Gray, Sir Alexander, 280
Greene, Graham, 322, 323
Gregory, Horace, 190

565

Grierson, John, 79
Grierson, Sir Herbert, 280
Grieve, (James) Michael Trevlyn, ix, xviii, xxi–xxiii, xxvii; 53–534 *passim*; notably, *alcohol* 361; *birth* 53; *car crashes* 281, 382, 383, 384; *conscientious objection to WWII* 268, 270, 271, 272, 274, 283, 295; *executor of CMG estate* 521, 528, 533; *health* 107, 119, 122, 123, 161, 177, 202, 203, 206, 211, 216, 231, 241, 276, 303, 404, 444; *journalism* 284, 286, 287, 311, 343, 366, 380, 432, 434, 455, 473, 530; *politics* 428, 432, 491; *schooling* 97, 172, 198, 199, 223, 225, 226, 228, 229, 238, 246
Grieve, Andrew Graham, x, xv, xvii, xix–xxi, xxv, 3, 5, 6, 8, 11, 19, 25, 40, 41, 52, 59, 62, 69, 71, 72, 76, 78, 81, 92, 95, 98, 101, 102, 103, 107, 129, 170, 172, 177, 178, 180, 198, 199, 200, 203, 204, 208, 210, 214, 217, 222, 229, 234, 235, 237, 351, 379, 475, 531
Grieve, Angela, 379, 392, 517
Grieve, Angus, 41, 42, 62, 93, 98, 108, 130, 172, 173, 178, 179, 181, 198, 199, 204, 208, 214, 217, 229, 233, 531
Grieve, Ann, 390, 505, 524
Grieve, Archibald Murray, 530
Grieve, Christine ('Chryssie'), 25, 41, 52, 53, 60, 62, 69, 76, 79, 93, 129, 177, 178, 181
Grieve, Christine Elizabeth Margaret, *see also* MacIntosh, Christine, xviii, xix, 25, 41, 42, 43, 46, 102, 103, 106, 115, 127, 128, 136, 145, 149, 151, 170
Grieve, Christopher Murray Trevlyn, 362, 379, 380, 386, 390, 397, 494, 530

Grieve, Deirdre, 138, 338, 343, 344, 346, 347, 348, 349, 350, 351, 355, 357, 358, 359, 360, 361, 362, 363, 380, 385, 386, 390, 397, 404, 436, 438, 469, 478, 479, 488, 512, 516, 529, 534
Grieve, Dorian, 530
Grieve, Elizabeth née Graham, *see also* Dawson, Elizabeth, xvii, xx, xi, 23, 531
Grieve, Henry, 531
Grieve, Isabella Jane, née Charlton, 531
Grieve, James ('Jimmy'), 531
Grieve, James, xix–xxi, 172, 392, 473, 531
Grieve, Jane, 517
Grieve, John ('Bacca'), 392, 531
Grieve, Judith, *see also* Behagg, Judith, 379, 488, 517
Grieve, Kate, 517
Grieve, Liza, 531
Grieve, Lucien, 404, 436, 530
Grieve, Margaret Cunningham Thomson, née Skinner, ('Peggy'), xiii–xviii, xx, xxi, xxv, 3, 6, 14, 19, 23, 25, 31, 32, 33, 34, 39, 40, 41, 42, 43, 70, 100, 102, 103, 105, 108, 109, 115, 124, 127, 128, 132, 133, 135, 139, 145, 146, 148, 149, 150, 168, 373
Grieve, Morag, *see also* Enticknap, Morag, 25, 62, 98, 108, 130, 172, 173, 178, 179, 181, 198, 199, 203, 204, 205, 206, 208, 214, 217, 225, 237, 351
Grieve, Provost James (of Langholm), 465, 488
Grieve, Robert, 531
Grieve, Thomas, 531
Grieve, Valda, *see also* Trevlyn, Valda, ix, xiii; 81–534 *passim*; notably, *car crash* 357, 358; *executor of CMG estate* 521, 528; *finances* 101, 201, 219, 224, 225, 228,

229, 231, 232, 233, 238, 243, 251, 252, 341, 343, 424, 468; *health* 87, 98, 107, 180, 202, 348, 369, 426, 436, 443, 481, 490, 514, 522, 524; *marriage* 81, 530; *politics* 282, 285; *portrait of* 417; *travel* 345, 347, 398, 425, 427, 431, 437, 454, 455, 456, 457, 481, 484, 486, 487, 497, 504, 508, 517, 534
Grieve, Walter Ross, xviii, xix, 31, 34, 42, 103, 127, 133, 136, 145, 149, 150, 151, 249, 303, 390, 392, 396, 397, 455, 479, 488, 505, 517, 524, 529, 530
Grieves, Henry (Harry), 530
Guillan, Nicholas, 310
Guillevic, Eugène, 365
Gunn, Neil, 57, 144, 182, 243, 372, 477

Haba, Alois, 414, 416
Habart, Michel, 320, 459
Haldane, Richard, 429
Hall, Robin, 382
Halliday, J.L., 488
Hamilton, Colin, 368, 435, 453, 454, 457, 472, 518, 521
Hamilton, General Sir Ian, xv, 4, 5
Hamilton, Matthew, 192, 193, 195
Hardie, (James) Keir, 265, 266, 285
Hardy, Frank, 407, 408
Harewood, Lord G.H.H.L., 382
Harris, Joel Chandler, xxiii
Harris, Max, 408
Harte, Bret, 83
Hawthorn, Jeremy, 402
Hay, George Campbell, 5, 157, 159, 160, 182, 183, 184, 192, 224, 225, 242, 434
Hay, J. McDougall, 4
Haynes, Jim, 368, 395, 398
Heaney, Seamus, xxix–xxxi, 484
Heath, Edward, 403
Heine, Heinrich, 476, 496
Henderson, Hamish, 300, 301, 316, 317, 350, 394, 395, 474

Henderson, Thomas, 91
Hendry, J.F., 154, 159
Henry, Claude, 388
Henryson, Robert, 278, 472, 478
Herman, Joseph, 217, 435, 436
Hewett, Dorothy, 408
Higgins, F.R., 163, 180
Hikmet, Nazim, 290, 440, 450
Hills, Fiona, 346, 348, 349, 350, 356, 358
Hitler, Adolf, 325
Hogg, James, 388
Holan, Vladimir, 472
Holliday, Frank, 293
Holub, Miroslav, 472, 482
Honeyman, T.J., 296
Honig, Camille R., 411
Hood, John, 179, 180
Hopkins, Gerard Manley, 291
Hopkins, H.O.V., 263
Horne, J.C.W., 365
Horne, Robert, 30
Hudson, Flexmore, 408
Hughes, Emrys, 281, 283, 285
Hughson, Mary, 202, 204, 206, 218, 234
Hugo, Victor, 187
Hume, David, 367, 469, 482
Hunter, Captain Michael John, 77
Hutchison, Ina, 122
Hutchison, Isabel K., 5
Hutchison, Pearse, 377, 378

Ibsen, Henrik, xvii
Insh, George Pratt, 90
Iqbal, Sir Muhammad, 450
Ireland, Kevin, 346
Irvine of Saltness, John ('Glybie'), 111
Irvine, Kirsty, 111
Isaacs, Jack, 456
Izanev, Stefan ('Stefan Dorba'), 347

Jackson, Mrs, 326, 338, 339, 341, 358, 360
Jacob, Violet, xv, 5
James VI, 132, 278
James, D.G., 159
Jamieson, Storm, 375
Jarrell, Randall, 316
Jeffrey, William, 87

John, Augustus, 221
Johnson, Dr Samuel, 83, 405
Johnson, Julia Grieve, 530
Johnston, Annie, 147
Johnston, Thomas, 165
Johnston, Thomas, Rt. Hon., 191
Johnstone, Mary, 450, 481, 497, 498, 533
Johnstone, Sarah, 450, 481, 498, 533
Johnstone, William, 44, 46, 185, 221, 389, 394, 396, 402, 417, 430, 449, 480, 497, 498, 533
Jones, David, 501
Jones, Gwyn, 509
Jósef, Attila, 348, 351, 364, 365, 393, 450
Joyce, James, xxi, xxiv, xxviii, xxx, 34, 123, 159, 186, 292, 304, 306, 307, 308, 312, 313, 314, 316, 317, 318, 319, 320, 388, 396, 467, 472, 475, 476, 478, 505

Kahane, Jack, 123
Kahlau, Heinz, 408
Kahn, Otto Hermann, 24
Kain, Richard M., 313
Kavanagh, Patrick, 370
Keats, John, 83, 187
Keith, Arthur Berriesdale, 158, 160
Kennedy, Aidan, 525
Kennedy, John F., xi, 422
Kennedy, Ludovic, 424
Kerr, Roderick Watson, xv, 3, 5, 8
Kerrigan, Catherine, xix
Kerrigan, Peter, 108, 166
Kierkegaard, Sören, 254
Kingston, William, 234
Kirkorian, Tamara, 480
Kirkwood, David, 246
Knight, G. Wilson, 209
Knight, Laura, 212
Knox, John, 296, 441, 515
Kocmanova, Jessie, 340, 368, 472, 481
Kunert, Gunter, 408
Kushnir, Danny, 474, 525

Lahr, Charles, 73, 78, 81, 140, 209, 217, 242, 281
Lahr, Esther, née Archer, 209
'Laidlaw, Alister K.', 4, 6,
12, 39, 157, 160, 164
Laidlaw, John, xxv, 12, 13, 24, 71, 358, 366, 379, 383, 384, 385, 386, 387
Laidlaw, Maggie, née Cairns, 13, 14
Laidlaw, Nellie, 13–14
Laidlaw, Robert, 70
Laidlaw, Willie, 13–14
Lamb, William, 45, 47
Lambie, Bailie Brian, 431, 463
Lamont, Archie, 197
Landis, Bernie, 332
Lane, Margaret (Lady Huntingdon), 323, 325, 327, 329, 330
Larkin, Philip, 501
Larsen, Christopher, 520
Lathen, Emma, 473
Lauchlan, Bill, 401
Lauder, Harry, xi
Lauder, Sir Thomas Dick, 158
Laughlin, James, 191
Laughlin, William, 289
Lauwerys, Joseph Albert, 322
Law, T.S., 420, 527
Lawrence, D.H., 151, 209
Le Roux, Louis N., xvii, 105, 106
Leask, Jimmie, 111
Leavis, F.R., 184, 382
Lee, Jenny, 441
Lee, Joseph, 3, 5, 20
Leland, Mary, 454, 455
Lenin, Vladimir Ilyich, xxix, xxx, 45, 47, 57, 86, 98, 153, 272, 290, 451, 460, 494, 495, 503, 523
Lenya, Lotte, 469, 470, 471
Leslie, Arthur, 434
Levy, Hyman, 291
Lewin, Ronald, 419
Lewis, Cecil Day, 93, 159
Lewis, Saunders, 143, 477, 487
Lewis, Wyndham, 459
Lincoln, Abraham, xxiii
Lindsay, Jack, 330, 375
Lindsay, Joyce, 497
Lindsay, Maurice, 357, 372, 404, 497, 508, 510, 532
Lingard, Joan, 477
Linklater, Eric, xxiii, xxvi, 93
Lithgow, Henry, 197
Lithgow, Sir James, 196

Littlewood, Joan, 269
Livesay, Dorothy, 507
Livingstone, William, 80, 179
Lloyd-George, David, xxiii
Lochhead, Liz, 480
Lom, Iain, 192
Longfellow, Henry Wadsworth, xxiii, 323
Lorimer, Robin, 380, 419
Lowenfels, Walter, 407, 408
Lucie-Smith, Edward, 414
Lukacs, Georg, 290, 412

MacAlister, George, 315
MacAoidh, Rob Donn, 80
MacArthur, Bessie J.B., 215
McAskill, George, 423
MacBeth, George, 501
MacBride, Sean, 523
MacCaig, Isabel, 322, 326, 358, 458
MacCaig, Norman, xiii, xxii, xxxi, 159, 297, 300, 305, 307, 322, 326, 341, 351, 355, 356, 360, 372, 422, 423, 425, 437, 453, 454, 458, 468, 469, 492, 503, 512, 529
McCance, Mrs W., 26, 27
McCance, William, 25, 26, 360, 463, 464, 465
McCarthy, Mary, xi
MacCodrum, Ian, 80
MacColl, Ewan, 269, 275, 276, 277, 319, 320, 321, 322, 337, 338
MacColl, Jean, 322
MacColl, W.D., 144, 147, 152, 257
Mac Colla, Fionn, *see* MacDonald, Thomas Douglas
McCormack, Count John, 34
MacCormick, John MacDonald, xxvii, xxviii, 35, 51, 257
McCreath, Mr, 29
McCrindle, Alex, 295, 300, 303, 350, 362, 477, 503, 523
McCrindle, Honor, 300, 350, 420, 477, 478
McCrindle, Jean, 350
McCrorie, Charles, 355
MacCulloch, Rev. Canon, 50
McCulloch, Margery, 158

MacDonagh, Donagh, 154
Macdonald, (James) Ramsay, 30, 64, 106
MacDonald, Alexander (Alasdair MacMhaighstir Alasdair), 80, 86, 144, 179, 192
Macdonald, Callum, 305, 307
MacDonald, Flora, 44, 46, 147
MacDonald, M., 308, 312, 319, 320
MacDonald, Mamie, 373
MacDonald, Mary, 493
MacDonald, Mrs C., 306, 307
MacDonald, Thomas Douglas ('Fionn Mac Colla'), 89, 105, 373, 462, 493
MacFarlane, George, 349
McDownall, Hugo, 93
McElroy, Kate, 108, 118, 138
McElroy, William, xvii, 42, 71, 74, 105, 108, 117, 118, 127, 132, 134, 135, 137, 139, 146, 148, 150, 169
McEwan, Sydney, 532
McEwen, Betty, 529
McFie, Ronald Campbell, 4
McGavin, Robert H., 308
MacGillivray, (James) Pittendrigh, 23, 160
McGonagall, William, 87
McGregor, Alisdair Alpin, 164
McGregor, Jimmie, 382
McGuffie, Jessie, 376
Macintosh, Alison, 379, 391, 469, 479, 514, 530
Macintosh, Alistair, 302, 304, 337, 362, 390, 391, 392, 396, 423, 424, 425, 426, 427, 428, 438, 439, 442, 461, 486, 488, 502, 503, 504, 507, 525, 530
Macintosh, Anne, 517, 525
Macintosh, Christine, *see also* Grieve, Christine Elizabeth Margaret, 298, 302, 303, 304, 337, 362, 390, 391, 395, 396, 422, 423, 424, 427, 428, 430, 435, 438, 439, 455, 461, 469, 478, 479, 486, 488, 502, 503, 504, 507, 514, 517, 525, 526, 529, 530, 532, 534
Macintosh, Donald, 299, 302, 304, 337, 379, 391, 425, 479, 502, 514, 517, 525, 530
Macintosh, Elspeth, 299, 302, 304, 337, 379, 390, 391, 425, 428, 438, 474, 479, 514, 525, 530
McIntosh, Hamish, 271
Macintosh, Rory, 379, 391, 397, 469, 479, 514, 517, 525, 530
MacIntyre, Angus, 506
MacIntyre, Duncan Bàn, 80, 390, 414
MacIntyre, Robert Donald, 206, 215
Mackay, A. Katherine, 400
Mackay, Christian, 400
Mackay, Eneas, 13, 14, 45, 46, 50, 57, 158
MacKechnie, James, 276, 319, 474
MacKechnie, Rev. John, 192
McKellar, Kenneth, 382
Mackenzie, Agnes Mure, 57, 78, 95, 254
Mackenzie, Compton, xvii, xxvi–xxviii, 30, 31, 32, 34, 35, 39, 46, 48, 49, 89, 145, 147, 161, 168, 246, 248, 257, 295, 393, 508, 509, 510
Mackenzie, Kenneth, 320
Mackie, A.D., 188, 286, 287
Mackie, Mrs A.D., 286, 287
MacLaren, James, 44, 83
McLaren, Moray, 48, 91, 295
MacLaurin, Charles, 39, 131
MacLean, Calum Iain, 112, 180
Maclean, Campbell, 515
Maclean, John, 152, 153, 180
Maclean, John, 152, 179, 182, 249, 250, 266, 417, 418, 419, 484
MacLean, Renée, 377, 524
MacLean, Sorley (Somhairle Mac Ghill-Eaithain), xxii, 79, 80, 96, 106, 110, 112, 128, 147, 152, 153, 179, 180,

189, 244, 256, 258, 377,
378, 458, 492, 520, 523
MacLellan, Dolina, 503
MacLellan, Robert, 253,
281
MacLellan, Sadie, 217, 253
MacLellan, William, 258,
275, 339, 352, 397, 500,
504
McLennan, Gordon, 401
MacLeod (of Skeabost),
144, 145
Macleod, Mary, 80
Macleod, Norman, 122,
159
McMillan, Alex, 355
MacMillan, Father John,
145, 147
MacNamara, Francis, 232
MacNeice, Louis, 159, 166,
190, 297
MacNeill, Flos, 246
Macpherson, James, xxiii
McQueen, John, 388, 420
McQuillan, Ruth, 437,
457, 487, 492, 511
MacSween, Chrissie, 49,
248
Mailer, Norman, xi
Mairet, Philip, 146
Malinowski, Ivan, 481
Manifold, John, 408
Manson, John, 167, 440,
443
Mao Tse-Tung, 324
Mardersteig, Giovanni,
435, 436, 457, 521
Marshak, Samuil
Yakovlevich, 424
Marshall, Alan, 408
Marshall, Herbert, 467
Martin, David, 211, 217
Martin, Graham, 505
Martin, John Smellie, 159
Martin, Kingsley, 140, 141
Martin, Rev. W.J.B., 339
Martinson, Harry, 352,
363, 364, 367
Marwick, Ernest, 93
Marx, Karl, xxvii, 290, 318,
494
Mary, Queen of Scots, 132,
281
Maschiwitz, Eric, 39
Masereel, Franz, 435, 436,
443, 456
Matisse, Henri, 360
Maxton, Jimmy, 222, 417
Mayakovsky, Vladimir
Vladimirovich, 291,

351, 375, 431, 440, 450,
467
Meier, Henk, 534
Meier, Jeanine, 534
Mickiewicz, Adam, 375
Migdale, Lord, 404
Miller (Wheeler), Harry
(James Harrison), 189,
191, 194, 196, 204, 211,
215, 216, 222
Miller, Karl, 437, 457
Miller, Liam, 421
Milne, Ewart, 370
Milner, Ian, 324, 332, 337,
339, 341, 345, 347, 368,
396, 407, 414, 416, 471,
472, 481
Milner, Jarmila, 333, 369,
408, 415, 472, 481
Milner, Linda, 408, 415,
482
Milnes, Humphrey, 424,
428, 469
Milton, John, 164, 464, 476
Mirsky, Prince Dmitri S.,
47, 78, 89, 186
Mistral, Frédéric, 161
Mitchell, David, 492
Mitchell, Jack, 407
Mitchell, James Leslie, see
also Gibbon, Lewis
Grassic, 65, 78, 89, 416,
417
Mitchell, Rhea, 92, 302,
377
Mitchell, Rosslyn, 39
Mitchison, Naomi, 47, 69,
87, 89, 243, 244
Moffat, Abe, 355
Moffat, Alan, 389, 533
Molotov, Vyacheslav
Mikhailovich, 291
Montague, Evelyn, 461,
484, 522
Montague, John, 370, 421,
442, 460, 462, 484, 486,
521
Montale, Eugenio, 352
Montalk, Count Potocki
de, 140, 141
Montgomerie, William, 87
Montrose, Duke of, xxvi,
257
Moore, Hugo, 309, 334,
375, 429
Moore, Thomas Sturge, 42
Mordrell, Oliver, 506
Morgan, Edwin, 300, 306,
308, 310, 318, 320, 333,
351, 352, 363, 364, 366,

381, 393, 394, 467, 505,
513, 515
Morris, Barbara, 347
Morris, Margaret, 211
Morris, Max, 347
Morris, Rev. W.J., 334,
335, 336
Morrison, David, 493
Morrison, Herbert Stanley,
264
Morrison, John, 408
Morrison, Roderick, 80
Morton, John, 267
Morvi, Princess Maya of,
516
Moser, Lida, 263
Mosley, Oswald, 285
Mottram, Eric, 467
Moulton, Matthew J., 82,
83
Muggeridge, Malcolm,
369, 370, 440, 441
Muir, Bob, 480, 534
Muir, Douglas, 493
Muir, Edwin, xxii, 26, 27,
85, 87, 97, 127, 184,
185, 186, 190, 307, 419,
431, 493, 522
Muir, Gavin, xxii, xxiii,
493
Muir, Kenneth, 87
Muir, Thomas, 182
Muir, Willa, née Anderson,
xvi, xvii, xxii, 26, 27,
97, 185, 217
Muirhead, R.E., xxvi,
xxviii, 14, 17, 20, 21,
22, 29, 32, 217, 270,
271, 283, 292, 293
Muller, H.J., 125
Munro, Hector Hugh
('Saki'), xxvi
Munro, Ian S., 416, 417
Munro, Neil, xv, 3, 5, 84,
117
Murdoch, Bryden, 480
Murison, David, 222, 434,
513
Murray, Charles, 3, 406
Murray, Sir William, 488
Murray, Tom, 340, 460

Nairn, Edward, 360
Napier, Roisin, 484, 500
Needham, Joseph, 290
Neill A.S., 225
Neill, Willie ('Will
O'Gallowa'), 434
Neish, Alex, 368
Neruda, Pablo, 290, 450,

569

472, 482, 515
Nicholas, T.E., 159
Nicol, Ian, 382, 389
Nicoll, Charles, 244, 378, 489, 519
Nicoll, Mrs C., 244, 379, 490, 519
Nietzsche, F.W., xiv, 505
Niven, Barbara, 164, 167, 318, 320, 322, 324, 337, 338, 341, 374, 394, 401, 405, 415, 416, 439, 462, 469
Noble, William, 532
Nott, James Michael, 66
Nott, Kathleen, 307
Nott, Rosemary, 66
Nott, Stanley, 44, 57, 65, 66, 84, 277

O'Brien, Conor Cruise, 523
O'Casey, Eileen, 118
O'Casey, Sean, 117, 299, 330, 370
O'Connell, Daniel, xxiii
'O'Connor, Frank' (O'Donovan, Michael), 163, 284
O'Faolain, Sean, 44
O'Grady, Desmond, 489
O'Hegarty, Patrick Sarsfield, 44
O'Keefe, Timothy, 533
O'Mahoney, Eoin, 283
O'Sullivan, Maurice, 84
O'Sullivan, Seumus, xxvi, 44, 45, 253, 370
Ogden, Denis, 400
Ogdon, John, 352, 365, 374, 389, 408, 409
Ogilvie, George, xv, xix–xxi, 4
Ogilvie, Will ('Cholly'), 6, 8
Olivier, Laurence, 206
Orage, A.R., 28, 84, 173
Orr, Alex, 246
Orr, Christine, 93
Orr, David, 52, 53, 54, 57, 61, 97, 98, 99, 100, 103, 104, 109, 110, 111, 112, 113, 115, 119, 120, 121, 126, 129, 144, 153, 159, 167, 177, 180, 213, 214, 216, 217, 224, 246, 256, 326, 341, 350, 356, 425
Orr, John, 250
Orr, Marjorie, 350
Orr, Stephens, 480

Orwell, Sonia, 368

Pape, A.G., xxvi, 35
Parandowski, Jan, 375
Park, Mungo, 65
Parsons, Leonard, 3
Pasternak, Boris, 431, 496
Patchen, Kenneth, 334
Paterson, A.J.B., 82, 86, 89, 94, 97, 100, 101, 112
Pavey, Leonard Arthur, 3
Pears, Peter, 443, 471
Peddie, Mary K., 400
Perrie, Walter, 492
Perrins, Charles William Dyson, xiv, 133
Peterkin, Norman, 518
Peto, Michael, 376
Peyre, Sully André, 271
Phibbs, Geoffrey, 163
Phillips, Delwyn, 263
Pickard, Tom, 444
Picton, Harold, 163
Pitter, Ruth, 308
Pödör, László, 365
Poe, Edgar Allen, 83
Polevoi, Boris, 410
Portello, Jesualdo, 310
Porteus, Hugh Gordon, 320
Potts, Paul, 207, 209, 211, 213, 214, 215, 216, 217, 393
Pound, Ezra, 28, 49, 275, 291, 382, 405, 406, 417, 445, 457, 458, 476, 482, 485, 487, 489, 501, 515
Pound, Mrs E., 457, 458
Pound, Omar, 485
Powell, Michael, 206
Power, William, 168, 205, 280
Powys, John Cowper, 151, 164, 513
Pressburger, Emeric, 206
Pritchard, Sadie, *see also* MacLellan, Sadie, 253, 260
Pritchard, Walter, 217, 249, 253, 260
'Pteleon', 272
Punton, Minnie, ix–xiii, xvii

Rachewiltz, Walter de, 485
Rago, Henry, 373
Ramsay, Mary, 224, 225, 246
Randall, A.W.G., 66
Ranger, S.J., 264

Ratter, Mr, 131, 159, 163, 231
Read, Sir Herbert, 412
Reavey, George, 467
Reid, Alexander, 336
Reid, Charles, 356
Reid, George, 499
Reid, John MacNair, 33, 143, 168, 253
Reinfrank, Arno, 407, 442
Reinfrank, Helen, 443
Renzio, Toni del, 223
Rexroth, Kenneth, 334
Rhine, Joseph Banks, 313
Rhys, Ioan, 433
Rhys, Keidrych, 154
Riach, Alan, 244, 269, 292, 376, 405, 435, 519, 520
Rice, Estelle, 360
Richard III, 318
Richards, David, 520
Richelieu, A.J.D., xxiii
Riddell, Alan, 305
Rilke, Rainer Maria, 5, 66, 67, 68, 291, 355, 434
Rimbaud, Arthur, 291
Ritchie, John, 383
Robert II, 158
Roberton, Sir Hugh, 222, 512
Roberts, Michael, 207
Robertson, Fred, 247
Robertson, R.R., 350
Robertson, Stanley, 47, 101
Robertson, Thomas, 55, 263
Robeson, Paul, 286, 503
Rodker, John, 112
Romains, Jules, 111, 125
Romilly, Esmond, 217
Rosebery, Earl of, 247
Rosenthal, M.L., 382, 389, 424
Ross, Father Anthony, 382, 515
Ross, Robert Baldwin, 141
Ross, Sir Ronald, xv, 5, 160, 161
Ross, William (Uilleam Ros), 80
Rossetti, Dante Gabriel, 162
Rothstein, Andrew, 281
Rousselot, Jean, 365
Roy, Ross, 388
Rudge, Olga, 485
Rukeyser, Muriel, 389, 390
Russell, Bertrand, 440
Russell, George William ('A.E.'), 34, 44, 46, 47, 85, 154, 173, 190, 424

Russell, Peter, 275, 310
Ryan, Desmond, 106, 284
Rydla, Lucjana, 497

Sackville-West, Edward, 66, 294
Sackville-West, Vita, 66
Sankhara, 290
Sarraute, Nathalie, 371
Sarsanedas, Jordi, 378
Sartre, Jean-Paul, 371
Saunders, Mrs R.C., 305
Saunders, R. Crombie, 304, 307
Saurat, Denis, 19, 97, 173, 183, 184, 186, 187, 313
Scarfe, Francis, 370
Schlapp, Professor, 66
Schoenmann, Ralph, 440
Schotz, Benno, 250, 350, 417
Schubert, Elspeth Harley, 352
Scott, Alexander, 306, 336, 432, 472, 478, 510
Scott, F.G., xxv, 13, 24, 26, 27, 28, 32, 43, 46, 48, 59, 71, 83, 92, 97, 98, 99, 101, 103, 104, 134, 155, 156, 173, 179, 183, 184, 186, 200, 202, 204, 205, 221, 222, 226, 231, 232, 233, 237, 290, 293, 294, 295, 312, 351, 366, 374, 382, 389, 409, 413, 415, 532, 533
Scott, Hope, 533
Scott, Lilias ('Lovey'), 205, 231, 233, 351, 397
Scott, Burgess (Mrs F.G.), 71, 231, 233, 295, 351, 397, 532
Scott, Mrs T., 420
Scott, Sir Walter, 160, 164
Scott, Tom, 355, 388, 419, 420, 453
Scott-Moncrieff, George, 88, 95
Sealy, Douglas, 435
Seghers, Anna, 290
Semerakova, Jagmilla, 332, 340
Shadbolt, Maurice, 346
Shakespear, Dorothy, 485
Shakespeare, William, 318, 391, 403
Shand, Jimmy, 382
Shaw, Ben, 32
Shaw, George Bernard, xxviii, 28, 186, 393, 429

Shearer, Johnnie, 212
Shearer, Mary, 202, 206, 234
Shelley, Percy Bysshe, 83, 187
Shepherd, Alison, 143, 145, 185
Shinwell, Emmanuel, 285
Shostakovich, Dmitry, 419
Sickert, Walter, 221
Silver, R.S., 296
Simon, Lord, 195
Simpson, Louis, 388, 390, 391, 458
Sinclair, Donald, 55, 80, 145, 147
Sinclair, J.G., 287, 398
Sinclair, Neil, 145, 147
Sinclair, W. Angus, 163
Singer, James Burns, 209, 372, 376
Sitwell, Edith, 297
Sitwell, Sacheverell, 518
Skinner, David, 146
Skinner, Ina, 148, 170, 439, 479, 517
Sleath, Fred, 249, 254, 256
Sloan, Alex, 216
Smeaton, Jessie B., 321
Smeaton, Mary S., 321
Smith, Brian, 166
Smith, Charles, 479, 502
Smith, Iain Crichton, 307, 437, 438
Smith, Janet Adam, 419
Smith, Naomi Royde, 190
Smith, Norman Kemp, 146, 336
Smith, Sydney Goodsir, xxii, 216, 234, 249, 256, 258, 297, 300, 307, 308, 309, 355, 356, 370, 372, 429
Smith, W. Gordon, 481
Solomon, Yonty, 518
Solzenitsyn, Aleksandr Isayevich, 496
Sorabji, Kaikhosru Shapurji, xxv, 27, 173, 207, 293, 294, 312, 313, 365, 366, 374, 390, 408, 415, 518
Soutar, William, 87, 99, 246, 336
Speirs, John, 184, 185, 186
Spence, Lewis, xxviii, 5, 20
Spender, Sir Stephen Harold, 166, 316
Spitteler, Carl, 5
Squair, Olive M., 496, 500, 504

Squire, Sir John Collings, 3, 11
Stalin, Josef, 108, 157, 182, 290, 325, 496
Steiner, George, 505
Stephens, Meic, 476, 477, 485, 487
Stevenson, Gerda, 471
Stevenson, Marjorie, 352, 366, 382, 397, 403, 406, 413, 416, 419, 444
Stevenson, Robert Louis, xx, 12, 419
Stevenson, Ronald, 352, 365, 374, 382, 390, 397, 402, 406, 407, 408, 409, 413, 414, 415, 416, 418, 443, 469, 470, 515
Stevenson, Sir Daniel Macaulay, 21, 22, 23
Stewart Thomson, T.B., 334, 335
Stewart, Andrew, 91
Stewart, Douglas, 195
Stewart, Jock, 147
Stewart, John, 490
Stewart, Willie, 265
Stieg, William, 288
Stock, Noel, 405
Stoneham, Lord, 404
Stott, Sir Gordon, 274
Stoyanoff, Istavan, 342, 344
Strachey, (Evelyn) John St Loe, 26, 166, 285
Stubbs, S.G. Blaxford, 131
Sun Yat-sen, 330
Sutherland, Robert Garioch, 179, 180, 307, 420, 474, 520

Tannahill, Andrew, 270, 271
Tarn, Nathaniel, 440
Taylor, A.J.P., 259
Taylor, Henry Grant, 74, 151, 157, 161, 166, 168, 180, 183, 201, 202, 209, 233, 234, 474
Tempest, Brigita, 337, 344
Tempest, Peter, 337
Theiner, George, 472
Thomas, Caitlin, 232
Thomas, Dylan, 232, 259, 281, 373, 486
Thomas, Susan, 479
Thomas, Vincent, 479, 486
Thompson, Francis, 11
Thompson, J.W.W., 517, 528

Thomson, David Cleghorn, 39, 48, 91
Thomson, George Malcolm, 4, 29, 84
Thomson, Lord, 488
Thomson, Morgan, 265, 266
Thomson, Roy, 344
Thorndike, Sybil, 64
Tillyard, E.M.W., 168
Todd, George, 307
Todd, Ruthven, 154
Tóibín, Colm, 484
Tolstoy, Count L.N., 494
Tonge, John, 185, 309, 350
Toynbee, Arnold, 503
Tremayne, Sydney, 307
Trevlyn, Valda, *see also* Grieve, Valda, xvii, xviii, xxi, 44, 53, 55, 56, 57, 60, 63, 66, 71, 72, 73, 74, 75, 76, 77, 112
Trocchi, Alexander, xi, 395, 398, 411
Truine, Holy, 81
Truman, Harry, 287
Tschiffely, A.F., 151
Tucker, Martin, 422, 424
Turnbull, Gael, 317, 333
Turnbull, J.D., 101
Turnbull, William, 481
Tweedie, Mrs, 341, 360
Tzara, Tristan, 310, 370

Ulbricht, Walter, 440
Urlov, S.A., 410

Valentine, James, 99, 100, 257
Valentine, Rev. L.E., 143
Vallejo, César, 450
Vesper, Margory, 529
Vickers, F.B., 408
Vivante, Leone, 131
Voroshilov, Klimenti Efremovich, 324

Wagner, Geoffrey Atheling, 288, 302
Wain, John, 370
Walker, Agnes, 294, 397
Wallace, Edgar, 160
Wallace, William, xxiv, 238

Walton, Eda Lou, 171
Wannau, Bill, 408
Warburg, Frederic, 86, 97
Wasserman, Jakob, 173
Waten, Judah, 407, 408
Watson, Celia, 506
Watson, Hon. David, 295, 298
Watson, J. Carmichael, 80
Watson, Roderick, 505, 506
Watt, Rev. Lauchlan MacLean, 6, 50
Waugh, Evelyn, 511
Waugh, Hilary, 473
Wedgwood, C.V., 375
Weigel-Brecht, Helene, 407
Weill, Kurt, 406, 469, 470, 471
Weir, Molly, 276
Wells, H.G., 28
Werner-Buerton, Ruth, 407
Weston, Jack, 424, 453, 460
Weston, John C., 437, 456, 458
Westwater, (Robert H.) Peter, 303, 373
Wheatley, Lord John, 491
Wheldon, Sir Huw, 459
Whistler, James A. M., 223
White, Betty, *née* Kelly, 387
White, Eric W., 392
White, Ernest George, 312
White, Jean, xxv, 24, 358, 367, 371, 380, 383, 384, 385, 386, 387, 399, 404, 428, 431, 433, 470, 475, 487, 492, 520, 528, 531, 534
White, Jim, 24, 358, 368, 371, 384, 387, 404
White, John, 358
White, Margaret Helen ('Maggie'), *née* Laidlaw, 24, 358, 531
White, William, 162
White, William, 358, 368, 371, 384, 404
Whitman, Walt, 316, 476
Whyte, James H., 57, 61, 75, 122, 186

Wild, Sir Ernest, 140, 141
Wilde, Oscar, 141
Wilder, Thornton, 313
Wilkie, Helen, 267, 284
Wilkie, Robert Blair, 245, 267, 270, 271, 284, 350
Willett, Henry, 222
Williams, Caerwyn, 487
Williams, D.J., 143
Williams, Galen, 422
Williams, Ifor, 487
Williams, J.L., 264
Williams, Jonathan, 488
Williamson, (Little) Mary Jean, 124, 204
Wilson, Edmund, 190
Wilson, Harold, 404
Wilson, James ('Pearlie'), 285
Wilson, Joan, 475
Wilson, Joyce, 488
Wilson, Norman, 522
Wolf, Hugo, 83
Wolfe, Alexander Stewart, 158, 160, 196
Wordsworth, Dorothy, 83
Wordsworth, William, xv
Wright, David, 345, 357, 458
Wright, Gordon, 115, 462, 515

X, Malcolm, 404

Yeats, William Butler, xxvi–xxix, 34, 128, 156, 163, 173, 190, 291, 340, 370, 452
Yevtushenko, Yevegeny Aleksandrovich, 371, 375, 498
Young, (Alexander Bell) Filson, 39
Young, David, 356
Young, Douglas, xxvii, 158, 160, 182, 183, 192, 205, 224, 270, 280, 336, 351
Young, James D., 301, 417

Zinsser, Hans, 92
Zlatarev, Paul, 347